Rising Threats, Enduring Challenges

Readings in U.S. Foreign Policy

Andrew Price-Smith

Colorado College

New York   Oxford

OXFORD UNIVERSITY PRESS

Oxford University Press is a department of the University of Oxford. It furthers the University's objective of excellence in research, scholarship, and education by publishing worldwide.

Oxford   New York
Auckland   Cape Town   Dar es Salaam   Hong Kong   Karachi
Kuala Lumpur   Madrid   Melbourne   Mexico City   Nairobi
New Delhi   Shanghai   Taipei   Toronto

With offices in
Argentina   Austria   Brazil   Chile   Czech Republic   France   Greece
Guatemala   Hungary   Italy   Japan   Poland   Portugal   Singapore
South Korea   Switzerland   Thailand   Turkey   Ukraine   Vietnam

Copyright © 2015 by Oxford University Press.

For titles covered by Section 112 of the US Higher Education Opportunity Act, please visit www.oup.com/us/he for the latest information about pricing and alternate formats.

Published in the United States of America by
Oxford University Press
198 Madison Avenue, New York, NY 10016
http://www.oup.com

Library of Congress Cataloging-in-Publication Data
Rising threats, enduring challenges : readings in U.S. foreign policy / [edited by] Andrew Price-Smith.
    pages cm
Includes index.
ISBN 978-0-19-989763-6 (pbk.)
1. United States--Foreign relations. 2. United States--Foreign relations--Sources. I. Price-Smith, Andrew T.
E183.7.R57 2013
327.73--dc23
                                                                2013031900

Printing number: 9 8 7 6 5 4 3 2 1

Printed in the United States of America
on acid-free paper

BRIEF CONTENTS

CONTENTS

The study of the conduct of U.S. foreign policy takes many forms, from diplomatic history, to the international relations theory, to policy analysis. In my opinion, the student of U.S. foreign policy requires materials from multiple approaches to gain a substantive command of the subject. Exposure to only one facet of the complex problems that confront the U.S.A.'s conduct of foreign policy will provide the student with only a partial capacity to comprehend the events occurring around them.

This project resulted from many years of teaching U.S. foreign policy, and from my conclusion that students required something more than the standard textbook. In selecting the readings for this anthology, I felt it imperative to combine certain crucial historical readings with articles that form the theoretical bedrock of the discipline of international relations. These theories span the levels of analysis that underpin the discipline, and reflect dominant perspectives such as Realism, Liberalism, bureaucratic politics, and political psychology. The inclusion of a section on institutions and processes incorporated many debates on the role of public opinion, interest groups, the media, labor, and business interests in influencing the direction of U.S. foreign policy.

This anthology also includes a section on U.S. relations with key states, from China, Russia, India to Iran, Afghanistan, Pakistan, and Latin America. Finally, this volume includes a section on rising threats and challenges to U.S. national and international interests including cyberattacks, nuclear proliferation, terrorism, energy scarcity, climate change, the Arab Spring, and imperial overstretch. Many of the readings herein are seminal to the discipline of international relations, and several are rather controversial. In my opinion, this diversity of theory and opinion is absolutely essential to the stimulation of intellectual debate.

ACKNOWLEDGMENTS

This volume is the result of teaching courses on U.S. foreign policy for many years, and the result of my recognition that my students would benefit from a challenging collection of readings that illustrated the core premises of international relations. I am grateful to my colleagues at Colorado College, particularly to Tom Cronin, David Hendrickson, and John Gould for their helpful advice. Moreover I am indebted to Jennifer Carpenter, executive editor for Politics, and Maegan Sherlock, associate editor, Roxanne Klaas, and the production staff of Oxford University Press, who were invaluable in the preparation of this volume.

Further, I should like to thank the reviewers who provided helpful feedback and constructive critiques of the volume: Thomas P. Dolan, Columbus State University; David Dreyer, Lenoir-Rhyne University; Andrew Flibbert, Trinity College; Steven Hill, University of Wisconsin-Eau Claire; Edward Kwon, Northern Kentucky University; Mary Fran Malone, University of New Hampshire; Khalil Marrar, DePaul University; Samuel Cary Nailling III, University of Tennessee, Knoxville; Evan N. Resnick, Yeshiva College of Yeshiva University; John W. Sutherlin, University of Louisiana at Monroe; Chris Van Aller, Winthrop University; Leo J. Weeks, University of West Florida; Joel H. Westra, Calvin College.

Finally, I would like to thank my dear wife Janell, who patiently endured weeks of editing and writing, helped me prepare documents, and scanned data. I also thank my mother Cynthia McLeod, and my stepfather Jack McLeod for his wisdom and helpful critiques over the years. This book is dedicated to my son William Thomas Price-Smith. May we learn from the lessons of the past, surmount the challenges of the present, and create a brighter future for all humanity.

Andrew T. Price-Smith
Colorado College

Our daily lives are profoundly influenced by foreign policy decision making, even though we may not recognize it immediately. Many of the items that we use, from cellphones to computers, clothing and cars, are manufactured elsewhere and shipped to us through global trade networks. The costly wars in Iraq and Afghanistan have touched our lives, either directly through family and friends, or indirectly through the media, or through the taxes we will all ultimately pay to finance those conflicts. Prospects of a confrontation with Iran over its nuclear programs drive up the global price of oil, increasing the cost of gasoline for everyone, which in turn drives up the cost of goods. Nations come together to try to deal with global issues that concern us, such as averting global climate change, preventing terrorism, rescuing the global economy, or dealing with soaring energy prices. Ultimately, we are all entangled in an economic, ecological, and strategic web that links our lives to those of other peoples around the world. So, the conduct of U.S. foreign policy with those nations influences our lives in ways that are both profound and often poorly understood.

The terrible attacks of September 11, 2001 marked the first decade of the 21st century as one of conflict and turmoil. Shadowy terrorist networks such as al Qaeda showed that nonstate actors represented significant threats to powerful nations. Osama bin Laden and his jihadist followers created bases in failed states such as Afghanistan, where they were protected by the fundamentalist Islamic theocracy of the Taliban. September 11th vividly demonstrated how such networks could employ strategies of asymmetrical warfare, using low-tech weapons in the form of jet planes and box-cutters, to strike at the American heartland. With a mixture of shock, fury, and fear, Americans felt acutely vulnerable to this new threat of terrorism.

In response to the attacks, the U.S.A. plunged into difficult wars in Afghanistan (2001–present) and Iraq (2003–2011) resulting in a decade of war that saw substantial U.S. casualties, and a considerable drain of U.S. resources. Despite the death of Osama bin Laden in Afghanistan in 2011 the threat of terrorism endures, although al Qaeda's power is now somewhat diminished.

Despite the end of the Iraq War and the death of Osama bin Laden, Washington still confronts a broad spectrum of challenges in the years ahead. The United States faces a constellation of rising powers that may seek to displace it from its position of dominance over the rest of the globe. The rise of China, India, and a resurgent Russia presents interesting tests for U.S. diplomacy in the decades to come. The growing threat from "rogue states" such as Iran and North Korea, and persistent instability in Afghanistan, Pakistan, and Mexico are also clouds on the horizon. The U.S.A. also faces a range of emerging threats, ranging from nuclear proliferation, to energy scarcity, climate change, pandemics, cyberwarfare, and an Arab world in disorder.

The rapid increase in American power over the past century has resulted in the relentless expansion of Washington's international interests and commitments. The U.S.A.'s enormous global military presence and its expansive diplomatic interests, now represent a considerable drain on the economic vitality of the U.S.A. Many analysts now question the U.S.A.'s ability to maintain its position as the dominant power in the world, given the country's reckless spending and economic fragility, indebtedness to China, and commitments to multiple wars over the past decade.

Despite these challenges the U.S.A. has faced enormous trials in the past, and overcome them: defeating the threats of Nazi Germany and Imperial Japan during the Second World War and outlasting the Soviet Union during the Cold War era. Through all of these great contests the U.S.A. has always emerged as a strong and more resilient nation.

The analysis of U.S. foreign policy is often cast as either a historical or theoretical exercise. However, the study of U.S. foreign policy requires a balanced perspective, one that integrates the historical and theoretical domains with policy analysis. An understanding of the theories presented in this volume is crucial, as it provides us with a way of interpreting history, data, and the actions of policymakers in the present. Theory offers the tools to make sense of the bewildering flurry of events that surrounds us in any given year. History without theory makes much of U.S. diplomatic behavior incomprehensible. Similarly, theoretical analyses devoid of historical context and data are often lacking in practical application to real-world concerns. Policy analyses devoid of history and theory are often simply snapshots in time, and thus incapable of providing analysis of institutions and processes as they evolve and change.

We cannot understand the conduct of modern U.S. foreign policy without some basic comprehension of the history of U.S. diplomacy as it puts modern policy in its proper context. The behavior of modern institutions often reflects trajectories or pathways that were determined in decades past. Thus, it is folly to discuss modern U.S. foreign policy vis-à-vis the nations of Latin America without some reference to the Monroe Doctrine and the Roosevelt Corollary. Similarly, one cannot hope to understand the Cold War without reference to Kennan's famous "X" article, nor modern U.S. foreign policy in the Persian Gulf without some understanding of the history of U.S. diplomacy in the region, particularly the Carter Doctrine.

Theories are like the glasses that many of us use to drive or to read. If we do not wear our glasses while driving, our perception of reality is dimmed and distorted. Without our glasses we may very well miss certain signposts, and as a result lose our way, or we may be ignorant of threats or obstacles on the road ahead, such as a herd of deer or a car accident. In a similar way theories operate as lenses that influence, and often enhance, our perception of political "reality." People often say that "the facts speak for themselves," but they do not. The facts are mute. They must be interpreted by theory that will give them context and significance. Without theory, we can only look at the facts and ask "so what?" and wonder about their implications and consequences. What you see will be influenced by which lens of theory you look through.

In this manner if we put on our Realist glasses we will see human nature as self-interested, power-hungry, unchanging, and seeking dominance over one another. We will see the international environment as hostile and anarchical, driven to aggressive competition, arms races, and perennial violence between nations. Realists confronted by such a dog-eat-dog world realize that survival of one's state is the penultimate goal, and that the only way to ensure survival is through the maximization of our power (typically through military capability). Realists acknowledge that today's friend is tomorrow's enemy, and argue that one cannot afford to be naïve in such a brutal and competitive environment. Further, Realists argue that sovereign states are the only actors in the international system that possess any significance, and that one should ideally focus on the relations between the Great Powers. Political reality, as viewed through our Realist lenses, is grim and foreboding. Yet our lenses (i.e., our theories) will help us to navigate this hostile environment.

According to Realism, uncertainty regarding the intentions of others induces fear, which combines with anarchy to generate what we call the *security dilemma*. Simply put, sovereign states caught up in the security dilemma all fear for their survival, and they cannot know the intentions of their neighbors, so they will invest in the maximization of power—often through the buildup of military forces. Even though nation A may see its own buildup of forces as defensive in nature, nations B and C may perceive it as offensive in nature and correspondingly increase their forces. This will in turn increase the anxiety of A as it may see the armaments of B and C as offensive in nature as well. Thus, the inability to know the intentions of the other often leads to problems of misperception, insecurity, and anxiety. Ultimately, this generates a spiral of militarization that we call an *arms race*. Modern arms races are underway in many regions of the world including East Asia, South Asia, and the Persian Gulf.

The theory that informs modern Realism begins with the Greek historian Thucydides, who wrote of the war between Athens and Sparta in his *History of the Peloponnesian War*. He argued that the war resulted from Sparta's growing fear of Athenian power. The Realist tradition is also informed by the writings of Niccolo Machiavelli who wrote *The Prince* and *The Discourses*. Machiavelli argued that the political world is driven by the forces of competitive self-interest, and that the principal aim of the leader of a state is to seek power. Other authors that influenced the development of modern Realism include Sun Tzu, Kautilya, Thomas Hobbes, Carl von Clausewitz, and Otto von Bismarck who coined the term *balance of power*. In the era since World War II prominent Realists include George F. Kennan, Henry Kissinger, Hans Morgenthau,[i] Kenneth Waltz,[ii] John Mearsheimer,[iii] Robert Jervis,[iv] Stephen Walt,[v] and Andrew J. Bacevich.[vi]

Conversely, if we put on our Liberal glasses, our perception of political "reality" changes significantly. We see other humans not as evil but as potentially good, as capable of learning from past mistakes and often engaged in cooperation. Viewed through Liberal lenses the

---

[i] See Hans Morgenthau, *Politics Among Nations*, New York: Knopf, 1967.

[ii] Kenneth Waltz, *Man, the State, and War*, revised ed., New York: Columbia University Press, 2001; and Kenneth Waltz, *Theory of International Politics*, Long Grove, IL: Waveland, 2010.

[iii] John Mearsheimer, *Tragedy of Great Power Politics*, New York: Norton, 2002; John Mearsheimer and Steven Walt, *The Israel Lobby and U.S. Foreign Policy*, New York: Farrar, Strauss and Giroux 2008; and John Mearsheimer, *Why Leaders Lie*, New York: Oxford University Press, 2011.

[iv] Jervis is known for integrating aspects of political psychology with Realism. See for example, Robert Jervis, *Perception and Misperception in International Politics*, Princeton, NJ: Princeton University Press, 1976; *The Logic of Images in International Politics*, New York: Columbia University Press, 1989.

[v] Stephen M Walt, *Taming American Power*, New York: Norton, 2006; and Stephen M. Walt, *The Origins of Alliances*, Ithaca, NY: Cornell University Press, 1990.

[vi] Andrew J. Bacevich, *The New American Militarism*, New York: Oxford University Press, 2006.

international environment remains anarchic, but the quality of anarchy changes from competition to cooperation. The dominant mode of interaction between peoples is no longer violence but trade and cooperation, and the nations of the world discover that it is in their own self-interest to trade and form what Hedley Bull called a "society of states."[vii]

According to Liberal international relations theory many actors may influence political outcomes, including sovereign states, international organizations, multinational corporations, and nongovernmental organizations. This proliferation of actors in the international game increases the complexity of our analysis, but is arguably more explanatory (at least according to Liberal theorists). Liberal theorists also argue that international law will provide a powerful check on the behavior of nations. Political reality, as viewed through Liberal lenses, is relatively peaceful and benign.

Ostensibly Liberal internationalism begins with the writings of the German philosopher Immanuel Kant, and the work of the Scottish economist Adam Smith. Kant's classic work in this vein is his *Treatise on Perpetual Peace*, where he argued that democracies will not fight one other as they share important democratic norms that work to mitigate conflict. Furthermore, the citizens of democracies will not want to bear the burden of "blood and treasure" to support war, in that the citizens bear the costs of war by surrendering both their lives and their wealth in the form of taxes. Thus, citizens of democracies will not go to war with each other. Conversely, Kant argued that democracies *would* go to war with authoritarian regimes, largely out of a desire to extend democracy to other peoples, and consequently expand what Kant called the "zone of peace." Collectively, these ideas are contained within what we call *Democratic Peace Theory*.

In his work the *Wealth of Nations*, the economist Adam Smith (and his protégé David Ricardo) argued that it made sense for nations to specialize in the production of certain goods that they could produce at less cost than other nations, and then trade those goods with other peoples. This is essentially the principal of comparative advantage. Thus, processes of trade would encourage the pacific cooperation of nations in the realm of economics, and states would find it increasingly costly (and thus irrational) to make war on each other to obtain materials and goods. In this sense we can think of variable-sum games, wherein the size of a pie (indicating the global economy) expands through economic cooperation, and thereby leads to peace. Conversely, the lack of trade and cooperation causes the pie to shrink, thereby increasing the probability of conflict between nations. Modern concepts of complex interdependence are the extension of this work by Smith and Ricardo.

Liberal theories of IR also have been influenced by the work of the British political scientist Hedley Bull who argued that even under conditions of international anarchy a "society of states" would emerge. Sovereign states would rationally recognize that it was in their mutual benefit to focus on peace, prosperity, and stability.[viii] Furthermore, American political scientists Robert Keohane and Joseph Nye wrote extensively on the concepts of *complex interdependence* and soft power.[ix] American political scientist G. John Ikenberry has written on the concept of American benign hegemony in the shaping of the modern

---

[vii]Hedley Bull, *The Anarchical Society*, London: Macmillan, 1976.

[viii]See Hedley Bull, *The Anarchical Society*, London: Macmillan Press, 1974.

[ix]See for example Robert O. Keohane, *After Hegemony*, Princeton, NJ: Princeton University Press, 1984; Robert Keohane and Joseph Nye, *Power and Interdependence*, 4th ed., Upper Saddle River, NJ: Pearson, 2011; and Joseph Nye, *The Future of Power*, New York: Public Affairs, 2011.

world order, cast in the form of international organizations, international trade networks, and mechanisms of collective security.[x]

However, theories serve as more than perceptual filters, they also frequently act as guides to action. In this way practitioners of Realism often see potential enemies all around them and act accordingly, typically maximizing their relative power by arming themselves to ensure their survival. Conversely, a Liberal theorist will instead typically see themselves among a number of potential friends, and seek to link themselves to these others through webs of interaction, typically trade and institutional linkages.

Thus, the Realist may perceive (and act on) a much darker world than the Liberal theorist standing right beside her, looking at exactly the same set of "facts." The same information may be interpreted in very different ways, depending on the theories being employed by the observer. If we employ our bureaucratic politics lenses our perceptions of political reality will focus on variables at the domestic level (within the U.S.A.) to explain our foreign policy behavior. Conversely, if we wear our political psychology glasses that focus on the individual level, our analyses will focus on the importance of perception and misperception, images, operational codes and cognitive effects.

One fascinating thing about U.S. foreign policy is the relative constancy in its display of both Liberal and Realist behavior, and the persistent influence of both Liberal and Realist ideas. The aggressive power politics associated with Realism was practiced in the era of Manifest Destiny and the early expansion of the republic. It was also evident in the Monroe Doctrine, the Mexican American War, the War of 1812, and the Spanish American War. Realism also played a crucial role in the "containment" of the Soviet Union during the Cold War, numerous U.S. military inventions in Central and South America, the Vietnam War, illiberal alliances with dictatorships during the Cold War era, Nixon's opening to China, the first Persian Gulf War (1991), and in the Afghan War (2001–present). The Realism practiced by Teddy Roosevelt and James Polk found modern manifestations in the policy of Harry Truman; Dwight Eisenhower; Richard Nixon, and his advisor Henry Kissinger; Ronald Reagan; and the presidency of the elder George Bush.

The Liberal tradition also pervades the conduct of U.S. foreign policy, flourishing under Woodrow Wilson who sought to develop international institutions for peace in the wake of the First World War. President Wilson's novel concept for the League of Nations was an attempt to bind countries together through a web of institutional linkages to facilitate cooperation, and avoid the scourge of war. During the Second World War, the United States fought with other Liberal Democracies (Britain, Canada, Australia) against the menace of fascism, embodied in the monstrous cruelties of the Axis Powers (Nazi Germany, Imperial Japan, and Fascist Italy). Following WWII, President Franklin Roosevelt presided over the creation of the United Nations, the institutional heir to Wilson's Liberal vision as expressed in the League of Nations. In this FDR sought to bind the nations of the world together through webs of diplomacy, trade, and commerce, and thereby reduce the probability of war. Liberalism also pervades the U.S.A.'s push for economic globalization, and the creation of comprehensive trade agreements between nations, such as the North American Free Trade Agreement. Liberal theory forms the core of decision making for many modern administrations from Carter, to Clinton, to that of President Obama.

---

[x]See for example G. John Ikenberry, *After Victory*, Princeton, NJ: Princeton University Press, 2001; and G. John Ikenberry, *Liberal Leviathan*, Princeton, NJ: Princeton University Press, 2011.

Interestingly, the *neoconservativism* that came to dominate U.S. foreign policy in the aftermath of the Cold War is actually a nationalistic twist on this longstanding Liberal tradition. With the dissolution of the Soviet Union in 1992 and the end of the Cold War era, the U.S.A. stood alone as the remaining superpower. Francis Fukuyama was so bold as to declare it the "end of history," based on the perceived triumph of democracy and Liberalism.[xi] Following his lead the 'neocons' (particularly journalist Charles Krauthammer, etc.) extolled the merits of American hegemony, of unipolarity, and the virtues of a benign liberal empire. The term neoconservatism is a misnomer, as the ideas underpinning this concept are actually derived from the Liberal visions of the German philosopher Immanuel Kant.[xii] Recall that Kant argued that democracies will make war against authoritarian nations to defeat such oppressive regimes and install democratic governments. The resulting expansion of democracy, coupled with Kant's argument that democracies do not fight one another, would thereby generate a *zone of peace*. The relentless expansion of this zone of peace would ultimately relegate war between nations to the history books. The neoconservative vision that was derived from Kantian logic held that the U.S.A. had the right, even the obligation, to use its pre-eminent power to push the spread of democracy, through the use of military force if necessary.[xiii] This logic underpinned much of the policies of the administration of George W. Bush, particularly the invasion of Iraq in 2003.

The U.S.A. now finds its position of dominance increasingly challenged as it faces a number of rising powers that may become peer competitors. Of these rising powers the greatest tests to U.S. dominance are likely to come from a rapidly growing China and a resurgent Russia. Authoritarian China poses the greatest potential to become a rival with its surging economy, mounting soft power, and the rapid growth of its military. Moreover, China's behavior in East Asia is increasingly belligerent as it seeks to test contentious historical claims to sovereignty throughout the South China Sea and East China Sea. Certain "rogue" states also present growing challenges to U.S. interests and national security, notably fundamentalist Iran, which is developing its nuclear capacity. The perennially unstable regime in North Korea, which has developed nuclear weapons and rudimentary ballistic missile technologies, also presents U.S. decision makers with persistent concerns in the theater of East Asia. Furthermore, the U.S. remains mired in the quagmire of Central Asia, where the intractable conflict in Afghanistan, and an increasingly unreliable ally in Pakistan have forced many to question the viability of the U.S. presence in the region.

The collection of works in this volume provides students with the sound fundamentals to investigate the history, theory and practice of U.S. foreign policy. I hope that students of international relations in general, and of foreign policy decision making in particular, find this collection of works valuable.

Andrew T. Price-Smith
Colorado College
Colorado Springs, CO

[xi]Francis Fukuyama, *The End of History and the Last Man*, New York: Penguin, 1992.

[xii]Immanuel Kant, *Perpetual Peace and Other Essays*, New York: Hackett, 1983.

[xiii]See the neoconservative arguments made by Charles Krauthammer, The Unipolar Moment, Foreign Affairs, 1990, http://www.foreignaffairs.com/articles/46271/charles-krauthammer/the-unipolar-moment

I

Historical Perspectives

"If you would understand anything, observe its beginning and its development."
—*Aristotle*

"Whoever wishes to foresee the future must consult the past; for human events ever resemble those of preceding times. This arises from the fact that they are produced by men who ever have been, and ever shall be, animated by the same passions, and thus they necessarily have the same results."
—*Niccolo Machiavelli*

"We should not look back unless it is to derive useful lessons from past errors, and for the purpose of profiting by dearly bought experience."
—*George Washington*

Much of the body of international political theory is grounded in historical sources and observations, and lessons gleaned from the past both illuminate the present and offer paths to the future. For example, a significant proportion of the modern principles of Realist theory are grounded in Thucydides' classic *History of the Peloponnesian War*.[1] The political historian John Gaddis argued against what he viewed as the artificial divorce of political science from history. "[W]e have been known, from time to time, to construct the intellectual equivalent of fortified trenches from which we fire artillery back and forth, dodging shrapnel even as we sink ever more deeply into mutual incomprehension."[2] Gaddis argued, correctly, that history and political science share a common intellectual ancestry, and he laments the "narcissism of minor differences" that has driven the disciplines apart over the past century. The political scientist Harvey Mansfield echoes this view: "(Political science) needs to open its eyes and admit to its curriculum the help of . . . history. It should be unafraid to risk considering what is ignored by science and may lack the approval of science."[3]

This section introduces students to the basic tenets of U.S. diplomatic history, as told through a number of original historical documents. In this, I hope that readers will form their own opinions of these documents, and how the principles and ideas expressed therein have influenced the conduct of U.S. foreign policy over the centuries.

The documents range from George Washington's call to avoid foreign entanglements, to the Monroe Doctrine and the Roosevelt Corollary that jointly served as a rationale for frequent U.S. intervention throughout Central and South America, and the Caribbean. This denotes the shift from an early policy that was relatively noninterventionist to the current U.S. policy of global interventionism.

This section also includes George Kennan's influential article on the "Sources of Soviet Conduct" that articulated the drivers of Soviet foreign policy during the Cold War, and Dwight Eisenhower's prophetic warning that Americans should be wary of the Military-Industrial Complex and its propensity to drag the American people into needless wars. I also include the Carter Doctrine, Reagan's speech in Berlin, George W. Bush's "Graduation Speech at West Point" that outlined the Bush Doctrine, and Barack Obama's humanitarian argument for U.S. intervention in the Libyan Civil War of 2011.

Notes

1. Thucydides. 1980. *History of the Peloponnesian War*. New York: Penguin.
2. Gaddis, J. 1997. "History, theory, and common ground." *International Security* 22, no. 1, p. 75.
3. Harvey Mansfield, as quoted in Jennifer Howard, "In Jefferson Lecture, Harvey Mansfield reflects on what the humanities can teach science and political science," *Chronicle of Higher Education*, May 9, 2007.

Farewell Address (1796)

GEORGE WASHINGTON

In the wake of domestic pressures to side with France during its hostilities with Britain, President Washington counseled that the U.S.A. should refrain from engaging in foreign alliances. Washington called for just and fair conduct in U.S. diplomacy with other nations, but also warned that the republic should avoid long-term animosity or friendship with other countries, and to take care to avoid foreign influence in our politics. He argued that such alliances could draw the U.S.A. into unnecessary wars. Modern isolationists often refer to Washington's speech as an argument for the US to withdraw from its active involvement in foreign affairs.

Observe good faith and justice toward all nations. Cultivate peace and harmony with all. Religion and morality enjoin this conduct. And can it be that good policy does not equally enjoin it? It will be worthy of a free, enlightened, and at no distant period a great nation to give to mankind the magnanimous and too novel example of a people always guided by an exalted justice and benevolence. Who can doubt that in the course of time and things the fruits of such a plan would richly repay any temporary advantages which might be lost by a steady adherence to it? Can it be that Providence has not connected the permanent felicity of a nation with its virtue? The experiment, at least, is recommended by every sentiment which ennobles human nature. Alas! Is it rendered impossible by its vices?

In the execution of such a plan nothing is more essential than that permanent, inveterate antipathies against particular nations and passionate attachments for others should be excluded, and that in place of them just and amicable feelings toward all should be cultivated. The nation which indulges toward another an habitual hatred or an habitual fondness is in some degree a slave. It is a slave to its animosity or to its affection, either of which is sufficient to lead it astray from its duty and its interest. Antipathy in one nation against another disposes each more readily to offer insult and injury, to lay hold of slight causes of umbrage, and to be haughty and intractable when accidental or trifling occasions of dispute occur.

So, likewise, a passionate attachment of one nation for another produces a variety of evils. Sympathy for the favorite nation, facilitating the illusion of an imaginary common interest in cases where no real common interest exists, and infusing into one the enmities of the other, betrays the former into a participation in the quarrels and wars of the latter without adequate inducement or justification. It leads also to concessions to the favorite nation of privileges denied to others, which is apt doubly to injure the nation making the concessions by unnecessarily parting with what ought to have been retained, and by exciting jealousy, ill will, and a disposition to retaliate in the parties from whom equal privileges are withheld; and it gives to ambitious, corrupted, or deluded citizens (who devote themselves to the favorite nation) facility to betray or sacrifice the interests of their own country without odium, sometimes even with popularity, gilding with the appearances of a virtuous sense of obligation, a commendable deference for public opinion, or a laudable zeal for public good the base or foolish compliances of ambition, corruption, or infatuation. . . .

Against the insidious wiles of foreign influence (I conjure you to believe me, fellow-citizens) the jealousy of a free people ought to be constantly awake, since history and experience prove that foreign influence is one of the most baneful foes of republican government. But that jealousy, to be useful, must be impartial, else it becomes the instrument of the very influence to be avoided, instead of a defense against it. Excessive partiality for one foreign nation and excessive dislike of another cause those whom they actuate to see danger only on one side, and serve to veil and even second the arts of influence on the other. Real patriots who may resist the intrigues of the favorite are liable to become suspected and odious, while its tools and dupes usurp the applause and confidence of the people to surrender their interests.

The great rule of conduct for us in regard to foreign nations is, in extending our commercial relations to have with them as little political connection as possible. So far as we have already formed engagements let them be fulfilled with perfect good faith. Here let us stop.

Europe has a set of primary interests which to us have none or a very remote relation. Hence she must be engaged in frequent controversies, the causes of which are essentially foreign to our concerns. Hence, therefore, it must be unwise in us to implicate ourselves by artificial ties in the ordinary vicissitudes of her politics or the ordinary combinations and collisions of her friendships or enmities.

Our detached and distant situation invites and enables us to pursue a different course. If we remain one people, under an efficient government, the period is not far off when we may defy material injury from external annoyance; when we may

take such an attitude as will cause the neutrality we may at any time resolve upon to be scrupulously respected; when belligerent nations, under the impossibility of making acquisitions upon us, will not lightly hazard the giving us provocation; when we may choose peace or war, as our interest, guided by justice, shall counsel.

Why forego the advantages of so peculiar a situation? Why quit our own to stand upon foreign ground? Why, by interweaving our destiny with that of any part of Europe, entangle our peace and prosperity in the toils of European ambition, rivalship, interest, humor, or caprice?

It is our true policy to steer clear of permanent alliances with any portion of the foreign world, so far, I mean, as we are now at liberty to do it, for let me not be understood as capable of patronizing infidelity to existing engagements. I hold the maxim no less applicable to public than to private affairs that honesty is always the best policy. I repeat, therefore, let those engagements be observed in their genuine sense. But in my opinion it is unnecessary and would be unwise to extend them.

Taking care always to keep ourselves by suitable establishments on a respectable defensive posture, we may safely trust to temporary alliances for extraordinary emergencies.

Harmony, liberal intercourse with all nations are recommended by policy, humanity, and interest. But even our commercial policy should hold an equal and impartial hand, neither seeking nor granting exclusive favors or preferences; consulting the natural course of things; diffusing and diversifying by gentle means the streams of commerce, but forcing nothing; establishing with powers so disposed, in order to give trade a stable course, to define the rights of our merchants, and to enable the Government to support them, conventional rules of intercourse, the best that present circumstances and mutual opinion will permit, but temporary and liable to be from time to time abandoned or varied as experience and circumstances shall dictate; constantly keeping in view that it is folly in one nation to look for disinterested favors from another; that it must pay with a portion of its independence for whatever it may accept under that character; that by such acceptance it may place itself in the condition of having given equivalents for nominal favors, and yet of being reproached with ingratitude for not giving more. There can be no greater error than to expect or calculate upon real favors from nation to nation. It is an illusion which experience must cure, which a just pride ought to discard. . . .

George Washington, Farewell Address, October 19, 1796.

The Monroe Doctrine (1823)

JAMES MONROE

During this speech President Monroe established a policy of exclusion that would prevent any further expansion of European powers in the Western Hemisphere. He stated that existing European colonies would be allowed to remain, but that further European imperialism in the Western hemisphere would no longer be tolerated by the U.S.A. The Doctrine was specifically directed toward Spain and Portugal, while the young U.S.A. looked to the British and their naval power to assist with the enforcement of the Doctrine. The Doctrine designated North and South America and the Caribbean basin as permanently residing within the "sphere of influence" of the U.S.A. The Doctrine also established the basis for an interventionist U.S. foreign policy in Latin America, one in which the U.S.A., as the dominant power, protected the region from hostile external powers. Unfortunately, the Monroe Doctrine has also served as a pretext for frequent U.S. military intervention throughout Latin America and the Caribbean, often to fulfill its own goals of regional hegemony.

Note: The Monroe Doctrine was expressed during President Monroe's seventh annual message to Congress, December 2, 1823:

. . . At the proposal of the Russian Imperial Government, made through the minister of the Emperor residing here, a full power and instructions have been transmitted to the minister of the United States at St. Petersburg to arrange, by amicable negotiation, the respective rights and interests of the two nations on the northwest coast of this continent. A similar proposal has been made by His Imperial Majesty to the Government of Great Britain, which has likewise been acceded to. The Government of the United States has been desirous by this friendly proceeding of manifesting the great value which they have invariably attached to the friendship of the Emperor and their solicitude to cultivate the best understanding with his Government. In the discussions to which this interest has given rise, and in the arrangements by which they may terminate, the occasion has been judged proper for asserting, as a principle in which the rights and interests of the United States are involved, that the American continents, by the free and independent condition which they have assumed and maintain, are henceforth not to be considered as subjects for future colonization by any European powers . . .

It was stated at the commencement of the last session that a great effort was then making in Spain and Portugal to improve the condition of the people of those countries, and that it appeared to be conducted with extraordinary moderation. It need scarcely be remarked that the results have been so far very different from what was then anticipated. Of events in that quarter of the globe, with which we have so much intercourse and from which we derive our origin, we have always been anxious and interested spectators. The citizens of the United States cherish sentiments the most friendly in favor of the liberty and happiness of their fellow-men on that side of the Atlantic. In the wars of the European powers in matters relating to themselves we have never taken any part, nor does it comport with our policy to do so. It is only when our rights are invaded or seriously menaced that we resent injuries or make preparation for our defense. With the movements in this hemisphere we are of necessity more immediately connected, and by causes which must be obvious to all enlightened and impartial observers. The political system of the allied powers is essentially different in this respect from that of America. This difference proceeds from that which exists in their respective Governments; and to the defense of our own, which has been achieved by the loss of so much blood and treasure, and matured by the wisdom of their most enlightened citizens, and under which we have enjoyed unexampled felicity, this whole nation is devoted. We owe it, therefore, to candor and to the amicable relations existing between the United States and those powers to declare that we should consider any attempt on their part to extend their system to any portion of this hemisphere as dangerous to our peace and safety. With the existing colonies or dependencies of any European power we have not interfered and shall not interfere. But with the Governments who have

declared their independence and maintain it, and whose independence we have, on great consideration and on just principles, acknowledged, we could not view any interposition for the purpose of oppressing them, or controlling in any other manner their destiny, by any European power in any other light than as the manifestation of an unfriendly disposition toward the United States. In the war between those new Governments and Spain we declared our neutrality at the time of their recognition, and to this we have adhered, and shall continue to adhere, provided no change shall occur which, in the judgment of the competent authorities of this Government, shall make a corresponding change on the part of the United States indispensable to their security.

The late events in Spain and Portugal shew that Europe is still unsettled. Of this important fact no stronger proof can be adduced than that the allied powers should have thought it proper, on any principle satisfactory to themselves, to have interposed by force in the internal concerns of Spain. To what extent such interposition may be carried, on the same principle, is a question in which all independent powers whose governments differ from theirs are interested, even those most remote, and surely none of them more so than the United States. Our policy in regard to Europe, which was adopted at an early stage of the wars which have so long agitated that quarter of the globe, nevertheless remains the same, which is, not to interfere in the internal concerns of any of its powers; to consider the government de facto as the legitimate government for us; to cultivate friendly relations with it, and to preserve those relations by a frank, firm, and manly policy, meeting in all instances the just claims of every power, submitting to injuries from none. But in regard to those continents circumstances are eminently and conspicuously different.

It is impossible that the allied powers should extend their political system to any portion of either continent without endangering our peace and happiness; nor can anyone believe that our southern brethren, if left to themselves, would adopt it of their own accord. It is equally impossible, therefore, that we should behold such interposition in any form with indifference. If we look to the comparative strength and resources of Spain and those new Governments, and their distance from each other, it must be obvious that she can never subdue them. It is still the true policy of the United States to leave the parties to themselves, in hope that other powers will pursue the same course. . . .

James Monroe, The Monroe Doctrine, December 2, 1823.

Corollary to the Monroe Doctrine (1904)

THEODORE ROOSEVELT

The Corollary is an extension of the Monroe Doctrine, amplifying the U.S.A.'s sphere of influence in the Western Hemisphere. Roosevelt proclaimed that the U.S.A. had the right to intervene in Latin American countries in cases of "flagrant and chronic wrongdoing." Essentially, the U.S.A. would henceforth intervene in unstable nations to prevent the European powers from intervening. This extension of U.S. power and commitments throughout the hemisphere made the U.S.A. the hegemonic force of the Americas. Ultimately, the Corollary led to multiple U.S. interventions throughout the Americas including invasions of Cuba, Haiti, Nicaragua, and the Dominican Republic. Many citizens in Latin American nations regarded the Corollary with distaste, and argued that it served as a pretext for a bellicose U.S. foreign policy of "Yankee Imperialism."

Note: (Excerpted from Theodore Roosevelt's Annual Message to Congress, December 6, 1904)

. . . It is not merely unwise, it is contemptible, for a nation, as for an individual, to use high-sounding language to proclaim its purposes, or to take positions which are ridiculous if unsupported by potential force, and then to refuse to provide this force. If there is no intention of providing and keeping the force necessary to back up a strong attitude, then it is far better not to assume such an attitude.

The steady aim of this Nation, as of all enlightened nations, should be to strive to bring ever nearer the day when there shall prevail throughout the world the peace of justice. There are kinds of peace which are highly undesirable, which are in the long run as destructive as any war. Tyrants and oppressors have many times made a wilderness and called it peace. Many times peoples who were slothful or timid or shortsighted, who had been enervated by ease or by luxury, or misled by false teachings, have shrunk in unmanly fashion from doing duty that was stern and that needed self-sacrifice, and have sought to hide from their own minds their shortcomings, their ignoble motives, by calling them love of peace. The peace of tyrannous terror, the peace of craven weakness, the peace of injustice, all these should be shunned as we shun unrighteous war. The goal to set before us as a nation, the goal which should be set before all mankind, is the attainment of the peace of justice, of the peace which comes when each nation is not merely safe-guarded in its own rights, but scrupulously recognizes and performs its duty toward others. Generally peace tells for righteousness; but if there is conflict between the two, then our fealty is due first to the cause of righteousness. Unrighteous wars are common, and unrighteous peace is rare; but both should be shunned. The right of freedom and the responsibility for the exercise of that right cannot be divorced. One of our great poets has well and finely said that freedom is not a gift that tarries long in the hands of cowards. Neither does it tarry long in the hands of those too slothful, too dishonest, or too unintelligent to exercise it. The eternal vigilance which is the price of liberty must be exercised, sometimes to guard against outside foes; although of course far more often to guard against our own selfish or thoughtless shortcomings.

If these self-evident truths are kept before us, and only if they are so kept before us, we shall have a clear idea of what our foreign policy in its larger aspects should be. It is our duty to remember that a nation has no more right to do injustice to another nation, strong or weak, than an individual has to do injustice to another individual; that the same moral law applies in one case as in the other. But we must also remember that it is as much the duty of the Nation to guard its own rights and its own interests as it is the duty of the individual so to do. Within the Nation the individual has now delegated this right to the State, that is, to the representative of all the individuals, and it is a maxim of the law that for every wrong there is a remedy. But in international law we have not advanced by any means as far as we have advanced in municipal law. There is as yet no judicial way of enforcing a right in international law. When one nation wrongs another or wrongs many others, there is no tribunal before which the wrongdoer can be brought. Either it is necessary supinely to acquiesce in the wrong, and thus put a premium upon brutality and aggression, or else it is necessary for the aggrieved nation valiantly to

stand up for its rights. Until some method is devised by which there shall be a degree of international control over offending nations, it would be a wicked thing for the most civilized powers, for those with most sense of international obligations and with keenest and most generous appreciation of the difference between right and wrong, to disarm. If the great civilized nations of the present day should completely disarm, the result would mean an immediate recrudescence of barbarism in one form or another. Under any circumstances a sufficient armament would have to be kept up to serve the purposes of international police; and until international cohesion and the sense of international duties and rights are far more advanced than at present, a nation desirous both of securing respect for itself and of doing good to others must have a force adequate for the work which it feels is allotted to it as its part of the general world duty. Therefore it follows that a self-respecting, just, and far-seeing nation should on the one hand endeavor by every means to aid in the development of the various movements which tend to provide substitutes for war, which tend to render nations in their actions toward one another, and indeed toward their own peoples, more responsive to the general sentiment of humane and civilized mankind; and on the other hand that it should keep prepared, while scrupulously avoiding wrongdoing itself, to repel any wrong, and in exceptional cases to take action which in a more advanced stage of international relations would come under the head of the exercise of the international police. A great free people owes it to itself and to all mankind not to sink into helplessness before the powers of evil.

It is not true that the United States feels any land hunger or entertains any projects as regards the other nations of the Western Hemisphere save such as are for their welfare. All that this country desires is to see the neighboring countries stable, orderly, and prosperous. Any country whose people conduct themselves well can count upon our hearty friendship. If a nation shows that it knows how to act with reasonable efficiency and decency in social and political matters, if it keeps order and pays its obligations, it need fear no interference from the United

States. Chronic wrongdoing, or an impotence which results in a general loosening of the ties of civilized society, may in America, as elsewhere, ultimately require intervention by some civilized nation, and in the Western Hemisphere the adherence of the United States to the Monroe Doctrine may force the United States, however reluctantly, in flagrant cases of such wrongdoing or impotence, to the exercise of an international police power. If every country washed by the Caribbean Sea would show the progress in stable and just civilization which with the aid of the Piatt Amendment Cuba has shown since our troops left the island, and which so many of the republics in both Americas are constantly and brilliantly showing, all question of interference by this Nation with their affairs would be at an end. Our interests and those of our southern neighbors are in reality identical. They have great natural riches, and if within their borders the reign of law and justice obtains, prosperity is sure to come to them. While they thus obey the primary laws of civilized society they may rest assured that they will be treated by us in a spirit of cordial and helpful sympathy. We would interfere with them only in the last resort, and then only if it became evident that their inability or unwillingness to do justice at home and abroad had violated the rights of the United States or had invited foreign aggression to the detriment of the entire body of American nations. It is a mere truism to say that every nation, whether in America or anywhere else, which desires to maintain its freedom, its independence, must ultimately realize that the right of such independence can not be separated from the responsibility of making good use of it.

In asserting the Monroe Doctrine, in taking such steps as we have taken in regard to Cuba, Venezuela, and Panama, and in endeavoring to circumscribe the theater of war in the Far East, and to secure the open door in China, we have acted in our own interest as well as in the interest of humanity at large. There are, however, cases in which, while our own interests are not greatly involved, strong appeal is made to our sympathies. Ordinarily it is very much wiser and more useful for us to concern ourselves with striving for our own moral and material betterment here at home than to concern ourselves with trying to better the condition of things in other nations. We have plenty of sins of our own to war against, and under ordinary circumstances we can do more for the general uplifting of humanity by striving with heart and soul to put a stop to civic corruption, to brutal lawlessness and violent race prejudices here at home than by passing resolutions and wrongdoing elsewhere. Nevertheless there are occasional crimes committed on so vast a scale and of such peculiar horror as to make us doubt whether it is not our manifest duty to endeavor at least to show our disapproval of the deed and our sympathy with those who have suffered by it. The cases must be extreme in which such a course is justifiable. There must be no effort made to remove the mote from our brother's eye if we refuse to remove the beam from our own. But in extreme cases action may be justifiable and proper. What form the action shall take must depend upon the circumstances of the case; that is, upon the degree of the atrocity and upon our power to remedy it. The cases in which we could interfere by force of arms as we interfered to put a stop to intolerable conditions in Cuba are necessarily very few. Yet it is not to be expected that a people like ours, which in spite of certain very obvious shortcomings, nevertheless as a whole shows by its consistent practice its belief in the principles of civil and religious liberty and of orderly freedom, a people among whom even the worst crime, like the crime of lynching, is never more than sporadic, so that individuals and not classes are molested in their fundamental rights—it is inevitable that such a nation should desire eagerly to give expression to its horror on an occasion like that of the massacre of the Jews in Kishenef, or when it witnesses such systematic and long-extended cruelty and oppression as the cruelty and oppression of which the Armenians have been the victims, and which have won for them the indignant pity of the civilized world.

Theodore Roosevelt, Corrollary to the Monroe Doctrine, December 6, 1904.

Fourteen Points Speech (1918)

WOODROW WILSON

During this speech, President Wilson assured the American people of the moral certainty of their fight against Germany and Austria-Hungary during World War I. In this expression of idealism Wilson emphasized the principles of free trade, freedom of the seas, disarmament, self-determination of peoples, democracy, and diplomatic transparency. The fourteen points also called for the creation of international institutions, notably the League of Nations that served as the predecessor to the modern United Nations. As such the Fourteen Points serve as the bedrock for modern Liberal institutionalism.

Gentlemen of the Congress . . .

It will be our wish and purpose that the processes of peace, when they are begun, shall be absolutely open and that they shall involve and permit henceforth no secret understandings of any kind. The day of conquest and aggrandizement is gone by; so is also the day of secret covenants entered into in the interest of particular governments and likely at some unlooked-for moment to upset the peace of the world. It is this happy fact, now clear to the view of every public man whose thoughts do not still linger in an age that is dead and gone, which makes it possible for every nation whose purposes are consistent with justice and the peace of the world to avow now or at any other time the objects it has in view.

We entered this war because violations of right had occurred which touched us to the quick and made the life of our own people impossible unless they were corrected and the world secured once for all against their recurrence. What we demand in this war, therefore, is nothing peculiar to ourselves. It is that the world be made fit and safe to live in; and particularly that it be made safe for every peace-loving nation which, like our own, wishes to live its own life, determine its own institutions, be assured of justice and fair dealing by the other peoples of the world as against force and selfish aggression. All the peoples of the world are in effect partners in this interest, and for our own part we see very clearly that unless justice be done to others it will not be done to us. The program of the world's peace, therefore, is our program; and that program, the only possible program, as we see it, is this:

I. Open covenants of peace, openly arrived at, after which there shall be no private international understandings of any kind but diplomacy shall proceed always frankly and in the public view.

II. Absolute freedom of navigation upon the seas, outside territorial waters, alike in peace and in war, except as the seas may be closed in whole or in part by international action for the enforcement of international covenants.

III. The removal, so far as possible, of all economic barriers and the establishment of an equality of trade conditions among all the nations consenting to the peace and associating themselves for its maintenance.

IV. Adequate guarantees given and taken that national armaments will be reduced to the lowest point consistent with domestic safety.

V. A free, open-minded, and absolutely impartial adjustment of all colonial claims, based upon a strict observance of the principle that in determining all such questions of sovereignty the interests of the populations concerned must have equal weight with the equitable claims of the government whose title is to be determined.

XIV. A general association of nations must be formed under specific covenants for the purpose of affording mutual guarantees of political independence and territorial integrity to great and small states alike.

In regard to these essential rectifications of wrong and assertions of right we feel ourselves to be intimate partners of all the governments and peoples associated together against the Imperialists. We cannot be separated in interest or divided in purpose. We stand together until the end.

For such arrangements and covenants we are willing to fight and to continue to fight until they are achieved; but only because we wish the right to prevail and desire a just and stable peace such as can be secured only by removing the chief provocations to war, which this program does not remove. We have no jealousy of German greatness, and there is nothing in this program that impairs it. We grudge her no achievement or distinction of learning or of pacific enterprise such as have made her record very bright and very enviable. We do not wish to injure her or to block in any way her legitimate influence or power. We do not wish to fight her either with arms or with hostile arrangements of trade if she is willing to associate herself with us and the other peace-loving nations of the world in covenants of justice and law and fair dealing. We wish her only to accept a place of equality among the peoples of the world,—the new world in which we now live,—instead of a place of mastery.

Neither do we presume to suggest to her any alteration or modification of her institutions. But it is necessary, we must frankly say, and necessary as a preliminary to any intelligent dealings with her on our part, that we should know whom her spokesmen speak for when they speak to us, whether for the Reichstag majority or for the military party and the men whose creed is imperial domination.

We have spoken now, surely, in terms too concrete to admit of any further doubt or question. An evident principle runs through the whole program I have outlined. It is the principle of justice to all peoples and nationalities, and their right to live on equal terms of liberty and safety with one another, whether they be strong or weak. Unless this principle be made its foundation no part of the structure of international justice can stand. The people of the United States could act upon no other principle; and to the vindication of this principle they are ready to devote their lives, their honor, and everything that they possess. The moral climax of this the culminating and final war for human liberty has come, and they are ready to put their own strength, their own highest purpose, their own integrity and devotion to the test.

Woodrow Wilson, Fourteen Points, January 8, 1918.

The Sources of Soviet Conduct[1]

"X" [GEORGE KENNAN]

George Kennan, a U.S. diplomat and historian, argued that the Marxist-Leninist ideology of the Soviet Union was inherently expansionist in nature. Therefore, the U.S.A. and its allies should try to contain Soviet expansion through the use of hard power at key geopolitical points. This article articulated the U.S. doctrine of "containment" during the early years of the Cold War era, and illustrated the Truman Administration's hard line policy toward Moscow. It is typically understood as the basis of a Realist stratagem to use force to ensure Soviet containment.

The political personality of Soviet power as we know it today is the product of ideology and circumstances: ideology inherited by the present Soviet leaders from the movement in which they had their political origin, and circumstances of the power which they now have exercised for nearly three decades in Russia. There can be few tasks of psychological analysis more difficult than to try to trace the interaction of these two forces and the relative role of each in the determination of official Soviet conduct. Yet the attempt must be made if that conduct is to be understood and effectively countered.

It is difficult to summarize the set of ideological concepts with which the Soviet leaders came into power. Marxian ideology, in its Russian-Communist projection, has always been in process of subtle evolution. The materials on which it bases itself are extensive and complex. But the outstanding features of Communist thought as it existed in 1916 may perhaps be summarized as follows: (a) that the central factor in the life of man, the factor which determines the character of public life and the "physiognomy of society," is the system by which material goods are produced and exchanged; (b) that the capitalist system of production is a nefarious one which inevitably leads to the exploitation of the working class by the capital-owning class and is incapable of developing adequately the economic resources of society or of distributing fairly the material goods produced by human labor; (c) that capitalism contains the seeds of its own destruction and must, in view of the inability of the capital-owning class to adjust itself to economic change, result eventually and inescapably in a revolutionary transfer of power to the working class; and (d) that imperialism, the final phase of capitalism, leads directly to war and revolution.

The rest may be outlined in Lenin's own words: "Unevenness of economic and political development is the inflexible law of capitalism. It follows from this that the victory of Socialism may come originally in a few capitalist countries or even in a single capitalist country. The victorious proletariat of that country, having expropriated the capitalists and having organized Socialist production at home, would rise against the remaining capitalist world, drawing to itself in the process the oppressed classes of other countries."[2] It must be noted that there was no assumption that capitalism would perish without proletarian revolution. A final push was needed from a revolutionary proletariat movement in order to tip over the tottering structure. But it was regarded as inevitable that sooner or later that push be given.

The circumstances of the immediate postrevolution period—the existence in Russia of civil war and foreign intervention, together with the obvious fact that the Communists represented only a tiny minority of the Russian people—made the establishment of dictatorial power a necessity. The experiment with "war Communism" and the abrupt attempt to eliminate private production and trade had unfortunate economic consequences and caused further bitterness against the new revolutionary regime. While the temporary relaxation of the effort to communize Russia, represented by the New Economic Policy, alleviated some of this economic distress and thereby served its purpose, it also made it evident that the "capitalistic sector of society" was still prepared to profit at once from any relaxation of governmental pressure, and would, if permitted to continue to exist, always constitute a powerful opposing element to the Soviet regime and a serious rival for influence in the country. Somewhat the same situation prevailed with respect to the individual peasant who, in his own small way, was also a private producer.

Lenin, had he lived, might have proved a great enough man to reconcile these conflicting forces to the ultimate benefit of Russian society, though this is questionable. But be that as it may, Stalin, and those whom he led in the struggle for succession to Lenin's position of leadership, were not the men to tolerate rival political forces in the sphere of power which they coveted. Their sense of insecurity was too great. Their particular brand of fanaticism, unmodified by any of the Anglo-Saxon traditions of compromise, was too fierce and too jealous to envisage any permanent sharing of power. From the Russian-Asiatic world out of which they had emerged they carried with them a skepticism as to the possibilities of permanent and peaceful coexistence of rival forces. Easily persuaded of their own doctrinaire "rightness," they insisted on the submission or destruction of all competing power.

Now the outstanding circumstance concerning the Soviet regime is that down to the present day this process of political consolidation has never been completed and the men in the Kremlin have continued to be predominantly absorbed with the struggle to secure and make absolute the power which they seized in November 1917. They have endeavored to secure it primarily against forces at home, within Soviet society itself. But they have also endeavored to secure it against the outside world. For ideology, as we have seen, taught them that the outside world was hostile and that it was their duty eventually to overthrow the political forces beyond their borders. The powerful hands of Russian history and tradition reached up to sustain them in this feeling. Finally, their own aggressive intransigence with respect to the outside world began to find its own reaction; and they were soon forced, to use another Gibbonesque phrase, "to chastise the contumacy" which they themselves had provoked. It is an undeniable privilege of every man to prove himself right in the thesis that the world is his enemy; for if lie reiterates it frequently enough and makes it the background of his conduct he is bound eventually to be right.

Now it lies in the nature of the mental world of the Soviet leaders, as well as in the character of their ideology, that no opposition to them can be officially recognized as having any merit or justification whatsoever. Such opposition can flow, in theory, only from the hostile and incorrigible forces of dying capitalism. As long as remnants of capitalism were officially recognized as existing in Russia, it was possible to place on them, as an internal element, part of the blame for the maintenance of a dictatorial form of society. But as these remnants were liquidated, little by little, this justification fell away; and when it was indicated officially that they had been finally destroyed, it disappeared altogether. And this fact created one of the most basic of the compulsions which came to act upon the Soviet régime: since capitalism no longer existed in Russia and since it could not be admitted that there could be serious or widespread opposition to the Kremlin springing spontaneously from the liberated masses under its authority, it became necessary to justify the retention of the dictatorship by stressing the menace of capitalism abroad.

This began at an early date. In 1924 Stalin specifically defended the retention of the "organs of suppression," meaning, among others, the army and the secret police, on the ground that "as long as there is a capitalist encirclement there will be danger of intervention with all the consequences that flow from that danger." In accordance with that theory, and from that time on, all internal opposition forces in Russia have consistently been portrayed as the agents of foreign forces of reaction antagonistic to Soviet power.

Now the maintenance of this pattern of Soviet power, namely, the pursuit of unlimited authority domestically, accompanied by the cultivation of the semi-myth of implacable foreign hostility, has gone far to shape the actual machinery of Soviet power as we know it today. Internal organs of administration which did not serve this purpose withered on the vine. Organs which did serve this purpose became vastly swollen. The security of Soviet power came to rest on the iron discipline of the Party, on the severity and ubiquity of the secret police, and on the uncompromising economic monopolism of the state. The "organs of suppression," in which the Soviet leaders had sought security from rival forces, became in large measure the masters of those whom they were designed to serve. Today the major part of the structure of Soviet power is committed to the perfection of the dictatorship and to the maintenance of the concept of Russia as in a state of siege, with the enemy lowering beyond the walls. And the millions of human beings who form that part of the structure of power must defend at all costs this concept of Russia's position, for without it they are themselves superfluous.

II

So much for the historical background. What does it spell in terms of the political personality of Soviet power as we know it today?

Of the original ideology, nothing has been officially junked. Belief is maintained in the basic badness of capitalism, in the inevitability of its destruction, in the obligation of the proletariat to assist in that destruction and to take power into its own hands. But stress has come to be laid primarily on those concepts which relate most specifically to the Soviet regime itself: to its position as the sole truly Socialist regime in a dark and misguided world, and to the relationships of power within it.

The first of these concepts is that of the innate antagonism between capitalism and Socialism. We have seen how deeply that concept has become imbedded in foundations of Soviet power. It has profound implications for Russia's conduct as a member of international society. It means that there can never be on Moscow's side any sincere assumption of a community of aims between the Soviet Union and powers which are regarded as capitalist. It must invariably be assumed in Moscow that the aims of the capitalist world are antagonistic to the Soviet regime, and therefore to the interests of the peoples it controls. If the Soviet Government occasionally sets its signature to documents which would indicate the contrary, this is to be regarded as a tactical manoeuvre permissible in dealing with the enemy (who is without honor) and should be taken in the spirit of *caveat emptor*. Basically, the antagonism remains. It is postulated. And from it flow many of the phenomena which we find disturbing in the Kremlin's conduct of foreign policy:

the secretiveness, the lack of frankness, the duplicity, the wary suspiciousness, and the basic unfriendliness of purpose. These phenomena are there to stay, for the foreseeable future. There can be variations of degree and of emphasis. When there is something the Russians want from us, one or the other of these features of their policy may be thrust temporarily into the background; and when that happens there will always be Americans who will leap forward with gleeful announcements that "the Russians have changed," and some who will even try to take credit for having brought about such "changes." But we should not be misled by tactical manoeuvres. These characteristics of Soviet policy, like the postulate from which they flow, are basic to the internal nature of Soviet power, and will be with us, whether in the foreground or the background, until the internal nature of Soviet power is changed.

This means that we are going to continue for a long time to find the Russians difficult to deal with. It does not mean that they should be considered as embarked upon a do-or-die program to overthrow our society by a given date. The theory of the inevitability of the eventual fall of capitalism has the fortunate connotation that there is no hurry about it. The forces of progress can take their time in preparing the final *coup de grâce*. Meanwhile, what is vital is that the "Socialist fatherland"—that oasis of power which has been already won for Socialism in the person of the Soviet Union—should be cherished and defended by all good Communists at home and abroad, its fortunes promoted, its enemies badgered and confounded. The promotion of premature, "adventuristic" revolutionary projects abroad which might embarrass Soviet power in any way would be an inexcusable, even a counter-revolutionary act. The cause of Socialism is the support and promotion of Soviet power, as defined in Moscow.

This brings us to the second of the concepts important to contemporary Soviet outlook. That is the infallibility of the Kremlin. The Soviet concept of power, which permits no focal points of organization outside the Party itself, requires that the Party leadership remain in theory the sole repository of truth. For if truth were to be found elsewhere, there would be justification for its expression in organized activity. But it is precisely that which the Kremlin cannot and will not permit.

This means that truth is not a constant but is actually created, for all intents and purposes, by the Soviet leaders themselves. It may vary from week to week, from month to month. It is nothing absolute and immutable—nothing which flows from objective reality. It is only the most recent manifestation of the wisdom of those in whom the ultimate wisdom is supposed to reside, because they represent the logic of history.

But we have seen that the Kremlin is under no ideological compulsion to accomplish its purposes in a hurry. Like the Church, it is dealing in ideological concepts which are of long-term validity, and it can afford to be patient. It has no right to risk the existing achievements of the revolution for the sake of vain baubles of the future. The very teachings of Lenin himself require great caution and flexibility in the pursuit of Communist purposes. Again, these precepts are fortified by the lessons of Russian history: of centuries of obscure battles between nomadic forces over the stretches of a vast unfortified plain. Here caution, circumspection, flexibility and deception are the valuable qualities; and their value finds natural appreciation in the Russian or the oriental mind. Thus the Kremlin has no compunction about retreating in the face of superior force. And being under the compulsion of no timetable, it does not get panicky under the necessity for such retreat. Its political action is a fluid stream which moves constantly, wherever it is permitted to move, toward a given goal. Its main concern is to make sure that it has filled every nook and cranny available to it in the basin of world power. But if it finds unassailable barriers in its path, it accepts these philosophically and accommodates itself to them. The main thing is that there should always be pressure, unceasing constant pressure, toward the desired goal. There is no trace of any feeling in Soviet psychology that that goal must be reached at any given time.

These considerations make Soviet diplomacy at once easier and more difficult to deal with than the diplomacy of individual aggressive leaders like Napoleon and Hitler. On the one hand it is more sensitive to contrary force, more ready to yield on individual sectors of the diplomatic front when that force is felt to be too strong, and thus more rational in the logic and rhetoric of power. On the other hand it cannot be easily defeated or discouraged by a single victory on the part of its opponents. And the patient persistence by which it is animated means that it can be effectively countered not by sporadic acts which represent the momentary whims of democratic opinion but only by highly intelligent long-range policies on the part of Russia's adversaries—policies no less steady in their purpose, and no less variegated and resourceful in their application, than those of the Soviet Union itself.

In these circumstances it is clear that the main element of any United States policy toward the Soviet Union must be that of a long-term, patient but firm and vigilant containment of Russian expansive tendencies. It is important to note, however, that such a policy has nothing to do with outward histrionics: with threats or blustering or superfluous gestures of outward "toughness." While the Kremlin is basically flexible in its reaction to political realities, it is by no means unamenable to considerations of prestige. Like almost any other government, it can be placed by tactless and threatening gestures in a position where it cannot afford to yield even though this might be dictated by its sense of realism. The Russian leaders are keen judges of human psychology, and as such they are highly conscious that loss of temper and of self-control is never a source of strength in political affairs. They are quick to exploit such evidences of weakness. For these reasons, it is a *sine qua non* of successful dealing with Russia that the foreign government in question should remain at all times cool and collected and that its demands on Russian policy should be put forward in such a manner as to leave the way open for a compliance not too detrimental to Russian prestige.

III

In the light of the above, it will be clearly seen that the Soviet pressure against the free institutions of the Western world is something that can be contained by the adroit and vigilant application of counter-force at a series of constantly shifting geographical and political points, corresponding to the shifts and manoeuvres of Soviet policy, but which cannot be charmed or talked out of existence. The Russians look forward to a duel of infinite duration, and they see that already they have scored great successes. It must be borne in mind that there was a time when the Communist Party represented far more of a minority in the sphere of Russian national life than Soviet power today represents in the world community.

But if ideology convinces the rulers of Russia that truth is on their side and that they can therefore afford to wait, those of us on whom that ideology has no claim are free to examine objectively the validity or that premise. The Soviet thesis not only implies complete lack of control by the West over its own economic destiny, it likewise assumes Russian unity, discipline and patience over an infinite period. Let us bring this apocalyptic vision down to earth, and suppose that the Western world finds the strength and resourcefulness to contain Soviet power over a period of ten to fifteen years. What does that spell for Russia itself?

The Soviet leaders, taking advantage of the contributions of modern technique to the arts of despotism, have solved the question of obedience within the confines of their power. Few challenge their authority; and even those who do are unable to make that challenge valid as against the organs of suppression of the state.

The Kremlin has also proved able to accomplish its purpose of building up in Russia, regardless of the interests of the inhabitants, an industrial foundation of heavy metallurgy, which is, to be sure, not yet complete but which is nevertheless continuing to grow and is approaching those of the other major industrial countries. All of this, however, both the maintenance of internal political security and the building of heavy industry, has been carried out at a terrible cost in human life and in human hopes and energies. It has necessitated the use of forced labor on a scale unprecedented in modern times under conditions of peace. It has involved the neglect or abuse of other phases of Soviet economic life, particularly agriculture, consumers' goods production, housing and transportation.

Thus the future of Soviet power may not be by any means as secure as Russian capacity for self-delusion would make it appear to the men in the Kremlin. That they can keep power themselves, they have demonstrated. That they can quietly and easily turn it over to others remains to be proved. Meanwhile, the hardships of their rule and the vicissitudes of international life have taken a heavy toll of the strength and hopes of the great people on whom their power rests. It is curious to note that the ideological power of Soviet authority is strongest today in areas beyond the frontiers of Russia, beyond the reach of its police power. But the possibility remains (and in the opinion of this writer it is a strong one) that Soviet power, like the capitalist world of its conception, bears within it the seeds of its own decay, and that sprouting of these seeds is well advanced.

IV

It is clear that the United States cannot expect in the foreseeable future to enjoy political intimacy with the Soviet regime. It must continue to regard the Soviet Union as a rival, not a partner, in the political arena. It must continue to expect that Soviet policies will reflect no abstract love of peace and stability, no real faith in the possibility of a permanent happy coexistence of the Socialist and capitalist worlds, but rather a cautious, persistent pressure toward the disruption and weakening of all rival influence and rival power.

Balanced against this are the facts that Russia, as opposed to the Western world in general, is still by far the weaker party, that Soviet policy is highly flexible, and that Soviet society may well contain deficiencies which will eventually weaken its own total potential. This would of itself warrant the United States entering with reasonable confidence upon a policy of firm containment, designed to confront the Russians with unalterable counter-force at every point where they show signs of encroaching upon the interests of a peaceful and stable world.

But in actuality the possibilities for American policy are by no means limited to holding the line and hoping for the best. It is entirely possible for the United States to influence by its actions the internal developments, both within Russia and throughout the international Communist movement, by which Russian policy is largely determined. This is not only a question of the modest measure of informational activity which this government can conduct in the Soviet Union and elsewhere, although this, too, is important. It is rather a question of the degree to which the United States can create among the peoples of the world generally the impression of a country which knows what it wants, which is coping successfully with the problems of its internal life and with the responsibilities of a World Power, and which has a spiritual vitality capable of holding its own among the major ideological currents of the time. To the extent that such an impression can be created and maintained, the aims of Russian Communism must appear sterile and quixotic, the hopes and enthusiasm of Moscow's supporters must wane, and added strain must be imposed on the Kremlin's foreign policies. For the palsied decrepitude of the capitalist world is the keystone of Communist philosophy. Even the failure of the United States to experience the early economic depression which the ravens of the Red Square have been predicting with such complacent confidence since hostilities ceased would have deep and important repercussions throughout the Communist world.

By the same token, exhibitions of indecision, disunity and internal disintegration within this country have an exhilarating effect on the whole Communist movement. At each evidence of these tendencies, a thrill of hope and excitement goes through the Communist world; a new jauntiness can be noted in the Moscow tread; new groups of foreign supporters climb on to what they can only view as the band wagon of international politics; and Russian pressure increases all along the line in international affairs.

It would be an exaggeration to say that American behavior unassisted and alone could exercise a power of life and death over the Communist movement and bring about the early fall of Soviet power in Russia. But the United States has it in its power to increase enormously the strains under which Soviet policy must operate, to force upon the Kremlin a far greater degree of moderation and circumspection than it has had to observe in recent years, and in this way to promote tendencies which must eventually find their outlet in either the breakup or the gradual mellowing of Soviet power. For no mystical, Messianic movement—and particularly not that of the Kremlin—can face frustration indefinitely without eventually adjusting itself in one way or another to the logic of that state of affairs.

Thus the decision will really fall in large measure in this country itself. The issue of Soviet-American relations is in essence a test of the overall worth of the United States as a nation among nations. To avoid destruction the United States need only measure up to its own best traditions and prove itself worthy of preservation as a great nation.

Surely, there was never a fairer test of national quality than this. In the light of these circumstances, the thoughtful observer of Russian-American relations will find no cause for complaint in the Kremlin's challenge to American society. He will rather experience a certain gratitude to a Providence which, by providing the American people with this implacable challenge has made their entire security as a nation dependent on their pulling themselves together and accepting the responsibilities of moral and political leadership that history plainly intended them to bear.

Notes

1. X [George Kennan], "The Sources of Soviet Conduct," *Foreign Affairs* 25 (July 1947) 566–582.
2. "Concerning the Slogans of the United States of Europe." August 1915. Official Soviet edition of Lenin's works.

Fireside Chat 19: On the War with Japan (1941)

FRANKLIN DELANO ROOSEVELT

Following the Japanese sneak attack on Pearl Harbor of 7 December 1941, President Roosevelt explained to the American people the dire need to make war on Japan, and to check the nefarious designs of the other Axis powers (Germany and Italy). To support his case Roosevelt laid out a timeline of acts of aggression by the Axis powers against peaceful nations, casting America's enemies as lawless bandits bent on global conquest. The Second World War was a classic example of the benign use of U.S. military power to stop the destructive expansion of the Axis powers, and to put an end to their genocidal ambitions.

A mericans:

The sudden criminal attacks perpetrated by the Japanese in the Pacific provide the climax of a decade of international immorality.

Powerful and resourceful gangsters have banded together to make war upon the whole human race. Their challenge has now been flung at the United States of America. The Japanese have treacherously violated the longstanding peace between us. Many American soldiers and sailors have been killed by enemy action. American ships have been sunk; American airplanes have been destroyed.

The Congress and the people of the United States have accepted that challenge.

Together with other free peoples, we are now fighting to maintain our right to live among our world neighbors in freedom, in common decency, without fear of assault.

I have prepared the full record of our past relations with Japan, and it will be submitted to the Congress. It begins with the visit of Commodore Parry to Japan eighty-eight years ago. It ends with the visit of two Japanese emissaries to the Secretary of State last Sunday, an hour after Japanese forces had loosed their bombs and machine guns against our flag, our forces and our citizens.

I can say with utmost confidence that no Americans today or a thousand years hence, need feel anything but pride in our patience and in our efforts through all the years toward achieving a peace in the Pacific which would be fair and honorable to every nation, large or small. And no honest person, today or a thousand years hence, will be able to suppress a sense of indignation and horror at the treachery committed by the military dictators of Japan, under the very shadow of the flag of peace borne by their special envoys in our midst.

The course that Japan has followed for the past ten years in Asia has paralleled the course of Hitler and Mussolini in Europe and in Africa. Today, it has become far more than a parallel. It is actual collaboration so well calculated that all the continents of the world, and all the oceans, are now considered by the Axis strategists as one gigantic battlefield.

In 1931, ten years ago, Japan invaded Manchukuo—without warning.

In 1935, Italy invaded Ethiopia—without warning.

In 1938, Hitler occupied Austria—without warning.

In 1939, Hitler invaded Czechoslovakia—without warning.

Later in '39, Hitler invaded Poland—without warning.

In 1940, Hitler invaded Norway, Denmark, the Netherlands, Belgium and Luxembourg—without warning.

In 1940, Italy attacked France and later Greece—without warning.

And this year, in 1941, the Axis Powers attacked Yugoslavia and Greece and they dominated the Balkans—without warning.

In 1941, also, Hitler invaded Russia—without warning.

And now Japan has attacked Malaya and Thailand—and the United States—without warning.

It is all of one pattern.

We are now in this war. We are all in it—all the way. Every single man, woman and child is a partner in the most tremendous undertaking of our American history. We must share together the bad news and the good news, the defeats and the victories—the changing fortunes of war.

So far, the news has been all bad. We have suffered a serious setback in Hawaii. Our forces in the Philippines, which include the brave people of that Commonwealth, are taking punishment, but are defending themselves vigorously. The reports from Guam and Wake and Midway Islands are still confused, but we must be prepared for the announcement that all these three outposts have been seized.

The casualty lists of these first few days will undoubtedly be large. I deeply feel the anxiety of all of the families of the men in our armed forces and the relatives of people in cities which have been bombed. I can only give them my solemn promise that they will get news just as quickly as possible.

This Government will put its trust in the stamina of the American people, and will give the facts to the public just as soon as two conditions have been fulfilled: first, that the information has been definitely and officially confirmed; and, second, that the release of the information at the time it is received will not prove valuable to the enemy directly or indirectly.

It must be remembered by each and every one of us that our free and rapid communication these days must be greatly restricted in wartime. It is not possible to receive full and speedy and accurate reports front distant areas of combat. This is particularly true where naval operations are concerned. For in these days of the marvels of the radio it is often impossible for the commanders of various units to report their activities by radio at all, for the very simple reason that this information would become available to the enemy and would disclose their position and their plan of defense or attack.

Now a word about the recent past and the future. A year and a half has elapsed since the fall of France, when the whole world first realized the mechanized might which the Axis nations had been building up for so many years. America has used that year and a half to great advantage. Knowing that the attack might reach us in all too short a time, we immediately began greatly to increase our industrial strength and our capacity to meet the demands of modern warfare.

Precious months were gained by sending vast quantities of our war material to the nations of the world still able to resist Axis aggression. Our policy rested on the fundamental truth that the defense of any country resisting Hitler or Japan was in the long run the defense of our own country. That policy has been justified. It has given us time, invaluable time, to build our American assembly lines of production.

Assembly lines are now in operation. Others are being rushed to completion. A steady stream of tanks and planes, of guns and ships and shells and equipment—that is what these eighteen months have given us.

But it is all only a beginning of what still has to be done. We must be set to face a long war against crafty and powerful bandits. The attack at Pearl Harbor can be repeated at any one of many points, points in both oceans and along both our coast lines and against all the rest of the Hemisphere.

It will not only be a long war, it will be a hard war. That is the basis on which we now lay all our plans. That is the yardstick by which we measure what we shall need and demand; money, materials, doubled and quadrupled production—ever-increasing. The production must be not only for our own Army and Navy and air forces. It must reinforce the other armies and navies and air forces fighting the Nazis and the war lords of Japan throughout the Americas and throughout the world.

I repeat that the United States can accept no result save victory, final and complete. Not only must the shame of Japanese treachery be wiped out, but the sources of international brutality, wherever they exist, must be absolutely and finally broken.

In my Message to the Congress yesterday I said that we "will make very certain that this form of treachery shall never endanger us again." In order to achieve that certainty, we must begin the great task that is before us by abandoning once and for all the illusion that we can ever again isolate ourselves from the rest of humanity.

In these past few years—and, most violently, in the past three days—we have learned a terrible lesson.

It is our obligation to our dead—it is our sacred obligation to their children and to our children—that we must never forget what we have learned.

And what we have learned is this:

There is no such thing as security for any nation—or any individual—in a world ruled by the principles of gangsterism.

There is no such thing as impregnable defense against powerful aggressors who sneak up in the dark and strike without warning.

We have learned that our ocean-girt hemisphere is not immune from severe attack—that we cannot measure our safety in terms of miles on any map any more.

We may acknowledge that our enemies have performed a brilliant feat of deception, perfectly timed and executed with great skill. It was a thoroughly dishonorable deed, but we must face the fact that modern warfare as conducted in the Nazi manner is a dirty business. We don't like it—we didn't want to get in it—but we are in it and we're going to fight it with everything we've got.

I do not think any American has any doubt of our ability to administer proper punishment to the perpetrators of these crimes.

Your Government knows that for weeks Germany has been telling Japan that if Japan did not attack the United States, Japan would not share in dividing the spoils with Germany when peace came. She was promised by Germany that if she came in she would receive the complete and perpetual control of the whole of the Pacific area—and that means not only the Far East, but also all of the Islands in the Pacific, and also a stranglehold on the west coast of North, Central and South America.

We know also that Germany and Japan are conducting their military and naval operations in accordance with a joint plan. That plan considers all peoples and nations which are not helping the Axis powers as common enemies of each and every one of the Axis powers.

That is their simple and obvious grand strategy. And that is why the American people must realize that it can be matched only with similar grand strategy. We must realize for example that Japanese successes against the United States in the Pacific are helpful to German operations in Libya; that any German success against the Caucasus is inevitably an assistance to Japan in her operations against the Dutch East Indies; that a German attack against Algiers or Morocco opens the way to a German attack against South America and the Canal.

On the other side of the picture, we must learn also to know that guerilla warfare against the Germans in, let us say Serbia or Norway, helps us; that a successful Russian offensive against the Germans helps us; and that British successes on land or sea in any part of the world strengthen our hands.

Remember always that Germany and Italy, regardless of any formal declaration of war, consider themselves at war with the United States at this moment just as much as they consider themselves at war with Britain or Russia. And Germany puts all the other Republics of the Americas into the same category of enemies. The people of our sister Republics of this Hemisphere can be honored by that fact.

The true goal we seek is far above and beyond the ugly field of battle. When we resort to force, as now we must, we are determined that this force shall be directed toward ultimate good as well as against immediate evil. We Americans are not destroyers—we are builders.

We are now in the midst of a war, not for conquest, not for vengeance, but for a world in which this nation, and all that this nation represents, will be safe for our children. We expect to eliminate the danger from Japan, but it would serve us ill if we accomplished that and found that the rest of the world was dominated by Hitler and Mussolini.

So we are going to win the war and we are going to win the peace that follows.

And in the difficult hours of this day—through dark days that may be yet to come—we will know that the vast majority of the members of the human race are on our side. Many of them are fighting with us. All of them are praying for us. But, in representing our cause, we represent theirs as well—our hope and their hope for liberty under God.

Franklin Delano Roosevelt, Fireside Chat 19: On the War with Japan, December 9, 1941

The Truman Doctrine (1947)

HARRY S. TRUMAN

This speech by Truman is often regarded as the formal beginning of the Cold War between the U.S.A. and the Soviet Union. Truman declared that the U.S.A. would supply economic and military aid to Greece and Turkey to suppress communist insurgencies in those nations. This was done to prevent these nations from falling into the orbit of the Soviet Union. The Truman Doctrine shifted U.S. foreign policy toward Moscow from a state of détente to one of active containment. This latter policy was largely based on the arguments of George Kennan.

Mr. President, Mr. Speaker, Members of the Congress of the United States:

The gravity of the situation which confronts the world today necessitates my appearance before a joint session of the Congress. The foreign policy and the national security of this country are involved.

One aspect of the present situation, which I wish to present to you at this time for your consideration and decision, concerns Greece and Turkey.

The United States has received from the Greek Government an urgent appeal for financial and economic assistance. Preliminary reports from the American Economic Mission now in Greece and reports from the American Ambassador in Greece corroborate the statement of the Greek Government that assistance is imperative if Greece is to survive as a free nation.

I do not believe that the American people and the Congress wish to turn a deaf ear to the appeal of the Greek Government.

Greece is not a rich country. Lack of sufficient natural resources has always forced the Greek people to work hard to make both ends meet. Since 1940, this industrious and peace loving country has suffered invasion, four years of cruel enemy occupation, and bitter internal strife.

When forces of liberation entered Greece they found that the retreating Germans had destroyed virtually all the railways, roads, port facilities, communications, and merchant marine. More than a thousand villages had been burned. Eighty-five per cent of the children were tubercular. Livestock, poultry, and draft animals had almost disappeared. Inflation had wiped out practically all savings.

As a result of these tragic conditions, a militant minority, exploiting human want and misery, was able to create political chaos which, until now, has made economic recovery impossible.

The very existence of the Greek state is today threatened by the terrorist activities of several thousand armed men, led by Communists, who defy the government's authority at a number of points, particularly along the northern boundaries. A Commission appointed by the United Nations Security Council is at present investigating disturbed conditions in northern Greece and alleged border violations along the frontier between Greece on the one hand and Albania, Bulgaria, and Yugoslavia on the other.

Meanwhile, the Greek Government is unable to cope with the situation. The Greek army is small and poorly equipped. It needs supplies and equipment if it is to restore the authority of the government throughout Greek territory. Greece must have assistance if it is to become a self-supporting and self-respecting democracy.

The United States must supply that assistance. We have already extended to Greece certain types of relief and economic aid but these are inadequate.

There is no other country to which democratic Greece can turn.

No other nation is willing and able to provide the necessary support for a democratic Greek government.

The British Government, which has been helping Greece, can give no further financial or economic aid after March 31. Great Britain finds itself under the necessity of reducing or liquidating its commitments in several parts of the world, including Greece.

We have considered how the United Nations might assist in this crisis. But the situation is an urgent one requiring immediate action and the United Nations and its related organizations are not in a position to extend help of the kind that is required.

It is important to note that the Greek Government has asked for our aid in utilizing effectively the financial and other assistance we may give to Greece, and in improving its public administration. It is of the utmost importance that we supervise the use of any funds made available to Greece; in such a manner that each dollar spent will count toward making Greece self-supporting, and will help to build an economy in which a healthy democracy can flourish.

The Greek Government has been operating in an atmosphere of chaos and extremism. It has made mistakes. The extension of aid by this country does not mean that the United States condones everything that the Greek Government has done or will do. We have condemned in the past, and we condemn now, extremist measures of the right or the left. We have in the past advised tolerance, and we advise tolerance now.

Greece's neighbor, Turkey, also deserves our attention.

The future of Turkey as an independent and economically sound state is clearly no less important to the freedom-loving peoples of the world than the future of Greece. The circumstances in which Turkey finds itself today are considerably different from those of Greece. Turkey has been spared the disasters that have beset Greece. And during the war, the United States and Great Britain furnished Turkey with material aid.

One of the primary objectives of the foreign policy of the United States is the creation of conditions in which we and other nations will be able to work out a way of life free from coercion. This was a fundamental issue in the war with Germany and Japan. Our victory was won over countries which sought to impose their will, and their way of life, upon other nations.

To ensure the peaceful development of nations, free from coercion, the United States has taken a leading part in establishing the United Nations. The United Nations is designed to make possible lasting freedom and independence for all its members. We shall not realize our objectives, however, unless we are willing to help free peoples to maintain their free institutions and their national integrity against aggressive movements that seek to impose upon them totalitarian regimes. This is no more than a frank recognition that totalitarian regimes imposed on free peoples, by direct or indirect aggression, undermine the foundations of international peace and hence the security of the United States.

The peoples of a number of countries of the world have recently had totalitarian regimes forced upon them against their will. The government of the United States has made frequent protests against coercion and intimidation, in violation of the Yalta agreement, in Poland, Rumania, and Bulgaria. I must also state that in a number of other countries there have been similar developments.

At the present moment in world history nearly every nation must choose between alternative ways of life. The choice is too often not a free one.

One way of life is based upon the will of the majority, and is distinguished by free institutions, representative government, free elections, guarantees of individual liberty, freedom of speech and religion, and freedom from political oppression.

The second way of life is based upon the will of a minority forcibly imposed upon the majority. It relies upon terror and oppression, a controlled press and radio; fixed elections, and the suppression of personal freedoms.

I believe that it must be the policy of the United States to support free peoples who are resisting attempted subjugation by armed minorities or by outside pressures.

I believe that we must assist free peoples to work out their own destinies in their own way.

I believe that our help should be primarily through economic and financial aid which is essential to economic stability and orderly political processes.

The world is not static, and the status quo is not sacred. But we cannot allow changes in the status quo in violation of the Charter of the United Nations by such methods as coercion, or by such subterfuges as political infiltration. In helping free and independent nations to maintain their freedom, the United States will be giving effect to the principles of the Charter of the United Nations.

It is necessary only to glance at a map to realize that the survival and integrity of the Greek nation are of grave importance in a much wider situation. If Greece should fall under the control of an armed minority, the effect upon its neighbor, Turkey, would be immediate and serious. Confusion and disorder might well spread throughout the entire Middle East.

Moreover, the disappearance of Greece as an independent state would have a profound effect upon those countries in Europe whose peoples are struggling against great difficulties to maintain their freedoms and their independence while they repair the damages of war.

It would be an unspeakable tragedy if these countries, which have struggled so long against overwhelming odds, should lose that victory for which they sacrificed so much. Collapse of free institutions and loss of independence would be disastrous not only for them but for the world. Discouragement and possibly failure would quickly be the lot of neighboring peoples striving to maintain their freedom and independence.

Should we fail to aid Greece and Turkey in this fateful hour, the effect will be far reaching to the West as well as to the East.

We must take immediate and resolute action.

I therefore ask the Congress to provide authority for assistance to Greece and Turkey in the amount of $400,000,000 for the period ending June 30, 1948. In requesting these funds, I have taken into consideration the maximum amount of relief assistance which would be furnished to Greece out of the $350,000,000 which I recently requested that the Congress authorize for the prevention of starvation and suffering in countries devastated by the war.

In addition to funds, I ask the Congress to authorize the detail of American civilian and military personnel to Greece and Turkey, at the request of those countries, to assist in the tasks of reconstruction, and for the purpose of supervising the use of such financial and material assistance as may be furnished. I recommend that authority also be provided for the instruction and training of selected Greek and Turkish personnel.

Finally, I ask that the Congress provide authority which will permit the speediest and most effective use, in terms of needed commodities, supplies, and equipment, of such funds as may be authorized.

This is a serious course upon which we embark.

I would not recommend it except that the alternative is much more serious. The United States contributed $341,000,000,000 toward winning World War II. This is an investment in world freedom and world peace.

The assistance that I am recommending for Greece and Turkey amounts to little more than 1 tenth of 1 percent of this investment. It is only common sense that we should safeguard this investment and make sure that it was not in vain.

The seeds of totalitarian regimes are nurtured by misery and want. They spread and grow in the evil soil of poverty and strife. They reach their full growth when the hope of a people for a better life has died. We must keep that hope alive.

The free peoples of the world look to us for support in maintaining their freedoms.

If we falter in our leadership, we may endanger the peace of the world—and we shall surely endanger the welfare of our own nation.

Harry S. Truman, The Truman Doctrine, March 12, 1947.

Farewell Address (1961)

DWIGHT D. EISENHOWER

In this speech, President Eisenhower warned the American people of the growing power of the "military-industrial complex," which consisted of powerful domestic interests that sought to undermine American democracy, and he warned of the undue influence of the military. Eisenhower argued that this hawkish alliance of domestic factions (i.e., industrial, political, and military interest groups) would drive the U.S.A. into unnecessary wars, enriching themselves at the expense of the American people, and representing a threat to American democracy.

My fellow Americans:

Three days from now, after half a century in the service of our country, I shall lay down the responsibilities of office as, in traditional and solemn ceremony, the authority of the Presidency is vested in my successor.

This evening I come to you with a message of leave-taking and farewell, and to share a few final thoughts with you, my countrymen.

We now stand ten years past the midpoint of a century that has witnessed four major wars among great nations. Three of these involved our own country. Despite these holocausts America is today the strongest, the most influential and most productive nation in the world. Understandably proud of this pre-eminence, we yet realize that America's leadership and prestige depend, not merely upon our unmatched material progress, riches and military strength, but on how we use our power in the interests of world peace and human betterment.

III

Throughout America's adventure in free government, our basic purposes have been to keep the peace; to foster progress in human achievement, and to enhance liberty, dignity and integrity among people and among nations. To strive for less would be unworthy of a free and religious people. Any failure traceable to arrogance, or our lack of comprehension or readiness to sacrifice would inflict upon us grievous hurt both at home and abroad.

Progress toward these noble goals is persistently threatened by the conflict now engulfing the world. It commands our whole attention, absorbs our very beings. We face a hostile ideology global in scope, atheistic in character, ruthless in purpose, and insidious in method. Unhappily the danger it poses promises to be of indefinite duration. To meet it successfully, there is called for, not so much the emotional and transitory sacrifices of crisis, but rather those which enable us to carry forward steadily, surely, and without complaint the burdens of a prolonged and complex struggle—with liberty at stake. Only thus shall we remain, despite every provocation, on our charted course toward permanent peace and human betterment.

Crises there will continue to be. In meeting them, whether foreign or domestic, great or small, there is a recurring temptation to feel that some spectacular and costly action could become the miraculous solution to all current difficulties. A huge increase in newer elements of our defense; development of unrealistic programs to cure every ill in agriculture; a dramatic expansion in basic and applied research—these and many other possibilities, each possibly promising in itself, may be suggested as the only way to the road we wish to travel.

But each proposal must be weighed in the light of a broader consideration: the need to maintain balance in and among national programs—balance between the private and the public economy, balance between cost and hoped for advantage—balance between the clearly necessary and the comfortably desirable; balance between our essential requirements as a nation and the duties imposed by the nation upon the individual; balance between action of the moment and the national welfare of the future. Good judgment seeks balance and progress; lack of it eventually finds imbalance and frustration.

The record of many decades stands as proof that our people and their government have, in the main, understood these truths and have responded to them well, in the face of stress and threat. But threats, new in kind or degree, constantly arise. I mention two only.

IV

A vital element in keeping the peace is our military establishment. Our arms must be mighty, ready for instant action, so that no potential aggressor may be tempted to risk his own destruction.

Our military organization today bears little relation to that known by any of my predecessors in peace time, or indeed by the fighting men of World War II or Korea.

Until the latest of our world conflicts, the United States had no armaments industry. American makers of plowshares could, with time and as required, make swords as well. But now we can no longer risk emergency improvisation of national defense; we have been compelled to create a permanent armaments industry of vast proportions. Added to this, three and a half million men and women are directly engaged in the defense establishment. We annually spend on military security more than the net income of all United State corporations.

This conjunction of an immense military establishment and a large arms industry is new in the American experience. The total influence—economic, political, even spiritual—is felt in every city, every Statehouse, every office of the Federal government. We recognize the imperative need for this development. Yet we must not fail to comprehend its grave implications. Our toil, resources and livelihood are all involved; so is the very structure of our society.

In the councils of government, we must guard against the acquisition of unwarranted influence, whether sought or unsought, by the military-industrial complex. The potential for the disastrous rise of misplaced power exists and will persist.

We must never let the weight of this combination endanger our liberties or democratic processes. We should take nothing for granted only an alert and knowledgeable citizenry can compel the proper meshing of huge industrial and military machinery of defense with our peaceful methods and goals, so that security and liberty may prosper together.

Akin to, and largely responsible for the sweeping changes in our industrial-military posture, has been the technological revolution during recent decades.

In this revolution, research has become central; it also becomes more formalized, complex, and costly. A steadily increasing share is conducted for, by, or at the direction of, the Federal government.

Today, the solitary inventor, tinkering in his shop, has been overshadowed by task forces of scientists in laboratories and testing fields. In the same fashion, the free university, historically the fountainhead of free ideas and scientific discovery, has experienced a revolution in the conduct of

research. Partly because of the huge costs involved, a government contract becomes virtually a substitute for intellectual curiosity. For every old blackboard there are now hundreds of new electronic computers.

The prospect of domination of the nation's scholars by Federal employment, project allocations, and the power of money is ever present and is gravely to be regarded.

Yet, in holding scientific research and discovery in respect, as we should, we must also be alert to the equal and opposite danger that public policy could itself become the captive of a scientific-technological elite.

It is the task of statesmanship to mold, to balance, and to integrate these and other forces, new and old, within the principles of our democratic system—ever aiming toward the supreme goals of our free society.

Dwight D. Eisenhower, Farewell Address, January 17, 1961.

State of the Union Address (1980)

January 23, 1980

JIMMY CARTER

The Carter Doctrine was a warning by President Carter that any outside power that tried to gain dominion over the oilfields of the Persian Gulf would be seen as a direct threat to U.S. national security interests, and would be repelled by various means including the use of force. It was based on the (inaccurate) premise that the Soviet invasion of Afghanistan in 1979 was an attempt by Moscow to project force into the Persian Gulf and seize the oil fields of the region. The Carter Doctrine explicitly notes the centrality of Persian Gulf oil to U.S. national security, and it articulates Washington's long-standing desire to control the oil resources of the region, and ensure the flow of oil to the global market. Following the articulation of the Carter Doctrine in 1979, the U.S. established the Rapid Deployment Joint Task Force (RDJTF; March 1980). The RDJTF then became Central Command (Centcom) under President Reagan in January 1983. Centcom subsequently expanded as it protected

U.S. interests in the Gulf region throughout the Tanker War in the mid-1980s (when both Iraq and Iran were firing on oil tankers). Thereafter Centcom assumed a dominant role in the region, clearly in evidence during Operation Desert Shield and Desert Storm in 1990/91, and the later invasion of Iraq by U.S. forces in 2003. Unfortunately, the Doctrine's interpretation by Carter's successors has resulted in long term, detrimental impacts on U.S. foreign policy such as the intense militarization of the Persian Gulf by U.S. forces.

This last few months has not been an easy time for any of us. As we meet tonight, it has never been more clear that the state of our Union depends on the state of the world. And tonight, as throughout our own generation, freedom and peace in the world depend on the state of our Union.

The 1980s have been born in turmoil, strife, and change. This is a time of challenge to our interests and our values and it's a time that tests our wisdom and our skills.

At this time in Iran, fifty Americans are still held captive, innocent victims of terrorism and anarchy. Also at this moment, massive Soviet troops are attempting to subjugate the fiercely independent and deeply religious people of Afghanistan. These two acts—one of international terrorism and one of military aggression—present a serious challenge to the United States of America and indeed to all the nations of the world. Together, we will meet these threats to peace.

I'm determined that the United States will remain the strongest of all nations, but our power will never be used to initiate a threat to the security of any nation or to the rights of any human being. We seek to be and to remain secure—a nation at peace in a stable world. But to be secure we must face the world as it is.

Three basic developments have helped to shape our challenges: the steady growth and increased projection of Soviet military power beyond its own borders; the overwhelming dependence of the Western democracies on oil supplies from the Middle East; and the press of social and religious and economic and political change in the many nations of the developing world, exemplified by the revolution in Iran.

Each of these factors is important in its own right. Each interacts with the others. All must be faced together, squarely and courageously. We will face these challenges, and we will meet them with the best that is in us. And we will not fail.

In response to the abhorrent act in Iran, our Nation has never been aroused and unified so greatly in peacetime. Our position is clear. The United States will not yield to blackmail.

We continue to pursue these specific goals: first, to protect the present and long-range interests of the United States; secondly, to preserve the lives of the American hostages and to secure, as quickly as possible, their safe release, if possible, to avoid bloodshed which might further endanger the lives of our fellow citizens; to enlist the help of other nations in condemning this act of violence, which is shocking and violates the moral and the legal standards of a civilized world; and also to convince and to persuade the Iranian leaders that the real danger to their nation lies in the North, in the Soviet Union and from the Soviet troops now in Afghanistan, and that the unwarranted Iranian quarrel with the United States hampers their response to this far greater danger to them.

We superpowers also have the responsibility to exercise restraint in the use of our great military force. The integrity and the independence of weaker nations must not be threatened. They must know that in our presence they are secure.

But now the Soviet Union has taken a radical and an aggressive new step. It's using its great military power against a relatively defenseless nation. The implications of the Soviet invasion of Afghanistan could pose the most serious threat to the peace since the Second World War.

The vast majority of nations on Earth have condemned this latest Soviet attempt to extend its colonial domination of others and have demanded the immediate withdrawal of Soviet troops. The Moslem world is especially and justifiably outraged by this aggression against an Islamic people. No action of a world power has ever been so quickly and so overwhelmingly condemned. But verbal condemnation is not enough. The Soviet Union must pay a concrete price for their aggression.

The region which is now threatened by Soviet troops in Afghanistan is of great strategic importance: It contains more than two-thirds of the world's exportable oil. The Soviet effort to dominate Afghanistan has brought Soviet military forces to within 300 miles of the Indian Ocean and close to the Straits of Hormuz, a waterway through which most of the world's oil must flow. The Soviet Union is now attempting to consolidate a strategic position, therefore, that poses a grave threat to the free movement of Middle East oil.

This situation demands careful thought, steady nerves, and resolute action, not only for this year but for many years to come. It demands collective efforts to meet this new threat to security in the Persian Gulf and in Southwest Asia. It demands the participation of all those who rely on oil from the Middle East and who are concerned with global peace and stability. And it demands consultation and close cooperation with countries in the area which might be threatened.

Meeting this challenge will take national will, diplomatic and political wisdom, economic sacrifice, and, of course, military capability. We must call on the best that is in us to preserve the security of this crucial region.

Let our position be absolutely clear: An attempt by any outside force to gain control of the Persian Gulf region will be regarded as an assault on the vital interests of the United States of America, and such an assault will be repelled by any means necessary, including military force.

In repressive regimes, popular frustrations often have no outlet except through violence. But when peoples and their governments can approach their problems together through open, democratic methods, the basis for stability and peace is far more solid and far more enduring. That is why our support for human rights in other countries is in our own national interest as well as part of our own national character.

Peace—a peace that preserves freedom— remains America's first goal. In the coming years, as a mighty nation we will continue to pursue peace. But to be strong abroad we must be strong at home. And in order to be strong, we must continue to face up to the difficult issues that confront us as a nation today.

The crises in Iran and Afghanistan have dramatized a very important lesson: Our excessive dependence on foreign oil is a clear and present danger to our Nation's security. The need has never been more urgent. At long last, we must have a clear, comprehensive energy policy for the United States.

As you well know, I have been working with the Congress in a concentrated and persistent way over the past 3 years to meet this need. We have made progress together. But Congress must act promptly now to complete final action on this vital energy legislation. Our Nation will then have a major conservation effort, important initiatives to develop solar power, realistic pricing based on the true value of oil, strong incentives for the production of coal and other fossil fuels in the United States, and our Nation's most massive peacetime investment in the development of synthetic fuels.

The American people are making progress in energy conservation. Last year we reduced overall petroleum consumption by 8 percent and gasoline consumption by 5 percent below what it was the year before. Now we must do more.

After consultation with the Governors, we will set gasoline conservation goals for each of the 50 States, and I will make them mandatory if these goals are not met.

I've established an import ceiling for 1980 of 8.2 million barrels a day—well below the level of foreign oil purchases in 1977. I expect our imports to be much lower than this, but the ceiling will be enforced by an oil import fee if necessary. I'm prepared to lower these imports still further if the other oil-consuming countries will join us in a fair and mutual reduction. If we have a serious shortage, I will not hesitate to impose mandatory gasoline rationing immediately.

The single biggest factor in the inflation rate last year, the increase in the inflation rate last year, was from one cause: the skyrocketing prices of OPEC oil. We must take whatever actions are necessary to reduce our dependence on foreign oil—and at the same time reduce inflation.

As individuals and as families, few of us can produce energy by ourselves. But all of us can conserve energy—every one of us, every day of our lives. Tonight I call on you—in fact, all the people of America—to help our Nation. Conserve energy. Eliminate waste. Make 1980 indeed a year of energy conservation.

Our material resources, great as they are, are limited. Our problems are too complex for simple slogans or for quick solutions. We cannot solve them without effort and sacrifice. Walter Lippmann once reminded us, "You took the good things for granted. Now you must earn them again. For every right that you cherish, you have a duty which you must fulfill. For every good which you wish to preserve, you will have to sacrifice your comfort and your ease. There is nothing for nothing any longer."

Together as one people, let us work to build our strength at home, and together as one indivisible union, let us seek peace and security throughout the world.

Together let us make of this time of challenge and danger a decade of national resolve and of brave achievement.

Thank you very much.

Jimmy Carter, The Carter Doctrine, January 23, 1980.

Remarks on East-West Relations at the Brandenburg Gate in West Berlin (1987)

June 12, 1987

RONALD REAGAN

In the waning years of the Cold War, President Reagan challenged Soviet Premier Gorbachev to tear down the Berlin Wall. The Wall was a powerful symbol of the communist oppression of the peoples of Eastern Europe. Reagan's speech stands as an important moment in the history of the Cold War, as the Wall was finally opened by the East German government on 9 November 1989, allowing for democracy to spread and flourish among the peoples of Eastern Europe.

Behind me stands a wall that encircles the free sectors of this city, part of a vast system of barriers that divides the entire continent of Europe. From the Baltic, south, those barriers cut across Germany in a gash of barbed wire, concrete, dog runs, and guardtowers. Farther south, there may be no visible, no obvious wall. But there remain armed guards and checkpoints all the same—still a restriction on the right to travel, still an instrument to impose upon ordinary men and women the will of a totalitarian state. Yet it is here in Berlin where the wall emerges most clearly; here, cutting across your city, where the news photo and the television screen have imprinted this brutal division of a continent upon the mind of the world. Standing before the Brandenburg Gate, every man is a German, separated from his fellow men. Every man is a Berliner, forced to look upon a scar.

President von Weizsacker has said: "The German question is open as long as the Brandenburg Gate is closed." Today I say: As long as this gate is closed, as long as this scar of a wall is permitted to stand, it is not the German question alone that remains open, but the question of freedom for all mankind. Yet I do not come here to lament. For I find in Berlin a message of hope, even in the shadow of this wall, a message of triumph.

In the 1950s, Khrushchev predicted: "We will bury you." But in the West today, we see a free world that has achieved a level of prosperity and well-being unprecedented in all human history. In the Communist world, we see failure, technological backwardness, declining standards of health, even want of the most basic kind—too little food. Even today, the Soviet Union still cannot feed itself. After these four decades, then, there stands before the entire world one great and inescapable conclusion: Freedom leads to prosperity. Freedom replaces the ancient hatreds among the nations with comity and peace. Freedom is the victor.

And now the Soviets themselves may, in a limited way, be coming to understand the importance of freedom. We hear much from Moscow about a new policy of reform and openness. Some political prisoners have been released. Certain foreign news broadcasts are no longer being jammed. Some economic enterprises have been permitted to operate with greater freedom from state control. Are these the beginnings of profound changes in the Soviet state? Or are they token gestures, intended to raise false hopes in the West, or to strengthen the Soviet system without changing it? We welcome change and openness; for we believe that freedom and security go together, that the advance of human liberty can only strengthen the cause of world peace.

There is one sign the Soviets can make that would be unmistakable, that would advance dramatically the cause of freedom and peace. General Secretary Gorbachev, if you seek peace, if you seek prosperity for the Soviet Union and Eastern Europe,

if you seek liberalization: Come here to this gate! Mr. Gorbachev, open this gate! Mr. Gorbachev, tear down this wall!

I understand the fear of war and the pain of division that afflict this continent—and I pledge to you my country's efforts to help overcome these burdens. To be sure, we in the West must resist Soviet expansion. So we must maintain defenses of unassailable strength. Yet we seek peace; so we must strive to reduce arms on both sides. Beginning 10 years ago, the Soviets challenged the Western alliance with a grave new threat, hundreds of new and more deadly SS-20 nuclear missiles, capable of striking every capital in Europe. The Western alliance responded by committing itself to a counterdeployment unless the Soviets agreed to negotiate a better solution; namely, the elimination of such weapons on both sides.

For many months, the Soviets refused to bargain in earnestness. As the alliance, in turn, prepared to go forward with its counterdeployment, there were difficult days—days of protests like those during my 1982 visit to this city—and the Soviets later walked away from the table.

But through it all, the alliance held firm. And I invite those who protested then—I invite those who protest today—to mark this fact: Because we remained strong, the Soviets came back to the table. And because we remained strong, today we have within reach the possibility, not merely of limiting the growth of arms, but of eliminating, for the first time, an entire class of nuclear weapons from the face of the Earth. As I speak, NATO ministers are meeting in Iceland to review the progress of our proposals for eliminating these weapons. At the talks in Geneva, we have also proposed deep cuts in strategic offensive weapons. And the Western allies have likewise made far-reaching proposals to reduce the danger of conventional war and to place a total ban on chemical weapons.

While we pursue these arms reductions, I pledge to you that we will maintain the capacity to deter Soviet aggression at any level at which it might occur. And in cooperation with many of our allies, the United States is pursuing the Strategic Defense Initiative—research to base deterrence not on the threat of offensive retaliation, but on defenses that truly defend; on systems, in short, that will not target populations, but shield them. By these means we seek to increase the safety of Europe and all the world. But we must remember a crucial fact: East and West do not mistrust each other because we are armed; we are armed because we mistrust each other. And our differences are not about weapons but about liberty. When President Kennedy spoke at the City Hall those 24 years ago, freedom was encircled, Berlin was under siege. And today, despite all the pressures upon this city, Berlin stands secure in its liberty. And freedom itself is transforming the globe.

Perhaps this gets to the root of the matter, to the most fundamental distinction of all between East and West. The totalitarian world produces backwardness because it does such violence to the spirit, thwarting the human impulse to create, to enjoy, to worship. The totalitarian world finds even symbols of love and of worship an affront. Years ago, before the East Germans began rebuilding their churches, they erected a secular structure: the television tower at Alexander Platz. Virtually ever since, the authorities have been working to correct what they view as the tower's one major flaw, treating the glass sphere at the top with paints and chemicals of every kind. Yet even today when the Sun strikes that sphere—that sphere that towers over all Berlin—the light makes the sign of the cross. There in Berlin, like the city itself, symbols of love, symbols of worship, cannot be suppressed.

As I looked out a moment ago from the Reichstag, that embodiment of German unity, I noticed words crudely spray-painted upon the wall, perhaps by a young Berliner, "This wall will fall. Beliefs become reality." Yes, across Europe, this wall will fall. For it cannot withstand faith; it cannot withstand truth. The wall cannot withstand freedom.

Ronald Reagan, Speech at Brandenburg Gate, June 12, 1987.

Graduation Speech at West Point (2002)

United States Military Academy West Point, New York

GEORGE W. BUSH

This speech at West Point by George W. Bush marks the beginning of the Bush Doctrine. Bush argued that the realities of the post-Cold War era called for America to undertake pre-emptive strikes against its adversaries. Thus, the U.S.A. abandoned its historical policy of containment for one of pre-emption or preventive war under the Bush Administration. The speech also justified American hegemony, unilateralism, and the use of power by the U.S.A. to attack nations that harbored terrorists.

This war will take many turns we cannot predict. Yet I am certain of this: Wherever we carry it, the American flag will stand not only for our power, but for freedom. (Applause.) Our nation's cause has always been larger than our nation's defense. We fight, as we always fight, for a just peace—a peace that favors human liberty. We will defend the peace against threats from terrorists and tyrants. We will preserve the peace by building good relations among the great powers. And we will extend the peace by encouraging free and open societies on every continent.

Building this just peace is America's opportunity, and America's duty. From this day forward, it is your challenge, as well, and we will meet this challenge together. (Applause.) You will wear the uniform of a great and unique country. America has no empire to extend or Utopia to establish. We wish for others only what we wish for ourselves—safety from violence, the rewards of liberty, and the hope for a better life.

In defending the peace, we face a threat with no precedent. Enemies in the past needed great armies and great industrial capabilities to endanger the American people and our nation. The attacks of September the 11th required a few hundred thousand dollars in the hands of a few dozen evil and deluded men. All of the chaos and suffering they caused came at much less than the cost of a single tank. The dangers have not passed. This government and the American people are on watch, we are ready, because we know the terrorists have more money and more men and more plans.

The gravest danger to freedom lies at the perilous crossroads of radicalism and technology. When the spread of chemical and biological and nuclear weapons, along with ballistic missile technology—when that occurs, even weak states and small groups could attain a catastrophic power to strike great nations. Our enemies have declared this very intention, and have been caught seeking these terrible weapons. They want the capability to blackmail us, or to harm us, or to harm our friends—and we will oppose them with all our power. (Applause.)

For much of the last century, America's defense relied on the Cold War doctrines of deterrence and containment. In some cases, those strategies still apply. But new threats also require new thinking. Deterrence—the promise of massive retaliation against nations—means nothing against shadowy terrorist networks with no nation or citizens to defend. Containment is not possible when unbalanced dictators with weapons of mass destruction

can deliver those weapons on missiles or secretly provide them to terrorist allies.

We cannot defend America and our friends by hoping for the best. We cannot put our faith in the word of tyrants, who solemnly sign nonproliferation treaties, and then systemically break them. If we wait for threats to fully materialize, we will have waited too long. (Applause.)

Homeland defense and missile defense are part of stronger security, and they're essential priorities for America. Yet the war on terror will not be won on the defensive. We must take the battle to the enemy, disrupt his plans, and confront the worst threats before they emerge. (Applause.) In the world we have entered, the only path to safety is the path of action. And this nation will act. (Applause.)

Our security will require the best intelligence, to reveal threats hidden in caves and growing in laboratories. Our security will require modernizing domestic agencies such as the FBI, so they're prepared to act, and act quickly, against danger. Our security will require transforming the military you will lead—a military that must be ready to strike at a moment's notice in any dark corner of the world. And our security will require all Americans to be forward looking and resolute, to be ready for preemptive action when necessary to defend our liberty and to defend our lives. (Applause.)

The work ahead is difficult. The choices we will face are complex. We must uncover terror cells in 60 or more countries, using every tool of finance, intelligence and law enforcement. Along with our friends and allies, we must oppose proliferation and confront regimes that sponsor terror, as each case requires. Some nations need military training to fight terror, and we'll provide it. Other nations oppose terror, but tolerate the hatred that leads to terror—and that must change. (Applause.) We will send diplomats where they are needed, and we will send you, our soldiers, where you're needed. (Applause.)

All nations that decide for aggression and terror will pay a price. We will not leave the safety of America and the peace of the planet at the mercy of a few mad terrorists and tyrants. (Applause.)

We will lift this dark threat from our country and from the world.

Because the war on terror will require resolve and patience, it will also require firm moral purpose. In this way our struggle is similar to the Cold War. Now, as then, our enemies are totalitarians, holding a creed of power with no place for human dignity. Now, as then, they seek to impose a joyless conformity, to control every life and all of life.

America confronted imperial communism in many different ways—diplomatic, economic, and military. Yet moral clarity was essential to our victory in the Cold War. When leaders like John F. Kennedy and Ronald Reagan refused to gloss over the brutality of tyrants, they gave hope to prisoners and dissidents and exiles, and rallied free nations to a great cause.

Some worry that it is somehow undiplomatic or impolite to speak the language of right and wrong. I disagree. (Applause.) Different circumstances require different methods, but not different moralities. (Applause.) Moral truth is the same in every culture, in every time, and in every place. Targeting innocent civilians for murder is always and everywhere wrong. (Applause.) Brutality against women is always and everywhere wrong. (Applause.) There can be no neutrality between justice and cruelty, between the innocent and the guilty. We are in a conflict between good and evil, and America will call evil by its name. (Applause.) By confronting evil and lawless regimes, we do not create a problem, we reveal a problem. And we will lead the world in opposing it. (Applause.)

As we defend the peace, we also have an historic opportunity to preserve the peace. We have our best chance since the rise of the nation state in the 17th century to build a world where the great powers compete in peace instead of prepare for war. The history of the last century, in particular, was dominated by a series of destructive national rivalries that left battlefields and graveyards across the Earth. Germany fought France, the Axis fought the Allies, and then the East fought the West, in proxy wars and tense standoffs, against a backdrop of nuclear Armageddon.

Competition between great nations is inevitable, but armed conflict in our world is not. More and more, civilized nations find ourselves on the same side—united by common dangers of terrorist violence and chaos. America has, and intends to keep, military strengths beyond challenge—(applause)—thereby, making the destabilizing arms races of other eras pointless, and limiting rivalries to trade and other pursuits of peace.

Today the great powers are also increasingly united by common values, instead of divided by conflicting ideologies. The United States, Japan and our Pacific friends, and now all of Europe, share a deep commitment to human freedom, embodied in strong alliances such as NATO. And the tide of liberty is rising in many other nations.

Generations of West Point officers planned and practiced for battles with Soviet Russia. I've just returned from a new Russia, now a country reaching toward democracy, and our partner in the war against terror. (Applause.) Even in China, leaders are discovering that economic freedom is the only lasting source of national wealth. In time, they will find that social and political freedom is the only true source of national greatness. (Applause.)

When the great powers share common values, we are better able to confront serious regional conflicts together, better able to cooperate in preventing the spread of violence or economic chaos. In the past, great power rivals took sides in difficult regional problems, making divisions deeper and more complicated. Today, from the Middle East to South Asia, we are gathering broad international coalitions to increase the pressure for peace. We must build strong and great power relations when times are good; to help manage crisis when times are bad. America needs partners to preserve the peace, and we will work with every nation that shares this noble goal. (Applause.)

And finally, America stands for more than the absence of war. We have a great opportunity to extend a just peace, by replacing poverty, repression, and resentment around the world with hope of a better day. Through most of history, poverty was persistent, inescapable, and almost universal. In the last few decades, we've seen nations from Chile to South Korea build modern economies and freer societies, lifting millions of people out of despair and want. And there's no mystery to this achievement.

The 20th century ended with a single surviving model of human progress, based on non-negotiable demands of human dignity, the rule of law, limits on the power of the state, respect for women and private property and free speech and equal justice and religious tolerance. America cannot impose this vision—yet we can support and reward governments that make the right choices for their own people. In our development aid, in our diplomatic efforts, in our international broadcasting, and in our educational assistance, the United States will promote moderation and tolerance and human rights. And we will defend the peace that makes all progress possible.

When it comes to the common rights and needs of men and women, there is no clash of civilizations. The requirements of freedom apply fully to Africa and Latin America and the entire Islamic world. The peoples of the Islamic nations want and deserve the same freedoms and opportunities as people in every nation. And their governments should listen to their hopes. (Applause.)

A truly strong nation will permit legal avenues of dissent for all groups that pursue their aspirations without violence. An advancing nation will pursue economic reform, to unleash the great entrepreneurial energy of its people. A thriving nation will respect the rights of women, because no society can prosper while denying opportunity to half its citizens. Mothers and fathers and children across the Islamic world, and all the world, share the same fears and aspirations. In poverty, they struggle. In tyranny, they suffer. And as we saw in Afghanistan, in liberation they celebrate. (Applause.)

America has a greater objective than controlling threats and containing resentment. We will work for a just and peaceful world beyond the war on terror.

George W. Bush, Graduation Speech at West Point, June 1, 2002.

Speech on Libya (2011)

"A Responsibility to Act" March 28, 2011

BARACK H. OBAMA

In this speech, President Obama argued that the U.S.A. has the responsibility to intervene in other nations to protect civilians from genocide or war crimes. It was made in response to the violence that Moammar Qaddafi directed against the democratic uprising in Libya during the Arab Spring revolutions of 2011. During the Libyan intervention of 2011, the U.S.A. worked with NATO allies (France and Britain in particular) to destroy much of the military infrastructure of the Qaddafi regime. Ultimately, the NATO intervention tipped the balance of power in favor of the prodemocracy forces. Unfortunately, the US has not always acted in such fashion to prevent the violent actions of other predatory governments against their own citizens (e.g., the Syrian civil war of 2011–13).

Note: The text of President Obama's speech Monday night at the National Defense University at Fort McNair in Washington, DC.

Tonight, I'd like to update the American people on the international effort that we have led in Libya—what we've done, what we plan to do, and why this matters to us.

For generations, the United States of America has played a unique role as an anchor of global security and as an advocate for human freedom. Mindful of the risks and costs of military action, we are naturally reluctant to use force to solve the world's many challenges. But when our interests and values are at stake, we have a responsibility to act. That's what happened in Libya over the course of these last six weeks.

Libya sits directly between Tunisia and Egypt—two nations that inspired the world when their people rose up to take control of their own destiny. For more than four decades, the Libyan people have been ruled by a tyrant—Moammar Gadhafi. He has denied his people freedom, exploited their wealth, murdered opponents at home and abroad, and terrorized innocent people around the world—including Americans who were killed by Libyan agents.

Last month, Gadhafi's grip of fear appeared to give way to the promise of freedom. In cities and towns across the country, Libyans took to the streets to claim their basic human rights. As one Libyan said, "For the first time we finally have hope that our nightmare of 40 years will soon be over."

Faced with this opposition, Gadhafi began attacking his people. As President, my immediate concern was the safety of our citizens, so we evacuated our embassy and all Americans who sought our assistance. Then we took a series of swift steps in a matter of days to answer Gadhafi's aggression. We froze more than $33 billion of Gadhafi's regime's assets. Joining with other nations at the United Nations Security Council, we broadened our sanctions, imposed an arms embargo, and enabled Gadhafi and those around him to be held accountable for their crimes. I made it clear that Gadhafi

had lost the confidence of his people and the legitimacy to lead, and I said that he needed to step down from power.

In the face of the world's condemnation, Gadhafi chose to escalate his attacks, launching a military campaign against the Libyan people. Innocent people were targeted for killing. Hospitals and ambulances were attacked. Journalists were arrested, sexually assaulted, and killed. Supplies of food and fuel were choked off. Water for hundreds of thousands of people in Misurata was shut off. Cities and towns were shelled, mosques were destroyed, and apartment buildings reduced to rubble. Military jets and helicopter gunships were unleashed upon people who had no means to defend themselves against assaults from the air.

Confronted by this brutal repression and a looming humanitarian crisis, I ordered warships into the Mediterranean. European allies declared their willingness to commit resources to stop the killing. The Libyan opposition and the Arab League appealed to the world to save lives in Libya. And so at my direction, America led an effort with our allies at the United Nations Security Council to pass a historic resolution that authorized a no-fly zone to stop the regime's attacks from the air, and further authorized all necessary measures to protect the Libyan people.

Ten days ago, having tried to end the violence without using force, the international community offered Gadhafi a final chance to stop his campaign of killing, or face the consequences. Rather than stand down, his forces continued their advance, bearing down on the city of Benghazi, home to nearly 700,000 men, women and children who sought their freedom from fear.

At this point, the United States and the world faced a choice. Gadhafi declared he would show "no mercy" to his own people. He compared them to rats, and threatened to go door to door to inflict punishment. In the past, we have seen him hang civilians in the streets, and kill over a thousand people in a single day. Now we saw regime forces on the outskirts of the city. We knew that if we wanted—if we waited one more day, Benghazi, a city nearly the size of Charlotte, could suffer a massacre that would have reverberated across the region and stained the conscience of the world.

It was not in our national interest to let that happen. I refused to let that happen. And so nine days ago, after consulting the bipartisan leadership of Congress, I authorized military action to stop the killing and enforce U.N. Security Council Resolution 1973.

We struck regime forces approaching Benghazi to save that city and the people within it. We hit Gadhafi's troops in neighboring Ajdabiya, allowing the opposition to drive them out. We hit Gadhafi's air defenses, which paved the way for a no-fly zone. We targeted tanks and military assets that had been choking off towns and cities, and we cut off much of their source of supply. And tonight, I can report that we have stopped Gadhafi's deadly advance.

In this effort, the United States has not acted alone. Instead, we have been joined by a strong and growing coalition. This includes our closest allies—nations like the United Kingdom, France, Canada, Denmark, Norway, Italy, Spain, Greece, and Turkey—all of whom have fought by our sides for decades. And it includes Arab partners like Qatar and the United Arab Emirates, who have chosen to meet their responsibilities to defend the Libyan people.

To summarize, then: In just one month, the United States has worked with our international partners to mobilize a broad coalition, secure an international mandate to protect civilians, stop an advancing army, prevent a massacre, and establish a no-fly zone with our allies and partners. To lend some perspective on how rapidly this military and diplomatic response came together, when people were being brutalized in Bosnia in the 1990s, it took the international community more than a year to intervene with air power to protect civilians. It took us 31 days.

Moreover, we've accomplished these objectives consistent with the pledge that I made to the American people at the outset of our military operations.

I said that America's role would be limited; that we would not put ground troops into Libya; that we would focus our unique capabilities on the front end of the operation and that we would transfer responsibility to our allies and partners. Tonight, we are fulfilling that pledge.

Our most effective alliance, NATO, has taken command of the enforcement of the arms embargo and the no-fly zone. Last night, NATO decided to take on the additional responsibility of protecting Libyan civilians. This transfer from the United States to NATO will take place on Wednesday. Going forward, the lead in enforcing the no-fly zone and protecting civilians on the ground will transition to our allies and partners, and I am fully confident that our coalition will keep the pressure on Gadhafi's remaining forces.

In that effort, the United States will play a supporting role—including intelligence, logistical support, search and rescue assistance, and capabilities to jam regime communications. Because of this transition to a broader, NATO-based coalition, the risk and cost of this operation—to our military and to American taxpayers—will be reduced significantly.

So for those who doubted our capacity to carry out this operation, I want to be clear: The United States of America has done what we said we would do.

That's not to say that our work is complete. In addition to our NATO responsibilities, we will work with the international community to provide assistance to the people of Libya, who need food for the hungry and medical care for the wounded. We will safeguard the more than $33 billion that was frozen from the Gadhafi regime so that it's available to rebuild Libya. After all, the money doesn't belong to Gadhafi or to us—it belongs to the Libyan people. And we'll make sure they receive it.

Now, despite the success of our efforts over the past week, I know that some Americans continue to have questions about our efforts in Libya. Gadhafi has not yet stepped down from power, and until he does, Libya will remain dangerous. Moreover, even after Gadhafi does leave power, 40 years of tyranny has left Libya fractured and without strong civil institutions. The transition to a legitimate government that is responsive to the Libyan people will be a difficult task. And while the United States will do our part to help, it will be a task for the international community and—more importantly—a task for the Libyan people themselves.

In fact, much of the debate in Washington has put forward a false choice when it comes to Libya. On the one hand, some question why America should intervene at all—even in limited ways—in this distant land. They argue that there are many places in the world where innocent civilians face brutal violence at the hands of their government, and America should not be expected to police the world, particularly when we have so many pressing needs here at home.

It's true that America cannot use our military wherever repression occurs. And given the costs and risks of intervention, we must always measure our interests against the need for action. But that cannot be an argument for never acting on behalf of what's right. In this particular country—Libya—at this particular moment, we were faced with the prospect of violence on a horrific scale. We had a unique ability to stop that violence: an international mandate for action, a broad coalition prepared to join us, the support of Arab countries, and a plea for help from the Libyan people themselves. We also had the ability to stop Gadhafi's forces in their tracks without putting American troops on the ground.

To brush aside America's responsibility as a leader and—more profoundly—our responsibilities to our fellow human beings under such circumstances would have been a betrayal of who we are. Some nations may be able to turn a blind eye to atrocities in other countries. The United States of America is different. And as President, I refused to wait for the images of slaughter and mass graves before taking action.

Moreover, America has an important strategic interest in preventing Gadhafi from overrunning those who oppose him. A massacre would have driven thousands of additional refugees across Libya's borders, putting enormous strains on the peaceful—yet fragile—transitions in Egypt and Tunisia. The democratic impulses that are dawning across the region would be eclipsed by the darkest form of dictatorship, as repressive leaders concluded that violence is the best strategy to cling to power. The writ of the United Nations Security Council would have been shown to be little more than empty words, crippling that institution's future credibility to uphold global peace and security. So while I will never minimize the costs involved in military action, I am convinced that a failure to act in Libya would have carried a far greater price for America.

Now, just as there are those who have argued against intervention in Libya, there are others who have suggested that we broaden our military mission beyond the task of protecting the Libyan people, and do whatever it takes to bring down Gadhafi and usher in a new government.

Of course, there is no question that Libya—and the world—would be better off with Gadhafi out of power. I, along with many other world leaders, have embraced that goal, and will actively pursue it through non-military means. But broadening our military mission to include regime change would be a mistake.

The task that I assigned our forces—to protect the Libyan people from immediate danger, and to establish a no-fly zone—carries with it a U.N. mandate and international support. It's also what the Libyan opposition asked us to do. If we tried to overthrow Gadhafi by force, our coalition would splinter. We would likely have to put U.S. troops on the ground to accomplish that mission, or risk killing many civilians from the air. The dangers faced by our men and women in uniform would be far greater. So would the costs and our share of the responsibility for what comes next.

To be blunt, we went down that road in Iraq. Thanks to the extraordinary sacrifices of our troops and the determination of our diplomats, we are hopeful about Iraq's future. But regime change there took eight years, thousands of American and Iraqi lives, and nearly a trillion dollars. That is not something we can afford to repeat in Libya.

As the bulk of our military effort ratchets down, what we can do—and will do—is support the aspirations of the Libyan people. We have intervened to stop a massacre, and we will work with our allies and partners to maintain the safety of civilians. We will deny the regime arms, cut off its supplies of cash, assist the opposition, and work with other nations to hasten the day when Gadhafi leaves power. It may not happen overnight, as a badly weakened Gadhafi tries desperately to hang on to power. But it should be clear to those around Gadhafi, and to every Libyan, that history is not on Gadhafi's side. With the time and space that we have provided for the Libyan people, they will be able to determine their own destiny, and that is how it should be.

Let me close by addressing what this action says about the use of America's military power, and America's broader leadership in the world, under my presidency.

As Commander-in-Chief, I have no greater responsibility than keeping this country safe. And no decision weighs on me more than when to deploy our men and women in uniform. I've made it clear that I will never hesitate to use our military swiftly, decisively, and unilaterally when necessary to defend our people, our homeland, our allies and our core interests. That's why we're going after al Qaeda wherever they seek a foothold. That is why we continue to fight in Afghanistan, even as we have ended our combat mission in Iraq and removed more than 100,000 troops from that country.

There will be times, though, when our safety is not directly threatened, but our interests and our values are. Sometimes, the course of history poses challenges that threaten our common humanity and our common security—responding to natural disasters, for example; or preventing genocide and keeping the peace; ensuring regional security, and maintaining the flow of commerce. These may not be America's problems alone, but they are important to us. They're problems worth solving. And in these circumstances, we know that the United States, as the world's most powerful nation, will often be called upon to help.

In such cases, we should not be afraid to act— but the burden of action should not be America's alone. As we have in Libya, our task is instead to mobilize the international community for collective action. Because contrary to the claims of some, American leadership is not simply a matter of going it alone and bearing all of the burden ourselves. Real leadership creates the conditions and coalitions for others to step up as well; to work with allies and partners so that they bear their share of the burden and pay their share of the costs; and to see that the principles of justice and human dignity are upheld by all.

Yes, this change will make the world more complicated for a time. Progress will be uneven, and change will come differently to different countries. There are places, like Egypt, where this change will inspire us and raise our hopes. And then there will be places, like Iran, where change is fiercely suppressed. The dark forces of civil conflict and sectarian war will have to be averted, and difficult political and economic concerns will have to be addressed.

The United States will not be able to dictate the pace and scope of this change. Only the people of the region can do that. But we can make a difference.

I believe that this movement of change cannot be turned back, and that we must stand alongside those who believe in the same core principles that have guided us through many storms: our opposition to violence directed at one's own people; our support for a set of universal rights, including the freedom for people to express themselves and choose their leaders; our support for governments that are ultimately responsive to the aspirations of the people.

Born, as we are, out of a revolution by those who longed to be free, we welcome the fact that history is on the move in the Middle East and North Africa, and that young people are leading the way. Because wherever people long to be free, they will find a friend in the United States. Ultimately, it is that faith—those ideals—that are the true measure of American leadership.

My fellow Americans, I know that at a time of upheaval overseas—when the news is filled with conflict and change—it can be tempting to turn away from the world. And as I've said before, our strength abroad is anchored in our strength here at home. That must always be our North Star—the ability of our people to reach their potential, to make wise choices with our resources, to enlarge the prosperity that serves as a wellspring for our power, and to live the values that we hold so dear.

But let us also remember that for generations, we have done the hard work of protecting our own people, as well as millions around the globe. We have done so because we know that our own future is safer, our own future is brighter, if more of mankind can live with the bright light of freedom and dignity.

Tonight, let us give thanks for the Americans who are serving through these trying times, and the coalition that is carrying our effort forward. And let us look to the future with confidence and hope not only for our own country, but for all those yearning for freedom around the world.

Thank you. God bless you, and may God bless the United States of America.

Barack H. Obama, A Responsibility to Act, March 28, 2011.

Part One: Historical Perspectives

a. Washington warned the young republic against foreign entanglements and permanent alliances with other nations. Do you find his argument compelling? Explain.

b. To what extent did the Monroe Doctrine illustrate the U.S.'s expansionist, and perhaps illiberal tendencies? How did the Doctrine affect the trajectory of relations between the United States and the nations of Latin America? To what extent did the U.S.'s enforcement of the Doctrine exclude other great powers from the Americas?

c. The Roosevelt Corollary established the role of the U.S. as the "police power" of the Western Hemisphere. What are the implications of this for modern U.S. foreign affairs?

d. In Wilson's Fourteen Points, he envisioned the creation of international institutions to diminish the probability of war. Name several institutions that evolved out of Wilson's vision, and discuss their impact on U.S. foreign policy.

e. In Kennan's "Long Telegram," he argued that while the Soviets were resistant to reason, they were very sensitive to the logic of force, or hard power. Were the Soviets capable of seeing a future of peaceful coexistence between capitalism and communism?

f. What was the significance of the strategy of containment implied by Kennan and President Truman? Was it effective?

g. President Eisenhower warned about the rise of the military-industrial complex, and its pernicious influence on the conduct of foreign affairs. To what extent has his warning come true?

h. The Carter Doctrine was a response to the Soviet invasion of which country in 1979? Which strategic region did the Doctrine seek to protect from Soviet influence, and why? Did it establish a pattern of behavior in U.S. foreign policy? Was this behavior productive or counterproductive?

i. Was Reagan's speech at Brandenburg Gate transformative or important? Explain.

j. Bush's speech at West Point established the Bush Doctrine, and the strategy of pre-emptive war. Has this change in US strategy been effective or problematic? Explain.

k. Obama's speech regarding the Libyan Intervention differed from the principles put forth in the Bush Doctrine, but did it mark a significant change in the trajectory of U.S. foreign policy?

II

Theory and Grand Strategy

Students of U.S. foreign policy will encounter many different theories and explanations of the U.S.A.'s behavior in this anthology. While every theory discussed in this volume has some capacity to explain U.S. behavior, students will find that some theories seem more illuminating and compelling than others. As I argued, theories operate as lenses that allow us to perceive different aspects of political "reality." Just as certain prisms refract different wavelengths of light, different theories allow us to perceive and then act on different facets of political world.

First, the article by Jack Snyder and Henry Nau presents a basic overview of several of the main theoretical perspectives for students of foreign policy analysis, Realism, Liberal theory, and Constructivism. Students also are introduced to levels of analysis, a tool used to analyze foreign policy decision making. There are three levels of analysis. The top level is called the systems level. At this level the international system is best represented as a billiard table, and all the sovereign states are like billiard balls that collide and interact with each other within the context of the system. At this level we explore two dominant theories, Realism and Liberalism, and both of them argue that sovereign states are rational maximizers of utility who conduct cost-benefit analyses based on available information, and operate under the constraints of international anarchy. In this section of the anthology we have articles by John Mearsheimer on the utility of Realism, and by Joseph Nye on Liberalism.

Domestic level scholars criticize systems level theory, arguing that it is not as explanatory as it should be. If we crack open the billiard ball (i.e. the state) to see if internal factors are truly driving the foreign conduct of states we then have dropped down to the domestic level of analysis. At this level we examine the internal drivers of foreign policy decision making within the state. Samuel Huntington presents his argument that the future will be riven by competition and war between different "civilizations," that much of this conflict may occur both within states, and between states, and that the major sources of conflict in the modern era are religion, language, and culture.

At the individual level of analysis, we study factors such as the role of perception and misperception in the conduct of U.S. foreign policy, and examine different styles of leadership and decision making. At this level we include Robert Jervis' classic arguments regarding the influence of psychological factors on foreign policy decision making.

This section also introduces students to the concept of polarity in the international system. In other words the number of poles of power that exist in the international system is thought to have an effect on the stability of that system, affecting the frequency of war. Unipolar systems exhibit one dominant pole of power, or one hegemonic state. Bipolar systems are governed by two dominant powers, a good example being the U.S.A. and the Soviet Union during the Cold War era. Bipolar systems are thought to be inherently relatively stable, and therefore relatively peaceful, although they certainly may generate tensions. Multipolar systems, or systems with three or more Great Powers, are thought to be the most dangerous types of systems, highly prone to instability and war. Richard Haass argues that we have now entered a period of nonpolarity as a function of globalization, and this decline of polarity will usher in a period marked by extreme instability. Conversely, John Mearsheimer argues that China's rise as a strategic competitor to the USA has eroded the unipolar order that has existed since the end of the Cold War. Thus, the rise of China will restructure the international system into a bipolar mode that may be fraught with growing tensions between Washington and Beijing.

One World, Rival Theories

JACK SNYDER

Snyder's article provides an excellent introduction to Liberal, Realist, and Constructivist theories of international relations. He also provides a brief introduction to theories of the Democratic peace, and links the latter to theories that operate at the domestic level.

The U.S. government has endured several painful rounds of scrutiny as it tries to figure out what went wrong on Sept. 11, 2001. The intelligence community faces radical restructuring; the military has made a sharp pivot to face a new enemy; and a vast new federal agency has blossomed to coordinate homeland security. But did September 11 signal a failure of theory on par with the failures of intelligence and policy? Familiar theories about how the world works still dominate academic debate. Instead of radical change, academia has adjusted existing theories to meet new realities. Has this approach succeeded? Does international relations theory still have something to tell policymakers?

Six years ago, political scientist Stephen M. Walt published a much-cited survey of the field. He sketched out three dominant approaches: realism, liberalism, and an updated form of idealism called "constructivism." Walt argued that these theories shape both public discourse and policy analysis. Realism focuses on the shifting distribution of power among states. Liberalism highlights the rising number of democracies and the turbulence of democratic transitions. Idealism illuminates the changing norms of sovereignty, human rights, and international justice, as well as the increased potency of religious ideas in politics.

The influence of these intellectual constructs extends far beyond university classrooms and tenure committees. Policymakers and public commentators invoke elements of all these theories when articulating solutions to global security dilemmas. President George W. Bush promises to fight terror by spreading liberal democracy to the Middle East and claims that skeptics "who call themselves 'realists'. . . have lost contact with a fundamental reality" that "America is always more secure when freedom is on the march." Striking a more eclectic tone, National Security Advisor Condoleezza Rice, a former Stanford University political science professor, explains that the new Bush doctrine is an amalgam of pragmatic realism and Wilsonian liberal theory. During the recent presidential campaign, Sen. John Kerry sounded remarkably similar: "Our foreign policy has achieved greatness," he said, "only when it has combined realism and idealism."

International relations theory also shapes and informs the thinking of the public intellectuals who translate and disseminate academic ideas. During the summer of 2004, for example, two influential framers of neoconservative thought, columnist Charles Krauthammer and political scientist Francis Fukuyama, collided over the implications of these conceptual paradigms for U.S. policy in Iraq.

Backing the Bush administration's Middle East policy, Krauthammer argued for an assertive amalgam of liberalism and realism, which he called "democratic realism." Fukuyama claimed that Krauthammer's faith in the use of force and the feasibility of democratic change in Iraq blinds him to the war's lack of legitimacy, a failing that "hurts both the realist part of our agenda, by diminishing our actual power, and the idealist portion of it, by undercutting our appeal as the embodiment of certain ideas and values."

Indeed, when realism, liberalism, and idealism enter the policymaking arena and public debate, they can sometimes become intellectual window dressing for simplistic worldviews. Properly understood, however, their policy implications are subtle and multifaceted. Realism instills a pragmatic appreciation of the role of power but also warns that states will suffer if they overreach. Liberalism highlights the cooperative potential of mature democracies, especially when working together through effective institutions, but it also notes democracies' tendency to crusade against tyrannies and the propensity of emerging democracies to collapse into violent ethnic turmoil. Idealism stresses that a consensus on values must underpin any stable political order, yet it also recognizes that forging such a consensus often requires an ideological struggle with the potential for conflict.

Each theory offers a filter for looking at a complicated picture. As such, they help explain the assumptions behind political rhetoric about foreign policy. Even more important, the theories act as a powerful check on each other. Deployed effectively, they reveal the weaknesses in arguments that can lead to misguided policies.

Is Realism Still Realistic?

At realism's core is the belief that international affairs is a struggle for power among self-interested states. Although some of realism's leading lights, notably the late University of Chicago political scientist Hans J. Morgenthau, are deeply pessimistic about human nature, it is not a theory of despair. Clearsighted states can mitigate the causes of war by finding ways to reduce the danger they pose to each other. Nor is realism necessarily amoral; its advocates emphasize that a ruthless pragmatism about power can actually yield a more peaceful world, if not an ideal one.

In liberal democracies, realism is the theory that everyone loves to hate. Developed largely by European émigrés at the end of World War II, realism claimed to be an antidote to the naive belief that international institutions and law alone can preserve peace, a misconception that this new generation of scholars believed had paved the way to war. In recent decades, the realist approach has been most fully articulated by U.S. theorists, but it still has broad appeal outside the United States as well. The influential writer and editor Josef Joffe articulately comments on Germany's strong realist traditions. (Mindful of the overwhelming importance of U.S. power to Europe's development, Joffe once called the United States "Europe's pacifier.") China's current foreign policy is grounded in realist ideas that date back millennia. As China modernizes its economy and enters international institutions such as the World Trade Organization, it behaves in a way that realists understand well: developing its military slowly but surely as its economic power grows, and avoiding a confrontation with superior U.S. forces.

Realism gets some things right about the post-9/11 world. The continued centrality of military strength and the persistence of conflict, even in this age of global economic interdependence, does not surprise realists. The theory's most obvious success is its ability to explain the United States' forceful military response to the September 11 terrorist attacks. When a state grows vastly more powerful than any opponent, realists expect that it will eventually use that power to expand its sphere of domination, whether for security, wealth, or other motives. The United States employed its military power in what some deemed an imperial fashion in large part because it could.

It is harder for the normally state-centric realists to explain why the world's only superpower announced a war against al Qaeda, a nonstate terrorist organization. How can realist theory account for the importance of powerful and violent individuals in a world of states? Realists point out that the central battles in the "war on terror" have been fought against two states (Afghanistan and Iraq), and that states, not the United Nations or Human Rights Watch, have led the fight against terrorism.

Even if realists acknowledge the importance of nonstate actors as a challenge to their assumptions, the theory still has important things to say about the behavior and motivations of these groups. The realist scholar Robert A. Pape, for example, has argued that suicide terrorism can be a rational, realistic strategy for the leadership of national liberation movements seeking to expel democratic powers that occupy their homelands. Other scholars apply standard theories of conflict in anarchy to explain ethnic conflict in collapsed states. Insights from political realism—a profound and wide-ranging intellectual tradition rooted in the enduring philosophy of Thucydides, Niccolò Machiavelli, and Thomas Hobbes—are hardly rendered obsolete because some nonstate groups are now able to resort to violence.

Post-9/11 developments seem to undercut one of realism's core concepts: the balance of power. Standard realist doctrine predicts that weaker states will ally to protect themselves from stronger ones and thereby form and reform a balance of power. So, when Germany unified in the late 19th century and became Europe's leading military and industrial power, Russia and France (and later, Britain) soon aligned to counter its power. Yet no combination of states or other powers can challenge the United States militarily, and no balancing coalition is imminent. Realists are scrambling to find a way to fill this hole in the center of their theory. Some theorists speculate that the United States' geographic distance and its relatively benign intentions have tempered the balancing instinct. Second-tier powers tend to worry more about their immediate neighbors and even see the United States as a helpful source of stability in regions such as East Asia. Other scholars insist that armed resistance by U.S. foes in Iraq, Afghanistan, and elsewhere, and foot-dragging by its formal allies actually constitute the beginnings of balancing against U.S. hegemony. The United States' strained relations with Europe offer ambiguous evidence: French and German opposition to recent U.S. policies could be seen as classic balancing, but they do not resist U.S. dominance militarily. Instead, these states have tried to undermine U.S. moral legitimacy and constrain the superpower in a web of multilateral institutions and treaty regimes—not what standard realist theory predicts.

These conceptual difficulties notwithstanding, realism is alive, well, and creatively reassessing how its root principles relate to the post-9/11 world. Despite changing configurations of power, realists remain steadfast in stressing that policy must be based on positions of real strength, not on either empty bravado or hopeful illusions about a world without conflict. In the run-up to the recent Iraq war, several prominent realists signed a public letter criticizing what they perceived as an exercise in American hubris. And in the continuing aftermath of that war, many prominent thinkers called for a return to realism. A group of scholars and public intellectuals (myself included) even formed the *Coalition for a Realistic Foreign Policy*, which calls for a more modest and prudent approach. Its statement of principles argues that "the move toward empire must be halted immediately." The coalition, though politically diverse, is largely inspired by realist theory. Its membership of seemingly odd bedfellows—including former Democratic Sen. Gary Hart and Scott McConnell, the executive editor of the *American Conservative* magazine—illustrates the power of international relations theory to cut through often ephemeral political labels and carry debate to the underlying assumptions.

The Divided House of Liberalism

The liberal school of international relations theory, whose most famous proponents were German philosopher Immanuel Kant and U.S. President Woodrow Wilson, contends that realism has a stunted vision that cannot account for progress in relations between nations. Liberals foresee a slow but inexorable journey away from the anarchic world the realists envision, as trade and finance forge ties between nations, and democratic norms spread. Because elected leaders are accountable to the people (who bear the burdens of war), liberals expect that democracies will not attack each other and will regard each other's regimes as legitimate and nonthreatening. Many liberals also believe that the rule of law and transparency of democratic processes make it easier to sustain international cooperation, especially when these practices are enshrined in multilateral institutions.

Liberalism has such a powerful presence that the entire U.S. political spectrum, from neoconservatives to human rights advocates, assumes it as largely self-evident. Outside the United States, as well, the liberal view that only elected governments are legitimate and politically reliable has taken hold. So it is no surprise that liberal themes are constantly invoked as a response to today's security dilemmas. But the last several years have also produced a fierce tug-of-war between disparate strains of liberal thought. Supporters and critics of the Bush administration, in particular, have emphasized very different elements of the liberal canon.

For its part, the Bush administration highlights democracy promotion while largely turning its back on the international institutions that most liberal theorists champion. The U.S. National Security Strategy of September 2002, famous for its support of preventive war, also dwells on the need to promote democracy as a means or fighting terrorism and promoting peace. The Millennium Challenge program allocates part of U.S. foreign aid according to how well countries improve their performance on several measures of democratization and the rule of law. The White House's steadfast support for promoting democracy in the Middle East—even with turmoil in Iraq and rising anti-Americanism in the Arab world—demonstrates liberalism's emotional and rhetorical power.

In many respects, liberalism's claim to be a wise policy guide has plenty of hard data behind it. During the last two decades, the proposition that democratic institutions and values help states cooperate with each other is among the most intensively studied in all of international relations, and it has held up reasonably well. Indeed, the belief that democracies never fight wars against each other is the closest thing we have to an iron law in social science.

But the theory has some very important corollaries, which the Bush administration glosses over as it draws upon the democracy-promotion element of liberal thought. Columbia University political scientist Michael W. Doyle's articles on democratic peace warned that, though democracies never fight each other, they are prone to launch messianic struggles against warlike authoritarian regimes to "make the world safe for democracy." It was precisely American democracy's tendency to oscillate between self-righteous crusading and jaded isolationism that prompted early Cold War realists' call for a more calculated, prudent foreign policy.

Countries transitioning to democracy, with weak political institutions, are more likely than other states to get into international and civil wars. In the last 15 years, wars or large-scale civil violence followed experiments with mass electoral democracy in countries including Armenia, Burundi, Ethiopia, Indonesia, Russia, and the former Yugoslavia. In part, this violence is caused by ethnic groups' competing demands for national self-determination, often a problem in new, multiethnic democracies. More fundamental, emerging democracies often have nascent political institutions that cannot channel popular demands in constructive directions or credibly enforce compromises among rival groups. In this setting, democratic accountability works imperfectly, and nationalist politicians can hijack public debate. The violence that is vexing the experiment with democracy in Iraq is just the latest chapter in a turbulent story that began with the French Revolution.

Contemporary liberal theory also points out that the rising democratic tide creates the presumption that all nations ought to enjoy the benefits of self-determination. Those left out may undertake violent campaigns to secure democratic rights. Some of these movements direct their struggles against democratic or semidemocratic states that they consider occupying powers—such as in Algeria in the 1950s, or Chechnya, Palestine, and the Tamil region of Sri Lanka today. Violence may also be directed at democratic supporters of oppressive regimes, much like the U.S. backing of the governments of Saudi Arabia and Egypt. Democratic regimes make attractive targets for terrorist violence by national liberation movements precisely because they are accountable to a cost-conscious electorate.

Nor is it clear to contemporary liberal scholars that nascent democracy and economic liberalism can always cohabitate. Free trade and the multifaceted globalization that advanced democracies promote often buffet transitional societies. World markets' penetration of societies that run on patronage and protectionism can disrupt social relations and spur strife between potential winners and losers. In other cases, universal free trade can make separatism look attractive, as small regions such as Aceh in Indonesia can lay claim to lucrative natural resources. So far, the trade-fueled boom in China has created incentives for improved relations with the advanced democracies, but it has also set the stage for a possible showdown between the relatively wealthy coastal entrepreneurs and the still impoverished rural masses.

While aggressively advocating the virtues of democracy, the Bush administration has shown little patience for these complexities in liberal thought—or for liberalism's emphasis on the importance of international institutions. Far from trying to assure other powers that the United States would adhere to a constitutional order, Bush "unsigned" the International Criminal Court statute, rejected the Kyoto environmental agreement, dictated take-it-or-leave-it arms control changes to Russia, and invaded Iraq despite opposition at the United Nations and among close allies.

Recent liberal theory offers a thoughtful challenge to the administration's policy choices. Shortly before September 11, political scientist G. John Ikenberry studied attempts to establish international order by the victors of hegemonic struggles in 1815, 1919, 1945, and 1989. He argued that even the most powerful victor needed to gain the willing cooperation of the vanquished and other weak states by offering a mutually attractive bargain, codified in an international constitutional order. Democratic victors, he found, have the best chance of creating a working constitutional order, such as the Bretton Woods system after World War II, because their transparency and legalism make their promises credible.

Does the Bush administration's resistance to institution building refute Ikenberry's version of liberal theory? Some realists say it does, and that recent events demonstrate that international institutions cannot constrain a hegemonic power if its preferences change. But international institutions can nonetheless help coordinate outcomes that are in the long-term mutual interest of both the hegemon and the weaker states. Ikenberry did not contend that hegemonic democracies are immune from mistakes. States can act in defiance of the incentives established by their position in the international system, but they will suffer the consequences and probably learn to correct course. In response to Bush's unilateralist stance, Ikenberry wrote that the incentives for the United States to take the lead in establishing a multilateral constitutional order remain powerful. Sooner or later, the pendulum will swing back.

Idealism's New Clothing

Idealism, the belief that foreign policy is and should be guided by ethical and legal standards, also has a long pedigree. Before World War II forced the United States to acknowledge a less pristine reality, Secretary of State Henry Stimson denigrated espionage on the grounds that "gentlemen do not read each other's mail." During the Cold War, such naive idealism acquired a bad name in the Kissingerian corridors of power and among hardheaded academics. Recently, a new version of idealism—called constructivism by its scholarly adherents—returned to a prominent place in debates on international relations theory. Constructivism, which holds that social reality is created through debate about values, often echoes the themes that human rights and international justice activists sound. Recent events seem to vindicate the theory's resurgence; a theory that emphasizes the role of ideologies, identities, persuasion, and transnational networks is highly relevant to understanding the post-9/11 world.

The most prominent voices in the development of constructivist theory have been American, but Europe's role is significant. European philosophical currents helped establish constructivist theory, and the *European Journal of International Relations* is one of the principal outlets for constructivist work. Perhaps most important, Europe's increasingly legalistic approach to international relations, reflected in the process of forming the European Union out of a collection of sovereign states, provides fertile soil for idealist and constructivist conceptions of international politics.

Whereas realists dwell on the balance of power and liberals on the power of international trade and democracy, constructivists believe that debates about ideas are the fundamental building blocks of international life. Individuals and groups become powerful if they can convince others to adopt their ideas. People's understanding of their interests depends on the ideas they hold. Constructivists find absurd the idea of some identifiable and immutable "national interest," which some realists cherish. Especially in liberal societies, there is overlap between constructivist and liberal approaches, but the two are distinct. Constructivists contend that their theory is deeper than realism and liberalism because it explains the origins of the forces that drive those competing theories.

For constructivists, international change results from the work of intellectual entrepreneurs who proselytize new ideas and "name and shame" actors whose behavior deviates from accepted standards. Consequently, constructivists often study the role of transnational activist networks—such as Human Rights Watch or the International Campaign to Ban Landmines—in promoting change. Such groups typically uncover and publicize information about violations of legal or moral standards at least rhetorically supported by powerful democracies, including "disappearances" during the Argentine military's rule in the late 1970s, concentration camps in Bosnia, and the huge number of civilian deaths from land mines. This publicity is then used to press governments to adopt specific remedies, such as the establishment of a war crimes tribunal or the adoption of a landmine treaty. These movements often make pragmatic arguments as well as idealistic ones, but their distinctive power comes from the ability to highlight deviations from deeply held norms of appropriate behavior.

Progressive causes receive the most attention from constructivist scholars, but the theory also helps explain the dynamics of illiberal transnational forces, such as Arab nationalism or Islamist extremism. Professor Michael N. Barnett's 1998 book *Dialogues in Arab Politics: Negotiations in Regional Order* examines how the divergence between state borders and transnational Arab political identities requires vulnerable leaders to contend for legitimacy with radicals throughout the Arab world—a dynamic that often holds moderates hostage to opportunists who take extreme stances.

Constructivist thought can also yield broader insights about the ideas and values in the current international order. In his 2001 book, *Revolutions in Sovereignty: How Ideas Shaped Modern International Relations,* political scientist Daniel Philpott demonstrates how the religious ideas of the Protestant Reformation helped break down the medieval political order and provided a conceptual basis for the modern system of secular sovereign states. After September 11, Philpott focused on the challenge to the secular international order posed by political Islam. "The attacks and the broader resurgence of public religion," he says, ought to lead international relations scholars to "direct far more energy to understanding the impetuses behind movements across the globe that are reorienting purposes and policies." He notes that both liberal human rights movements and radical Islamic movements have transnational structures and principled motivations that challenge the traditional supremacy of self-interested states in international politics. Because constructivists believe that ideas and values helped shape the modern state system, they expect intellectual constructs to be decisive in transforming it—for good or ill.

When it comes to offering advice, however, constructivism points in two seemingly incompatible directions. The insight that political orders arise from shared understanding highlights the need for dialogue across cultures about the appropriate rules of the game.

This prescription dovetails with liberalism's emphasis on establishing an agreed international constitutional order. And, yet, the notion of cross-cultural dialogue sits awkwardly with many idealists' view that they already know right and wrong. For these idealists, the essential task is to shame rights abusers and cajole powerful actors into promoting proper values and holding perpetrators accountable to international (generally Western) standards. As with realism and liberalism, constructivism can be many things to many people.

Stumped by Change

None of the three theoretical traditions has a strong ability to explain change—a significant weakness in such turbulent times. Realists failed to predict the end of the Cold War, for example. Even after it happened, they tended to assume that the new system would become multipolar ("back to the future," as the scholar John J. Mearsheimer put it). Likewise, the liberal theory of democratic peace is stronger on what happens after states become democratic than in predicting the timing of democratic transitions, let alone prescribing how to make transitions happen peacefully. Constructivists are good at describing changes in norms and ideas, but they are weak on the material and institutional circumstances necessary to support the emergence of consensus about new values and ideas.

With such uncertain guidance from the theoretical realm, it is no wonder that policymakers, activists, and public commentators fall prey to simplistic or wishful thinking about how to effect change by, say, invading Iraq or setting up an International Criminal Court. In lieu of a good theory of change, the most prudent course is to use the insights of each of the three theoretical traditions as a check on the irrational exuberance of the others. Realists should have to explain whether policies based on calculations of power have sufficient legitimacy to last. Liberals should consider whether nascent democratic institutions can fend off powerful interests that oppose them, or how international institutions can bind a hegemonic power inclined to go its own way. Idealists should be asked about the strategic, institutional, or material conditions in which a set of ideas is likely to take hold.

Theories of international relations claim to explain the way international politics works, but each of the currently prevailing theories falls well short of that goal. One of the principal contributions that international relations theory can make is not predicting the future but providing the vocabulary and conceptual framework to ask hard questions of those who think that changing the world is easy.

Jack Snyder, "One World, Rival Theories," Foreign Policy 145 (2004), pp.52–62. © 2004, Foreign Policy.

Why We Fight Over Foreign Policy

HENRY R. NAU

Henry Nau argues that we simplify reality by constructing models to explain international politics, but that such oversimplification can generate problems. Different models and theories allow people to focus on different sets of "facts." Therefore, Nau contends that disputes about foreign policy are often about one's "perspective and judgment." He presents a brief summary of Realism, Liberalism, and Constructivism and uses these theories to critique the Bush Administration's decision to invade Iraq in 2003.

Different perspectives yield different conclusions.

Why do we disagree so stridently about foreign policy? An easy answer is because leaders lie about events abroad.[1] Take the decision to invade Iraq. Didn't Tony Blair say before the war that Iraq could assemble a nuclear weapon in 45 minutes? He was obviously lying, right? Or what about George W. Bush, whose CIA director said at the time that it was a "slam dunk" that Iraq had nuclear weapons? He obviously knew better. Didn't he?

Well, maybe. But what if we disagree not because leaders are wicked and lie but because they, like we, see the world differently and assemble and emphasize different facts that lead to different conclusions? Saddam Hussein evaded U.N. inspectors. That's a fact. But was he hiding something like weapons of mass destruction (WMD)? Or was he behaving as might any leader of a country that comes under external threat? Answers to those questions are interpretations. Some looked at Iraq's glass and saw it was half full of WMD; others concluded that it was half empty.

Simplify But Not Simple

No subject in the world is as complex as foreign affairs. You are dealing not just with natural facts, such as disasters and disease, but also with social facts such as human beings who change their minds and behave creatively. Natural facts—like a virus—don't do that. They behave according to fixed laws. Further, social facts are embedded in different cultures. People from different cultures interpret the same facts differently. What does a devout Muslim see when he or she walks by a Christian church? In some cases, an infidel institution. Not exactly what a devout Christian sees. Individual human beings and diverse cultures create multiple meanings from the same set of facts. Given this enormous complexity, how do we make any sense at all out of international affairs?

We simplify. We approach the world with labels and models that direct us toward a particular slice of reality, We can't see it all, so we use our learning, experience, and judgment to select a

direction, to look for certain facts that are important to us in terms of how we believe the world works. Surveying the material for his biography of Abraham Lincoln, Carl Sandburg wrote that "anyone dealing with the vast actual evidence cannot use the whole of it . . . therefore . . . he . . . picks what is plain, moving, and important."[2] We have to neglect some facts not because we are ignorant or ideological but precisely because we can know something only if we exclude something else. If we knew everything, we'd know nothing until we knew what was important to us—and what's important to us is a matter of personal perspective and judgment. Thus, we emphasize certain facts, and our opponents often emphasize other facts, perhaps the very ones we deemphasize. We reach different conclusions not because we dissemble and lie but because we see the world differently and judge different facts to be more important.

Consider four facts related to North Korea's development of nuclear weapons—the accumulation of weapons-grade plutonium before 1994, the 1994 agreement which froze the plutonium production program, the start-up in the late 1990s of a separate uranium enrichment program, and the termination of the 1994 agreement in 2002. Those who believe that direct negotiation with North Korea is the best way to handle this issue emphasize the second and fourth facts. The freeze agreement prevented further production of plutonium and thus capped the amount of weapons-grade materials available to produce nuclear weapons. The termination of the agreement allowed North Korea to resume plutonium production and test a bomb in October 2005. Thus, from this point of view, the termination of the agreement was a mistake even though North Korea had begun a separate enrichment project because that program was still a long way from producing weapons-grade materials.[3] Those who believe that sanctions and isolation are the best way to deal with the problem emphasize the first and third facts. North Korea already had weapons-grade material before 1994 and could have tested a bomb at any time with that material.

Moreover, it broke the 1994 agreement by starting up the enriched uranium program. So terminating the 1994 agreement did nothing except make explicit what was going on anyway, a stealth program to acquire nuclear weapons. Better from this point of view to rally allies and isolate North Korea until it disclosed and dismantled all nuclear weapons programs.

Are these positions just partisan—the one supporting President Clinton's policy of negotiation, the other President Bush's policy of isolation? Possibly, but I'd wager they are also the product of different perspectives about what causes things to happen in international affairs. One believes that North Korea can be persuaded to give up nuclear programs by inclusion and negotiated compromise, the other that North Korea can be dissuaded from nuclear weapons primarily by isolation and material sanctions. The first is not unwilling to threaten force, as Clinton reportedly did in 1994, and the second is not unwilling to consider negotiations, as Bush did in 2005 (reaching the most recent agreement announced in February 2007). But the relative difference in emphasis is clear.

Thus, all leaders, analysts and citizens simplify when they debate foreign affairs. And therein lies our problem. We forget that we are simplifying and claim veracity and truth for our insights. Our opponents must be depraved or incompetent if they do not agree with us. How many people say today they hate George Bush or, in the 1990s, Bill Clinton? Emotions take over for common sense. Since we have to simplify to make any sense of world affairs, why not go all the way? Make the world really simple and divide it into two groups, those who are good and agree with us and those who are evil and disagree with us. We're all guilty of this. Bush oversimplified when he said after 9/11, "those who are not with us are against us." But Democrats, who deplore Bush's comment, oversimplify when they say Bush is evil and lied to us about the Iraq War.

In this essay, I try to show that the Iraq War and almost all foreign policy issues are not in the first instance about brilliant and stupid or honest and mendacious people. They are rather matters of perspective and judgment. People struggle to simplify and make sense of an extraordinarily complex world. In the process they emphasize different facts even when they see the same facts. For example, proponents of the Iraq War saw the incomplete facts about Saddam Hussein's weapons of mass destruction as evidence of what he was hiding. Opponents of the war saw the same facts as evidence of what he did not have.

In the end, people take responsibility for how they see the world. That we simplify and emphasize different aspects of reality does not excuse us from moral accountability. Some people do lie. We have to make judgments about good and evil. But before we denounce each other as evil, which seems to come earlier and earlier in our foreign policy debates, wouldn't it be nice if we knew more about the different ways in which people legitimately see the world and differ in their emphasis and interpretation of the facts, often the same ones?

Three Perspectives

Theorists of international relations have long recognized three principal ways to think about the world and select and evaluate facts. The realist perspective thinks about the world primarily in terms of a struggle for power, alliances, and the threat and use of force. The liberal perspective looks at it more in terms of expanding cooperation and complex interdependence through trade, negotiations, and international institutions. The ideational or what political scientists today call constructivist or identity perspective sees it largely in terms of what people and states believe—the ideas, norms, and values they share that shape their discourse and identity. Many of us are familiar with these perspectives or simplified versions of international relations theories (the theories themselves become endlessly complex), but we may not fully understand how directly they influence our day-to-day debates.

In the realist outlook, people and states worry most about their survival and seek sufficient military power and wealth to protect themselves against would-be adversaries. Because states exist separately, they have to look out for their own security. There is no single center of legitimate power, a World 911, that they can call upon when attacked. The United Nations, in this sense, is not a world government. A domestic government has a monopoly on the legitimate use of force. No domestic group can take up arms legitimately against the state. But the United Nations has no such monopoly. It can use force only with the consent of the great powers on the Security Council, and Article 51 of the U.N. Charter gives all states the right to use force to defend themselves whether or not the United Nations approves. State power decides the way international institutions work and defends the nation's values or identity.

Thus the world from this perspective works through a contest and balancing of military and economic power to protect national security. Weak states unite against strong states and do what they can to prevent might from making right. The terrorist attacks against the United States on September 11, 2001, appear from this perspective as "a war in which the weak turned the guns of the strong against them . . . showing . . . that in the end there is no such thing as a universal civilization of which we all too easily assume we are the rightful leaders."[4] The realist perspective interprets this event as a contest between the weak and the strong in which there is no rightful universal authority except that which each state decides.

The liberal perspective sees the world in terms of institutional cooperation and world order, not material struggle and balancing. It asks why international life cannot be similar to domestic life in which a single authority does exist and enforces common rules and law. After all, the scope of governmental authority has expanded since the beginning of time. Villages became towns, towns cities, cities merged into states, and today states constitute nations and unions such as the European Union. Why can't society eventually become global, and common institutions and laws prevail at the international level just as they do today at the domestic level?

Modernization pushes us in this direction. The world is becoming smaller through the interdependence of communications (diplomacy), transportation (trade), professional societies (epistemic communities), urbanization and industrialization (bureaucracies), common problem solving (law), and environmental protection (planet earth). The habit of cooperation slowly diminishes the significance of power and ideological differences.

From this perspective, states don't just seek power to survive. They also seek to form more perfect unions. Thus, the attacks of 9/11 represented not another cycle in the struggle between the weak and strong but a failure of the international community to include the weak and address their grievances. As Caryle Murphy commented about 9/11 in the *Washington Post* (September 16, 2001), "if we want to avoid creating more terrorists, we must end the Israeli-Palestinian conflict in a way both sides see as fair." Ignoring oppression and marginalizing people create conflict. What deters conflict, then, is not balancing forces but removing the alienation that prompts the conflict in the first place.

The identity perspective sees the world in terms of dialogue and dispute about values, norms, and identities. How groups and states envision themselves and others drives their use of power and their behavior in common institutions. States don't just seek to survive; they seek to survive as a particular kind of society—for example, a democratic or a theocratic society—and they use international institutions to shape a common discourse and develop shared identities. Ideas influence power and institutions, not the other way around.

From this perspective, the attacks of September 11 are the consequence neither of a power struggle nor unresolved grievances but of incompatible or insufficiently shared identities. As Jim Hoagland wrote in his *Washington Post* column nearly a year after the 9/11 attacks (August 1, 2002), "The removal of Saddam Hussein and Yasser Arafat are necessary but not sufficient conditions [to resolve the Middle East conflict] . . . [and] the administration cannot rely . . . on a now discredited peace process. . . . Only a level and clarity of American commitment to democratic change . . . will calm an ever more deadly conflict." The argument deemphasizes the use of force—the removal of certain leaders by force is not enough—and does not expect much from negotiations or diplomacy—cannot rely on the discredited peace process. Only a change in the identity of regimes in the Middle East that creates a more common dialogue can discipline the use of force and realize the promises of diplomacy.

Which Perspective Matters More?

People and political leaders apply these perspectives simultaneously. Serious people look at the world in multiple ways. They collect and evaluate facts from different perspectives. But when they act, they have to choose. Why? Because we can't focus on everything and get anything specific done, and we don't have unlimited resources to do everything.

So, let's say the president of the United States needs your advice today about the next steps in Iraq. Do you agree with his plan to surge troops in Baghdad to defeat the sectarian extremists, or do you believe negotiations within as well as outside Iraq are more urgent than ever, as the Iraq Study Group recommended? Or do you remind him that neither military force nor negotiations can succeed without less corrupt and more democratic countries in the region, as he argued in his inaugural address in 2005?

Well, you say, all of these things are necessary, and President Bush himself has implemented policies to address all of them. But some policies conflict and others come first. "In a choice of evils," Abraham Lincoln once said, "[war] may not always be the worst."[5] Nevertheless, war increases instability, and makes democracy in Iraq more, not less, difficult. Negotiations to end the Arab-Israeli dispute may lessen terrorism, but then terrorism may make negotiations useless. President Clinton mediated an Arab-Israeli agreement in December 2000 only to see it blown up six weeks later by Palestinian extremists (intifada) and Israeli hardliners

(election of Ariel Sharon). However worthy that agreement was, extremists who held the balance of forces on the ground torpedoed it.

So you have to tell the president which policy matters more and how the country can afford it. And you do that by judging one policy to be more important than another. As one example, you advise the president that prosecuting the war in Baghdad is a priority to weaken extremists in Iraq and elsewhere in the Middle East, eventually enabling moderate governments to negotiate a peace settlement that can stick and encourage longer-term economic development and democratic progress. This judgment is realist. It doesn't ignore liberal (negotiations) and identity (democracy) factors, it just says that the use of force is needed to quell extremism as a way to improve the situation on the ground and facilitate negotiations and longer term developments (preventing a repeat of Clinton's experience). Or, as a counterexample, you advise the president, as the Iraq Study Group recently did, that negotiating a regional solution to the Iraq problem and a wider Middle East peace settlement takes priority over defeating extremists because it will alleviate the grievances that fuel extremism, enabling moderates to regain control of security and military forces, shut down terrorism, and open the way to economic growth and political reforms. This judgment is liberal. Again, it doesn't ignore realist (extremists) and identity (reforms) factors, it just says that negotiations to achieve fairness and equity among Iraqis and between Palestinians and Israelis will legitimatize existing governments, empowering them to end violence, pursue economic development, and promote democratic reforms.

Where, you might ask, is the concern in these two recommendations for human rights in the Middle East, especially women's rights? Must women be long suffering and wait for the defeat of extremists or the fruits of negotiations before they can expect democratic reforms? An identity perspective offers a third line of advice to the president which emphasizes democracy over security and negotiations: promote constitutional reforms and elections to make governments in Iraq and the

Middle East more transparent and accountable, exposing extremism and corruption and building trust to negotiate lasting prosperity and peace. This is the policy the Bush administration actually pursued from 2003 to 2006 (remember the ink-stained fingers of people who voted), while critics, taking a more realist or liberal perspective, complained that security was being neglected or that diplomatic negotiations were being postponed.

These alternative perspectives illuminate the contours of the Iraq debate. The neoconservatives, who dominated policy in 2003–2005, advocated the need to overthrow the government (regime change) to end the pursuit of WMD in Iraq and set the stage for wider negotiations in the Middle East. This identity perspective is now in retreat. Realist strategists opposed the invasion in 2003 because they feared the instability that would result from the change of governments. They stressed containment and balancing power to resolve conflicts, whatever the ideology of governments. They are now back in fashion. And liberal strategists, who criticized the failure to avoid war by negotiations and then to push negotiations after the war when America was strong, now push talks with Syria and Iran when the United States is weak. They see negotiations as a way out of the war even as U.S. forces draw down and radical regimes such as Iran and Syria gain influence. Each perspective advocates a different key (cause) to unlock the riddle of Iraq—ideas such as democracy, balancing such as containment, and negotiations to facilitate compromise.

Perspectives illuminate other debates. Take the issue of how to deal with China. Liberal approaches say, negotiate with an authoritarian China to integrate it into the world economy, thereby reforming China's economy and eventually opening up its political system. What if in the meantime you make China stronger and it remains or becomes hostile? Realist perspectives worry about this and advise strengthening military alliances with Japan and South Korea and balancing China's military buildup, especially in the Taiwan Strait. Where in either the liberal or realist judgment, one might ask, is an emphasis on human rights and protection of dissidents in China? Well, it's not there or not there as much as it would be in a judgment made from an identity perspective. In this case, you would advise the president to give higher priority to democratic reforms in China, backing moderates in Beijing to temper aggressive foreign policies toward Taiwan, improve the regional climate for common trade and investment opportunities, and eventually transcend territorial and military disputes. In this case, ideas change institutions and ultimately resolve military conflicts, rather than institutional factors (e.g., détente, arms control, etc.) managing military tensions and later changing political ideas. Which factors—material (power), interactive (institutions), or political (ideas)—cause other factors is a crucial judgment, and people of good will and high intelligence differ in the judgments they make.

Let's look more closely at two controversial cases of differing judgments in the Iraq War—the question of links between Iraq and al Qaeda, and the issue of Iraq's weapons of mass destruction.

Links between Iraq and Al Qaeda

Gathering intelligence illustrates vividly the reality of facts and perspectives. Information does not exist in a vacuum or pop up on the computer screen because it is there. You have to ask for it or click the mouse in certain places to discover it. I learned this lesson firsthand while serving on the National Security Council in the White House. An intelligence officer paid me a first visit. Naively, I expected him to give me a briefing on the facts in my area of responsibility (which was international economic affairs). Instead he asked me what I was interested in. It was the right question. He could have given me a briefing based on what he thought was most important. But as a good civil servant (there are still many) he recognized that I was part of a newly elected administration that had the right by democratic process to set priorities. Either way, the intelligence officer or I would select and go look for certain facts depending upon what we were interested in.

And so it was with intelligence gathered about contacts between al Qaeda and Iraq and Iraq's WMD. Various intelligence agencies (there are many) went after specific facts. In the first instance they did not do this because they were political. They did it because they had to. Where would they start without some question (bias)? Some civil servants, to be sure, are outright political and leak policies when they oppose them, just as appointed officials are sometimes dogmatic and insist on facts that are consistent with what they are looking for. But most civil servants and political appointees are not ideological. They are simply interested in different things, because they have to be interested in something to gather and evaluate any facts at all.

Fortunately, these differences make for good intelligence. You want as many different people or agencies gathering facts from as many different perspectives as possible. Clearly they need to communicate with one another and share these different facts. That was a shortcoming in the intelligence gathering before 9/11, both during the eight years of the Clinton administration, when a self-imposed legal wall separated domestic and foreign intelligence gathering, and the eight months of the Bush administration when a new administration viewed the policies of the previous administration with skepticism and took several months to get its own act in order. But that shortcoming has been corrected. The one thing you cannot expect or correct from this competitive gathering of intelligence is agreement. If that's the objective of the director of national intelligence, the new structure will fail. Intelligence will always be discordant and muddied. There are no slam dunks in intelligence. As the *Washington Post* columnist Jim Hoagland wisely notes (July 29, 2004), "Most of the time you are not going to have perfect knowledge for making decisions. . . . The key point is always going to be the judgment you then make from what is almost always imperfect intelligence."

On the issues of contacts between al Qaeda and Iraq, policymakers made different judgments based on the same facts. Policymakers in the Defense Department made too much of al Qaeda contacts with Iraq, but critics in Congress and elsewhere made too little of these contacts. Here's what the 9/11 Commission said in its report issued in summer

2004, a report widely regarded as objective even though it seemed to blame Bush more for eight months of dawdling on the terrorist threat than Clinton for eight years:

> around this time [1997] Bin Laden sent out a number of feelers to the Iraqi regime, offering some cooperation. None are reported to have received a significant response.

> In mid-1998, the situation reversed: it was Iraq that reportedly took the initiative. In March 1998, after Bin Laden's public fatwa [the declaration of a holy war] against the United States, two al Qaeda members reportedly went to Iraq to meet with Iraqi intelligence. In July, an Iraqi delegation traveled to Afghanistan to meet first with the Taliban and then with Bin Laden. Sources reported that one, or perhaps both, of these meetings were apparently arranged through Bin Laden's Egyptian deputy, Zawahiri, who had ties of his own to the Iraqis.

> Similar meetings between Iraqi officials and Bin Laden may have occurred in 1999 during a period of some reported strains with the Taliban. According to the reporting, Iraqi officials offered Bin Laden safe haven in Iraq. Bin Laden declined, apparently judging that his circumstances in Afghanistan remained more favorable than the Iraqi circumstances. The reports describe friendly contacts and indicate some common themes in both sides' hatred of the United States. But to date we have seen no evidence that these or the earlier contacts ever developed into a collaborative operational relationship. Nor have we seen evidence indicating that Iraq cooperated with al Qaeda in developing or carrying out any attacks against the United States.[6]

Opponents of the decision to go to war did not hesitate to emphasize the conclusion that "no collaborative operational relationship" existed between Iraq and al Qaeda. But supporters of the decision wondered about the contacts that did exist, especially the offer by Iraq in 1999 to give bin Laden safe haven in Iraq. Although bin Laden declined that offer at the time, the offer suggested a very substantial motivation to collaborate. After all, Iraq was offering to become another Taliban government to harbor and support bin Laden and al Qaeda. And, although bin Laden said no, if Iraq offered safe haven once, might it not do so again? Moreover, what constitutes collaboration in the shadowy world of nonstate actors? What is that threshold and how do we know when it is crossed? Is it unreasonable to conclude from this intelligence that Iraq and al Qaeda might collaborate operationally in the future? Is it unreasonable to conclude that they won't? Both seem like reasoned judgments of the facts made from different perspectives.

My purpose here is not to resolve this dispute but, on the contrary, to note that it cannot be resolved, especially not by claiming that the facts either way are a "slam dunk." Perspectives influenced these judgments as much as facts. Those looking at this intelligence from a liberal perspective, which emphasizes interdependent relationships between al Qaeda and Iraq, would be looking for repetitive interactions and joint behavior. No concrete intelligence that connects the two parties operationally, no connection warranted. Those looking at it from a realist perspective would pay more attention to the broader strategic context in which these relationships existed. Al Qaeda and Iraq had a common enemy in the United States and thought once to collaborate against that enemy. Might they not do so again, especially after 9/11 (the earlier offer of safe haven came in 1999)? The first would see no significant interactions between al Qaeda and Iraq; the second would see a potential alliance and common adversary against the United States.

Still others, it might be recalled, argued that Iraq and al Qaeda would never collaborate because one was secular and the other sectarian. Although made by some realist commentators, this judgment is not realist. It is an identity judgment. Iraq and al Qaeda cannot collaborate because their political identities are too dissimilar. Realist judgments would never argue that ideological factors are more important than strategic ones. Yet, in this statement, ideological differences (identity) between

Iraq and al Qaeda are driving them apart more than strategic (realist) antagonisms toward the United States are bringing them together.

Weapons of Mass Destruction

The intelligence about Iraq's weapons of mass destruction provides another instance of differing judgments about the same facts. We can't possibly do justice to the whole issue here. But consider the following. Not only American, but all the major intelligence services (British, French, German, Russian, Chinese, Australian, etc.) concluded in early 2003 that Saddam Hussein possessed weapons of mass destruction.[7] Hans Blix, the head of the U.N. inspection effort in Iraq, reported as much to the Security Council two weeks before the invasion began: "intelligence agencies have expressed the view the proscribed programs [in Iraq] have continued or restarted in this period [since 1998]." "It is further contended," he noted, "that proscribed programs and items are located in underground facilities . . . and that proscribed items are being moved around Iraq." From this information, Blix himself drew the judgment that, although Iraq had undertaken "a substantial measure of disarmament," Iraq's actions, "three to four months into the new resolution [referring to U.N. Resolution 1441], cannot be said to constitute immediate cooperation, nor do they necessarily cover all areas of relevance."[8]

These were the facts before the invasion. There is no doubt that some policymakers went beyond the facts. They concluded, as Director of Central Intelligence George Tenet did, that the evidence Saddam Hussein had WMD was a slam dunk. But critics make the same slam dunk assessment when they claim (in retrospect) that the facts were clear he did not have WMD. To be sure, there were dissenting views about Saddam's weapons within intelligence agencies. As I have already noted, there always are. Nevertheless, intelligence agencies, like decision makers, have to make judgments because the facts alone do not decide. All major western intelligence agencies made the same judgment that Saddam Hussein had weapons of mass destruction. That suggests the evidence before the invasion was fairly convincing. Fair-minded analysts acknowledge as much. As columnist Jim Hoagland noted in the *Washington Post* (July 29, 2004), "If you look at the way Saddam Hussein acted, any reasonable person would have concluded that he was hiding those weapons, just from what he said and did."

After the invasion (and one might argue only because the invasion allowed a thorough search of Iraq for WMD), we now know that Saddam Hussein did not have any actual weapons, although he did have some related capabilities to make such weapons. So what happened? Did political leaders deliberately manipulate or manufacture the facts? Although Congressional investigations thus far (additional ones are coming under the new Democratic Congress) have found no evidence that Bush and other administration officials pressured the intelligence agencies to come up with the facts they wanted, many today conclude that these officials did just that.[9] Many in Britain believe Blair did the same thing, especially when he highlighted the intelligence dossier that claimed Iraq might be able to assemble a bomb within 45 minutes. Partisanship and politics drive such conclusions. Do we gain anything by arguing that such weighty decisions are driven by political perfidy? Not very much. If the intelligence services of France, Germany, and Russia also concluded that Saddam Hussein had WMD, did their leaders too manipulate the facts? Hardly, since these leaders opposed the war. More likely, leaders on both sides of the issue simply interpreted the same facts differently. Perspective, not politics, drove leaders' decisions.

Bush officials defined the problem as waging the war on terror and preventing rogue states from acquiring WMD, which they might pass on to terrorists. In their view (and more than a decade of Iraqi obstinacy supports it), diplomacy and international sanctions had failed. Iraq kicked out U.N. inspectors in 1998, and aside from firing a few errant missiles, the U.S. and U.N. did nothing about it. If diplomacy was to have another chance, force would have to be used to get the inspectors back into Iraq and then to threaten Iraq with invasion if it did not

fully cooperate. It's possible that the neocons had a plan from the very beginning to attack Baghdad and correct the mistake they believed Bush's father made in 1991 by not getting rid of Saddam Hussein. Maybe foreign policy is all about blood feuds and personal elite politics. But maybe it is not. The Bush administration may have honestly believed, based on a realist assessment of what drives behavior in international affairs, that a much stronger utilization of force was necessary to make diplomacy and international institutions work.

And in a significant way they were right. Deploying an invasion force in the Persian Gulf in fall 2002 achieved what missile firings in 1998 failed to achieve. Inspectors returned to Iraq. Diplomacy was given another chance. Now the issue was how much time to give the inspectors to track down suspected WMD and whether in the end to trust Saddam Hussein and the judgment of the Security Council that Iraq had fully and verifiably disarmed. Complicating matters further, as war supporters saw it, was the fact that France and Russia, each of which has a veto on Security Council action, had substantial economic stakes in Iraq, both legitimate in the form of commercial contracts and illegitimate in the form of bribes extracted under the U.N. oil-for-food program.

Opponents of the decision to go to war made the case for continuing inspections and requiring international agreement in the Security Council to legitimize the use of force. They were not opposed to the use of force, any more than Bush or Blair officials were opposed to the role of inspectors and diplomacy. But, assessing the situation more from a liberal perspective that emphasizes diplomacy and international agreement, they believed, as Hans Blix intimated in his report, that Saddam Hussein had gone a long way to satisfy the international community that he had no WMD and would clarify remaining uncertainties if he was given enough time. They were more willing to trust Saddam and more eager to use international institutions, namely the veto system in the Security Council, to delay the use of force. If the United States was suspect in its desire for diplomacy—just a way station toward war, as critics contended—U.N. officials and war opponents were suspect in their willingness to use force—not a last but a past resort (no longer applicable in modern-day international affairs). Critics of the war never acknowledged that an invasion force was necessary to retrieve the diplomatic option of U.N. inspectors. But, equally, supporters of the war never made clear what evidence from inspections would ultimately satisfy them that Iraq had fully disarmed. The reluctance of both opponents and supporters of war to come clean reflects their relative preference for the use of diplomacy and force. It is a matter of emphasis and perspective, not of bad faith and politics.

Other analysts emphasize the role of actor identities and see the war determined largely by Saddam's paranoia. Was Saddam really bent on acquiring nuclear weapons when we find out he had none? Was he eventually willing to comply with international inspections and rules when he danced around the inspectors so many times? Maybe the issue for Saddam was not WMD per se, as realist perspectives saw it, or complying with international rules, as liberal perspectives saw it, but Iraq operating according to an ideological and normative code that alienated it from the rest of the world. Iraq, in short, acted in accordance with the dictates of its paranoid politics and ruler rather than an intention to acquire WMD or eventually satisfy U.N. inspectors.

Some evidence for this ideational view of Iraq's behavior exists. One of the great mysteries of the Iraq war is why Saddam Hussein gave up everything, including eventually his life, for nothing, since he had no WMD. This is something realists said he would never do, He was a survivor, not suicidal. Yet, if he knew he did not have WMD, why did he risk his regime pretending he did? A bluff may be rational, but not if it is pressed to the point of being called. Perhaps he did not know whether he had WMD, which then suggests he was disconnected from his own regime as well as the international community. Or perhaps he just didn't believe the U.S. and its allies would attack, or that France, Russia, and other supporters would let them attack. Diplomacy would save his regime. But all of these speculations suggest that he was out of touch; that,

as identity perspectives argue, there was no significant shared discourse or knowledge between Saddam Hussein and other players that might have led to a peaceful resolution of the dispute through common understandings. Liberal and realist factors—diplomacy and even rational deterrence by force—never had a chance to work because identity factors overrode them.

The same identity perspective, of course, can be used to explain U.S. behavior. The neocons were out of touch and never seriously considered how big the threat was and how many troops would be needed to contend with it, which realist perspectives stressed, or what specific results of the inspection process they would accept, which liberal perspectives stressed. They were driven all along by an ideological view of the world that distrusted other states and international negotiators unless they were similarly ideologically oriented. This identity perspective, it might be argued, also drives the Bush doctrine of democratizing Iraq and the Middle East region. A peaceful solution to WMD or serious political disputes, such as the Arab-Israeli dispute, is unlikely, according to this view, unless the governments in the region share more fundamental values including pluralism, human rights, and the rule of law.

Analysts employing a liberal perspective assume diplomacy and institutions can work in spite of such ideological or regime differences, indeed, they argue, that's the whole point of diplomacy. As the Iraq Study Group argued, you talk with your enemies in particular. Analysts who see the world more in identity than institutional terms, however, wonder which countries can be counted on to ensure that diplomatic agreements are implemented, especially in institutions that are divided among countries of different ideological persuasions and affinities. Still other analysts, who see the world in realist terms, conclude that all the talk about ideology and democracy is just that, talk. Ideas are epiphenomenal and other interests matter more. Neocons and Bush simply disguised their real motives—to depose Hussein and settle old scores—with a lot of rationalization about WMD and democracy. When no WMD were found, they shifted their rationale to promoting freedom and democracy.

Compare, Evaluate, Prioritize

Perspectives provide a powerful tool for understanding why we disagree about foreign policy. They illuminate not only contemporary but historical debates.[10] People of good faith differ in the judgments they make about the principal causes of world events. Serious analysts consider all perspectives and gather as many facts from each perspective as they can. But they can never gather all the facts, and they must still interpret which facts are more important than others. Just as they are condemned to select something in order to understand anything, they are also condemned to make different judgments and thus to disagree.

Yes, it is possible and necessary to narrow disagreements, to formulate hypotheses from different perspectives about how the world works, and to look for new facts that can adjudicate between alternative propositions. That is the scientific method, and all serious people use it. But scientific method is not truth. It is a tool to analyze in a rationalist or positivist manner an infinitely complicated world. Even natural scientists demur from declaring that they have discovered the truth. They may demonstrate that a proposition is not false, that is, it seems to be consistent with the way the world is. But all good natural scientists know that their propositions do not capture the real world as it actually is. An alternative proposition may also be consistent with their results. In physics, quantum mechanics explains subatomic phenomena on the basis of probability, while Newtonian mechanics explains planetary phenomena on the basis of fixed bodies. Both theories work within their domains, but the worlds they postulate are completely incompatible. The actual world is obviously something different from either theory. So physicist and mathematicians are looking for another theory that might tell us about a world which accounts for both Newtonian and quantum mechanics and much more. That's string theory, but there's no guarantee that it will be the final word either. If we have that much trouble knowing the way the natural world actually

works, whose parts do not have a will of their own, shouldn't we be more modest about what we can know about the social world of international politics?

The social sciences, especially world affairs, are much more complicated. The subjects they study— human beings—do have minds of their own, and they can and do often change their minds on a whim. How do we capture the laws by which such a world works? For the most part, we don't. We adopt different perspectives, gather facts suggested by those perspectives, compare, evaluate, and ultimately prioritize those facts. In the process we make different judgments and give weight to different perspectives. The miracle is that we don't disagree more than we actually do.

Politics works against the recognition of the role of perspectives. Each side insists that the facts speak for themselves when the facts favor its interpretation. Lee Hamilton, a respected former Democratic congressman and co-chair of the 9/11 Commission, gave a recent example. Appearing at a September 11, 2006, press conference with his Republican co-chair of the 9/11 Commission, Thomas Kean, Hamilton said: "Facts are not Republican, and they're not Democratic. They're not ideological. Facts are facts." But, revealingly, he made this comment to rebuke his Republican co-chair; they were having a dispute about the facts in an ABC docudrama, "The Path to 9/11." Facts may not be Republican or Democratic, but they have to be interpreted by Republicans and Democrats. Hamilton said what we all say when we want to claim the facts for our point of view. We say the facts are a slam dunk. But they never are.

Given these complexities, could we be more modest? Could we tone down the personalization of debate, as well as all attempts to beat each other up with "the" facts. Our opponents on an issue are not stupid or evil. They speak from a different perspective, and we can listen carefully to them to divine how and where they emphasize and evaluate facts differently than we do. David Brooks, the respected *New York Times* columnist, demonstrates how we all use perspectives when we present our own conclusions. Asking about current leaders in Iran, he wrote (September 21, 2006):

> Do they respond to incentives and follow the dictates of what we call self-interest? . . . Or, alternatively, are they playing an entirely different game? Are the men who occupy the black hole that is the Iranian power elite engaged in a religious enterprise based on an eschatological time frame and driven by supernatural longings we can't begin to fathom?

Brooks is addressing and contrasting the realist (material self-interest) and identity (religious aspirations) perspectives on Iranian leadership, in the same article, he mentions a third perspective, the liberal one. Many intellectual elites, he writes, counsel a code of caution toward the Iranian leadership; "Be tolerant of cultural differences, seek to understand the responses of people who feel oppressed, don't judge groups, never criticize somebody else's religion." These are all respectable ways to address an enormously complicated problem. But they are not compatible with one another. We have to choose. Brooks makes his choices:

> The Muslim millenarians possess a habit of mind that causes them to escalate conflicts. . . . They seem confident they can prevail, owing to their willingness to die for their truth. They don't seem to feel marginalized but look down on us as weak, and doubt our ability to strike back. . . . With America exhausted by Iraq, . . . Western policy is drifting toward the option . . . that is containment. . . . In other words, a policy that was designed to confront a secular, bureaucratic foe—the Soviets—will now be used to confront a surging, jihadist one.

For Brooks, "a habit of mind," "a surging, jihadist one," an identity perspective drives Muslim fundamentalists. The millenarians do not feel "marginalized" because they are weak or excluded by international diplomacy and institutions, as a liberal point of view might emphasize. Rather they feel strong and empowered by their ideas, "their truth," and are willing to die for it. So they won't be stopped by realist strategies that try to contain or

counterbalance them. Their ideas preclude compromise and deterrence.

Others will certainly disagree with Brooks. But they will do so by making different judgments about the same facts. They may argue that the jihadist mind-set comes from marginalization of Islamic grievances in the past and may be alleviated by inclusion and compromise in the future. Or they may conclude that ideological mind-sets do eventually respond to containment and material counterpressures, just as George Kennan predicted in 1947 that communist fundamentalists would eventually mellow if the United States contained Soviet expansion in Europe.

These differing judgments are all logical and can be understood without disparaging our political opponents. Indeed, one can even argue they are all necessary if we are going to see the world in as many different ways as possible, because we cannot see it as it actually is. While each of us, as a moral human being, has to make a choice, all of us together can benefit from the differences. We can thank the people we disagree with because they remind us that none of us has a corner on the true nature of the world we inhabit, especially the world of foreign affairs.

Notes

1. "Bush lied about Iraq" brings up 1.26 million hits on Google; "Blair lied about Iraq" brings up 1.13 million.
2. Carl Sandburg, *Abraham Lincoln: The War Years Volume 1* (Harcourt Brace and World, 1939), vii.
3. See Nicholas D. Kristof, "Talking to Evil," *New York Times* (August 13, 2006).
4. Ronald Steel, "The Weak at War with the Strong," *New York Times* (September 14, 2001).
5. Sandburg, *Abraham Lincoln,* 90.
6. *The 9/11 Commission Report: Final Report of the National Commission on Terrorist Attacks upon the United States,* authorized edition (W.W. Norton, 2004), 66.
7. A *New York Times* editorial (November 15, 2005) disputed the claim that other intelligence agencies agreed with U.S. intelligence. The White House fired back the same day with a fact sheet supporting the

claim. Perhaps the best adjudicator of this dispute is a former CIA agent who was in the intelligence community in spring 2003 before he left the CIA and became a sharp critic of the administration. Paul Pillar wrote in "Intelligence, Policy, and the War in Iraq," *Foreign Affairs* 85:2 (March/April 2006): "the Bush administration was quite right: its perception of Saddam's weapons capacities was shared by the Clinton administration, congressional Democrats, and most other Western governments and intelligence services." See also Mortimer B. Zuckerman, "Foul-ups—Not Felonies," *U.S. News and World Report* (November 14, 2005).

8. "In a Chief Inspector's Words: A Substantial Measure of Disarmament," excerpts from reports by Hans Blix and Mohammed El Baradei to the U.N. Security Council, *New York Times* (March 8, 2003).

9. For example, the bipartisan report by the Senate Intelligence Committee in 2005 concluded that it "did not find any evidence that administration officials attempted to coerce, influence, or pressure analysts to change their judgment related to Iraq's WMD." And the Robb-Silverman report was equally clear: there was "no evidence of political pressure to influence the intelligence community's prewar assessments of Iraq's weapons programs" or "to skew or alter any . . . analytical judgments."

10. See the debates on eighteenth- and nineteenth-century European wars, World Wars I and II, and the Cold War in my book, *Perspectives on International Relations: Power, institutions, and Ideas.*

Hypotheses on Misperception

ROBERT JERVIS

Jervis analyzes the role of psychological factors in the decision making processes of policy makers, particularly the role of perception and misperception. He discusses the importance of belief structures and images, cognitive consistency, and cognitive dissonance as factors that may undermine rationality. He also analyzes impediments to effective learning by policymakers, and notes how they often engage in wishful thinking and false analogies. Finally Jervis discusses problems with the effective signaling of one's intent to policymakers in another state.

In determining how he will behave, an actor must try to predict how others will act and how their actions will affect his values. The actor must therefore develop an image of others and of their intentions. This image may, however, turn out to be an inaccurate one; the actor may, for a number of reasons, misperceive both others' actions and their intentions. In this research note I wish to discuss the types of misperceptions of other states' intentions which states tend to make. The concept of intention is complex, but here we can consider it to comprise the ways in which the state feels it will act in a wide range of future contingencies. These ways of acting usually are not specific and well-developed plans. For many reasons a national or individual actor may not know how he will act under given conditions, but this problem cannot be dealt with here.

I. Previous Treatments of Perception in International Relations

Although diplomatic historians have discussed misperception in their treatments of specific events, students of international relations have generally ignored this topic. However, two sets of scholars have applied content analysis to the documents that flowed within and between governments in the six weeks preceding World War I. But the data have been put into quantitative form in a way that does not produce accurate measures of perceptions and intentions and that makes it impossible to gather useful evidence on misperception.[1]

The second group of theorists who have explicitly dealt with general questions of misperception in international relations consists of those, like Charles Osgood, Amitai Etzioni, and, to a lesser extent, Kenneth Boulding and J. David Singer, who have analyzed the cold war in terms of a spiral of misperception.[2] This approach grows partly out of the mathematical theories of L. F. Richardson[3] and partly out of findings of social and cognitive psychology, many of which will be discussed in this research note.

These authors state their case in general, if not universal, terms, but do not provide many historical cases that are satisfactorily explained by their theories. Furthermore, they do not deal with any of the numerous instances that contradict their notion of the self-defeating aspects of the use of power. They ignore the fact that states are not individuals and that the findings of psychology can be applied to organizations only with great care. Most important, their theoretical analysis is for the most part of reduced value because it seems largely to be a product of their assumption that the Soviet Union is a basically status-quo power whose apparently aggressive behavior is a product of fear of the West.

Yet they supply little or no evidence to support this view. Indeed, the explanation for the differences of opinion between the spiral theorists and the proponents of deterrence lies not in differing general views of international relations, differing values and morality,[4] or differing methods of analysis,[5] but in differing perceptions of Soviet intentions.

II. Theories—Necessary and Dangerous

Despite the limitations of their approach, these writers have touched on a vital problem that has not been given systematic treatment by theorists of international relations. The evidence from both psychology and history overwhelmingly supports the view (which may be labeled Hypothesis I) that decision-makers tend to fit incoming information into their existing theories and images. Indeed, their theories and images play a large part in determining what they notice. In other words, *actors tend to perceive what they expect.* Furthermore (Hypothesis Ia), a theory will have greater impact on an actor's interpretation of data (a) the greater the ambiguity of the data and (b) the higher the degree of confidence with which the actor holds the theory.[6]

For many purposes we can use the concept of differing levels of perceptual thresholds to deal with the fact that it takes more, and more unambiguous, information for an actor to recognize an unexpected phenomenon than an expected one. An experiment by Bruner and Postman determined "that the recognition threshold for . . . incongruous playing cards (those with suits and color reversed) is significantly higher than the threshold for normal cards."[7] Not only are people able to identify normal (and therefore expected) cards more quickly and easily than incongruous (and therefore unexpected) ones, but also they may at first take incongruous cards for normal ones.

However, we should not assume, as the spiral theorists often do, that it is necessarily irrational for actors to adjust incoming information to fit more closely their existing beliefs and images. ("Irrational" here describes acting under pressures that the actor would not admit as legitimate if he were conscious of them.) For example, Osgood claims that psycho-logic is displayed when the Soviets praise a man or a proposal and people in the West react by distrusting the object of this praise.[8] But if a person believes that the Russians are aggressive, it is logical for him to be suspicious of their moves. When we say that a decision-maker "dislikes" another state this usually means that he believes that that other state has policies conflicting with those of his nation. Reasoning and experience indicate to the decision-maker that the "disliked" state is apt to harm his state's interests. Thus in these cases there is no need to invoke "psychologic," and it cannot be claimed that the cases demonstrate the substitution of "emotional consistency for rational consistency."[9]

The question of the relations among particular beliefs and cognitions can often be seen as part of the general topic of the relation of incoming bits of information to the receivers' already established images. The need to fit data into a wider framework of beliefs, even if doing so does not seem to do justice to individual facts, is not, or at least is not only, a psychological drive that decreases the accuracy of our perceptions of the world, but is "essential to the logic of inquiry."[10] Facts can be interpreted, and indeed identified, only with the aid of hypotheses and theories. Pure empiricism is impossible, and it would be unwise to revise theories in the light of every bit of information that does not easily conform to them.[11] No hypothesis can be expected to account for all the evidence, and if a prevailing view is supported by many theories and by a large pool of findings it should not be quickly altered. Too little rigidity can be as bad as too much.[12]

This is as true in the building of social and physical science as it is in policy-making.[13]

Thus it is important to see that the dilemma of how "open" to be to new information is one that inevitably plagues any attempt at understanding in any field. Instances in which evidence seems to be ignored or twisted to fit the existing theory can often be explained by this dilemma instead of by illogical or nonlogical psychological pressures toward consistency. This is especially true of decision-makers' attempts to estimate the intentions of other states, since they must constantly take account of the danger that the other state is trying to deceive them.

The theoretical framework discussed thus far, together with an examination of many cases, suggests Hypothesis 2: scholars and decision-makers are apt to err by being too wedded to the established view and too closed to new information, as opposed to being too willing to alter their theories.[14] Another way of making this point is to argue that *actors tend to establish their theories and expectations prematurely*. In politics, of course, this is often necessary because of the need for action. But experimental evidence indicates that the same tendency also occurs on the unconscious level. Bruner and Postman found that "perhaps the greatest single barrier to the recognition of incongruous stimuli is the tendency for perceptual hypotheses to fixate after receiving a minimum of confirmation. . . . Once there had occurred in these cases a partial confirmation of the hypothesis . . . it seemed that nothing could change the subject's report."[15]

However, when we apply these and other findings to politics and discuss kinds of misperception, we should not quickly apply the label of cognitive distortion. We should proceed cautiously for two related reasons. The first is that the evidence available to decision-makers almost always permits several interpretations. It should be noted that there are cases of visual perception in which different stimuli can produce exactly the same pattern on an observer's retina. Thus, for an observer using one eye the same pattern would be produced by a sphere the size of a golf ball which was quite close to the observer, by a baseball-sized sphere that was further away, or by a basketball-sized sphere still further away. Without other clues, the observer cannot possibly determine which of these stimuli he is presented with, and we would not want to call his incorrect perceptions examples of distortion. Such cases, relatively rare in visual perception, are frequent in international relations. The evidence available to decision-makers is almost always very ambiguous since accurate clues to others' intentions are surrounded by noise[16] and deception. In most cases, no matter how long, deeply, and "objectively" the evidence is analyzed, people can differ in their interpretations, and there are no general rules to indicate who is correct.

The second reason to avoid the label of cognitive distortion is that the distinction between perception and judgment, obscure enough in individual psychology, is almost absent in the making of inferences in international politics. Decision-makers who reject information that contradicts their views—or who develop complex interpretations of it—often do so consciously and explicitly. Since the evidence available contains contradictory information, to make any inferences requires that much information be ignored or given interpretations that will seem tortuous to those who hold a different position.

Indeed, if we consider only the evidence available to a decision-maker at the time of decision, the view later proved incorrect may be supported by as much evidence as the correct one—or even by more. Scholars have often been too unsympathetic with the people who were proved wrong. On closer examination, it is frequently difficult to point to differences between those who were right and those who were wrong with respect to their openness to new information and willingness to modify their views. Winston Churchill, for example, did not open-mindedly view each Nazi action to see if the explanations provided by the appeasers accounted for the data better than his own beliefs. Instead, like Chamberlain, he fitted each bit of ambiguous information into his own hypotheses. That he was correct should not lead us to overlook the fact that his methods of analysis and use of theory to produce cognitive consistency did not basically differ from those of the appeasers.[17]

A consideration of the importance of expectations in influencing perception also indicates that the widespread belief in the prevalence of "*wishful thinking*" may be incorrect, or at least may be based on inadequate data. The psychological literature on the interaction between affect and perception is immense and cannot be treated here, but it should be noted that phenomena that at first were considered strong evidence for the impact of affect on perception often can be better treated as demonstrating the influence of expectations.[18] Thus, in international relations, cases like the United States' misestimation of the political climate in Cuba in April 1961, which may seem at first glance to have been instances of wishful thinking, may instead be more adequately explained by the theories held by the decision-makers (e.g., Communist governments are unpopular). Of course, desires may have an impact on perception by influencing expectations, but since so many other factors affect expectations, the net influence of desires may not be great.

There is evidence from both psychology[19] and international relations that when expectations and desires clash, expectations seem to be more important. The United States would like to believe that North Vietnam is about to negotiate or that the USSR is ready to give up what the United States believes is its goal of world domination, but ambiguous evidence is seen to confirm the opposite conclusion, which conforms to the United States' expectations. Actors are apt to be especially sensitive to evidence of grave danger if they think they can take action to protect themselves against the menace once it has been detected.

III. Safeguards

Can anything then be said to scholars and decision-makers other than "Avoid being either too open or too closed, but be especially aware of the latter danger"? Although decision-makers will always be faced with ambiguous and confusing evidence and will be forced to make inferences about others which will often be inaccurate, a number of safeguards may be suggested which could enable them to minimize their errors. First, and most obvious, decision-makers should be aware that they do not make "unbiased" interpretations of each new bit of incoming information, but rather are inevitably heavily influenced by the theories they expect to be verified. They should know that what may appear to them as a self-evident and unambiguous inference often seems so only because of their preexisting beliefs. To someone with a different theory the same data may appear to be unimportant or to support another explanation. Thus many events provide less independent support for the decision-makers' images than they may at first realize. Knowledge of this should lead decision-makers to examine more closely evidence that others believe contradicts their views.

Second, decision-makers should see if their attitudes contain consistent or supporting beliefs that are not logically linked. While it is not logically surprising nor is it evidence of psychological pressures to find that people who believe that Russia is aggressive are very suspicious of any Soviet move, other kinds of consistency are more suspect. For example, most people who feel that it is important for the United States to win the war in Vietnam also feel that a meaningful victory is possible. And most people who feel defeat would neither endanger U.S. national security nor be costly in terms of other values also feel that we cannot win. Although there are important logical linkages between the two parts of each of these views (especially through theories of guerrilla warfare), they do not seem strong enough to explain the degree to which the opinions are correlated. Similarly, in Finland in the winter of 1939, those who felt that grave consequences would follow Finnish agreement to give Russia a military base also believed that the Soviets would withdraw their demand if Finland stood firm. And those who felt that concessions would not lead to loss of major values also believed that Russia would fight if need be.[20] In this country, those who favored a nuclear test ban tended to argue that fallout was very harmful, that only limited improvements in technology would flow from further testing, and that a test ban would increase the chances for peace and security. Those who opposed the test ban were apt to disagree on all three points. This does not mean, of course, that the people holding such sets of supporting views were necessarily wrong in any one element. The Finns who wanted to make concessions to the USSR were probably correct in both parts of their argument. But decision-makers should be suspicious if they hold a position in which elements that are not logically connected support the same conclusion. This condition is psychologically comfortable and makes decisions easier to reach (since competing values do not have to be balanced off against each other). The chances are thus considerable that at least part of the reason why a person holds some of these views is related to psychology and not to the substance of the evidence.

Decision-makers should also be aware that actors who suddenly find themselves having an important shared interest with other actors have a tendency to overestimate the degree of common interest involved. This tendency is especially strong for those actors (e.g., the United States, at least before 1950) whose beliefs about international relations and morality imply that they can cooperate only with "good" states and that with those states there will be no major conflicts. On the other hand, states that have either a tradition of limited cooperation with others (e.g., Britain) or a strongly held theory that differentiates occasional from permanent allies[21] (e.g., the Soviet Union) find it easier to resist this tendency and need not devote special efforts to combating its danger.

A third safeguard for decision-makers would be to make their assumptions, beliefs, and the predictions that follow from them as explicit as possible. An actor should try to determine, before events occur, what evidence would count for and against his theories. By knowing what to expect he would know what to be surprised by, and surprise could indicate to that actor that his beliefs needed revaluation.[22]

A fourth safeguard is more complex. The decision-maker should try to prevent individuals and organizations from letting their main task, political future, and identity become tied to specific theories and images of other actors.[23] If this occurs, subgoals originally sought for their contribution to higher ends will take on value of their own, and information indicating possible alternative routes to the original goals will not be carefully considered. For example, the U.S. Forest Service was unable to carry out its original purpose as effectively when it began to see its distinctive competence not in promoting the best use of lands and forests but rather in preventing all types of forest fires.[24]

Organizations that claim to be unbiased may not realize the extent to which their definition of their role has become involved with certain beliefs about the world. Allen Dulles is a victim of this lack of understanding when he says, "I grant that we are all creatures of prejudice, including CIA officials, but by entrusting intelligence coordination to our central intelligence service, which is excluded from policy-making and is married to no particular military hardware, we can avoid, to the greatest possible extent, the bending of facts obtained through intelligence to suit a particular occupational viewpoint."[25] This statement overlooks the fact that the CIA has developed a certain view of international relations and of the cold war which maximizes the importance of its information-gathering, espionage, and subversive activities. Since the CIA would lose its unique place in the government if it were decided that the "back alleys" of world politics were no longer vital to U.S. security, it is not surprising that the organization interprets information in a way that stresses the continued need for its techniques.

Fifth, decision-makers should realize the validity and implications of Roberta Wohlstetter's argument that "a willingness to play with material from different angles and in the context of unpopular as well as popular hypotheses is an essential ingredient of a good detective, whether the end is the solution of a crime or an intelligence estimate."[26] However, it is often difficult, psychologically and politically, for any one person to do this. Since a decision-maker usually cannot get "unbiased" treatments of data, he should instead seek to structure conflicting biases into the decision-making process. The decision-maker, in other words, should have devil's advocates around. Just as, as Neustadt points out,[27] the decision-maker will want to create conflicts among his subordinates in order to make appropriate choices, so he will also want to ensure that incoming information is examined from many different perspectives with many different hypotheses in mind. To some extent this kind of examination will be done automatically through the divergence of goals, training, experience, and information that exists in any large organization. But in many cases this divergence will not be sufficient. The views of those analyzing the data will still

be too homogeneous, and the decision-maker will have to go out of his way not only to cultivate but to create differing viewpoints.

While all that would be needed would be to have some people examining the data trying to validate unpopular hypotheses, it would probably be more effective if they actually believed and had a stake in the views they were trying to support. If in 1941 someone had had the task of proving the view that Japan would attack Pearl Harbor, the government might have been less surprised by the attack. And only a person who was out to show that Russia would take objectively great risks would have been apt to note that several ships with especially large hatches going to Cuba were riding high in the water, indicating the presence of a bulky but light cargo that was not likely to be anything other than strategic missiles. And many people who doubt the wisdom of the administration's Vietnam policy would be somewhat reassured if there were people in the government who searched the statements and actions of both sides in an effort to prove that North Vietnam was willing to negotiate and that the official interpretation of such moves as the Communist activities during the Têt truce of 1967 was incorrect.

Of course all these safeguards involve costs. They would divert resources from other tasks and would increase internal dissension. Determining whether these costs would be worth the gains would depend on a detailed analysis of how the suggested safeguards might be implemented. Even if they were adopted by a government, of course, they would not eliminate the chance of misperception. However, the safeguards would make it more likely that national decision-makers would make conscious choices about the way data were interpreted rather than merely assuming that they can be seen in only one way and can mean only one thing. Statesmen would thus be reminded of alternative images of others just as they are constantly reminded of alternative policies.

These safeguards are partly based on Hypothesis 3: actors can more easily assimilate into their established image of another actor information contradicting that image if the information is transmitted and considered bit by bit than if it comes all at once. In the former case, each piece of discrepant data can be coped with as it arrives and each of the conflicts with the prevailing view will be small enough to go unnoticed, to be dismissed as unimportant, or to necessitate at most a slight modification of the image (e.g., addition of exceptions to the rule). When the information arrives in a block, the contradiction between it and the prevailing view is apt to be much clearer and the probability of major cognitive reorganization will be higher.

IV. Sources of Concepts

An actor's perceptual thresholds—and thus the images that ambiguous information is apt to produce—are influenced by what he has experienced and learned about.[28] If one actor is to perceive that another fits in a given category he must first have, or develop, a concept for that category. We can usefully distinguish three levels at which a concept can be present or absent. First, the concept can be completely missing. The actor's cognitive structure may not include anything corresponding to the phenomenon he is encountering. This situation can occur not only in science fiction, but also in a world of rapid change or in the meeting of two dissimilar systems. Thus China's image of the Western world was extremely inaccurate in the mid-nineteenth century, her learning was very slow, and her responses were woefully inadequate. The West was spared a similar struggle only because it had the power to reshape the system it encountered. Once the actor clearly sees one instance of the new phenomenon, he is apt to recognize it much more quickly in the future.[29] Second, the actor can know about a concept but not believe that it reflects an actual phenomenon. Thus Communist and Western decision-makers are each aware of the other's explanation of how his system functions, but do not think that the concept corresponds to reality. Third, the actor may hold a concept, but not believe that another actor fills it at the present moment. Thus the British and French statesmen of the 1930s held a concept of states with unlimited ambitions. They realized that Napoleons were possible, but they did not think Hitler belonged in that category.

Hypothesis 4 distinguishes these three cases: misperception is most difficult to correct in the case of a missing concept and least difficult to correct in the case of a recognized but presumably unfilled concept. All other things being equal (e.g., the degree to which the concept is central to the actor's cognitive structure), the first case requires more cognitive reorganization than does the second, and the second requires more reorganization than the third.

However, this hypothesis does not mean that learning will necessarily be slowest in the first case, for if the phenomena are totally new the actor may make such grossly inappropriate responses that he will quickly acquire information clearly indicating that he is faced with something he does not understand. And the sooner the actor realizes that things are not—or may not—be—what they seem, the sooner he is apt to correct his image.[30]

Three main sources contribute to decision-makers' concepts of international relations and of other states and influence the level of their perceptual thresholds for various phenomena. First, an actor's beliefs about his own domestic political system are apt to be important. In some cases, like that of the USSR, the decision-makers' concepts are tied to an ideology that explicitly provides a frame of reference for viewing foreign affairs. Even where this is not the case, experience with his own system will partly determine what the actor is familiar with and what he is apt to perceive in others. Louis Hartz claims, "It is the absence of the experience of social revolution which is at the heart of the whole American dilemma. . . . In a whole series of specific ways it enters into our difficulty of communication with the rest of the world. We find it difficult to understand Europe's 'social question'. . . .We are not familiar with the deeper social struggles of Asia and hence tend to interpret even reactionary regimes as 'democratic.'"[31] Similarly, George Kennan argues that in World War I the Allied powers, and especially America, could not understand the bitterness and violence of others' internal conflicts: ". . . The inability of the Allied statesmen to picture to themselves the passions of the Russian civil war [was partly caused by the fact that] we represent . . . a society in which the manifestations of evil have been carefully buried and sublimated in the social behavior of people, as in their very consciousness. For this reason, probably, despite our widely traveled and outwardly cosmopolitan lives, the mainsprings of political behavior in such a country as Russia tend to remain concealed from our vision."[32]

Second, concepts will be supplied by the actor's previous experiences. An experiment from another field illustrates this. Dearborn and Simon presented business executives from various divisions (e.g., sales, accounting, production) with the same hypothetical data and asked them for an analysis and recommendations from the standpoint of what would be best for the company as a whole. The executives' views heavily reflected their departmental perspectives.[33] Similarly it has been argued that Chamberlain was slow to recognize Hitler's intentions partly because of the limiting nature of his personal background and business experiences.[34] The impact of training and experience seems to be demonstrated when the background of the appeasers is compared to that of their opponents. One difference stands out: "A substantially higher percentage of the anti-appeasers (irrespective of class origins) had the kind of knowledge which comes from close acquaintance, mainly professional, with foreign affairs."[35] Since members of the diplomatic corps are responsible for meeting threats to the nation's security before these grow to major proportions and since they have learned about cases in which aggressive states were not recognized as such until very late, they may be prone to interpret ambiguous data as showing that others are aggressive. It should be stressed that we cannot say that the professionals of the 1930s were more apt to make accurate judgments of other states. Rather, they may have been more sensitive to the chance that others were aggressive. They would then rarely take an aggressor for a status-quo power, but would more often make the opposite error.[36] Thus in the years before World War I the permanent officials in the British Foreign Office overestimated German aggressiveness.[37]

A third source of concepts, which frequently will be the most directly relevant to a decision-maker's perception of international relations, is international history. As Henry Kissinger points out, one reason why statesmen were so slow to recognize the threat posed by Napoleon was that previous events had accustomed them only to actors who wanted to modify the existing system, not overthrow it.[38] The other side of the coin is even more striking: historical traumas can heavily influence future perceptions. They can either establish a state's image of the other state involved or can be used as analogies. An example of the former case is provided by the fact that for at least ten years after the Franco-Prussian War most of Europe's statesmen felt that Bismarck had aggressive plans when in fact his main goal was to protect the status quo. Of course the evidence was ambiguous. The post-1871 Bismarckian maneuvers, which were designed to keep peace, looked not unlike the pre-1871 maneuvers designed to set the stage for war. But that the post-1871 maneuvers were seen as indicating aggressive plans is largely attributable to the impact of Bismarck's earlier actions on the statesmen's image of him.

A state's previous unfortunate experience with a type of danger can sensitize it to other examples of that danger. While this sensitivity may lead the state to avoid the mistake it committed in the past, it may also lead it mistakenly to believe that the present situation is like the past one. Santayana's maxim could be turned around: "Those who remember the past are condemned to make the opposite mistakes."

The application of the Munich analogy to various contemporary events has been much commented on, and I do not wish to argue the substantive points at stake. But it seems clear that the probabilities that any state is facing an aggressor who has to be met by force are not altered by the career of Hitler and the history of the 1930s. Similarly the probability of an aggressor's announcing his plans is not increased (if anything, it is decreased) by the fact that Hitler wrote *Mein Kampf*. Yet decision-makers are more sensitive to these possibilities, and thus more apt to perceive ambiguous evidence as indicating they apply to a given case, than they would have been had there been no Nazi Germany.

Historical analogies often precede, rather than follow, a careful analysis of a situation (e.g., Truman's initial reaction to the news of the invasion of South Korea was to think of the Japanese invasion of Manchuria). Noting this precedence, however, does not show us which of many analogies will come to a decision-maker's mind. Truman could have thought of nineteenth-century European wars that were of no interest to the United States. Several factors having nothing to do with the event under consideration influences what analogies a decision-maker is apt to make. One factor is the number of cases similar to the analogy with which the decision-maker is familiar. Another is the importance of the past event to the political system of which the decision-maker is a part. The more times such an event occurred and the greater its consequences were, the more a decision-maker will be sensitive to the particular danger involved and the more he will be apt to see ambiguous stimuli as indicating another instance of this kind of event. A third factor is the degree of the decision-maker's personal involvement in the past case—in time, energy, ego, and position. The last-mentioned variable will affect not only the event's impact on the decision-maker's cognitive structure, but also the way he perceives the event and the lesson he draws. Greater personal involvement will usually give the event greater impact, especially if the decision-maker's own views were validated by the event. One need not accept a total application of learning theory to nations to believe that "nothing fails like success."[39] It also seems likely that if many critics argued at the time that the decision-maker was wrong, he will be even more apt to see other situations in terms of the original event. A fourth factor is the degree to which the analogy is compatible with the rest of his belief system. A fifth is the absence of alternative concepts and analogies. Individuals and states vary in the amount of direct or indirect political experience they have had which can provide different ways of interpreting data. Decision-makers who are aware of multiple possibilities of states' intentions may be less likely to seize on an analogy prematurely. The perception of citizens of nations like the United States which have relatively little history of international politics may be more apt to be heavily influenced by the few major international events that have been important to their country.

The first three factors indicate that an event is more apt to shape present perceptions if it occurred in the recent rather than the remote past. If it occurred recently, the statesman will then know about it at first hand even if he was not involved in the making of policy at the time. Thus if generals are prepared to fight the last war, diplomats may be prepared to avoid the last war. Part of the Anglo-French reaction to Hitler can be explained by the prevailing beliefs that the First World War was to a large extent caused by misunderstandings and could have been avoided by farsighted and non-belligerent diplomacy. And part of the Western perception of Russia and China can be explained by the view that appeasement was an inappropriate response to Hitler.[40]

V. The Evoked Set

The way people perceive data is influenced not only by their cognitive structure and theories about other actors but also by what they are concerned with at the time they receive the information. Information is evaluated in light of the small part of the person's memory that is presently active—the "evoked set." My perceptions of the dark streets I pass walking home from the movies will be different if the film I saw had dealt with spies than if it had been a comedy. If I am working on aiding a country's education system and I hear someone talk about the need for economic development in that state, I am apt to think he is concerned with education, whereas if I had been working on, say, trying to achieve political stability in that country, I would have placed his remarks in that framework.[41]

Thus Hypothesis 5 states that when messages are sent from a different background of concerns and information than is possessed by the receiver, misunderstanding is likely. Person A and person B will read the same message quite differently if A has seen several related messages that B does not know about. This difference will be compounded if, as is frequently the case, A and B each assume that the other has the same background he does. This means that misperception can occur even when deception is neither intended nor expected. Thus Roberta Wohlstetter found not only that different parts of the United States government had different perceptions of data about Japan's intentions and messages partly because they saw the incoming information in very different contexts, but also that officers in the field misunderstood warnings from Washington: "Washington advised General Short [in Pearl Harbor] on November 27 to expect 'hostile action' at any moment, by which it meant 'attack on American possessions from without,' but General Short understood this phrase to mean 'sabotage.'"[42] Washington did not realize the extent to which Pearl Harbor considered the danger of sabotage to be primary, and furthermore it incorrectly believed that General Short had received the intercepts of the secret Japanese diplomatic messages available in Washington which indicated that surprise attack was a distinct possibility. Another implication of this hypothesis is that if important information is known to only part of the government of state A and part of the government of state B, international messages may be misunderstood by those parts of the receiver's government that do not match, in the information they have, the part of the sender's government that dispatched the message.[43]

Two additional hypotheses can be drawn from the problems of those sending messages. Hypothesis 6 states that when people spend a great deal of time drawing up a plan or making a decision, they tend to think that the message about it they wish to convey will be clear to the receiver.[44] Since they are aware of what is to them the important pattern in their actions, they often feel that the pattern will be equally obvious to others, and they overlook the degree to which the message is apparent to them only because they know what to look for. Those who have not participated in the endless meetings may not understand what information the sender is trying to convey. George Quester has shown how the German and, to a lesser extent, the British desire to maintain target limits on bombing in the first eighteen months of World War II was undermined partly by the fact that each side knew the limits it was seeking and its own reasons for any

apparent "exceptions" (e.g., the German attack on Rotterdam) and incorrectly felt that these limits and reasons were equally clear to the other side.[45]

Hypothesis 7 holds that actors often do not realize that actions intended to project a given image may not have the desired effect because the actions themselves do not turn out as planned. Thus even without appreciable impact of different cognitive structures and backgrounds, an action may convey an unwanted message. For example, a country's representatives may not follow instructions and so may give others impressions contrary to those the home government wished to convey. In such cases both sides will believe that the other is reading hostility into a policy of theirs which is friendly. Similarly, Quester's study shows that the attempt to limit bombing referred to above failed partly because neither side was able to bomb as accurately as it thought it could and thus did not realize the physical effects of its actions.[46]

VI. Further Hypotheses from the Perspective of the Perceiver

From the perspective of the perceiver several other hypotheses seem to hold. Hypothesis 8 is that there is an overall tendency for decision-makers to see other states as more hostile than they are.[47] There seem to be more cases of statesmen incorrectly believing others are planning major acts against their interest than of statesmen being lulled by a potential aggressor. There are many reasons for this which are too complex to be treated here (e.g., some parts of the bureaucracy feel it is their responsibility to be suspicious of all other states; decision-makers often feel they are "playing it safe" to believe and act as though the other state were hostile in questionable cases; and often, when people do not feel they are a threat to others, they find it difficult to believe that others may see them as a threat). It should be noted, however, that decision-makers whose perceptions are described by this hypothesis would not necessarily further their own values by trying to correct for this tendency. The values of possible outcomes as well as their probabilities must be considered, and it may be that the probability of an unnecessary arms-tension cycle arising out of misperceptions, multiplied by the costs of such a cycle, may seem less to decision-makers than the probability of incorrectly believing another state is friendly, multiplied by the costs of this eventuality.

Hypothesis 9 states that actors tend to see the behavior of others as more centralized, disciplined, and coordinated than it is. This hypothesis holds true in related ways. Frequently, too many complex events are squeezed into a perceived pattern. Actors are hesitant to admit or even see that particular incidents cannot be explained by their theories.[48] Those events not caused by factors that are important parts of the perceiver's image are often seen as though they were. Further, actors see others as more internally united than they in fact are and generally overestimate the degree to which others are following a coherent policy. The degree to which the other side's policies are the product of internal bargaining,[49] internal misunderstandings, or subordinates' not following instructions is underestimated. This is the case partly because actors tend to be unfamiliar with the details of another state's policy-making processes. Seeing only the finished product, they find it simpler to try to construct a rational explanation for the policies, even though they know that such an analysis could not explain their own policies.[50]

Familiarity also accounts for Hypothesis 10: because a state gets most of its information about the other state's policies from the other's foreign office, it tends to take the foreign office's position for the stand of the other government as a whole. In many cases this perception will be an accurate one, but when the other government is divided or when the other foreign office is acting without specific authorization, misperception may result. For example, part of the reason why in 1918 Allied governments incorrectly thought "that the Japanese were preparing to take action [in Siberia], if need be, with agreement with the British and French alone, disregarding the absence of American consent,"[51] was that Allied ambassadors had talked mostly with Foreign Minister Motono, who was among the minority of the Japanese favoring this policy.

Hypothesis 11 states that actors tend to overestimate the degree to which others are acting in response to what they themselves do when the others behave in accordance with the actor's desires; but when the behavior of the other is undesired, it is usually seen as derived from internal forces. If the *effect* of another's action is to injure or threaten the first side, the first side is apt to believe that such was the other's *purpose*. The second part of Hypothesis 11 is illustrated by the tendency of actors to believe that the hostile behavior of others is to be explained by the other side's motives and not by its reaction to the first side. Thus Chamberlain did not see that Hitler's behavior was related in part to his belief that the British were weak. More common is the failure to see that the other side is reacting out of fear of the first side, which can lead to self-fulfilling prophecies and spirals of misperception and hostility.

This difficulty is often compounded by an implication of Hypothesis 12: when actors have intentions that they do not try to conceal from others, they tend to assume that others accurately perceive these intentions. Only rarely do they believe that others may be reacting to a much less favorable image of themselves than they think they are projecting.[52]

Hypothesis 13 suggests that if it is hard for an actor to believe that the other can see him as a menace, it is often even harder for him to see that issues important to him are not important to others. While he may know that another actor is on an opposing team, it may be more difficult for him to realize that the other is playing an entirely different game. This is especially true when the game he is playing seems vital to him.[53]

The final hypothesis, Hypothesis 14, is as follows: actors tend to overlook the fact that evidence consistent with their theories may also be consistent with other views. When choosing between two theories we have to pay attention only to data that cannot be accounted for by one of the theories. But it is common to find people claiming as proof of their theories data that could also support alternative views. We should be careful lest we forget that a piece of information seems in many cases to confirm a certain hypothesis only because we already believe that hypothesis to be correct and that the information can with as much validity support a different hypothesis. For example, one of the reasons why the German attack on Norway took both that country and England by surprise, even though they had detected German ships moving toward Norway, was that they expected not an attack but an attempt by the Germans to break through the British blockade and reach the Atlantic. The initial course of the ships was consistent with either plan, but the British and Norwegians took this course to mean that their predictions were being borne out.[54] This is not to imply that the interpretation made was foolish, but only that the decision-makers should have been aware that the evidence was also consistent with an invasion and should have had a bit less confidence in their views.

The longer the ships would have to travel the same route whether they were going to one or another of two destinations, the more information would be needed to determine their plans. Taken as a metaphor, this incident applies generally to the treatment of evidence. Thus as long as Hitler made demands for control only of ethnically German areas, his actions could be explained either by the hypothesis that he had unlimited ambitions or by the hypothesis that he wanted to unite all the Germans. But actions against non-Germans (e.g., the takeover of Czechoslovakia in March 1938) could not be accounted for by the latter hypothesis. And it was this action that convinced the appeasers that Hitler had to be stopped. It is interesting to speculate on what the British reaction would have been had Hitler left Czechoslovakia alone for a while and instead made demands on Poland similar to those he eventually made in the summer of 1939. The two paths would then still not have diverged, and further misperception could have occurred.

Notes

1. See, for example, Ole Holsti, Robert North, and Richard Brody, "Perception and Action in the 1914 Crisis," in J. David Singer, ed., *Quantitative International Politics* (New York 1968). For a fuller discussion of the Stanford content analysis studies and the general problems of quantification, see my "The Costs of the Quantitative Study of International Relations," in Klaus Knorr and James N. Rosenau, eds., *Contending Approaches to International Politics* (forthcoming).

2. See, for example, Osgood, *An Alternative to War or Surrender* (Urbana 1962); Etzioni, *The Hard Way to Peace* (New York 1962); Boulding, "National Images and International Systems," *Journal of Conflict Resolution,* iii (June 1959), 120–31; and Singer, *Deterrence, Arms Control, and Disarmament* (Columbus 1962).

3. *Statistics of Deadly Quarrels* (Pittsburgh 1960) and *Arms and Insecurity* (Chicago 1960). For non-mathematicians a fine summary of Richardson's work is Anatol Rapoport's "L. F. Richardson's Mathematical Theory of War," *Journal of Conflict Resolution,* I (September 1957), 249–99.

4. See Philip Green, *Deadly Logic* (Columbus 1966); Green, "Method and Substance in the Arms Debate," *World Politics,* XVI (July 1964), 642–67; and Robert A. Levine, "Fact and Morals in the Arms Debate," *World Politics,* xiv (January 1962), 239–58.

5. See Anatol Rapoport, *Strategy and Conscience* (New York 1964).

6. Floyd Allport, *Theories of Perception and the Concept of Structure* (New York 1955), 382; Ole Holsti, "Cognitive Dynamics and Images of the Enemy," in David Finlay, Ole Holsti, and Richard Fagen, *Enemies in Politics* (Chicago 1967), 70.

7. Jerome Bruner and Leo Postman, "On the Perceptions of Incongruity: A Paradigm," in Jerome Bruner and David Krech, eds., *Perception and Personality* (Durham, N.C., 1949), 210.

8. P. 27.

9. *Ibid.,* 26.

10. I have borrowed this phrase from Abraham Kaplan, who uses it in a different but related context in *The Conduct of Inquiry* (San Francisco 1964), 86.

11. The spiral theorists are not the only ones to ignore the limits of empiricism. Roger Hilsman found that most consumers and producers of intelligence felt that intelligence should not deal with hypotheses, but should only provide the policy-makers with "all the facts" (*Strategic Intelligence and National Decisions* [Glencoe 1956], 46). The close interdependence between hypotheses and facts is overlooked partly because of the tendency to identify "hypotheses" with "policy preferences."

12. Karl Deutsch interestingly discusses a related question when he argues, "Autonomy . . . requires both intake from the present and recall from

memory, and selfhood can be seen in just this continuous balancing of a limited present and a limited past. . . . No further self-determination is possible if either openness or memory is lost. . . . To the extent that [systems cease to be able to take in new information], they approach the behavior of a bullet or torpedo: their future action becomes almost completely determined by their past. On the other hand, a person without memory, an organization without values or policy . . .—all these no longer steer, but drift: their behavior depends little on their past and almost wholly on their present. Driftwood and the bullet are thus each the epitome of another kind of loss of self-control. . ." (*Nationalism and Social Communication* [Cambridge, Mass., 1954], 167–68).

13. Raymond Bauer, "Problems of Perception and the Relations between the U.S. and the Soviet Union," *Journal of Conflict Resolution,* v (September 1961), 223–29.

14. Requirements of effective political leadership may lead decision-makers to voice fewer doubts than they have about existing policies and images, but this constraint can only partially explain this phenomenon. Similar calculations of political strategy may contribute to several of the hypotheses discussed below.

15. P. 221. Similarly, in experiments dealing with his subjects' perception of other people, Charles Dailey found that "premature judgment appears to make new data harder to assimilate than when the observer withholds judgment until all data are seen. It seems probable . . . that the observer mistakes his own inferences for facts" ("The Effects of Premature Conclusion Upon the Acquisition of Understanding of a Person," *Journal of Psychology,* XXX [January 1952], 149–50).

16. For a use of this concept in political communication, see Roberta Wohlstetter, *Pearl Harbor* (Stanford 1962).

17. Similarly, Robert Coulondre, the French ambassador to Berlin in 1939, was one of the few diplomats to appreciate the Nazi threat. Partly because of his earlier service in the USSR, "he was painfully sensitive to the threat of a Berlin-Moscow agreement. He noted with foreboding that Hitler had not attacked Russia in his *Reichstag* address of April 28. . . . So it went all spring and summer, the ambassador relaying each new evidence of the impending diplomatic revolution and adding to his admonitions his pleas for decisive counteraction" (Franklin Ford and Carl Schorske, "The Voice in the Wilderness: Robert Coulondre," in Gordon Craig and Felix Gilbert, eds., *The Diplomats,* Vol. III [New York 1963] 573–74). His hypotheses were correct, but it is difficult to detect differences between the way he and those ambassadors who were incorrect, like Neville Henderson, selectively noted and interpreted information. However, to the extent that the fear of war influenced the appeasers' perceptions of Hitler's intentions, the appeasers' views did have an element of psycho-logic that was not present in their opponents' position.

18. See, for example, Donald Campbell, "Systematic Error on the Part of Human Links in Communications Systems," *Information and Control,* I (1958), 346–50; and Leo Postman, "The Experimental Analysis of Motivational Factors in Perception," in Judson S. Brown, ed., *Current Theory and Research in Motivation* (Lincoln, Neb., 1953), 59–108.

19. Dale Wyatt and Donald Campbell, "A Study of Interviewer Bias as Related to Interviewer's Expectations and Own Opinions," *International Journal of Opinion and Attitude Research,* IV (Spring 1950), 77–83.

20. Max Jacobson, *The Diplomacy of the Winter War* (Cambridge, Mass., 1961), 136–39.

21. Raymond Aron, *Peace and War* (Garden City 1966), 29.

22. Cf. Kuhn, *The Structure of Scientific Revolution,* 65. A fairly high degree of knowledge is needed before one can state precise expectations. One indication of the lack of international relations theory is that most of us are not sure what "naturally" flows from our theories and what constitutes either "puzzles" to be further explored with the paradigm or "anomalies" that cast doubt on the basic theories.

23. See Philip Selznick, *Leadership in Administration* (Evanston 1957).

24. Ashley Schiff, *Fire and Water: Scientific Heresy in the Forest Service* (Cambridge, Mass., 1962). Despite its title, this book is a fascinating and valuable study.

25. *The Craft of Intelligence* (New York 1963), 53.

26. P. 302. See Beveridge, 93, for a discussion of the idea that the scientist should keep in mind as many hypotheses as possible when conducting and analyzing experiments.

27. *Presidential Power* (New York 1960).

28. Most psychologists argue that this influence also holds for perception of shapes. For data showing that people in different societies differ in respect to their predisposition to experience certain optical illusions and for a convincing argument that this difference can be explained by the societies' different physical environments, which have led their people to develop different patterns of drawing inferences from ambiguous visual cues, see Marshall Segall, Donald Campbell, and Melville Herskovits, *The Influence of Culture on Visual Perceptions* (Indianapolis 1966).

29. Thus when Bruner and Postman's subjects first were presented with incongruous playing cards (i.e., cards in which symbols and colors of the suits were not matching, producing red spades or black diamonds), long exposure times were necessary for correct identification. But once a subject correctly perceived the card and added this type of card to his repertoire of categories, he was able to identify other incongruous cards much more quickly. For an analogous example—in this case, changes in the analysis of aerial reconnaissance photographs of an enemy's secret weapons-testing facilities produced by the belief that a previously unknown object may be present—see David Irving, *The Mare's Nest* (Boston 1964), 66–67, 274–75.

30. Bruner and Postman, 220.

31. *The Liberal Tradition in America* (New York 1955), 306.

32. *Russia and the West under Lenin and Stalin* (New York 1962), 142–43.

33. DeWitt Dearborn and Herbert Simon, "Selective Perception: A Note on the Departmental Identification of Executives," *Sociometry*, XXI (June 1958), 140–44.

34. Hugh Trevor-Roper puts this point well: "Brought up as a business man, successful in municipal politics, [Chamberlain's] outlook was entirely parochial. Educated Conservative aristocrats like Churchill, Eden, and Cranborne, whose families had long been used to political responsibility, had seen revolution and revolutionary leaders before, in their own history, and understood them correctly; but the Chamberlains, who had run from radical imperialism to timid conservatism in a generation of life in Birmingham, had no such understanding of history or the world: to them the scope of human politics was limited by their own parochial horizons, and Neville Chamberlain could not believe that Hitler was fundamentally different from himself. If Chamberlain wanted peace, so must Hitler" ("Munich—Its Lessons Ten Years Later," in Francis Loewenheim, ed., *Peace or Appeasement?* [Boston 1965], 152–53). For a similar view see A. L, Rowse, *Appeasement* (New York 1963), 117.

35. *Ibid.*, 15.

36. During a debate on appeasement in the House of Commons, Harold Nicolson declared, "I know that those of us who believe in the traditions of our policy, . . . who believe that one great function of this country is to maintain moral standards in Europe, to maintain a settled pattern of international relations, not to make friends with people who are demonstrably evil . . .—I know that those who hold such beliefs are accused of possessing the Foreign Office mind. I thank God that I possess the Foreign Office mind" (quoted in Martin Gilbert, *The Roots of Appeasement* [New York 1966], 187). But the qualities Nicolson mentions and applauds may be related to a more basic attribute of "the Foreign Office mind"—suspiciousness.

37. George Monger, *The End of Isolation* (London 1963). I am also indebted to Frederick Collignon for his unpublished manuscript and several conversations on this point.

38. *The Power of Small States* (Chicago 1959), 81.

39. William Inge, *Outspoken Essays,* First Series (London 1923), 88.

40. Of course, analogies themselves are not "unmoved movers." The interpretation of past events is not automatic and is informed by general views of international relations and complex judgments. And just as beliefs about the past influence the present, views about the present influence interpretations of history. It is difficult to determine the degree to which the United States' interpretation of the reasons it went to war in 1917 influenced American foreign policy in the 1920s and 1930s and how much the isolationism of that period influenced the histories of the war.

41. For some psychological experiments on this subject, see Jerome Bruner and A. Leigh Minturn,

"Perceptual Identification and Perceptual Organization," *Journal of General Psychology*, LIII (July 1955), 22–28; Seymour Feshbach and Robert Singer, "The Effects of Fear Arousal and Suppression of Fear Upon Social Perception," *Journal of Abnormal and Social Psychology*, LV (November 1957), 283–88; and Elsa Sippoal, "A Group Study of Some Effects of Preparatory Sets," *Psychology Monographs*, XLVI, No. 210 (1935), 27–28. For a general discussion of the importance of the perceiver's evoked set, see Postman, 87.

42. Pp. 73–74.

43. For example, Roger Hilsman points out, "Those who knew of the peripheral reconnaissance flights that probed Soviet air defenses during the Eisenhower administration and the U-2 flights over the Soviet Union itself . . . were better able to understand some of the things the Soviets were saying and doing than people who did not know of these activities" (*To Move a Nation* [Garden City 1967], 66). But it is also possible that those who knew about the U-2 flights at times misinterpreted Soviet messages by incorrectly believing that the sender was influenced by, or at least knew of, these flights.

44. I am grateful to Thomas Schelling for discussion on this point.

45. *Deterrence Before Hiroshima* (New York 1966), 105–22.

46. *Ibid.*

47. For a slightly different formulation of this view, see Holsti, 27.

48. The Soviets consciously hold an extreme version of this view and seem to believe that nothing is accidental. See the discussion in Nathan Leites, *A Study of Bolshevism* (Glencoe 1953), 67–73.

49. A. W. Marshall criticizes Western explanations of Soviet military posture for failing to take this into account. See his "Problems of Estimating Military Power," a paper presented at the 1966 Annual Meeting Political Science Association, 16.

50. It has also been noted that in labor-management disputes both sides may be apt to believe incorrectly that the other is controlled from above, either from the international union office or from the company's central headquarters (Robert Blake, Herbert Shepard, and Jane Mouton, *Managing Intergroup Conflict in Industry* [Houston 1964], 182). It has been further noted that both Democratic and Republican members of the House tend to see the other party as the one that is more disciplined and united (Charles Clapp, The *Congressman* [Washington 1963], 17–19).

51. George Kennan, *Russia Leaves the War* (New York 1967), 484.

52. Herbert Butterfield notes that these assumptions can contribute to the spiral of "Hobbesian fear. . . . You yourself may vividly feel the terrible fear that you have of the other party, but you cannot enter into the other man's counter-fear, or even understand why he should be particularly nervous. For you know that you yourself mean him no harm, and that you want nothing from him save guarantees for your own safety; and it is never possible for you to realize or remember properly that since he cannot see the inside of your mind, he can never have the same assurance of your intentions that you have" (*History and Human Conflict* [London 1951], 20).

53. George Kennan makes clear that in 1918 this kind of difficulty was partly responsible for the inability of either the Allies or the new Bolshevik government to understand the motivations of the other side; "There is . . . nothing in nature more egocentrical than the embattled democracy. . . . It . . . tends to attach to its own cause an absolute value which distorts its own vision of everything else. . . . It will readily be seen that people who have got themselves into this frame of mind have little understanding for the issues of any contest other than the one in which they are involved. The idea of people wasting time and substance on any *other* issue seems to them preposterous" (*Russia and the West*, 11–12).

54. Johan Jorgen Holst, "Surprise, Signals, and Reaction: The Attack on Norway," *Cooperation and Conflict*, No. i (1966), 34. The Germans made a similar mistake in November 1942 when they interpreted the presence of an Allied convoy in the Mediterranean as confirming their belief that Malta would be resupplied. They thus were taken by surprise when landings took place in North Africa (William Langer, *Our Vichy Gamble* [New York 1966], 365).

Robert Jervis, "Hypotheses on Misperception," World Politics 20:3 (1968), pp. 454–479. Reproduced with permission of Cambridge University Press.

The Clash of Civilizations?

SAMUEL P. HUNTINGTON

In this seminal article, Huntington argues that the processes of globalization have brought formerly distant cultures into increasing contact, resulting in misunderstanding, resentment, and ultimately conflict. Thus, he postulates that differences in culture and identity between groups will become the primary drivers of conflict in the 21st century. As a result the dominant mode of conflict will shift from within civilizations to between different civilizations, and thus the West, the Arab nations, and China will increasingly engage in culturally-based conflict with one another.

The Next Pattern of Conflict

World politics is entering a new phase, and intellectuals have not hesitated to proliferate visions of what it will be—the end of history, the return of traditional rivalries between nation states, and the decline of the nation state from the conflicting pulls of tribalism and globalism, among others. Each of these visions catches aspects of the emerging reality. Yet they all miss a crucial, indeed a central, aspect of what global politics is likely to be in the coming years.

It is my hypothesis that the fundamental source of conflict in this new world will not be primarily ideological or primarily economic. The great divisions among humankind and the dominating source of conflict will be cultural. Nation states will remain the most powerful actors in world affairs, but the principal conflicts of global politics will occur between nations and groups of different civilizations. The clash of civilizations will dominate global politics. The fault lines between civilizations will be the battle lines of the future.

Conflict between civilizations will be the latest phase in the evolution of conflict in the modern world. For a century and a half after the emergence of the modern international system with the Peace of Westphalia, the conflicts of the Western world were largely among princes—emperors, absolute monarchs and constitutional monarchs attempting to expand their bureaucracies, their armies, their mercantilist economic strength and, most important, the territory they ruled. In the process they created nation states, and beginning with the French Revolution the principal lines of conflict were between nations rather than princes. In 1793, as R. R. Palmer put it, "The wars of kings were over; the wars of peoples had begun." This nineteenth-century pattern lasted until the end of World War I. Then, as a result of the Russian Revolution and the reaction against it, the conflict of nations yielded to the conflict of ideologies, first among communism, fascism-Nazism and liberal democracy, and then between communism and liberal democracy. During the Cold War, this latter conflict became embodied in the struggle between the two superpowers, neither of which was a nation state in the classical European sense and each of which defined its identity in terms of its ideology.

These conflicts between princes, nation states and ideologies were primarily conflicts within Western civilization, "Western civil wars," as William Lind has labeled them. This was as true of the Cold War as it was of the world wars and the earlier wars of the seventeenth, eighteenth and nineteenth centuries. With the end of the Cold War, international politics moves out of its Western phase, and its centerpiece becomes the interaction between the West and non-Western civilizations and among non-Western civilizations. In the politics of civilizations, the peoples and governments of non-Western civilizations no longer remain the objects of history as targets of Western colonialism but join the West as movers and shapers of history.

The Nature of Civilizations

During the cold war the world was divided into the First, Second and Third Worlds. Those divisions are no longer relevant. It is far more meaningful now to group countries not in terms of their political or economic systems or in terms of their level of economic development but rather in terms of their culture and civilization.

What do we mean when we talk of a civilization? A civilization is a cultural entity. Villages, regions, ethnic groups, nationalities, religious groups, all have distinct cultures at different levels of cultural heterogeneity. The culture of a village in southern Italy may be different from that of a village in northern Italy, but both will share in a common Italian culture that distinguishes them from German villages. European communities, in turn, will share cultural features that distinguish them from Arab or Chinese communities. Arabs, Chinese and Westerners, however, are not part of any broader cultural entity. They constitute civilizations. A civilization is thus the highest cultural grouping of people and the broadest level of cultural identity people have short of that which distinguishes humans from other species. It is defined both by common objective elements, such as language, history, religion, customs, institutions, and by the subjective self-identification of people. People have levels of identity: a resident of Rome may define himself with varying degrees of intensity as a Roman, an Italian, a Catholic, a Christian, a European, a Westerner. The civilization to which he belongs is the broadest level of identification with which he intensely identifies. People can and do redefine their identities and, as a result, the composition and boundaries of civilizations change.

Civilizations may involve a large number of people, as with China ("a civilization pretending to be a state," as Lucian Pye put it), or a very small number of people, such as the Anglophone Caribbean. A civilization may include several nation states, as is the case with Western, Latin American and Arab civilizations, or only one, as is the case with Japanese civilization. Civilizations obviously blend and overlap, and may include subcivilizations. Western civilization has two major variants, European and North American, and Islam has its Arab, Turkic and Malay subdivisions. Civilizations are nonetheless meaningful entities, and while the lines between them are seldom sharp, they are real. Civilizations are dynamic; they rise and fall; they divide and merge. And, as any student of history knows, civilizations disappear and are buried in the sands of time.

Westerners tend to think of nation states as the principal actors in global affairs. They have been that, however, for only a few centuries. The broader reaches of human history have been the history of civilizations. In *A Study of History,* Arnold Toynbee identified 21 major civilizations; only six of them exist in the contemporary world.

Why Civilizations Will Clash

Civilization identity will be increasingly important in the future, and the world will be shaped in large measure by the interactions among seven or eight major civilizations. These include Western, Confucian, Japanese, Islamic, Hindu, Slavic-Orthodox, Latin American and possibly African civilization. The most important conflicts of the future will occur along the cultural fault lines separating these civilizations from one another.

Why will this be the case?

First, differences among civilizations are not only real; they are basic. Civilizations are differentiated from each other by history, language, culture, tradition and, most important, religion. The people of different civilizations have different views on the relations between God and man, the individual and the group, the citizen and the state, parents and children, husband and wife, as well as differing views of the relative importance of rights and responsibilities, liberty and authority, equality and hierarchy. These differences are the product of centuries. They will not soon disappear. They are far more fundamental than differences among political ideologies and political regimes. Differences do not necessarily mean conflict, and conflict does not necessarily mean violence. Over the centuries, however, differences among civilizations have generated the most prolonged and the most violent conflicts.

Second, the world is becoming a smaller place. The interactions between peoples of different civilizations are increasing; these increasing interactions intensify civilization consciousness and awareness of differences between civilizations and commonalities within civilizations. North African immigration to France generates hostility among Frenchmen and at the same time increased receptivity to immigration by "good" European Catholic Poles. Americans react far more negatively to Japanese investment than to larger investments from Canada and European countries. Similarly, as Donald Horowitz has pointed out, "An Ibo may be . . . an Owerri Ibo or an Onitsha Ibo in what was the Eastern region of Nigeria. In Lagos, he is simply an Ibo. In London, he is a Nigerian. In New York, he is an African." The interactions among peoples of different civilizations enhance the civilization-consciousness of people that, in turn, invigorates differences and animosities stretching or thought to stretch back deep into history.

Third, the processes of economic modernization and social change throughout the world are separating people from longstanding local identities. They also weaken the nation state as a source of identity. In much of the world religion has moved in to fill this gap, often in the form of movements that are labeled "fundamentalist." Such movements are found in Western Christianity, Judaism, Buddhism and Hinduism, as well as in Islam. In most countries and most religions the people active in fundamentalist movements are young, college-educated, middle-class technicians, professionals and business persons. The "unsecularization of the world," George Weigel has remarked, "is one of the dominant social facts of life in the late twentieth century." The revival of religion, "la revanche de Dieu," as Gilles Kepel labeled it, provides a basis for identity and commitment that transcends national boundaries and unites civilizations.

Fourth, the growth of civilization-consciousness is enhanced by the dual role of the West. On the one hand, the West is at a peak of power. At the same time, however, and perhaps as a result, a return to the roots phenomenon is occurring among non-Western civilizations. Increasingly one hears references to trends toward a turning inward and "Asianization" in Japan, the end of the Nehru legacy and the "Hinduization" of India, the failure of Western ideas of socialism and nationalism and hence "re-Islamization" of the Middle East, and now a debate over Westernization versus Russianization in Boris Yeltsin's country. A West at the peak of its power confronts non-Wests that increasingly have the desire, the will and the resources to shape the world in non-Western ways.

In the past, the elites of non-Western societies were usually the people who were most involved with the West, had been educated at Oxford, the Sorbonne or Sandhurst, and had absorbed Western attitudes and values. At the same time, the populace in non-Western countries often remained deeply imbued with the indigenous culture. Now, however, these relationships are being reversed. A de-Westernization and indigenization of elites is occurring in many non-Western countries at the same time that Western, usually American, cultures, styles and habits become more popular among the mass of the people.

Fifth, cultural characteristics and differences are less mutable and hence less easily compromised and resolved than political and economic ones. In the former Soviet Union, communists can become democrats, the rich can become poor and the poor rich, but Russians cannot become Estonians and Azeris cannot become Armenians. In class and ideological conflicts, the key question was "Which side are you on?" and people could and did choose sides and change sides. In conflicts between civilizations, the question is "What are you?" That is a given that cannot be changed. And as we know, from Bosnia to the Caucasus to the Sudan, the wrong answer to that question can mean a bullet in the head. Even more than ethnicity, religion discriminates sharply and exclusively among people. A person can be half-French and half-Arab and simultaneously even a citizen of two countries. It is more difficult to be half-Catholic and half-Muslim.

Finally, economic regionalism is increasing. The proportions of total trade that were intraregional rose between 1980 and 1989 from 51 percent to 59 percent in Europe, 33 percent to 37 percent in East Asia, and 32 percent to 36 percent in North America. The importance of regional economic blocs is likely to continue to increase in the future. On the one hand, successful economic regionalism will reinforce civilization-consciousness. On the other hand, economic regionalism may succeed only when it is rooted in a common civilization. The European Community rests on the shared foundation of European culture and Western Christianity. The success of the North American Free Trade Area depends on the convergence now underway of Mexican, Canadian and American cultures. Japan, in contrast, faces difficulties in creating a comparable economic entity in East Asia because Japan is a society and civilization unique to itself. However strong the trade and investment links Japan may develop with other East Asian countries, its cultural differences with those countries inhibit and perhaps preclude its promoting regional economic integration like that in Europe and North America.

Common culture, in contrast, is clearly facilitating the rapid expansion of the economic relations between the People's Republic of China and Hong Kong, Taiwan, Singapore and the overseas Chinese communities in other Asian countries. With the Cold War over, cultural commonalities increasingly overcome ideological differences, and mainland China and Taiwan move closer together. If cultural commonality is a prerequisite for economic integration, the principal East Asian economic bloc of the future is likely to be centered on China. This bloc is, in fact, already coming into existence. As Murray Weidenbaum has observed,

> Despite the current Japanese dominance of the region, the Chinese-based economy of Asia is rapidly emerging as a new epicenter for industry, commerce and finance. This strategic area contains substantial amounts of technology and manufacturing capability (Taiwan), outstanding entrepreneurial, marketing and services acumen (Hong Kong), a fine communications network (Singapore), a tremendous pool of financial capital (all three), and very large endowments of land, resources and labor (mainland China). . . . From Guangzhou to Singapore, from Kuala Lumpur to Manila, this influential network—often based on extensions of the traditional clans—has been described as the backbone of the East Asian economy.[1]

Culture and religion also form the basis of the Economic Cooperation Organization, which brings together ten non-Arab Muslim countries: Iran, Pakistan, Turkey, Azerbaijan, Kazakhstan, Kyrgyzstan, Turkmenistan, Tadjikistan, Uzbekistan and Afghanistan. One impetus to the revival and expansion of this organization, founded originally in the 1960s by Turkey, Pakistan and Iran, is the realization by the leaders of several of these countries that they had no chance of admission to the European Community. Similarly, Caricom, the Central American Common Market and Mercosur rest on common cultural foundations. Efforts to build a broader Caribbean-Central American economic entity bridging the Anglo-Latin divide, however, have to date failed.

As people define their identity in ethnic and religious terms, they are likely to see an "us" versus "them" relation existing between themselves and people of different ethnicity or religion. The end of ideologically defined states in Eastern Europe and the former Soviet Union permits traditional ethnic identities and animosities to come to the fore. Differences in culture and religion create differences over policy issues, ranging from human rights to immigration to trade and commerce to the environment. Geographical propinquity gives rise to conflicting territorial claims from Bosnia to Mindanao. Most important, the efforts of the West to promote its values of democracy and liberalism as universal values, to maintain its military predominance and to advance its economic interests engender countering responses from other civilizations. Decreasingly able to mobilize support and form coalitions on the basis of ideology, governments and groups will increasingly attempt to mobilize support by appealing to common religion and civilization identity.

The clash of civilizations thus occurs at two levels. At the micro-level, adjacent groups along the fault lines between civilizations struggle, often violently, over the control of territory and each other. At the macro-level, states from different civilizations compete for relative military and economic power, struggle over the control of international institutions and third parties, and competitively promote their particular political and religious values.

The Fault Lines between Civilizations

The fault lines between civilizations are replacing the political and ideological boundaries of the Cold War as the flash points for crisis and bloodshed. The Cold War began when the Iron Curtain divided Europe politically and ideologically. The Cold War ended with the end of the Iron Curtain. As the ideological division of Europe has disappeared, the cultural division of Europe between Western Christianity, on the one hand, and Orthodox Christianity and Islam, on the other, has reemerged. The most significant dividing line in Europe, as William Wallace has suggested, may well be the eastern boundary of Western Christianity in the year 1500. This line runs along what are now the boundaries between Finland and Russia and between the Baltic states and Russia, cuts through Belarus and Ukraine separating the more Catholic western Ukraine from Orthodox eastern Ukraine, swings westward separating Transylvania from the rest of Romania, and then goes through Yugoslavia almost exactly along the line now separating Croatia and Slovenia from the rest of Yugoslavia. In the Balkans this line, of course, coincides with the historic boundary between the Hapsburg and Ottoman empires. The peoples to the north and west of this line are Protestant or Catholic; they shared the common experiences of European history—feudalism, the Renaissance, the Reformation, the Enlightenment, the French Revolution, the Industrial Revolution; they are generally economically better off than the peoples to the east; and they may now look forward to increasing involvement in a common European economy and to the consolidation of democratic political systems. The peoples to the east and south of this line are Orthodox or Muslim; they historically belonged to the Ottoman or Tsarist empires and were only lightly touched by the shaping events in the rest of Europe; they are generally less advanced economically; they seem much less likely to develop stable democratic political systems. The Velvet Curtain of culture has replaced the Iron Curtain of ideology as the most significant dividing line in Europe. As the events in Yugoslavia show, it is not only a line of difference; it is also at times a line of bloody conflict.

Conflict along the fault line between Western and Islamic civilizations has been going on for 1,300 years. After the founding of Islam, the Arab and Moorish surge west and north only ended at Tours in 732. From the eleventh to the thirteenth century the Crusaders attempted with temporary success to bring Christianity and Christian rule to the Holy Land. From the fourteenth to the seventeenth century, the Ottoman Turks reversed the balance, extended their sway over the Middle East and the Balkans, captured Constantinople, and twice laid siege to Vienna. In the nineteenth and early twentieth centuries as Ottoman power declined Britain, France, and Italy established Western control over most of North Africa and the Middle East.

After World War II, the West, in turn, began to retreat; the colonial empires disappeared; first Arab nationalism and then Islamic fundamentalism manifested themselves; the West became heavily dependent on the Persian Gulf countries for its energy; the oil-rich Muslim countries became money-rich and, when they wished to, weapons-rich. Several wars occurred between Arabs and Israel (created by the West). France fought a bloody and ruthless war in Algeria for most of the 1950s; British and French forces invaded Egypt in 1956; American forces went into Lebanon in 1958; subsequently American forces returned to Lebanon, attacked Libya, and engaged in various military encounters with Iran; Arab and Islamic terrorists, supported by at least three Middle Eastern governments, employed the weapon of the weak and bombed Western planes and installations and seized Western hostages. This warfare between Arabs and the West culminated in 1990, when the United States sent a massive army to the Persian Gulf to defend some Arab countries against aggression by another. In its aftermath nato planning is increasingly directed to potential threats and instability along its "southern tier."

This centuries-old military interaction between the West and Islam is unlikely to decline. It could become more virulent. The Gulf War left some Arabs feeling proud that Saddam Hussein had attacked Israel and stood up to the West. It also left many feeling humiliated and resentful of the West's military presence in the Persian Gulf, the West's overwhelming military dominance, and their apparent inability to shape their own destiny. Many Arab countries, in addition to the oil exporters, are reaching levels of economic and social development where autocratic forms of government become inappropriate and efforts to introduce democracy become stronger. Some openings in Arab political systems have already occurred. The principal beneficiaries of these openings have been Islamist movements. In the Arab world, in short, Western democracy strengthens anti-Western political forces. This may be a passing phenomenon, but it surely complicates relations between Islamic countries and the West.

Those relations are also complicated by demography. The spectacular population growth in Arab countries, particularly in North Africa, has led to increased migration to Western Europe. The movement within Western Europe toward minimizing internal boundaries has sharpened political sensitivities with respect to this development. In Italy, France and Germany, racism is increasingly open, and political reactions and violence against Arab and Turkish migrants have become more intense and more widespread since 1990.

On both sides the interaction between Islam and the West is seen as a clash of civilizations. The West's "next confrontation," observes M. J. Akbar, an Indian Muslim author, "is definitely going to come from the Muslim world. It is in the

sweep of the Islamic nations from the Maghreb to Pakistan that the struggle for a new world order will begin." Bernard Lewis comes to a similar conclusion:

> We are facing a mood and a movement far transcending the level of issues and policies and the governments that pursue them. This is no less than a clash of civilizations—the perhaps irrational but surely historic reaction of an ancient rival against our Judeo-Christian heritage, our secular present, and the worldwide expansion of both.[2]

Historically, the other great antagonistic interaction of Arab Islamic civilization has been with the pagan, animist, and now increasingly Christian black peoples to the south. In the past, this antagonism was epitomized in the image of Arab slave dealers and black slaves. It has been reflected in the on-going civil war in the Sudan between Arabs and blacks, the fighting in Chad between Libyan-supported insurgents and the government, the tensions between Orthodox Christians and Muslims in the Horn of Africa, and the political conflicts, recurring riots and communal violence between Muslims and Christians in Nigeria. The modernization of Africa and the spread of Christianity are likely to enhance the probability of violence along this fault line. Symptomatic of the intensification of this conflict was the Pope John Paul II's speech in Khartoum in February 1993 attacking the actions of the Sudan's Islamist government against the Christian minority there.

On the northern border of Islam, conflict has increasingly erupted between Orthodox and Muslim peoples, including the carnage of Bosnia and Sarajevo, the simmering violence between Serb and Albanian, the tenuous relations between Bulgarians and their Turkish minority, the violence between Ossetians and Ingush, the unremitting slaughter of each other by Armenians and Azeris, the tense relations between Russians and Muslims in Central Asia, and the deployment of Russian troops to protect Russian interests in the Caucasus and Central Asia. Religion reinforces the revival of ethnic identities and restimulates Russian fears about the security of their southern borders. This concern is well captured by Archie Roosevelt:

> Much of Russian history concerns the struggle between the Slavs and the Turkic peoples on their borders, which dates back to the foundation of the Russian state more than a thousand years ago. In the Slavs' millennium-long confrontation with their eastern neighbors lies the key to an understanding not only of Russian history, but Russian character. To understand Russian realities today one has to have a concept of the great Turkic ethnic group that has preoccupied Russians through the centuries.[3]

The conflict of civilizations is deeply rooted elsewhere in Asia. The historic clash between Muslim and Hindu in the subcontinent manifests itself now not only in the rivalry between Pakistan and India but also in intensifying religious strife within India between increasingly militant Hindu groups and India's substantial Muslim minority. The destruction of the Ayodhya mosque in December 1992 brought to the fore the issue of whether India will remain a secular democratic state or become a Hindu one. In East Asia, China has outstanding territorial disputes with most of its neighbors. It has pursued a ruthless policy toward the Buddhist people of Tibet, and it is pursuing an increasingly ruthless policy toward its Turkic-Muslim minority. With the Cold War over, the underlying differences between China and the United States have reasserted themselves in areas such as human rights, trade and weapons proliferation. These differences are unlikely to moderate. A "new cold war," Deng Xaioping reportedly asserted in 1991, is under way between China and America.

The same phrase has been applied to the increasingly difficult relations between Japan and the United States. Here cultural difference exacerbates economic conflict. People on each side allege racism on the other, but at least on the American side the antipathies are not racial but cultural. The basic values, attitudes, behavioral patterns of the two societies could hardly be more different. The economic issues between the United States and Europe are no less serious than those between the United States and Japan, but they do not have the same political salience and emotional intensity because the differences between American culture and European culture are so much less than those between American civilization and Japanese civilization.

The interactions between civilizations vary greatly in the extent to which they are likely to be characterized by violence. Economic competition clearly predominates between the American and European subcivilizations of the West and between both of them and Japan. On the Eurasian continent, however, the proliferation of ethnic conflict, epitomized at the extreme in "ethnic cleansing," has not been totally random. It has been most frequent and most violent between groups belonging to different civilizations. In Eurasia the great historic fault lines between civilizations are once more aflame. This is particularly true along the boundaries of the crescent-shaped Islamic bloc of nations from the bulge of Africa to central Asia. Violence also occurs between Muslims, on the one hand, and Orthodox Serbs in the Balkans, Jews in Israel, Hindus in India, Buddhists in Burma and Catholics in the Philippines. Islam has bloody borders.

Civilization Rallying: The Kin-Country Syndrome

Groups or states belonging to one civilization that become involved in war with people from a different civilization naturally try to rally support from other members of their own civilization. As the post-Cold War world evolves, civilization commonality, what H. D. S. Greenway has termed the "kin-country" syndrome, is replacing political ideology and traditional balance of power considerations as the principal basis for cooperation and coalitions. It can be seen gradually emerging in the post-Cold War conflicts in the Persian Gulf, the Caucasus and Bosnia. None of these was a full-scale war between civilizations, but each involved some elements of civilizational rallying, which seemed to become more important as the conflict continued and which may provide a foretaste of the future.

First, in the Gulf War one Arab state invaded another and then fought a coalition of Arab, Western and other states. While only a few Muslim governments overtly supported Saddam Hussein, many Arab elites privately cheered him on, and he was highly popular among large sections of the Arab publics. Islamic fundamentalist movements universally supported Iraq rather than the Western-backed governments of Kuwait and Saudi Arabia. Forswearing Arab nationalism, Saddam Hussein explicitly invoked an Islamic appeal. He and his supporters attempted to define the war as a war between civilizations. "It is not the world against Iraq," as Safar Al-Hawali, dean of Islamic Studies at the Umm Al-Qura University in Mecca, put it in a widely circulated tape. "It is the West against Islam." Ignoring the rivalry between Iran and Iraq, the chief Iranian religious leader, Ayatollah Ali Khamenei, called for a holy war against the West: "The struggle against American aggression, greed, plans and policies will be counted as a jihad, and anybody who is killed on that path is a martyr." "This is a war," King Hussein of Jordan argued, "against all Arabs and all Muslims and not against Iraq alone."

The rallying of substantial sections of Arab elites and publics behind Saddam Hussein caused those Arab governments in the anti-Iraq coalition to moderate their activities and temper their public statements. Arab governments opposed or distanced themselves from subsequent Western efforts to apply pressure on Iraq, including enforcement of a no-fly zone in the summer of 1992 and the bombing of Iraq in January 1993. The Western-Soviet-Turkish-Arab anti-Iraq coalition of 1990 had by 1993 become a coalition of almost only the West and Kuwait against Iraq.

Muslims contrasted Western actions against Iraq with the West's failure to protect Bosnians against Serbs and to impose sanctions on Israel for violating U.N. resolutions. The West, they alleged, was using a double standard. A world of clashing civilizations, however, is inevitably a world of double standards: people apply one standard to their kin-countries and a different standard to others.

Conflicts and violence will also occur between states and groups within the same civilization. Such conflicts, however, are likely to be less intense and less likely to expand than conflicts between civilizations. Common membership in a civilization reduces the probability of violence in situations where it might otherwise occur. In 1991 and 1992 many people were alarmed by the possibility of violent conflict between Russia and Ukraine over territory, particularly Crimea, the Black Sea fleet, nuclear weapons and economic issues. If civilization is what counts, however, the likelihood of violence between Ukrainians and Russians should be low. They are two Slavic, primarily Orthodox peoples who have had close relationships with each other for centuries. As of early 1993, despite all the reasons for conflict, the leaders of the two countries were effectively negotiating and defusing the issues between the two countries. While there has been serious fighting between Muslims and Christians elsewhere in the former Soviet Union and much tension and some fighting between Western and Orthodox Christians in the Baltic states, there has been virtually no violence between Russians and Ukrainians.

Civilization rallying to date has been limited, but it has been growing, and it clearly has the potential to spread much further. As the conflicts in the Persian Gulf, the Caucasus and Bosnia continued, the positions of nations and the cleavages between them increasingly were along civilizational lines. Populist politicians, religious leaders and the media have found it a potent means of arousing mass support and of pressuring hesitant governments. In the coming years, the local conflicts most likely to escalate into major wars will be those, as in Bosnia and the Caucasus, along the fault lines between civilizations. The next world war, if there is one, will be a war between civilizations.

The West versus the Rest

The west is now at an extraordinary peak of power in relation to other civilizations. Its superpower opponent has disappeared from the map. Military conflict among Western states is unthinkable, and Western military power is unrivaled. Apart from Japan, the West faces no economic challenge. It dominates international political and security institutions and with Japan international economic institutions. Global political and security issues are effectively settled by a directorate of the United

States, Britain and France, world economic issues by a directorate of the United States, Germany and Japan, all of which maintain extraordinarily close relations with each other to the exclusion of lesser and largely non-Western countries. Decisions made at the U.N. Security Council or in the International Monetary Fund that reflect the interests of the West are presented to the world as reflecting the desires of the world community. The very phrase "the world community" has become the euphemistic collective noun (replacing "the Free World") to give global legitimacy to actions reflecting the interests of the United States and other Western powers.[4] Through the IMF and other international economic institutions, the West promotes its economic interests and imposes on other nations the economic policies it thinks appropriate. In any poll of non-Western peoples, the imf undoubtedly would win the support of finance ministers and a few others, but get an overwhelmingly unfavorable rating from just about everyone else, who would agree with Georgy Arbatov's characterization of imf officials as "neo-Bolsheviks who love expropriating other people's money, imposing undemocratic and alien rules of economic and political conduct and stifling economic freedom."

Western domination of the U.N. Security Council and its decisions, tempered only by occasional abstention by China, produced U.N. legitimation of the West's use of force to drive Iraq out of Kuwait and its elimination of Iraq's sophisticated weapons and capacity to produce such weapons. It also produced the quite unprecedented action by the United States, Britain and France in getting the Security Council to demand that Libya hand over the Pan Am 103 bombing suspects and then to impose sanctions when Libya refused. After defeating the largest Arab army, the West did not hesitate to throw its weight around in the Arab world. The West in effect is using international institutions, military power and economic resources to run the world in ways that will maintain Western predominance protect Western interests and promote Western political and economic values.

That at least is the way in which non-Westerners see the new world, and there is a significant element of truth in their view. Differences in power and struggles for military, economic and institutional power are thus one source of conflict between the West and other civilizations. Differences in culture, that is basic values and beliefs, are a second source of conflict. V. S. Naipaul has argued that Western civilization is the "universal civilization" that "fits all men." At a superficial level much of Western culture has indeed permeated the rest of the world. At a more basic level, however, Western concepts differ fundamentally from those prevalent in other civilizations. Western ideas of individualism, liberalism, constitutionalism, human rights, equality, liberty, the rule of law, democracy, free markets, the separation of church and state, often have little resonance in Islamic, Confucian, Japanese, Hindu, Buddhist or Orthodox cultures. Western efforts to propagate such ideas produce instead a reaction against "human rights imperialism" and a reaffirmation of indigenous values, as can be seen in the support for religious fundamentalism by the younger generation in non-Western cultures. The very notion that there could be a "universal civilization" is a Western idea, directly at odds with the particularism of most Asian societies and their emphasis on what distinguishes one people from another. Indeed, the author of a review of 100 comparative studies of values in different societies concluded that "the values that are most important in the West are least important worldwide."[5] In the political realm, of course, these differences are most manifest in the efforts of the United States and other Western powers to induce other peoples to adopt Western ideas concerning democracy and human rights. Modern democratic government originated in the West. When it has developed in non-Western societies it has usually been the product of Western colonialism or imposition.

The central axis of world politics in the future is likely to be, in Kishore Mahbubani's phrase, the conflict between "the West and the Rest" and the responses of non-Western civilizations to Western power and values.[6] Those responses generally take one or a combination of three forms. At one extreme, non-Western states can, like Burma and North Korea, attempt to pursue a course of isolation, to insulate their societies from penetration or "corruption" by the West, and, in effect, to opt out of participation in the Western-dominated global community. The costs of this course, however, are high, and few states have pursued it exclusively. A second alternative, the equivalent of "bandwagoning" in international relations theory, is to attempt to join the West and accept its values and institutions. The third alternative is to attempt to "balance" the West by developing economic and military power and cooperating with other non-Western societies against the West, while preserving indigenous values and institutions; in short, to modernize but not to Westernize.

The Torn Countries

In the future, as people differentiate themselves by civilization, countries with large numbers of peoples of different civilizations, such as the Soviet Union and Yugoslavia, are candidates for dismemberment. Some other countries have a fair degree of cultural homogeneity but are divided over whether their society belongs to one civilization or another. These are torn countries. Their leaders typically wish to pursue a bandwagoning strategy and to make their countries members of the West, but the history, culture and traditions of their countries are non-Western.

During the past decade Mexico has assumed a position somewhat similar to that of Turkey. Just as Turkey abandoned its historic opposition to Europe and attempted to join Europe, Mexico has stopped defining itself by its opposition to the United States and is instead attempting to imitate the United States and to join it in the North American Free Trade Area. Mexican leaders are engaged in the great task of redefining Mexican identity and have introduced fundamental economic reforms that eventually will lead to fundamental political change. In 1991 a top adviser to President Carlos Salinas de Gortari described at length to me all the changes the Salinas government was making. When he finished, I remarked: "That's most impressive. It seems to me that basically you want to change Mexico from a Latin American country into a North American country." He looked at me with surprise and exclaimed: "Exactly! That's

precisely what we are trying to do, but of course we could never say so publicly." As his remark indicates, in Mexico as in Turkey, significant elements in society resist the redefinition of their country's identity. In Turkey, European-oriented leaders have to make gestures to Islam (Özal's pilgrimage to Mecca); so also Mexico's North American-oriented leaders have to make gestures to those who hold Mexico to be a Latin American country (Salinas' Ibero-American Guadalajara summit).

For the United States, Mexico is the most immediate torn country. Globally the most important torn country is Russia. The question of whether Russia is part of the West or the leader of a distinct Slavic-Orthodox civilization has been a recurring one in Russian history. That issue was obscured by the communist victory in Russia, which imported a Western ideology, adapted it to Russian conditions and then challenged the West in the name of that ideology. The dominance of communism shut off the historic debate over Westernization versus Russification. With communism discredited Russians once again face that question.

To redefine its civilization identity, a torn country must meet three requirements. First, its political and economic elite has to be generally supportive of and enthusiastic about this move. Second, its public has to be willing to acquiesce in the redefinition. Third, the dominant groups in the recipient civilization have to be willing to embrace the convert. All three requirements in large part exist with respect to Mexico. The first two in large part exist with respect to Turkey. It is not clear that any of them exist with respect to Russia's joining the West. The conflict between liberal democracy and Marxism-Leninism was between ideologies which, despite their major differences, ostensibly shared ultimate goals of freedom, equality and prosperity. A traditional, authoritarian, nationalist Russia could have quite different goals. A Western democrat could carry on an intellectual debate with a Soviet Marxist. It would be virtually impossible for him to do that with a Russian traditionalist. If, as the Russians stop behaving like Marxists, they reject liberal democracy and begin behaving like Russians but not like Westerners, the relations between Russia and the West could again become distant and conflictual.[8]

Implications for the West

This article does not argue that civilization identities will replace all other identities, that nation states will disappear, that each civilization will become a single coherent political entity, that groups within a civilization will not conflict with and even fight each other. This paper does set forth the hypotheses that differences between civilizations are real and important; civilization-consciousness is increasing; conflict between civilizations will supplant ideological and other forms of conflict as the dominant global form of conflict; international relations, historically a game played out within Western civilization, will increasingly be de-Westernized and become a game in which non-Western civilizations are actors and not simply objects; successful political, security and economic international institutions are more likely to develop within civilizations than across civilizations; conflicts between groups in different civilizations will be more frequent, more sustained and more violent than conflicts between groups in the same civilization; violent conflicts between groups in different civilizations are the most likely and most dangerous source of escalation that could lead to global wars; the paramount axis of world politics will be the relations between "the West and the Rest"; the elites in some torn non-Western countries will try to make their countries part of the West, but in most cases face major obstacles to accomplishing this; a central focus of conflict for the immediate future will be between the West and several Islamic-Confucian states.

This is not to advocate the desirability of conflicts between civilizations. It is to set forth descriptive hypotheses as to what the future may be like. If these are plausible hypotheses, however, it is necessary to consider their implications for Western policy. These implications should be divided between short-term advantage and long-term accommodation. In the short term it is clearly in the interest of the West to promote greater cooperation and unity within its own civilization, particularly between its European and North American components; to

incorporate into the West societies in Eastern Europe and Latin America whose cultures are close to those of the West; to promote and maintain cooperative relations with Russia and Japan; to prevent escalation of local inter-civilization conflicts into major inter-civilization wars; to limit the expansion of the military strength of Confucian and Islamic states; to moderate the reduction of Western military capabilities and maintain military superiority in East and Southwest Asia; to exploit differences and conflicts among Confucian and Islamic states; to support in other civilizations groups sympathetic to Western values and interests; to strengthen international institutions that reflect and legitimate Western interests and values and to promote the involvement of non-Western states in those institutions.

In the longer term other measures would be called for. Western civilization is both Western and modern. Non-Western civilizations have attempted to become modern without becoming Western. To date only Japan has fully succeeded in this quest. Non-Western civilizations will continue to attempt to acquire the wealth, technology, skills, machines and weapons that are part of being modern. They will also attempt to reconcile this modernity with their traditional culture and values. Their economic and military strength relative to the West will increase. Hence the West will increasingly have to accommodate these non-Western modern civilizations whose power approaches that of the West but whose values and interests differ significantly from those of the West. This will require the West to maintain the economic and military power necessary to protect its interests in relation to these civilizations. It will also, however, require the West to develop a more profound understanding of the basic religious and philosophical assumptions underlying other civilizations and the ways in which people in those civilizations see their interests. It will require an effort to identify elements of commonality between Western and other civilizations. For the relevant future, there will be no universal civilization, but instead a world of different civilizations, each of which will have to learn to coexist with the others.

Notes

1. Murray Weidenbaum, *Greater China: The Next Economic Superpower?*, St. Louis: Washington University Center for the Study of American Business, Contemporary Issues, Series 57, February 1993, pp. 2–3.

2. Bernard Lewis, "The Roots of Muslim Rage," *The Atlantic Monthly*, vol. 266, September 1990, p. 60; *Time*, June 15, 1992, pp. 24–28.

3. Archie Roosevelt, *For Lust of Knowing*, Brown: Little, Brown, 1988, pp. 332–333.

4. Almost invariably Western leaders claim they are acting on behalf of "the world community." One minor lapse occurred during the run-up to the Gulf War. In an interview on "Good Morning America," Dec. 21, 1990, British Prime Minister John Major referred to the actions "the West" was talking against Saddam Hussein. He quickly corrected himself and subsequently referred to "the world community." He was, however, right when he erred.

5. Harry C. Triandis, *The New York Times*, Dec. 25, 1990, p. 41, and "Cross-Cultural Studies of Individualism and Collectivism," Nebrasaka Symposium on Motivation, vol. 37, 1989, pp. 41–133.

6. Kishore Mahbubani, "The West and the Rest," *The National Interest*, Summer 1992, pp. 3–13.

7. Sergei Stankevich, "Russia in Search of Itself," *The National Interest,*Summer 1992, pp. 47–51; Daniel Schneider, "A Russian Movement Rejects Western Tilt," *Christian Science Monitor*, Feb. 5,1993, pp. 5–7.

8. Owen Harries has pointed out that Australia is trying (unwisely in his view) to become a torn country in reverse. Although it has been a full member not only of the West but also of the ABCA military and intelligence core of the West, its current leaders are in effect proposing that it defect from the West, redefine itself as an Asian country and cultivate close ties with its neighbors. Australia's future, they argue, is with the dynamic economies of East Asia. But, as I have suggested, close economic cooperation normally requires a common cultural base. In addition, none of the three conditions necessary for a torn country to join another civilization is likely to exist in Australia's case.

Public Diplomacy and Soft Power

JOSEPH S. NYE, JR.

Nye articulates several core principles of Liberal theory, and takes issue with various facets of Realism. Nye argues that the U.S. can attain its foreign policy goals more efficiently if it abandons strategies of coercion and adopts a more pacific strategy of attracting and co-opting other countries to adopt U.S. goals. Thus, he argues that the U.S.A. may benefit more from projecting the merits of its values, culture, institutions, and policies than from its projection of hard power, or military force.

Power is the ability to affect others to obtain the outcomes you want. One can affect others' behavior in three main ways: threats of coercion ("sticks"), inducements and payments ("carrots"), and attraction that makes others want what you want. A country may obtain the outcomes it wants in world politics because other countries want to follow it, admiring its values, emulating its example, and/or aspiring to its level of prosperity and openness. In this sense, it is important to set the agenda and attract others in world politics, and not only to force them to change through the threat or use of military or economic weapons. This soft power—getting others to want the outcomes that you want—co-opts people rather than coerces them.[1]

Soft power rests on the ability to shape the preferences of others. At the personal level, we all know the power of attraction and seduction. Political leaders have long understood the power that comes from setting the agenda and determining the framework of a debate. Soft power is a staple of daily democratic politics. The ability to establish preferences tends to be associated with intangible assets such as an attractive personality, culture, political values and institutions, and policies that are seen as legitimate or having moral authority. If I can get you to want to do what I want, then I do not have to force you to do what you do *not* want.

Soft power is not merely influence, though it is one source of influence. Influence can also rest on the hard power of threats or payments. And soft power is more than just persuasion or the ability to move people by argument, though that is an important part of it. It is also the ability to entice and attract. In behavioral terms, soft power is attractive power. In terms of resources, soft power resources are the assets that produce such attraction. Whether a particular asset is an attractive soft power resource can be measured through polls or focus groups. Whether that attraction in turn produces desired policy outcomes has to be judged in each particular case. But the gap between power measured as resources and power judged by the outcomes of behavior is not unique to soft power. It occurs with all forms of power. Before the fall of France in 1940, for example, Britain and France had

more tanks than Germany, but that advantage in military power resources did not accurately predict the outcome of the battle.

This distinction between power measured in behavioral outcomes and power measured in terms of resources is important for understanding the relationship between soft power and public diplomacy. In international politics, the resources that produce soft power arise in large part from the values an organization or country expresses in its culture, in the examples it sets by its internal practices and policies, and in the way it handles its relations with others. Public diplomacy is an instrument that governments use to mobilize these resources to communicate with, and attract the publics of other countries, rather then merely their governments. Public diplomacy tries to attract by drawing attention to these potential resources through broadcasting, subsidizing cultural exports, arranging exchanges, and so forth. But if the content of a country's culture, values, and policies are not attractive, public diplomacy that "broadcasts" them cannot produce soft power. It may produce just the opposite. Exporting Hollywood films full of nudity and violence to conservative Muslim countries may produce repulsion rather than soft power. And Voice of America (VOA) broadcasts that extol the virtues of government policies that are seen by others as arrogant will be dismissed as mere propaganda and not produce the soft power of attraction.

Governments sometimes find it difficult to control and employ soft power, but that does not diminish its importance. It was a former French foreign minister who observed that Americans are powerful because they can "inspire the dreams and desires of others, thanks to the mastery of global images through film and television and because, for these same reasons, large numbers of students from other countries come to the United States to finish their studies" (Vedrine and Moisi 2001, 3).

Soft power is an important reality. Those self-styled realists who deny the importance of soft power are like people who do not understand the power of seduction. They succumb to the "concrete fallacy" that espouses that something is not a power resource unless you can drop it on a city or on your foot.[2] During a meeting with President John F.

Kennedy, senior statesman John J. McCloy exploded in anger about paying attention to popularity[7] and attraction in world politics: "'world opinion?' I don't believe in world opinion. The only thing that matters is power." But as Arthur Schlesinger noted, "like Woodrow Wilson and Franklin Roosevelt, Kennedy understood that the ability to attract others and move opinion was an element of power" (McCloy and Schlesinger, as quoted in Haefele 2001, 66). The German editor Josef Joffe once argued that America's soft power was even larger than its economic and military assets. "U.S. culture, lowbrow or high, radiates outward with an intensity last seen in the days of the Roman Empire—but with a novel twist. Rome's and Soviet Russia's cultural sway stopped exactly at their military borders. America's soft power, though, rules over an empire on which the sun never sets" (Joffe 2001, 43). But cultural soft power can be undercut by policies that are seen as illegitimate. In recent years, particularly after the invasion of Iraq, American soft power has declined. For example, a 2007 BBC opinion poll reported that across twenty-five countries, half of those polled said the United States played a mainly negative role in the world (*New York Times* 2007).

The Development of Public Diplomacy

The soft power of a country rests primarily on three resources: its culture (in places where it is attractive to others), its political values (when it lives up to them at home and abroad), and its foreign policies (when they are seen as legitimate and having moral authority). Culture is the set of practices that create meaning for a society, and it has many manifestations. It is common to distinguish between high culture such as literature, art, and education, which appeals to elites; and popular culture, which focuses on mass entertainment. After its defeat in the Franco-Prussian War, the French government sought to repair the nation's shattered prestige by promoting its language and literature through the Alliance Francaise created in 1883. "The projection of French culture abroad thus became a significant component of French diplomacy" (Pells 1997, 31). Italy, Germany, and others soon followed suit. World War I saw a rapid acceleration of efforts to

deploy soft power, as most of those governments established offices to propagandize their cause. The United States not only established its own office but was a central target of other countries. During the early years before American entry into the war, Britain and Germany competed to create favorable images in American public opinion.

The United States was a relative latecomer to the idea of using information and culture for the purposes of diplomacy. In 1917, President Woodrow Wilson established a Committee on Public Information directed by his friend, the newspaperman George Creel. In Creel's words, his task was "a vast enterprise in salesmanship, the world's greatest adventure in advertising" (Rosenberg 1982, 79). Creel insisted that his office's activities did not constitute propaganda and were merely educational and informative. But the facts belied his denials. Among other things, Creel organized tours, churned out pamphlets on "the Gospel of Americanism," established a government-run news service, made sure that motion picture producers received wartime allotments of scarce materials, and saw to it that the films portrayed America in a positive light. The office aroused suspicions sufficient enough that it was abolished shortly after the return of peace.

The advent of radio in the 1920s led many governments into the arena of foreign-language broadcasting, and in the 1930s, communists and fascists competed to promote favorable images to foreign publics. In addition to its foreign-language radio broadcasts, Nazi Germany perfected the propaganda film. As Britain's Foreign Secretary Anthony Eden realized about the new communications in 1937, "It is perfectly true, of course, that good cultural propaganda cannot remedy the damage done by a bad foreign policy, but it is no exaggeration to say that even the best of diplomatic policies may fail if it neglects the task of interpretation and persuasion which modern conditions impose" (as quoted in Wagnleitner 1994, 50).

By the late 1930s, the Roosevelt administration was convinced that "America's security depended on its ability to speak to and to win the support of people in other countries" (Pells 1997, 33). President Roosevelt was particularly concerned about

German propaganda in Latin America. In 1938, the State Department established a Division of Cultural Relations, and supplemented it two years later with an Office of Inter-American Affairs that, under Nelson Rockefeller, actively promoted information about America and its culture to Latin America. In 1939, Germany beamed seven hours of programming a week to Latin America, and the United States about twelve. By 1941, the United States broadcast around the clock.

After America's entry into the war, the government's cultural offensive became global in scope. In 1942, Roosevelt created an Office of Wartime Information (OWI) to deal in presumably accurate information, while an intelligence organization, the Office of Strategic Service, included among its functions the dissemination of disinformation. The OWI even worked to shape Hollywood into an effective propaganda tool, suggesting additions and deletions to many films and denying licenses to others. And Hollywood executives were happy to cooperate out of a mixture of patriotism and self-interest. Well before the cold war, "American corporate and advertising executives, as well as the heads of Hollywood studios, were selling not only their products but also America's culture and values, the secrets of its success, to the rest of the world" (Pells 1997, xiii). Wartime soft power resources were created partly by the government and in part independently. What became known as the Voice of America grew rapidly during World War II. Modeled after the BBC, by 1943 it had twenty-three transmitters delivering news in twenty-seven languages.

With the growth of the Soviet threat in the cold war, public diplomacy continued to expand, but so did a debate about the extent to which it should be a captive purveyor of government information or an independent representative of American culture. Special radios were added such as Radio Liberty and Radio Free Europe, which used exiles to broadcast to the Eastern bloc. More generally, as the cold war developed, there was a division between those who favored the slow media of cultural diplomacy—art, books, exchanges—which had a "trickle down effect," and those who favored the

fast information media of radio, movies, and newsreels, which promised more immediate and visible "bang for the buck." Although the tension has never fully been resolved to this day, public diplomacy of both sorts helped to erode faith in communism behind the Iron Curtain.[3] When the Berlin Wall finally went down in 1989, it collapsed under the assault of hammers and bulldozers, not an artillery barrage.

With the end of the cold war, Americans were more interested in budget savings than in investments in soft power. From 1963 to 1993, the federal budget grew fifteen-fold, but the United States Information Agency (USIA) budget grew only six and a half times larger. The USIA had more than 12,000 employees at its peak in the mid-1960s but only 9,000 in 1994 and 6,715 on the eve of its takeover by the U.S. State Department (U.S. Department of State n.d.). Soft power seemed expendable. Between 1989 and 1999, the budget of the USIA, adjusted for inflation, decreased 10 percent. While government-funded radio broadcasts reached half the Soviet population every week and between 70 and 80 percent of the populace of Eastern Europe during the cold war, at the beginning of the new century, a mere 2 percent of Arabs heard the VOA (Blinken 2003, 287). Resources for the USIA mission in Indonesia, the world's largest Muslim nation, were cut in half. From 1995 to 2001, academic and cultural exchanges dropped from forty-five thousand to twenty-nine thousand annually, while many accessible downtown cultural centers and libraries were closed (Johnson and Dale 2003, 4). In comparison, the BBC World Service had half again as many weekly listeners around the globe as did the VOA. Public diplomacy had become so identified with fighting the cold war that few Americans noticed that with an information revolution occurring, soft power was becoming mere rather than less important. Government policies reflected popular attitudes. For example, the percentage of foreign affairs articles on the front page of U.S. newspapers dropped by nearly half (Hiatt 2007). Only after September 2001 did Americans begin to rediscover the importance of investing in the instruments of soft power.

Public Diplomacy in an Information Age

Promoting positive images of one's country is not new, but the conditions for projecting soft power have transformed dramatically in recent years. For one thing, nearly half the countries in the world are now democracies. The competitive cold war model has become less relevant as a guide for public diplomacy. While there is still a need to provide accurate information to populations in countries like Burma or Syria, where the government controls information, there is a new need to garner favorable public opinion in countries like Mexico and Turkey, where parliaments can now affect decision making. For example, when the United States sought support for the Iraq war, such as Mexico's vote in the UN or Turkey's permission for American troops to cross its territory, the decline of American soft power created a disabling rather than an enabling environment for its policies. Shaping public opinion becomes even more important where authoritarian governments have been replaced. Public support was not so important when the United States successfully sought the use of bases in authoritarian countries, but it turned out to be crucial under the new democratic conditions in Mexico and Turkey. Even when foreign leaders are friendly, their leeway may be limited if their publics and parliaments have a negative image of the United States. In such circumstances, diplomacy aimed at public opinion can become as important to outcomes as the traditional classified diplomatic communications among leaders.

Information is power, and today a much larger part of the world's population has access to that power. Long gone are the days when "small teams of American foreign service officers drove Jeeps to the hinterlands of Latin America and other remote regions of the world to show reel-to-reel movies to isolated audiences" (Ross 2003, 252). Technological advances have led to a dramatic reduction in the cost of processing and transmitting information. The result is an explosion of information, and that has produced a "paradox of plenty" (Simon 1998, 30–33). Plenty of information leads to scarcity of attention. When people are overwhelmed with the volume of information confronting them, it is hard to know what to focus on. Attention rather than information becomes the scarce resource, and those who can distinguish valuable information from background clutter gain power. Editors and cue-givers become more in demand, and this is a source of power for those who can tell us where to focus our attention.

Among editors and cue-givers, credibility is the crucial resource and an important source of soft power. Reputation becomes even more important than in the past, and political struggles occur over the creation, and destruction of credibility. Governments compete for credibility not only with other governments but with a broad range of alternatives including news media, corporations, nongovernmental organizations (NGOs), intergovernmental organizations, and networks of scientific communities.

Politics has become a contest of competitive credibility. The world of traditional power politics is typically about whose military or economy wins. Politics in an information age "may ultimately be about whose story wins" (Arquila and Ronfeldt 1999). Governments compete with each other and with other organizations to enhance their own credibility' and weaken that of their opponents. Witness the struggle between Serbia and NATO to frame the interpretation of events in Kosovo in 1999 and the events in Serbia a year later. Prior to the demonstrations that led to the overthrow of Slobodan Milosevic in October 2000, 45 percent of Serb adults were tuned to Radio Free Europe and VOA. In contrast, only 31 percent listened to the state-controlled radio station. Radio Belgrade (Kaufman 2003). Moreover, the domestic alternative radio station, B92, provided access to Western news, and when the government tried to shut it down, it continued to provide such news on the Internet.

Reputation has always mattered in world politics, but the role of credibility becomes an even more important power resource because of the "paradox of plenty." Information that appears to be propaganda may not only be scorned, but it may also turn out to be counterproductive if it undermines a country's reputation for credibility. Exaggerated claims about Saddam Hussein's weapons of mass destruction and ties to Al Qaeda may have helped mobilize domestic support for the Iraq war, but the subsequent disclosure of the exaggeration dealt a costly blow to American credibility. Similarly, the treatment of prisoners at Abu Ghraib and Guantanamo in a manner inconsistent with American values led to perceptions of hypocrisy that could not be reversed by broadcasting pictures of Muslims living well in America. In fact, the slick production values of the new American satellite television station Alhurra did not make it competitive in the Middle East, where it was widely regarded as an instrument of government propaganda. Under the new conditions of the information age, more than ever, the soft sell may prove more effective than the hard sell. Without underlying national credibility, the instruments of public diplomacy cannot translate cultural resources into the soft power of attraction. The effectiveness of public diplomacy is measured by minds changed (as shown in interviews or polls), not dollars spent or slick production packages.

The Dimensions of Current Public Diplomacy

In 1963, Edward R. Murrow, the noted broadcaster who was director of the USIA in the Kennedy administration, defined public diplomacy as interactions not only with foreign governments but primarily with nongovernmental individuals and organizations, and often presenting a variety of private views in addition to government views (as cited in Leonard 2002). Skeptics who treat the term *public diplomacy* as a mere euphemism for propaganda miss the point. Simple propaganda often lacks credibility and thus is counterproductive as public diplomacy. Good public diplomacy has to go beyond propaganda. Nor is public diplomacy merely public relations campaigns. Conveying information and selling a positive image is part of it, but public diplomacy also involves building long-term relationships that create an enabling environment for government policies.

The mix of direct government information with long-term cultural relationships varies with three dimensions of public diplomacy, and all three are

important (Leonard 2002). The first and most immediate dimension is daily communications, which involves explaining the context of domestic and foreign policy decisions. After making decisions, government officials in modern democracies usually devote a good deal of attention to what and how to tell the press. But they generally focus on the domestic press. The foreign press has to be an important target for the first stage of public diplomacy. The first stage must also involve preparation for dealing with crises. A rapid response capability means that false charges or misleading information can be answered immediately. For example, when Al Jazeera broadcast Osama bin Laden's first videotape on October 7, 2001, U.S. officials initially sought to prevent both Al Jazeera and American networks from broadcasting further messages from bin Laden. But in the modern information age, such action is not only as frustrating as stopping the tide, but it runs counter to the value of openness that America wants to symbolize. A better response would be to prepare to flood Al Jazeera and other networks with American voices to counter bin Laden's hate speech. While Al Jazeera and other foreign networks are hardly free of bias, they also need content. As their Washington bureau chief invited, "Please come talk to us, exploit us" (as quoted in Blinken 2003).

The second dimension is strategic communication, which develops a set of simple themes much as a political or advertising campaign does. The campaign plans symbolic events and communications over the course of the next year to reinforce central themes or to advance a particular government policy. Special themes focus on particular policy initiatives. For example, when the Reagan administration decided to implement NATO's two-track decision of deploying missiles while negotiating to remove existing Soviet intermediate-range missiles, the Soviet Union responded with a concerted campaign to influence European opinion and make the deployment impossible. The United States's themes stressed the multilateral nature of the NATO decision, encouraged European governments to take the lead when possible, and used nongovernmental American participants effectively to counter Soviet arguments. Even though polls in Germany showed residual concerns about the policy, they also showed that the German public was pro-American by a two-thirds majority. As former secretary of state George Schultz later concluded, "I don't think we could have pulled it off if it hadn't been for a very active program of public diplomacy. Because the Soviets were very-active all through 1983 . . . with peace movements and all kinds of efforts to dissuade our friends in Europe from deploying" (as quoted in Tuch 1990).

The third dimension of public diplomacy is the development of lasting relationships with key individuals over many years through scholarships, exchanges, training, seminars, conferences, and access to media channels. Over time, about seven hundred thousand people, including two hundred heads of governments, have participated in American cultural and academic exchanges, and these exchanges helped to educate world leaders like Anwar Sadat, Helmut Schmidt, and Margaret Thatcher. Other countries have similar programs. For example, Japan has developed an interesting exchange program bringing six thousand young foreigners from forty countries each year to teach their languages in Japanese schools, with an alumni association to maintain the bonds of friendship that develop.[4]

Each of these three dimensions of public diplomacy plays an important role in helping to create an attractive image of a country that can improve its prospects for obtaining its desired outcomes. But even the best advertising cannot sell an unpopular product. Policies that appear as narrowly self-serving or arrogantly presented are likely to prohibit rather than produce soft power. At best, longstanding friendly relationships may lead others to be slightly more tolerant in their responses. Sometimes friends will give you the benefit of the doubt or forgive more willingly. This is what is meant by an enabling or a disabling environment for policy.

A communications strategy cannot work if it cuts against the grain of policy. Actions speak louder than words, and public diplomacy that appears to be mere window dressing for hard power

projection is unlikely to succeed. In 2003, former speaker of the House of Representatives Newt Gingrich attacked the State Department for failing to sell America's policy (Gingrich 2003). But selling requires paying attention to your markets, and on that dimension, the fault did not rest with the State Department. For example, Gingrich complained about America's removal from the UN Human Rights Commission in 2001. But that was in retaliation for America's failure to pay its UN dues (a policy that originated in the U.S. Congress) and the unilateral policies of the new Bush administration (that often originated in other executive departments despite the warnings of the State Department). As Republican Senator Charles Hagel noted, after 9/11 many people in Washington were suddenly talking about the need for renewed public diplomacy to "get our message out." But, he pointed out, "Madison Avenue-style packaging cannot market a contradictory or confusing message. We need to reassess the fundamentals of our diplomatic approach. . . . Policy and diplomacy must match, or marketing becomes a confusing and transparent barrage of mixed messages" (Hagel 2003).

Effective public diplomacy is a two-way street that involves listening as well as talking. We need to understand better what is going on in the minds of others and what values we share. That is why exchanges are often more effective than mere broadcasting. By definition, soft power means getting others to want the same outcomes you want, and that requires an understanding of how they are hearing your messages and adapting them accordingly. It is crucial to understand the target audience. Yet research on foreign public opinion is woefully underfunded.

Preaching at foreigners is not the best way to convert them. Too often, political leaders think that the problem is simply that others lack information, and that if they simply knew what we know, they would see things our way. But all information goes through cultural filters, and declamatory statements are rarely heard as intended. Telling is far less influential than actions and symbols that show as well as tell. That is why the Bush administration initiatives on increasing development assistance or combating HIV/AIDS were potentially important before they vanished under the burdens of Iraq. It is interesting that provision of Tsunami relief to Indonesia in 2004 helped to reverse in part the precipitous slide in America's standing in Indonesian polls that began after the Iraq war.

Broadcasting is important but needs to be supplemented by effective "narrowcasting" via the Internet. While the Internet reaches only the elites in many parts of the world where most people are too poor to own a telephone (much less a computer), its flexibility and low cost allows for the targeting of messages to particular groups. It also provides a way to transfer information to countries where the government blocks traditional media. And the Internet can be used interactively and in combination with exchanges. Face-to-face communications remain the most effective, but they can be supplemented and reinforced by the Internet. For example, a combination of personal visits and Internet resources can create both virtual and real networks of young people who want to learn about each other's cultures. Or the United States might learn a lesson from Japan and pay young foreigners to spend a year teaching their language and culture in American schools. The alumni of these programs could then form associations that would remain connected over the Internet.

Some countries accomplish almost all of their public diplomacy through actions rather than broadcasting. Norway is a good example. It has only 5 million people, lacks an international language or transnational culture, is not a central location or hub of organizations or multinational corporate brands, and is not a member of the European Union. Nonetheless, it has developed a voice and presence out of proportion to its modest size and resources "through a ruthless prioritization of its target audiences and its concentration on a single message—Norway as a force for peace in the world" (Leonard 2002, 53). The relevant activities include conflict mediation in the Middle East, Sri Lanka, and Colombia, as well as its large aid budget and its frequent participation in peacekeeping missions. Of course, not all Norwegian actions are consistent in their message. The domestic politics of whaling sometimes strikes a discordant note

among environmentalists, but overall, Norway shows how a small country can exploit a diplomatic niche that enhances its image and role.

Not only do actions need to reinforce words, it is important to remember that the same words and images that are most successful in communicating to a domestic audience may have negative effects on a foreign audience. When President Bush used the term *axis of evil* to refer to Iraq, Iran, and North Korea in his 2002 State of the Union address, it was well received domestically. However, foreigners reacted against lumping together disparate diplomatic situations under a moralistic label. Similarly, while declaring a "war on terrorism" helped mobilize public and congressional support after 9/11, many foreign publics believed that the United States was making cooperative efforts against terrorism more difficult, particularly when the idea of a war of indefinite duration could be used to incarcerate prisoners at Guantanamo without full legal rights. In 2006, the British Foreign Office prohibited its diplomats from using the phrase because they believed that it played into Al Qaeda's narrative of global jihad (Nye 2007).

Even when policy and communications are "in sync," wielding soft power resources in an information age is difficult. For one thing, as mentioned earlier, government communications are only a small fraction of the total communications among societies in an age that is awash in information. Hollywood movies that offend religious fundamentalists in other countries or activities by American missionaries that appear to devalue Islam will always be outside the control of government. Some skeptics have concluded that Americans should accept the inevitable and let market forces take care of the presentation of the country's culture and image to foreigners. Why pour money into VOA when CNN, MSNBC, or Fox can do the work for free? But such a conclusion is too facile. Market forces portray only the profitable mass dimensions of American culture, thus reinforcing foreign images of a one-dimensional country.

Developing long-term relationships is not always profitable in the short term, and thus leaving it simply to the market may lead to underinvestment.

While higher education may pay for itself, and non-profit organizations can help, many exchange programs would shrink without government support. Private companies must respond to market forces to stay in business. If there is no market for broadcasting in Serbo-Croatian or Pashtu, companies will not broadcast in those languages. And sometimes private companies will cave in to political pressures from foreign governments if that is better for profits—witness the way Rupert Murdoch dropped the BBC and its critical messages from his satellite television broadcasts to China in the 1990s.

At the same time, postmodern publics are generally skeptical of authority, and governments are often mistrusted. Thus, it often behooves governments to keep in the background and to work with private actors. Some NGOs enjoy more trust than governments do, and though they are difficult to control, they can be useful channels of communication. American foundations and NGOs played important roles in the consolidation of democracy in Eastern Europe after the end of the cold war. Similarly, for countries like Britain and the United States, which enjoy significant immigrant populations, such diasporas can provide culturally sensitive and linguistically skilled connections. Building relationships between political parties in different countries was pioneered by Germany, where the major parties have foundations for foreign contacts that are partly supported by government funds. During the Reagan administration, the United States followed suit when it established the National Endowment for Democracy, which provided funds for the National Democratic Institute and the International Republican Institute, as well as trade unions and chambers of commerce, to promote democracy and civil society overseas.

American companies can also play an important role. Their representatives and brands directly touch the lives of far more people than government representatives do. Some public-spirited businesspeople have suggested that companies develop and share sensitivity and communications training for corporate representatives before they are sent abroad. Companies can also take the lead in sponsoring specific public diplomacy projects such as "a technology company working with Sesame Workshop and a Lebanese broadcaster to co-produce an English language children's program centered on technology, an area of American achievement that is universally admired" (Reinhard 2003, 30).

Another benefit to indirect public diplomacy is that it is often able to take more risks in presenting a range of views. It is sometimes domestically difficult for the government to support presentation of views that are critical of its own policies. Yet such criticism is often the most effective way of establishing credibility. Part of America's soft power grows out of the openness of its society and polity and the fact that a free press, Congress, and courts can criticize and correct policies. When the government instruments avoid such criticism, they not only diminish their own credibility but also fail to capitalize on an important source of attraction for foreign elites (even when they are fiercely critical of government policies). In fact, some observers have suggested that the United States would get a better return on its investment if it turned Alhurra into an international C-SPAN that broadcasts seminars, town meetings, and congressional debates.

The military can sometimes play an important role in the generation of soft power. In addition to the aura of power that is generated by its hard power capabilities, the military has a broad range of officer exchanges, joint training, and assistance programs with other countries in peacetime. The Pentagon's international military and educational training programs include sessions on democracy and human rights along with military training. In wartime, military psychological operations ("psyops") are an important way to influence foreign behavior. An enemy outpost, for example, can be destroyed by a cruise missile or captured by ground forces, or enemy soldiers can be convinced to desert and leave the post undefended. Such psyops often involve deception and disinformation that is effective in war but counterproductive in peace. The dangers of a military role in public diplomacy arise when it tries to apply wartime tactics in ambiguous situations. This is particularly tempting in the current ill-defined war on terrorism that blurs the distinction between normal

Table 1 Soft Power Sources, Referees, and Receivers

Sources of Soft Power	Referees for Credibility or Legitimacy	Receivers of Soft Power
Foreign policies	Governments, media, nongovernmental organizations (NGOs), intergovernmental organizations (IGOs)	Foreign governments and publics
Domestic values and policies	Media. NGOs, IGOs	Foreign governments and publics
High culture	Governments, NGOs, IGOs	Foreign governments and publics
Pop culture	Media, markets	Foreign publics

civilian activities and traditional war. The net result of such efforts is to undercut rather than create soft power.

Finally, it is a mistake to see public diplomacy simply in adversarial terms. Sometimes there is a competition of "my information versus your information," but often there can be gains for both sides. German public diplomacy during the cold war is a good example. In contrast to French public diplomacy, which sought to demonstrate independence from the United States, a key theme of German public diplomacy was to portray itself as a reliable ally in American eyes. Thus, German and American policy information goals were mutually reinforcing. Political leaders may share mutual and similar objectives—for example, the promotion of democracy and human rights. In such circumstances, there can be joint gains from coordination of public diplomacy programs. Cooperative public diplomacy can also help take the edge off suspicions of narrow national motives.

In addition, there are times when cooperation, including enhancement of the public image of multilateral institutions like NATO or the UN, can make it easier for governments to use such instruments to handle difficult tasks like peacekeeping, promoting democracy, or countering terrorism. For example, during the cold war, American public diplomacy in Czechoslovakia was reinforced by the association of the United States with international conventions that fostered human rights. In 1975, the multilateral Helsinki Conference on Security and Cooperation in Europe (CSCE) legitimized discussion of human rights behind the Iron Curtain and had consequences that were unforeseen by those who signed its Final Act. As former CIA director Robert Gates concluded, despite initial American resistance, "the Soviets desperately wanted the CSCE, they got it, and it laid the foundations for the end of their empire" (as quoted in Thomas 2003, 257).

Conclusions

Power in a global information age, more than ever, will include a soft dimension of attraction as well as the hard dimensions of coercion and inducement. The ability to combine hard and soft power effectively is "smart power." The United States managed to deploy smart power throughout much of the cold war. It has been less successful in melding soft and hard power in the period since 9/11. The current struggle against transnational terrorism is a struggle over winning hearts and minds, and the current overreliance on hard power alone is not the path to success. Public diplomacy is an important tool in the arsenal of smart power, but smart public diplomacy requires an understanding of the role of credibility, self-criticism, and the role of civil society in generating soft power. Public diplomacy that degenerates into propaganda not only fails to convince, but can undercut soft power.

Notes

1. I first introduced this concept in *Bound to Lead: The Changing Nature of American Power* (Nye 1990). It builds on what Peter Bachrach and Morton Baratz (1963) called the "second face of power." I developed the concept more fully in *Soft Power: The Means to Success in World Politics* (Nye 2004).
2. The term is from Steven Lukes (2005).
3. See Yale Richmond (2003). Also, see Nye (2004, chap. 2).
4. See David McConnell (forthcoming).

References

Arquila, John, and D. Ronfeldt. 1999. *The Emergence of Neopolitik: Toward an American Information Strategy.* Santa Monica. CA: RAND.

Bachrach, Peter, and Morton Baratz. 1963. Decisions and Nondecisions: An Analytical Framework. *American Political Science Review* 57 (September): 632–42.

Blinken, Anthony J. 2003. Winning the War of Ideas. In *The Battle for Hearts and Minds: Using Soft Power to Undermine Terrorist Networks,* ed. Alexander T. J. Lennon. Cambridge, MA: MIT Press.

Gingrich, Newt. 2003. Rogue State Department. *Foreign Policy* (July): 42.

Haefele, Mark. 2001. John K Kennedy, USIA, and World Public Opinion. *Diplomatic History* 23 (1): 66.

Hagel, Senator Chuck. 2003. *Challenges of World Leadership.* Speech given to the National Press Club, June 19, Washington, DC.

Hiatt, Fred. 2007. The Vanishing Foreign Correspondent. *Washington Post* (January 29).

Joffe, Josef. 2001. Who's Afraid of Mr. Big? *The National Interest* 64 (Summer): 43.

Johnson, Stephen, and Helle Dale. 2003. How to Reinvigorate U.S. Public Diplomacy. *The Heritage Foundation Backgrounder* 1645 (April 23), p. 4.

Kaufman, Edward. 2003. A Broadcasting Strategy to Win Media Wars. In *TheBattle for Hearts and Minds.* Washington, DC: Center for Strategic and International Studies.

Leonard, Mark. 2002. *Public Diplomacy.* London: Foreign Policy Centre.

Lukes, Steven. 2005. *Power: A Radical View.* 2nd ed. London: Palgrave.

McConnell, David. Forthcoming. Japan's Image Problem and the Soft Power Solution: The JET Program as Cultural Diplomacy. In *Soft Power Influx: National Assets in Japan and the United States,* ed. Yasushi Watanabe and David McConnell. Armonk, NY: Sharpe.

New York Times. 2007. Global View of U.S. Worsens, Poll Shows (January 23).

Nye, Joseph. 1990. *Bound to Lead: The Changing Nature of American Power.* New York: Basic Books.

———. 2004. *Soft Power: The Means to Success in World Politics.* New York: Public Affairs.

———. 2007. Just Don't Mention the War on Terrorism. *International Herald Tribune* (February 8).

Pells, Richard. 1997. *Not Like Us.* New York: Basic Books.

Reinhard, Keith. 2003. Restoring Brand America. *Advertising Age* (June 23), p. 30.

Richmond, Yale. 2003. *Cultural Exchange and the Cold War.* University Park: Pennsylvania State University Press.

Rosenberg, Emily. 1982. *Spreading the American Dream.* New York: Hill & Wang.

Ross, Christopher. 2003. Public Diplomacy Comes of Age. In *The Battle for Hearts and Minds.* Washington, DC: Center for Strategic and International Studies.

Simon, Herbert A. 1998. Information 101: It's Not What You Know, It's How You Know It. *Journal for Quality and Participation* (July–August): 30–33.

Thomas, Daniel C. 2001. *The Helsinki Effect: International Norms, Human Rights, and the Demise of Communism.* Princeton, NJ: Princeton University Press.

Tuch, Hans N. 1990. *Communicating with the World: U.S. Public Diplomacy Overseas* (chap. 12). New York: St. Martin's.

U.S. Department of State. n.d. *History of the Department of State during the Clinton Presidency (1993–2001).* Washington, DC: Office of the Historian, Bureau of Public Affairs.

Vedrine, Hubert, and Dominique Moisi. 2001. *France in an Age of Globalization.* Washington, DC: Brookings Institutions Press.

Wagnleitner, Reinhold. 1994. *Coca Colonization and the Cold War.* Chapel Hill: University of North Carolina Press.

Joseph S. Nye, Jr., "Public Diplomacy and Soft Power," The Annals of the American Academy of Political and Social Science 616:1 (2008), pp. 94–109, copyright © 2008 by SAGE Publications. Reprinted by permission of SAGE Publications.

The Age of Nonpolarity

What Will Follow U.S. Dominance

RICHARD N. HAASS

Haass asserts that the "unipolar moment" that existed in the decades after the Cold War is now finished. The depletion of U.S. power is the result of multiple pressures including the intensification of globalization, a nonexistent energy policy, and the costly war in Iraq. Further, Haass contends that sovereign states have lost much of their historical monopoly over power, and that power is increasingly diffused among many nations and nonstate actors. Thus, he argues that the international system is now marked by its "nonpolarity."

SUMMARY

The United States' unipolar moment is over. International relations in the twenty-first century will be defined by nonpolarity. Power will be diffuse rather than concentrated, and the influence of nation-states will decline as that of nonstate actors increases. But this is not all bad news for the United States; Washington can still manage the transition and make the world a safer place.

The principal characteristic of twenty-first-century international relations is turning out to be nonpolarity: a world dominated not by one or two or even several states but rather by dozens of actors possessing and exercising various kinds of power. This represents a tectonic shift from the past.

The twentieth century started out distinctly multipolar. But after almost 50 years, two world wars, and many smaller conflicts, a bipolar system emerged. Then, with the end of the Cold War and the demise of the Soviet Union, bipolarity gave way to unipolarity—an international system dominated by one power, in this case the United States. But today power is diffuse, and the onset of nonpolarity raises a number of important questions. How does nonpolarity differ from other forms of international order? How and why did it materialize? What are its likely consequences? And how should the United States respond?

Newer World Order

In contrast to multipolarity—which involves several distinct poles or concentrations of power—a nonpolar international system is characterized by numerous centers with meaningful power.

In a multipolar system, no power dominates, or the system will become unipolar. Nor do concentrations of power revolve around two positions, or the system will become bipolar. Multipolar systems can be cooperative, even assuming the form of a concert of powers, in which a few major powers work together on setting the rules of the game and disciplining those who violate them. They can also be more competitive, revolving around a balance of power, or conflictual, when the balance breaks down.

At first glance, the world today may appear to be multipolar. The major powers—China, the European Union (EU), India, Japan, Russia, and the United States—contain just over half the world's people and account for 75 percent of global GDP and 80 percent of global defense spending. Appearances, however, can be deceiving. Today's world differs in a fundamental way from one of classic multipolarity: there are many more power centers, and quite a few of these poles are not nation-states. Indeed, one of the cardinal features of the contemporary international system is that nation-states have lost their monopoly on power and in some domains their preeminence as well. States are being challenged from above, by regional and global organizations; from below, by militias; and from the side, by a variety of nongovernmental organizations (NGOs) and corporations. Power is now found in many hands and in many places.

In addition to the six major world powers, there are numerous regional powers: Brazil and, arguably, Argentina, Chile, Mexico, and Venezuela in Latin America; Nigeria and South Africa in Africa; Egypt, Iran, Israel, and Saudi Arabia in the Middle East; Pakistan in South Asia; Australia, Indonesia, and South Korea in East Asia and Oceania. A good many organizations would be on the list of power centers, including those that are global (the International Monetary Fund, the United Nations, the World Bank), those that are regional (the African Union, the Arab League, the Association of Southeast Asian Nations, the EU, the Organization of American States, the South Asian Association for Regional Cooperation), and those that are functional (the International Energy Agency, OPEC, the Shanghai Cooperation Organization, the World Health Organization). So, too, would states within nation-states, such as California and India's Uttar Pradesh, and cities, such as New York, Sao Paulo, and Shanghai. Then there are the large global companies, including those that dominate the worlds of energy, finance, and manufacturing. Other entities deserving inclusion would be global media outlets (al Jazeera, the BBC, CNN), militias (Hamas, Hezbollah, the Mahdi Army, the Taliban), political parties, religious institutions and movements, terrorist organizations (al Qaeda), drug cartels, and NGOs of a more benign sort (the Bill and Melinda Gates Foundation, Doctors Without Borders, Greenpeace). Today's world is increasingly one of distributed, rather than concentrated, power.

In this world, the United States is and will long remain the largest single aggregation of power. It spends more than $500 billion annually on its military—and more than $700 billion if the operations in Afghanistan and Iraq are included—and

boasts land, air, and naval forces that are the world's most capable. Its economy, with a GDP of some $14 trillion, is the world's largest. The United States is also a major source of culture (through films and television), information, and innovation. But the reality of American strength should not mask the relative decline of the United States' position in the world—and with this relative decline in power an absolute decline in influence and independence. The U.S. share of global imports is already down to 15 percent. Although U.S. GDP accounts for over 25 percent of the world's total, this percentage is sure to decline over time given the actual and projected differential between the United States' growth rate and those of the Asian giants and many other countries, a large number of which are growing at more than two or three times the rate of the United States.

GDP growth is hardly the only indication of a move away from U.S. economic dominance. The rise of sovereign wealth funds—in countries such as China, Kuwait, Russia, Saudi Arabia, and the United Arab Emirates—is another. These government-controlled pools of wealth, mostly the result of oil and gas exports, now total some $3 trillion. They are growing at a projected rate of $1 trillion a year and are an increasingly important source of liquidity for U.S. firms. High energy prices, fueled mostly by the surge in Chinese and Indian demand, are here to stay for some time, meaning that the size and significance of these funds will continue to grow. Alternative stock exchanges are springing up and drawing away companies from the U.S. exchanges and even launching initial public offerings (IPOs). London, in particular, is competing with New York as the world's financial center and has already surpassed it in terms of the number of IPOs it hosts. The dollar has weakened against the euro and the British pound, and it is likely to decline in value relative to Asian currencies as well. A majority of the world's foreign exchange holdings are now in currencies other than the dollar, and a move to denominate oil in euros or a basket of currencies is possible, a step that would only leave the U.S. economy more vulnerable to inflation as well as currency crises.

U.S. primacy is also being challenged in other realms, such as military effectiveness and diplomacy. Measures of military spending are not the same as measures of military capacity. September 11 showed how a small investment by terrorists could cause extraordinary levels of human and physical damage. Many of the most costly pieces of modern weaponry are not particularly useful in modern conflicts in which traditional battlefields are replaced by urban combat zones. In such environments, large numbers of lightly armed soldiers can prove to be more than a match for smaller numbers of highly trained and better-armed U.S. troops.

Power and influence are less and less linked in an era of nonpolarity. U.S. calls for others to reform will tend to fall on deaf ears, U.S. assistance programs will buy less, and U.S.-led sanctions will accomplish less. After all, China proved to be the country best able to influence North Korea's nuclear program. Washington's ability to pressure Tehran has been strengthened by the participation of several western European countries—and weakened by the reluctance of China and Russia to sanction Iran. Both Beijing and Moscow have diluted international efforts to pressure the government in Sudan to end its war in Darfur. Pakistan, meanwhile, has repeatedly demonstrated an ability to resist U.S. entreaties, as have Iran, North Korea, Venezuela, and Zimbabwe.

The trend also extends to the worlds of culture and information. Bollywood produces more films every year than Hollywood. Alternatives to U.S.-produced and disseminated television are multiplying. Web sites and blogs from other countries provide further competition for U.S.-produced news and commentary. The proliferation of information is as much a cause of nonpolarity as is the proliferation of weaponry.

Farewell to Unipolarity

Charles Krauthammer was more correct than he realized when he wrote in these pages nearly two decades ago about what he termed "the unipolar moment." At the time, U.S. dominance was real. But it lasted for only 15 or 20 years. In historical terms, it was a moment. Traditional realist theory would have predicted the end of unipolarity and the dawn of a multipolar world. According to this line of reasoning, great powers, when they act as great powers are wont to do, stimulate competition from others that fear or resent them. Krauthammer, subscribing to just this theory, wrote, "No doubt, multipolarity will come in time. In perhaps another generation or so there will be great powers coequal with the United States, and the world will, in structure, resemble the pre-World War I era."

But this has not happened. Although anti-Americanism is widespread, no great-power rival or set of rivals has emerged to challenge the United States. In part, this is because the disparity between the power of the United States and that of any potential rivals is too great. Over time, countries such as China may come to possess GDPs comparable to that of the United States. But in the case of China, much of that wealth will necessarily be absorbed by providing for the country's enormous population (much of which remains poor) and will not be available to fund military development or external undertakings. Maintaining political stability during a period of such dynamic but uneven growth will be no easy feat. India faces many of the same demographic challenges and is further hampered by too much bureaucracy and too little infrastructure. The EU's GDP is now greater than that of the United States, but the EU does not act in the unified fashion of a nation-state, nor is it able or inclined to act in the assertive fashion of historic great powers. Japan, for its part, has a shrinking and aging population and lacks the political culture to play the role of a great power. Russia may be more inclined, but it still has a largely cash-crop economy and is saddled by a declining population and internal challenges to its cohesion.

The fact that classic great-power rivalry has not come to pass and is unlikely to arise anytime soon is also partly a result of the United States' behavior, which has not stimulated such a response. This is not to say that the United States under the leadership of George W. Bush has not alienated other nations; it surely has. But it has not, for the most part, acted in a manner that has led other states to conclude that the United States constitutes a threat to their vital national interests. Doubts about the wisdom and legitimacy of U.S. foreign policy are pervasive, but this has tended to lead more to denunciations (and an absence of cooperation) than outright resistance.

A further constraint on the emergence of great-power rivals is that many of the other major powers are dependent on the international system for their economic welfare and political stability. They do not, accordingly, want to disrupt an order that serves their national interests. Those interests are closely tied to cross-border flows of goods, services, people, energy, investment, and technology—flows in which the United States plays a critical role. Integration into the modern world dampens great-power competition and conflict.

But even if great-power rivals have not emerged, unipolarity has ended. Three explanations for its demise stand out. The first is historical. States develop; they get better at generating and piecing together the human, financial, and technological resources that lead to productivity and prosperity. The same holds for corporations and other organizations. The rise of these new powers cannot be stopped. The result is an ever larger number of actors able to exert influence regionally or globally.

A second cause is U.S. policy. To paraphrase Walt Kelly's Pogo, the post-World War II comic hero, we have met the explanation and it is us. By both what it has done and what it has failed to do, the United States has accelerated the emergence of alternative power centers in the world and has weakened its own position relative to them. U.S. energy policy (or the lack thereof) is a driving force behind the end of unipolarity. Since the first oil shocks of the 1970s, U.S. consumption of oil has grown by approximately 20 percent, and, more important, U.S. imports of petroleum products have more than doubled in volume and nearly doubled as a percentage of consumption. This growth in demand for foreign oil has helped drive up the world price of oil from just over $20 a barrel to over $100 a barrel in less than a decade. The result is an enormous transfer of wealth and leverage to those states with energy reserves. In short, U.S. energy policy has helped bring about the emergence of oil and gas producers as major power centers.

U.S. economic policy has played a role as well. President Lyndon Johnson was widely criticized for simultaneously fighting a war in Vietnam and increasing domestic spending. President Bush has fought costly wars in Afghanistan and Iraq, allowed discretionary spending to increase by an annual rate of eight percent, and cut taxes. As a result, the United States' fiscal position declined from a surplus of over $100 billion in 2001 to an estimated deficit of approximately $250 billion in 2007. Perhaps more relevant is the ballooning current account deficit, which is now more than six percent of GDP. This places downward pressure on the dollar, stimulates inflation, and contributes to the accumulation of wealth and power elsewhere in the world. Poor regulation of the U.S. mortgage market and the credit crisis it has spawned have exacerbated these problems.

The war in Iraq has also contributed to the dilution of the United States' position in the world. The war in Iraq has proved to be an expensive war of choice—militarily, economically, and diplomatically as well as in human terms. Years ago, the historian Paul Kennedy outlined his thesis about "imperial overstretch," which posited that the United States would eventually decline by overreaching, just as other great powers had in the past. Kennedy's theory turned out to apply most immediately to the Soviet Union, but the United States—for all its corrective mechanisms and dynamism—has not proved to be immune. It is not simply that the U.S. military will take a generation to recover from Iraq; it is also that the United States lacks sufficient military assets to continue doing what it is doing in Iraq, much less assume new burdens of any scale elsewhere.

Finally, today's nonpolar world is not simply a result of the rise of other states and organizations or of the failures and follies of U.S. policy. It is also an inevitable consequence of globalization. Globalization has increased the volume, velocity, and importance of cross-border flows of just about everything, from drugs, e-mails, greenhouse gases, manufactured goods, and people to television and radio signals, viruses (virtual and real), and weapons.

Globalization reinforces nonpolarity in two fundamental ways. First, many cross-border flows take place outside the control of governments and without their knowledge. As a result, globalization dilutes the influence of the major powers. Second, these same flows often strengthen the capacities of nonstate actors, such as energy exporters (who are experiencing a dramatic increase in wealth owing to transfers from importers), terrorists (who use the Internet to recruit and train, the international banking system to move resources, and the global transport system to move people), rogue states (who can exploit black and gray markets), and Fortune 500 firms (who quickly move personnel and investments). It is increasingly apparent that being the strongest state no longer means having a near monopoly on power. It is easier than ever before for individuals and groups to accumulate and project substantial power.

Nonpolar Disorder

The increasingly nonpolar world will have mostly negative consequences for the United States and for much of the rest of the world as well. It will make it more difficult for Washington to lead on those occasions when it seeks to promote collective responses to regional and global challenges. One reason has to do with simple arithmetic. With so many more actors possessing meaningful power and trying to assert influence, it will be more difficult to build collective responses and make institutions work. Herding dozens is harder than herding a few. The inability to reach agreement in the Doha Round of global trade talks is a telling example.

Nonpolarity will also increase the number of threats and vulnerabilities facing a country such as the United States. These threats can take the form of rogue states, terrorist groups, energy producers that choose to reduce their output, or central banks whose action or inaction can create conditions that affect the role and strength of the U.S. dollar. The Federal Reserve might want to think twice before continuing to lower interest rates, lest it precipitate a further move away from the dollar. There can be worse things than a recession.

Iran is a case in point. Its effort to become a nuclear power is a result of nonpolarity. Thanks more than anything to the surge in oil prices, it has become another meaningful concentration of power, one able to exert influence in Iraq, Lebanon, Syria, the Palestinian territories, and beyond, as well as within OPEC. It has many sources of technology and finance and numerous markets for its energy exports. And due to nonpolarity, the United States cannot manage Iran alone. Rather, Washington is dependent on others to support political and economic sanctions or block Tehran's access to nuclear technology and materials. Nonpolarity begets nonpolarity.

Still, even if nonpolarity was inevitable, its character is not. To paraphrase the international relations theorist Hedley Bull, global politics at any point is a mixture of anarchy and society. The question is the balance and the trend. A great deal can and should be done to shape a nonpolar world. Order will not just emerge. To the contrary, left to its own devices, a nonpolar world will become messier over time. Entropy dictates that systems consisting of a large number of actors tend toward greater randomness and disorder in the absence of external intervention.

The United States can and should take steps to reduce the chances that a nonpolar world will become a cauldron of instability. This is not a call for unilateralism; it is a call for the United States to get its own house in order. Unipolarity is a thing of the past, but the United States still retains more capacity than any other actor to improve the quality of the international system. The question is whether it will continue to possess such capacity.

Energy is the most important issue. Current levels of U.S. consumption and imports (in addition to their adverse impact on the global climate) fuel nonpolarity by funneling vast financial resources to oil and gas producers. Reducing consumption would lessen the pressure on world prices, decrease U.S. vulnerability to market manipulation by oil suppliers, and slow the pace of climate change. The good news is that this can be done without hurting the U.S. economy.

Strengthening homeland security is also crucial. Terrorism, like disease, cannot be eradicated. There will always be people who cannot be integrated into societies and who pursue goals that cannot be realized through traditional politics. And sometimes, despite the best efforts of those entrusted with homeland security, terrorists will succeed. What is needed, then, are steps to make society more resilient, something that requires adequate funding and training of emergency responders and more flexible and durable infrastructure. The goal should be to reduce the impact of even successful attacks.

Resisting the further spread of nuclear weapons and unguarded nuclear materials, given their destructive potential, may be as important as any other set of undertakings. By establishing internationally managed enriched-uranium or spent-fuel banks that give countries access to sensitive nuclear materials, the international community could help countries use nuclear power to produce electricity rather than bombs. Security assurances and defensive systems can be provided to states that might otherwise feel compelled to develop nuclear programs of their own to counter those of their neighbors. Robust sanctions—on occasion backed by armed force—can also be introduced to influence the behavior of would-be nuclear states.

Even so, the question of using military force to destroy nuclear or biological weapons capabilities remains. Preemptive strikes—attacks that aim to stop an imminent threat—are widely accepted as a form of self-defense. Preventive strikes—attacks on capabilities when there is no indication of imminent use—are something else altogether. They should not be ruled out as a matter of principle, but nor should they be depended on. Beyond questions of feasibility, preventive strikes run the risk of making a nonpolar world less stable, both because they might actually encourage proliferation (governments could see developing or acquiring nuclear weapons as a deterrent) and because they would weaken the long-standing norm against the use of force for purposes other than self-defense.

Combating terrorism is also essential if the nonpolar era is not to turn into a modern Dark Ages. There are many ways to weaken existing terrorist organizations by using intelligence and law enforcement resources and military capabilities. But this is a loser's game unless something can be done

to reduce recruitment. Parents, religious figures, and political leaders must delegitimize terrorism by shaming those who choose to embrace it. And more important, governments must find ways of integrating alienated young men and women into their societies, something that cannot occur in the absence of political and economic opportunity.

Trade can be a powerful tool of integration. It gives states a stake in avoiding conflict because instability interrupts beneficial commercial arrangements that provide greater wealth and strengthen the foundations of domestic political order. Trade also facilitates development, thereby decreasing the chance of state failure and alienation among citizens. The scope of the World Trade Organization must be extended through the negotiation of future global arrangements that further reduce subsidies and both tariff and nontariff barriers. Building domestic political support for such negotiations in developed countries will likely require the expansion of various safety nets, including portable health care and retirement accounts, education and training assistance, and wage insurance. These social policy reforms are costly and in some cases unwarranted (the cause of job loss is far more likely to be technological innovation than foreign competition), but they are worth providing nonetheless given the overall economic and political value of expanding the global trade regime.

A similar level of effort might be needed to ensure the continued flow of investment. The goal should be to create a World Investment Organization that would encourage capital flows across borders so as to minimize the chances that "investment protectionism" gets in the way of activities that, like trade, are economically beneficial and build political bulwarks against instability. A WIO could encourage transparency on the part of investors, determine when national security is a legitimate reason for prohibiting or limiting foreign investment, and establish a mechanism for resolving disputes.

Finally, the United States needs to enhance its capacity to prevent state failure and deal with its consequences. This will require building and maintaining a larger military, one with greater capacity to deal with the sort of threats faced in Afghanistan and Iraq. In addition, it will mean establishing a civilian counterpart to the military reserves that would provide a pool of human talent to assist with basic nation-building tasks. Continuing economic and military assistance will be vital in helping weak states meet their responsibilities to their citizens and their neighbors.

The Not-So-Lonely Superpower

Multilateralism will be essential in dealing with a nonpolar world. To succeed, though, it must be recast to include actors other than the great powers. The UN Security Council and the G-8 (the group of highly industrialized states) need to be reconstituted to reflect the world of today and not the post-World War II era. A recent meeting at the United Nations on how best to coordinate global responses to public health challenges provided a model. Representatives of governments, UN agencies, NGOs, pharmaceutical companies, foundations, think tanks, and universities were all in attendance. A similar range of participants attended the December 2007 Bali meeting on climate change. Multilateralism may have to be less formal and less comprehensive, at least in its initial phases. Networks will be needed alongside organizations. Getting everyone to agree on everything will be increasingly difficult; instead, the United States should consider signing accords with fewer parties and narrower goals. Trade is something of a model here, in that bilateral and regional accords are filling the vacuum created by a failure to conclude a global trade round. The same approach could work for climate change, where agreement on aspects of the problem (say, deforestation) or arrangements involving only some countries (the major carbon emitters, for example) may prove feasible, whereas an accord that involves every country and tries to resolve every issue may not. Multilateralism à la carte is likely to be the order of the day.

Nonpolarity complicates diplomacy. A nonpolar world not only involves more actors but also lacks the more predictable fixed structures and relationships that tend to define worlds of unipolarity, bipolarity, or multipolarity. Alliances, in particular, will lose much of their importance, if only because alliances require predictable threats, outlooks, and obligations, all of which are likely to be in short supply in a nonpolar world. Relationships will instead become more selective and situational. It will become harder to classify other countries as either allies or adversaries; they will cooperate on some issues and resist on others. There will be a premium on consultation and coalition building and on a diplomacy that encourages cooperation when possible and shields such cooperation from the fallout of inevitable disagreements. The United States will no longer have the luxury of a "You're either with us or against us" foreign policy.

Nonpolarity will be difficult and dangerous. But encouraging a greater degree of global integration will help promote stability. Establishing a core group of governments and others committed to cooperative multilateralism would be a great step forward. Call it "concerted nonpolarity." It would not eliminate nonpolarity, but it would help manage it and increase the odds that the international system will not deteriorate or disintegrate.

Imperial by Design

JOHN J. MEARSHEIMER

Mearsheimer provides a Realist critique of both the neoconservative and Liberal institutionalist visions that have guided U.S. foreign policy through the early years of the 21st century. Through the lens of "offensive Realism" he argues that the neoconservatism of the Bush Administration, and the "liberal empire" of the Clinton and Obama Administrations have pushed the U.S.A. into costly wars in Iraq and Afghanistan and resulted in the deterioration of American power. He argues that the U.S.A. should adopt a policy of "offshore balancing" that would be less costly and refrain from alienating other nations.

In the first years after the Cold War ended, many Americans had a profound sense of optimism about the future of international politics. President Bill Clinton captured that mood when he told the UN General Assembly in September 1993:

> It is clear that we live at a turning point in human history. Immense and promising changes seem to wash over us every day. The Cold War is over. The world is no longer divided into two armed and angry camps. Dozens of new democracies have been born. It is a moment of miracles.

The basis of all this good feeling was laid out at the time in two famous articles by prominent neoconservatives. In 1989, Francis Fukuyama argued in "The End of History?" that Western liberal democracy had won a decisive victory over communism and fascism and should be seen as the "final form of human government."[1] One consequence of this "ideological evolution," he argued, was that large-scale conflict between the great powers was "passing from the scene," although "the vast bulk of the Third World remains very much mired in history, and will be a terrain of conflict for many years to come." Nevertheless, liberal democracy and peace would eventually come to the Third World as well, because the sands of time were pushing inexorably in that direction.

One year later, Charles Krauthammer emphasized in "The Unipolar Moment" that the United States had emerged from the Cold War as by far the most powerful country on the planet.[2] He urged American leaders not to be reticent about using that power "to lead a unipolar world, unashamedly laying down the rules of world order and being prepared to enforce them." Krauthammer's advice fit neatly with Fukuyama's vision of the future: the United States should take the lead in bringing democracy to less developed countries the world over. After all, that shouldn't be an especially difficult task given that America had awesome power and the cunning of history on its side.

U.S. grand strategy has followed this basic prescription for the past twenty years, mainly because most policy makers inside the Beltway have agreed with the thrust of Fukuyama's and Krauthammer's early analyses.

The results, however, have been disastrous. The United States has been at war for a startling two out of every three years since 1989, and there is no end in sight. As anyone with a rudimentary knowledge of world events knows, countries that continuously fight wars invariably build powerful national-security bureaucracies that undermine civil liberties and make it difficult to hold leaders accountable for their behavior; and they invariably end up adopting ruthless policies normally associated with brutal dictators. The Founding Fathers understood this problem, as is clear from James Madison's observation that "no nation can preserve its freedom in the midst of continual warfare." Washington's pursuit of policies like assassination, rendition and torture over the past decade, not to mention the weakening of the rule of law at home, shows that their fears were justified.

To make matters worse, the United States is now engaged in protracted wars in Afghanistan and Iraq that have so far cost well over a trillion dollars and resulted in around forty-seven thousand American casualties. The pain and suffering inflicted on Iraq has been enormous. Since the war began in March 2003, more than one hundred thousand Iraqi civilians have been killed, roughly 2 million Iraqis have left the country and 1.7 million more have been internally displaced. Moreover, the American military is not going to win either one of these conflicts, despite all the phony talk about how the "surge" has worked in Iraq and how a similar strategy can produce another miracle in Afghanistan. We may well be stuck in both quagmires for years to come, in fruitless pursuit of victory.

The United States has also been unable to solve three other major foreign-policy problems. Washington has worked overtime—with no success—to shut down Iran's uranium-enrichment capability for fear that it might lead to Tehran acquiring nuclear weapons. And the United States, unable to prevent North Korea from acquiring nuclear weapons in the first place, now seems incapable of compelling Pyongyang to give them up. Finally, every post-Cold War administration has tried and failed to settle the Israeli-Palestinian conflict; all indicators are that this problem will deteriorate further as the West Bank and Gaza are incorporated into a Greater Israel.

The unpleasant truth is that the United States is in a world of trouble today on the foreign-policy front, and this state of affairs is only likely to get worse in the next few years, as Afghanistan and Iraq unravel and the blame game escalates to poisonous levels. Thus, it is hardly surprising that a recent Chicago Council on Global Affairs survey found that "looking forward 50 years, only 33 percent of Americans think the United States will continue to be the world's leading power." Clearly, the heady days of the early 1990s have given way to a pronounced pessimism.

This regrettable situation raises the obvious questions of what went wrong? And can America right its course?

The downward spiral the United States has taken was anything but inevitable. Washington has always had a choice in how to approach grand strategy. One popular option among some libertarians is *isolationism*. This approach is based on the assumption that there is no region outside the Western Hemisphere that is strategically important enough to justify expending American blood and treasure. Isolationists believe that the United States is remarkably secure because it is separated from all of the world's great powers by two giant moats—the Atlantic and Pacific Oceans—and on top of that it has had nuclear weapons—the ultimate deterrent—since 1945. But in truth, there is really no chance that Washington will adopt this policy, though the United States had strong isolationist tendencies until World War II. For since then, an internationalist activism, fostered by the likes of the Rockefeller Foundation, has thoroughly delegitimized this approach. American policy makers have come to believe the country should be militarily involved on the world stage. Yet though no mainstream politician would dare advocate isolationism at this point, the rationale for this grand strategy shows just how safe the United States is. This means, among other things, that it will always be a challenge to motivate the U.S. public to want to run the world and especially to fight wars of choice in distant places.

Offshore balancing, which was America's traditional grand strategy for most of its history, is but another option. Predicated on the belief that there are three regions of the world that are strategically important to the United States—Europe, Northeast Asia and the Persian Gulf—it sees the United States' principle goal as making sure no country dominates any of these areas as it dominates the Western Hemisphere. This is to ensure that dangerous rivals in other regions are forced to concentrate their attention on great powers in their own backyards rather than be free to interfere in America's. The best way to achieve that end is to rely on local powers to counter aspiring regional hegemons and otherwise keep U.S. military forces over the horizon. But if that proves impossible, American troops come from offshore to help do the job, and then leave once the potential hegemon is checked.

Selective engagement also assumes that Europe, Northeast Asia and the Persian Gulf are the only areas of the world where the United States should be willing to deploy its military might. It is a more ambitious strategy than offshore balancing in that it calls for permanently stationing U.S. troops in those regions to help maintain peace. For selective engagers, it is not enough just to thwart aspiring hegemons. It is also necessary to prevent war in those key regions, either because upheaval will damage our economy or because we will eventually get dragged into the fight in any case. An American presence is also said to be valuable for limiting nuclear proliferation. But none of these strategies call for Washington to spread democracy around the globe—especially through war.

The root cause of America's troubles is that it adopted a flawed grand strategy after the Cold War. From the Clinton administration on, the United States rejected all these other avenues, instead pursuing *global dominance,* or what might alternatively be called global hegemony, which was not just doomed to fail, but likely to backfire in dangerous ways if it relied too heavily on military force to achieve its ambitious agenda.

Global dominance has two broad objectives: maintaining American primacy, which means making sure that the United States remains the most powerful state in the international system; and spreading democracy across the globe, in effect, making the world over in America's image. The underlying belief is that new liberal democracies will be peacefully inclined and pro-American, so the more the better. Of course, this means that Washington must care a lot about every country's politics. With global dominance, no serious attempt is made to prioritize U.S. interests, because they are virtually limitless.

This grand strategy is "imperial" at its core; its proponents believe that the United States has the right as well as the responsibility to interfere in the politics of other countries. One would think that such arrogance might alienate other states, but most American policy makers of the early nineties and beyond were confident that would not happen, instead believing that other countries—save for so-called rogue states like Iran and North Korea—would see the United States as a benign hegemon serving their own interests.

There is, however, an important disagreement among global dominators about how best to achieve their strategy's goals. On one side are the neoconservatives, who believe that the United States can rely heavily on armed force to dominate and transform the globe, and that it can usually act unilaterally because American power is so great. Indeed, they tend to be openly contemptuous of Washington's traditional allies as well as international institutions, which they view as forums where the Lilliputians tie down Gulliver. Neoconservatives see spreading democracy as a relatively easy task. For them, the key to success is removing the reigning tyrant; once that is done, there is little need to engage in protracted nation building.

On the other side are the liberal imperialists, who are certainly willing to use the American military to do social engineering. But they are less confident than the neoconservatives about what can be achieved with force alone. Therefore, liberal imperialists believe that running the world requires the United States to work closely with allies and international institutions. Although they think that democracy has widespread appeal, liberal imperialists are usually less sanguine than the neoconservatives about the ease of exporting it to other states. As we set off to remake the world after the fall of the Berlin Wall, these principles of global dominance set the agenda.

Bill Clinton was the first president to govern exclusively in the post-Cold War world, and his administration pursued global dominance from start to finish. Yet Clinton's foreign-policy team was comprised of liberal imperialists; so, although the president and his lieutenants made clear that they were bent on ruling the world—blatantly reflected in former-Secretary of State Madeleine Albright's well-known comment that "if we have to use force, it is because we are America; we are the indispensable nation. We stand tall and we see further than other countries into the future"—they employed military force reluctantly and prudently. They may have been gung ho about pushing the unipolar moment onward and upward, but for all their enthusiasm, even these democracy promoters soon saw that nation building was no easy task.

During his first year in office, Clinton carelessly allowed the United States to get involved in nation building in Somalia. But when eighteen American soldiers were killed in a firefight in Mogadishu in October 1993 (famously rendered in *Black Hawk Down*), he immediately pulled U.S. troops out of the country. In fact, the administration was so spooked by the fiasco that it refused to intervene during the Rwandan genocide in the spring of 1994, even though the cost of doing so would have been small. Yes, Clinton did commit American forces to Haiti in September 1994 to help remove a brutal military regime, but he had to overcome significant congressional opposition and he went to great lengths to get a UN resolution supporting a multinational intervention force. Most of the American troops were out of Haiti by March 1996, and at no time was there a serious attempt at nation building.

Clinton did talk tough during the 1992 presidential campaign about using American power against Serbia to halt the fighting in Bosnia, but after taking office, he dragged his feet and only used airpower in 1995 to end the fighting. He went to war against Serbia for a second time in 1999—this time over Kosovo—and once again would only rely on airpower, despite pressure to deploy ground forces from his NATO commander, General Wesley Clark, and then-British Prime Minister Tony Blair.

By early 1998, the neoconservatives were pressuring Clinton to use military force to remove Saddam Hussein. The president endorsed the long-term goal of ousting the Iraqi leader, but he refused to go to war to make that happen. The United States under Bill Clinton was, as Richard Haass put it, a "reluctant sheriff."

Although the Clinton administration made little progress toward achieving global hegemony during its eight-year reign, it at least managed to avoid any major foreign-policy disasters. It seemed to understand the inherent difficulties of nation building and devoted neither much blood nor much treasure in its pursuit.

Nevertheless, given the American public's natural reluctance to engage in foreign adventures, by the 2000 presidential campaign, many were unhappy with even this cautious liberal imperialism. George W. Bush tried to capitalize on this sentiment by criticizing Clinton's foreign policy as overzealous—and as it turns out, ironically, especially for doing too much nation building. The Republican candidate called for the United States to scale back its goals and concentrate on reinvigorating its traditional Cold War alliances. The main threat facing the United States, he argued, was a rising China; terrorism was paid little attention. In effect, Bush was calling for a grand strategy of selective engagement. Not surprisingly, his opponent, Vice President Al Gore, called for pursuing global dominance, albeit in a multilateral guise.

When Bush won, it appeared that the United States was about to adopt a less ambitious grand strategy. But that did not happen because the new Bush administration drastically altered its approach to the world after 9/11.

There was never any question that Washington would treat terrorism as its main threat after that horrific day. But it was not clear at first how the administration would deal with the problem. Over the course of the next year, Bush turned away from selective engagement and embraced global dominance. Unlike his predecessor in the White House, however, he adopted the neoconservative formula for ruling the world. And that meant relying primarily on the unilateral use of American military force. From the early days of Afghanistan onward, America was to enter the age of the "Bush Doctrine," which was all about using the U.S. military to bring about regime change across the Muslim and Arab world. It is easy to forget now, but Iraq was supposed to be a step in the remarkably far-reaching plan to sow democracy in an area of the world where it was largely absent, thereby creating peace. President Bush put the point succinctly in early 2003 when he said, "By the resolve and purpose of America, and of our friends and allies, we will make this an age of progress and liberty. Free people will set the course of history, and free people will keep the peace of the world."

By pursuing this extraordinary scheme to transform an entire region at the point of a gun, President Bush adopted a radical grand strategy that has no parallel in American history. It was also a dismal failure.

The Bush administration's quest for global dominance was based on a profound misunderstanding of the threat environment facing the United States after 9/11. And the president and his advisers overestimated what military force could achieve in the modern world, in turn greatly underestimating how difficult it would be to spread democracy in the Middle East. This triumvirate of errors doomed Washington's effort to dominate the globe, undermined American values and institutions on the home front, and threatened its position in the world.

With the attacks on the World Trade Center and the Pentagon, the Bush administration all of a sudden was forced to think seriously about terrorism. Unfortunately, the president—and most Americans for that matter—misread what the country was dealing with in two important ways: greatly exaggerating the threat's severity, and failing to understand why al-Qaeda was so enraged at the United States. These mistakes led the administration to adopt policies that made the problem worse, not better.

In the aftermath of 9/11, terrorism was described as an existential threat. President Bush emphasized that virtually every terrorist group on the planet—including those that had no beef with Washington—was our enemy and had to be eliminated if we hoped to win what became known as the global war on terror (GWOT). The administration also maintained that states like Iran, Iraq and Syria were not only actively supporting terrorist organizations but were also likely to provide terrorists with weapons of mass destruction (WMD). Thus, it was imperative for the United States to target these rogue states if it hoped to win the GWOT—or what some neoconservatives like Norman Podhoretz called World

War IV. Indeed, Bush said that any country which "continues to harbor or support terrorism will be regarded by the United States as a hostile regime." Finally, the administration claimed that it was relatively easy for groups like al-Qaeda to infiltrate and strike the homeland, and that we should expect more disasters like 9/11 in the near future. The greatest danger for sure would be a WMD attack against a major American city.

This assessment of America's terrorism problem was flawed on every count. It was threat inflation of the highest order. It made no sense to declare war against groups that were not trying to harm the United States. They were not our enemies; and going after all terrorist organizations would greatly complicate the daunting task of eliminating those groups that did have us in their crosshairs. In addition, there was no alliance between the so-called rogue states and al-Qaeda. In fact, Iran and Syria cooperated with Washington after 9/11 to help quash Osama bin Laden and his cohorts. Although the Bush administration and the neoconservatives repeatedly asserted that there was a genuine connection between Saddam Hussein and al-Qaeda, they never produced evidence to back up their claim for the simple reason that it did not exist.

The fact is that states have strong incentives to distrust terrorist groups, in part because they might turn on them someday, but also because countries cannot control what terrorist organizations do, and they may do something that gets their patrons into serious trouble. This is why there is hardly any chance that a rogue state will give a nuclear weapon to terrorists. That regime's leaders could never be sure that they would not be blamed and punished for a terrorist group's actions. Nor could they be certain that the United States or Israel would not incinerate them if either country merely suspected that they had provided terrorists with the ability to carry out a WMD attack. A nuclear handoff, therefore, is not a serious threat.

When you get down to it, there is only a remote possibility that terrorists will get hold of an atomic bomb. The most likely way it would happen is if there were political chaos in a nuclear-armed state, and terrorists or their friends were able to take advantage of the ensuing confusion to snatch a loose nuclear weapon. But even then, there are additional obstacles to overcome: some countries keep their weapons disassembled, detonating one is not easy and it would be difficult to transport the device without being detected. Moreover, other countries would have powerful incentives to work with Washington to find the weapon before it could be used. The obvious implication is that we should work with other states to improve nuclear security, so as to make this slim possibility even more unlikely.

Finally, the ability of terrorists to strike the American homeland has been blown out of all proportion. In the nine years since 9/11, government officials and terrorist experts have issued countless warnings that another major attack on American soil is probable—even imminent. But this is simply not the case.[3] The only attempts we have seen are a few failed solo attacks by individuals with links to al-Qaeda like the "shoe bomber," who attempted to blow up an American Airlines flight from Paris to Miami in December 2001, and the "underwear bomber," who tried to blow up a Northwest Airlines flight from Amsterdam to Detroit in December 2009. So, we do have a terrorism problem, but it is hardly an existential threat. In fact, it is a minor threat. Perhaps the scope of the challenge is best captured by Ohio State political scientist John Mueller's telling comment that "the number of Americans killed by international terrorism since the late 1960s . . . is about the same as the number killed over the same period by lightning, or by accident-causing deer, or by severe allergic reactions to peanuts."

One might argue that there has been no attack on American soil since 9/11 because the GWOT has been a great success. But that claim is undermined by the fact that al-Qaeda was trying hard to strike the United States in the decade before 9/11, when there was no GWOT, and it succeeded only once. In February 1993, al-Qaeda exploded a truck bomb in a garage below the World Trade Center, killing six people. More than eight years passed before the group struck that same building complex for the second time. None of this is to deny that 9/11 was a spectacular success for the terrorists, but it was no

Pearl Harbor, which launched the United States into battles against Imperial Japan and Nazi Germany, two truly dangerous adversaries. Roughly 50 million people—the majority of them civilians—died in that conflict. It is absurd to compare al-Qaeda with Germany and Japan, or to liken the GWOT to a world war.

This conspicuous threat inflation has hurt the American effort to neutralize al-Qaeda. By foolishly widening the scope of the terrorism problem, Washington has ended up picking fights with terrorist groups and countries that otherwise had no interest in attacking the United States, and in some cases were willing to help us thwart al-Qaeda. Enlarging the target set has also led American policy makers to take their eyes off our main adversary. Furthermore, defining the terrorist threat so broadly, coupled with the constant warnings about looming attacks that might be even more deadly than 9/11, has led U.S. leaders to wage war all around the globe and to think of this struggle as lasting for generations. This is exactly the wrong formula for dealing with our terrorism problem. We should instead focus our attention wholly on al-Qaeda and any other group that targets the United States, and we should treat the threat as a law-enforcement problem rather than a military one that requires us to engage in large-scale wars the world over. Specifically, we should rely mainly on intelligence, police work, carefully selected covert operations and close cooperation with allies to neutralize the likes of al-Qaeda.

To deal effectively with terrorism, it is imperative to understand what motivates al-Qaeda to target the United States in the first place. One also wants to know why large numbers of people in the Arab and Muslim world are so angry with America that they support, or at least sympathize with, these types of terrorist groups. Simply put, why do they hate us?

There are two possible answers to this question. One possibility is that al-Qaeda and its supporters loathe us because of who we are; in other words, this is a clash of civilizations that has arisen because these extremists hate Western values in general and liberal democracy in particular. Alternatively, these groups may hate us because they are furious with our Middle East policies. There is an abundance of survey data and anecdotal evidence that shows the second answer is the right one. Anger and hatred toward the United States among Arabs and Muslims is largely driven by Washington's policies, not by any deep-seated antipathy toward the West.[4] The policies that have generated the most anti-Americanism include Washington's support for Israel's treatment of the Palestinians; the presence of American troops in Saudi Arabia after the 1991 Gulf War; U.S. support for repressive regimes in countries like Egypt; American sanctions on Baghdad after the First Gulf War, which are estimated to have caused the deaths of about five hundred thousand Iraqi civilians; and the U.S. invasion and occupation of Iraq.

None of this is to say that the hard-core members of al-Qaeda like or respect American values and institutions because surely most of them do not. But there is little evidence that they dislike them so much that they would be motivated to declare war on the United States. The case of Khalid Shaikh Mohammed—who the 9/11 Commission described as "the principal architect of the 9/11 attacks"—tells us a great deal. The Palestinian issue, not hatred of the American way of life, motivated him. In the commission's words, "By his own account, KSM's animus toward the United States stemmed not from his experiences there as a student, but rather from his violent disagreement with U.S. foreign policy favoring Israel." The commission also confirmed that bin Laden was motivated in good part by America's support for Israel's behavior toward the Palestinians.

Not surprisingly, President Bush and his advisers rejected this explanation of 9/11, because accepting it would effectively have been an admission that the United States bore considerable responsibility for the events of that tragic day. We would be acknowledging that it was our Middle East policies that were at the heart of it all. Instead, right after 9/11 happened the president stated, "They hate our freedoms: our freedom of religion, our freedom of speech, our freedom to vote and assemble and disagree with each other." Despite all the evidence to

the contrary, this argument sold well in America—at least for a few years. But what were the policy implications of portraying the fight with al-Qaeda as a clash between two different ways of life?

There was no chance that the United States was going to change its basic character to solve its terrorism problem. Instead, the Bush administration decided to carry out social engineering on a grand scale. No lessons learned from the dismal record of nation building in the Clinton years. Yes! We would bring liberal democracy and Western values to the Arabs and the Iranians, and our troubles with terrorism would go away. "The world has a clear interest in the spread of democratic values," the president said, "because stable and free nations do not breed the ideologies of murder."

Given American military might and the belief that democracy was sweeping the globe, the Bush administration and its supporters reasoned that it would be relatively easy to remake the Arab and Muslim world in America's image. They were wrong, of course, for the Bush administration failed to understand the limits of what American military power could do to transform the Middle East.

The faulty assumption that America could perform social engineering through its indomitable military might—beyond the lofty theorizing of the neoconservatives—found its roots in Afghanistan. By December 2001, it appeared that the U.S. military had won a quick and stunning victory against the Taliban and installed a friendly regime in Kabul that would be able to govern the country effectively for the foreseeable future. Very importantly, the war was won with a combination of American airpower, local allies and small Special Forces units. How easy it seemed to deliver that country its freedom. There was no need for a large-scale invasion, so when the fighting ended, the United States did not look like an occupier. Nor did it seem likely to become one, because Hamid Karzai was expected to keep order in Afghanistan without much U.S. help.

The perception of a stunning triumph in Afghanistan was significant because leaders rarely initiate wars unless they think that they can win quick and decisive victories. The prospect of fighting a protracted conflict makes policy makers gun-shy, not just because the costs are invariably high, but also because it is hard to tell how long wars will come to an end. But by early 2002, it seemed that the United States had found a blueprint for winning wars in the developing world quickly and decisively, thus eliminating the need for a protracted occupation. It appeared that the American military could exit a country soon after toppling its regime and installing a new leader, and move on to the next target. It looked like the neoconservatives had been vindicated. This interpretation convinced many people in the foreign-policy establishment that the road was now open for using the U.S. military to transform the Middle East and dominate the globe.

And with this hubris firmly in place, America attacked Iraq on March 19, 2003. Within a few months, it looked like the "Afghan model" had proved its worth again. Saddam was in hiding and President Bush landed on the USS *Abraham Lincoln* with a big banner in the background that announced: "Mission Accomplished." It seemed at the time that it would not be long before the next war began, maybe against Iran or Syria, and then the other states in the region might be so scared of America that merely threatening them with an attack would be enough to cause regime change.

It all turned out to be a mirage, of course, as Iraq quickly became a deadly quagmire with Afghanistan following suit a few years later.

Indeed, what initially appeared to be a dazzling victory in Afghanistan was not. There was little chance that the United States would avoid a protracted occupation, since we faced two insurmountable problems. While it was relatively easy to topple the Taliban from power, it was not possible for the American military and its allies to decisively defeat that foe. When cornered and facing imminent destruction, Taliban fighters melted away into the countryside or across the border into Pakistan, where they could regroup and eventually come back to fight another day. This is why insurgencies with external sanctuaries have been especially difficult to stamp out in the past.

Furthermore, the Karzai government was doomed to fail, not just because its leader was put in power by Washington, and not just because Afghanistan has always had a weak central government, but also because Karzai and his associates are incompetent and corrupt. This meant that there would be no central authority to govern the country and check the Taliban when it came back to life. And that meant the United States would have to do the heavy lifting. American troops would have to occupy the country and fight the Taliban, and they would have to do so in support of a fragile government with little legitimacy outside of Kabul. As anyone familiar with the Vietnam War knows, this is a prescription for defeat.

If more evidence is needed that the "Afghan model" does not work as advertised, Iraq provides it. Contrary to what the neoconservatives claimed before the invasion, the United States could not topple Saddam and avoid a long occupation, unless it was willing to put another dictator in charge. Not only did Baghdad have few well-established political institutions and a weak civil society, the removal of Saddam was certain to unleash powerful centrifugal forces that would lead to a bloody civil war in the absence of a large American presence. In particular, the politically strong Sunnis were sure to resist losing power to the more numerous Shia, who would benefit the most from the U.S. invasion. There were also profound differences among various Shia groups, and the Kurds did not even want to be ruled by Baghdad. On top of all that, al-Qaeda in Mesopotamia eventually emerged on the scene. (Of course, the United States did not face a terrorist threat from Iraq before the invasion.) All of this meant that a protracted American occupation would be necessary to keep the country from tearing itself apart.

And long, messy occupations were always inevitable. For though one might argue that the United States would have succeeded in Afghanistan had it not invaded Iraq and instead concentrated on building a competent government in Kabul that could keep the Taliban at bay, even if this were true (and I have my doubts), it still would have taken a decade or more to do the job. During this time the U.S. military would have been pinned down in Afghanistan and thus unavailable to invade Iraq and other countries in the Middle East. The Bush Doctrine, however, was dependent on winning quick and decisive victories, which means that even a drawn-out success in Afghanistan would have doomed the strategy.

Alternatively, one might argue that the main problem in Afghanistan and Iraq was that the U.S. military had a flawed counterinsurgency doctrine during the early stages of those conflicts. According to this story, the United States eventually found the right formula with the December 2006 edition of the U.S. Army and Marine Corps *Counterinsurgency Field Manual 3-24* (FM 3-24). Indeed, the purported success of the Iraq surge is often ascribed to the implementation of the new rules of engagement. Some even claim that it has helped us achieve victory in Iraq. The problem with this argument is that President Bush made clear when the surge was launched in January 2007 that tamping down the violence was a necessary but not sufficient condition for success. He wisely emphasized that it was also essential that rival Iraqi groups ameliorate their differences and find a workable system for sharing political power. But to this day there has been little progress in fixing Iraq's fractured society and building an effective political system, as evidenced by the difficulty Iraqi politicians have had forming a government in the wake of the March 7, 2010, parliamentary elections. Hence, the surge has not been a success. This failure is not for lack of trying; nation building is a daunting task. The scope of the challenge is still greater in Afghanistan. So even if one believes that the American military now has a smart counterinsurgency doctrine, the fact is that it has yet to succeed.

There is no question that it is possible to defeat an insurgency, but it is almost never quick or easy, and there is no single formula for success. As FM 3-24 warns, "Political and military leaders and planners should never underestimate its scale and complexity." Even in a best-case scenario like the Malayan Emergency, where the British faced a numerically weak and unpopular Communist guerrilla force based in the small Chinese minority, pacification still took roughly a dozen years. What makes the enterprise so difficult is that victory usually requires more than just defeating the insurgents in firefights. It usually demands nation building as well because it is essential to fix the political and social problems that caused the insurgency in the first place; otherwise, it is likely to spring back to life. So even if it was a sure bet that the United States could succeed at counterinsurgency with the right people and doctrine, it would still take many years to achieve decisive results. "Insurgencies," as FM 3-24 notes, "are protracted by nature." This means that when the American military engages in this kind of war fighting, it will end up pinned down in a lengthy occupation. And when that happens, the Bush Doctrine cannot work.

But the Bush administration and its neoconservative supporters badly miscalculated how easy it would be to create free, stable societies in the Middle East. They thought that beheading regimes was essentially all that was needed for democracy to take hold.

It is hard to believe that any policy maker or student of international affairs could have believed that democracy would spring forth quickly and easily once tyrants like Saddam Hussein were toppled. After all, it is clear from the historical record that imposing democracy on another country is an especially difficult task that usually fails.[5] Jeffrey Pickering and Mark Peceny, who investigated the democratizing consequences of interventions by liberal states from 1946 to 1996, conclude that "liberal intervention . . . has only very rarely played a role in democratization since 1945."[6]

The United States in particular has a rich history of trying and failing to impose democracy on other countries. New York University professors Bruce Bueno de Mesquita and George Downs report in the *Los Angeles Times* that:

> Between World War II and the present, the United States intervened more than 35 times in developing countries around the world. . . . In only one case—Colombia after the American decision in 1989 to engage in the war on drugs—did a full-fledged, stable democracy . . . emerge within 10 years. That's a success rate of less than 3%.

Pickering and Peceny similarly find only a single case—Panama after the removal of Manuel Noriega—in which American intervention clearly resulted in the emergence of a consolidated democracy. Furthermore, William Easterly and his colleagues at NYU looked at how U.S. and Soviet interventions during the Cold War affected the prospects for a democratic form of government. They found that "superpower interventions are followed by significant declines in democracy, and that the substantive effects are large."

None of this is to say that it is impossible for the United States to impose democracy abroad. But successes are the exception rather than the rule, and as is the case with democratization in general, externally led attempts to implant such a governing structure usually occur in countries with a particular set of internal characteristics. It helps greatly if the target state has high levels of ethnic and religious homogeneity, a strong central government, reasonably high levels of prosperity and some experience with democracy. The cases of post-World War II Germany and Japan, which are often held up as evidence that the United States can export democracy to the Middle East, fit these criteria. But those examples are highly unusual, which is why the United States has failed so often in its freedom-spreading quest.

Even Eastern Europe circa 1989 does not provide a useful precedent. Democracy quickly sprouted there when communism collapsed and the autocrats who ruled in the region fell from power. These cases, however, have little in common with what the United States has been trying to do in the Muslim world. Democracy was not imposed on the countries of Eastern Europe; it was homegrown in every instance, and most of these countries possessed many of the necessary preconditions for democratization. There is no question that the United States has tried to help nurture these nascent democracies, but these are not cases where Washington successfully exported popular rule to foreign lands, which is what the Bush Doctrine was all about.

A good indicator of just how imprudent the Bush administration and the neoconservatives were to think that the United States could impose

democracy with relative ease is that Francis Fukuyama did not believe it could be done and therefore did not support the Iraq War. Indeed, by 2006 he had publicly abandoned neoconservatives and adopted the mantle of liberal imperialism.[7] Fukuyama did not ditch his core belief that democracy was ineluctably spreading across the globe. What he rejected was his former compatriots' belief that the process could be accelerated by invading countries like Iraq. America, he maintained, could best pursue its interests "not through the exercise of military power," but through its ability "to shape international institutions."

Moreover, it is worth noting that even if the United States was magically able to spread democracy in the Middle East, it is not clear that the new regimes would always act in ways that met with Washington's approval. The leaders of those new democratic governments, after all, would have to pay attention to the views of their people rather than take orders from the Americans. In other words, democracies tend to have minds of their own. This is one reason why the United States, when it has toppled democratically elected regimes that it did not like—as in Iran (1953), Guatemala (1954) and Chile (1973)—helped install dictators rather than democrats, and why Washington helps to thwart democracy in countries where it fears the outcome of elections, as in Egypt and Saudi Arabia.

If all of this were not enough, global dominance, especially the Bush administration's penchant for big-stick diplomacy, negatively affects nuclear proliferation as well. The United States is deeply committed to making sure that Iran does not acquire a nuclear arsenal and that North Korea gives up its atomic weapons, but the strategy we have employed is likely to have the opposite effect.

The main reason that a country acquires nuclear weapons is that they are the ultimate deterrent. It is extremely unlikely that any state would attack the homeland of a nuclear-armed adversary because of the fear that it would prompt nuclear retaliation. Therefore, any country that feels threatened by a dangerous rival has good reason to want a survivable nuclear deterrent. This basic logic explains why the United States and the Soviet Union built formidable stockpiles during the Cold War. It also explains why Israel acquired atomic weapons and refuses to give them up.

All of this tells you that when the United States places Iran, Iraq and North Korea on the "axis of evil" and threatens them with military force, it gives those countries a powerful incentive to acquire a nuclear deterrent. The Bush administration, for example, would not have invaded Iraq in March 2003 if Saddam had an atomic arsenal because the Iraqi leader probably would have used it, since he almost certainly was going to die anyway. It is not clear whether Iran is pursuing nuclear weapons today, but given that the United States and Israel frequently hint that they might attack it nevertheless, the regime has good reason to want a deterrent to protect itself. Similarly, Pyongyang would be foolish to give up its nuclear capability in the absence of some sort of rapprochement with Washington.

And there is no good reason to think that spreading democracy would counter proliferation either. After all, five of the nine nuclear-armed states are democracies (Britain, France, India, Israel and the United States), and two others (Pakistan and Russia) are borderline democracies that retain significant authoritarian features.

In short, the Bush administration's fondness for threatening to attack adversaries (oftentimes with the additional agenda of forced democratization) encouraged nuclear proliferation. The best way for the United States to maximize the prospects of halting or at least slowing down the spread of nuclear weapons would be to stop threatening other countries because that gives them a compelling reason to acquire the ultimate deterrent. But as long as America's leaders remain committed to global dominance, they are likely to resist this advice and keep threatening states that will not follow Washington's orders.

The United States needs a new grand strategy. Global dominance is a prescription for endless trouble—especially in its neoconservative variant. Unfortunately, the Obama administration is populated from top to bottom with liberal imperialists who remain committed to trying to govern the world, albeit with less emphasis on big-stick diplomacy and more emphasis on working with allies and international institutions. In effect, they want to bring back Bill Clinton's grand strategy.

The Obama team's thinking was clearly laid out in Secretary of State Hillary Clinton's speech to the Council on Foreign Relations this past September. Sounding very much like Madeleine Albright, Clinton said:

> I think the world is counting on us today as it has in the past. When old adversaries need an honest broker or fundamental freedoms need a champion, people turn to us. When the earth shakes or rivers overflow their banks, when pandemics rage or simmering tensions burst into violence, the world looks to us.

Recognizing that many Americans are in dire straits these days and not enthusiastic about trying to run the world, Clinton reminded them that:

> Americans have always risen to the challenges we have faced. . . . It is in our DNA. We do believe there are no limits on what is possible or what can be achieved. . . . For the United States, global leadership is both a responsibility and an unparalleled opportunity.

President Obama is making a serious mistake heading down this road. He should instead return to the grand strategy of offshore balancing, which has served this country well for most of its history and offers the best formula for dealing with the threats facing America—whether it be terrorism, nuclear proliferation or a traditional great-power rival.

In general terms, the United States should concentrate on making sure that no state dominates Northeast Asia, Europe or the Persian Gulf, and that it remains the world's only regional hegemon. This is the best way to ensure American primacy. We should build a robust military to intervene in those areas, but it should be stationed offshore or back in the United States. In the event a potential hegemon comes on the scene in one of those regions, Washington should rely on local forces to counter it and only come onshore to join the fight when it appears that they cannot do the job themselves. Once the potential hegemon is checked, American troops should go back over the horizon.

Offshore balancing does not mean that the United States should ignore the rest of the world. But it should maintain a substantially lower profile outside of Northeast Asia, Europe and the Gulf, and it should rely on diplomacy and economic statecraft, not military force, to protect its interests in areas of little strategic importance. Washington should also get out of the business of trying to spread democracy around the globe, and more generally acting as if we have the right and the responsibility to interfere in the domestic politics of other countries. This behavior, which violates the all-important principle of self-determination, not only generates resentment toward the United States, but also gets us involved in nation building, which invariably leads to no end of trouble.

Specifically, offshore balancing is the best grand strategy for ameliorating our terrorism problem. Placing American troops in the Arab and Muslim world is a major cause of terrorist attacks against the United States, as University of Chicago professor Robert Pape's research shows. Remember what happened after President Ronald Reagan sent marines into Beirut in 1982? A suicide bomber blew up their barracks the following year, killing 241 service members. Reagan had the good sense to quickly pull the remaining marines out of Lebanon and keep them offshore. And it is worth noting that the perpetrators of this act did not pursue us after we withdrew.

Reagan's decision was neither surprising nor controversial, because the United States had an offshore-balancing strategy in the Middle East during this period. Washington relied on Iraq to contain Iran during the 1980s, and kept the rapid-deployment force—which was built to intervene in the Gulf if the local balance of power collapsed—at the ready should it be needed. This was smart policy.

After Iraq invaded Kuwait in August 1990, the United States, once again acting as an offshore balancer, moved large numbers of troops into Saudi Arabia to liberate Kuwait. After the war was won and victory was consolidated, those troops should

have been pulled out of the region. But that did not happen. Rather, Bill Clinton adopted a policy of dual containment—checking both Iran and Iraq instead of letting them check one another. And lest we forget, the resulting presence of U.S. forces in Saudi Arabia was one of the main reasons that Osama bin Laden declared war on the United States. The Bush administration simply made a bad situation even worse.

Sending the U.S. military into countries in the Arab and Muslim world is helping to cause our terrorism problem, not solve it. The best way to fix this situation is to follow Ronald Reagan's example and pull all American troops out of Afghanistan and Iraq, then deploy them over the horizon as part of an offshore-balancing strategy. To be sure, the terrorist challenge would not completely disappear if the United States went back to offshore balancing, but it would be an important step forward.

Next is to address the other causes, like Washington's unyielding support for Israel's policies in the occupied territories. Indeed, Bill Clinton recently speculated that the Israeli-Palestinian conflict is responsible for about half of the terrorism we face. Of course, this is why the Obama administration says it wants to achieve a two-state solution between Israel and the Palestinians. But given the lack of progress in solving that problem, and the fact that it is going to take at least a few years to get all of the American troops out of Afghanistan and Iraq, we will be dealing with al-Qaeda for the foreseeable future.

Offshore balancing is also a better policy than global dominance for combating nuclear proliferation. It has two main virtues. It calls for using military force in only three regions of the world, and even then, only as a matter of last resort. America would still carry a big stick with offshore balancing but would wield it much more discreetly than it does now. As a result, the United States would be less threatening to other countries, which would lessen their need to acquire atomic weapons to protect themselves from a U.S. attack.

Furthermore, because offshore balancing calls for Washington to help local powers contain aspiring regional hegemons in Northeast Asia, Europe and the Gulf, there is no reason that it cannot extend its nuclear umbrella over its allies in those areas, thus diminishing their need to have their own deterrents. Certainly, the strategy is not perfect: some allies will want their own nuclear weapons out of fear that the United States might not be there for them in a future crisis; and some of America's adversaries will still have powerful incentives to acquire a nuclear arsenal. But all things considered, offshore balancing is still better than global dominance for keeping proliferation in check.

Oddly enough, before being blown off course by 9/11, the Bush administration realized the most serious challenge that the United States is likely to face in the decades ahead is dealing with a rising China. If the People's Republic grows economically over the next thirty years the way it has in recent decades, it is likely to translate its economic might into military power and try to dominate Asia as the United States dominates the Western Hemisphere. But no American leader will accept that outcome, which means that Washington will seek to contain Beijing and prevent it from achieving regional hegemony. We can expect the United States to lead a balancing coalition against China that includes India, Japan, Russia, Singapore, South Korea and Vietnam, among others.

Of course, America would check China's rise even if it were pursuing global dominance. Offshore balancing, however, is better suited to the task. For starters, attempting to dominate the globe encourages the United States to fight wars all around the world, which not only wears down its military in peripheral conflicts, but also makes it difficult to concentrate its forces against China. This is why Beijing should hope that the American military remains heavily involved in Afghanistan and Iraq for many years to come. Offshore balancing, on the other hand, is committed to staying out of fights in the periphery and concentrating instead on truly serious threats.

Another virtue of offshore balancing is its emphasis on getting other countries to assume the burden of containing an aspiring regional hegemon. Global dominators, in contrast, see the United States as the indispensable nation that must do almost all of the heavy lifting to make containment work. But this is not a smart strategy because the human and economic price of checking a powerful adversary can be great, especially if war breaks out. It almost always makes good sense to get other countries to pay as many of those costs as possible while preserving one's own power. The United States will have to play a key role in countering China, because its Asian neighbors are not strong enough to do it by themselves, but an America no longer weakened by unnecessary foreign intervention will be far more capable of checking Beijing's ambitions.

Offshore balancing costs considerably less money than does global dominance, allowing America to better prepare for the true threats it faces. This is in good part because this strategy avoids occupying and governing countries in the developing world and therefore does not require large armies trained for counterinsurgency. Global dominators naturally think that the United States is destined to fight more wars like Afghanistan and Iraq, making it essential that we do counterinsurgency right the next time. This is foolish thinking, as both of those undertakings were unnecessary and unwinnable. Washington should go to great lengths to avoid similar future conflicts, which would allow for sharp reductions in the size of the army and marine corps. Instead, future budgets should privilege the air force and especially the navy, because they are the key services for dealing with a rising China. The overarching goal, however, should be to take a big slice out of the defense budget to help reduce our soaring deficit and pay for important domestic programs. Offshore balancing is simply the best grand strategy for dealing with al-Qaeda, nuclear proliferators like North Korea and the potential threat from China.

Perhaps most importantly, moving toward a strategy of offshore balancing would help us tame our fearsome national-security state, which has grown alarmingly powerful since 9/11. Core civil liberties are now under threat on the home front and the United States routinely engages in unlawful behavior abroad. Civilian control of the military is becoming increasingly problematic as well. These worrisome trends should not surprise us; they are precisely what one expects when a country engages in a broadly defined and endless global war against terror and more generally commits itself to worldwide hegemony. Never-ending militarization invariably leads to militarism and the demise of cherished liberal values. It is time for the United States to show greater restraint and deal with the threats it faces in smarter and more discerning ways. That means putting an end to America's pursuit of global dominance and going back to the time-honored strategy of offshore balancing.

Notes

1. Francis Fukuyama, "The End of History?" *The National Interest* (Summer 1989).
2. Charles Krauthammer, "The Unipolar Moment," *Foreign Affairs* 70, no. 1 (1990/1991).
3. Ian S. Lustick, *Our Own Strength Against Us: The War on Terror as a Self-inflicted Disaster* (Oakland, CA: The Independent Institute, 2008).
4. Office of the Under Secretary of Defense for Acquisition, Technology, and Logistics, *Report of the Defense Science Board Task Force on Strategic Communication* (Washington, DC: Government Printing Office, September 2004); John Zogby and James Zogby, "Impressions of America 2004: How Arabs View America; How Arabs Learn about America" (Washington, DC: Zogby International, 2004).
5. Andrew Enterline and J. Michael Greig, "The History of Imposed Democracy and the Future of Iraq and Afghanistan," *Foreign Policy Analysis* 4, no. 4 (October 2008). In an examination of forty-three cases of imposed democratic regimes between 1800 and 1994, it was found that 63 percent failed.
6. Jeffrey Pickering and Mark Peceny, "Forging Democracy at Gunpoint," *International Studies Quarterly* 50, no. 3 (September 2006).
7. Francis Fukuyama, *America at the Crossroads* (New Haven, CT: Yale University Press, 2006).

John J. Mearsheimer, "Imperial by Design," The National Interest 111 (2011), pp. 16–34. Reprinted by permission of Center for the National Interest.

Part Two: Theory and Grand Strategy

Jack Snyder, One World, Rival Theories

1. Can you articulate the defining characteristics of Realism? Of Liberalism? Of Constructivism?
2. According to Snyder what are the primary challenges to Realism in the 21st century?
3. How did facets of Liberal theory serve as an impetus to the US War in Iraq (2003–2011)?
4. How might the promotion of democracy abroad lead to war? Why?
5. Why do the "three traditions" have a difficult time explaining political change?
6. To what degree do power, institutions, and ideas interact in explaining the U.S. intervention in Libya in 2011?
7. Would you describe President Obama as a Realist? As a Liberal? Explain.

Henry R. Nau, Why We Fight Over Foreign Policy

1. How do simplifications and models of the complex political world help us to make decisions?
2. What are some of the negative consequences that arise from theoretical oversimplification?
3. Which perspective—Realist, Liberal, or Constructivist—best explains the attacks of September 2001 by al Qaeda? Explain.
4. Nau argued that an ideational perspective drove the neoconservatives (and the Bush Administration) to invade Iraq in 2003. Do you agree with his conclusion? Explain.
5. What are some of the limitations of social science?

Robert Jervis, Hypotheses on Misperception

1. How do policymakers' pre-existing belief structures affect their perception of other information?
2. Give a modern example of *cognitive consistency* resulting in poor decision making.
3. Give an example of *wishful thinking* by policymakers.
4. What are the impediments to effective *learning* by policymakers?
5. What impedes one country's effective *signaling* of its intent to another nation?

Samuel P. Huntington, The Clash of Civilizations?

1. Is Huntington's definition of *civilization* adequate? If not, how would you improve on it?
2. Given that this article was written in 1993, has the actual record of conflict since that point supported Huntington's conclusions? Are most wars in the modern era intercivilizational conflicts, or do they result from other factors?
3. Has the locus of conflict shifted from *within* civilizations to *between* civilizations? Give examples to support your position.
4. Processes of *globalization* bring previously distal cultures into increasing contact, causing resentment and misunderstanding. Is globalization then a driver of conflict between civilizations?
5. Huntington argued that the "revival of religion," and schisms between religions, will function as a driver of war between civilizations. Is there evidence to support this conclusion? Explain.
6. Huntington argued that Islam possesses "bloody borders." Does the data since 1993 support this conclusion? If so, why would Islam's relations with other cultures be so prone to conflict?
7. Is there increasing evidence of "civilizational commonality?" In Islam? In East Asia? In the Americas? Explain.
8. Huntington argued that conflicts within civilizations will be less lethal than conflicts between civilizations. Does the evidence support this conclusion?

Joseph S. Nye, Jr., Public Diplomacy and Soft Power

1. Nye argued that the invasion of Iraq in 2003 eroded the *soft power* of the U.S.A. Do you agree? If so, what were the consequences for Washington?
2. According to Nye the soft power of a nation rests on three resources. Name them, and explain their significance.
3. How would you distinguish between soft power and propaganda?
4. Do you agree with Nye's assertion that the "paradox of plenty" may lead to suboptimal outcomes? Explain.
5. Is there tension between Nye's position and Huntington's argument regarding the "clash of civilizations?" Explain.
6. Are there any difficulties in using soft power to change the preferences of others, and to set the political agenda? Explain.

Richard N. Haass, The Age of Nonpolarity: What Will Follow U.S. Dominance

1. Are we now in an age of unipolarity, bipolarity, or multipolarity? What are the consequences for U.S. foreign policy?
2. Haass argued that U.S. power is in a relative decline. Is this accurate? If so, what are the implications of such a decline?
3. Is the U.S. now subject to what Paul Kennedy called *imperial overstretch*?
4. To what extent has globalization diluted U.S. power? Provide examples.

John J. Mearsheimer, Imperial by Design

1. What was Mearsheimer's principle critique of the neoconservative position espoused by Krauthammer and Fukuyama?
2. What does Mearsheimer mean by *offshore balancing*? What are the strengths and weaknesses of this strategy?
3. Mearsheimer argued that following the September 11th attacks the Bush Administration's assessment of the terrorist threat was inaccurate. What were these inaccurate observations and calculations?
4. Mearsheimer argued that Washington, DC has engaged in *threat inflation* regarding the threat posed by terrorists. Do you agree? Explain.
5. How does *threat inflation* undermine U.S. national security?
6. Mearsheimer argued that the "clash of civilizations" argument is not explanatory, rather that the Arab and Muslim world is reacting to Washington's policies. Do you agree? Explain your position.
7. How did the "Afghan Model" of the conduct of war prove misleading to U.S. policymakers? What are the perils of this model? Give examples.
8. Why is it so difficult to defeat an insurgency?
9. Mearsheimer argued that the forcible spread of democracy abroad by the U.S.A. is actually counterproductive to U.S. national security. Do you agree? Explain your position.

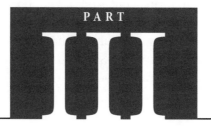

Institutions and Processes

In this section we analyze the influence of domestic institutions, factions, and forces on the conduct of U.S. foreign policy. Readers will examine the role of the presidency and the departments within the executive branch through the lens of the bureaucratic politics model that emphasizes competition between elements within the government. Nongovernmental actors include the mass media, scientific experts, and domestic factions (interest groups) that lobby the government. We also examine the role of public opinion on foreign policy decision making.

Jacobs and Page analyze the influence of various groups (media, business, labor) on the formulation of U.S. foreign policy. They conclude that international business interests are in fact the principal driver of U.S. foreign policy decisions. This is followed by Patrick Haney's article on the advising processes that influenced decision making within the George W. Bush Administration, through the lens of a bureaucratic politics model. Further readings deal with Congress and the influence of electoral politics on the conduct of foreign affairs. Baum and Potter's article regarding the role of the mass media and public opinion on foreign policy decision making argues that the mass media acts as an intervening factor in decision making. Collectively, these articles allow for an interesting debate on the importance of public opinion on foreign policy decision making.

Stephen Walt and John Mearsheimer follow with their controversial article on the Israel Lobby, arguing that this lobby exerts a profound influence on U.S. foreign policy in the Middle East and Persian Gulf, and has driven the U.S.A. to undertake needless wars in those regions. Andrew Bacevich argues that economic and moral weakness at the domestic level, coupled with the rise of the dangerous ethos of *Liberal imperialism*, constitute clear and present dangers to the Republic. The section concludes with Loch Johnson's analysis of the intelligence process, and its relationship to foreign policy decision making.

Who Influences U.S. Foreign Policy?

LAWRENCE R. JACOBS AND BENJAMIN I. PAGE

In this article Jacobs and Page analyze the role of domestic actors on the foreign policy decision-making process. They explore the role of various domestic level factions that hypothetically drive foreign policy, organized business and labor, public opinion, and experts. They conclude that the group with the greatest influence on U.S. foreign policy decision making is international business.

Research in international relations has identified a variety of actors who appear to influence U.S. foreign policy, including experts and "epistemic communities," organized interests (especially business and labor), and ordinary citizens or "public opinion." This research, however, has often focused on a single factor at a time, rather than systematically testing the relative importance of alternative possible influences. Using extensive survey data gathered over three decades we conduct a comparative test, attempting to account for the expressed foreign policy preferences of policy makers by means of the preferences of the general public and those of several distinct sets of elites. The results of cross-sectional and time-lagged analyses suggest that U.S. foreign policy is most heavily and consistently influenced by internationally oriented business leaders, followed by experts (who, however, may themselves be influenced by business). Labor appears to have significant but smaller impacts. The general public seems to have considerably less effect, except under particular conditions. These results generally hold over several different analytical models (including two-observation time series) and different clusters of issues (economic, military, and diplomatic), with some variations across different institutional settings (the U.S. House, Senate, and executive branch).

Do organized interest groups seeking narrow benefits for their members drive American foreign policy? Or is policy more influenced by the views of epistemic communities that use their expertise to identify the national interest? Alternatively, do the collective preferences of ordinary citizens shape U.S. foreign policy? Do the wielders of influence vary by issue domain, the level of issue salience, or the particular government institutions involved in policy making?

Such questions touch on the classical "Who governs?" query that has animated much research in American and comparative politics (Dahl 1961). But they are even more central to debates in international relations. They relate to the democratic character of American conduct internationally, the extent to which calculations of national interest do or do not drive U.S. foreign policy, and the general nature of domestic sources of foreign policy. To answer fundamental empirical questions about who influences government officials may help pave the way for developing broader theory regarding the determinants of international behavior.

These questions also have bearing on important normative issues. Democratic theories emphasizing popular sovereignty and electoral accountability argue that government policy ought to reflect the views of ordinary citizens (e.g., Dahl 1989). Adherents of these relatively "populistic" democratic theories would presumably applaud findings of strong public influence on U.S. foreign policy. On the other hand, more elite-oriented theories of democracy (Burke 1949; Sartori 1987; Schumpeter 1976), as well as realist theories of international relations (Kennan 1951; Lippmann 1955; Morgenthau 1973) would sound an alarm. They question the competence of citizens and assert that the quality of foreign policy is likely to suffer if the mass public is allowed to have much direct impact. Evidence that experts and members of "epistemic communities" significantly affect U.S. foreign policy would be applauded by some as holding out the best hope for objectively identifying and advancing the national interest in an increasingly complex global environment (Adler and Haas 1992; Haas 1992; Hall 1989), Alternatively, findings that organized interest groups drive U.S. foreign policy would raise troubling questions about a possible "bias in representation" toward particularistic groups (Moravcsik 1997, 530).

Competing Views of Who Influences U.S. Foreign Policy

Three prominent, empirically based views of who influences U.S. foreign policy suggest sharply different predictions.

Neoliberalism and Organized Groups

Many scholars who take a neoliberal approach to international politics emphasize the decisive influence of organized interest groups on foreign policy (e.g., Keohane 1984). In this view, executive and legislative officials with foreign policy authority bargain with domestic groups that use their members' votes, campaign contributions, threatened or actual capital flight, labor strikes, and other tools to affect the electoral benefits and costs to elected officials of choosing alternative policies (e.g., Frieden 1991; Gourevitch 1986; Rogowski 1989). For instance, Keohane and

Milner (1996) trace targeted government subsidies and trade protections to the influence of well-organized and financed groups; Snyder (1991) attributes defense policy to logrolling coalitions.

Organized labor and, perhaps even more so, business corporations possess critical resources for pressuring policy makers. Given their mission to protect the jobs and benefits of its members, "[labor] leaders have spoken out often on foreign affairs" (Galenson 1986, 62). In addition to addressing foreign policies that affect its bread and butter interests at home, organized labor in the United States has historically also spoken out on such matters as anticommunism, the Vietnam war, defense spending, and U.S.-Soviet relations, perhaps changing stands as the Cold War ended and the AFL-CIO's blue-collar base was challenged by an influx of civil service and other unions representing white-collar, professional, and service occupations (Lipset 1986). Despite the substantial political resources of U.S. organized labor, however, including its financial contributions, volunteers, and voters in many congressional districts, there is some disagreement about whether it exerts significant policy influence (Gottschalk 2001) or not (Esping-Anderson 1990).

Some neoliberal analysts of international politics have singled out business corporations and business associations as exerting particular influence on American foreign policy because of their effects on the economy and their capacity to prompt voters to punish the incumbent political party (Milner 1997). A number of studies have reported influence by business on specific types of foreign policy: Rogowski (1989) traces economic policies to powerful domestic economic interests; Trubowitz (1998) points to uneven economic growth and struggles for regional economic advantage to explain a variety of foreign policies; and Grossman and Helpman (1994, 1995) link industry lobbying and campaign contributions to international trade relations and, specifically, increased tariffs for politically organized industries. Some argue that pressures on governments to tailor foreign policy to please business have increased over the past three decades with the emergence of an open world economy characterized by rapid international movement of capital and greater exposure to global economic competition (Bates and Lien 1985; Winters 1996).

This line of research suggests that different policy-making institutions may vary in their susceptibility to organized pressures. Executive branch officials, who play a central part in national security and foreign policy, have been said to focus on identifying collective gains in pursuing the "national interest" and therefore to be somewhat resistant to organized pressure (Art 1973; Krasner 1972, 1978; Wildavsky 1991). Organized groups may be particularly influential with Congress, where senators and, especially, Representatives (elected in relatively small districts) may be acutely responsive to demands for concentrated benefits from narrowly based groups of constituents and campaign donors (Milner 1997).

In short, interest group-oriented scholars suggest that labor and, especially, business should exert a strong influence on U.S. foreign policy.

Epistemic Communities and Knowledge-Based Experts

Research on "epistemic communities" indicates that the growing complexity and uncertainty of global problems has "led policy makers to turn to new and different channels of advice" and specifically to new "networks of knowledge-based experts" in the academy, think tanks, and other repositories of technocratic expertise in order to articulate the objective causes of international problems, the "real" stakes or interests of states affected by those problems, and appropriate policy remedies (Haas, 1992, 12; cf. Hall 1989 and Nelkin 1979). In the introduction to an influential special volume of *International Organization*, Peter Haas (1992) argued that the "epistemic community members' professional training, prestige, and reputation for expertise . . . accord them access to the political system and . . . influence over policy debates" through agenda setting and the formulation of policy alternatives in the executive and legislative branches (2–3, 17; Adler and Haas 1992).

Research on epistemic communities has two implications that are important for us. First, it suggests that experts equip government officials to conduct analyses and reach decisions that can be independent of direct pressures from organized groups or citizens. The implication, then, is that business and labor may exert relatively little direct influence on the foreign policy decisions of government officials.

Second, epistemic communities may serve as concrete mechanisms for identifying and addressing the objective interests of states that may ultimately be defined, as classical and structural realists emphasize, by interstate competition and the structure of the international system (Walt 1987; Waltz 1959, 1979; but cf. Rose 1998). Students of epistemic communities argue that realists incorrectly "assume that a state's interests are clear and that the ways in which its interests may be most efficaciously pursued are equally clear" (Adler and Haas 1992, 367–69; Haas 1992, 13–14). Instead, they maintain, technical experts are the vehicle for the interpretation of international structures, the identification of the "imperatives" facing the state, and the articulation of state interests in international politics. In short, research on epistemic communities suggests that conditions of uncertainty produce strong incentives for government officials charged with making foreign policy to respond to experts from think tanks, the academy, and other reservoirs of highly trained specialists and professionals.

Median Voter Theory and the Influence of Public Opinion

Median voter theory predicts that actual or anticipated electoral competition motivates holders of government office to minimize the distance between their policy stands and the policy preferences of voters, thus responding strongly to the public's preferences, (in the case of unidimensional, two-party competition, parties are predicted to converge exactly at the position of the median voter [Downs 1957].) Empirical evidence of public influence on foreign policy has been reported in a large and growing body of research by students of international relations and foreign policy (e.g., Hartley and Russett 1992; Holsti 1996; Nincic 1990; Russett 1990; Sobel 1993, 2001; Wittkopf 1990). Effects of the public have also been found in quantitative analyses by students of public opinion, who have reported, for example, that 62% of U.S. foreign policies *changed* in the same direction in which public opinion had previously changed (Page and Shapiro 1983, 182) and that congressional district-level public support for military spending was related to Congress members' votes on military spending bills during the presidency of Ronald Reagan (Bartels 1991; see also Monroe 1979, 1998). This and other evidence of influence by the public is now recognized in broader debates about international relations (e.g., Putnam 1988, 432, 436) and national security policy, which Miroslav Nincic (1990) found to be "tethered to domestic electoral calculations," especially when elections approach (395).

The idea of government responsiveness to public opinion has also informed research on the "democratic peace" which has found a tendency for individual democratic states and, especially, pairs of democratic states to be more pacific on average than nondemocratic states (Russett and Oneal 2001; cf. Elman, 1997, 10–20). One line of thinking in democratic peace research argues that competitive elections "makes democratic leaders . . . sensitive to public opinion" because politicians either anticipate electoral punishment or are thrown out of office for being unresponsive: "Citizens in a democratic state can influence governmental policy directly, through public opinion, or indirectly, through their representatives."[1]

Salience may be an important condition affecting the extent of public influence. E. E. Schattschneider's (1960) analysis of the "scope of conflict" indicates that the general public should have its greatest impact on highly salient issues that draw intense attention from the media and voters and thereby pose the most direct threat of electoral punishment for government officials who are unresponsive. In contrast, narrow, well-organized interests may dominate on less visible issues. Some empirical evidence seems to support the prediction of greater public influence when salience is high (e.g., Page and Shapiro 1983, 181).

There are also indications that the characteristics of different government institutions may produce different degrees of influence by the public. For example, members of the House of Representatives, which the Federalist Papers labeled the "people's House" due to their frequent election in small and decentralized districts, were expected to be especially sensitive to public opinion, while officials in the executive branch and Senate were expected to be less responsive due to their insulation from the public by longer terms in office and originally indirect elections.

An ample body of qualitative and quantitative research, then, indicates that U.S. foreign policy and the policy preferences of government officials are substantially influenced by public opinion. Apparently accepting such influence as an empirical fact, a long line of observers including classical realists has urged policy makers *not* to respond to the preferences of citizens, because of concerns that the general public engages in "simple moralistic and legalistic" thinking, is detached from the reality of international politics, exhibits unstable shifting "moods," and hungers for "quick results" (Morgenthau 1973, pp. 135, 146–48; cf. Almond 1950 and Kennan 1951). Walter Lippmann (1955) warned that following public opinion would create a "morbid derangement of the true functions of power" and produce policies "deadly to the very survival of the state as a free society" (15, 20, 26–27).

Problems with Past Research

Previous research concerning the impact of organized groups, epistemic communities, and public opinion on U.S. foreign policy has produced an impressive body of results that point in diverse directions regarding who influences government officials. It has not, however, definitely sorted out the relative impact of different factors on U.S. foreign policy. Even excellent case studies that disentangle causal mechanisms and trace processes of policy making usually leave open the issue of how well they generalize beyond those particular cases. Perhaps even more importantly, lack of definitiveness has also resulted from two problems related to the scholarly division of labor: omitted variables and lack of comparative testing. Understandably, each of the three main approaches we have reviewed has tended to focus on a set of variables of particular interest to it, rarely investigating and testing competing explanations at the same time. Most studies of public opinion and government policy, including foreign affairs (some of which were conducted by the present authors [Jacobs and Shapiro 1994; Page and Shapiro 1983; but cf. Jacobs 1992, 1993, 231–33, and Page 2002]), have failed to include any independent variables *other* than public opinion. However understandable this research strategy may be, it runs the risk that other important influences may be neglected. It may lead each approach to overestimate the importance of its own favorite factors and to offer little or no estimate of the *relative* impact of different possible influences.

What is now needed, we believe, is *comparative* analysis, based on a large number of diverse cases, of the relative influence on U.S. foreign policy of several key actors, including organized interest groups (especially business and labor), epistemic communities from think tanks and the academy, and mass public opinion. The present paper attempts to take a first step in that direction.

Data and Methods

We have analyzed a set of data that are uniquely well suited to this purpose, drawn from eight quadrennial pairs of surveys that that were sponsored from 1974 through 2002 by the Chicago Council on Foreign Relations (CCFR) and implemented by the Gallup and Harris organizations.[2] These surveys, covering a large and diverse set of foreign policy issues, elicited the policy preferences of the general public and also the preferences of several distinct sets of "foreign policy leaders," including policy makers (government officials in the executive branch, the House of Representatives, and the Senate), members of critical interest groups (especially business and Labor), and members of epistemic communities (educators and leaders of private foreign policy organizations or think tanks).[3]

These parallel surveys of the mass public and foreign policy leaders have both strengths and limitations. The government officials and other elites were not randomly selected for interviews; they were chosen from institutional positions involving foreign policy responsibilities or expertise.[4] Although a total of 2,916 elites were interviewed in the eight leadership surveys, the number of each specific type of elite interviewed in any single year was not very large.[5] (The surveys of the general public were based on random, relatively large samples of about 1,550 respondents each.)[6]

Despite their limitations, the CCFR surveys provide what are, so far as we know, the best available data on comparably measured foreign policy preferences of ordinary citizens, interest groups, epistemic communities, and U.S. government officials. They cover a wide range of foreign policy issues over a lengthy period of time, both during and after the Cold War. Data on large numbers of key policy makers are very difficult to obtain (but cf. Holsti and Rosenau 1984), especially from samples that are comparable over multiple years.[7] The CCFR elite samples have the advantage of being drawn in a consistent manner across years, because of continuity in survey organizations and research teams as well as conscious efforts to produce comparable data. In addition, the private and confidential nature of the interviews with respected survey organizations probably helped to discourage public posturing and encourage relatively candid expression of views.

A crucial advantage of these survey data is that they permit us to analyze relationships using precise, directly comparable measures of the policy preferences of policy makers and those of the public, members of interest groups, and experts. These measures are based on responses to identical questions asked of the various groups at the same time. Previous researchers have generally lacked such comparable measures and have had to struggle with the question of exactly how close a given policy did or did not come to the wishes of particular actors.

A clear message from all four models is that business is a consistently effective influence on policy makers. Its absolute and relative influence does appear to vary, though, based on how the different models treat the passage of time. The contrast between the cross-sectional and the time-lag models suggest that business leaders may exert strong effects quite rapidly, perhaps through phone calls and other direct contacts with officials.

Experts

Experts, judging by some of our models, also appear to be a potent force affecting the views of policy makers. According to cross-sectional Models 1 and 2, experts have the second strongest contemporaneous influence (next to business) on policy makers' preferences. This finding, which at least partly fits the expectations of researchers on epistemic communities, applies with nearly equal magnitude to all policy makers taken together and also to those from each of the three institutional settings analyzed separately. But according to the time series analysis of Model 3, experts did not exert any significant influence at all. This suggests either that experts' impact is extremely quick, fully embodied in policy makers' previously measured preferences, or (perhaps more plausibly) that the expressed preferences of experts are largely effects rather than causes of policy makers' stands, That is, the substantial estimated effects in cross-sectional Models 1 and 2 may be inflated by simultaneity bias. The same problem may affect the results of Model 4, which indicates that *changes* in experts' and policy makers' preferences over the same time period tend to go in the same direction. Since these changes are measured between the same two time points (previous and current surveys), we cannot be sure which change actually preceded or caused the other. Still, we cannot dismiss the possibility that experts and epistemic communities have substantial influence on officials.

The Public

Perhaps the most surprising finding in this whole set of analyses is the apparent weakness of public opinion. Even with these reduced and refined models, the public does not appear to exert substantial, consistent influence on the makers of foreign policy. In none of the 16 regression analyses, applying our four models to four sets of decision makers, was the public opinion coefficient dominant over those of the elite actors. The contemporaneous Model 1 estimate for

the effect of public preferences on officials in the House of Representatives was statistically significant but weak ($b = .10$); the public had no significant effects, even by a one-tailed test or the loose $p < .10$ standard, in Model 2.[8] The *negative* coefficients for public opinion in the time series analysis (Model 3), if taken seriously, actually indicate that—controlling for the past views of governmental and nongovernmental elites—officials tend perversely to move *away* from public opinion. A more plausible interpretation of these borderline-significant coefficients, however, is that the public simply has no effect at all. According to Model 4, public opinion resurfaces as a notable but secondary influence on policy makers overall and on House officials, with no significant effect on Senate or administration officials. But even this degree of public influence may be overstated by the simultaneous-change analysis of Model 4: If policy makers have reciprocal effects on the public, a simultaneity bias may inflate the estimates.

Taken together, these findings hint at partial confirmation of the Founders' expectations about the House of Representatives as "the people's" chamber. More importantly, however, they run against the thrust of much past research that has found substantial impacts of public opinion.

Labor

Labor leaders are estimated by Models 1 and 2 to exert contemporaneous influence on foreign policy decision makers, but only weakly ($b = 16$ for all policy makers taken together in both Model 1 and Model 2), and mainly on the legislative rather than the executive branch. Research on the role of interest groups in the making of U.S. foreign policy generally anticipates just such a modest role for organized labor. What is surprising, though, is that in the Model 3 time series analysis labor emerges as the second strongest influence (next only to the inertia effect of officials themselves) on policy makers as a whole, with particular impact on officials in the House of Representatives. Model 3, making use of time asymmetries, offers particularly strong evidence regarding causation. Labor, despite its limited contemporaneous influence, is apparently able—perhaps owing to its active presence in states and localities—to apply delayed pressure on government officials, especially House members, who may be particularly sensitive to organized pressure within their decentralized districts. (Another possibility, as we will see, is that labor indirectly impacts the national agenda through experts.) This evidence of delayed effects is consistent with the absence of significant labor coefficients in Model 4, because delayed effects of *changes* in labor's stands will presumably show up only later, not in simultaneous changes by policy makers.

We also used the same four regression models to explore possible variations in influence on policy makers during different time periods and across three domains of foreign policy—defense, diplomacy, and economic issues. Separate analyses for each of the eight survey years produced results that generally paralleled those we have displayed for all years combined, with some apparently random variation in coefficients due to the smaller numbers of cases. For the different issue domains, too, the same pattern of findings generally held: substantial business influence, contemporaneous but not lagged effects by experts, and delayed effects by labor, with little impact from the public, In the Economic realm, however, where foreign policy cuts close to home, public opinion did appear to have significant contemporaneous influence on policy makers: a modest coefficient of .17 in Model 1 but a more substantial .36 in Model 2 and a remarkable .93 in same period–change Model 4 (all significant at $p < .01$). (In the Model 3 time series analysis, however, the public's coefficient did not come close to significance.) With regard to defense policy there were some indications, consistent with previous literature (e.g., Snyder 1991), that business has a particularly strong effect on policy makers. Because of the limited number of cases, interpretation of the issue-specific results requires caution.

Searching for Public Influence on Government Officials

Given the surprisingly weak estimates of influence by public opinion (with the partial exceptions of effects on House members and in economic policy), we were concerned that real public influence might be masked by the inclusion in the analysis of labor leaders, who we found to have a moderate influence on policy makers and whose preferences were fairly strongly correlated with those of the public ($r = .82$). In order to provide the best possible opportunity for public opinion to display effects, we dropped the labor variable and regressed the preferences of policy makers only on the preferences of the general public, business, and experts.

The proportion of variance accounted for was virtually the same as in the earlier analyses, indicating that the public and labor can indeed be substituted for each other without losing much predictive power. But even with these rather generous—and somewhat implausible—causal assumptions (namely, that labor leaders have *no* independent impact on foreign policy at all but merely act as statistical proxies for the general public), the estimated influence of public opinion on the preference of government officials remained, at best modest.

Other results hinted at support for the Schattschneider (1960) view that the public has more influence on high-salience than low-salience issues, but estimates of public impact remained modest even for the very highest-salience issues, where—according to all four models—the estimated impact of both business and experts remained substantially greater than that of the public.[9]

In short, in spite of generous model specifications, the effect of public opinion on the preferences of foreign policy makers appears to be—at best—modest, when critical competing variables are controlled for. In general, public opinion takes a back seat to business and experts. These results challenge research that has suggested a generally strong public impact on foreign policy.

Still, we are not suggesting that public opinion has no effect at all on U.S. foreign policy. We have noted indications of significant public impact on members of the House of Representatives, on economic policy, and (perhaps) on issues of especially high salience. The public may play a substantial part in highly salient questions of war and peace, such as those analyzed by Sobel (2001). Further, we have not explored possible effects by the public on agenda setting, or on decision makers' anticipation of later, *retrospective* public opinion, or on the rhetorical packaging of policy choices (Jacobs and Shapiro 2000). (The makers of foreign policy may for example, work hard to avoid high levels of military casualties that could provoke electoral punishment; see Mueller 1973.) But it is worth emphasizing that our measurements of public opinion, based on large sample surveys, are quite good; any attenuation of coefficients due to measurement error should affect elite groups more than the public. And this sort of result is not likely to result from model misspecification due to causal ambiguities. An erroneous finding of *non* influence by the public is considerably less likely to result from simultaneity bias than is an excessively large estimate of its influence.[10]

All in all, the implications of our findings for previous research connecting public opinion and policy making are sobering.

Indirect Business and Labor Influence through Experts?

The substantial influence of experts suggested by our cross-sectional models and the simultaneous-change Model 4, though in line with past research on epistemic communities, is subject to doubt about its causal status. Even if one sets aside the possibility of reciprocal influences by officials on experts that would tend to inflate their apparent impact on officials (a possibility highlighted by the null findings from the Model 3 over-time analyses), there remains the question of whether the preferences of experts are a truly independent variable or whether they function in an intervening role. For example, experts might themselves be influenced by business or labor and, in turn, transmit the preferences of those groups to officials.

Researchers on epistemic communities sometimes assume that policy makers are guided by independent, objective analysis from new "knowledge-based elites": that experts are not merely vehicles for pressing officials on behalf of organized interests. Yet the widespread funding of think tanks by business—and, to a much lesser extent, by organized labor—suggests that interest groups may sometimes affect who becomes a recognized expert and what such experts

say. Thus experts might not be autonomous influences on policy makers but, instead, might—in whole or in part—convey, to officials the preferences of others.

The results suggest that organized groups do influence experts and that this impact is quite substantial. If we set aside the time series findings of no expert effects on policy makers, and accept the cross-sectional estimates of substantial contemporaneous effects, we can go on to estimate indirect effects that business and labor may have on public officials through their influence on experts. For example, if a l-percentage point increase in business support for some policy generally leads to a .61-percentage point increase in experts' support for that policy, and if such a .61-percentage point increase for experts would then lead to a .183 (.30 × .61)-percentage point increase in officials' support, business would obtain a small but not irrelevant increment of indirect clout. This estimated indirect impact of .183 can be added to the direct impact of business on policy makers (estimated at .52 points), yielding a total business impact of slightly over .70. That is to say, a 10-percentage point increase in business support for a given policy may lead to a 7-point, rather than 5-point, increase in officials' support for that policy.[11]

Similar calculations for labor based on Model 1 cross-sectional analyses indicate a .126 indirect effect of labor on officials, Adding that to the estimated direct effect of .16, the total impact of labor on foreign policy officials is about .29, nearly double the size of the direct effect alone.[12] This amounts to a surprisingly strong impact, given labor's reputation for general ineffectiveness in American politics. It is an impact that appears to occur with, some delay over time and to depend significantly on indirect influence through experts. Even so, the estimated total effect on foreign policy of business is more than twice that of labor.

Foreign Policy, The National Interest, and Democracy

Our analyses using four distinct types of statistical models indicate that internationally oriented business leaders exercise strong, consistent, and perhaps lopsided influence on the makers of U.S. foreign policy. The estimates of strong business influence hold up under different models, for different political and institutional conditions, and for different time periods. They hold for high- as well as low-salience issues, for a variety of substantive issue areas, and with respect to different institutional groups of policy makers (though especially for executive branch and Senate officials). These findings tend to confirm theoretical expectations and empirical research from the organized interest group literature in international relations.

The estimated impacts of experts on policy makers do not generally match those of business, but they, too, are quite substantial, according to three of our four models (though not the Model 3 analyses of impact over time). This lends some credence to claims by analysts of epistemic communities. Our further investigation, of who influences experts suggests, however, that organized groups—not just independent, objective evaluations of complex international realities—may color the views of experts. These findings indicate that the direct foreign policy clout of business and labor may be augmented by an indirect influence on policy makers that works through experts.

Labor, even taking into account its possible indirect influence through experts, has less impact on the makers of U.S. foreign policy than business does. This finding, too, fits with some previous work by international relations scholars who focus on organized interest groups. Nonetheless, labor leaders do appear to exert a surprisingly consistent (if secondary) influence on policy makers, especially on members of the House of Representatives and concerning particular types of issues.

The findings from our cross-sectional and simultaneous-change analyses, as contrasted with the time series analyses using lagged independent variables, suggest that the influence of business tends to be fairly quick, while labor's influence tends to be delayed and is exerted over time as labor makes its presence in congressional districts felt. Although labor's effect on foreign policy has been downplayed by some international relations scholars, our evidence of labor's impact is consistent

with recent revaluations of its nested impact on US. social welfare policy (Gottschaulk 2001).

To our surprise, public opinion—the aggregate foreign policy preferences of ordinary citizens—was repeatedly estimated by our Models 1–3 to have little or no significant effect on government officials. When effects of public opinion emerged in these models (namely, on economic issues, on members of the House of Representatives, and perhaps on very high-salience issues), the absolute and relative magnitudes of effects were generally modest. These findings of little influence by public opinion are generally immune to issues of model specification and causal ambiguity that may affect some of our other results. On the other hand, the moderately strong estimates of public influence using Model 4 (based on same-period changes) may be inflated by simultaneity bias and should probably be taken as establishing an upper bound on public effects. Even those estimates were generally smaller than for business or experts. These results contradict expectations drawn from a large body of previous research.

If one accepts the survey-measured aggregate policy preferences of foreign policy decision makers as satisfactory indicators of actual policy (and we have argued that it is reasonable to do so), our findings have several important implications for understanding U.S. foreign policy, international affairs, and American democratic governance.

First, these findings underline the continuing importance of moving from monocausal explanations to multi-causal explanations in international relations scholarship (see Keohane 1989 and Putnam 1988). Although recent work in international relations (e.g., Moravcsik 1997; Russett and Oneal 2001; Snyder 1991) has shown substantial progress in this respect, there is still a pressing need for comprehensive examinations of multiple possible determinants of U.S. foreign policy across a range of issues.

Our evidence suggests that business may exert the most consistent influence on government officials but that policy makers' views may also be affected by labor, experts, and, to a lesser extent, public opinion. These results suggest that three of the most prominent lines of analysis of foreign policy—the interest group, epistemic community, and public opinion approaches—each have some merit. But at the same time, research along each of these lines has tended to omit critical alternative variables. It has seldom systematically examined the relative impact of competing influences. This risks artificially inflating estimates of the importance of particular factors of interest.

This hazard seems particularly serious for quantitative analyses of the effect of public opinion, not only on foreign policy (see, however, Hartley and Russett 1992 and Ostrom and Marra 1986, which take steps to be multivariate) but also on U.S. domestic policy. For instance, Erikson, MacKuen, and Stimson's widely discussed *Macro Polity* (2002) concludes that domestic policy is highly responsive to public opinion, yet it comes to that conclusion without considering the possible impact of organized interests. In our analyses, a very strong bivariate relationship between public opinion and the preferences of policy makers crumbled away almost completely when we included data on organized interests and experts in multivariate regressions. To be sure, foreign policy may be quite different from domestic (Art 1973; Wildavsky 1991), but we cannot be certain of this until comparable research is conducted that includes relevant variables and potentially complex causal dynamics (Bartels 2002; Jacobs and Shapiro 2000; Page 2002; see also Druckman, Jacobs, and Ostermeier 2004 and Jacobs and Burns 2004).

Second, our results have some troubling normative implications. The apparently weak influence of the public will presumably disappoint those adherents of democratic theory (e.g., Dahl 1989) who advocate substantial government responsiveness to the reasoned preferences of citizens (Page and Shapiro 1992). Our findings indicate that the gravitational pull on foreign policy decision makers by the "foreign policy establishment" (especially business leaders and experts) tends to be stronger than the attraction of public opinion. This is consistent with the pattern of extensive and persistent "gaps" that Chicago Council studies have found between the foreign policy preferences of the public and those of policy makers. For example, ordinary Americans, more than policy makers or other elites, have repeatedly expressed stronger support for protecting Americans' jobs, stopping the inflow of illegal drugs, and reducing illegal immigration, as well as for a multilateral, cooperative foreign policy based on bolstering the United Nations, working closely with allies, and participating in international treaties and agreements (Bouton and Page 2002; Jacobs and Page 2003).

Comparatively muted influence by the mass public might initially please classical realist critics of citizen input into foreign affairs, who consider public opinion to be ill-informed and capricious (e.g., Lippmann 1955). Yet those same critics would want to see policy makers rise above the politics of organized interest groups in order to pursue the "national interest" perhaps as identified by independent, objective experts. Our finding of a substantial impact on foreign policy by business—generally a greater impact than by experts—suggests that purely technocratic calculations do not always predominate in the making of foreign policy. Competing political interests continue to fight over the national interest, and business often wins that competition.

Notes

1. See Peterson 1995, 10–11, and Russett and Oneal 2001, 274; also cf. Russett 1996, 100. Alternatively, the democratic peace has been attributed to liberal norms that promote nonviolent resolution of conflict, international law and shared membership in intergovernmental organizations, and economic interdependence that puts a premium on stable, ongoing commercial relations (Doyle 1983; Elman 1997; Owen 1994; Russett and Oneal 2001).

2. The 2002 study was cosponsored by the German Marshall Fund of the United States. Gallup conducted the surveys in 1978, 1982, 1986, 1990, 1994, and 1998, the Harris organization conducted them in 1974, and Harris Interactive did so in 2002. See Rielly (1975 et seq.).

3. Of less interest to the present analysis, the leadership surveys also included respondents from the media, religious leaders, special interest groups

relevant to foreign policy, and (in 1974) leaders of minority groups. As discussed below, we created a single category of "experts" by combining "educators" (i.e., faculty who teach in the area of foreign affairs and presidents and chancellors of major universities), "special foreign policy organizations" (i.e., think tanks), and "private foreign policy groups" (i.e., leaders of major foreign policy organizations), after analyzing each group separately.

4. Senators and Representatives, for example, were chosen (at least through 1990) from the membership of committees and subcommittees related to foreign policy. Administration officials came from the Department of State and from internationally oriented units of the commerce, treasury, agriculture, and other departments, though rarely from the Department of Defense or the National Security Council. Business respondents were sampled mainly from corporate vice presidents for international affairs, and labor respondents from high-level union officials oriented toward foreign affairs.

5. The average number interviewed each year was about 76 for government officials, 58 for business, 28 for labor, and 79 for experts. Although the categories of respondents were generally quite stable across surveys, the 1974 survey combined officials from the House, Senate, and administration, added minority groups, and did not survey think tank members. For 1978 through 2002, the average numbers of policy makers interviewed were 19 from the Senate, 36 from the House, and 23 from the administration.

6. In 2002, 2,862 respondents were interviewed by telephone and 400 were interviewed in person. This made it possible to assess comparability with the previous in-person surveys. We use the combined telephone and in-person data set. Interviews were typically conducted in the fall but in 2002 were carried out in June.

7. Holsti and Rosenau (1984) report an outstanding study of a wide range of U.S. decision makers and foreign policy leaders, including high-ranking military officers (unfortunately excluded from the Chicago Council, surveys).

8. We are reluctant to reply on the loose $p < .10$ criterion for statistical significance because, when many tests are performed, it can produce a number of false positives. By the same token, we hesitate to rely on one-tailed tests at the $p < .05$ level (equivalent to two-tailed tests at $p < .10$), because we are not sufficiently confident that the possibility of real negatively signed influences can be altogether ruled out theoretically. Still, we must also avoid the possibility of false negatives, e.g., dismissing public opinion as having "no effect" just because its coefficients do not pass our relatively stringent tests. For that reason, all tables include (along with standard errors) information on significance at the $p < .10$ level by two-tailed test, which readers are free to interpret as they will.

9. In regressions limited to the most highly salient issue cases (those with 4% or fewer "don't know" responses), coefficients for the public neared or attained statistical significance only under Model 1 ($.21^{**}$) and Model 4 ($.33+$). The coefficients for different salience categories are highly unstable because of small Ns.

10. Reciprocal effects of government officials on public opinion, for example, would bias our cross-sectional and contemporaneous-change estimates of the public's influence on officials *upward* rather than downward.

11. By similar calculations, Model 2 (including a lagged dependent variable) produced estimates of a total business impact on policy makers of .56: an indirect impact through experts of .115 ($.24 \times .48$) plus a direct impact of .44.

12. According to Model 2 analyses with a lagged dependent variable, labor has a slightly smaller total impact of .22: a .06 indirect effect through experts ($.24 \times .27$), combined with a direct effect of .16.

References

Adler, Emanuel, and Peter Haas. 1992. Conclusion: Epistemic Communities, World Order, and the Creation of a Reflective Research Program. *International Organization* 46 (Winter): 367–90.

Almond, Gabriel. 1950. *The American People and Foreign Policy.* New York: Harcourt, Brace.

Art, Robert. 1973. Bureaucratic Politics and American. Foreign Policy: A Critique. *Policy Sciences* 4 (Dec.): 467–90.

Bartels, Larry. 1991. Constituency Opinion and Congressional Policy Making: The Reagan Defense Buildup. *American Political Science Review* 85 (June): 457–74.

———. 2002. *Economic Inequality and Political Representation.* Paper presented at the 2002 annual meeting of the American Political Science Association, Boston.

Bates, Robert, and Da-Hsiang Lien. 1985. A Note on Taxation, Development, and Representative Government. *Politics and Society* 14 (Mar.): 53–70.

Bennett, W. Lance. 1990. Toward a Theory of Press-State Relations in the United States. *Journal of Communications* 40 (Spring): 103–25.

———. 1994. The Media and the Foreign Policy Process. In *The New Politics of American Foreign Policy,* ed. D. Deese, pp. 168–88. New York: St. Martin's Press.

Bouton, Marshall M., and Benjamin I. Page, eds. 2002. *World-Views 2002: American Public Opinion and Foreign Policy.* Chicago: Chicago Council on Foreign Relations.

Burke, Edmund. 1949. Speech to the Electors of Bristol. In *Burke's Politics: Selected Writings and Speeches,* ed. R. Hoffmann and P. Levack. New York: Alfred Knopf.

Chatterjee, Samprit, and Bertram Price. 1991. *Regression Analysis by Example.* 2nd ed. New York: Wiley.

Dahl, Robert A. 1961. *Who Governs? Democracy and Power in an American City.* New Haven, CT: Yale University Press.

———. A. 1989. *Democracy and Its Critics.* New Haven, CT: Yale University Press.

Downs, Anthony. 1957. *An Economic Theory of Democracy.* New York: Harper and Row.

Doyle, Michael. 1983. Kant, Liberal Legacies, and Foreign Affairs. *Philosophy and Public Affairs* 12 (3): 205–35; 12 (4): 323–53.

Druckman, James N., Lawrence R. Jacobs, and Eric Ostermeier. 2004. Candidate Strategies to Prime Issues and Image. *Journal of Politics.*

Elman, Mariam Fendius. 1997. Introduction: The Need for a Qualitative Test of the Democratic Peace Theory. In *Paths to Peace: Is Democracy the Answer?,* ed. M. F. Elman. Cambridge, MA: MIT Press.

Entman, Robert M. 2004. *Projections of Power: Framing News, Public Opinion, and U.S. Foreign Policy.* Chicago: University of Chicago Press.

Erikson, Robert S., Michael B. MacKuen, and James A. Stimson. 2002 *The Macro Polity.* New York: Cambridge University Press.

Esping-Andersen, Gosta. 1990. *The Three Worlds of Welfare Capitalism.* Princeton, NJ: Princeton University Press.

Freeman, John. 1983. Granger Causality and the Time Series Analysis of Political Relationships. *American Journal of Political Science* 27 (May): 327–58.

Frieden, Jeffry A. 1991. Invested Interests: The Politics of National Economic Policies in a World of Global Finance. *International Organization* 45 (Autumn): 425–51.

Galenson, Walter. 1986. The Historical Role of American Trade Unionism. In *Unions in Transition: Entering the Second Century,* ed. S. M. Lipset. San Francisco: Institute for Contemporary Studies.

Gottschalk, Marie. 2001. *In the Shadow of the Welfare State.* Ithaca, NY: Cornell University Press.

Gourevitch, Peter. 1986. *Politics in Hard Tunes.* Ithaca, NY: Cornell University Press.

Grossman, Gene M., and Elhanan Helpman. 1994. Protection for Sale. *American Economic Review* 84 (Sept.): 833–50.

———. 1995. Trade Wars and Trade Talks. *Journal of Political Economy* 103 (Aug.): 675–708.

Haas, Peter. 1992. "Introduction: Epistemic Communities and International Policy Coordination." *International Organization* 46 (Winter): 1–35.

Hall, Peter. 1989. *The Political Power of Economic Ideas: Keynesianism across Nations.* Princeton, NJ: Princeton University Press.

Hallin, Daniel C. 1986. *The "Uncensored War": The Media and Vietnam.* New York: Oxford University Press.

Hartley, Thomas, and Bruce Russett. 1992. "Public Opinion and the Common Defense: Who Governs Military Spending in the United States?" *American Political Science Review* 86 (December): 905–15.

Herman, Edward, and Noam Chomsky. 1988. *Manufacturing Consent: The Political Economy of the Mass Media.* New York: Pantheon Books.

Holsti, Oli. 1996. *Public Opinion and American Foreign Policy.* Ann Arbor: University of Michigan Press.

Holsti, Oli, and James N. Rosenau. 1984. *American Leadership in World Affairs: Vietnam and the Breakdown of Consensus.* London: Allen and Unwin.

Jacobs, Lawrence. 1993. *The Health of Nations: Public Opinion and the Making of Health Policy in the U.S. and Britain.* Ithaca, NY: Cornell University Press.

———. 1992. Institutions and Culture: Health Policy and Public Opinion in the U.S. and Britain. *World Politics* 44 (Jan.): 179–209.

Jacobs, Lawrence, and Melanie Burns. 2004. The Second Face of the Public Presidency: Presidential Polling and the Shift from Policy to Personality Polling. *Presidential Studies Quarterly* 34 (Sept.): 536–56.

Jacobs, Lawrence, and Benjamin Page. 2003. The Disconnect of American Foreign Policy Makers from Public Opinion: International Relations Theory and Practice. Paper presented at the 2003 annual meeting of the Midwest Political Science Association.

Jacobs, Lawrence, and Robert Y. Shapiro. 1994. Issues, Candidate Image and Priming: The Use of Private Polls in Kennedy's 1960 Presidential Campaign. *American Political Science Review* 88 (Sept.): 527–40.

———. 2000. *Politicians Don't Pander: Political Manipulation and the Loss of Democratic Responsiveness.* Chicago: University of Chicago Press.

Kennan, George. 1951. *American Diplomacy, 1900–1950.* Chicago: University of Chicago Press.

Keohane, Robert. 1984. *After Hegemony: Cooperation and Discord in the World Political Economy.* Princeton, NJ: Princeton University Press.

———. 1989. *International Institutions and State Power.* Boulder, CO: Westview Press.

Keohane, Robert, and Helen Milner, eds. 1996. *Internationalization and Domestic Politics.* Cambridge: Cambridge University Press.

Krasner, Stephen. 1972. Are Bureaucracies Important? (or Allison Wonderland). *Foreign Policy* 7 (Summer): 159–79.

———. 1978. *In Defense of the National Interest: Raw Materials, Investments, and U.S. Foreign Policy.* Princeton, NJ: Princeton University Press.

Lippmann, Walter. 1955. *Essays in the Public Philosophy.* Boston: Little, Brown.

Lipset, Seymour Martin. 1986. *Unions in Transition: Entering the Second Century.* San Francisco: Institute for Contemporary Studies.

Milner, Helen. 1997. *Interests, Institutions, and Information: Domestic Politics and International Relations.* Princeton, NJ: Princeton University Press.

Monroe, Alan D. 1979. Consistency between Public Preferences and National Policy Decisions. *American Politics Quarterly* 7 (Jan.): 3–19.

———. 1998. American Public Opinion and Public Policy, 1980–1993. *Public Opinion Quarterly* 62 (Spring): 6–28.

Moravcsik, Andy. 1997. Taking Preferences Seriously: A Liberal Theory of International Politics. *International Organization* 51 (Autumn): 513–53.

Morgenthau, Hans. 1973. *Politics among Nations.* New York: Knopf.

Mueller, John E. 1973. *War, Presidents and Public Opinion.* New York: Wiley.

Nacos, Brigette, Robert Shapiro, and Pierangelo Isernia. 2000. *Decision Making in a Glass House: Mass Media, Public Opinion, and American and European Foreign Policy in the 21st Century.* New York: Rowan and Littlefield.

Nelkin, Dorothy. 1979. Scientific Knowledge, Public Policy, and Democracy. *Knowledge, Creation, Diffusion, Utilization* 1 (Sept.): 106–22.

Nincic, Miroslav. 1990. U.S. Soviet Policy and the Electoral Connection. *World Politics* 42: 370–96.

Ostrom, Charles W., Jr., and Robin E. Marra. 1986. U.S. Defense Spending and the Soviet Estimate. *American Political Science Review* 80 (Sept.): 819–41.

Owen, John. 1994. How Liberalism Produces Democratic Peace. *International Security* 19 (Fall): 87–125.

Page, Benjamin. 2002. The Semi-Sovereign Public. In *Navigating Public Opinion; Polls, Policy, and the Future of American Democracy,* ed. Jeff Manza, Fay Lomax Cook, and Benjamin Page. New York: Oxford University Press.

Page, Benjamin L, and Robert Y. Shapiro. 1983. Effects of Public Opinion on Policy. *American Political Science Review 77* (Mar.): 175–90.

———. 1992. *The Rational Public: Fifty Years of Trends in Americans' Policy Preferences* Chicago: University of Chicago Press.

Peterson, Susan. 1995. How Democracies Differ: Public Opinion, State Structure, and the Lessons of the Fashoda Crisis. *Security Studies* 5 (Autumn): 3–37.

Putnam, Robert. 1988. Diplomacy and Domestic Politics: The Logic of Two-Level Games. *International Organization* 42 (Summer): 427–60.

Rielly, John. 1975. *American Public Opinion and U.S. Foreign Policy, 1975.* Chicago: Chicago Council on Foreign Relations (Corresponding studies published in 1979, 1983, 1987, 1991, 1995, and 1999.)

Rogowski, Ronald. 1989. *Commerce and Coalitions.* Princeton, NJ: Princeton University Press.

Rose, Gideon. 1998. Neoclassical Realism and Theories of Foreign Policy. *World Politics* 51 (Oct.): 144–72.

Russett, Bruce. 1990. *Controlling the Sword: The Democratic Governance of National Security.* Cambridge, MA: Harvard University Press.

———. 1996. Why Democratic Peace? In *Debating the Democratic Peace,* ed. M. Brown, S. Lynn-Jones, and S. Miller, 82–115. Cambridge, MA: MIT Press.

Russett, Bruce, and John Oneal. 2001. *Triangulating Peace: Democracy, Interdependence, and International Organizations.* New York: Norton.

Sartori, Giovanni. 1987. *The Theory of Democracy Revisited.* Chatham, NJ: Chatham House.

Schattschneider, E. E. 1960. *The Semi-Sovereign People: A Realist's View of Democracy in America.* New York: Holt, Rinehart and Winston.

Schumpeter, Joseph. 1950. *Capitalism, Socialism, and Democracy.* New York: Harper.

Sigal, Leon V. 1973. *Reporters and Officials: The Organization and Politics of Newsmaking.* Lexington, MA: D. C. Heath.

Snyder, Jack. 1991. *Myths of Empire: Domestic Politics and International Ambition.* Ithaca, NY: Cornell University Press.

Sobel, Richard. 2001. *The Impact of Public Opinion on U.S. Foreign Policy since Vietnam.* Ithaca, New York: Oxford University Press.

———. (ed.). 1993. *Public Opinion in U.S. Foreign Policy: The Controversy over Contra Aid.* Lanham, MD: Rowman &. Littlefield.

Trubowitz, Peter. 1998. *Defining the National Interest: Conflict and Change in American Foreign Policy.* Chicago: University of Chicago Press.

Walt, Stephen M. 1987. *The Origins of Alliances.* Ithaca, NY: Cornell University Press.

Waltz, Kenneth. 1959. *Man, the State, and War: A Theoretical Analysis.* New York: Columbia University Press.

———. 1979. *Theory of International Politics.* Reading, MA: Addison–Wesley.

Wildavsky, Aaron. 1975. *Budgeting: A Comparative Theory of Budgetary Processes.* Boston: Little, Brown.

———. 1991. The Two Presidencies. In *The Two Presidencies: A Quarter Century Assessment,* ed. S. Shull. Chicago: Nelson-Hall, 11–25.

Winters, Jeffrey A. 1996. *Power in Motion:* Ithaca, NY: Cornell University Press.

Wittkopf, E. 1990. *Faces of Internationalism: Public Opinion and American Foreign Policy.* Durham, NC: Duke University Press.

Lawrence R. Jacobs and Benjamin I. Page, "Who Influences U.S. Foreign Policy," American Political Science Review 99:1 (2005), pp. 107–123. Reproduced with permission of Cambridge University Press.

Foreign-Policy Advising: Models and Mysteries from the Bush Administration

PATRICK J. HANEY

Haney examines the process of presidential decision making in foreign policy through the lens of the Bush Doctrine. Specifically, he analyzes the Bush Administration's decisions regarding both the Iraq War and the continuing embargo of Cuba. He analyzes the effectiveness of the bureaucratic politics model and the role of groupthink in decisionmaking. Haney concludes that, despite the fact that presidents are bound by powerful domestic actors and institutions, they may also take surprisingly unilateral actions on occasion.

There is a wide range of scholarly approaches to studying presidents, advisers, and foreign-policy making, all aiming to capture the genesis of policy, the "essence of decision." While we have made some progress in capturing the complexity of how presidents construct foreign-policy advisory processes, and the kinds of ways they wield power so as to control the policy process, our conceptual models may not be keeping up with practice. While a range of theories exists to explain foreign-policy cases of a variety of types, and may do so in discrete ways, we are less able to come to terms with how the foreign-policy process can be both open to a vast range of forces from inside and outside the White House and dominated by the president using unilateral mechanisms of power all at the same time. I use U.S. policy toward Cuba and in Iraq during the first administration of George W. Bush to illustrate this empirical challenge to our conceptual models.

There is a long tradition in the analysis of U.S. foreign policy to study how presidents assemble teams of advisers to help make decisions. Starting especially in the 1970s, a series of new works helped push our understanding of how presidents put these teams together, how they do their work, and what effects the structuring of decision making has on the process of reaching decisions and policy. Exploring the links among decision structure, process, and outcomes has been a consistent theme in the literature. While we have seen a diverse set of approaches to studying these questions in the last twenty or so years, they all trace themselves back in one way or another to the seminal works by Graham Allison (1971), *Essence of Decision*;Richard T. Johnson (1974), *Managing the White House*;Alexander George (1980), *Presidential Decisionmaking in Foreign Policy: The Effective Use of Information and Advice*;and Irving Janis (1972), *Victims of Groupthink*.

In this article, I try to highlight some of the conceptual developments we see in the literature in understanding presidents and their advisory structures since these works. I do so not in the form of an exhaustive review of the literature but rather by pointing to several examples of the kind of scholarship that has developed around these issues in the domain of foreign policy. Then I use two heuristic cases from the present Bush administration to show how the literature helps us understand some things about the policy process and the role of the president in it but frankly leaves us unable to fully grasp some others. U.S. policy toward Cuba and policy in Iraq, I argue, are interesting because many of the models from the literature are helpful in understanding how President Bush and his advisers work in a broader policy environment to craft foreign policy. But they also show the limits of what we can understand. We have models that help us see the president caught in a vast bureaucracy or porous policy environment rife with congressional and interest group activism where presidents must lead through persuasion; and we have models that help us see the president as the dominant foreign-policy player who leads by fiat. In short, though, what we have yet to develop are theories that help us understand how the president can be both of these things at the same time in the same policy domain. Analysts of foreign-policy decision making have long understood small-group processes, and have perhaps more recently come to appreciate the impact of institutions and domestic politics on decision making, but now must take into account the increasing power of the president to act alone, even when in the midst of a dizzying array of political forces that constrain the White House.

Models of the Foreign-Policy Process

Research that attempts to understand how U.S. presidents have organized the White House for policy making has long explored the possible effects of those structures on policy making. Probably the most well-known study of the process of decision making is Janis's *Victims of Groupthink* (1972). Janis was motivated to explain performance failures, such as the American fiasco at the Bay of Pigs, by examining the internal dynamics or group processes that lead ultimately to group decisions. "Groupthink" is when individuals within cohesive groups seek unanimity or concurrence to such an extent that they cease to vigilantly perform the tasks of decision making. Janis hypothesized that the presence of groupthink during the process of decision making might lead to policy failures. While a psychological phenomenon that cannot be directly observed, Janis argued that groupthink produces behavioral consequences or symptoms that can be observed—and that can be avoided with proper planning.

Richard Johnson takes a more structural approach to these issues; he explores how the president "manage[s] a team of men to provide him with information, staff out his alternatives, and otherwise extend his reach" (1974, xxii) so that the

president can be successful at leadership and policy making. Johnson focuses on how the White House is organized for general policy making. He identifies three generic models of organization that presidents have used—a formalistic, a competitive, and a collegial model of decision making. Alexander George (1980) picks up here and applies Johnson's models to the foreign-policy domain to discuss how modern U.S. presidents structure advisory networks and the impact of that on information processing.

Graham Allison's (1971) approach is to explore how organizational structures and bureaucratic games shape the policy-making process and direct policy outputs or outcomes. This bureaucratic politics approach, or family of approaches, opened the "black box" of decision making to analysis and to explore the ways that internal political processes affect foreign-policy making. An emphasis on the ways that organizational processes and procedures (Allison's Model II) and bureaucratic bargaining and infighting (Allison's Model III) affect the decisions reached by groups is central to this approach. Allison examines these components in American decision making during the October 1962 Cuban Missile Crisis.

A variety of recent approaches to understanding how presidents construct a foreign-policy process are worth mentioning, each representing a broader strain of theoretical and empirical research. In *Organizing the Presidency* (2002), Hess and Pfiffner track the ways that modern U.S. presidents have structured White House operations. Besides describing the organizational styles of each administration, they discuss how presidents learn from the perceived organizational mistakes of each former president in an effort to fine-tune the structure of policy making. Burke and Greenstein (1989) examine the importance of advisory groups as well as presidential personality and the political environment during two cases of American decision making about Vietnam: Eisenhower in 1954 and Johnson in 1964–65. They seek to explain why two presidents who were faced with very similar problems responded in such very different ways. Their analysis indicates that the way presidents organize advisory groups may have an important impact on the process of decision making, but that the individual president's style and the political climate also affect the process of decision making. In my own work (Haney 2002), I tried to take the models developed by Johnson (1974), applied to foreign policy by George (1980), and apply them specifically to foreign-policy crises, showing how presidents constructed hybrids of the ideal types to suit their needs.

In *The Institutional Presidency* (1992), Burke argues that studies of the U.S. presidency need to begin to examine in more depth the nexus between the enduring institutional (structural) features of the presidency and the management strategies and styles of particular presidents, and the implications of each for the other. He attempts to move in this direction by showing how modern U.S. presidents have dealt with these issues. In a similar vein, Ponder explores how presidents have tried to control policy making by centralizing the process inside the White House. He focuses particular importance on the use of staff to help the president. Bringing some of the "new institutionalism" into this domain, he also views the White House as an institution whose rules are determined endogenously, thus open to presidential influence (2000, 176–77). Garrison (1999) also follows in this general approach, examining what she calls the structural, procedural, and interpersonal influence maneuvers used in policy making by different advisers.

Picking up on the evolutionary model of Hult and Walcott (2003), Newmann tracks the development of policy-making structures over time in an administration. He shows how the initial decision-making structures represent what he calls a president's administrative theory—the president's preferences about the methods and goals for foreign-policy making, and the president's beliefs about what is the proper relationship to have with advisers. He shows how these structures change over the course of an administration, and argues that while each president is unique, there are patterns of evolution across administrations (Newmann 2003, 24–25). Newmann shows a general narrowing of participants as the president seeks

advice from an ever smaller number of individuals. He also shows that for policies on which the president places a high priority, he is likely to try to exert more control—by managing the pace of the process; defining policy content; and by excluding participants.

Preston (2001) pursues these issues by asking what difference the personality, leadership style, and policy experience of the president makes for foreign policy. Or, under what circumstances do these factors matter? He uses the "personality at a distance" technique developed by Margaret G. Hermann to "type" leaders along two dimensions of personality and political experience: (1) the need for power or control and the level of presidential involvement in policy making, and (2) the president's need for information (cognitive complexity) and the president's attentiveness to the external environment. This approach also feeds off the earlier effort to show how different foreign-policy decisions are likely made by different kinds of "ultimate decision units." By "decision unit," we mean whether a decision can be reached by a single dominant leader, by a small group, or the result of bargaining among multiple autonomous actors (Hermann, Hermann, and Hagan 1987), and what difference that may make not just for understanding the processes involved but potentially what impact it has on outcomes as well.

In a study that picks up from Janis's work on groupthink more than Johnson's (1974) or George's (1980), Herek, Janis, and Huth (1987) use a case survey methodology to try to study the relationship between decision-making processes and crisis outcomes across a variety of cases in American foreign policy. They show that in general, the greater the number of decision-making process defects there are, the more likely the decision reached is to lead to a policy failure—thus drawing attention to the importance of constructing sound or vigilant foreign-policy advisory processes.

While each of the examples of newer literature on foreign-policy advising rakes its own unique approach, there is a common ground among these otherwise diverse works—progressing from the starting points laid out by Allison, Janis, Johnson, and George. I would argue that increasingly work in this area also shares a basic acceptance of the "new institutionalism," summarized by March and Olsen in their argument that institutions affect the flow of political life through them. They take as their basic assumption that the organization of political life matters, that institutions "define the framework within which politics takes place" (March and Olsen 1989, 18). Our models of understanding the interplay among psychology, interpersonal dynamics, and decision structures have become more sophisticated. Our understanding of the dangers of flawed processes has become more certain. And our capacity for taking into account not just the broad political environment but the broader institutional environment within which presidents and their advisers must work has also increased. These theoretical and empirical developments help us understand much about the presidency and foreign-policy making today, but as the two cases to which I turn now suggest, we are still faced with serious empirical challenges.

Tightening the Grip on Cuba (Policy)

The policy process that surrounds the U.S. embargo of Cuba is one that has evolved over time from an era of tight presidential control in the Eisenhower and Kennedy era to one that is now widely recognized as infused with domestic political and electoral interests and congressional and interest group activism. If policy toward the island was run out of the Oval Office in the 1960s, by the 1980s it was largely driven by the powerful ethnic interest group, the Cuban American National Foundation, which had close ties to the Reagan campaign and White House. But in the 1990s, Congress became much more involved in setting the course of policy toward Cuba, ultimately codifying the embargo into law in the controversial Helms-Burton Act in 1996. President Clinton tried to reassert presidential control by using "licensing" power embedded in the law to allow certain kinds of exchange with the island in 1998 and 1999, thus essentially ignoring Helms-Burton and daring Congress to do something about it. His efforts to establish a "blue ribbon" commission to study and make recommendations on U.S.

policy toward Cuba, however, were thwarted by domestic political considerations when Cuban Americans in south Florida began calling the commission the "Gore Commission"—a sure sign of electoral danger for the Democrats in Florida in 2000. Many saw the idea of such a commission as a way for the Clinton-Gore administration to get political cover for loosening if not calling for an end to the embargo.

The response from many in Congress who were moving to a more negative view of the embargo but who nevertheless wanted to continue to set policy toward Cuba, led by business interests and farm state Republicans, interestingly, began to allow the sale of food and medicine to Cuba in 2000. At the same time, many in Congress began to set their sights on killing the "travel ban" that prevents U.S. citizens from visiting the island and spending money by eliminating money for its enforcement from the Treasury Department budget (see Bardach 2002; Brenner, Haney, and Vanderbush 2002; Fisk 2000, 2001; Haney and Vanderbush, 2005; Kaplowitz 1998; Kiger 1997; Morley and McGillion 2002; Torres 1999).

The point of this brief review is to suggest that the policy process around U.S. Cuba policy had largely escaped the firm grasp of the White House by the time President George W. Bush came to office. The range of actors involved in Cuba policy, and its center of gravity on the Hill rather than in the White House, had come to make the Cuba policy process look more like a domestic-policy issue than a foreign-policy one. And momentum was shifting away from the embargo and toward increased openness with the island. As George W. Bush came to Washington, Cuba policy did not seem an area ripe for tight presidential control as one might expect in other foreign-policy cases. Even after the attacks of September 11, when the Bush administration suggested that Cuba was not playing a productive role in the war against terrorism and that Cuba had a biological weapons capacity, the range of anti-embargo—and especially anti-travel ban—forces continued to grow (Davies and Tamayo 2002; Miller 2002). Bush had to resort to the use of a "recess appointment" to put his preferred person at the State Department as assistant secretary for the Western Hemisphere, Otto Reich, whom the Senate would not confirm.

Bush made no moves to change the "wet foot/dry foot" immigration policy that Clinton established. And he did not allow the lawsuits against foreign companies for "trafficking" in stolen property in Cuba that had belonged to U.S. nationals to proceed. This right to sue is provided in Helms-Burton but was waived by Clinton every six months. Candidate Bush seemed to indicate he might allow the suits to proceed, but in the face of heavy pressure from allies (whose companies would be the objects of the lawsuits), he has continued to exercise the waiver that blocks the suits, including in January 2005—the first such opportunity since his reelection. In other words, Cuba policy can at first glance seem largely outside of the president's control. Advised on Cuba policy by his brother Jeb Bush, the Governor of Florida with close ties to the conservative Cuban-American community, Congressman Lincoln Diaz-Balart (R-FL), and others, Bush has mostly not engaged in Cuba policy except to try to fight back efforts to end the travel ban (including threatening to veto a spending bill that did not include money for the enforcement of the travel ban).

Thus, this first look at the Cuba policy process seems to show a porous process with little opportunity for firm presidential control. Such a process would seem not well-suited to a type of analysis that examines the president's advisory system as if it were the genesis of policy. And I would argue that this look does reflect one reality about the Cuba policy process. But there is another policy and process that must be balanced against this view—one dominated by President Bush and a relatively small group of like-minded insiders. This policy process would seem ripe for exactly the type of analysis for which Cuba policy seemed inappropriate before.

Many of the most hard-line anti-Castro Cuban Americans in Miami, those who worked hard for Bush's election in 2000 and his brother's in 2002, were less than thrilled with what little effort the administration made to reverse some of the policies from the Clinton administration with which they disagreed, such as the wet foot/dry foot and the lack of full implementation of Helms-Burton. With respect to Bush's Cuba policy, one noted analyst, Damian Fernandez, commented: "He's tiptoeing around the margins. . . . The question is one of heightened expectations. For many in the Cuban American community, it's 'We voted for you; you won Florida; you promised—where are the deliverables'" (quoted in Bumiller 2003).

In an effort to court these voters in Florida—voters who turn out to the polls in extremely high numbers—for the 2004 election, Bush formed the President's Commission for Assistance to a Free Cuba. The commission released its report in May 2004, and called for tightening the embargo by limiting family visits to the island, for redefining "family" to mean only *immediate* family, and for a reduction in the amount of money that could be spent during family visits, among other things. President Bush took a number of their suggestions, including the more limited definition of what constitutes a family for the purposes of sending money home to "family," and announced new limits on family travel (now only one visit every three years instead of one per year, with no exceptions) and remittances, as well as a $45 million increase in funds to promote a democratic transition on the island (San Martin and Ross 2004). Some suggested that the moves would cost Bush votes from moderate members of the exile community whose travel to Cuba and ability to help members of their family still living on the island was made more difficult by these reforms (see Yanez 2004). Perhaps in response to this potential loss of support, the Bush administration did not immediately move to enforce the restrictions on travel and spending by Cuban Americans, though they eventually did (see Tyler 2004).

In this case, we see the president enacting a set of reforms that were unpopular with many, though very popular with a select few. While there was a veneer of "inclusion" in the process, in the form of the commission, it appears the policy was the result of a small group of policy/political advisers and the president himself. What was really more an interagency committee than a "commission" of experts was chaired by Secretary of State Colin Powell and

Secretary of Housing and Urban Development, and Cuban American, Mel Martinez. The merging of politics and policy, and the effort by the White House to take control of policy and create a process that existed alongside yet largely separate from the dynamics with which we had become accustomed for Cuba policy, is striking.

Cuba policy under President Bush has certainly been affected by his political advisers' calculations about Cuban-American voters, but that is only one of a variety of factors that currently shape U.S. policy toward Cuba. U.S. economic interests, including both the larger desire to maintain global trade momentum and the particular interests of various domestic economic groups, are also part of the story. Institutional interests are also on display as members of the legislature compete with the executive for control over policy (see Haney and Vanderbush 2005). All this serves to remind us that understanding the policy process today is not just about understanding the president and his policy and advisory preferences. Nor is it only about trying to build a type of explanation that can account for the impact of forces in the larger political and institutional environment on the president. Rather, it is trying to find ways to study both at the same time, even when that seems paradoxical. How can the president be both a virtual policy bystander, or perhaps a "first among equals," and a driving force at the center of decisions at the same time? Or put another way, how can a policy domain be characterized as being driven by a "predominant leader," "multiple autonomous actors," and "small groups" (Hermann, Hermann, and Hagan 1987), all at the same time? I would argue that coming to terms with this complexity is perhaps the central challenge of studying presidents, advisers, and foreign-policy making today.

The Vulcans, the Exiles, the Reporters, and Iraq

The decision to invade Iraq, and to thus put the Bush Doctrine into full effect, is a similarly puzzling mix of a porous policy environment alongside a strikingly powerful president. In an era when we had become accustomed to seeing presidents unable to cut through the bureaucracy at State or Defense, or to escape the oversight of Congress, President Bush both reflected those expectations and at other times entirely destroyed them. How a handful of people were able to wrest control of the bureaucracy and outmaneuver Congress and the public to move forward with a war in Iraq is no easy question to handle. Even Richard Haass, then director of Policy Planning at the State Department, has trouble answering how this came about. "I will go to my grave not knowing that. I can't answer it. I can't explain the strategic obsession with Iraq—why it rose to the top of people's priority list" (Lemann 2004, 157).

One thing is certain: the policy process involved in Iraq policy was run by a small, tightly controlled group of loyalists, who Mann calls the "Vulcans," and yet at the same time the process was surrounded by a wide range of outsiders and outside interests pushing in all directions. On the porous side of the equation, there were outside groups such as the Iraqi National Congress and its leader Ahmed Chalabi pushing for regime change in Iraq, and of course Congress and even the Clinton administration had called for such a change. The Project for a new American Century had called for such a policy as prelude to a wider remaking of the Middle East. Chalabi had close ties to Richard Perle, then chairman of the Defense Policy Board, a nongovernmental advisory panel for the secretary of defense. And former Director of Central Intelligence James Woolsey had become a mainstay on television calling for Saddam's ouster (Mann 2004, 334–36; Hersh 2004, 168). These were outsiders but their close personal connections linked them in important ways to those inside the administration.

But the group around the president was (and is) small. Richard Clarke said that Bush "doesn't reach out, typically, for a lot of experts. He has a very narrow, regulated, highly regimented set of channels to get advice" (quoted in Lemann 2004). Woodward also said that Bush told him, with respect to Iraq, "I have no outside advice. Anybody who says they're an outside adviser of this administration on this particular matter is not telling the truth" (quoted in Lemann 2004).

The vision that tied the group around Bush together was that of an "unchallengeable America, a United States whose military power was so awesome that it no longer needed to make compromises or accommodations (unless it chose to do so) with any other nation or groups of countries" (Mann 2004, xii). Insiders included Bush, Vice President Cheney, his chief of staff Lewis "Scooter" Libby, National Security Adviser Condoleezza Rice, Secretary of Defense Donald Rumsfeld, his deputy Paul Wolfowitz, the Undersecretary for Policy Douglas Feith, Secretary of State Colin Powell, and his deputy Richard Armitage and undersecretary Marc Grossman, Rice's deputy Stephen Hadley, the NSC's regional specialist for Iraq Zalmay Khalilzad, the NSC counterterrorism expert General Wayne Downing, DCI George Tenet, Deputy Director of the CIA John McLaughlin, and the chairman and vice chairman of the Joint Chiefs of State. They all agreed that containment was not a viable plan for Saddam and wanted regime change (Mann 2004, 332–33).

This group of insiders also worked to make it clear that dissent would not be tolerated. Richard Clarke recalls that the day following the 9/11 attacks Bush said to him: "Look, I know you have a lot to do and all . . . but I want you, as soon as you can, to go back over everything, everything. See if Saddam did this. See if he's linked in any way." After an effort to assure the president that there is no good evidence there, Bush said testily, "Look into Iraq, Saddam" (Clarke 2004, 32). When General Eric Shinseki, then chief of staff of the Army, testified before Congress in February 2003 and in response to a question about force levels expressed concern that present force levels were too low, his view was quickly repudiated at the Pentagon and his successor—with Shinseki still months from retirement—was named by the administration (Daalder and Lindsay 2003, 150; Clarke 2004, 270).

In another example, according to Hersh, in the summer of 2001 a career officer at the Pentagon was assigned the task of rethinking the assumptions of the Vulcans about Saddam's ouster, a "what could go wrong?" study. But the officer found that no one cared, and he was told that the Pentagon's leadership "wanted to focus not on what could go wrong but what would go right" (2004, 168–69). In another example, a group called the Pentagon's Office of Special Plans was established to go back through all the intelligence available about Iraq, weapons of mass destruction (WMD), and terrorism, including data from the Iraqi National Congress, and assemble a picture that would be persuasive to the public (Hersh 2004, 207–11). According to Hersh, they called themselves "the cabal" (2004, 207). Before long the public discourse was dominated by the view that Saddam would easily be overthrown and U.S. forces would be greeted as liberators with flowers and chocolates.[1]

The record seems mixed on from whence came the genesis of the policy shift toward the Bush Doctrine and the war in Iraq and away from the tenets of containment and realism. What is clear is that many came to the administration with not just a long history with Saddam but with a formed opinion that he should go and American military power should be used to accomplish this, even in the form of an all-out invasion. Clarke asserts that "the Administration began with Iraq on the agenda" (2004, 264). Many of the people now inside the administration were part of a group actively calling for his overthrow during the Clinton administration. And Cheney, Rumsfeld, and Wolfowitz had long been part of the wing of the Republican Party that had been less accepting of détente and containment in the Cold War; with that gone, they began to assert a new more powerful role for the United States, led by military power, to reshape the political map. Then the attacks of September 11 helped underscore the realities of this new system and the potential for American power to reshape it (Mann 2004, 339). The question many ask is, "Where was Bush on September 10th?" Was he with the neoconservative Vulcans, or not? The view in PBS's *Frontline* (2003) suggests he may not have been, that the attacks provided the opportunity for Cheney, Rumsfeld, and Wolfowitz to win the president's ear over Powell and others seen as more "realists" and less as neoconservatives. But Daalder and Lindsay disagree: "September 11 did more to reaffirm Bush's view of the world than to transform it" (2003, 79). This view

included the key points that "the world is a dangerous place. . . . International agreements and institutions could not protect the American people; that
only the might of the American military could"
(2003, 80).

Having set their sights on Iraq, starting on at
least September 12 according to Clarke, the administration sold its case that Iraq posed a test case of
the Bush Doctrine: a case for preemptive military
action against an imminent threat from WMD
either delivered directly or indirectly by giving the
weapons to al Qaeda. Because no WMD stockpiles
were found in Iraq, or even advanced programs to
develop the weapons, many have begun to point to
a range of other reasons for the now clearly preventive war in Iraq (see Mandelbaum 1995; Daalder
and Lindsay 2003, 127). But even Haass admits that
"the only serious argument for war was weapons of
mass destruction" (quoted in Lemann 2004, 158).
And there is reason to believe that at the upper
levels of the government they *knew* Saddam had no
such weapons. Richard Clarke argues Bush and his
advisers "had to know there was no imminent
threat" from Iraq (2004, 268). The uranium tubes
story and the African uranium story both seemed
flimsy at best. But the press was not well situated to
confront Bush and his advisers. In his book *Plan of
Attack,* Woodward concedes that he had his doubts
about the intelligence on WMD, but nevertheless
he was in no position to take on the administration:
"I did not feel I had enough information to effectively challenge the official conclusions about Iraq's
alleged WMD. In light of subsequent events, I
should have pushed for a page one story, even on
the eve of war, presenting more forcefully what our
sources were saying" (2004, 355–56). Other journalists pushed stories that highlighted certain intelligence, only to have it turn out to be false as well
(see, e.g., Editors 2004; Jackson 2003).

Within this porous political environment the
president was nonetheless able to act with great unilateral and relatively unchecked power. Another
domain in which this story played itself out was with
respect to the way prisoners suspected of being terrorists could be treated under U.S. law. The White
House developed a very broad interpretation of what

constitutes torture and the process involved in drafting that ruling perhaps looks familiar. White House
Counsel Alberto R. Gonzales, "working closely with
a small group of conservative legal officials at the
White House, the Justice Department and the Defense Department—and overseeing deliberations
that generally excluded potential dissenters—helped
chart other legal paths in the handling and imprisonment of suspected terrorists and the applicability
of international conventions to U.S. military and law
enforcement activities" (Smith and Eggen 2005).

And of course there is more to be written in the
future on how the president, in the midst of an en-
tangling web of powerful actors, nonetheless acts
with great unilateral authority. According to Hersh,
President Bush has made the decision to expand
the war on terrorism to Iran through covert means
(for now) and has placed such actions under the
Pentagon's control. "The President has signed a
series of findings and executive orders authorizing
secret commando groups and other Special Forces
units to conduct covert operations against suspected terrorist targets in as many as ten nations in
the Middle East and South Asia." By assigning the
job to the Defense Department rather than the
CIA, Bush "enables Rumsfeld to run the operations
off the books—free from legal restrictions imposed
on the C.I.A." (Hersh 2005).

Two standard theories of foreign-policy advising seem to explain some of this pattern. First, the
bureaucratic politics explanation, with its focus on
players in position who vie to win the game of
policy, seems to have some traction here. Inside the
Bush administration are a core of actors who have
long held a different view of the role of American
power in world affairs, and a strong view about
Saddam. Once inside government not at a tertiary
level but as key players, and aided by the changed
political environment after the attacks of 9/11, these
actors seized the day and changed the direction of
American foreign policy, one might argue. Depending on one's view, President Bush was either
always with this group or was persuaded to join
them after 9/11. The versions of the policy process
found in Woodward (2004), Daalder and Lindsay
(2003), and Clarke (2004), and most other versions

of the emergence of the Bush Doctrine and the war in Iraq, all seem to reflect versions of this bureaucratic politics explanation. Lemann's counterfactual about how the administration would not only be staffed differently but would perhaps not have gone into Iraq had Cheney not joined the ticket, but instead someone like former Senator John Danforth (R-MO), for example, also seems energized by such a perspective (2004, 150). Perhaps the thing that the bureaucratic politics approach helps us see best is the way that solutions can wait for years until the right problem emerges. The neoconservatives had long pushed for regime change in Iraq, bur after 9/11 their policy had its day.

But such a focus may put too much emphasis on players in position and not enough on the power of ideas. One can see in Mann (2004) and Daalder and Lindsay (2003) a strong core set of beliefs about the role of U.S. power in the world that predated the end of the Cold War and that came to fruition after 9/11. Foreign-policy analysis has begun to take into account this competition of ideas, and I would argue this perspective helps lend insight into the current policy process.

Another view of the advisory process and its link to the lack of WMD in Iraq and the underestimation of the level of violence in postwar Iraq that is worth some consideration in this case is Janis's groupthink hypothesis. The team of advisers around President Bush would seem to fit Janis's description of relatively small, cohesive, and like minded. There appears to have been some pressure exerted on dissenters in this case, and an overestimation of the ability to find WMD and to bring about security and democracy in Iraq. This all fits in Janis's model of the organizational prerequisites for group-think and some of the behavioral symptoms of groupthink that could contribute to policy failure. But on the WMD side of the equation, there is perhaps some reason to believe that many in the administration knew, or suspected, there were no such weapons in Iraq. While it appears true that DCI George Tenet told the president that with respect to WMD in Iraq it was a "slam dunk case," Clarke suggests that many knew the case was not so clear-cut and that this clarity, and the mushroom

cloud imagery, was part of a public relations strategy more than it was policy analysis. My view would be that it cannot be groupthink if they knew there were no WMD in Iraq. Only with the passage of more time will we be able to come to more satisfying answers about how this policy process developed, what was an intelligence failure, what was a conceptual error, and what was incompetence, and what may have been purposeful deception. In any event, the answers to these questions have great significance not just for our understanding of the policy advising process but also for the health of the republic.

Models and Mysteries: Studying a Different Kind of Power?

In *Essence of Decision,* Allison was not only making a point about the policy process; he was making a powerful statement about the *study* of the policy process. Analysts, Allison argued, needed to add these new conceptual models to their analytic tool kit so as to be able to see these things when they happened. Without understanding how presidential power and policy making might work, we would not even know it if we saw it. I would argue that those who study presidents, advisers, and foreign policy have largely taken Allison's warning to heart, but the Cuba and Iraq cases suggest that while we can see and understand much, our models have not mastered political reality. Having settled on the idea, for example, that a policy might be driven by a "small group," by a "single dominant leader," or by "multiple autonomous actors" (Hermann, Hermann, and Hagan 1987), we have yet to capture how a policy might be driven by two or even three of these constructs all at the same time. How can the president be so weak, so embedded in a range of powerful actors, and yet still also act—in the same policy domain—with striking unilateral power with few if any checks?

In recent books, Louis Fisher (2000) and Gordon Silverstein (1997) each make compelling arguments that since World War II the president has garnered significant unilateral control over much of foreign policy and war power, often with the unwitting (and even witting) help of Congress.

Mayer makes a similar point with his new institutional approach, which "begins with the assumption that presidents seek control over policy and process" (2001, 24). For Mayer, the politics of the presidency is about getting control of the institutions that create and implement policy. While the conventional wisdom is that the presidency is weak and thus leadership must rest in Neustadt-like persuasion, Mayer argues that throughout U.S. history presidents have relied on their executive authority to make unilateral policy without interference from either Congress or the courts. While both Cuba policy and policy with respect to the war in Iraq are policy domains in which President Bush is encased in interested and powerful actors and institutions, often left relatively powerless among them, he at other times has been able to act with surprising strength and without constraint. Kelley (forthcoming) devotes an edited volume to the different ways presidents have come to rely on their command powers to control policy unto themselves. And Ponder makes the point too: just because other institutions are out there does not mean the presidency is weak (2000, 199).

If in the 1970s the central challenge for those who studied foreign-policy advising was to take into account a new literature from psychology and organizational theory and apply it to foreign-policy cases, and if over time that challenge became broadened to include an appreciation for how Congress, interest groups, and public opinion also set the political environment in which presidents and advisers work, then the central challenge for us today is to take into account the growing literature on the unilateral executive. This challenge, though, is not just to take into account another new (or renewed) line of theory, it is to find ways to see this powerful unilateral president as existing alongside the more powerless one we see when we embed the president in an array of other powerful forces. How can the president be both Gulliver, tied down by the Lilliputians, and the Puppetmaster, pulling the strings, at the same time?

As Allison reminds us, we must know what we *might* see if we are to see it at all. Many of our approaches to understanding presidents and advisers

in foreign-policy making are perhaps too narrow; others may be too imprecise. The challenge of the Bush Doctrine for us as analysts is not only that it represents a potentially dramatic policy change, but also that it underscores the limits of our models. We know enough from our models as they stand that the foreign-policy process we see today is extraordinary in a variety of ways, and we need to keep up if we are to truly understand just how extraordinary it may be.

Notes

1. Today many of the same actors call the insurgents in Iraq just a few hundred (or perhaps a few thousand) "dead-enders," contrary to the report released by the National Intelligence Council that calls Iraq the new central training ground for the next generation of professional terrorists (see Priest 2005, A01).

References

Allison, Graham T. 1971. *Essence of Decision*. Boston; Little, Brown.

Bardach, Anne Louise. 2002. *Cuba Confidential: Love and Vengeance in Miami and Havana*. New York: Random House.

Brenner, Phillip, Patrick J. Haney, and Walt Vanderbush. 2002. The Confluence of Domestic and International Interests: U.S. Policy toward Cuba, 1998–2001. *International Studies Perspectives* 3 (May): 192–208.

Bumiller, Elisabeth. 2003. Bush Promises Cuban Americans to Keep Up Pressure on Castro. *New York Times* (Oct. 11), p. A5.

Burke, John P. 1992. *The Institutional Presidency*. Baltimore: Johns Hopkins University Press.
Burke, John P., and Fred I. Greenstein. 1989. *How Presidents Test Reality*. New York: Sage.

Clarke, Richard A. 2004. *Against All Enemies: Inside America's War on Terror*. New York: Free Press.

Daalder, Ivo H., and James M. Lindsay. 2003. *America Unbound: The Bush Revolution on Foreign Policy*. Washington, DC: Brookings.

Davies, Frank, and Juan O. Tamayo. 2002. Cuba Hampers War on Terror, U.S. Says. *Miami Herald* (September 18). Available at http://www .hermanos.org/docs/tmh091802.htm.

Editors of the *New York Times*. 2004. The Times and Iraq. *New York Times* (May 16). Available at http://www.nytimes.com/2004/05/26/international/middleeast/26FTE_NOTE.html.

Fisher, Louis. 2000. *Congressional Abdication on War and Spending*. College Station: Texas A&M Press.

Fisk, Daniel W. 2000. Economic Sanctions: The Cuba Embargo Revisited. In *Sanctions as Economic Statecraft*, ed. Steve Chan and A. Cooper Drury, pp. 65–85. New York: St. Martin's.

———. 2001. Cuba: The End of an Era. *Washington Quarterly* 24(Winter): 93–107.

Frontline. 2003. *The War Behind Closed Doors* (Feb. 20). Available at http://www.pbs.org/wgbh/pages/frontline/shows/Iraq/.

Garrison, Jean A. 1999. *Games Advisors Play: Foreign Policy in the Nixon and Carter Administrations*. College Station: Texas A&M Press.

George, Alexander L. 1980. *Presidential Decision Making in Foreign Policy: The Effective Use of Information and Advice*. Boulder, CO: Westview Press.

Haney, Patrick J. 2002. *Organizing for Foreign Policy: Presidents, Advisers, and the Management of Decision Making*. 2nd ed. Ann Arbor, MI: University of Michigan Press.

Haney, Patrick J., and Walt Vanderbush. 2005. *The Cuban Embargo: The Domestic Politics of an American Foreign Policy*. Pittsburgh, PA: University of Pittsburgh Press.

Herek, Gregory M., Irving L. Janis, and Paul Huth. 1987. Decision Making during International Crises. *Journal of Conflict Resolution* 31 (2): 203–26.

Hermann, Margaret G., Charles F. Hermann, and Joe D. Hagan. 1987. How Decision Units Shape Foreign Policy Behavior. In *New Directions in the Study of Foreign Policy,* ed. Charles F. Hermann, Charles W. Kegley, and James N. Rosenau, pp. 309–36. Boston: Unwin Hyman.

Hersh, Seymour M. 2004. *Chain of Command: The Road from 9/11 to Abu Ghraib*. New York: Harper Collins.

———. 2005. The Coming Wars. *The New Yorker* (Jan. 24). Available at http://www.newyorker.com/fact/content/?050124fa_fact.

Hess, Stephen, and James P. Pfiffner. 2002. *Organizing the Presidency*. 3rd ed. Washington, DC: Brookings.

Hult, Karen M., and Charles E. Walcott. 2003. *Empowering the White House: Governance under Nixon. Ford, and Carter*. Lawrence: University Press of Kansas.

Jackson, William E., Jr. 2003. Miller's Star Fades (Slightly) at "NY Times." *Editor & Publisher* (Oct. 2). Available at http://www.editorandpublisher.com/eandp/news/article_display.jsp?vnu_content_id=1991338.

Janis, Irving L. 1972. *Victims of Groupthink: A Psychological Study of Foreign-Policy Decisions and Fiascoes*. Boston: Houghton Mifflin.

Johnson, Richard T. 1974. *Managing the White House*. New York: Harper & Row.

Kaplowitz, Donna Rich. 1998. *Anatomy of a Failed Embargo: US Sanctions against Cuba*. Boulder, CO: Lynne Rienner.

Kelley, Christopher S., ed. Forthcoming. *Executing the Constitution: Putting the President Back into the Constitution*. Albany: State University of New York Press.

Kiger, Patrick J. 1997. *Squeeze Play: The United States, Cuba, and the Helms-Burton Act*. Washington, DC: Center for Public Integrity.

Lemann, Nicholas. 2004. Remember the Alamo: How George W. Bush Reinvented Himself. *The New Yorker* (Oct. 18): 148–61.

Mandelbaum, Michael. 1995. Lessons of the Next Nuclear War. *Foreign Affairs* 74 (Mar./April): 22–37.

Mann, James. 2004. *Rise of the Vulcans: A History of Bush's War Cabinet*. New York: Viking. March, James G., and Johan P. Olsen. 1989. *Rediscovering Institutions*. New York: Free Press. Mayer, Kenneth R. 2001. *With the Stroke of a Pen: Executive Orders and Presidential Power*. Princeton, NJ: Princeton University Press.

Miller, Judith. 2002. Washington Accuses Cuba of Germ-Warfare Research. *New York Times* (May 7), p. A6.

Morley, Morris H., and Chris McGillion. 2002. *Unfinished Business: America and Cuba after the Cold War, 1989–2001*. New York: Cambridge University Press.

Newmann, William W. 2003. *Managing National Security Policy: The President and the Process.* Pittsburgh, PA: University of Pittsburgh Press.

Ponder, Daniel E. 2000. *Good Advice: Information and Policy Making in the White House.* College Station: Texas A&M Press.

Preston, Thomas. 2001. *The President and his Inner Circle.* New York: Columbia University Press.

Priest, Dana. 2005. Iraq New Terror Breeding Ground: War Created Haven, CIA Advisers Report. *Washington Post* (Jan. 14), p. A01.

San Martin, Nancy, and Karl Ross. 2004. Bush to Tighten Cuba Sanctions, Seek New Funds. *Miami Herald. Herald,* May 7, p. 1A.

Silverstein, Gordon. 1997. *Imbalance of Powers.* New York: Oxford University Press.

Smith, R. Jeffrey, and Dan Eggen, 2005. Gonzales Helped Set the Course for Detainees: Justice Nominee's Hearings Likely to Focus On interrogation Policies. *Washington Post* (Jan. 5), p. A01.

Torres, Maria de los Angeles. 1999. *In the Land of Mirrors: Cuban Exile Politics in the United States.* Ann Arbor: University of Michigan Press.

Tyler, Jeff. 2004. Getting Along with Cuba. *National Public Radio: Marketplace* (June 8). Available at http://marketplace.publicradio.org/shows/2004/06/08_mpp.html.

Woodward, Bob. 2004. *Plan of Attack.* New York: Simon & Schuster.

Yanez, Luisa. 2004. Policy on Cuba Will Cost Bush Votes, Group Warns. *Miami Herald* (May 11), p. 5B.

The Relationships between Mass Media, Public Opinion, and Foreign Policy

Toward a Theoretical Synthesis

MATTHEW A. BAUM AND PHILIP B. K. POTTER

Baum and Potter consider the role of public opinion on the decision making of foreign policy elites, and examine the role of the mass media in moderating that relationship. They discuss the "rally round the flag" phenomenon, casualty aversion, "wag the dog" diversions, and the "CNN effect." They argue that the mass media actually serves as an autonomous and strategic actor in its influence on U.S. foreign policy decision making.

Democracy requires that citizens' opinions play some role in shaping policy outcomes, including in foreign policy. Yet, although the literature on public opinion and foreign policy has made great progress in recent decades, scholars have reached no consensus concerning what the public thinks, or thinks about, with respect to foreign policy; how it comes to hold those opinions; or whether those opinions influence (or even should influence) foreign policy. In this article, we first review the extensive gains in scholarly knowledge in the area of public opinion and foreign policy over the past several decades, emphasizing relatively recent work. We then suggest a framework, based on the concept of market equilibrium, aimed at synthesizing the disparate research programs that constitute the literature on public opinion and foreign policy. To do so, in addition to considering the relationship between leaders and the public, we incorporate a third strategic actor, the mass media, which we believe plays a critical role alongside citizens and elites in shaping the public's attitudes about, and influence on, foreign policy. Our goal is to clarify the multifaceted relationships between these actors and foreign policy outcomes.

Introduction

Following the invasion of Iraq in March 2003, members of Congress from both parties, and the Bush administration, complained that biased media coverage was turning public opinion against the war. Congressman James Marshall (D-GA) opined that reporters were painting a "falsely bleak picture" that "weakens our national resolve" (Marshall 2003). President Bush struck a similar chord, claiming, "We're making good progress in Iraq. Sometimes it's hard to tell when you listen to the filter [media]" (Bush 2003). Defense Secretary Donald Rumsfeld added that "the news media seem to want to carry the negative" (Rumsfeld 2005). These statements reflect two assumptions widely shared by decision makers of all political perspectives: First, that the mass media often fail to deliver the messages policy makers think they should convey, and second, that the media shape public opinion about foreign policy.

Yet, although political leaders routinely assume that the media wield independent influence on public opinion and policy, most political science scholarship reduces the media's role to a "conveyor belt" that passively transports elite views (e.g., Jentleson 1992, Brody 1991)—particularly the views of the most powerful elites (Zaller & Chiu 2000, Bennett et al. 2006)—to the public. In contrast, a parallel literature in political communication (Kuypers 1997, Graber 2002, Paletz 2002) details the processes by which the media shape political opinions. This literature does not consistently link the relationship between media coverage and public opinion to policy outcomes.

There is, however, an emerging recognition among scholars who study the interactions of the public, leaders, and the media that these actors are interdependent and that exclusive attention to one or two of the three may distort theoretical predictions and empirical findings (Entman 2000, Nacos et al. 2000, Holsti 2004).

In this article, we first review the extensive gains in scholarly knowledge in this area over the past several decades, with emphasis on relatively recent work. We then begin to synthesize into a more coherent framework the disparate research programs that constitute the literature on public opinion and foreign policy. Our goal is to clarify the multifaceted relationships between these actors and link them to foreign policy outcomes. Although many of the insights from this literature are intended to be general, until quite recently scholarship—and especially empirical research—has largely focused on the U.S. case. Hence, this is our primary, albeit not our exclusive, focus.

The key to such a synthesis lies in determining how to fit the mass media into this complex set of interrelationships. Are the media a causal or a caused variable, an intervening variable between public opinion and foreign policy, or primarily a conveyor belt for messages from the elite to the public, as the political science literature often implies?[1]

In our view, the media are engaged in a constant process of framing the news in response to the often competing requirements of leaders and the public.

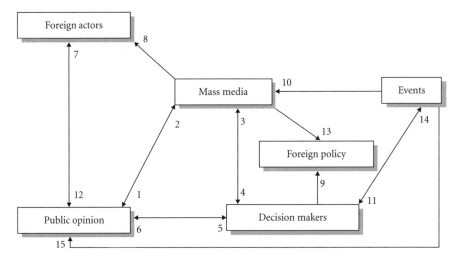

1) Paletz 2002, Graber 2002, Reese 2001, Baum 2003
2) Hamilton 2003, Zaller unpublished manuscript
3) Cohen 1963, Sigal 1973, Bennett 1990, Brody 1991
4) Powlick 1995, Denham 1997, Merril 1995, Malek 1996
5) Powlick 1991, Eisinger 2003, Meuller 1995
6) Zaller 1992, Lewis 2001, Brody 2001, Jentleson 1992
7) Evans, Jacobson, & Putnam 1993
8) Finel & Lord 1999

9) Hermann & Hermann 1989, Mintz 2004, Kolodziej 1981
10) Gartner 2004, Graber 1997, Tifft & Jones 1999
11) Behr & Iyengar 1985, Andrade & Young 1996
12) Manheim & Albritton 1984, Zhang & Cameron 2003
13) Sharkey 1993, Wolfsfeld 2004, Stetch 1994, Rotberg & Weiss 1996
14) DeRound & Peake 2000, Clark 2003, James & Oneal 1991, Meernik 2004
15) Feaver & Gelpi 2004, Mueller 1973, Slantchev 2004, Kull & Ramsay 2001

Figure 1. **Prior specifications of causality in relationship(s) between the mass media, public opinion, and foreign policy. The citations associated with each arrow are illustrative rather than exhaustive. They represent simplifications of the authors' arguments, intended to highlight the absence of a clear causal chain across the broader system.**

Consequently—although, consistent with indexing theories (e.g., Hallin 1986, Bennett 1990, Zaller & Chiu 2000), political elites clearly influence news media content—we believe the mass media are nonetheless more accurately characterized as a discrete strategic actor. As such, the media's framing of elite rhetoric has an independent causal effect on public perceptions of conflict characteristics, and through this process, on foreign policy.

Indeed, we argue that the media influence nearly every aspect of the relationship between public opinion and foreign policy. Hence, any comprehensive theoretical framework attempting to account for either public opinion regarding foreign policy or the effects of public opinion on foreign policy requires an interdisciplinary approach that incorporates public opinion, elite preferences, and the mass media as independent strategic actors with distinct preferences and incentives.

The literature outlines a dizzying array of interactions between the public, leaders, and the media, the complexity of which is evident in **Figure 1**. Even this highly stylized representation of the literature reveals studies maintaining that the media influence public opinion, public opinion influences the media, public opinion influences decision makers, decision makers influence public opinion, decision makers influence the media, foreign policy influences public opinion, decision makers influence events, and the media influence foreign policy. This is further complicated by feedback from both foreign actors and the emerging "facts on the ground." In short, scholars have investigated every conceivable causal link between the public, decision makers (foreign and domestic), and the media. We believe this web of causal arrows has become so dense that further investigation into these narrow individual pathways is likely to produce diminishing returns.

The early stages of many research programs are characterized by scholarly emphasis on delineating causal pathways among the constituent elements within a broader theoretical framework. This is frequently how knowledge accumulates. Eventually, enough of the linear relationships become illuminated that the proverbial "hidden face within the picture" emerges. However, that face can also be obscured by the very foundational research aimed at revealing it. Some scholars have observed such a pattern in the scientific study of public opinion and foreign policy (e.g., Robinson 2000, Entman 2003).

We argue that a clearer understanding of the media-opinion-foreign policy nexus emerges when, rather than exploring static snapshots of bilateral relationships between foreign policy actors, we consider them together as coequal players within a market that produces foreign policy outcomes through dynamic interaction.[2] The circularity of the relationships between leaders, the media, and public opinion in the foreign policy arena is in many respects analogous to the classical economic notions of supply and demand, and of producers and consumers in a marketplace. This foreign policy marketplace is driven primarily by the distribution of the key market commodity—information—among

these three actors. Typically, information favors leadership; however, certain dynamics can lead the public to overcome its informational disadvantage, producing different short- and long-term equilibria. This distinction guides much of the discussion that follows.

Figure 2 illustrates the process through which differing short- and long-term equilibria can arise. It traces the typical path of the foreign policy information gap, that is, the informational advantage that leaders enjoy over the public. As the primary traders of information in the marketplace—simultaneously beholden to leaders for their supply of this key commodity and to the public for demand—the media play a central role in narrowing this information gap over time.

Typically, public attention to foreign policy (and consequently demand for foreign policy news) is very low, resulting in an equilibrium favorable to leaders. This is especially true in the early stages of a military conflict, where, in **Figure 2**, IG_{t_1} represents the relatively large information gap at time t_1. However, several factors—including casualties, elite discord, and evidence that leaders have "spun" the facts beyond credulity (a concept we term the elasticity of reality)—can prompt the public to

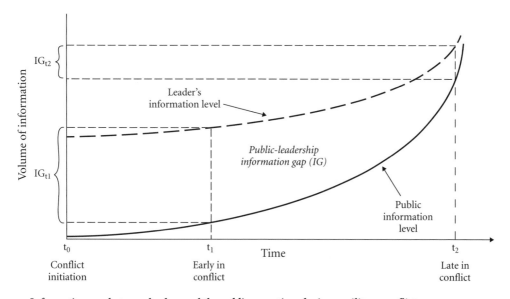

Figure 2. Information gap between leaders and the public, over time during a military conflict.

increase its demand for information from the media, thereby narrowing the information gap. This becomes more likely as a conflict drags on, represented in **Figure 2** by the smaller information gap (IG_{t_2}) at time t_2. The media play a crucial role because they produce this dynamism. If there were no third actor controlling the flow of information, or if such an actor were merely a passive conveyor belt, leaders would have less incentive to respond to changes in the public's demand for information (except perhaps near an election).

Economists rarely ask whether supply causes demand or whether consumers cause producers. Rather, in attempting to understand markets, scholars focus on the concept of equilibrium—how to identify it and determine when it is likely to shift. We believe this is also a useful way to conceptualize the process of foreign policy formulation. Present knowledge about the relationships between actors in the foreign policy marketplace emerges from static snapshots. Yet, each of these snapshots suggests a common, and perhaps interesting, market equilibrium. For example, in the "rally round the flag" literature (discussed below), the well-documented short-term market equilibrium (time t_1 in **Figure 2**) favors leaders. However, the literature on the public's response to casualties (also discussed below) implies the presence of another long-term equilibrium (time t_2 in **Figure 2**) where public opinion can shape, or at least constrain, policy.

This is the task we undertake in this article. We begin with a review of the state of knowledge concerning the three main actors in the foreign policy marketplace: the public, their leaders, and the media.

The Actors

The Public

The public's capacity to gather and retain information, and to use it to formulate coherent opinions, is arguably integral to the functioning of democracy. Madison, Hamilton, and other like-minded federalists were suspicious of the public's capacity to contribute constructively to political decision making, especially in foreign policy. In contrast, a long liberal tradition—with origins in the work of Kant, Rousseau, Bentham, and Mill, and more recently manifested in the vast literature on the democratic peace (e.g., Doyle 1986, Russett & Oneal 2001)—views citizen engagement as crucial to well-considered policy and peaceful international relations. Contemporary democratic theorists (e.g., Habermas 1996) also consider responsiveness to the public to be a cornerstone of democratic governance. However, despite the theoretical importance of the public's engagement with foreign policy, social scientists have struggled to consistently characterize the public's actual role in the foreign policy process.

The question of the public's informational capacity is a crucial foundation underlying our understanding of the foreign policy marketplace. Research suggests a consensus around two key points: (a) Citizens are typically at a significant informational disadvantage vis-à-vis leadership elites, and (b) they compensate by employing heuristic cues that allow them to make reasoned judgments with small amounts of information.

Most scholars draw a clear distinction between public opinion on foreign policy in general, on the one hand, and public opinion in relation to conflicts or crises, on the other. Whereas the public is typically not closely attuned to the details of international politics, crises often appear to attract public attention. This has prompted scholars to ask what role, if any, public opinion actually plays in specific American foreign policy crises. For instance, some research suggests public opinion influenced U.S. policy toward Nicaragua (Sobel 2001), Somalia (Klarevas 2002), and Iraq (Larson & Savych 2005).

As noted, there is a conceptual divide between studies emphasizing short- versus long-term opinion dynamics. In the near term, the public tends to rally behind presidential foreign policy initiatives, thereby giving presidents considerable influence over public opinion (Mueller 1973, Brody 1991); over the longer term, a separate body of research (Sobel 2001, Baum 2004a, Canes-Wrone 2006) suggests that public opinion can constrain foreign policy. We argue that these previously distinct literatures can be unified within a market framework.

After all, the longer a conflict lasts, the greater the opportunity for the public to accumulate sufficient information to overcome—or at least reduce—its informational disadvantage. To clarify this relationship, we next consider short- and long-term opinion dynamics.

The rally-round-the-flag phenomenon.   Political observers have long noted that the public often responds positively in the short term to military engagements abroad, and a voluminous literature has investigated the validity and magnitude of the rally phenomenon. Lee (1977, p. 253) notes, "the average man's reaction [to engagement abroad] will include a feeling of patriotism in supporting presidential actions." Most empirical updates and tests confirm the existence of a short-term rally effect to a greater or lesser extent, and under at least some circumstances (James & Oneal 1991, Oneal & Bryan 1995). Others, however, counter that rallies tend to be infrequent and ephemeral and thus rarely of political consequence (Stoll 1984; Oneal et al. 1996).

Further demonstrating the importance of perceived common interests in determining individual responses to the use of force, Baum (2002), in a study of major U.S. uses of force between 1953 and 1998, finds stark differences in individuals' rally responses depending on their party affiliations and the partisan configuration of government. He finds that rallies are mostly limited to opposition party identifiers and Independents. The reason is that typically a president's fellow partisans already approve of his performance prior to a rally event, so they cannot re-evaluate the president's performance upwards. Just such a rally pattern emerged following 9/11; nearly all of George W. Bush's record 36-point gain in approval ratings occurred among Democrats and Independents, majorities of whom had disapproved of his performance prior to 9/11.

The presence of a rally effect seems to suggest a "knee-jerk" public reaction to the use of force abroad. How can we reconcile this with the view of public opinion as largely rational and coherent? The likely answer, reinforced by an emerging body of research, is that rallies, or the absence thereof, may be rational responses to the interaction of pre-existing individual preferences with the information environment.

This suggests that in the face of a significant informational disadvantage, the public uses elite positions—and particularly those of fellow-partisan elites—as a critical cognitive shortcut. However, they do so only absent evidence undercutting the reliability of this shortcut. The rally effect results from a market equilibrium characterized by highly informed leaders and a public at a significant informational disadvantage.

Casualty aversion.   In contrast to the rally literature, research on the longer-term relationship between public opinion and foreign policy primarily explores the characteristics of the conflicts themselves, particularly the casualties they engender (Mueller 1973, Gartner & Segura 2000) or public perceptions regarding their relative success (Feaver & Gelpi 2004, Gelpi et al. 2005; Eichenberg 2005).

Prior findings on the public's reaction to casualties are consistent with our conception of foreign policy formulation as a market process centered on the exchange of information. As we have seen, the public appears to tolerate casualties more readily in the presence of elite consensus, multilateral support, and traditional missions—all clear informational cues indicating that a mission is likely to be worthwhile. The reciprocal circumstance is equally suggestive: Public support tends to be more fragile when the public has less experience with the mission and thus requires greater information to assess it. In such cases, the public may react quickly and negatively to the information produced by elite discord, while being especially responsive to the higher information content of local casualties.

The missing link between the rally and casualty-aversion literatures lies in the realization that the various actors in our marketplace gather information in different ways and, even more significantly, at different rates. As we have seen, the public's informational disadvantage makes it susceptible to the framing of information by elites. However, if this disadvantage wanes, as in a protracted conflict, tolerance for the framing preferred by elites begins to break down, and the public asserts itself in the foreign policy arena.

This is, of course, a highly stylized representation of a vastly complex reality. Yet, we argue that, in part because of its simplicity, it better captures the dynamics of the foreign policy marketplace than the static snapshots that have previously dominated research.

Decision Makers

We have considered the dynamics of public behavior in the foreign policy marketplace and found that outcomes are driven, in part, by the supply of and demand for information. The public's influence on foreign policy appears to be lowest when it is informationally weakest (typically in early stages of conflicts) but somewhat higher in longer conflicts as the information gap dissipates. We next consider how leaders respond to these market dynamics and constraints.

The diversionary use of force. Leaders' expectations complicate the short-term relationship between public opinion and foreign policy. Ample evidence suggests leaders recognize their informational advantage early in conflicts. This recognition can produce an incentive—especially in democracies—to use conflict to manipulate public opinion. This is the key insight of the diversionary-war literature. The link to the rally phenomenon is clear; a diversionary war aimed at distracting attention from domestic problems or bolstering electoral prospects—popularly known as a "wag the dog" scenario—is only likely to tempt a leader who anticipates a rally response from the electorate (Baum 2004a). If leaders act on such expectations in systematic ways, this effectively reverses the causal relationship between public opinion and foreign policy.

In our conception of the foreign policy marketplace, the diversionary argument is the mirror image of the rally phenomenon. The prospect of a short war may occasionally tempt leaders who gamble that the conflict will not outlast the rally. However, the ever-present possibility that a conflict may drag on makes using force particularly risky, in part because the public may respond negatively to the casualties such extended conflicts frequently engender.

We suspect that the mixed evidence regarding the diversionary use of force stems from some of the market mechanisms discussed above. Conflict tends to narrow the information gap between the public and their leaders unless it can be concluded rapidly (often an elusive goal). The nontraditional, aggressive, or unilateral missions leaders might initiate to "wag the dog," in turn, are the very types of conflict most likely to provide cues (such as partisan elite discord) that tend to turn the public against a military engagement. In short, the discrepancy between the empirically well-documented rally effect and the ambiguous empirical evidence regarding the (logically compelling) diversionary war theory becomes less puzzling when both are considered within the broader context of a foreign policy marketplace.

Still, our picture of this marketplace is not yet complete. How do these informational cues travel from leaders to the public? How do leaders monitor public opinion? Such questions appear to open a window for the mass media to mediate the relationship between public opinion and foreign policy leadership as a discrete third actor in the foreign policy marketplace.

Mass Media

We have outlined how information asymmetry largely dictates the dynamics between the public and its leaders in the foreign policy marketplace—specifically the degree to which the public is informationally disadvantaged, thereby allowing leaders to sustain their preferred frames on information. The media play the crucial role of collecting, framing, and distributing information—the key market commodity.

Without question, leaders place great value on controlling this commodity. Bryan G. Whitman, Deputy Assistant Secretary of Defense for Media Operations, observed with respect to the Pentagon's policy of embedding reporters within U.S. combat units in Iraq in 2003, "Our goal was to dominate the information market . . ." (Carr 2003).

The traditional view of the media—especially in political science—as a mostly accommodating conduit for elite messages is built on a simplifying assumption that the media serve primarily as a linkage mechanism rather than as an independent, strategic actor in the policy-making process (Malek 1996, Brody 1991, Bloch & Lehman-Wilzig 2002). The best-known variant of this perspective holds that the media "index" their coverage to elite rhetoric in Washington (Hallin 1986, Bennett 1990, Bennett et al. 2006). Some research from outside political science, however, suggests that the media may be more proactive than indexing theories suggest. For example, the political communication "gatekeeper" literature (White 1950, Galtung & Ruge 1965, Patterson 1993) shows that journalists shape news by determining the newsworthiness of stories. This suggests the media may well present an unrepresentative sample of elite rhetoric. This potential for bias increases with the heightened prominence of more-partisan "new" media outlets (Baum & Groeling, unpublished manuscript).

The indexing hypothesis has proven durable in part because media do frequently transmit elite messages with largely intact frames. As noted, the public is typically ill-informed and so unmotivated to object. Thus, the information equilibrium tends to favor leaders, and, hence, the media are more responsive to leaders' preferences than to those of the public. Consequently, although indexing theories are well-supported when the criterion for evaluation is the frequency with which the media transmit elite messages, this overlooks the market dynamic through which the prevailing equilibrium can shift from one favoring leaders to one favoring the public.

In contrast to the passive-media assumption implicit in much of the indexing literature, in the foreign policy market the media play a critical role in these shifts when they occur. In fact, as the primary link between leaders and the public, the media are a central actor in the foreign policy marketplace. The nature of this link is not well captured by the conveyor-belt analogy. Within the market framework, the media are more aptly characterized as a middleman or trader of information, simultaneously beholden to two actors whose interests often

conflict: leaders and the public. The media primarily rely on leaders for access to information, that is, for their supply of the key market commodity. However, this information usually comes prepackaged in a frame that leaders would prefer that the media retain.

Of course, the media are equally reliant on the demand of the public as the ultimate consumers of this information. In their role as democratic citizens, members of the public have an interest in obtaining unframed (i.e., objective) information. Understanding how the media respond to these competing market pressures is the key to unlocking the foreign policy process as a dynamic phenomenon.

As when we sought to account for short- and long-term public opinion, we argue that the market framework can account for both the relatively passive media that seem to predominate under many circumstances and the more proactive media that sometimes emerge. The equilibrium between leaders and the public in the foreign policy marketplace accounts for this variance.

Despite a widely held belief in the media's mission to inform (e.g., Bennett 1997, Patterson 2000), they do not consistently act to remedy the informational inequities in the foreign policy marketplace. Rather, they react in ways that tend to exacerbate the prevailing trend. Early in conflicts—and especially major conflicts (Baker & Oneal 2001, Chapman & Reiter 2004)—when the public is informationally disadvantaged and thus most inclined to rally 'round the flag, the media are least likely to naysay; to the contrary, the media provide what the market equilibrium dictates. The public is sold the rally message it is predisposed to buy, while the media preserve their relationship with leaders who prefer that they retain the rally frame. In this light, the market framework seems consistent with Zaller & Chiu's (2000) finding that the media often rally along with the public when conflicts arise because of their dependence on authoritative sources for information—primarily the White House and executive agencies. Similarly, the market framework seems consonant with Entman's (2003) argument that the media are most likely to independently influence foreign policy when leaders debate over what he terms contestable frames for a given policy action—that is, culturally ambiguous frames subject to multiple interpretations (e.g., whether the Iraq War and its aftermath constitute liberation or occupation). In contrast, the media are least likely to exert independent influence when leaders employ culturally congruent frames—that is, frames congruent with schemas habitually employed by most citizens. An example is President Bush's post-9/11 characterization of Osama bin Laden and al Qaeda as "evil doers." Such culturally congruent frames are extremely difficult for the media to challenge (Entman 2003).

When leaders employ culturally congruent frames, the public's information disadvantage is exacerbated by the one-dimensional tone of media coverage. The media provide what the market demands: coverage consonant with a dominant and culturally congruent frame offered by the administration. In contrast, when leaders debate over contestable frames, the media hasten the dissipation of the public's informational disadvantage, as the "framing war" (i.e., elite debate) exposes citizens to more and more varied information. In the absence of a clear market demand for a single, dominant frame, the media offer multiple frames to satisfy diverse consumer preferences. In doing so, they narrow the information gap between leaders and the public, thereby increasing the potential for the public to influence policy. This understanding of the media's role makes it possible to synthesize a variety of literatures on the media within one coherent conceptual framework.

The CNN effect. Some scholars and journalists have argued that recent technical changes, culminating in the 24-hour news cycle, have fundamentally altered the relationship between public opinion and foreign policy—a phenomenon commonly referred to as the "CNN effect" (Gilboa 2005).[3] According to early proponents of this perspective (Sharkey 1993, Maren 1994), citizens, shocked by dramatic, real-time television images of suffering and hardship, may demand that their leaders "do something" to alleviate the problem, thereby pressuring politicians to

act in circumstances where they otherwise would not. A closely related corollary holds that the 24-hour news cycle pressures leaders to react more rapidly to events than in prior eras, in order to appear responsive to the public and in control of the situation (Robinson 2000, 2001). Such pressures could compromise traditional diplomacy, especially in situations where deliberate, or "quiet," diplomacy is most crucial (Wolfsfeld 2004).

Integral to this argument is the belief that the 24-hour news cycle is fundamentally different from previous formats because it transmits dramatic, vivid images to consumers in near-real time. In the context of the market framework, scholars were concerned that the CNN effect might fundamentally alter the market equilibrium; however, the reality seems not to have proven so stark.

In theory, the CNN effect could be expected to shift the market equilibrium in favor of the public by more rapidly providing information, thereby undermining elite frames. Thus, the duration and magnitude of the public's informational disadvantage—during periods when the media primarily transmit officially framed information—could be expected to shrink as the speed and volume of news increases. Similarly, the need to fill airtime with varied content might lead the media to move beyond government-framed information more quickly.

For those seeking to precisely define and measure a CNN effect, the major challenge lies not in determining whether the relationship between media and policy is changing (most agree that it is), but in elucidating the nature of the change and in determining whether the 24-hour news cycle is responsible for it. A number of other changes in the international system are discussed as competing candidate explanations. Entman (2003) argues that the relationship between decision-making elites and the media has changed considerably since the end of the Cold War. Others have suggested that 9/11 produced a similar transition (Zelizer & Allan 2002).

Hindman (2004) applies "media system dependency theory" to the analysis of public opinion regarding the performance of both the media and the president before and after 9/11. He finds that partisan differences become stronger predictors of presidential approval after terrorist attacks. Hutcheson et al. (2004) find that following 9/11, governing elites articulated particularly nationalistic themes. They suggest that this emphasis was explicitly aimed at uniting public opinion behind the war on terror. Similarly, Robinson (2005) argues that current events (e.g., the war on terror and the war in Iraq), combined with strengthened media management by the government, have undermined the CNN effect and reinstated some of the media deference that characterized the Cold War.

The implication seems to be that the CNN effect, to the extent it ever existed, was a temporary phenomenon made possible by the coincidental confluence of new technology and the absence of a coherent geopolitical threat. These arguments likely combine to explain why the CNN effect seems to have had a significantly less transformative effect than early scholarship anticipated.

Elite media and media as an elite.   Several authors have suggested a distinction between the elite and the popular media, which may respond in different ways to the forces outlined above (Paletz 2002, Baum 2003). It is perhaps unsurprising that there might be a division in the media along this faultline, given the sometimes wide opinion gaps between elites and the public (Page & Barabas 2000, Page & Bouton 2006). Such a possibility complicates the stylized market framework, which treats the media as unitary. However, relaxing this assumption might help further account for the media's tendency toward deference to elites, at least under many circumstances.

Elite media are thought to play a more active role in the shaping of elite opinion and, through it, foreign policy. For example, Tifft & Jones (1999) find that leaders often lack independent access to news and information and so rely on the media to inform them of important emerging events (see also Powlick 1995). More directly, the editorial content of elite publications such as the *Wall Street Journal* and *Foreign Affairs* influences the thinking of leaders about foreign policy issues. Decision makers rely on these sources for factual

information as well as informed opinion (Ferre 1980, Malek 1996).

The records of former presidents are replete with examples of media shaping the information and opinions of leaders. We see this in the extensive newspaper clippings found in archives of past decision makers as well as in more direct correspondence. For instance, at the height of the 1956 Suez Crisis, Merrill Mueller, an NBC correspondent and host, wrote the following to President Eisenhower:

> Because I feel the attached [notes from an interview with British Foreign Secretary Selwyn Lloyd] is so important to our government at this time, I send you herewith one of my own copies of a report of mine that is now being distributed. . . . [W]henever I stumble on anything as critical as the attached you will hear from me. (Mueller 1956)

Mueller's letter illustrates how the media can, at least sometimes, directly influence the information available to and hence opinions of leadership, even at the highest level. It also suggests that the distinction between decision-making and media elites is less clear than most theoretical models imply. In the above-cited letter, Mueller is clearly nominating himself for a position in the administration, and although he himself did not make this leap, others have. A prominent recent example is Tony Snow, who left his position as an anchor on the FOX News Channel to become White House Press Secretary. The academic literature has noted this cross-fertilization and its implications for the capacity of the media to function as the "fourth estate" (Holsti & Rosenau 1984, Reilly 1995).

The mass news audience demands local human-interest stories, political stories that can be framed as a "horserace," and so-called "soft news" (Baum 2003, Hamilton 2003); the general public does not typically demand to be informed about foreign policy. However, as noted, scholars (e.g., Patterson 2000) have long argued that the media has a partly self-imposed, but also constitutionally prescribed, mission to inform the public. When this mission complements the ability to sell, the media are likely to use the salable story as peg to inform. However, the degree to which informing and selling coincide depends largely on whether the media are able to frame the news in a way that appeals to its buyers: the public.

Hallin (1986) suggests that the media do not report on items on which there is near universal agreement; nor do they report on ideas that lie beyond the "sphere of legitimate controversy" Others have suggested that an issue is likely to resonate with the public if large segments of the citizenry perceive it as affecting them. Neuman et al. (1992) find that the electorate's relative lack of interest in foreign relations results from the perceived distance between overseas events and their day-to-day lives.

Some of the lessons learned in the communication literature about public preferences in media coverage help explain why the public occasionally takes interest in a given foreign policy issue and why the media periodically begin to report on it. For example, as discussed above, casualties may both attract people's attention to foreign policy and turn them sharply against it. The mechanisms by which this occurs remain somewhat unclear, but viewing the media as an actor in a broader foreign policy market clarifies some of them. For instance, the media tend to frame casualties in terms of local losses, flag-draped caskets, and grieving American families. In short, casualties transform a foreign engagement into a domestic issue, making foreign crises seem close to home and to local communities (Aldrich et al. 1989). This attention then acts as a peg on which the media can hang more general stories on the conflict that had previously seemed distant to the public, thereby priming the public to assess whether an engagement is worth the cost.

Synthesis: Defining the Foreign Policy Market

Our market formulation builds on other recent work that incorporates the interactions of the media, leadership, and public opinion into a single model. Examples include "activation" models of public opinion (Powlick & Katz 1998) and "cascade" models (Entman 2003). In this section, we argue that gaining additional insight into foreign policy formulation requires moving from episodic

to consistent incorporation of the role of media into our theoretical models.

Previous Attempts at Synthesis

As we have seen, absent the market framework or some other unifying concept, it is difficult to delineate clear relationships between leadership, the media, and public opinion. The seeming circularity of these interactions has inspired work questioning, "Who leads whom?" For instance, Canes-Wrone (2006) argues that presidents typically appeal to public opinion on issues the public is likely to support, but do so primarily when they themselves advocate such issues. Presidents aim such appeals at gaining leverage vis-à-vis Congress. She sees this as a benign process by which both the public interest and the president's policy preferences become law, at least when the two coincide. Domke et al. (2006) explore the role of "going public" in the passage of the Patriot Act. They argue that political elites' capacity to manipulate the media messages that reach the public is greatest in times of national crisis or upheaval.

In perhaps the most comprehensive analysis of the dynamic interactions between the actors in the foreign policy market, Entman's (2003) cascade model attempts to clarify how elites pass information to the media, and subsequently to the public, and the inevitable pushback that occurs in the process. Entman observes that much of the literature incorporates an implicit model, along the following lines: (1) government interacts with the media; (2) the media tell people what to believe; and (3) people provide minor feedback to the media.

However, he argues that reality does not fit these stylized assumptions well. Historically, the media have varied from lapdog to watchdog with some regularity. The traditional model has difficulty explaining these transitions. Entman's more complex model attempts to account for the interactions between the White House, the rhetoric that reaches the media, the media's framing of this rhetoric, and the public response. All this is further complicated by feedback loops and interactions.

Entman shows that the present alignment between the media, the public, and the administration is far less reliable and stable than the more rigid framework of the Cold War. He argues that variations in cultural congruence, power, strategy, and motivation imply a continuum in the media-administration relationship, ranging from instances where the media essentially distribute the administration's message, at one end, to cases where they are quite critical and emphasize a contrary frame, at the other. This overall assessment is not reassuring for those who believe public opinion can or should positively influence foreign policy. In Entman's (2003) model, elite framing and spin remain dominant despite recent events and advances in technology that some suggest have favored the public (see above).

These studies have taken important steps toward synthesizing the interrelated literatures we consider here, and are therefore in many respects the forebears of our market framework.[4] For example, in order to underscore the empirical observation that the media only occasionally assert an independent frame on administration rhetoric, and do so only under a fairly restrictive set of conditions, Entman (2003) models the media as a periodic actor in his cascade. Our dynamic market framework takes this arrangement as a starting point. However, by incorporating the role of information in determining market equilibria, it captures the media's ubiquitous presence in the foreign policy process—either as lapdog or watchdog. In short, the market framework builds on prior research, offering additional insight into the dynamic nature of foreign policy process by introducing the concept of market equilibrium and thereby accounting for the seemingly contrasting roles of leaders, the public, and the media identified by previous scholars.

The Foreign Policy Marketplace

As noted, much of the difficulty in developing a coherent model of the foreign policy process results from conceptualizing leadership, public opinion, or the media independently from the broader context of the foreign policy marketplace. The difficulty increases when we try to model these relationships as sequential actions. Doing so blurs a dynamic characterized by expectations, anticipated reactions,

and constant updating. Consequently, we have outlined some of the ways in which the foreign policy process shares important elements in common with marketplaces as we understand them in the study of economics. Both contexts involve the convergence of actors and information on points of equilibrium, rather than linear causal chains. We have traced the rough outline of how this market might work; we now offer a more concise summation.

Of the three primary actors in the foreign policy marketplace, two—the public and its leaders—are interested in creating policy that suits their interests and preferences, which are sometimes at odds. When these interests are at odds, the ability to influence policy varies with the relative amount of information (again, the primary market commodity) held by each actor. In a democracy, the electorate holds fundamental power. Yet, in international affairs, leaders typically enjoy a substantial informational advantage. In many cases, this allows them to effectively dictate foreign policy.

As the third actor in the marketplace, the media act as traders of information. On the supply side, they are beholden to leaders for much of the content of the news (their product) and therefore are under pressure to preserve elites' preferred framing of information. However, on the demand side, they are equally beholden to the public as the consumers of this information, and the public's interest frequently lies in seeing beyond these very frames. Thus, the media walk a fine line—paying enough deference to elite frames to maintain access, while deviating enough to generate and maintain public interest in the news. Foreign policy outcomes result from the delicate equilibrium that emerges between these competing forces. In theory, we should be able to understand and scientifically analyze these equilibria—just as we do the equilibria between supply and demand in traditional economic markets—by observing the relative distribution of information among the primary market actors.

Such a market formulation of the foreign policy process accounts for the fact that decision-making elites and the media are motivated by goals other than the dispassionate transmission of objective information to the electorate. Many communication scholars (e.g., Bennett 1997, Patterson 2000) view such transmission as a key ingredient of a functional democracy, and the political science literature (e.g., Jentleson 1992, Zaller 1992, Brody 1991) often assumes such a function. Yet, the government has little political or institutional incentive to provide "unframed" information, and because news content is determined by the vicissitudes of the marketplace, the news media are arguably not well suited for this role (Hamilton 2003; Zaller 2003 and unpublished manuscript).

Nonetheless, elite messages are necessarily about something. Hence, on some level, and to at least some degree, objective reality or facts must enter the marketplace. Of course, in the interaction between the elites who supply framed messages and the media that transmit them, the precise nature of reality is nearly always subject to debate. We refer to this as the elasticity of reality, which we define as the range within which events can be spun, or framed, without inducing a significant backlash from the public. Similarly, Rosenau (1961, p. 36) writes of the "outer limits within which decision makers and opinion makers feel constrained to operate."

The public is typically slow to demand accountability on foreign policy issues (Rosenau 1961, Zaller 1994a), but when it finds that reality has been stretched too far, the reaction can be swift and severe. The costs are very high for leaders who provide, and the media that transmit, messages that overstretch the elasticity of reality. This does not imply that, over time, reality trumps framing. The public rarely observes reality directly, especially in the realm of foreign affairs. Rather, the public observes and responds to a framed representation of reality, in both the short and longer term (Baum & Groeling 2007).

In the initial stages of a foreign policy event, when elites have a substantial informational advantage, the public's perception of reality is very elastic. This frequently allows a president to dominate the so-called "framing war." Over time, as events unfold and the public gathers more information, the degree of elasticity diminishes, opening a space for alternative frames to influence public opinion. If some entrepreneurs (e.g., journalists) elect to proffer an alternative frame, it stands a better chance of competing with the president's preferred frame, so long as it does not stray beyond the ever-shrinking elasticity of reality.

Events surrounding the conflict in Iraq provide a case in point. Whatever the "truth," the public, over time, arrived at a seemingly firm conviction that the Bush administration's justifications for the war exceeded the elasticity of reality. The resulting fallout took the form of plummeting approval ratings for President Bush and the loss by his party of the Congress in the 2006 midterm election. Evidence of a preemptive media effort to prevent a comparable antimedia backlash can be seen in the New York Times' wave of introspection—following the revelation that there were no weapons of mass destruction in Iraq—concerning how and why it had accepted the administration's preferred frames so uncritically.

Slantchev (2006) shows why the ever-present and implicit threat of public backlash might consistently, rather than sporadically, influence the behavior of leaders via anticipation of public reactions. His formal model links the electorate's theoretical capacity to sanction leaders (given full information) to the logic of domestic audience costs (Fearon 1994). Slantchev (2006) argues that because an independent media can function as a relatively unbiased, and hence credible, information source, it can facilitate public monitoring—the ultimate source of audience costs (Schultz 2001, Baum 2004a)—of leaders' foreign policy actions. This makes it easier to determine when a leader should be punished for a policy failure. In other words, a free press narrows the information gap between leaders and the public.

Slantchev's theory represents an important contribution to the process of delineating the mechanisms underlying our hypothesized foreign policy market. However, additional theoretical and empirical work remains to first concretely establish and then fully explicate the functions and policy implications of this market process.

Conclusion

The next important scholarly step forward in explicating the relationship between public opinion and foreign policy requires an important conceptual refinement. Models of the policy formulation process must elevate the mass media from the role of a conveyor belt to that of an independent, strategic actor (as some of the communications literature does). Additionally, rather than continuing to represent this process through standard linear models that (with relatively few exceptions) predominate in the literature, we believe a market equilibrium approach is more conceptually faithful and thus will ultimately prove more empirically fruitful.

In the early stages of research on the relationships between the public, leaders, and the media in the foreign policy arena, scholars concentrated on delineating the causal pathways among these actors. This approach yielded many important insights, but the broader theoretical framework remained obscured. We believe this framework is best characterized as a marketplace in which the relative distribution of information among these three actors in large part determines their relative influence on foreign policy. The market framework allows us to synthesize many disparate findings in the literature, thereby revealing the proverbial "hidden face in the picture."

However, this synthesis represents only a preliminary step. A number of avenues for future research remain. For example, to enhance analytic traction, we treated the media as a unitary actor. This is obviously not descriptively accurate, and especially not in the contemporary era of 24-hour cable news networks, Internet blogs, and soft news (Baum 2003; Hamilton 2003; Baum & Groeling, unpublished manuscript). Yet, as noted, most research on public opinion and foreign policy treats "the mass media" as precisely that: an undifferentiated mass.

A potentially fruitful avenue for future research would thus entail unpacking this unitary-actor assumption, to consider the implications, only briefly alluded to herein, of increasingly niche-oriented and sometimes overtly partisan new media outlets. For instance, media fragmentation increasingly allows citizens to primarily expose themselves to information that reinforces their pre-existing beliefs. In an unpublished manuscript, Baum & Groeling conjecture that self-selection by citizens into ideologically "friendly" media environments may complicate future presidents' efforts to forge sustainable bipartisan consensus behind their foreign policy initiatives. In the context of the foreign policy marketplace, such selective exposure may slow the narrowing of the information gap between leaders and the public, and hence also slow the tightening of the elasticity of reality.

This review has primarily focused on the United States, largely because the literature is centered on the American context. However, the dynamics we describe have obvious implications for the relationship between the media, public opinion, and foreign policy in other nations. In fact, comparative research in this area is rapidly proliferating (e.g., Risse-Kappen 1991, Arian et al. 1992, Cohen 1995, Morgan & Anderson 1999, Isernia et al. 2002). Such an extension is long overdue, as it will enhance our understanding of foreign policy in other countries and provide a more generalized conceptualization of the ways in which media interact with public opinion to produce foreign policy in democracies.

Scholars have paid comparatively little attention to the role of the media in autocracies. Yet some recent research (Stein, unpublished manuscript) suggests that, at least under some circumstances, the media can play an important role in the public policy process even in autocracies.

In another potential avenue for future research suggested by our market framework, recent real-world cases indicate that the information gap between the public and its leaders can narrow at very different rates depending (presumably) on the nature of the crisis and the rhetoric that surrounds it. We have identified some potential cues that might affect this rate (e.g., casualties and elite discord). More work is needed, however, to explicate the relationship between these factors and this narrowing process. What motivates the public to acquire and incorporate new information across a broad range of foreign policy situations?

Scholars have learned a great deal about the interrelationship between the mass media, public opinion, and elite decision makers. Yet, as we have described, the daunting—and in some respects perhaps impossible—task of delineating clear causal pathways has constrained this advance. Recent research (e.g., Entman 2003, Powlick & Katz 1998) has begun to move beyond the limitations imposed by linear causal frameworks. Our proposed market framework is aimed at breaking through this conceptual wall once and for all, in the hope of facilitating a new avenue of research in this critically important aspect of democratic politics.

Notes

1. To enhance analytic traction, we treat the media—analytically, but not grammatically—as a unitary actor. Of course, we recognize that the mass media consist of a diverse array of distinct actors with varying incentives. (In the conclusion, we consider the implications of relaxing this assumption.)
2. In a similar argument, Hamilton (2003, p. 19) asserts that "newsworthiness" is a "function of the number of consumers and their value in the marketplace."
3. The term "CNN effect" emerged before competing 24-hour news networks (e.g., FOX, MSNBC) appeared. Recent studies use it as shorthand to refer to a wide array of news outlets.
4. However, it is important to bear in mind exactly what each attempt at synthesis is attempting to accomplish. Entman's (2003) cascade model more closely approaches a fully formed theory than our conceptual framework, which does not make any specific claims of cause and effect. (Indeed, we argue that causality is typically multi-directional.) Powlick & Katz (1998) also do not propose a theory of cause and effect, but rather a framework for understanding media activation in the opinion-policy relationship. In this regard, our enterprise more closely resembles that of Powlick & Katz.

Literature Cited

Aldrich, J. H., C. Gelpi, P. Feaver, J. Reifler, and K. T. Sharp. 2006. Foreign Policy and the Electoral Connection. *Annual Review of Political Science* 9: 477–502.

Aldrich, J. H., J. L. Sullivan, and E. Borgida. 1989. Foreign Affairs and Issue Voting: Do Presidential Candidates "Waltz Before a Blind Audience"? *American Political Science Review* 83 (1): 123–41.

Almond, G. A. 1950. *The American People and Foreign Policy*. New York: Harcourt Brace.

Arian, A., M. Shamir, and R. Venura. 1992. Public Opinion and Political Change—Israel and the Intifada. *Comparative Politics* 24 (3): 317–34.

Baker, W. D., and J. R. Oneal. 2001. Patriotism or Opinion Leadership?: The Nature and Origins of the "Rally 'round the Flag" Effect. *Journal of Conflict Resolution* 44 (5): 661–87.

Baum, M. A. 2002. The Constituent Foundations of the Rally-Round-the-Flag Phenomenon. *International Studies Quarterly* 46: 263–98.

———. 2003. *Soft News Goes to War: Public Opinion and American Foreign Policy in the New Media Age*. Princeton, NJ: Princeton University Press

———. 2004a. Going Private: Presidential Rhetoric, Public Opinion, and the Domestic Politics of Audience Costs in U.S. Foreign Policy Crises. *Journal of Conflict Resolution* 48: 603–31.

———. 2004b. How Public Opinion Constrains the Use of Force: The Case of Operation Restore Hope. *Presidential Studies Quarterly* 34: 187–226.

———. 2006. *Getting the Message: Information Transparency and the Domestic Politics of Militarized Disputes*. Presented at the annual meeting of the American Political Science Association, Philadelphia, PA.

Baum, M. A., and T. Groeling. 2007. *Crossing the Water's Edge: Elite Rhetoric, Media Coverage and the Rally-Round-the-Flag Phenomenon, 1979–2003*. John F. Kennedy School Government Faculty Research Work. Paper Series No. RWP07–013.

———. n.d. *Shot by the Messenger: An Experimental Examination of the Effects of Party Cues on Public Opinion Regarding National Security and War*. Unpublished manuscript.

Bennett, D. S., and A. C. Stam, III. 1998. The Declining Advantage of Democracy: A Combined Model of War Outcomes and Duration. *Journal of Conflict Resolution* 42 (3): 344–66.

Bennett, W. L. 1990. Toward a Theory of Press-State Relations in the United States. *Journal of Communications* 40: 103–25.

———. 1997. *News: The Politics of Illusion*, 3rd ed. New York: Longman.

Bennett, W. L., R. G. Lawrence, and S. Livingston. 2006. None Dare Call It Torture: Indexing and the Limits of Press Independence in the Abu Ghraib scandal. *Journal of Communication* 56: 467–85.

Berinsky, A. 2007. Assuming the Costs of War: Events, Elites, and American Public Support for Military Conflict. *Journal of Politics* 69: 975–97.

Bloch, Y., and S. Lehman-Wilzig. 2002. An Exploratory Model of Media-Government Relations. In *Media and Conflict*, ed. E. Gilboa, pp. 153–69. New York: Transnational.

Brody, R. A. 1991. *Assessing the President: The Media, Elite Opinion, and Public Support*. Stanford, CA: Stanford University Press.

Bush, G. W. 2003. *President Bush, Kenyan President Kibaki Discuss State Visit*. White House Press Transcript. Available at http://www.whitehouse.gov/news/releases/2003/10/20031006-3.html.

Campbell, A., P. E. Converse, W. E. Miller, and D. E. Stokes. 1960. *The American Voter*. New York: Wiley.

Canes-Wrone, B. 2006. *Who Leads Whom? Presidents, Policy, and the Public*. Chicago: University of Chicago Press.

Carr, D. 2003. War News from MTV and People Magazine. *New York Times* (March 27), p. B14.

Chapman, T. L., and D. Reiter. 2004. The United Nations Security Council and the Rally 'Round the Flag Effect. *Journal of Conflict Resolution* 48: 886–909.

Chiozza, G., and H. E. Goemans. 2004. International Conflict and the Tenure of Leaders: Is War Still Ex-Post Inefficient? *American Journal of Political Science* 48 (3): 604–19.

Choi, S. W., and P. James. 2006. Media Openness, Democracy and Militarized Interstate Disputes: An Empirical Analysis. *British Journal of Political Science* 37: 23–46.

Clark, D. H. 2003. Can Strategic Interaction Divert Diversionary Behavior? A Model of U.S. Conflict Propensity. *Journal of Politics* 65: 1013–39.

Cohen, B. C. 1963. *The Press and Foreign Policy*. Princeton, NJ: Princeton University Press.

———. 1995. *Democracies and Foreign Policy: Public Participation in the United States and the Netherlands*. Madison: University of Wisconsin Press.

Colaresi, M. 2007. The Benefit of the Doubt. *International Organization* 61 (1): 99–143.

Delli-Carpini, M., and S. Keeter. 1996. *What Americans Know About Politics and Why it Matters*. New Haven, CT: Yale University Press.

DeRouen, K., and J. Peake. 2002. The Dynamics of Diversion: The Domestic Implications of Presidential Use of Force. *International Interactions* 28: 191–211.

Destler, T. M. 2001. The Reasonable Public and the Polarized Policy Process. In *The Real and the Ideal: Essays on International Relations in Honor of Richard H. Ullman*, ed. A. Lake and D. Ochmanek, pp. 75–90. New York: Rowman & Littlefield.

Domke, D., E. S. Graham, K. Coe, S. L. John, and T. Coopman. 2006. Going Public as Political Strategy: The Bush Administration, an Echoing Press, and Passage of the Patriot Act. *Political Communication* 23 (3): 291–312.

Doyle, M. W. 1986. Liberalism and World Polities. *American Political Science Review* 80: 1151–69.

Druckman, J. N. 2001. The Implications of Framing Effects for Citizen Competence. *Political Behavior* 23: 225–56.

Eichenberg, R. C. 2005. Victory Has Many Friends: U.S. Public Opinion and the Use of Military Force. *International Security* 30: 140–77.

Entman, R. M. 2000. Media and Political Conflict: News from the Middle East. *American Political Science Review* 94 (2): 521–22.

———. 2003. *Projections of Power: Framing News, Public Opinion, and U.S. Foreign Policy*. Chicago: University of Chicago Press.

Fearon, J. D. 1994. Domestic Political Audiences and the Escalation of International Disputes. *American Political Science Review* 88: 577–92.

Feaver, P. D., and C. Gelpi. 2004. *Choosing Your Battles: American Civil-Military Relations and the Use of Force*. Princeton, NJ: Princeton University Press.

Ferre, J. P. 1980. Denominational Biases in the American Press. *Review of Religious Research* 21: 276–83.

Filson, D., and S. Werner. 2004. Bargaining and Fighting: The Impact of Regime Type on War Onset, Duration, and Outcomes. *American Journal of Political Science* 48 (2): 296–313.

Fordham, B. O. 1998. The Politics of Threat Perception and the Use of Force: A Political Economy Model of U.S. Uses of Force, 1949–1994. *International Studies Quarterly* 42: 567–90.

———. 2005. Strategic Conflict Avoidance and the Diversionary Use of Force. *Journal of Politics* 67: 132–53.

Fordham, B. O., and C. C. Sarver. 2001. Militarized Interstate Disputes and United States Uses of Force. *International Studies Quarterly* 45: 455–66.

Galtung, J., and M. H. Ruge. 1965. The Structure of Foreign News. *Journal of Peace Resolution* 2: 64–91.

Gartner, S. 2006. *Casualties and Public Support: An Experimental Analysis.* Presented at the annual meeting of the American Political Science Association, Philadelphia, PA.

Gartner, S., and G. M. Segura. 1998. Race, Casualties, and Opinion in the Vietnam War. *Journal of Politics* 62 (1): 115–46.

———. 2000. War, Casualties and Public Opinion. *Journal of Conflict Resolution* 42 (3): 278–300.

Gelpi, C., P. D. Feaver, and J. Reifler. 2005. Success Matters—Casualty Sensitivity and the War in Iraq. *International Security* 30 (3): 7–46.

Gelpi, C., and Grieco, J. 2008. Democracy, Interdependence and the Sources of the Liberal Peace. *Journal of Peace Research.* In press.

Gilboa, E. 2005. The CNN Effect: The Search for a Communication Theory of International Relations. *Political Communications* 22 (1): 27–44.

Graber, D. A. 2002. *Mass Media and American Politics,* 6th ed. Washington, DC: CQ Press.

Habermas, J. 1996. *Between Facts and Norms: Contributions to a Discourse Theory of Law and Democracy.* Cambridge, MA: MIT Press.

Hallin, D. C. 1986. *The "Uncensored War."* Berkeley: University of California Press.

Hallin, D., and P. Mancini. 2004. *Comparing Media Systems: Three Models of Media and Politics.* Cambridge: Cambridge University Press.

Hamilton, J. T, 2003. *All the News That's Fit to Sell: How the Market Transforms Information into News.* Princeton, NJ: Princeton University Press.

Hess, G. D., and A. Orphanides. 1995. War Politics—An Economic, Rational-Voter Framework. *American Economic Review* 85: 828–46.

Hindman, D. B. 2004. Media System Dependency and Public Support for the Press and President. *Mass Communication and Society* 7: 29–42.

Holsti, O. R. 2004. *Public Opinion and American Foreign Policy.* Ann Arbor: University of Michigan Press.

Holsti, O. R., and J. Rosenau. 1984. *American Leadership in World Affairs: Vietnam and the Breakdown of Consensus.* Boston: Allen & Unwin.

Howell, W. G., and J. C. Pevehouse. 2005. Presidents, Congress, and the Use of Force. *International Organizations* 59: 209–32.

Hutcheson, J., D. Domke, A. Billeaudeaux, and P. Garland. 2004. U.S. National Identity, Political Elites, and a Patriotic Press Following September 11. *Political Communication* 21: 27–50.

Isernia, P., Z. Juhasz, and H. Rattinger. 2002. Foreign Policy and the Rational Public in Comparative Perspective. *Journal of Conflict Resolution* 46 (2): 201–24.

Iyengar, S., and D. R. Kinder. 1987. *News that Matters: Television and American Opinion.* Chicago: University of Chicago Press.

Iyengar, S., and R. Reeves. 1997. *Do the Media Govern: Politicians, Voters, and Reporters in America.* Thousand Oaks, CA: Sage.

Jacobs, L. R, and R. Y. Shapiro. 2000. *Politicians Don't Pander: Political Manipulation and the Loss of Democratic Responsiveness.* Chicago: University of Chicago Press.

Jacobson, G. 2006. *A Divider, Not a Uniter: George W. Bush and the American People.* New York: Longman.

James, P., and J. R. Oneal. 1991. The Influence of Domestic and International Politics on the President's Use of Force. *Journal of Conflict Resolution* 35: 307–32.

Jentleson, B. W. 1992. The Pretty Prudent Public—Post Post-Vietnam American Opinion on the Use of Military Force. *International Studies Quarterly* 36 (l): 49–74.

Jentleson, B. W., and R. L. Britton. 1998. Still Pretty Prudent: Post-Cold War American Public Opinion on the Use of Military Force. *Journal of Conflict Resolution* 42: 395–417.

Katz, A. Z. 2000. Public Opinion and the Contradictions of Jimmy Carter's Foreign Policy. *Presidential Studies Quarterly* 4 (30): 662–87.

Key, V. O. 1961. *Public Opinion and American Democracy.* New York: Knopf.

Klarevas, L. 2002. The "Essential Domino" of Military Operations: American Public Opinion and the Use of Force. *International Studies Perspective* 3: 417–37.

Krosnick, J. A., and D. R. Kinder. 1990. Altering the Foundations of Support for the President through Priming. *American Political Science Review* 84: 497–512.

Kull, S., and C. Ramsey. 2001. The Myth of the Reactive Public. In *Public Opinion and the International Use of Force,* ed. P. P. Everts and P. Isernia, pp. 205–28. London: Routledge.

Kuypers, J. A. 1997. *Presidential Crisis Rhetoric and the Press in the Post-Cold War World.* Westport, CT: Praeger.

Lai, B., and D. Reiter. 2005. Rally 'Round the Union Jack? Public Opinion and the Use of Force in the United Kingdom, 1948–2001. *International Studies Quarterly* 49 (2): 255–72.

Larson, E. V. 2000. Putting Theory to Work: Diagnosing Public Opinion on the U.S. Intervention in Bosnia. In *Being Useful: Policy Relevance and International Relations Theory,* ed. M. Nincic and J. Lepgold, pp. 174–233. Ann Arbor: University of Michigan Press.

Larson, E. V., and B. Savych. 2005. *American Public Support for US Military Operations from Mogadishu to Baghdad: Technical Appendixes.* Santa Monica, CA: RAND.

Lee, J. R. 1977. Rallying Around the Flag. *Presidential Studies Quarterly* 2: 252–56.

Levy, J. S. 1989. The Diversionary Theory of War: A Critique. In *Handbook of War Studies,* ed. M. I. Midlarsky, pp. 259–88. New York: Unwin-Hyman.

Lippmann, W., and C. Merz. 1920. *A List of the News.* New York: New Republic.

Lipser, S. M. 1966. The President, the Polls, and Vietnam. *Transactions* 3: 20–22.

Livingston, S., and L. Bennett. 2003. Gatekeeping, Indexing, and Live-Event News: Is Technology Altering the Construction of News? *Political Communications* 20: 363–80.

Livingston, S., and T. Eachus. 1995–1996. Humanitarian Crises and U.S. Foreign Policy: Somalia and the CNN Effect Reconsidered. *Political Communications* Winter.

Lupia, A., and M. D. McCubbins. 1998. *The Democratic Dilemma: Can Citizens Learn What, They Need to Know?* Cambridge: Cambridge University Press.

Malek, A. 1996. *New York Times* Editorial Position and US Foreign Policy: The Case of Iran Revisited. In *News Media and Foreign Relations,* ed. A. Malek, pp. 224–45. Norwood, NJ: Able.

Maren, M. 1994. Feeding a Famine. *Forbes Media Critic* 2.1 (Fall): 30–38.

Marshall, J. 2003. Falsely Bleak Reports Reduce Our Chance for Success in Iraq. *Atlanta Journal-Constitution* (Sep. 22): p. 11A.

Meernik, J. 2004. *The Political Use of Military Force in US Foreign Policy.* Aldershot, UK: Ashgate.

Mermin J. 1997. Television News and American Intervention in Somalia: The Myth of a Media-Driven Foreign Policy. *Political Science Quarterly* 112 (Fall): 385–404.

Moeller, S. 1999. *Compassion Fatigue: Flow the Media Sell Disease, Famine, War and Death.* New York: Routledge.

Moore, W. H., and D. J. Lanoue. 2003. Domestic Politics and U.S. Foreign Policy: A Study of Cold War Conflict Behavior. *Journal of Politics* 65: 376–96.

Moosbrugger, L. *Institutions, Information, and Political Sophistication: A Causal Model.* Unpublished manuscript.

Morgan, T. C., and C. J. Anderson. 1999. Domestic Support and Diversionary External Conflict in Great Britain, 1950–1992. *Journal of Politics* 61: 799–814.

Morgan, T. C., and K. N. Bickers. 1992. Domestic Discontent: And the Use of Force. *Journal of Conflict Resolution* 36: 25–52.

Mueller, J. E. 1973. *War Presidents and Public Opinion.* New York: Wiley.

Mueller, M. 1956. *Letter from Merrill Mueller of NBC to Dwight Eisenhower.* Eisenhower Presidential Library, Central Files, Suez Crisis Folder Box 5 11/16/1956.

Nacos, B. L., R. Y. Shapiro, and P. Isernia. 2000. *Decision-making in a Glass House.* New York: Rowman & Littlefield.

Neuman, R., M. R. Just, and A. N. Crigler. 1992. *Common Knowledge: News and the Construction of Political Meaning.* Chicago: University of Chicago Press.

Oneal, J. R., and A. L. Bryan. 1995. The Rally 'Round the Flag Effect in U.S. Foreign Policy Crises, 1950–1985. *Political Behavior* 17 (4): 379–401.

Oneal, J. R., B. Lian, and J. H. Joyner. 1996. Are the American People "Pretty Prudent"? Public Responses to US Uses of Force, 1950–1988. *International Studies Quarterly* 40 (2): 261–79.

Oneal, J. R., and B. M. Russett. 1997. The Classical Liberals Were Right: Democracy, Interdependence, and Conflict, 1950–1985. *International Studies Quarterly* 41 (2): 267–93.

Oneal, J. R., and J. Tir. 2006. Does the Diversionary Use of Force Threaten the Democratic Peace? Assessing the Effect of Economic Growth on Interstate Conflict, 1921–2001. *International Studies Quarterly* 50: 755–79.

Ostrom, C. W., and B. L. Job. 1986. The President Anti the Political Use of Force. *American Political Science Review* 80 (2): 541–66.

Page, B. I., and J. Barabas. 2000. Foreign Policy Gaps Between Citizens and Leaders. *International Studies Quarterly* 44 (3): 339–64.

Page, B. I., and M. M. Bouton. 2006. *The Foreign Policy Disconnect: What Americans Want from Our Leaders But Don't Get.* Chicago: University of Chicago Press.

Page, B. I., and R. Shapiro. 1992. *The Rational Public: Fifty Years of Trends in American Policy.* Chicago: University of Chicago Press.

Paletz, D. L. 2002. *The Media in American Politics.* New York: Longman.

Patterson, T. E. 1993. *Out of Order.* New York: Knopf.

———. 2000. The United States: News in a Free-Market Society. In *Democracy and the Media: A Comparative Perspective,* ed. A. Mughan, pp. 241–65. Cambridge: Cambridge University Press.

Popkin, S. L. 1993. Information Shortcuts and the Reasoning Voter. In *Information, Participation, and Choice: An Economic Theory of Democracy in Perspective,* ed. B. Grofman, pp. 17–35. Ann Arbor: University of Michigan Press.

———. 1994. *The Reasoning Voter: Communication and Persuasion in Presidential Campaigns.* Chicago: University of Chicago Press.

Potter, P. B. K. 2007. Does Experience Matter? American Presidential Experience, Age, and International Conflict. *Journal of Conflict Resolution* 51 (3): 351–78.

Powlick, P. J. 1995. The Sources of Public Opinion for American Foreign-Policy Officials. *International Studies Quarterly* 39: 427–51.

Powlick, P., and A. Z. Katz. 1998. Defining the American Public Opinion/Foreign Policy Nexus. *International Studies Quarterly* 42: 29–61.

Rahn, W. M. 1993. The Role of Partisan Stereotypes in Information Processing About Political Candidates. *American Journal of Political Science* 37: 472–96.

Reilly, J. 1995. *American Public Opinion and U.S. Foreign Policy.* Chicago: Chicago Council of Foreign Relations.

Reiter, D., and A. C. Stam, III. 2002. *Democracies at War.* Princeton, NJ: Princeton University Press.

Risse-Kappen, T. 1991. Public Opinion, Domestic Structure, and Foreign Policy in Liberal Democracies. *World Politics* 43 (4): 479–512.

Robinson, P. 2000. The Policy-Media Interaction Model: Measuring Media Power During Humanitarian Crisis. *Journal of Peace Research* 37 (5): 613–33.

———. 2001. Operation Restore Hope and the Illusion of a News Media Driven Intervention. *Political Studies* 49 (5): 941–56.

————. 2002. *The CNN Effect: The Myth of News Media, Foreign Polity and Intervention.* London: Routledge.

————. 2005. The CNN Effect Revisited. *Critical Studies in Mass Communications* 22: 344–49.

Rosenau, J. N. 1961. *Public Opinion and Foreign Policy.* New York: Random House.

Rumsfeld, D. 2005. Interview with Jerry Agar, KMBZ News Radio 980. Transcript available at http://www.defenselink.mil/transcripts/transcript.aspx?transcriptid=3246.

Russett, B. M., and J. R. Oneal. 2001. *Triangulating Peace: Democracy, Interdependence, and International Organizations.* New York: Norton.

Schmitt-Beck, R. 2003. Mass Communication, Personal Communication and Vote Choice: The Filter Hypothesis of Media Influence in Comparative Perspective. *British Journal of Political Science* 33: 233–59.

Schultz, K. A. 2001. *Democracy and Coercive Diplomacy.* Cambridge: Cambridge University Press.

Sharkey, J. 1993. When Pictures Drive Foreign Policy. *American Journalism Review* 15 (10): 14–19.

Slantchev, B. 2004. How Initiators End Their Wars: The Duration of Warfare and the Terms of Peace. *American Journal of Political Science* 48 (4): 813–29.

————. 2006. Politicians, the Media, and Domestic Audience Costs. *International Studies Quarterly* 50 (2): 445–77.

Sniderman, P. M., R. A. Brody, and P. E. Tetlock. 1991. *Reasoning and Choice.* Cambridge: Cambridge University Press.

Sobel, R. 2001. *The Impact of Public Opinion on U.S. Foreign Policy Since Vietnam.* New York: Oxford University Press.

Stein, E. The Dynamic Relationship of Elites, Media and Public Opinion in Authoritarian Brazil. Unpublished manuscript.

Stoll, R. J. 1984. The Guns of November: Presidential Reelections and the Use of Force, 1947–1982. *Journal of Conflict Resolution* 28: 231–46.

Tifft, S. E., and A. S. Jones. 1999. *The Trust: The Private and Powerful Family behind the New York Times.* Boston: Little Brown.

Verba, S., R. A. Brody, E. B. Parker, N. H. Nie, N. W. Polsby, et al. 1967. Public Opinion and War in Vietnam. *American Political Science Review* 61 (2): 317–33.

Weingast, B. R. 1984. The Congressional-Bureaucratic System: A Principal Agent Perspective (With Applications to the SEC). *Public Choice* 44 (1): 147–91.

White, D. M. 1950. The Gatekeeper. A Case Study in the Selection of News. *Journalism Quarterly* 27: 383–90.

Wolfsfeld, G. 2004. *Media and the Path to Peace.* Cambridge: Cambridge University Press.

Zaller, J. 1992. *The Nature and Origins of Mass Opinion.* New York: Cambridge University Press.

————. 1994a. Positive Constructs of Public Opinion. *Critical Studies in Mass Communication* 11: 276–87.

————. 1994b. Elite Leadership of Mass Opinion: New Evidence from the Gulf War. In *Taken by Storm: The Media, Public Opinion and U.S. Foreign Policy in the Gulf War,* ed. L. W. Bennett and D. L. Paletz, pp. 186–209. Chicago: University Chicago Press.

————. 2003. A New Standard of News Quality: Burglar Alarms for the Monitorial Citizen. *Political Communication* 20: 109–30.

————. n.d. *A Theory of Media Politics: How the Interests of Politicians, Journalists, and Citizens Shape the News.* Unpublished manuscript.

Zaller, J., and D. Chiu. 2000. Government's Little Helper: U.S. Press Coverage of Foreign Policy Crises, 1946–1999. In *Decisionmaking in a Glass House,* ed. B. L. Nacos, R. Y. Shapiro, and P. Isernia, pp. 61–84. New York: Rowman & Littlefield.

Zelizer, B., and S. Allan. 2002. *Journalism after September 11.* New York: Routledge.

The Israel Lobby and U.S. Foreign Policy

JOHN J. MEARSHEIMER AND STEPHEN M. WALT

In this highly controversial article, Walt and Mearsheimer argue that U.S. foreign policy is deeply beholden to the interests of other nations, principally through the process of lobbying by ethnically based interest groups or factions. The authors hold that "the Israel Lobby" has diverted American policy elites away from serving the national interest of the U.S.A. In so doing, they argue that 'the lobby' has driven us into needless wars in Iraq, fostered a short-sighted and inflammatory U.S. foreign policy approach in the Middle East, and created a range of suboptimal foreign policy outcomes for the U.S.A.

U.S. foreign policy shapes events in every corner of the globe. Nowhere is this truer than in the Middle East, a region of recurring instability and enormous strategic importance. Most recently, the Bush administration's attempt to transform the region into a community of democracies has helped produce a resilient insurgency in Iraq, a sharp rise in world oil prices, terrorist bombings in Madrid, London and Amman, and open warfare in Gaza and Lebanon. With so much at stake for so many, all countries need to understand the forces that drive U.S. Middle East policy.

The U.S. national interest should be the primary object of American foreign policy. For the past several decades, however, and especially since the Six-Day War in 1967. a recurring feature—and arguably the central focus—of U.S. Middle East policy has been its relationship with Israel. The combination of unwavering U.S. support for Israel and the related effort to spread democracy throughout the region has inflamed Arab and Islamic opinion and jeopardized U.S. security.

This situation has no equal in American political history. Why has the United States adopted policies that jeopardized its own security in order to advance the interests of another state? One might assume that the bond between the two countries is based on shared strategic interests or compelling moral imperatives. As we show below,

however, neither of those explanations can account for the remarkable level of material and diplomatic support that the United States provides to Israel.

Instead, the overall thrust of U.S. policy in the region is due primarily to U.S. domestic politics and especially to the activities of the "Israel lobby." Other special-interest groups have managed to skew U.S. foreign policy in directions they favored, but no lobby has managed to divert U.S. foreign policy as far from what the American national interest would otherwise suggest, while simultaneously convincing Americans that U.S. and Israeli interests are essentially identical.[1]

In the pages that follow, we describe how the Israel lobby has accomplished this feat and how its activities have shaped America's actions in this critical region. Given the strategic importance of the Middle East and its potential impact on others, both Americans and non-Americans need to understand and address the lobby's influence on U.S. policy.

Some readers will find this analysis disturbing, but most of the facts recounted here are not in serious dispute among scholars. Indeed, our account draws primarily on mainstream sources like *The New York Times*, *The Washington Post*, *Ha'aretz*, or *Forward*. It also relies on the work of Israeli scholars and journalists, who deserve great credit for shedding light on these issues. We also cite evidence provided by respected Israeli and international human-rights organizations. Similarly, our claims about the lobby's impact rely on testimony from the lobby's own members, as well as testimony from politicians who have worked with them. Readers may reject our conclusions, of course, but the evidence on which they rest is not controversial.

The Great Benefactor

Since the October War in 1973, Washington has provided Israel with a level of support dwarfing the amounts provided to any other state. It has been the largest annual recipient of direct U.S. economic and military assistance since 1976 and the largest total recipient since World War II. Total direct U.S. aid to Israel amounts to well over $140 billion in 2003 dollars.[2] Israel receives about $3 billion in direct foreign assistance each year, which is roughly one-fifth of America's foreign-aid budget. In per capita terms, the United States gives each Israeli a direct subsidy worth about $500 per year.[3] This largesse is especially striking when one realizes that Israel is now a wealthy industrial state with a per capita income roughly equal to that of South Korea or Spain.[4]

Israel also gets other special deals from Washington.[5] Other aid recipients get their money in quarterly installments, but Israel receives its entire appropriation at the beginning of each fiscal year and thus earns extra interest. Most recipients of American military assistance are required to spend all of it in the United States, but Israel can use roughly 25 percent of its aid allotment to subsidize its own defense industry. Israel is the only recipient that does not have to account for how the aid is spent, an exemption that makes it virtually impossible to prevent the money from being used for purposes the United States opposes, like building settlements in the West Bank.

Moreover, the United States has provided Israel with nearly $3 billion to develop weapons systems like the *Lavi* aircraft that the Pentagon did not want or need, while giving Israel access to top-drawer U.S. weaponry like Blackhawk helicopters and F-16 jets. Finally, the United States gives Israel access to intelligence that it denies its NATO allies and has turned a blind eye toward Israel's acquisition of nuclear weapons.[6]

In addition, Washington provides Israel with consistent diplomatic support. Since 1982, the United States has vetoed 33 United Nations Security Council resolutions that were critical of Israel, a number greater than the combined total of vetoes cast by all the other Security Council members.[7] It also blocks Arab states' efforts to put Israel's nuclear arsenal on the International Atomic Energy Agency's agenda.[8]

The United States also comes to Israel's rescue in wartime and takes its side when negotiating peace. The Nixon administration resupplied Israel during the October War and protected Israel from the threat of Soviet intervention. Washington was deeply involved in the negotiations that ended that war as well as the lengthy "step-by-step" process that followed, just as it played a key role in the negotiations that preceded and followed the 1993 Oslo accords.[9] There was occasional friction between U.S. and Israeli officials in both cases, but the United States coordinated its positions closely with Israel and consistently backed the Israeli approach to the negotiations. Indeed, one American participant at Camp David (2000) later said, "Far too often, we functioned . . . as Israel's lawyer."[10]

As discussed below, Washington has given Israel wide latitude in dealing with the Occupied Territories (the West Bank and Gaza Strip), even when its actions were at odds with stated U.S. policy. Moreover, the Bush administration's ambitious strategy to transform the Middle East—beginning with the invasion of Iraq—was partly intended to improve Israel's strategic situation. The Bush administration also took Israel's side during the recent war in Lebanon and initially opposed calls for a ceasefire in order to give Israel more time to go after Hezbollah. Apart from wartime alliances, it is hard to think of another instance where one country has provided another with a similar level of material and diplomatic support for such an extended period. America's support for Israel is, in short, unique.

This extraordinary generosity might be understandable if Israel were a vital strategic asset or if there were a compelling moral case for sustained U.S. backing. But neither rationale is convincing.

A Strategic Liability

According to the website of the American-Israel Public Affairs Committee (AIPAC), "The United States and Israel have formed a unique partnership to meet the growing strategic threats in the Middle East. . . . This cooperative effort provides significant benefits for both the United States and Israel."[11] This claim is an article of faith among Israel's supporters and is routinely invoked by Israeli politicians and pro-Israel Americans.

Israel may have been a strategic asset during the Cold War.[12] By serving as America's proxy after the 1967 war, Israel helped contain Soviet expansion in the region and inflicted humiliating defeats on Soviet clients like Egypt and Syria. Israel occasionally helped protect other U.S. allies (like Jordan's King Hussein), and its military prowess forced Moscow to spend more in backing its losing clients. Israel also gave the United States useful intelligence about Soviet capabilities.

Israel's strategic value during this period should not be overstated, however.[13] Backing Israel was not cheap, and it complicated America's relations with the Arab world. For example, the U.S. decision to give Israel $2.2 billion in emergency military aid during the October War triggered an Arab oil embargo and production decrease that inflicted considerable damage on Western economies. Moreover, Israel's military could not protect U.S. interests in the region. For example, the United States could not rely on Israel when the Iranian Revolution in 1979 raised concerns about the security of Persian Gulf oil supplies. Washington had to create its own "Rapid Deployment Force" instead.

Even if Israel was a strategic asset during the Cold War, the first Gulf War (1990–91) revealed that Israel was becoming a strategic burden. The United States could not use Israeli bases during the war without rupturing the anti-Iraq coalition, and it had to divert resources (e.g., Patriot missile batteries) to keep Tel Aviv from doing anything that

might fracture the alliance against Saddam. History repeated itself in 2003. Although Israel was eager for the United States to attack Saddam, President Bush could not ask it to help without triggering Arab opposition. So Israel stayed on the sidelines again.[14]

Beginning in the 1990s, and especially after 9/11, U.S. support for Israel has been justified by the claim that both states are threatened by terrorist groups originating in the Arab or Muslim world, and by a set of "rogue states" that back these groups and seek WMD. For many, this rationale implies that Washington should give Israel a free hand in dealing with the Palestinians and with groups like Hezbollah, and not press Israel to make concessions until all Palestinian terrorists are imprisoned or dead. It also implies that the United States should go after countries like the Islamic Republic of Iran, Saddam Hussein's Iraq and Bashar al-Asad's Syria. Israel is thus seen as a crucial ally in the war on terror because its enemies are said to be America's enemies.

This new rationale seems persuasive, but Israel is, in fact, a liability in the war on terror and the broader effort to deal with rogue states.

To begin with, "terrorism" is a tactic employed by a wide array of political groups; it is not a single unified adversary. The terrorist organizations that threaten Israel (e.g., Hamas or Hezbollah) do not threaten the United States, except when it intervenes against them (as in Lebanon in 1982). Moreover, Palestinian terrorism is not random violence directed against Israel or "the West"; it is largely a response to Israel's prolonged campaign to colonize the West Bank and Gaza Strip.

More important, saying that Israel and the United States are united by a shared terrorist threat has the causal relationship backwards. Rather, the United States has a terrorism problem in good part because it is so closely allied with Israel, not the other way around. U.S. support for Israel is hardly the only source of anti-American terrorism, but it is an important one, and it makes winning the war on terror more difficult.[15] There is no question, for example, that many al-Qaeda leaders, including Osama bin Laden, are motivated in part by Israel's presence in Jerusalem and the plight of the Palestinians. According to the U.S. 9/11 Commission, Bin Laden explicitly sought to punish the United States for its policies in the Middle East, including its support for Israel. He even tried to time the attacks to highlight this issue.[16]

Equally important, unconditional U.S. support for Israel makes it easier for extremists like Bin Laden to rally popular support and to attract recruits. Public-opinion polls confirm that Arab populations are deeply hostile to American support for Israel, and the U.S. State Department's Advisory Group on Public Diplomacy for the Arab and Muslim World found that "citizens in these countries are genuinely distressed at the plight of the Palestinians and at the role they perceive the United States to be playing."[17]

As for so-called rogue states in the Middle East, they are not a dire threat to vital U.S. interests, apart from the U.S. commitment to Israel itself. Although the United States does have important disagreements with these regimes, Washington would not be nearly as worried about Iran, Baathist Iraq or Syria were it not so closely tied to Israel. Even if these states acquire nuclear weapons—which is obviously not desirable—it would not be a strategic disaster for the United States. President Bush admitted as much, saying that "the threat from Iran is, of course, their stated objective to destroy our strong ally Israel."[18] Yet this danger is probably overstated in light of Israel's and America's own nuclear deterrents. Neither country could be blackmailed by a nuclear-armed rogue state, because the blackmailer could not carry out the threat without receiving overwhelming retaliation. The danger of a "nuclear handoff" to terrorists is equally remote. A rogue state could not be sure the transfer would be undetected or that it would not be blamed and punished afterwards.

Furthermore, the U.S. relationship with Israel makes it harder to deal effectively with these states. Israel's nuclear arsenal is one reason why some of its neighbors want nuclear weapons, and threatening these states with regime change merely increases that desire. Yet Israel is not much of an asset when the United States contemplates using force against these regimes, since it cannot participate in the fight.

In short, treating Israel as America's most important ally in the campaign against terrorism and assorted Middle East dictatorships both exaggerates Israel's ability to help on these issues and ignores the ways that Israel's policies make U.S. efforts more difficult.

Unquestioned support for Israel also weakens the U.S. position outside the Middle East. Foreign elites consistently view the United States as too supportive of Israel and think its tolerance of Israeli repression in the Occupied Territories is morally obtuse and a handicap in the war on terrorism.[19] In April 2004, for example, 52 former British diplomats sent Prime Minister Tony Blair a letter saying that the Israel-Palestine conflict had "poisoned relations between the West and the Arab and Islamic worlds" and warning that the policies of Bush and then-Prime Minister Ariel Sharon were "one-sided and illegal."[20] Unqualified U.S. support for Israel's recent assault on Lebanon has elicited similar criticism from many other countries as well.

A final reason to question Israel's strategic value is that it does not act like a loyal ally. Israeli officials frequently ignore U.S. requests and renege on promises made to top U.S. leaders (including past pledges to halt settlement construction and to refrain from "targeted assassinations" of Palestinian leaders).[21] Moreover, Israel has provided sensitive U.S. military technology to potential U.S. rivals like China, in what the U.S. State Department inspector-general called "a systematic and growing pattern of unauthorized transfers."[22] According to the U.S. General Accounting Office, Israel also "conducts the most aggressive espionage operations against the U.S. of any ally."[23] In addition to the case of Jonathan Pollard, who gave Israel large quantities of classified material in the early 1980s, a new controversy erupted in 2004, when it was revealed that a key Pentagon official (Larry Franklin) had passed classified information to an Israeli diplomat, allegedly aided by two AIPAC officials.[24] Israel is hardly the only country that spies on the United States, but its willingness to spy on its principal patron casts further doubt on its strategic value.

A Dwindling Moral Case

Apart from its alleged strategic value, Israel's backers also argue that it deserves unqualified U.S. support because 1) it is weak and surrounded by enemies; 2) it is a democracy, which is a morally preferable form of government; 3) the Jewish people have suffered from past crimes and therefore deserve special treatment; and 4) Israel's conduct has been morally superior to its adversaries' behavior.

On close inspection, however, each of these arguments is unpersuasive. There is a strong moral case for supporting Israel's existence, but that is fortunately not in jeopardy. Viewed objectively, Israel's past and present conduct offers little moral basis for privileging it over the Palestinians.

Backing the Underdog?

Israel is often portrayed as weak and besieged, a Jewish David surrounded by a hostile Arab Goliath. This image has been carefully nurtured by Israeli leaders and sympathetic writers, but the opposite image is closer to the truth. Contrary to popular belief, the Zionists had larger, better-equipped, and better-led forces during the 1947–49 War of Independence, except for a brief three- to four-week period in May-June 1948, when the Arab armies enjoyed a temporary advantage in equipment (but nothing else). Moreover, the Israel Defense Forces (IDF) won quick and easy victories against Egypt in 1956 and against Egypt, Jordan and Syria in 1967—*before* large-scale U.S. aid began flowing to Israel.[25] These victories offer eloquent evidence of Israeli patriotism, organizational ability and military prowess, but they also reveal that Israel was far from helpless even in its earliest years.

Today, Israel is the strongest military power in the Middle East. Its conventional forces are far superior to its neighbors', and it is the only state in the region with nuclear weapons. Egypt and Jordan signed peace treaties with Israel, and Saudi Arabia has offered to do so as well. Syria has lost its Soviet patron, Iraq has been decimated by three disastrous wars, and Iran is hundreds of miles away. The Palestinians barely have effective police, let alone a military that could threaten Israel's existence.

Despite the IDF's recent difficulties in Lebanon, it is still more than a match for any of the conventional forces in the region and none of its potential adversaries could defeat it on the battlefield and conquer Israeli territory. According to a 2005 assessment by Tel Aviv University's prestigious Jaffee Center for Strategic Studies, "The strategic balance decidedly favors Israel, which has continued to widen the qualitative gap between its own military capability and deterrence powers and those of its neighbors."[26] If backing the underdog were a compelling rationale, the United States would be supporting Israel's opponents.

Aiding a Fellow Democracy?

American backing is often justified by the claim that Israel is a fellow democracy surrounded by hostile dictatorships. This rationale sounds convincing, but it cannot account for the current level of U.S. support. After all, there are many democracies around the world, but none receives the level of support that Israel does. The United States has overthrown democratic governments in the past and supported dictators when this was thought to advance U.S. interests, and it has good relations with a number of dictatorships today. Thus, being democratic neither justifies nor explains America's support for Israel.

The "shared democracy" rationale is also weakened by aspects of Israeli democracy that are at odds with core American values. The United States is a liberal democracy where people of any race, religion or ethnicity are supposed to enjoy equal rights. By contrast, Israel was explicitly founded as a Jewish state, and whether a citizen is regarded as Jewish ordinarily depends on kinship (i.e., verifiable Jewish ancestry).[27] Given the priority attached to Israel's Jewish character (which explains its longstanding commitment to maintaining an unchallenged Jewish majority within its territory), it is not surprising that Israel's 1.3 million Arabs are treated as second-class citizens or that a recent Israeli government commission found that Israel behaves in a "neglectful and discriminatory" manner towards them.[28]

Similarly, Israel does not permit Palestinians who marry Israeli citizens to become citizens themselves and does not give these spouses the right to live in Israel. The Israeli human-rights organization *B'tselem* called this restriction "a racist law that determines who can live here according to racist criteria."[29] Such laws may be understandable, given Israel's founding principles, but they are not consistent with America's image of democracy.

Israel's democratic status is also undermined by its refusal to grant the Palestinians a viable state of their own. Israel controls the lives of about 3.8 million Palestinians in Gaza and the West Bank, while colonizing lands on which the Palestinians have long dwelt.[30] Israel is formally democratic, but the millions of Palestinians that it controls are denied full political rights, and the "shared democracy" rationale is correspondingly weakened.

Compensation for Past Crimes

A third moral justification is the history of Jewish suffering in the Christian West, especially the tragic experience of the Holocaust. Because Jews were persecuted for centuries and can only be safe in a Jewish homeland, many believe that Israel deserves special treatment from the United States.

There is no question that Jews suffered greatly from the despicable legacy of antisemitism, and that Israel's creation was an appropriate response to a long record of crimes. This history, as noted, provides a strong moral case for supporting Israel's existence. Israel's founding was also consistent with America's general commitment to national self-determination. But the creation of Israel also involved additional crimes against a largely innocent third party: the Palestinians.

The history of these events is well-documented. When political Zionism began in earnest in the late nineteenth century, there were only about 15,000 Jews in Palestine.[31] In 1893, for example, the Arabs comprised roughly 95 percent of the population, and, though under Ottoman control, they had been in continuous possession of this territory for 1,300 years.[32] Even when Israel was founded, Jews were only about 35 percent of Palestine's population and owned 7 percent of the land.[33]

The mainstream Zionist leadership was not interested in establishing a bi-national state or accepting a permanent partition of Palestine. The Zionist leadership was sometimes willing to accept partition as a first step, but this was a tactical maneuver and not their real objective. As David Ben-Gurion put it in the summer of 1937, "After the formation of a large army in the wake of the establishment of the state, we shall abolish partition and expand to the whole of Palestine."[34] This ambition did not change after 1937 or even after Israel was founded in 1947–48. According to Israeli historian Benny Morris, "Zionist mainstream thought had always regarded a Jewish state from the Mediterranean to the Jordan River as its ultimate goal. The vision of 'Greater Israel' as Zionism's ultimate objective did not end with the 1948 war."[35]

To achieve this goal, the Zionists had to expel large numbers of Arabs from the territory that would eventually become Israel. There was simply no other way to accomplish their objective, as the Arabs were unlikely to give up their land voluntarily. Ben-Gurion saw the problem clearly, writing in 1941 that "it is impossible to imagine general evacuation [of the Arab population] without compulsion, and brutal compulsion."[36] Or, as he wrote his son Amos in October 1937, "We shall organize a modern defense force, . . . and then I am certain that we will not be prevented from settling in other parts of the country, either by mutual agreement with our Arab neighbors or by some other means."[37] As Morris puts it, "The consensus or near consensus in support of transfer—voluntary if possible, compulsory if necessary—was clear. Nor, as some critics have contended, did interest in and support for transfer end or wane when the British government in effect dropped the idea . . . in October 1938."[38]

This opportunity came in 1947–48, when Jewish forces drove up to 700,000 Palestinians into exile.[39] Israeli officials have long claimed that the Arabs fled because their leaders told them to, but careful scholarship (much of it by Israeli historians like Morris) has demolished this myth. In fact, most Arab leaders urged the Palestinian population to stay home, but fear of violent death at the hands of Zionist forces led most of them to flee.[40] After the war, Israel barred the return of the Palestinian exiles.

The fact that the creation of Israel entailed a moral crime against the Palestinian people was well understood by Israel's leaders. As Ben-Gurion told Nahum Goldmann, president of the World Jewish Congress,

> If I was an Arab leader, I would never make terms with Israel. That is natural: we have taken their country. Sure, God promised it to us, but what does that matter to them? Our God is not theirs. We come from Israel, it's true, but two thousand years ago, and what is that to them? There has been antisemitism, the Nazis, Hitler, Auschwitz, but was that their fault? They only see one thing: we have come here and stolen their country. Why should they accept that?[41]

Since then, Israeli leaders have repeatedly sought to deny the Palestinians' national ambitions.[42] Prime Minister Golda Meir famously remarked that "there was no such thing as Palestinians," and even Prime Minister Yitzhak Rabin, who signed the 1993 Oslo accords, nonetheless opposed creating a full-fledged Palestinian state.[43] Pressure from extremist violence and the growing Palestinian population has forced subsequent Israeli leaders to disengage from some of the Occupied Territories and to explore territorial compromise, but no Israeli government has been willing to offer the Palestinians a viable state of their own. Even Prime Minister Ehud Barak's purportedly generous offer at Camp David in July 2000 would only have given the Palestinians a disarmed and dismembered set of "Bantustans" under *de facto* Israeli control.[44]

Europe's crimes against the Jews provide a strong moral justification for Israel's right to exist. But Israel's survival is not in doubt, even if some Islamic extremists harbor unrealistic hopes or make outrageous references to "erasing Israel from the map of time."[45] More important, the tragic history of the Jewish people does not obligate the United States to help Israel no matter what it does today.

"Virtuous Israelis" versus "Evil Arabs"

The final moral argument portrays Israel as a country that has sought peace at every turn and showed great restraint even when provoked. The Arabs, by contrast, are said to have acted with great wickedness. This narrative—which is endlessly repeated by Israeli leaders and American apologists such as Alan Dershowitz—is yet another myth.[46] In terms of actual behavior, Israel's conduct is not morally distinguishable from the actions of its opponents.

Israeli scholarship shows that the early Zionists were far from benevolent towards the Palestinian Arabs.[47] The Arab inhabitants did resist the Zionists' encroachments, which is hardly surprising given that the Zionists were trying to create their own state on Arab lands. The Zionists responded vigorously, and neither side owns the moral high ground during this period. This same scholarship also reveals that the creation of Israel in 1947–48 involved explicit acts of ethnic cleansing, including executions, massacres and rapes by Jews.[48] Such atrocities have taken place in many wars, of course, but their occurrence in this period undercuts Israel's claim to a special moral status.

Furthermore, Israel's subsequent conduct towards its Arab adversaries and its Palestinian subjects has often been brutal, belying any claim to morally superior conduct. Between 1949 and 1956, for example, Israeli security forces killed between 2,700 and 5,000 Arab infiltrators, the overwhelming majority of them unarmed.[49] The IDF conducted numerous cross-border raids against its neighbors in the early 1950s, and, though these actions were portrayed as defensive responses, they were actually part of a broader effort to expand Israel's borders. Israel's expansionist ambitions also led it to join Britain and France in attacking Egypt in 1956. Israel withdrew from the lands it had conquered only in the face of intense U.S. pressure.[50]

The IDF also murdered hundreds of Egyptian prisoners of war in both the 1956 and 1967 wars.[51] In 1967, it expelled between 100,000 and 260,000 Palestinians from the newly conquered West Bank and drove 80,000 Syrians from the Golan Heights.[52] It was also complicit in the massacre of 700 innocent Palestinians at the Sabra and Shatila refugee camps following its invasion of Lebanon in 1982. An Israeli investigatory commission found then-Defense Minister Sharon "personally responsible" for these atrocities.[53] The commission's willingness to hold a top official like Sharon accountable is admirable, but we should not forget that Israeli voters subsequently elected him prime minister.

Israeli personnel have tortured numerous Palestinian prisoners, systematically humiliated and inconvenienced Palestinian civilians, and used force indiscriminately against them on numerous occasions. During the first intifada (1987–91), for example, the IDF distributed truncheons to its troops and encouraged them to break the bones of Palestinian protestors. The Swedish "Save the Children" organization estimated that "23,600 to 29,900 children required medical treatment for their beating injuries in the first two years of the intifada," with nearly one-third sustaining broken bones. It also estimated that "nearly one-third of the beaten children were aged ten and under."[54]

Israel's response to the second intifada (2000–05) has been even more violent, leading *Ha'aretz* to declare that "the IDF . . . is turning into a killing machine whose efficiency is awe-inspiring, yet shocking."[55] The IDF fired one million bullets in the first days of the uprising, hardly a measured response.[56] Since then, Israel has killed 3.4 Palestinians for every Israeli lost, the majority of whom have been innocent bystanders; the ratio of Palestinian to Israeli children killed is even higher (5.7 to one).[57] Israeli forces have also killed several foreign peace activists, including a 23-year-old American woman crushed by an Israeli bulldozer in March 2003.[58]

These facts about Israel's conduct have been amply documented by numerous human-rights organizations—including prominent Israeli groups—and are not disputed by fair-minded observers. That is the reason four former officials of Shin Bet (the Israeli domestic-security organization) condemned Israel's conduct during the second intifada in November 2003. One of them declared, "We are behaving disgracefully," and another termed Israel's conduct "patently immoral."[59]

A similar pattern can be seen in Israel's response to the recent escalation in violence in Gaza and Lebanon. The killing of two Israeli soldiers (and the capture of a third) by Hamas led to a massive reprisal that killed dozens of Palestinians (most of them innocent civilians) and destroyed essential infrastructure throughout Gaza. Similarly, after Hezbollah units captured or killed several IDF soldiers near the Israeli-Lebanese border, Israel unleashed a massive air and artillery offensive that killed hundreds of innocent Lebanese civilians, forced hundreds of thousands more to flee their homes, and destroyed millions of dollars worth of property.

But isn't Israel entitled to do whatever it takes to protect its citizens? Doesn't the unique evil of terrorism justify continued U.S. support, even if Israel often responds harshly?

In fact, this argument is not a compelling moral justification either. Palestinians have used terrorism against their Israeli occupiers, and their willingness to attack innocent civilians is clearly wrong and should be roundly condemned. This behavior is not surprising, however, because the Palestinians have long been denied basic political rights and believe they have no other way to force Israeli concessions. As former Prime Minister Barak once admitted, had he been born a Palestinian, he "would have joined a terrorist organization."[60] If the situation were reversed, and the Israelis were under Arab occupation, they would undoubtedly be using similar tactics against their oppressors, just as other resistance movements around the world have done.

Indeed, terrorism was one of the key tactics the Zionists used when they were in a similarly weak position and trying to obtain their own state. Between 1944 and 1947, several Zionist organizations used terrorist bombings to drive the British from Palestine and took the lives of many innocent civilians along the way.[61] Israeli terrorists also murdered U.N. mediator Count Folke Bernadotte in 1948, because they opposed his proposal to internationalize Jerusalem.[62] Nor were the perpetrators of these acts isolated extremists: the leaders of the murder plot were eventually granted amnesty by the Israeli government; one of them was elected to the Knesset.

Another terrorist leader, who approved Bernadotte's murder but was not tried, was future Prime Minister Yitzhak Shamir. Indeed, Shamir openly argued that "neither Jewish ethics nor Jewish tradition can disqualify terrorism as a means of combat."

Rather, terrorism had "a great part to play . . . in our war against the occupier [Britain]."[63] If the Palestinians' use of terrorism is morally reprehensible today, so was Israel's reliance upon it in the past. Thus one cannot justify U.S. support for Israel on the grounds that its prior conduct was morally superior.[64]

Similarly, although Israel is clearly justified in responding to violent acts by groups like Hamas and Hezbollah, its willingness to inflict massive suffering on innocent civilians casts doubt on its repeated claims to a special moral status. Israel may not have acted worse than many other countries, but it clearly has not acted any better.

The Israel Lobby

If neither strategic nor moral arguments can account for America's support for Israel, how are we to explain it? The explanation lies in the political power of the Israel lobby. Were it not for the lobby's ability to work effectively within the American political system, the relationship between Israel and the United States would be far less intimate than it is today.

What Is the Lobby?

We use "the lobby" as a convenient short-hand term for the loose coalition of individuals and organizations that actively work to shape U.S. foreign policy in a pro-Israel direction. Our use of this term is not meant to suggest that "the lobby" is a unified movement with a central leadership or that individuals within it do not disagree on certain issues. The lobby is not a cabal or conspiracy, and its activities are essentially consistent with the interest-group tradition that has long governed American political life.

The core of the lobby consists of American Jews who make a significant effort in their daily lives to bend U.S. foreign policy so that it advances Israel's interests.[65] Their activities go beyond merely voting for candidates who are pro-Israel to include writing letters, contributing money and supporting pro-Israel organizations. But the lobby is not synonymous with American Jews. Israel is not a salient issue for many of them, and many do not support the lobby's positions. In a 2004 survey, for example, roughly 36 percent of Jewish-Americans said they were either "not very" or "not at all" emotionally attached to Israel.[66] Moreover, some groups that work on Israel's behalf—such as the "Christian Zionists" discussed below—are not Jewish.

Jewish-Americans also differ on specific Israeli policies. Many of the key organizations in the lobby, like AIPAC and the Conference of Presidents of Major Jewish Organizations, are run by hardliners who generally supported the expansionist policies of Israel's Likud party, including its hostility to the Oslo peace process. The bulk of U.S. Jewry, on the other hand, is more favorably disposed to making concessions to the Palestinians, and a few groups—such as Jewish Voice for Peace—strongly advocate such steps.[67] Despite these differences, the majority of organized groups in the American Jewish community favor steadfast U.S. support for Israel.

Not surprisingly, American Jewish leaders often consult with Israeli officials so that the former can maximize their influence in the United States. As one activist with a major Jewish organization wrote, "It is routine for us to say: 'This is our policy on a certain issue, but we must check what the Israelis think.' We as a community do it all the time."[68] There is also a strong norm against criticizing Israeli policy, and Jewish-American leaders rarely support putting pressure on Israel. Thus, Edgar Bronfman, Sr., the president of the World Jewish Congress, was accused of "perfidy" when he wrote a letter to President Bush in mid-2003 urging him to pressure Israel to curb construction of its controversial "security fence."[69] Critics declared, "It would be obscene at any time for the president of the World Jewish Congress to lobby the president of the United States to resist policies being promoted by the government of Israel."

Similarly, when Israel Policy Forum president Seymour Reich advised Secretary of State Condoleezza Rice to pressure Israel to reopen a critical border crossing in the Gaza Strip in November 2005, critics denounced his action as "irresponsible behavior" and declared, "There is absolutely no room in the Jewish mainstream for actively canvassing against the security-related policies . . . of

Israel."[70] Recoiling from these attacks, Reich proclaimed, "The word pressure is not in my vocabulary when it comes to Israel."

Jewish-Americans have formed an impressive array of organizations to influence American foreign policy, of which AIPAC is the most powerful and well-known. In 1997, *Fortune* magazine asked members of Congress and their staffs to list the most powerful lobbies in Washington.[71] AIPAC was ranked second behind the American Association of Retired People (AARP) but ahead of heavyweight lobbies like the AFL-CIO and the National Rifle Association (NRA). A *National Journal* study in March 2005 reached a similar conclusion, placing AIPAC in second place (tied with AARP) in Washington's "muscle rankings."[72]

The lobby also includes prominent Christian evangelicals like Gary Bauer, Jerry Falwell, Ralph Reed and Pat Robertson, as well as Dick Armey and Tom DeLay, former majority' leaders in the House of Representatives. These "Christian Zionists" believe Israel's rebirth is part of Biblical prophecy, support its expansionist agenda and think pressuring Israel is contrary to God's will.[73] In addition, the lobby also draws support from neoconservative gentiles such as John Bolton, the late *Wall Street Journal* editor Robert Bartley, former Secretary of Education William Bennett, former UN Ambassador Jeanne Kirkpatrick and columnist George Will.

Sources of Power

The United States has a divided government that offers many avenues for influencing the policy process. As a result, interest groups can shape policy in many different ways: lobbying elected representatives and members of the Executive Branch, making campaign contributions, voting in elections, molding public opinion, etc.[74]

Furthermore, special-interest groups enjoy disproportionate power when they are committed to a particular issue and the bulk of the population is indifferent. This is often the case in foreign affairs. Policy makers will tend to accommodate those who care about the issue in question, even if their numbers are small, confident that the rest of the population will not penalize them.

The Israel lobby's power flows from its unmatched ability to play this game of interest-group politics. In its basic operations, it is no different from the farm lobby, the NRA, steel and textile-workers groups, and other ethnic lobbies. What sets the Israel lobby apart is its extraordinary effectiveness. But there is nothing improper about American Jews and their Christian allies attempting to sway U.S. policy towards Israel. To repeat: the lobby's activities are not the sort of conspiracy depicted in antisemitic tracts like the *Protocols of the Elders of Zion*. For the most part, the individuals and groups that comprise the lobby are doing what other special-interest groups do, just much better. Moreover, pro-Arab interest groups are weak to non-existent, which makes the lobby's task even easier.[75]

Strategies for Success

The lobby pursues two broad strategies to promote U.S. support for Israel. First, it wields significant influence in Washington, pressuring both Congress and the Executive Branch to support Israel down the line. Whatever an individual lawmaker or policy maker's own views, the lobby tries to make supporting Israel the "smart" political choice.

Second, the lobby strives to ensure that public discourse about Israel portrays it in a positive light, by repeating myths about Israel and its founding and by publicizing Israel's side in the policy debates of the day. The goal is to prevent critical commentary about Israel from getting a fair hearing in the political arena. Controlling the debate is essential to guaranteeing U.S. support, because a candid discussion of U.S.-Israeli relations might lead Americans to favor a different policy.

Influencing Congress

A key pillar of the lobby's effectiveness is its influence in the U.S. Congress, where Israel is virtually immune from criticism. This is in itself a remarkable situation, because Congress almost never shies away from contentious issues. Whether the issue is abortion, affirmative action, health care or welfare, there is certain to be a lively debate on Capitol Hill. Where Israel is concerned, however, potential critics fall silent; there is hardly any debate at all.

One reason for the lobby's success with Congress is that some key members are "Christian Zionists" like Dick Armey, who said in September 2002, "My number-one priority in foreign policy is to protect Israel."[76] One would think that the number-one priority for any congressman would be to "protect America," but that is not what Armey said. There are also Jewish senators and congressmen who work to make U.S. foreign policy support Israel's interests.

Pro-Israel congressional staffers are another source of the lobby's power. As Morris Amitay, a former head of AIPAC, once noted, "There are a lot of guys at the working level up here [on Capitol Hill] . . . who happen to be Jewish, who are willing . . . to look at certain issues in terms of their Jewishness. . . . These are all guys who are in a position to make the decision in these areas for those senators. . . . You can get an awful lot done just at the staff level."[77]

It is AIPAC itself, however, that forms the core of the lobby's influence in Congress.[78] AIPAC's success is due to its ability to reward legislators and congressional candidates who support its agenda and to punish those who challenge it. Money is critical to U.S. elections (as the recent scandal over lobbyist Jack Abramoff's various shady dealings reminds us), and AIPAC makes sure that its friends get financial support from the myriad pro-Israel political action committees. Those seen as hostile to Israel, on the other hand, can be sure that AIPAC will direct campaign contributions to their political opponents. AIPAC also organizes letter-writing campaigns and encourages newspaper editors to endorse pro-Israel candidates.

There is no doubt about the potency of these tactics. To take but one example, in 1984, AIPAC helped defeat Senator Charles Percy from Illinois, who, according to one prominent lobby figure, had "displayed insensitivity and even hostility to our concerns." Thomas Dine, the head of AIPAC at the time, explained what happened: "All the Jews in America, from coast to coast, gathered to oust Percy. And the American politicians—those who hold public positions now, and those who aspire— got the message."[79] Other U.S. politicians who have fell AIPAC's wrath include former representatives

Paul Findley (R-IL), Pete McCloskey (R-CA), Cynthia McKinney (D-GA), and James Moran (D-VA), just to name a few.[80] One could also include Senator Hillary Clinton (D-NY), whose support for Palestinian statehood and public embrace of Suha Arafat (wife of Palestinian Liberation Organization Chairman Yasser Arafat) provoked strong criticism from groups in the lobby. Not surprisingly, Clinton became an ardent defender of Israel once she began running for office herself.[81] AIPAC prizes its reputation as a formidable adversary, of course, because this discourages anyone from questioning its agenda.

AIPAC's influence on Capitol Hill goes even further, however. According to Douglas Bloomfield, a former AIPAC staff member, "It is common for members of Congress and their staffs to turn to AIPAC first when they need information, before calling the Library of Congress, the Congressional Research Service, committee staff or administration experts."[82] More important, he notes that AIPAC is "often called upon to draft speeches, work on legislation, advise on tactics, perform research, collect co-sponsors and marshal votes."

The bottom line is that AIPAC, which bills itself as "America's Pro-Israel Lobby," has an unchallenged hold on the U.S. Congress.[83] Open debate about U.S. policy towards Israel does not occur there, even though that policy has important consequences for the entire world. Thus, one of the three main branches of the U.S. government is firmly committed to supporting Israel. As former Senator Ernest Hollings (D-SC) noted as he was leaving office, "You can't have an Israeli policy other than what AIPAC gives you around here."[84] Small wonder that former Israeli Prime Minister Ariel Sharon once told an American audience, "When people ask me how they can help Israel, I tell them—help AIPAC." His successor, Ehud Olmert, agrees, remarking, "Thank God we have AIPAC, the greatest supporter and friend we have in the whole world."[85]

Influencing the Executive

The lobby also has significant leverage over the Executive Branch. That power derives in part from the influence Jewish voters have on presidential elections. Despite their small numbers in the population (less than 3 percent), Jewish-Americans make large campaign donations to candidates from both parties. *The Washington Post* once estimated that Democratic presidential candidates "depend on Jewish supporters to supply as much as 60 percent of the money."[86] Furthermore, Jewish voters have high turn-out rates and are concentrated in key states like California, Florida, Illinois, New Jersey, New York and Pennsylvania. This increases their weight in determining electoral outcomes. Because they matter in close elections, presidential candidates try not to antagonize Jewish voters.

Key organizations in the lobby also directly target the administration in power. For example, pro-Israel forces make sure that critics of the Jewish state do not get important foreign-policy appointments. Jimmy Carter wanted to make George Ball his first secretary of state, but he knew that Ball was perceived as critical of Israel and that the lobby would oppose the appointment.[87] This litmus test encourages any aspiring policy maker to become an overt supporter of Israel (or at the very least, to refrain from criticizing U.S. support for Israel). Thus, public critics of Israeli policy have become an endangered species in the U.S. foreign policy establishment.

These constraints still operate today. When 2004 presidential candidate Howard Dean called for the United States to take a more "even-handed role" in the Arab-Israeli conflict, Senator Joseph Lieberman accused him of selling Israel down the river and said his statement was "irresponsible."[88] Virtually all of the top Democrats in the House of Representatives signed a hard-hitting letter to Dean criticizing his comments, and *The Chicago Jewish Star* reported that "anonymous attackers . . . are clogging the e-mail inboxes of Jewish leaders around the country, warning—without much evidence—that Dean would somehow be bad for Israel."[89]

This worry was absurd, however, because Dean is in fact quite hawkish on Israel.[90] His campaign co-chair was a former AIPAC president, and Dean said his own views on the Middle East more closely reflected those of AIPAC than of the more moderate Americans for Peace Now. Dean had merely suggested that to "bring the sides together," Washington should act as an honest broker. This is hardly a radical idea, but it is anathema to the lobby, which does not tolerate the idea of even-handedness when it comes to the Arab-Israeli conflict.

The lobby's goals are also served when pro-Israel individuals occupy important positions in the Executive Branch. During the Clinton administration, for example, Middle East policy was largely shaped by officials with close ties to Israel or to prominent pro-Israel organizations—including Martin Indyk, the former deputy director of research at AIPAC and co-founder of the pro-Israel Washington Institute for Near East Policy (WINEP); Dennis Ross, who joined WINEP after leaving government in 2001; and Aaron Miller, who has lived in Israel and often visits there.[91]

These men were among President Clinton's closest advisors at the Camp David summit in July 2000. Although all three supported the Oslo peace process and favored creation of a Palestinian state, they did so only within the limits of what would be acceptable to Israel.[92] In particular, the American delegation took most of its cues from Israeli Prime Minister Ehud Barak, coordinated negotiating positions with Israel in advance, and did not offer its own independent proposals for settling the conflict. Not surprisingly, Palestinian negotiators complained that they were "negotiating with two Israeli teams—one displaying an Israeli flag, and one an American flag."[93]

The situation is even more pronounced in the Bush administration, whose ranks have included fervently pro-Israel individuals like Elliot Abrams, John Bolton, Douglas Feith, I. Lewis ("Scooter") Libby, Richard Perle, Paul Wolfowitz and David Wurmser. As we shall see, these officials consistently pushed for policies favored by Israel and backed by organizations in the lobby.

Manipulating the Media

In addition to influencing government policy directly, the lobby strives to shape public perceptions about Israel and the Middle East. It does not want an open debate on issues involving Israel, because an open debate might cause Americans to question the level of support that they currently provide. Accordingly, pro-Israel organizations work hard to influence the media, think tanks and academia, institutions that are critical in shaping popular opinion.

The lobby's perspective on Israel is widely reflected in the mainstream media, in good part because most American commentators are pro-Israel. The debate among Middle East pundits, journalist Eric Alterman writes, is "dominated by people who cannot imagine criticizing Israel."[94] He lists 61 "columnists and commentators who can be counted upon to support Israel reflexively and without qualification." Conversely, Alterman found just five pundits who consistently criticize Israeli behavior or endorse pro-Arab positions. Newspapers occasionally publish guest op-eds challenging Israeli policy, but the balance of opinion clearly favors the other side.

This pro-Israel bias is reflected in the editorials of major newspapers. Robert Bartley, the late editor of the *Wall Street Journal*, once remarked, "Shamir, Sharon, Bibi—whatever those guys want is pretty much fine by me."[95] Not surprisingly, the *Journal*, along with other prominent newspapers like *The Chicago Sun-Times* and *The Washington Times,* regularly run editorials that are strongly pro-Israel and rarely publish editorials that criticize it. Magazines like *Commentary, The New Republic* and *The Weekly Standard* also zealously defend Israel at every turn.

Editorial bias is also found in papers like *The New York Times.* The *Times* occasionally criticizes Israeli policies and sometimes acknowledges that the Palestinians have legitimate grievances, but it is not even-handed.[96] In his memoirs, for example, former *Times* executive editor Max Frankel recounted the impact his own pro-Israel attitude had on his editorial choices: "I was much more deeply devoted to Israel than I dared to assert." He goes on, "Fortified by my knowledge of Israel and my friendships there, I myself wrote most of our Middle East commentaries. As more Arab than Jewish readers recognized, I wrote them from a pro-Israel perspective."[97]

The media's reporting of news events involving Israel is somewhat more even-handed than editorial commentary is, in part because reporters strive to be objective, but also because it is difficult to cover events in the Occupied Territories without acknowledging Israel's actual behavior. To discourage unfavorable reporting on Israel, the lobby organizes letter-writing campaigns, demonstrations and boycotts against news outlets whose content it considers anti-Israel. One CNN executive has said that he sometimes gets 6,000 e-mail messages in a single day complaining that a story is anti-Israel.[98] Similarly, the pro-Israel Committee for Accuracy in Middle East Reporting in America (CAMERA) organized demonstrations outside National Public Radio stations in 33 cities in May 2003. It also tried to convince contributors to withhold support from NPR until its Middle East coverage became more sympathetic to Israel." Boston's NPR station, WBUR, reportedly lost more than $1 million in contributions as a result of these efforts. Pressure on NPR has also come from Israel's friends in Congress, who have asked NPR for an internal audit as well as more oversight of its Middle East coverage.

These factors help explain why the American media offer few criticisms of Israeli policy, rarely question Washington's unconditional commitment to Israel, and only occasionally discuss the lobby's influence on U.S. policy.

Think Tanks That Think One Way

Pro-Israel forces predominate in U.S. think tanks, which play an important role in shaping public debate as well as actual policy. The lobby created its own think tank in 1985, when Martin Indyk helped found WINEP.[99] Although WINEP plays down its links to Israel and claims instead that it provides a "balanced and realistic" perspective on Middle East issues, this is not the case.[100] In fact, WINEP is funded and run by individuals who are deeply committed to advancing Israel's agenda.

The lobby's influence in the think-tank world extends well beyond WINEP. Over the past 25 years, pro-Israel forces have established a commanding presence at the American Enterprise Institute (AEI), the Brookings Institution, the Center for Security' Policy, the Foreign Policy Research Institute, the Heritage Foundation, the Hudson Institute, the Institute for Foreign Policy Analysis and the Jewish Institute for National Security Affairs (JINSA). These think tanks are decidedly pro-Israel and include few, if any, critics of U.S. support for the Jewish state.

A good indicator of the lobby's influence in the think-tank world is the evolution of the Brookings Institution. For many years, its senior expert on Middle East issues was William B. Quandt, a distinguished academic and former NSC official with a well-deserved reputation for evenhandedness regarding the Arab-Israeli conflict. Today, however, work on these issues at Brookings is conducted through its Saban Center for Middle East Studies, which is financed by Haim Saban, a wealthy Israeli-American businessman and ardent Zionist.[101] The director of the Saban Center is the ubiquitous Martin Indyk. Although it occasionally hosts Arab experts and tolerates some divergence of opinion, Saban Center publications never question U.S. support for Israel and rarely, if ever, offer significant criticisms of key Israeli policies. In sum, what was once a nonpartisan policy institute on Middle East matters has moved in a decidedly pro-Israel direction overtime.

Thus, the balance of power inside the Beltway strongly favors Israel. There are a few think tanks that are not reflexively pro-Israel (e.g., the New America Foundation, the CATO Institute, the Middle East Institute), but the largest and most visible think tanks usually take Israel's side and do not question the merits of unconditional U.S. support.

Policing Academia

The lobby has had the most difficulty stifling debate about Israel on college campuses, because academic freedom is a core value and because tenured professors are hard to threaten or silence. Even so, there was only mild criticism of Israel in the 1990s, when the Oslo peace process was underway. Criticism rose after that process collapsed and Ariel Sharon came to power in early 2001. It became especially intense when the IDF reoccupied the West Bank in spring 2002 and employed massive force against the second intifada.

The lobby moved aggressively to "take back the campuses." New groups sprang up, like the Caravan for Democracy, which brought Israeli speakers to U.S. colleges.[102] Established groups such as the Jewish Council for Public Affairs and Hillel jumped into the fray, and a new entity—the Israel on Campus Coalition—was formed to coordinate the many groups that now sought to make Israel's case on campus. Finally, AIPAC more than tripled its spending for programs to monitor university activities and to train young advocates for Israel, in order to "vastly expand the number of students involved on campus . . . in the national pro-Israel effort."[103]

The lobby also monitors what professors write and teach. In September 2002, for example, Daniel Pipes, a passionately pro-Israel neoconservative, established a website (Campus Watch) that posted dossiers on suspect academics and encouraged students to report comments or behavior that might be considered hostile to Israel.[104] This transparent attempt to blacklist and intimidate scholars prompted such a harsh reaction that Pipes later removed the dossiers, but the website still invites students to report alleged anti-Israel behavior at U.S. colleges.

Groups in the lobby also direct their fire at particular professors and the universities that hire them. Columbia University, which had the late Palestinian scholar Edward Said on its faculty, has been a frequent target of pro-Israel forces. Jonathan Cole, the former Columbia provost, reported, "One can be sure that any public statement in support of the Palestinian people by the preeminent literary critic Edward Said will elicit hundreds of e-mails, letters and journalistic accounts that call on us to denounce Said and to either sanction or fire him."[105] When Columbia recruited historian Rashid Khalidi from the University of Chicago, Cole says that "the complaints started flowing in from people who disagreed with the content of his political views." Princeton faced the same problem a few years later when it considered trying to woo Khalidi away from Columbia.[106]

A similar pattern occurred again in 2006, when the departments of History and Sociology at Yale University voted to appoint Professor Juan Cole, a distinguished historian at the University of Michigan. Cole is also the author of a prize-winning weblog ("Informed Comment") and has criticized a number of Israeli policies in recent years. His appointment was attacked by pro-Israel columnists in *The Wall Street Journal* and *The Washington Times.* The newspaper *Jewish Week* reported that several prominent Jewish donors called Yale officials in order to protest the appointment, which was subsequently overturned by the University's appointments committee. The impact of this alleged donor pressure is unknown, but the incident underscores the importance that Israel's supporters now attach to shaping discourse on campus.[107]

A classic illustration of the effort to police academia occurred in late 2004, when the "David Project" produced a propaganda film alleging that faculty in Columbia University's Middle East studies program were antisemitic and were intimidating Jewish students who defended Israel.[108] Columbia was raked over the coals in pro-Israel circles, but a faculty committee assigned to investigate the charges found no evidence of antisemitism. The only incident worth noting was the possibility that one professor had "responded heatedly" to a student's question.[109] The committee also discovered that the accused professors had been the target of an overt intimidation campaign.

Perhaps the most disturbing aspect of this campaign to eliminate criticism of Israel from college campuses is the effort by Jewish groups to push Congress to establish mechanisms that monitor what professors say about Israel.[110] Schools judged to have an anti-Israel bias would be denied federal funding. This effort to get the U.S. government to police campuses has not yet succeeded, but the attempt illustrates the importance pro-Israel groups place on controlling debate on these issues.

Finally, a number of Jewish philanthropists have established Israel studies programs (in addition to the roughly 130 Jewish Studies programs that already exist) so as to increase the number of Israel-friendly scholars on campus.[111] NYU announced the establishment of the Taub Center for Israel Studies on May 1, 2003, and similar programs have been established at other universities like Berkeley,

Brandeis and Emory. Academic administrators emphasize the pedagogical value of these programs, but they are intended in good part to promote Israel's image on campus. Fred Lafer, the head of the Taub Foundation, makes clear that his foundation funded the NYU center to help counter the "Arabic [sic] point of view" that he thinks is prevalent in NYU's Middle East programs.[112]

In sum, the lobby has gone to considerable lengths to protect Israel from criticism on college campuses. It has not been as successful in academia as it has been on Capitol Hill, but it has worked hard to stifle criticism of Israel by professors and students, and there is much less of it on campuses today.[113]

The Great Silencer

No discussion of how the lobby operates would be complete without examining one of its most powerful weapons: the charge of antisemitism. Anyone who criticizes Israeli actions or says that pro-Israel groups have significant influence over U.S. Middle East policy—an influence that AIPAC celebrates—stands a good chance of getting labeled an antisemite. In fact, anyone who says that there is an Israel lobby runs the risk of being charged with antisemitism, even though the Israeli media frequently refer to America's "Jewish lobby."[114] In effect, the lobby boasts of its own power and then attacks anyone who calls attention to it. This tactic is very effective; antisemitism is loathsome, and no responsible person wants to be accused of it.

Europeans have been more willing than Americans to criticize Israeli policy in recent years. Some attribute this to a resurgence of antisemitism in Europe. We are "getting to a point," the U.S. ambassador to the European Union said in early 2004, "where it is as bad as it was in the 1930s."[115] Measuring antisemitism is a complicated matter, but the weight of evidence points in the opposite direction. For example, in the spring of 2004, when accusations of European antisemitism filled the air in America, separate surveys of European public opinion conducted by the Anti-Defamation League and the Pew Research Center for the People and the Press showed that it was actually declining.[116]

Consider France, which pro-Israel forces often portray as the most antisemitic state in Europe. A poll of French citizens in 2002 found that: 89 percent could envisage living with a Jew; 97 percent believe making antisemitic graffiti is a serious crime; 87 percent think attacks on French synagogues are scandalous; and 85 percent of practicing French Catholics reject the charge that Jews have too much influence in business and finance.[117] It is unsurprising that the head of the French Jewish community declared in the summer of 2003 that "France is not more antisemitic than America."[118] According to a recent article in *Ha'aretz,* the French police report that antisemitic incidents in France declined by almost 50 percent in 2005, despite the fact that France has the largest Muslim population of any country in Europe.[119]

Finally, when a French Jew was brutally murdered by a Muslim gang in February 2006, tens of thousands of French demonstrators poured into the streets to condemn antisemitism. Moreover, President Jacques Chirac and Prime Minister Dominique de Villepin both attended the victim's memorial service in a public show of solidarity with French Jewry.[120] It is also worth noting that, in 2002, more Jews immigrated to Germany than Israel, making it "the fastest growing Jewish community in the world," according to an article in the Jewish newspaper *Forward.*[121] If Europe were really heading back to the 1930s, it is hard to imagine that Jews would be moving there in large numbers.

We recognize, however, that Europe is not free of the scourge of antisemitism. No one would deny that there are still some virulent autochthonous antisemites in Europe (as there are in the United States), but their numbers are small and their extreme views are rejected by the vast majority of Europeans. Nor would one deny that there is antisemitism among European Muslims, some of it provoked by Israel's behavior towards the Palestinians and some of it straightforwardly racist.[122] This problem is worrisome, but it is hardly out of control. Muslims constitute less than five percent of Europe's total population, and European governments are working hard to combat the problem.

Why? Because most Europeans reject such hateful views.[123] In short, when it comes to antisemitism, Europe today bears hardly any resemblance to Europe in the 1930s.

This is why pro-Israel forces, when pressed to go beyond assertion, claim that there is a "new antisemitism," which they equate with criticism of Israel.[124] In other words, criticize Israeli policy, and you are by definition an antisemite. When the synod of the Church of England voted to divest from Caterpillar Inc. on the grounds that the company manufactures the bulldozers used to demolish Palestinian homes, the Chief Rabbi complained that it would "have the most adverse repercussions on . . . Jewish-Christian relations in Britain," while Rabbi Tony Bayfield, the head of the Reform movement, said: "There is a clear problem of anti-Zionist—verging on anti-Semitic—attitudes emerging in the grass roots, and even in the middle ranks of the Church."[125] However, the Church was guilty of neither anti-Zionism nor antisemitism; it was merely protesting Israeli policy.[126]

Critics are also accused of holding Israel to an unfair standard or questioning its right to exist. But these are bogus charges too. Western critics of Israel hardly ever question its right to exist. Instead, they question its behavior towards the Palestinians. This is a legitimate criticism; Israelis question it themselves. Nor is Israel being judged unfairly. Rather, Israeli treatment of the Palestinians elicits criticism because it is contrary to widely accepted human-rights norms and international law, as well as the principle of national self-determination. And it is hardly the only state that has faced sharp criticism on these grounds.

This discussion of a powerful lobby working to move U.S. policy in a pro-Israel direction is bound to make some people uncomfortable, because it seems to invoke the spectre of "dual loyalty," a familiar antisemitic canard in old Europe. The charge, in its original incarnation, was that Jews were perpetual aliens who were only loyal to each other. They could not assimilate and become good patriots, so the argument went, because they were thought to be more loyal to their fellow Jews than to the societies in which they lived.

We reject this view wholeheartedly and do not believe that Americans who lobby on Israel's behalf are in any way disloyal. Rather, we recognize that all individuals have many attachments—to country, religion, family, employer, etc.—and that in the United States, it is legitimate to express these attachments in politics. In other words, it is neither improper nor illegitimate for Americans to advocate policies they believe will benefit both the United States and Israel.

But it is equally legitimate for others to point out that groups like AIPAC and the individuals who press Israel's case have a commitment to Israel that shapes their thinking about many foreign-policy issues. Why else would Malcolm Hoenlein, the driving force behind the powerful Conference of Presidents, describe his job as follows: "I devote myself to the security of the Jewish state"?[127] It should be legitimate for others to discuss the influence of these groups and to question whether their prescriptions are the right ones without being smeared as antisemites.

In sum, although there are a great many special-interest groups in the United States, most of them can only dream of having the political muscle that pro-Israel organizations possess. The question, therefore, is this: What effect does the Israel lobby have on U.S. foreign policy?

The Tail Wagging the Dog

If the lobby's impact were confined to U.S. economic aid to Israel, its influence might not be that worrisome. Foreign aid is valuable, but not as useful as having the world's only superpower bring its vast capabilities to bear on Israel's behalf. Accordingly, the lobby has also sought to shape the core elements of U.S. Middle East policy. In particular, it has worked successfully to convince American leaders to back Israel's continued repression of the Palestinians and to take aim at Israel's primary regional adversaries—Iran, Iraq, and Syria—as well as groups like Hezbollah.

Demonizing the Palestinians

It is now largely forgotten, but in the fall of 2001, and especially in the spring of 2002, the Bush administration made a brief attempt to reduce anti-American sentiment in the Arab world and undermine support for terrorist groups like al-Qaeda, by halting Israel's expansionist policies in the Occupied Territories and advocating the creation of a Palestinian state.

Bush had enormous potential leverage at his disposal. He could have threatened to reduce U.S. economic and diplomatic support for Israel, and the American people would almost certainly have supported him. A May 2003 poll reported that over 60 percent of Americans were willing to withhold aid to Israel if it resisted U.S. pressure to settle the conflict; that number rose to 70 percent among "politically active" Americans.[128] Indeed, 73 percent said that United States should not favor either side.

Yet the Bush administration failed to change Israel's policies, and Washington ended up backing Israel's hard-line approach instead. Over time, the administration also adopted Israel's justifications for this approach, so that U.S. and Israeli rhetoric became similar. By February 2003, a *Washington Post* headline summarized the situation: "Bush and Sharon Nearly Identical on Mideast Policy."[129] The lobby's influence was a central part of this switch.

The story begins in late September 2001, when President Bush began pressuring Israeli Prime Minister Sharon to show restraint in the Occupied Territories. He also pressed Sharon to allow Israeli Foreign Minister Shimon Peres to meet with Palestinian President Yasser Arafat, even though Bush was highly critical of Arafat's leadership.[130] Bush also said publicly that he supported a Palestinian state.[131] Alarmed by these developments, Sharon accused Bush of trying "to appease the Arabs at our expense," warning that Israel "will not be Czechoslovakia."[132]

Bush was reportedly furious at Sharon's likening him to Neville Chamberlain, and White House press secretary Ari Fleischer called Sharon's remarks "unacceptable."[133] The Israeli prime minister offered a pro forma apology, but he quickly joined forces with the lobby to convince the Bush administration and the American people that the United States and Israel faced a common threat from terrorism.[134] Israeli officials and lobby representatives repeatedly emphasized that there was no real difference between Arafat and Osama bin Laden, insisting that the United States and Israel should isolate the Palestinians' elected leader and have nothing to do with him.[135]

The lobby also went to work in Congress. On November 16, eighty-nine senators sent Bush a letter praising him for refusing to meet with Arafat, but also demanding that the United States not restrain Israel from retaliating against the Palestinians and insisting that the administration state publicly that it stood steadfastly behind Israel. According to *The New York Times,* the letter "stemmed from a meeting two weeks ago between leaders of the American Jewish community and key senators," adding that AIPAC was "particularly active in providing advice on the letter."[136]

By late November, relations between Tel Aviv and Washington had improved considerably. This was due in part to the lobby's efforts to bend U.S. policy in Israel's direction, but also to America's initial victory in Afghanistan, which reduced the perceived need for Arab support in dealing with al-Qaeda. Sharon visited the White House in early December and had a friendly meeting with Bush.[137]

Trouble erupted again in April 2002, however, after the IDF launched Operation Defensive Shield and resumed control of virtually all the major Palestinian areas on the West Bank.[138] Bush knew that Israel's action would damage America's image in the Arab and Islamic world and undermine the war on terrorism, so he demanded on April 4 that Sharon "halt the incursions and begin withdrawal." He underscored this message two days later, saying this meant "withdrawal without delay." On April 7, Bush's national security adviser, Condoleezza Rice, told reporters, "'Without delay' means without delay. It means now." That same day, Secretary of State Colin Powell set out for the Middle East to pressure all sides to stop fighting and start negotiating.[139]

Israel and the lobby swung into action. A key target was Powell, who began feeling intense heat from pro-Israel officials in Vice President Cheney's office and the Pentagon, as well as from neoconservative pundits like Robert Kagan and William Kristol, who accused him of having "virtually obliterated

the distinction between terrorists and those fighting terrorists."[140] A second target was Bush himself, who was being pressed by Jewish leaders and Christian evangelicals, the latter a key component of his political base. Tom DeLay and Dick Armey were especially outspoken about the need to support Israel, and DeLay and Senate Minority Leader Trent Lott visited the White House and personally warned Bush to back off.[141]

The first sign that Bush was caving came on April 11—only one week after he told Sharon to withdraw his forces—when Ari Fleischer said the president believes Sharon is "a man of peace."[142] Bush repeated this statement publicly upon Powell's return from his abortive mission, and he told reporters that Sharon had responded satisfactorily to his call for a full and immediate withdrawal.[143] Sharon had done no such thing, but the president of the United States was no longer willing to make an issue of it.

Meanwhile, Congress was also moving to back Sharon. On May 2, it overrode the administration's objections and passed two resolutions reaffirming support for Israel. (The Senate vote was 94–2; the House version passed 352–21.) Both resolutions emphasized that the United States "stands in solidarity with Israel" and that the two countries are, to quote the House resolution, "now engaged in a common struggle against terrorism." The House version also condemned "the ongoing support of terror by Yasir Arafat," who was portrayed as a central element of the terrorism problem.[144] A few days later, a bipartisan congressional delegation on a fact-finding mission in Israel publicly proclaimed that Sharon should resist U.S. pressure to negotiate with Arafat.[145] On May 9, a House appropriations subcommittee met to consider giving Israel an extra $200 million to fight terrorism. Secretary of State Powell opposed the package, but the lobby backed it, just as it had helped write the two congressional resolutions.[146] Powell lost.

In short, Sharon and the lobby took on the president of the United States and triumphed. Hemi Shalev, a journalist for the Israel newspaper *Ma'ariv,* reported that Sharon's aides "could not hide their satisfaction in view of Powell's failure. Sharon saw the white in President Bush's eyes, they bragged, and the president blinked first."[147] But it was the pro-Israel forces in the United States, not Sharon or Israel, that played the key role in defeating Bush.

The situation has changed little since then. The Bush administration refused to deal further with Arafat, who eventually died in November 2004. It subsequently embraced the new Palestinian leader, Mahmoud Abbas, but has done virtually nothing to help him gain a viable state. Sharon continued to develop his plans for unilateral "disengagement" from the Palestinians, based on withdrawal from Gaza coupled with continued expansion on the West Bank, which entails building the so-called "security fence," seizing Palestinian-owned land, and expanding settlement blocks and road networks. By refusing to negotiate with Abbas (who has recognized Israel, renounced terrorism and favors a negotiated settlement) and making it impossible for him to deliver tangible benefits to the Palestinian people, Sharon's strategy contributed directly to Hamas's electoral victory.[148] With Hamas in power, of course, Israel has another excuse not to negotiate. The administration has supported Sharon's actions (and those of his successor, Ehud Olmert), and Bush has even endorsed unilateral Israeli annexations in the Occupied Territories, reversing the stated policy of every president since Lyndon Johnson.[149]

U.S. officials have offered mild criticisms of a few Israeli actions but have done little to help create a viable Palestinian state. Former national security adviser Brent Scowcroft even declared in October 2004 that Sharon has President Bush "wrapped around his little finger."[150] If Bush tries to distance the United States from Israel, or even criticizes Israeli actions in the Occupied Territories, he is certain to face the wrath of the lobby and its supporters in Congress. Democratic party presidential candidates understand these facts of life too, which is why John Kerry went to great lengths to display his unalloyed support for Israel in 2004 and why John McCain and Hillary Clinton are doing the same thing today.[151]

Maintaining U.S. support for Israel's policies against the Palestinians is a core goal of the lobby, but its ambitions do not stop there. It also wants America to help Israel remain the dominant regional power. Not surprisingly, the Israeli government and pro-Israel groups in the United States worked together to shape the policy of the Bush administration towards Iraq, Syria and Iran, as well as its grand scheme for reordering the Middle East.

Israel and the Iraq War

Pressure from Israel and the lobby was not the only factor behind the U.S. decision to attack Iraq in March 2003, but it was a critical element. Some Americans believe that this was a "war for oil," but there is hardly any direct evidence to support this claim. Instead, the war was motivated in good part by a desire to make Israel more secure. According to Philip Zelikow, a member of the president's Foreign Intelligence Advisory Board (2001–03), executive director of the 9/11 Commission, and now counselor to Secretary of State Condoleezza Rice, the "real threat" from Iraq was not a threat to the United States.[152] The "unstated threat" was the "threat against Israel," Zelikow told a University of Virginia audience in September 2002, noting further that "the American government doesn't want to lean too hard on it rhetorically, because it is not a popular sell."[153]

On August 16, 2002, eleven days before Vice President Cheney kicked off the campaign for war with a hard-line speech to the Veterans of Foreign Wars, *The Washington Post* reported that "Israel is urging U.S. officials not to delay a military strike against Iraq's Saddam Hussein."[154] By this point, according to Sharon, strategic coordination between Israel and the United States had reached "unprecedented dimensions," and Israeli intelligence officials had given Washington a variety of alarming reports about Iraq's WMD programs.[155] As one retired Israeli general later put it, "Israeli intelligence was a full partner to the picture presented by American and British intelligence regarding Iraq's non-conventional capabilities."[156]

Israeli leaders were deeply distressed when President Bush decided to seek U.N. Security Council authorization for war in September, and even more worried when Saddam agreed to let U.N. inspectors back into Iraq, because these developments seemed to reduce the likelihood of war. Foreign Minister Shimon Peres told reporters in September 2002, "The campaign against Saddam Hussein is a must. Inspections and inspectors are good for decent people, but dishonest people can overcome easily inspections and inspectors."[157]

At the same time, former Prime Minister Ehud Barak wrote a *New York Times* op-ed warning that "the greatest risk now lies in inaction."[158] His predecessor, Benjamin Netanyahu, published a similar piece in *The Wall Street Journal* entitled "The Case for Toppling Saddam."[159]

Netanyahu declared, "Today nothing less than dismantling his regime will do," adding, "I believe I speak for the overwhelming majority of Israelis in supporting a preemptive strike against Saddam's regime." Or, as *Ha'aretz* reported in February 2003, "The [Israeli] military and political leadership yearns for war in Iraq."[160]

As Netanyahu suggests, however, the desire for war was not confined to Israel's leaders. Apart from Kuwait, which Saddam conquered in 1990, Israel was the only country in the world in which both the politicians and the public enthusiastically favored war.[161] As journalist Gideon Levy observed at the time, "Israel is the only country in the West whose leaders support the war unreservedly and where no alternative opinion is voiced."[162] In fact, Israelis were so gung-ho for war that their allies in America told them to damp down their hawkish rhetoric, lest it look as if the war was for Israel.[163]

The Lobby and the Iraq War

Within the United States, the main driving force behind the Iraq War was a small band of neoconservatives, many with close ties to Israel's Likud party.[164] In addition, key leaders of the lobby's major organizations lent their voices to the campaign for war.[165] According to *Forward*,

> As President Bush attempted to sell the . . . war in Iraq, America's most important Jewish organizations rallied as one to his defense. In statement after statement community leaders stressed the

need to rid the world of Saddam Hussein and his weapons of mass destruction.[166]

The editorial goes on to say that "concern for Israel's safety rightfully factored into the deliberations of the main Jewish groups."

Although neoconservatives and other lobby leaders were eager to invade Iraq, the broader American Jewish community was not.[167] In fact, Samuel Freedman reported just after the war started that "a compilation of nationwide opinion polls by the Pew Research Center shows that Jews are less supportive of the Iraq war than the population at large, 52% to 62%."[168] Thus, it would be wrong to blame the war in Iraq on "Jewish influence." Rather, the war was due in large part to the lobby's influence and especially that of the neoconservatives within it.

The neoconservatives were already determined to topple Saddam before Bush became president.[169] They caused a stir in early 1998 by publishing two open letters to President Clinton calling for Saddam's removal from power.[170] The signatories, many of whom had close ties to pro-Israel groups like JINSA or WINEP and whose ranks included Elliot Abrams, John Bolton, Douglas Feith, William Kristol, Bernard Lewis, Donald Rumsfeld, Richard Perle and Paul Wolfowitz, had little trouble convincing the Clinton administration to adopt the general goal of ousting Saddam.[171] But the neoconservatives were unable to sell a war to achieve that objective. Nor were they able to generate much enthusiasm for invading Iraq in the early months of the Bush administration.[172] As important as the neoconservatives were for making the Iraq war happen, they needed help to achieve their aim.

That help arrived with 9/11. Specifically, the events of that fateful day led Bush and Cheney to reverse course and become strong proponents of a preventive war to topple Saddam. Neoconservatives in the lobby—most notably Scooter Libby, Paul Wolfowitz and Princeton historian Bernard Lewis—reportedly played especially critical roles in persuading the president and vice president to favor war.

For the neoconservatives, 9/11 was a golden opportunity to make the case for war with Iraq. At a key meeting with Bush at Camp David on September 15, Wolfowitz advocated attacking Iraq before Afghanistan, even though there was no evidence that Saddam was involved in the attacks on the United States and Bin Laden was known to be in Afghanistan.[173] Bush rejected this advice and chose to go after Afghanistan instead, but war with Iraq was now regarded as a serious possibility. The president tasked U.S. military planners on November 21, 2001, with developing concrete plans for an invasion.[174]

Meanwhile, other neoconservatives were at work within the corridors of power. We do not have the full story yet, but scholars like Lewis and Fouad Ajami of John Hopkins University reportedly played key roles in convincing Vice President Cheney to favor the war.[175] Cheney's views were also heavily influenced by the neoconservatives on his staff, especially Eric Edelman, John Hannah and chief of staff Libby, one of the most powerful individuals in the administration.[176] The vice president's influence helped convince President Bush by early 2002. With Bush and Cheney on board, the die was cast for war.

Outside the administration, neoconservative pundits lost no time making the case that invading Iraq was essential to winning the war on terrorism. Their efforts were partly aimed at keeping pressure on Bush and partly intended to overcome opposition to the war both inside and outside of the government. On September 20, a group of prominent neoconservatives and their allies published another open letter, telling the president, "Even if evidence does not link Iraq directly to the [9/11] attack, any strategy aiming at the eradication of terrorism and its sponsors must include a determined effort to remove Saddam Hussein from power in Iraq."[177] The letter also reminded Bush that "Israel has been and remains America's staunchest ally against international terrorism." In the October 1 issue of *The Weekly Standard*, Robert Kagan and William Kristol called for regime change in Iraq immediately after the Taliban was defeated. That same day, Charles Krauthammer argued in *The Washington*

Post that after we were finished with Afghanistan, Syria should be next, followed by Iran and Iraq. "The war on terrorism," he argued, "will conclude in Baghdad," when we finish off "the most dangerous terrorist regime in the world."[178]

These salvos were the beginning of an unrelenting public-relations campaign to win support for invading Iraq.[179] A key part of this campaign was the manipulation of intelligence information so as to make Saddam look like an imminent threat. For example, Libby visited the CIA several times to pressure analysts to find evidence that would make the case for war. He also helped prepare a detailed briefing on the Iraq threat in early 2003 that was pushed on Colin Powell, then preparing his infamous presentation to the U.N. Security Council on that subject.[180] According to Bob Woodward, Powell "was appalled at what he considered overreaching and hyperbole. Libby was drawing only the worst conclusions from fragments and silky threads."[181] Although Powell discarded Libby's most outrageous claims, his U.N. presentation was still riddled with errors, as Powell now acknowledges.

The campaign to manipulate intelligence also involved two organizations that were created after 9/11 and reported directly to Undersecretary of Defense Douglas Feith.[182] The Policy Counterterrorism Evaluation Group was tasked with finding links between al-Qaeda and Iraq that the intelligence community supposedly missed. Its two key members were David Wurmser, a hard-core neoconservative, and Michael Maloof, a Lebanese-American who had close ties with Perle. The Office of Special Plans was tasked with finding evidence that could be used to sell war with Iraq. It was headed by Abram Shulsky, a neoconservative with longstanding ties to Wolfowitz, and its ranks included recruits from pro-Israel think tanks.[183]

Like virtually all the neoconservatives, Feith is deeply committed to Israel. He also has longstanding ties to the Likud party. He wrote articles in the 1990s supporting the settlements and arguing that Israel should retain the Occupied Territories.[184] More important, along with Perle and Wurmser, he wrote the famous "Clean Break" report in June 1996 for incoming Israeli Prime Minister Benjamin Netanyahu.[185] Among other things, it recommended that Netanyahu "focus on removing Saddam Hussein from power in Iraq—an important Israeli strategic objective in its own right." It also called for Israel to take steps to reorder the entire Middle East. Netanyahu did not implement their advice, but Feith, Perle and Wurmser were soon advocating that the Bush administration pursue those same goals. This situation prompted *Ha'aretz* columnist Akiva Eldar to warn that Feith and Perle "are walking a fine line between their loyalty to American governments . . . and Israeli interests."[186]

Wolfowitz is equally committed to Israel. *Forward* once described him as "the most hawkishly pro-Israel voice in the administration," and selected him in 2002 as the first among 50 notables who "have consciously pursued Jewish activism."[187] At about the same time, JINSA gave Wolfowitz its Henry M. Jackson Distinguished Service Award for promoting a strong partnership between Israel and the United States. *The Jerusalem Post*, describing him as "devoutly pro-Israel," named him "Man of the Year" in 2003.[188]

Finally, a brief word is in order about the neoconservatives' prewar support of Ahmed Chalabi, the unscrupulous Iraqi exile who headed the Iraqi National Congress (INC). They embraced Chalabi because he had worked to establish close ties with Jewish-American groups and had pledged to foster good relations with Israel once he gained power.[189] This was precisely what pro-Israel proponents of regime change wanted to hear, so they backed Chalabi in return. Journalist Matthew Berger laid out the essence of the bargain in the *Jewish Journal*:

> The INC saw improved relations as a way to tap Jewish influence in Washington and Jerusalem and to drum up increased support for its cause. For their part, the Jewish groups saw an opportunity to pave the way for better relations between Israel and Iraq, if and when the INC is involved in replacing Saddam Hussein's regime.[190]

Given the neoconservatives' devotion to Israel, their obsession with Iraq and their influence in the Bush administration, it is not surprising that many

Americans suspected that the war was designed to further Israeli interests. For example, Barry Jacobs of the American Jewish Committee acknowledged in March 2005 that the belief that Israel and the neoconservatives conspired to get the United States into a war in Iraq was "pervasive" in the U.S. intelligence community.[191] Yet few people would say so publicly, and most who did—including Senator Ernest Hollings (D-SC) and Representative James Moran (D-VA)—were condemned for raising the issue.[192] Journalist Michael Kinsley put the point well in late 2002, when he wrote, "The lack of public discussion about the role of Israel . . . is the proverbial elephant in the room: Everybody sees it, no one mentions it."[193] The reason for this reluctance, he observed, was fear of being labeled an antisemite.

To be sure, the groups and individuals that pushed for war did not operate in a vacuum, and they did not lead the United States to war by themselves. As noted, the war would probably not have occurred absent the September 11 attacks, which helped convince President Bush and Vice President Cheney to support it. Still, neoconservatives like Wolfowitz, then-deputy defense secretary, were quick to link Saddam Hussein with 9/11 (even though there was no evidence he was involved), and portray his overthrow as critical to winning the war on terror. Thus, the lobby's actions were a necessary but not sufficient condition for war. Without its efforts, the United States would have been far less likely to have gone to war in March 2003.

Dreams of Regional Transformation

The Iraq War was not supposed to be a costly debacle. Rather, it was intended as the first step in a larger plan to reorder the Middle East. This ambitious strategy was a dramatic departure from previous U.S. policy, and the lobby and Israel were critical driving forces behind this shift. This point was made clearly after the Iraq War began in a front-page story in *The Wall Street Journal*. The headline says it all: "President's Dream: Changing Not Just Regime but a Region: A Pro-U.S., Democratic Area Is a Goal That Has Israeli and Neoconservative Roots."[194]

Pro-Israel forces have long been interested in getting the U.S. military more directly involved in the Middle East, so that it could help protect Israel.[195] But they had limited success on this front during the Cold War, because America acted as an "off-shore balancer" in the region. Most U.S. forces designated for the Middle East, like the Rapid Deployment Force, were kept "over the horizon" and out of harm's way. Washington maintained a favorable balance of power by playing local powers off against each other. This is the reason the Reagan administration supported Saddam against revolutionary Iran during the Iran-Iraq War (1980–88).

Policy changed after the first Gulf War, when the Clinton administration adopted a strategy of "dual containment." It called for stationing substantial U.S. forces in the region to contain both Iran and Iraq, instead of using one to check the other. The father of dual containment was Martin Indyk, who first articulated the strategy in May 1993 at the pro-Israel think tank WINEP and then implemented it as director for Near East and South Asian affairs at the National Security Council.[196]

There was considerable dissatisfaction with dual containment by the mid-1990s. It made the United States the mortal enemy of two regimes that also hated each other, and it forced Washington to bear the burden of containing both of them.[197] Not surprisingly, the lobby worked actively in Congress to save the policy.[198] Pressed by AIPAC and other pro-Israel forces, Clinton toughened up the policy in the spring of 1995 by imposing an economic embargo on Iran. But AIPAC and company wanted more. The result was the 1996 Iran and Libya Sanctions Act, which imposed sanctions on any foreign companies investing more than $40 million to develop petroleum resources in Iran or Libya. As Ze'ev Schiff, the military correspondent for Ha'aretz, noted at the time, "Israel is but a tiny element in the big scheme, but one should not conclude that it cannot influence those within the Beltway."[199]

By the late 1990s, however, the neoconservatives were arguing that dual containment was not enough and that regime change in Iraq was now essential. By toppling Saddam and turning Iraq into a vibrant democracy, they argued, the United States

would trigger a far-reaching process of change throughout the Middle East. This line of thinking, of course, was evident in the "Clean Break" study the neoconservatives wrote for Netanyahu. By 2002, when invading Iraq had become a front-burner issue, regional transformation had become an article of faith in neoconservative circles.[200]

Charles Krauthammer describes this grand scheme as the brainchild of Natan Sharansky, the Israeli politician whose writings have impressed President Bush.[201] But Sharansky was hardly a lone voice in Israel. In fact, Israelis across the political spectrum believed that toppling Saddam would alter the Middle East to Israel's advantage. Aluf Benn reported in Ha'aretz (February 17, 2003), "Senior IDF officers and those close to Prime Minister Ariel Sharon, such as National Security Adviser Ephraim Halevy, paint a rosy picture of the wonderful future Israel can expect after the war. They envision a domino effect, with the fall of Saddam Hussein followed by that of Israel's other enemies. . . . Along with these leaders will disappear terror and weapons of mass destruction."[202]

In short, Israeli leaders, neoconservatives and the Bush administration all saw war with Iraq as the first step in an ambitious campaign to remake the Middle East. And in the first flush of victory, they turned their sights on Israel's other regional opponents.

Gunning for Syria

Israeli leaders did not push the Bush administration to put the screws on Syria before March 2003; they were too busy pushing for war against Iraq. But once Baghdad fell in mid-April, Sharon and his lieutenants began urging Washington to target Damascus.[203] On April 16, for example, Sharon and Shaul Mofaz, his defense minister, gave high-profile interviews in different Israeli newspapers. Sharon, in Yedioth Ahronoth, called for the United States to put "very heavy" pressure on Syria.[204] Mofaz told Ma'ariv, "We have a long list of issues that we are thinking of demanding of the Syrians, and it is appropriate that it should be done through the Americans."[205] Sharon's national security adviser, Ephraim Halevy, told a WINEP audience that it was now important for the United States to get rough with Syria. *The Washington Post* reported that Israel was "fueling the campaign" against Syria by feeding the United States intelligence reports about the actions of President Bashar al-Asad.[206]

Prominent members of the lobby made the same arguments after Baghdad fell.[207] Wolfowitz declared, "There has got to be regime change in Syria." Richard Perle told a journalist, "We could deliver a short message, a two-word message [to other hostile regimes in the Middle East]: 'You're next.'"[208] In early April, WINEP released a bipartisan report stating that Syria "should not miss the message that countries that pursue Saddam's reckless, irresponsible and defiant behavior could end up sharing his fate."[209] On April 15, Yossi Klein Halevi wrote a piece in *The Los Angeles Times* entitled "Next, Turn the Screws on Syria." The following day, Zev Chafets wrote an article for the *New York Daily News* entitled "Terror-Friendly Syria Needs a Change, Too." Not to be outdone, Lawrence Kaplan wrote in *The New Republic* on April 21 that Syrian leader Asad was a serious threat to America.[210]

Back on Capitol Hill, Congressman Eliot Engel (D-NY) had reintroduced the Syria Accountability and Lebanese Sovereignty Restoration Act on April 12.[211] It threatened sanctions against Syria if it did not withdraw from Lebanon, give up its WMD and stop supporting terrorism. It also called for Syria and Lebanon to take concrete steps to make peace with Israel. This legislation was strongly endorsed by the lobby—especially AIPAC—and "framed," according to the *Jewish Telegraph Agency,* "by some of Israel's best friends in Congress."[212] It had been on the back burner for some time, largely because the Bush administration had little enthusiasm for it. But the anti-Syrian act passed overwhelmingly (398–4 in the House; 89–4 in the Senate), and Bush signed it into law on December 12, 2003.[213]

Yet the Bush administration was still divided about the wisdom of targeting Syria at that time. Although the neoconservatives were eager to pick a fight with Damascus, the CIA and the State Department were opposed. Even after Bush signed the new law, he emphasized that he would go slowly in implementing it.[214]

Bush's ambivalence is understandable. First, the Syrian government had been providing the United States with important intelligence about al-Qaeda since 9/11 and had also warned Washington about a planned terrorist attack in the Gulf.[215] Syria had also given CIA interrogators access to Mohammed Zammar, the alleged recruiter of some of the 9/11 hijackers. Targeting the Asad regime would jeopardize these valuable connections and thus undermine the larger war on terrorism.

Second, Syria was not on bad terms with Washington before the Iraq War (it had even voted for U.N. Resolution 1441), and it was no threat to the United States. Playing hardball with Syria would make the United States look like a bully with an insatiable appetite for beating up Arab states. Finally, putting Syria on the American hit list would give Damascus a powerful incentive to cause trouble in Iraq. Even if one wanted to pressure Syria, it made good sense to finish the job in Iraq first.

Yet Congress insisted on putting the screws to Damascus, largely in response to pressure from Israeli officials and pro-Israel groups like AIPAC.[216] If there were no lobby, there would have been no Syria Accountability Act, and U.S. policy toward Damascus would have been more in line with the U.S. national interest.

Putting Iran in the Crosshairs

Although Israeli officials tend to describe every threat in the starkest terms, Iran is widely portrayed as their most dangerous enemy because it is the most likely to acquire nuclear weapons. Most Israelis regard an Islamic country in the Middle East with nuclear weapons as an existential threat. As Israeli Defense Minister Binyamin Ben-Eliezer remarked one year before the Iraq War: "Iraq is a problem. . . . But you should understand, if you ask me, today Iran is more dangerous than Iraq."[217]

Sharon began publicly pushing the United States to confront Iran in November 2002 in a high-profile interview in *The Times* (London).[218] Describing Iran as the "center of world terror" and bent on acquiring nuclear weapons, he declared that the Bush administration should put the strong arm on Iran "the day after" it conquered Iraq. In late April 2003,

Ha'aretz reported that the Israeli ambassador in Washington was now calling for regime change in Iran.[219] The overthrow of Saddam, he noted, was "not enough." In his words, America "has to follow through. We still have great threats of that magnitude coming from Syria, coming from Iran."

The neoconservatives also lost no time in making the case for regime change in Tehran.[220] On May 6, AEI cosponsored an all-day conference on Iran with the pro-Israel Foundation for the Defense of Democracies and the Hudson Institute.[221] The speakers were all strongly pro-Israel, and many called for the United States to replace the Iranian regime with a democracy. As usual, there followed a stream of articles by prominent neoconservatives making the case for going after Iran. For example, William Kristol wrote in *The Weekly Standard* on May 12, "The liberation of Iraq was the first great battle for the future of the Middle East. . . . But the next great battle—not, we hope, a military one— will be for Iran."[222]

The Bush administration has responded to the lobby's pressure by working overtime to shut down Iran's nuclear program. Iran seems determined to obtain a nuclear capability, however, and Washington has had little success in its attempts to thwart it. As a result, the lobby has intensified its pressure on the U.S. government, using all the strategies in its play book.[223] Op-eds and articles now warn of imminent dangers from a nuclear Iran, caution against any appeasement of a "terrorist" regime, and hint darkly of preventive action should diplomacy fail. The lobby is also pushing Congress to approve the Iran Freedom Support Act, which would expand existing sanctions on Iran. Israeli officials also warn that they may take preemptive action should Iran continue down the nuclear road, hints partly intended to keep Washington focused on this issue.

One might argue that Israel and the lobby have not had much influence on U.S. policy toward Iran, since the United States has its own reasons to keep Iran from going nuclear. This is partly true, but Iran's nuclear ambitions do not pose an existential threat to the United States. If Washington could live with a nuclear Soviet Union, a nuclear China or even a nuclear North Korea—regimes that were at one time regarded as fanatical and possibly undeterrable—then it can live with a nuclear Iran. This is the reason the lobby must keep constant pressure on U.S. politicians to confront Tehran. Iran and the United States would hardly be allies if the lobby did not exist, but U.S. policy would be more temperate, Iran's past overtures might well have been welcomed and pursued and preventive war would not be a serious option.

Summary

It is not surprising that Israel and its American supporters want the United States to deal with any and all threats to Israel's security. If their efforts to shape U.S. policy succeed, Israel's enemies get weakened or overthrown and Israel gets a free hand with the Palestinians. But, even if the United States fails to transform the Middle East and finds itself in conflict with an increasingly radicalized Arab and Islamic world, Israel still ends up protected by the world's only superpower.[224] This is not a perfect outcome from the lobby's perspective, but it is obviously preferable to Washington's distancing itself from Israel or using its leverage to force Israel to make peace with the Palestinians.

Conclusion

Can the lobby's power be curtailed? One would like to think so, given the Iraq debacle, the obvious need to rebuild America's image in the Arab and Islamic worlds, and the recent revelations about AIPAC officials passing U.S. government secrets to Israel. One might also think that Arafat's death and the election of the more moderate Mahmoud Abbas would have led Washington to press vigorously and even-handedly for a peace agreement. In short, there are ample grounds for U.S. leaders to distance themselves from the lobby and adopt a Middle East policy more consistent with broader U.S. interests. In particular, using American power to achieve a just peace between Israel and the Palestinians would help advance the broader goals of fighting extremism and promoting democracy in the Middle East.

But that is not going to happen anytime soon. AIPAC and its allies (including Christian Zionists) have no serious opponents in the struggle for influence in Washington. Although a few countervailing forces do exist, they are either significantly weaker (in the case of pro-Arab or pro-Islamic groups) or not interested in broad foreign-policy questions (in the case of oil companies and weapons manufacturers).[225] Organizations in the lobby know it has become more difficult to make Israel's case today, and they are responding by expanding their activities and staffs.[226] Moreover, American politicians remain acutely sensitive to campaign contributions and other forms of political pressure, and major media outlets are likely to remain sympathetic to Israel no matter what it does.

This situation is dangerous for the United States because the lobby's influence causes trouble on several fronts. It increases the terrorist danger that all states face, including America's various allies. By preventing U.S. leaders from pressuring Israel to make peace, the lobby has also made it impossible to end the Israeli-Palestinian conflict. This situation gives extremists a powerful recruiting tool, increases the pool of potential terrorists and sympathizers, and contributes to Islamic radicalism around the world.

Furthermore, the lobby's campaign for regime change in Iran and Syria could lead the United States to attack those countries, with potentially disastrous effects. We do not need another Iraq. At a minimum, the lobby's hostility toward these countries makes it especially difficult for Washington to enlist them against al-Qaeda and the Iraqi insurgency, where their help is badly needed.

There is a moral dimension here as well. Thanks to the lobby, the United States has become the de facto enabler of Israeli expansion in the Occupied Territories, making it complicit in the crimes perpetrated against the Palestinians. This situation undercuts Washington's efforts to promote democracy abroad and makes it look hypocritical when it presses other states to respect human rights. U.S. efforts to limit nuclear proliferation appear equally hypocritical, given its willingness to accept Israel's nuclear arsenal which encourages Iran and others to seek similar capabilities.

Moreover, the lobby's campaign to squelch debate about Israel is unhealthy for democracy. Silencing skeptics by organizing blacklists and boycotts—or by suggesting that critics are antisemites—violates the principle of open debate upon which democracy depends. The inability of the U.S. Congress to conduct a genuine debate on these vital issues paralyzes the entire process of democratic deliberation. Israel's backers should be free to make their case and to challenge those who disagree with them. But efforts to stifle debate by intimidation must be roundly condemned by those who believe in free speech and open discussion of important public issues.

Finally, the lobby's influence has been bad for Israel. Its ability to persuade Washington to support an expansionist agenda has discouraged Israel from seizing opportunities—including a peace treaty with Syria and a prompt and full implementation of the Oslo accords—that would have saved Israeli lives and shrunk the ranks of Palestinian extremists. Denying the Palestinians their legitimate political rights certainly has not made Israel more secure. The long campaign to kill or marginalize a generation of Palestinian leaders has empowered extremist groups like Hamas and reduced the number of Palestinian leaders who would be both willing to accept a fair settlement and able to make it work. This course raises the awful specter of Israel eventually occupying the pariah status once reserved for apartheid states like South Africa. Ironically, Israel itself would probably be better off if the lobby were less powerful and U.S. policy were more evenhanded.

Yet there is still a ray of hope. Although the lobby remains a powerful force, the adverse effects of its influence are increasingly difficult to hide. Powerful states can maintain flawed policies for quite some time, but reality cannot be ignored forever. What is needed, therefore, is a candid discussion of the lobby's influence and a more open debate about U.S. interests in this vital region. Israel's well-being is one of those interests, but its continued occupation of the West Bank and its broader regional agenda are not. Open debate will expose the limits of the strategic and moral case for one-sided U.S. support. It could also move the United States to a position more consistent with its own national interest, with the interests of the other states in the region, and with Israel's long-term interests as well.

Notes

1. Although the existence of individuals and groups lobbying on Israel's behalf does not prove that unconditional U.S. support for Israel is contrary to the national interest, it does suggest that this support would not be provided if the lobby were less powerful. If unconditional support were obviously the right policy, it probably would not take constant efforts by a powerful special-interest group to bring it about. As Richard Gephardt, the former House Minority Leader, told the American-Israel Public Affairs Committee (AIPAC). "Without [your] constant support . . . and all your fighting on a daily basis to strengthen that relationship, it would not be." Moreover, if the lobby were weaker, U.S. policy towards the Israeli-Palestinian peace process, Iran. Iraq and Syria would almost certainly be different. The Gephardt quotation was downloaded from the AIPAC website [http://wwvv.aipac.org/] on January 12, 2004. Also see Michael Kinsley, "J'Accuse, Sort Of," *Slate.com,* March 12, 2003.

2. According to the "Greenbook" of the U.S. Agency for International Development (USAID), which reports "overseas loans and grants," Israel has received $140,142,800,000 (in constant 2003 dollars) from the United States through 2003. "Greenbook" web site [http://qesdb.cdie.org/gbk/], November 8, 2005.

3. According to the "Greenbook," Israel received about $3.7 billion in direct aid from the United States in 2003. Israel's population according to the International Institute for Strategic Studies [IISS] and the CIA is 6,276,883. IISS, *The Military Balance. 2005–2006* (Routledge, 2005), p. 192; http://www.cia.gov/cia/publications/factbook/. That averages out to $589 per Israeli. If one assumes the same population size and $3 billion in total aid, each Israeli receives $478.

4. See http://www.cia.gov/cia/publications/factbook/; *World Bank Atlas* (Development Data Group, World Bank, September 2004), pp. 64–65.

5. For a discussion of the various special deals that Israel receives, see Clyde R. Mark, "Israel: U.S. Foreign Assistance," Issue Brief for Congress (Congressional Research Service, April 26, 2005).

6. Avner Cohen, *Israel and the Bomb* (Columbia University Press, 1999); Seymour M. Hersh, *The Samson Option: Israel's Nuclear Arsenal and American Foreign Policy* (Random House. 1991).

7. "Report of the Open-Ended Working Group on the Question of Equitable Representation on and Increase in the Membership of the Security Council and Other Matters Related to the Security Council," Annex III, U.N. General Assembly Official Records, 58th Session, Supplement No. 47, 2004, pp. 13–14; Donald Neff, "An Updated List of Vetoes Cast by the United States to Shield Israel from Criticism by the U.N. Security Council," *Washington Report on Middle East Affairs,* May/June 2005; Stephen Zunes, "U.S. Declares Open Season on UN Workers," *ConimonDreams.org,* January 10. 2003; "Meetings conducted/Actions taken by the Security Council in 2006," United Nations, June 26, 2006; from www.un.org/Depts/dhl/resguide/seact2006.htm. There were also many resolutions that never came to a vote because Security Council members knew that the United States would veto them.

8. Marc Perelman, "International Agency Eyes Israeli Nukes," *Forward,* September 5, 2003.

9. William B. Quandt, *Peace Process: American Diplomacy and the Arab-Israeli Conflict since 1967,* 3rd ed. (Brookings Institution Press, 2005), chapters 5–7, 10–12.

10. Nathan Guttman, "U.S. Accused of Pro-Israel Bias at 2000 Camp David," *Ha'aretz,* April 29, 2005. Also see Aaron D. Miller, "Israel's Lawyer," *The Washington Post,* May 23, 2005; "Lessons of Arab-Israeli Negotiating: Four Negotiators Look Back and Ahead," Transcript of panel discussion, Middle East Institute, April 25, 2005. For general discussions of how the United States consistently favors Israel over the Palestinians, see Noam Chomsky, *The Fateful Triangle: The United States, Israel and the Palestinians* (South End Press, 1999); Kathleen Christison, *Perceptions of Palestine: Their Influence on U.S. Middle East Policy* (University of California Press, 2001).

11. Downloaded from AIPAC's website [http://aipac.org/documents/unitedefforts.html] on January 12, 2006.

12. See, for example, Warren Bass, *Support Any Friend: Kennedy's Middle East and the Making of the US-Israel Alliance* (Oxford University Press, 2003); A.F.K. Organski, *The $36 Billion Bargain: Strategy and Politics in U.S. Assistance to Israel* (Columbia University Press, 1990); Steven L. Spiegel, "Israel as a Strategic Asset," *Commentary,* June 1983, pp. 51–55; Idem, *The Other Arab-Israeli Conflict: Making America's Middle East Policy, from Truman to Reagan* (University of Chicago Press, 1985).

13. This point was not lost on Moshe Dayan, who, remembering a talk he had with Henry Kissinger at the time of the October 1973 War, noted, "Though I happened to remark that the United States was the only country that was ready to stand by us, my silent reflection was that the United States would really rather support the Arabs." Moshe Dayan, *Moshe Dayan: Story of My Life* (William Morrow, 1976), pp. 512–513. Also see Zach Levey, "The United States' Skyhawk Sale to Israel, 1966: Strategic Exigencies of an Arms Deal," *Diplomatic History,* Vol. 28, No. 2 (April 2004), pp. 255–276.

14. Bernard Lewis wrote in 1992, "Whatever value Israel might have had as a strategic asset during the Cold War, that value obviously ended when the Cold War itself came to a close. The change was clearly manifested in the Gulf War last year, when what the United States most desired from Israel was to keep out of the conflict—to be silent, inactive and, as far as possible, invisible. . . . Israel was not an asset, but an irrelevance—some even said a nuisance. Some of the things that the Israeli government later said and did were unlikely to change this perception." "Rethinking the Middle East," *Foreign Affairs,* Vol. 71, No. 4 (Fall 1992), pp. 110–111.

15. According to Middle East expert Shibley Telhami, "No other issue resonates with the public in the Arab world, and many other parts of the Muslim world, more deeply than Palestine. No other issue shapes the regional perceptions of America more fundamentally than the issue of Palestine." *The Stakes: America and the Middle East* (Westview Press, 2002), p. 96.

16. National Commission on Terrorist Attacks against the United States, "Outline of the 9/11 Plot," Staff Statement No. 16, June 16, 2004. Also see Nathan Guttman, "Al-Qaida Planned Attacks during PM's Visit to White House," *Ha'aretz,* June 17, 2004; Marc Perelman, "Bin Laden Aimed to Link Plot to Israel," *Forward,* June 25, 2004.

17. *Changing Minds, Winning Peace: A New Strategic Direction for U.S. Public Diplomacy in the Arab and Muslim World. Report of the Advisory Group on Public Diplomacy for the Arab and Muslim World,* Submitted to the Committee on Appropriations, U.S. House of Representatives, October 1, 2003, p. 18.

18. "President Discusses War on Terror and Operation Iraqi Freedom," speech delivered at Renaissance Cleveland Hotel, March 20, 2006, Office of the White House Press Secretary.

19. See The Pew Global Attitudes Project, *America Admired, Yet Its New Vulnerability Seen As Good Thing, Say Opinion Leaders* (The Pew Research Center for the People and the Press, December 19. 2001); Pew Global Attitudes Project, *Views of a Changing World 2003,* p. 5.

20. For a copy of the letter, see "Doomed to Failure in the Middle East," *The Guardian,* April 27, 2004.

21. Consider, for example, the controversy that erupted in 2005 over Israel's decision to expand its settlements in the West Bank. See Aluf Benn, "We Can't Expect Explicit U.S. Okay to Build in Settlements," *Ha'aretz,* March 28, 2005; Akiva Eldar, "Bush: End Expansion of Settlements," *Ha'aretz,* May 27, 2005; "Bush Warns Israel over West Bank," *BBC News Online,* April 11, 2005; Donald Macintyre, "Sharon Vows to Defy Bush over Expansion of Israeli Settlements," *The Independent,* April 22, 2005.

22. Quoted in Duncan L. Clarke, "Israel's Unauthorized Arms Transfers," *Foreign Policy,* No. 99 (Summer 1995), p. 94. This article provides an excellent discussion of the problem. There was a bitter controversy in 2004–2005 between the United States and Israel over Israeli arms sales to China. See Aluf Benn and Amnon Barzilai, "Pentagon Official Wants Yaron Fired," *Ha'aretz,* December 16, 2004; Aluf Benn, "U.S. Keeps Israel Out of New Fighter-Jet Development Program," *Ha'aretz,* October 12, 2005.

23. Quoted in Duncan L. Clarke, "Israel's Economic Espionage in the United States," *Journal of Palestine Studies,* Vol. 27, No. 4 (Summer 1998), p. 21. Also

see Bob Drogin and Greg Miller, "Israel Has Long Spied on U.S. Say Officials," *The Los Angeles Times,* September 3, 2004; "FBI Says Israel a Major Player in Industrial Espionage," *Jewish Bulletin,* January 16, 1998; Clyde R. Mark, "Israeli-United States Relations," Issue Brief for Congress (Congressional Research Service, November 9, 2004), pp. 14–15; Joshua Mitnick, "U.S. Accuses Officials of Spying," *The Washington Times,* December 16, 2004.

24. On the Pollard affair, see Hersh, *Samson Option,* pp. 285–305; Idem, "The Traitor: Why Pollard Should Never Be Released," *The New Yorker,* Vol. 74, issue 42 (January 18, 1999), pp. 26–33.

25. Trevor N. Dupuy, *Elusive Victory: The Arab-Israeli Wars, 1947–1974* (Harper and Row, 1978), pp. 3–19, 121–125, 146–147, 212–214, 231–244, 333–340, 388–390, 597–605, 623–633; Simha Flapan, *The Birth of Israel: Myths and Realities* (Pantheon Books, 1987), pp. 189–199; Rashid Khalidi, "The Palestinians and 1948: The Underlying Causes of Failure," in Eugene L. Rogan and Avi Shlaim, eds., *The War for Palestine: Rewriting the History of 1948* (Cambridge University Press, 2001), pp. 12–36; Haim Levenberg, *Military Preparations of the Arab Community in Palestine, 1945–1948* (Frank Cass, 1993); Benny Morris, *The Birth of the Palestinian Refugee Problem Revisited* (Cambridge University Press, 2004), chapters 1, 3; Idem, *Righteous Victims: A History of the Zionist-Arab Conflict, 1881–1999* (Alfred Knopf 1999), pp. 187–189, 191–196, 217–223, 235–236, 241–242, 286–291, 311–313, 393–395; Idem, *1948 and After: Israel and the Palestinians* (Clarendon Press, 1990), pp. 13–16; Martin Van Creveld, *The Sword and the Olive: A Critical History of the Israeli Defense Forces* (Public Affairs, 1998), pp. 77–82, 137–138, 179–182.

26. Amos Harel, "Israel Maintains Its Strategic Advantage, Says Jaffee Center," *Ha'aretz,* November 23, 2005. Also see, Uri Bar-Joseph, "The Paradox of Israeli Power," *Survival,* Vol. 46, No. 4 (Winter 2004–05), pp. 137–156; Martin Van Creveld, "Opportunity Beckons," *The Jerusalem Post,* May 15, 2003.

27. For three instructive pieces on this matter from the Israeli press, see Amiram Baikal, "Majority of Israelis Are Opposed to Intermarriage, Survey Finds," *Ha'aretz,* September 15, 2003; Nicky Blackburn, "Better a Jew," *Ha'aretz,* April 21, 2004;

Lily Galili, "Hitting Below the Belt," *Ha'aretz,* August 8, 2004.

28. See "The Official Summation of the Or Commission Report," published in *Ha'aretz,* September 2, 2003. For evidence of how hostile many Israelis were to the report's findings and recommendations, see "No Avoiding the Commission Recommendations," *Ha'aretz,* September 4, 2003; Molly Moore, "Israeli Report Is Welcomed, Dismissed," *The Washington Post*, September 3, 2003. Also see Bernard Avishai, "Saving Israel from Itself: A Secular Future for the Jewish State," *Harper's Magazine,* January 2005.

29. Quoted in Justin Huggler, "Israel Imposes 'Racist' Marriage Law," *The Guardian,* August 1, 2003. Also see James Bennet, "Israel Blocks Palestinians from Marrying into Residency," *The New York Times,* July 31, 2003; "Racist Legislation," *Ha'aretz* editorial, July, 19, 2004; "Racist Legislation," *Ha'aretz* editorial, January 18, 2005. Even the Anti-Defamation League (ADL) criticized the legislation, albeit mildly, Nathan Guttman, Yair Ettinger, Sharon Sadeh, "ADL Criticizes Law Denying Citizenship to Palestinians," *Ha'aretz,* August 5, 2003.

30. Israel formally withdrew from Gaza in the summer of 2005, but continued to maintain substantial control over its residents. Specifically, Israel controls air, sea and land access, which means that the Palestinians are in effect prisoners within Gaza, able to enter or leave only with Israeli approval. Escalating violence in the summer of 2006 led Israel to reoccupy Gaza, and Israeli airstrikes and artillery fire have destroyed key buildings and bridges there.

31. The first wave of European Jews to come to Palestine is known as the First Aliyah, and it covers the years from 1882 to 1903. There were slightly more than 15,000 Jews in Palestine in 1882. Justin McCarthy, *The Population of Palestine: Population History and Statistics of the Late Ottoman Period and the Mandate* (Columbia University Press, 1990), p. 10, which has excellent data for the years from 1850 to 1915.

32. The total population of Palestine in 1893 was roughly 530,000, of whom about 19,000 were Jewish (3.6 percent). Arabs comprised the vast majority of the remaining population. McCarthy, *Population of Palestine,* p. 10.

33. Flapan, *Birth of Israel,* p. 44; Morris, *Righteous Victims,* p. 186.

34. Flapan, *Birth of Israel,* p. 22. Similarly, Ben-Gurion told his son, "Erect a Jewish State at once, even if it is not in the whole of the land. The rest will come in the course of time. It must come." Avi Shlaim, *The Iron Wall: Israel and the Arab World* (Norton, 2000), p. 21. Also see Flapan, *Birth of Israel,* pp. 13–53; Nur Masalah, *Expulsion of the Palestinians: The Concept of Transfer in Zionist Political Thought, 1882–1948* (Institute for Palestine Studies, 1992), chapter 2; Morris, *Righteous Victims,* pp. 138–139; Avi Shlaim, *The Politics of Partition: King Abdullah, the Zionists, and Palestine, 1921–1951* (Oxford University Press, 1999).

35. Benny Morris, *Israel's Border Wars, 1949–1956* (Oxford University Press, 1997), p. 11. According to Shabtai Teveth, "[M]ass immigration and military strength would serve still another purpose, at which Ben-Gurion only hinted. Only initiates knew that Ben-Gurion regarded the creation of a Jewish state in part of Palestine as a stage in the longer process toward a Jewish state in all of Palestine.... And so Ben-Gurion spoke in ambiguous tones about a state being but a step toward 'a complete solution for the Jewish people and a powerful instrument for the total fulfillment of Zionism, an instrument for the redemption of all the Land of Israel'.... In October 1938, he wrote to his children that 'I don't regard a state in part of Palestine as the final aim of Zionism, but as a means toward that aim.'" See Shabtai Teveth, *Ben-Gurion and the Palestinian Arabs: From Peace to War* (Oxford University Press, 1985), pp. 187–188. Ben-Gurion retained this view after independence, saying in early 1949 that "Before the founding of the state, on the eve of its creation, our main interest was *self-defense* . . . but now the issue at hand is conquest, not self defense. As for setting the borders—it's an open-ended matter. In the Bible as well as in our history there are all kinds of definitions of the country's borders, so there's no real limit." Quoted in Tom Segev, *1949: The First Israelis* (Henry Holt & Co., 1998) p. 6.

36. Masalha, *Expulsion of the Palestinians,* p. 128. Also see Morris, *Righteous Victims,* pp. 140, 142, 168–169. This statement is from a memorandum Ben-Gurion wrote prior to the Extraordinary Zionist Conference at New York's Biltmore Hotel in May 1942. After outlining the need for "brutal compulsion," Ben-Gurion also noted that "we should in no way make it part of our programme." Ben-Gurion was not rejecting this policy, however, he was simply noting that the Zionists should not openly proclaim it. Indeed, he went on to say that the Zionists should not "discourage other people, British or American, who favour transfer from advocating this course, but we should in no way make it part of our programme." Ben-Gurion would have preferred to consolidate Jewish control over Palestine in agreement with the Arabs, but he recognized that this was unlikely and that the Zionists would have to acquire a strong military force in order to achieve their aims. As he wrote Moshe Sharett in June 1937, "Were I an Arab . . . an Arab politically, nationally minded . . . I would rebel even more vigorously, bitterly, and desperately against the immigration that will one day turn Palestine and all its Arab residents over to Jewish rule." Quoted in Shabtai Teveth, *Ben-Gurion: The Burning Ground, 1886–1948* (Houghton Mifflin, 1987), p. 544. When combined with his other statements on this topic, it is clear that Ben-Gurion understood that a predominantly Jewish state was unlikely to be established without forcefully removing the Arab population.

37. Quoted in Michael Bar-Zohar, *Facing a Cruel Mirror: Israel's Moment of Truth* (Charles Scribner's Sons, 1990), p. 16.

38. Benny Morris, "Revisiting the Palestinian Exodus of 1948," in Rogan and Shlaim, *War for Palestine,* p 44. On the pervasiveness of transfer thinking among Zionists before Israel was established in 1948, see Masalha, *Expulsion of the Palestinians;* Morris, *Birth Revisited,* chapter 2; Idem, "A New Exodus for the Middle East?," *The Guardian,* October 3, 2002; Ari Shavit, "Survival of the Fittest," *Ha'aretz,* January 9, 2004.

39. Morris, *Birth Revisited,* provides a detailed account of this event. Also see Meron Benvenisti, *Sacred Landscape: The Buried History of the Holy Land since 1948,* trans. Maxine Kaufman-Lacusta (University of California Press, 2000), chapters 3–4. The only remaining debate of real significance regarding the expulsion of the Palestinians from their homeland is whether it was "born of war," as

Morris argues, or by design, as Norman Finkelstein argues in *Image and Reality of the Israel-Palestine Conflict* (London: Verso, 1995), chapter 3.

40. Erskine Childers, "The Other Exodus," *The Spectator*, May 12, 1961; Flapan, *Birth of Israel*, pp. 81–118; Walid Khalidi, "Why Did the Palestinians Leave Revisited," *Journal of Palestine Studies*, Vol. 34, No. 2 (Winter 2005), pp. 42–54; Idem, "The Fall of Haifa," *Middle East Forum*, Vol. 35, No. 10 (December, 1959), pp. 22–32; Morris, *Birth Revisited*.

41. Nahum Goldmann, *The Jewish Paradox*, trans. Steve Cox (Grosset and Dunlap, 1978), p. 99. Ze'ev Jabotinsky, the founding father of the Israeli right, made essentially the same point when he wrote, "Colonization is self-explanatory and what it implies is fully understood by every sensible Jew and Arab. There can only be one purpose in colonization. For the country's Arabs that purpose is essentially unacceptable. This is a natural reaction and nothing will change it." Quoted in Ian Lustick, "To Build and To Be Built By: Israel and the Hidden Logic of the Iron Wall," *Israel Studies*, Vol. 1, No. 1 (Spring 1996), p. 200.

42. See Geoffrey Aronson, *Israel, Palestinians, and the Intifada: Creating Facts on the West Bank* (Kegan Paul International, 1990); Amnon Barzilai, "A Brief History of the Missed Opportunity," *Ha'aretz*, June 5, 2002; Idem, "Some Saw the Refugees as the Key to Peace," *Ha'aretz*, June 11, 2002; Moshe Behar, "The Peace Process and Israeli Domestic Politics in the 1990s," *Socialism and Democracy*, Current Issue Number 32, Vol. 16, No. 2 (Summer-Fall 2002), pp. 34–47; Adam Hanieh and Catherine Cook, "A Road Map to the Oslo Cul-de-Sac," *Middle East Report Online*, May 15, 2003; "Israel's Interests Take Primacy: An Interview with Dore Gold," in *bitterlemons.org*, "What Constitutes a Viable Palestinian State?" March 15, 2004, Edition 10; Nur Masalha, *Imperial Israel and the Palestinians: The Politics of Expansion* (Pluto Press, 2000); Sara Roy, "Erasing the 'Optics' of Gaza," *The Daily Star Online*, February 14, 2004; "36 Years, and Still Counting," *Ha'aretz*, September 26, 2003.

43. Rashid Khalidi, *Palestinian Identity: The Construction of Modern National Consciousness* (Columbia University Press, 1997), p. 147. Meir also said, "It was not as though there was a Palestinian people in Palestine considering itself as a Palestinian people and we came and threw them out and took their country away from them. They did not exist." Masalha, *Imperial Israel*, p. 47. Rabin said in 1995, two years after signing the Oslo accords, "I seek peaceful coexistence between Israel as a Jewish state, not all over the land of Israel, or most of it; its capital, the united Jerusalem; its security border with Jordan rebuilt; next to it, a Palestinian entity, less than a state, that runs the life of Palestinians. . . . This is my goal, not to return to the pre-Six-Day War lines but to create two entities, a separation between Israel and the Palestinians who reside in the West Bank and the Gaza Strip." Hanieh and Cook, "Road Map." Also see Akiva Eldar, "On the Same Page, Ten Years On," *Ha'aretz*, November 5, 2005; David Grossman, "The Night Our Hope for Peace Died," *The Guardian*, November 4, 2005; Michael Jansen, "A Practice that Prevents the Emergence of a Palestinian State," *Jordan Times*, November 10, 2005. In the spring of 1998, Israel and its American supporters sharply criticized First Lady Hillary Clinton for saying, "It would be in the long-term interests of peace in the Middle East for there to be a state of Palestine, a functioning modern state that is on the same footing as other states." Tom Rhodes and Christopher Walker, "Congress Tells Israel to Reject Clinton's Pullout Plan," *The New York Times*, May 8, 1998. James Bennet, "Aides Disavow Mrs. Clinton on Mideast," *The New York Times*, May 8, 1998.

44. See Charles Enderlin, *Shattered Dreams: The Failure of the Peace Process in the Middle East, 1995–2002*, trans. Susan Fairfield (Other Press, 2003), pp. 201, 207–208; Jeremy Pressman, "Visions in Collision: What Happened at Camp David and Taba?" *International Security*, Vol. 28, No. 2 (Fall 2003), p. 17; Ron Pundak, "From Oslo to Taba: What Went Wrong?," *Survival*, Vol. 43, No. 3 (Autumn 2001), pp. 31–45; Jerome Slater, "What Went Wrong? The Collapse of the Israeli-Palestinian Peace Process," *Political Science Quarterly*, Vol. 116, No. 2 (July 2001), p. 184; Deborah Sontag, "Quest for Mideast Peace: How and Why It Failed," *The New York Times*, July 26, 2001; Clayton E. Swisher, *The Truth about Camp David: The Untold Story about the Collapse of the Peace Process* (Nation Books, 2004), pp. 284, 318, 325. Barak

himself said after Camp David that "the Palestinians were promised a continuous piece of sovereign territory except for a razor-thin Israeli wedge running from Jerusalem through from Maale Adumim to the Jordan River," which effectively would have been under Israel's control. Benny Morris, "Camp David and After: An Exchange (1. An Interview with Ehud Barak)," *The New York Review of Books*, Vol. 49, No. 10 (June 13, 2002), p. 44. Also see the map Israeli negotiators presented to the Palestinians during the early rounds at Camp David, a copy of which can be found in Roane Carey, ed., *The New Intifada: Resisting Israel's Apartheid* (Verso, 2001), p. 36. For other accounts of Camp David, see Shlomo Ben-Ami, *Scars of War: Wounds of Peace: The Israeli-Palestinian Tragedy* (Oxford University Press, 2006); Dennis Ross, *The Missing Peace: The Inside Story of the Fight for Middle East Peace* (Farrar Straus Giroux, 2004). Ben-Ami was a key participant at Camp David and is sharply critical of Yasser Arafat's handling of the negotiations. But even he later admitted, "If I were a Palestinian I would have rejected Camp David, as well." See "Norman Finkelstein & Former Israeli Foreign Minister Shlomo Ben-Ami Debate: Complete Transcript," *Democracy Now!* Radio and TV broadcast, February 14, 2006.

45. In a speech in October 2005, Iranian President Mahmoud Ahmadinejad reportedly called for Israel to be "wiped off the map," a statement widely interpreted as threatening the physical destruction of the Jewish state and its inhabitants. A more accurate translation of Ahmadinejad's statement is "the occupation regime over Jerusalem should vanish from the page of time" (or alternatively, "be eliminated from the pages of history"). Instead of calling for the physical destruction of Israel, Ahmadinejad was suggesting that Israel's control over Jerusalem should be seen as a temporary condition, like Soviet control of Eastern Europe or the shah's regime in Iran. While still provocative and highly objectionable, it was not a call for the physical liquidation of Israel or its population. See Ethan Bronner and Nazila Fathi, "Just How Far Did They Go, Those Words Against Israel?," *The New York Times*, June 11, 2006; Jonathan Steele, "Lost in Translation," *The Guardian*,

June 14, 2006; "Iranian President at Tehran Conference: 'Very Soon, This Stain of Disgrace [i.e. Israel] Will Be Purged From the Center of the Islamic World—and This is Attainable'," Middle East Media Research Institute, Special Dispatch Series No. 1013, October 25, 2005.

46. See Alan Dershowitz, *The Case for Israel* (John Wiley & Sons, 2003). For a telling critique of Dershowitz's book, see Norman G. Finkelstein, *Beyond Chutzpah: On the Misuse of Anti-Semitism and the Abuse of History* (University of California Press, 2005). Also see "Dershowitz v. Desch," *American Conservative*, January 16, 2005.

47. Morris, *Righteous Victims*, chapters 2–5.

48. Morris, *Birth Revisited*. It should be noted that many Israeli documents concerning the events of 1948 remain classified; Morris expects "that with respect to both expulsions and atrocities, we can expect additional revelations as the years pass and more Israeli records become available." Morris, "Revisiting the Palestinian Exodus," in Rogan and Shlaim, *War for Palestine*, p. 49. In fact, he maintains that the reported cases of rape he knows about are "just the tip of the iceberg." See Shavit, "Survival of the Fittest."

49. Morris, *Israel's Border Mars*, p. 432. Also see *ibid.*, pp. 126–153, 178–184. For evidence of similar behavior after the 1967 War, see Uri Avnery, "Crying Wolf?," *Counter Punch*, March 15, 2003; Ami Kronfeld, "Avnery on Ethnic Cleansing and a Personal Note," in Jewish Voice for Peace, *Jewish Peace News*, March 17, 2003; Katherine M. Metres, "As Evidence Mounts, Toll of Israeli Prisoner of War Massacres Grows," *Washington Report on Middle East Affairs*, February/March 1996, pp. 17, 104–105.

50. During his negotiations with the British and French governments over the launching of the 1956 war, Ben-Gurion proposed a grand plan for reordering the region that would have divided Jordan between Israel and Iraq, transferred all of Lebanon south of the Litani River to Israel, and given Israel portions of the Sinai as well. On Israel's policies in the 1950s, see Morris, *Israel's Border Wars*; Morris, *Righteous Victims*, chapter 6, especially pp. 289–290; Shlaim, *Iron Wall*, chapters 3–4, especially pp. 184–185; Kennett Love, *Suez: the Twice Fought War* (McGraw-Hill, 1969),

pp. 589–638; Michael Brecher, *Decisions in Israel's Foreign Policy* (Yale University Press, 1975), pp. 282–283.

51. Gabby Bron, "Egyptian POWs Ordered to Dig Graves, Then Shot by Israeli Army," *Yedioth Ahronoth,* August 17, 1995; Ronal Fisher, "Mass Murder in the 1956 Sinai War," *Ma'ariv,* August 8, 1995 [Copies of these two pieces can be found in *Journal of Palestine Studies,* Vol. 25, No. 3 (Spring 1996), pp. 148–155]; Galal Bana, "Egypt: We Will Turn to the International War Crimes Tribunal in the Hague if Israel Will Not Compensate Murdered Prisoners of War," *Ha'aretz,* July 24, 2002; Zehavat Friedman, "Personal Reminiscence: Remembering Ami Kronfeld," in Jewish Voice for Peace, *Jewish Peace News,* September 25, 2005; Metres, "As Evidence Mounts."

52. Avnery, "Crying Wolf"; Robert Blecher, "Living on the Edge: The Threat of 'Transfer' in Israel and Palestine," MERIP, Middle East Report 225, Winter 2002; Baruch Kimmerling, *Politicide: Ariel Sharon's War against the Palestinians* (Verso, 2003), p. 28. Also see Chomsky, *Fateful Triangle,* p. 97; Morris, *Righteous Victims,* pp. 328–329; Tanya Reinhart, *Israel/Palestine: How to End the War of 1948* (Seven Stories Press, 2002), p. 8. Morris reports (p. 329) that 120,000 Palestinians applied to return to their homes right after the 1967 War, but Israel allowed only about 17,000 to come back. Amnesty International estimated in mid-2003 that in the years since Israel had acquired the West Bank and the Gaza Strip, it had destroyed more than 10,000 Palestinian homes in those areas. Danny Rubinstein, "Roads, Fences and Outposts Maintain Control in the Territories," *Ha'aretz,* August 12, 2003.

53. "Report of the Commission of Inquiry into the Events at the Refugee Camps in Beirut," February 7, 1983. The report is commonly called "The Kalian Commission Report" after its chairman, Yitzhak Kalian.

54. Swedish Save the Children, "The Status of Palestinian Children during the Uprising in the Occupied Territories," Excerpted Summary Material, Jerusalem, 1990, in *Journal of Palestine Studies,* Vol. 19, No. 4 (Summer 1990), pp. 136–146. Also see Joshua Brilliant, "Officer Tells Court Villagers Were Bound, Gagged and Beaton, 'Not Guilty' Plea at 'Break Bones' Trial," *Jerusalem Post,* March 30, 1990; Joshua Brilliant, "'Rabin Ordered Beatings', Meir Tells Military Court," *Jerusalem Post,* June 22, 1990; Jackson Diehl, "Rights Group Accuses Israel of Violence Against Children in Palestinian Uprising," *The Washington Post,* May 17, 1990; James A. Graff, "Crippling a People: Palestinian Children and Israeli State Violence," *Alif,* No. 13 (1993), pp. 46–63; Ronald R. Stockton, "Intifada Deaths," *Journal of Palestine Studies,* Vol. 19, No. 4 (Summer 1990), pp. 86–95. Ehud Barak, the IDF's Deputy Chief of Staff during the First Intifada, said at the time. "We do not want children to be shot under any circumstances. . . . When you see a child you don't shoot." Nevertheless, the Swedish Save the Children report estimated that 6,500 to 8,000 children were wounded by gunfire during the first two years of the Intifada. Researchers investigated 66 of the 106 recorded cases of "child gunshot deaths." They concluded that almost all of them "were hit by directed—not random or ricochet—gunfire"; nearly twenty percent suffered multiple gunshot wounds; twelve percent were shot from behind; fifteen percent of the children were ten years of age or younger; "most children were not participating in a stone-throwing demonstration when shot dead"; and "nearly one-fifth of the children were shot dead while at home or within ten meters of their homes."

55. "Unbridled Force," *Ha'aretz* editorial, March 16, 2003. For other evidence, see Jonathan Cook, "Impunity on Both Sides of the Green Line," MERIP, Middle East Report Online, November 23, 2005; "When Everything Is Permissible," *Ha'aretz* editorial, June 6, 2005; "It Can Happen Here," *Ha'aretz* editorial, November 22, 2004; Chris McGreal, "Snipers with Children in Their Sights," *The Guardian,* June 28, 2005; Idem, "Israel Shocked by Image of Soldiers Forcing Violinist to Play at Roadblock," *The Guardian,* November 29, 2004; Greg Myre, "Former Israeli Soldiers Tell of Harassment of Palestinians," *The New York Times,* June 24, 2004; Reuven Pedatzur, "The Message to the Soldiers Was Clear," *Ha'aretz,* December 13, 2004; Conal Urquhart, "Israeli Soldiers Tell of Indiscriminate Killings by Army and A Culture of Impunity," *The Guardian,* September 6, 2005.

56. See Swisher, *Truth about Camp David*, p. 387.

57. According to *B'tselem*, between September 29, 2000, and December 31, 2005, 3,386 Palestinians were killed by the Israelis, of whom 676 were children. Of those 3,386 deaths, 1,185 were bystanders, 1,008 were killed while fighting the Israelis, and the circumstances of 563 deaths are unknown. During the same period, 992 Israelis were killed by the Palestinians, 118 of whom were children. Of those 992 deaths, 683 were civilians and 309 belonged to Israeli security forces. *B'tselem* press release, January 4, 2006.

58. Nathan Guttman, "'It's a Terrible Thing, Living with the Knowledge that You Crushed Our Daughter,'" *Ha'aretz*, April 30, 2004; Adam Shapiro, "Remembering Rachel Corrie," *The Nation*, March 18, 2004; Tsahar Rotem, "British Peace Activist Shot by IDF Troops in Gaza Strip," *Ha'aretz*, April 11, 2003.

59. Molly Moore, "Ex-Security Chiefs Turn on Sharon," *The Washington Post*, November 15, 2003. "Ex-Shin Bet Heads Warn of 'Catastrophe' without Peace Deal," *Ha'aretz*, November 15, 2003. These comments were based on an interview in the Israeli newspaper *Yedioth Ahronoth* on November 14, 2003. For a copy of that interview, see "We Are Seriously Concerned about the Fate of the State of Israel," The Alternative Information Center, December 1, 2003.

60. Bill Maxwell, "U.S. Should Reconsider Aid to Israel," *St. Petersburg Times*, December 16, 2001.

61. See J. Bowyer Bell, *Terror Out of Zion: The Fight for Israeli Independence* (Transaction Publishers, 1996); Joseph Heller, *The Stern Gang: Ideology, Politics and Terror, 1940–1949* (Frank Cass, 1995); Bruce Hoffmann, *The Failure of British Military Strategy within Palestine, 1939–1947* (Bar-Ilan University, 1983); Morris, *Righteous Victims*, pp. 173–180; Segev, *One Palestine*, pp. 468–486. According to Haim Levenberg, 210 of the 429 casualties from Jewish terrorism in Palestine during 1946 were civilians. The other 219 were police and soldiers. Levenberg, *Military Preparations*, p. 72. Furthermore, it was Jewish terrorists from the infamous Irgun who in late 1937 introduced the practice of placing bombs in buses and large crowds. Benny Morris speculates that, "The Arabs may well have learned the value of terrorist bombings from the Jews." *Righteous Victims*, pp. 147, 201. Also see Lenni Brenner, *The Iron Wall: Zionist Revisionism from Jabotinsky to Shamir* (Zed Books, 1984), p. 100; Yehoshua Porath, *The Palestinian Arab National Movement: from Riots to Rebellion, Vol. II, 1929–1939* (Frank Cass, 1977), p. 238. Finally, Morris notes that during the 1948 war the main Jewish terrorist groups "knowingly planted bombs in bus stops with the aim of killing non-combatants, including women and children." *Birth Revisited*, p. 80.

62. Bell, *Terror Out of Zion*, pp. 336–340.

63. Quoted in Chomsky, *Fateful Triangle*, pp. 485–486. Israeli Prime Minister Levi Eshkol used to call Menachem Begin "the terrorist." Barzilai, "Brief History." On Shamir, see Avishai Margalit, "The Violent Life of Yitzhak Shamir," *The New York Review of Books*, May 14, 1992, pp. 18–24.

64. Moreover, Israel's claim to a morally superior status is undermined by some of its other policies. Israel once cultivated close ties with apartheid-era South Africa and aided the white minority government's nuclear weapons program. Peter Liberman, "Israel and the South African Bomb," *The Nonproliferation Review*, Vol. II, No. 2 (Summer 2004), pp. 46–80. In 1954, Israeli intelligence forces bombed a U.S. diplomatic facility in Cairo in a bungled attempt to sow discord between Egypt and the United States. Shlaim, *Iron Wall*, pp. 110–113.

65. As with other special-interest groups, the boundaries of the Israel lobby cannot be defined precisely, which underscores the fact that it is not a hierarchical organization with a defined membership list. It has a core consisting of organizations whose declared purpose is to influence the U.S. government on Israel's behalf, but it also draws support from a penumbra of groups and individuals who are committed to steadfast U.S. support for Israel but who are not as energetically or consistently engaged as the core. Thus, an AIPAC lobbyist or an analyst at the Washington Institute for Near East Policy (WINEP) is part of the core, but an individual who occasionally writes pro-Israel letters to his or her Congressional representative or local newspaper is part of the broader network of supporters.

66. Steven M. Cohen, *The 2004 National Survey of American Jews*, sponsored by the Jewish Agency

for Israel's Department of Jewish-Zionist Education, February 24, 2005. The figure two years earlier was 28 percent. See Steven M. Cohen, *The 2002 National Survey of American Jews,* sponsored by the Jewish Agency for Israel's Department of Jewish-Zionist Education, conducted in November-December 2002. Also see Amiran Barkat, "Young American Jews Are More Ambivalent Toward Israel, Study Shows," *Ha'aretz,* March 7, 2005; Steven M. Cohen, "Poll: Attachment of U.S. Jews to Israel Falls in Past 2 Years," *Forward,* March 4, 2005; M. J. Rosenberg, "Letting Israel Sell Itself," Israel Policy Forum Issue Brief #218, March 18, 2005.

67. J. J. Goldberg, "Old Friend, Shattered Dreams," *Forward,* December 24, 2004: Esther Kaplan, "The Jewish Divide on Israel," *The Nation,* July 12, 2004; Michael Massing, "Conservative Jewish Groups Have Clout," *The Los Angeles Times,* March 10, 2002; Eric Yoffie. "Reform the Conference," *Forward,* August 2,2002.

68. Ori Nir, "FBI Probe: More Questions Than Answers," *Forward,* May 13, 2005.

69. Inigo Gilmore, "U.S. Jewish Leader Hit over Letter," *The London Sunday Telegraph,* August 12, 2003; Isi Liebler, "When Seymour Met Condi," *The Jerusalem Post,* November 24, 2005. Also see Sarah Bronson, "Orthodox Leader: U.S. Jews Have No Right to Criticize Israel," *Ha'aretz,* August 2, 2004.

70. Liebler, "When Seymour Met Condi": Ori Nir, "O.U. Chief Decries American Pressure on Israel," *Forward,* December 2, 2005; Idem, "Rice Trip Raises Concern over U.S. Pressure on Israel," *Forward,* November 18, 2005: Seymour D. Reich, "Listen to America," *The Jerusalem Post,* November 13, 2005.

71. Jeffrey H. Birnbaum, "Washington's Power 25," *Fortune,* December 8, 1997. AIPAC was ranked number 4 in a similar study conducted in 2001. See Jeffrey H. Birnbaum and Russell Newell, "Fat and Happy in D.C." *Fortune,* May 28, 2001.

72. Richard E. Cohen and Peter Bell, "Congressional Insiders Poll," *National Journal,* March 5, 2005; James D. Besser, "Most Muscle? It's NRA, Then AIPAC and AARP," *The Chicago Jewish Star,* March 11–24, 2005.

73. See Max Blumenthal, "Born-Agains for Sharon," *Salon.com,* October 30, 2004; Darrell L. Bock.

"Some Christians See a 'Road Map' to End Times," *The Los Angeles Times,* June 18, 2003; Nathan Guttman, "Wiping Out Terror, Bringing On Redemption," *Ha'aretz,* April 29, 2002; Tom Hamburger and Jim VandeHei, "Chosen People: How Israel Became a Favorite Cause of Christian Right," *The Wall Street Journal,* May 23, 2002; Paul Nussbaum, "Israel finds an Ally in American Evangelicals," *The Philadelphia Inquirer,* November 17, 2005. Daniel Pipes maintains that, "other than the Israel Defense Forces, America's Christian Zionists may be the Jewish state's ultimate strategic asset." "[Christian Zionism:] Israel's Best Weapon?" *The New York Post,* July 15, 2003.

74. On the role of interest groups in American politics, see David B. Truman, *The Governmental Process: Political Interests and Public Opinion* (Alfred Knopf, 1951); James Q. Wilson, *Political Organizations* (Basic Books, 1973); Frank R. Baumgartner and Beth L. Leech, *Basic Interests: The Importance of Groups in Politics and in Political Science* (Princeton University Press, 1998).

75. The weakness of the "Palestinian lobby" in the United States is captured in the headlines of these two articles: Nora Boustany, "Palestinians' Lone Hand in Washington," *The Washington Post,* April, 19, 2002; George Gedda, "PLO Loses D.C. Office Because of Unpaid Rent," *The Chicago Tribune,* April 12, 2002. On the weak impact of the "Arab lobby," see Ali A. Mazrui, "Between the Crescent and the Star-Spangled Banner: American Muslims and U.S. Foreign Policy," *International Affairs,* Vol. 72, No. 3 (July 1996), pp. 493–506; Nabeel A. Khoury, "The Arab Lobby: Problems and Prospects," *The Middle East Journal,* Vol. 41, No. 3 (Summer 1987), pp. 379–396; Andrea Barron, "Jewish and Arab Diasporas in the United States and Their Impact on U.S. Middle East Policy," in Yehuda Lukacs and Abdalla M. Battah. eds., *The Arab-Israeli Conflict: Two Decades of Change* (Westview, 1988), pp. 238–259.

76. Jake Tapper, "Questions for Dick Armey: Retiring, Not Shy," *The New York Times Magazine,* September 1, 2002. Also, former House Majority Leader Tom DeLay has called himself "an Israeli at heart." See James Bennet, "DeLay Says Palestinians Bear Burden for Achieving Peace," *The New York Times,* July 30, 2003.

77. Quoted in Mitchell Bard, "Israeli Lobby Power," *Midstream,* Vol. 33, No. 1 (January 1987), pp. 6–8.

78. For a detailed analysis of AIPAC's structure and operations, which complements the arguments offered here, see Michael Massing. "The Storm over the Israel Lobby," *The New York Review of Books,* Vol. 53, No. 10 (June 8, 2006). Also see Paul Findley, *They Dare to Speak Out: People and Institutions Confront Israel's Lobby,* 3rd ed. (Lawrence Hill Books, 2003); Michael Lind, "The Israel Lobby," *Prospect,* Issue No. 73 (April 2002**).**

79. Quoted in Edward Tivnan, *The Lobby: Jewish Political Power and American Foreign Policy* (Simon and Schuster, 1987), p. 191. J. J. Goldberg, the editor *of Forward,* said in 2002, "There is this image in Congress that you don't cross these people or they take you down." Quoted in John Diamond and Brianna B. Piec, "Pro-Israel Groups Intensify Political Front in U.S.," *The Chicago Tribune,* April 16, 2002.

80. See Findley, *They Dare to Speak Out,* chapter 3.

81. After Clinton appeared at a pro-Israel rally in July 2006 and expressed unqualified support for Israel's highly destructive retaliation in Lebanon, Helen Freedman, executive director of Americans for a Safe Israel, declared that "I thought her remarks were very good, especially in light of her history, and we can't forget her kiss to Suha." See Patrick Mealy, "Clinton Vows to Back Israel in Latest Mideast Conflict," *The New York Times,* July 18, 2006.

82. Quoted in Camille Mansour, *Beyond Alliance: Israel in U.S. Foreign Policy,* trans. James A. Cohen (Columbia University Press, 1994), p. 242.

83. Although AIPAC has been able to use its political muscle to avoid having to register as a foreign agent for another government, it is especially concerned about that problem today because of the Larry Franklin spy scandal, and thus it is going to considerable lengths to emphasize its "American side." See Ori Nir, "Leaders Fear Probe Will Force Pro-Israel Lobby to File as 'Foreign Agent' Could Fuel Dual Loyalty Talk," *Forward,* December 31, 2004; Idem, "Leaders Stress American Side of AIPAC," *Forward,* May 27, 2005.

84. "Sen. Hollings Floor Statement Setting the Record Straight on His Mideast Newspaper Column," May 20, 2004, originally posted on the former Senator's website (now defunct) but still available at www.shalomctr.org/node/620.

85. The Sharon quotation was printed in an AIPAC advertisement in *The Chicago Jewish Star,* August 29-September 11, 2000; the Olmert quotation is from "To Israel With Love," *The Economist,* August 5, 2006, p. 37. Sharon and Olmert are not alone in their appraisals of AIPAC's power. Senate Minority Leader Harry Reid says. "I can't think of a policy organization in the country as well-organized or respected [as AIPAC]," and former House Speaker Newt Gingrich called it "the most effective general-interest group . . . across the entire planet." Former President Bill Clinton described AIPAC as "stunningly effective" and "better than anyone else lobbying in this town." Quotations downloaded from the AIPAC website on January 14, 2005 [wwv.aipae.org/documents/vvhoweare.html#say].

86. Thomas B. Edsall and Alan Cooperman, "GOP Uses Remarks to Court Jews," *The Washington Post,* March 13, 2003. Also see James D. Besser, "Jews' Primary Role Expanding," *Jewish Week,* January 23, 2004; Alexander Bolton, "Jewish Defections Irk Democrats," *The Hill,* March 30, 2004; E. J. Kessler, "Ancient Woes Resurfacing as Dean Eyes Top Dem Post," *Forward,* January 28, 2005. Hamilton Jordan wrote a memorandum to President Jimmy Carter in June 1977, in which he said: "Out of 125 members of the Democratic National Finance Council, over 70 are Jewish; In 1976, over 60% of the large donors to the Democratic Party were Jewish; Over 60% of the monies raised by Nixon in 1972 was from Jewish contributors; Over 75% of the monies raised in Humphrey's 1968 campaign was from Jewish contributors; Over 90% of the monies raised by Scoop Jackson in the Democratic primaries was from Jewish contributors; In spite of the fact that you were a long shot and came from an area of the country where there is a smaller Jewish community, approximately 35% of our primary funds were from Jewish supporters. Wherever there is major political fundraising in this country, you will find American Jews playing a significant role." Hamilton Jordan, Confidential File, Box 34, File "Foreign Policy/Domestic Politics Memo, HJ Memo, 6/77," declassified June 12, 1990.

87. Douglas Brinkley, "Out of the Loop," *The New York Times,* December 29, 2002. Lawrence Kaplan reports that after Bruce Riedel, the Middle East expert on the National Security Council, left his job at the end of 2001, the Pentagon "held up the appointment of Riedel's designated successor, Middle East expert Alina Romanowski, whom Pentagon officials suspect of being insufficiently supportive of the Jewish state." "Torpedo Boat: How Bush Turned on Arafat," *The New Republic,* February 18, 2003. The position was eventually filled by Elliot Abrams, a fervent supporter of Israel. "Indeed, for the government of Israel," Nathan Guttman wrote, "it is a gift from heaven." See "From Clemency to a Senior Post," *Ha'aretz,* December 16, 2002.

88. E. J. Kessler, "Lieberman and Dean Spar Over Israel," *Forward,* September 9, 2003; Stephen Zunes, "Attacks on Dean Expose Democrats' Shift to the Right," *Tikkun,* November/December 2003.

89. Zunes, "Attacks on Dean"; James D. Besser, "Dean's Jewish Problem," *The Chicago Jewish Star,* December 19, 2003–January 8, 2004.

90. E. J. Kessler, "Dean Plans to Visit Israel, Political Baggage in Tow," *Forward,* July 8, 2005; Zunes, "Attacks on Dean."

91. Laura Blumenfeld, "Three Peace Suits: For These Passionate American Diplomats, a Middle East Settlement is the Goal of a Lifetime," *The Washington Post,* February 24, 1997.

92. Samuel ("Sandy") Berger, President Clinton's National Security Adviser, reports that at one point during the negotiations at Camp David (July 2000), Dennis Ross made the remarkable comment, "If Barak offers try anything more. I'll be against this agreement." Unedited transcript of "Comments by Sandy Berger at the Launch of *How Israelis and Palestinians Negotiate* (USIP Press, 2005)," U.S. Institute of Peace, Washington, DC, June 7, 2005.

93. Quoted in Blumenfeld, "Three Peace Suits."

94. Eric Alterman, "intractable Foes, Warring Narratives," *MSNBC.com,* March 28, 2002.

95. Quoted in Bret Stephens, "Eye on the Media by Bret Stephens: Bartley's Journal," *The Jerusalem Post,* November 21, 2002.

96. See Jerome N. Slater, "Muting the Alarm: *The New York Times* and the Israeli-Palestinian Conflict. 2000–2006," unpublished ms., State University of New York, Buffalo, 2006.

97. Max Frankel, *The Times of My Life And My Life with the Times* (Random House, 1999), pp. 401–403.

98. Felicity Barringer, "Some U.S. Backers of Israel Boycott Dailies Over Mideast Coverage That They Deplore," *The New York Times,* May 23, 2002.

99. Joel Beinin, "Money, Media and Policy Consensus: The Washington Institute for Near East Policy," *Middle East Report,* January-February 1993, pp. 10–15; Mark H. Milstein, "Washington Institute for Near East Policy: An AIPAC 'Image Problem,'" *Washington Report on Middle East Affairs,* July 1991.

100. Quoted in Milstein, "Washington Institute."

101. "Brookings Announces New Saban Center for Middle East Policy," Brookings Institution Press Release, May 9, 2002; Andrew Ross Sorkin, "Schlepping to Moguldom," *The New York Times,* September 5, 2004.

102. James D. Besser, "Turning up Heat in Campus Wars," *Jewish Week,* July 25, 2003; Ronald S. Lauder and Jay Schottenstein, "Back to School for Israel Advocacy," *Forward,* November 14, 2003: Rachel Pomerance, "Israel Forces Winning Campus Battle, Say Students Attending AIPAC Meeting," *JTA,* December 31, 2002. Jewish groups are also targeting high schools. See Max Gross, "Israel Advocacy Coalition Targeting High Schools," *Forward,* January 23, 2004; "New Pro-Israel Campaign Targets High School Students," *JTA,* June 2, 2004.

103. Besser, "Turning up Heat," In 2002 and 2003, AIPAC brought 240 college students to Washington, DC for intensive advocacy training, sending them back to school to win over campus leaders to Israel's cause. Besser, "Turning up Heat"; Pomerance, "Israel Forces Winning." In the spring of 2005, it hosted 100 student government presidents (80 of whom were not Jewish) at its annual conference. Nathaniel Popper, "Pro-Israel Groups: Campuses Improving," *Forward,* June 24, 2005.

104. Michael Dobbs, "Middle East Studies under Scrutiny in U.S.," *The Washington Post,* January 13, 2004; Michelle Goldberg, "Osama University?" *Salon.com,* November 6, 2003; Kristine McNeil, "The War on Academic Freedom," *The Nation,*

November 11, 2002; Zachary Lockman, "Behind the Battle over US Middle East Policy," *Middle East Report Online,* January 2004.

105. Jonathan R. Cole, "The Patriot Act on Campus: Defending the University Post—9/11," *The Boston Review,* Summer 2003.

106. Chanakya Sethi, "Khalidi Candidacy for New Chair Draws Fire," *The Daily Princetonian,* April 22, 2005; Idem, "Debate Grows over Khalidi Candidacy," *The Daily Princetonian,* April 28, 2005.

107. See Philip Weiss, "Burning Cole," *The Nation,* July 3, 2006; Liel Liebovitz, "Middle East Wars Flare Up at Yale," *Jewish Week,* June 2, 2006; and the symposium entitled "Posting Mortem," in *The Chronicle of Higher Education,* July 28, 2006.

108. Robert Gaines, "The Battle at Columbia University," *Washington Report on Middle East Affairs,* April, 2005, pp. 56–57; Caroline Glick, "Our World: The Columbia Disaster," *The Jerusalem Post,* April 4. 2005; Joseph Massad, "Witch Hunt at Columbia: Targeting the University," *CounterPunch,* June 3, 2005; Nathaniel Popper, "Columbia Students Say Firestorm Blurs Campus Reality," *Forward,* February 11, 2005; Scott Sherman, "The Mideast Comes to Columbia," *The Nation,* April 4, 2005; Chanan Weissman, "Columbia Unbecoming," *The Jerusalem Post,* February 6, 2005.

109. Columbia University Ad Hoc Grievance Committee, Final Report, New York, 28 March 2005 (excerpts)," in *The Journal of Palestine Studies,* Vol. 34, No. 4 (Summer 2005), pp. 90–100.

110. Goldberg, "Osama University?"; Ron Kampeas, "Campus Oversight Passes Senate as Review Effort Scores a Victory," *JTA,* November 22, 2005; Stanley Kurtz, "Reforming the Campus: Congress Targets Title VI," *National Review Online,* October 14, 2003; McNeil, "War on Academic Freedom"; Ori Nir, "Groups Back Bill to Monitor Universities," *Forward,* March 12, 2004; Sara Roy, "Short Cuts," *The London Review of Books,* April 1, 2004; Anders Strindberg, "The New Commissars," *The American Conservative,* February 2, 2004.

111. The number 130 comes from Mitchell G. Bard, "Tenured or Tenuous: Defining the Role of Faculty in Supporting Israel on Campus," report published by The Israel on Campus Coalition

and The American-Israeli Cooperative Enterprise, May 2004, p. 11. Also see Nacha Cattan, "NYU Center: New Addition to Growing Academic Field," *Forward,* May 2, 2003; Samuel G. Freedman, "Separating the Political Myths from the Facts in Israel Studies," *The New York Times,* February 16, 2005; Jennifer Jacobson, "The Politics of Israel Studies," *The Chronicle of Higher Education,* June 24, 2005, pp. 10–12; Michael C. Kotzin, "The Jewish Community and the Ivory Tower: An Urgent Need for Israel Studies," *Forward,* January 30, 2004; Nathaniel Popper, "Israel Studies Gain on Campus as Disputes Grow," *Forward,* March 25, 2005.

112. Quoted in Cattan, "NYU Center."

113. Jonathan Kessler, "Pro-Israel Activism Makes Comeback on Campus," *Forward,* December 26, 2003; Popper, "Campuses Improving"; Barry Silverman and Randall Kaplan, "Pro-Israel College Activists Quietly Successful on Campus," *JTA,* May 9, 2005; Chanan Tigay, "As Students Return to Campus, Activists Prepare a New Approach," *JTA,* September 1, 2005. Nevertheless, there are limits to the lobby's effectiveness on campuses. See Joe Eskenazi, "Book: College Campuses Quiet, but Anti-Israel Feeling Is Growing," *JTA,* November 29, 2005; Gary Rosenblatt, "U.S. Grad Students Seen Hostile to Israel," *Jewish Week,* June 17, 2005.

114. Not surprisingly, the baseless claim that we are antisemites was a common theme in a number of early responses to our original article and Working Paper.

115. Quoted in Tony Judt, "Goodbye to All That?," *The Nation,* January 3, 2005.

116. Anti-Defamation League (ADL), "Attitudes toward Jews, Israel and the Palestinian-Israeli Conflict in Ten European Countries," April 2004; The Pew Global Attitudes Project, *A Year After Iraq War: Mistrust of America in Europe Even Higher, Muslim Anger Persists* (The Pew Research Center for the People and the Press, March 16, 2004), pp. 4–5, 26. On the ADL survey, see "ADL Survey Finds Some Decrease in Anti-Semitic Attitudes in Ten European Countries," ADL Press Release, April 26, 2004; Shlomo Shamir, "Poll Shows Decrease in Anti-Semitic Views in Europe," *Ha'aretz,* April 27, 2004. These findings

had virtually no effect on pro-Israel pundits, who continued to argue that antisemitism was rampant in Europe. See, for example, Daniel J. Goldhagen, "Europe's Toothless Reply to Anti-Semitism: Conference Fails to Build Tools to Fight a Rising Sickness," *The Los Angeles Times,* April 30, 2004; Charles Krauthammer, "The Real Mideast 'Poison,'" *The Washington Post,* April 30, 2004.

117. Martin Peretz, the editor-in-chief of The New Republic, says, "The headquarters of anti-Semitic Europe today, just as during the Third Republic, is Paris." "Cambridge Diarist: Regrets," *The New Republic,* April 22, 2002, p. 50. The data in this paragraph are from "Anti-Semitism in Europe: Is It Really Rising?," *The Economist,* May 4, 2002.

118. Quoted in Marc Perelman, "Community Head: France No More Antisemitic Than U.S.," *Forward,* August, 1, 2003. Also see Francois Bujon de l'Estang, "A Slander on France," *The Washington Post,* June 22, 2002; "French President Accuses Israel of Conducting Anti-French Campaign," *Ha'aretz,* May 12, 2002.

119. "French Police: Anti-Semitism in France Sharply Decreased in 2005," *Ha'aretz,* January 19, 2006.

120. "French Protest for Murdered Jew," *BBC News Online,* February 26, 2006; Michel Zlotowski, "Large Memorial Held for Parisian Jew," *The Jerusalem Post,* February 23, 2006.

121. Avi Beker, "The Eternally Open Gate," *Ha'aretz,* January 11, 2005; Josef Joffe, "A Boom, if Not A Renaissance, in Modern-Day Germany," *Forward,* July 25, 2003; Nathaniel Popper, "Immigrant Policy Eyed as German Community Swells," *Forward,* July 25, 2003; Eliahu Salpeter, "Jews from the CIS Prefer Germany to the Jewish State," *Ha'aretz,* May 28, 2005. Also, *The Times* of London reported in the spring of 2005, that, "An estimated 100,000 Jews have returned to Russia in the past few years, sparking a dramatic renaissance of Jewish life in a country with a long history of anti-Semitism." Jeremy Page, "Once Desperate to Leave, Now Jews Are Returning to Russia, Land of Opportunity," *The Times,* April 28, 2005. Also see Lev Krichevsky, "Poll: Russians Don't Dislike Jews, and More Are against Anti-Semitism," *JTA,* February 2, 2006.

122. The chairman of the Education Department of the Jewish Agency recently said that "present day violent anti-Semitism originates from two separate sources: radical Islamists in the Middle East and Western Europe as well as the neo-Nazi youth element in Eastern Europe and Latin America." Jonathan Schneider, "Anti-Semitism Still a World Problem," *The Jerusalem Post,* January 26, 2006.

123. In the ADL's April 2004 survey, "Attitudes toward Jews, Israel and the Palestinian-Israeli Conflict in Ten European Countries," the following question was asked: "In your opinion, is it very important, somewhat important, somewhat unimportant or not important at all for our government to take a role in combating anti-Semitism in our country?" The percentages for those who strongly agree or somewhat agree were Italy (92), Britain (83), Netherlands (83), France (82), Germany (81), Belgium (81), Denmark (79), Austria (76), Switzerland (74), Spain (73). See p. 19.

124. Phyllis Chester, *The New Anti-Semitism: The Current Crisis and What We Must Do about It* (Jossey-Bass, 2003); Hillel Halkin, "The Return of Anti-Semitism: To Be against Israel Is to Be against the Jews," *The Wall Street Journal,* February 5, 2002; Barry Kosmin and Paul Iganski, "Judeophobia—Not Your Parent's Anti-Semitism," *Ha'aretz,* June 3, 2003; Amnon Rubinstein, "Fighting the New Anti-Semitism," *Ha'aretz,* December 2, 2003; Gabriel Schoenfeld, *The Return of Anti-Semitism* (Encounter Books, 2003); Natan Sharansky, "Anti-Semitism Is Our Problem," *Ha'aretz,* August 10, 2003; Yair Sheleg, "A World Cleansed of the Jewish State," *Ha'aretz,* April 18, 2002; Yair Sheleg, "Enemies, a Post-National Story," *Ha'aretz,* March, 8, 2003. For criticism of this perspective, see Akiva Eldar, "Anti-Semitism Can Be Self-Serving," *Ha'aretz,* May 3, 2002; Brian Klug, "The Myth of the New Anti-Semitism," *The Nation,* February 2, 2004; Ralph Nader, "Criticizing Israel is Not Anti-Semitism," *CounterPunch,* October 16/17, 2004; Henri Picciotto and Mitchell Plitnick, eds., *Refraining Anti-Semitism: Alternative Jewish Perspectives* (Jewish Voice for Peace, 2004); and especially Finkelstein, *Beyond Chutzpah,* chapters 1–3.

125. Helen Nugent, "Chief Rabbi Flays Church over Vote on Israel Assets," *Times Online*, February 17, 2006. Also see Bill Bowder, "Sacks Seeks Talks after Synod Vote on Disinvestment," *Church Times*, February 24, 2006; "Bulldozer Motion 'Based on Ignorance,'" in *ibid*; Ruth Gledhill, "Church Urged to Reconsider Investments with Israel," *Times Online,* May 28, 2005; Irene Lancaster, "Anglicans Have Betrayed the Jews," Downloaded from Moriel Ministries (UK) website, February 20, 2006; "U.K. Chief Rabbi Attacks Anglicans over Israel Divestment Vote," *Ha'aretz,* February 17, 2006.

126. That the Church of England was merely criticizing Israeli policy and not engaging in antisemitism is clearly reflected in the February 10, 2006, letter that the Archbishop of Canterbury (Rowan Williams) sent to England's Chief Rabbi (Jonathan Sacks) explaining the Church's decision on divestment. For a copy of the letter, see "Archbishop: Synod Call Was Expression of Concern," February 10, 2006. Downloaded from Church of England website, February 20, 2006.

127. Quoted in Michael Massing, "Deal Breakers," *The American Prospect,* Vol. 13, No. 5 (March 11, 2002).

128. Steven Kull (Principal Investigator), *Americans on the Middle East Road Map* (Program on International Policy Attitudes, University of Maryland, May 30, 2003), pp. 9–11, 18–19. Also see Steven Kull *et al., Americans on the Israeli-Palestinian Conflict* (Program on International Policy Attitudes, University of Maryland, May 6, 2002). A 2005 Anti-Defamation League public opinion survey found that 78 percent of Americans believe that their government should favor neither Israel nor the Palestinians. "American Attitudes toward Israel and the Middle East," Survey conducted on March 18–25, 2005, and June 19–23, 2005, by the Marttila Communications Group for the Anti-Defamation League.

129. Robert G. Kaiser, "Bush and Sharon Nearly Identical on Mideast Policy," *The Washington Post*, February, 9, 2003.

130. Lee Hockstader and Daniel Williams, "Israel Says It Won't 'Pay Price' of Coalition," *The Washington Post,* September 18, 2001; Jonathan Karp, "Sharon Cancels Peace Talks in Rebuff to U.S. Concerns," *The Wall Street Journal,* September 24, 2001; Thomas Oliphant, "A Delicate Balance," *The Boston Globe,* September, 18, 2001; "Israel's Opportunity," *The Los Angeles Times* editorial, September 18, 2001.

131. Kurt Eichenwald, "U.S. Jews Split on Washington's Shift on Palestinian State," *The New York Times,* October 5, 2001. At the same time, Prime Minister Tony Blair made "Britain's strongest endorsement yet of Palestinian statehood." Michael Dobbs, "Blair Backs Creation of Palestinian State," *The Washington Post,* October 16, 2001.

132. James Bennet, "Sharon Invokes Munich in Warning U.S. on 'Appeasement.'" *The New York Times*, October, 5, 2001; Jane Perlez and Katharine Q. Seelye, "U.S. Strongly Rebukes Sharon for Criticism of Bush. Calling it 'Unacceptable.'" *The New York Times,* October 6, 2001; Shlomo Shamir, "U.S. Jews: Sharon is 'Worried' by Terrorism Distinction," *Ha'aretz,* September 18, 2001; Alan Sipress and Lee Hockstader, "Sharon Speech Riles U.S.," *The Washington Post,* October 6, 2001. For evidence that other Israelis shared Sharon's fears, see Israel Harel, "Lessons from the Next War," *Ha'aretz,* October 6, 2001.

133. Jack Donnelly, "Nation Set to Push Sharon on Agreement," *The Boston Globe,* October 10, 2001; Hockstader and Sipress, "Sharon Speech Riles U.S."; Perlez and Seelye, "U.S. Strongly Rebukes Sharon."

134. Lee Hockstader, "Sharon Apologetic over Row with U.S.," *The Washington Post,* October 7, 2001; Serge Schmemann, "Raising Munich, Sharon Reveals Israeli Qualms," *The New York Times,* October 6, 2001.

135. Aluf Benn, "Analysis: Clutching at Straws," *Ha'aretz,* September 18, 2001; "Excerpts from Talk by Sharon," *The New York Times,* December 4, 2001; William Safire, "'Israel or Arafat,'" *The New York Times,* December 3, 2001.

136. Elaine Sciolino, "Senators Urge Bush Not to Hamper Israel," *The New York Times,* November 17, 2001.

137. Dana Milbank, "Bush Spokesman Gentle on Israeli Assault," *The Washington Post,* December 3, 2001; Safire, "Israel or Arafat"; David Sanger, "U.S. Walks a Tightrope on Terrorism in Israel," *The New York Times,* December 4, 2001.

138. Keith B. Richburg and Molly Moore, "Israel Rejects Demands to Withdraw Troops," *The Washington Post,* April 11, 2002. All quotes in this paragraph are from Fareed Zakaria, "Colin Powell's Humiliation: Bush Should Clearly Support His Secretary of State—Otherwise He Should Get a New One," *Newsweek,* April 29, 2002. Also sec Mike Allen and John Lancaster, "Defiant Sharon Losing Support in White House," *The Washington Post,* April 11, 2002, which describes the Bush administration's anger with Sharon.

139. It is worth noting that the American people were generally supportive of Bush's efforts to put pressure on Israel in the spring of 2002. A Time/CNN poll taken on April 10–11 found that 60 percent of Americans felt that U.S. aid to Israel should be cut off or reduced if Sharon refused to withdraw from the Palestinian areas he had recently occupied. "Poll: Americans Support Cutting Aid to Israel," Reuters News Release, April 12, 2002; AFP News Release, April 13, 2002. Also see *Israel and the Palestinians* (Program on International Policy Attitudes, University of Maryland, last updated on August 15, 2002). Moreover, 75 percent of those surveyed thought that Powell should meet with Arafat when he visited Israel. Regarding Sharon, only 35 percent found him trustworthy, while 35 percent thought he was a warmonger, 20 percent saw him as a terrorist, and 25 percent considered him an enemy of the United States.

140. William Kristol and Robert Kagan, "'Senior White House Aides:' Speak Up!," *The Weekly Standard,* April, 11, 2002. For a graphic description of the heat that the lobby put on Powell when he was in the Middle East, see Bob Woodward, *Bush at War* (New York: Simon and Schuster, 2002), pp. 323–326. Also see John Simpson, "Israeli Leader Has More Power in Washington than Powell," *The Sunday Telegraph* (London), April 14, 2002, which describes a joint press conference Powell and Sharon conducted by noting, "The Secretary of State's language, body and verbal, certainly were not that of the paymaster coming to call a client to account. Far from it. Mr. Powell seemed ingratiating, deferential; no doubt he realizes how much support Mr. Sharon has back in Washington and how much influence his friends have there with the President." It

is also worth noting that former Israeli Prime Minister Benjamin Netanyahu, who was making Israel's case in the United States at the time, said even before Powell arrived in Israel that his trip "won't amount to anything." Elaine Sciolino, "Netanyahu Says Powell Mission 'Won't Amount to Anything' and Urges Arafat's Exile," *The New York Times,* April 11, 2002.

141. James D. Besser, "No Tennessee Waltz," *Jewish Week,* December 27, 2002. Also see Mike Allen and Juliet Eilperin, "White House and DeLay at Odds," *The Washington Post,* April 26, 2002; Judith Eilperin and Helen Dewar, "Lawmakers Endorse Israel's Offensive," *The Washington Post,* May 3, 2002. Bush was feeling intense pressure not just from lawmakers, but from Jewish leaders and Christian evangelicals. See Mike Allen and John Lancaster, "Defiant Sharon Losing Support in White House," *The Washington Post,* April 11, 2002; Dan Balz, "Bush Statement on Mideast Reflects Tension in GOP," *The Washington Post,* April 7, 2003; Elisabeth Bumiller, "Bush Sends Aide to Speak at Rally to Quell a Growing Furor," *The New York Times,* April 16, 2002; Bradley Burston, "Background: Can Bush Afford to Press Sharon for Peace?," *Ha'aretz,* May 6, 2002; Akiva Eldar, "Bush and Israel, 1991 and 2002," *Ha'aretz,* May 6, 2002; Alison Mitchell, "U.S. Political Leaders Seek Unity on Mideast, for Now," *The Washington Post,* April 12, 2002; William Safire, "On Being an Ally," *The New York Times,* April 11, 2002; Alan Sipress, "Policy Divide Thwarts Powell in Mideast Effort," *The Washington Post,* April 26, 2002; and Alan Sipress and Karen DeYoung, "U.S. Presses Ahead with Peace Efforts," *The Washington Post,* May 9, 2002.

142. Randall Mikkelsen, "White House Calls Sharon 'Man of Peace'," Reuters, April 11, 2002; Bill Sammon, "White House Softens Tone with Israel," *The Washington Times,* April 12, 2002.

143. Peter Slevin and Mike Allen, "Bush: Sharon A 'Man of Peace'," *The Washington Post,* April 19, 2002; David Sanger, "President Praises Effort by Powell in the Middle East," *The New York Times,* April 19, 2002. For a transcript of the press conference, see "President Bush, Secretary Powell Discuss Middle East," White House, Office of the Press Secretary, April 18, 2002.

144. Eilperin and Dewar, "Lawmakers Endorse Israel's Offensive"; Juliet Eilperin and Mike Allen, "Hill Leaders Plan Votes on Pro-Israel Relations," *The Washington Post,* May 2, 2002; Alison Mitchell, "House and Senate Support Israel in Strong Resolutions," *The New York Times*, May 3, 2002. For copies of the two resolutions, see "2 Resolutions 'Expressing Solidarity with Israel,'" *The New York Times,* May 3, 2002. Also see Matthew E. Berger, "Bills in Congress Boost Israel, Treat Arafat as Terrorist," *The Jewish Bulletin,* April 26, 2002.

145. Arieh O'Sullivan, "Visiting Congressmen Advise Israel to Resist Administration Pressure to Deal with Arafat," *The Jerusalem Post,* May 6, 2002.

146. Eli Lake, "Israeli Lobby Wins $200 Million Fight," United Press International, May 11, 2002.

147. Quoted in Jefferson Morley, "Who's in Charge?" *The Washington Post,* April 26, 2002. As Akiva Eldar noted just before Sharon steamrolled Bush, "Sharon has a lot of experience sticking it to the Americans. . . . Ultimately, whether it was Palestinian terror, Arafat's mistakes, or domestic politics, the Americans were sent to the peanut gallery." See his "Words Are Not Enough," *Ha'aretz,* April 8, 2002. Nor was Bush's humiliation lost on commentators around the world. Spain's leading daily, *El Pais,* expressed the views of many outside observers when it commented, "If a country's weight is measured by its degree of influence on events, the superpower is not the USA but Israel." Quoted in Morlev, "Who's in Charge?"

148. Bradley Burston, "Hamas 'R' Us," *Ha'aretz,* January 18, 2006; Akiva Eldar, "Kadima to A New Middle East," *Ha'aretz,* December 19, 2005; Idem, "Who Needs Abu Mazen?," *Ha'aretz,* November 7, 2005: Ran HaCohen, "Hamas and Israel: Rival Twins," *AntiWar.com,* February 6, 2006; M. J. Rosenberg, "No Partner—As Always," *IFF Friday,* Issue No. 260, February 3, 2006; Danny Rubenstein, "All We Did Was Switch the Non-Partner," *Ha'aretz,* February 5, 2006; "Disarray Among the Palestinians," *The New York Times* editorial, January 17, 2006.

149. Regarding the views of previous Presidents, see Clyde R. Mark. "Israeli-United States Relations," Issue Brief for Congress (Congressional Research Service. August 29, 2002), p. 7. On April 14. 2004. Bush broke with his predecessors and proclaimed that Israel would not have to return all of the territories that it occupied in 1967, and that Palestinian refugees would not be allowed to return to their former homes in Israel, but would have to settle in a new Palestinian state. See "Statement by the President Regarding Israel-Arab Peace Process," April 14, 2004; and "President Bush's Letter to Prime Minister Sharon," April 14, 2004.

150. "US Scowcroft Criticizes Bush Admin's Foreign Policy," *The Financial Times,* October 13, 2004. Also see Glenn Kessler, "Scowcroft is Critical of Bush," *The Washington Post,* October 16, 2004.

151. On Kerry, see Gadi Dechter, "Analysis: President Kerry on Israel," United Press International press release, July 9. 2004; Nathan Guttman, "Kerry Position Paper Outlines Support for Israel," *Ha'aretz,* July 2, 2004; Nathan Guttman, "Kerry Jumps on Sharon Bandwagon in Favoring Gaza Disengagement Plan," *Ha'aretz,* April 25, 2004. On Clinton, see Adam Dickter, "Hillary: 'I Had A Lot to Prove'," *Jewish Week,* November 18, 2005; Kristen Lombardi, "Hillary Calls Israel a 'Beacon' of Democracy," *The Village Voice,* December 11, 2005; Sonia Verma, "Clinton Stressed U.S.-Israel Coalition," *Newsday,* November 15, 2005; Rachel Zabarkes Friedman, "Senator Israel," *National Review Online,* May 25, 2005.

152. Emad Mekay, "Iraq Was Invaded 'to Protect Israel'—US Official," *Asia Times Online,* March 31, 2004. Zelikow also served with Rice on the National Security Council when George H. W. Bush was President, and co-authored a book with her on German reunification. He was also one of the principal authors of the second Bush administration's 2002 *National Security Strategy,* the most comprehensive official presentation of the so-called Bush Doctrine.

153. Following publication of our original article. Zelikow challenged our use of this quotation and claimed that we had taken his remarks out of context. In particular, he suggested that he had been speaking primarily about the first Gulf War in 1990–91, and not about the 2003 war that was then being contemplated. A full record of his remarks shows that this claim is false and that he was clearly referring to the debate on whether the

United States should launch a preventive war against Iraq in 2002–03. For the exchange, which includes the text of the key passages of his September 2002 remarks, see the "Letters" section of *The London Review of Books,* Vol. 28, No. 10 (May 25, 2006).

154. Jason Keyser, "Israel Urges U.S. to Attack," *The Washington Post,* August 16, 2002. Also see Aluf Benn, "PM Urging U.S. Not to Delay Strike against Iraq," *Ha'aretz,* August 16, 2002; Idem, "PM Aide: Delay in U.S. Attack Lets Iraq Speed Up Arms Program," *Ha'aretz,* August 16, 2002; Reuven Pedhatzur, "Israel's Interest in the War on Saddam," *Ha'aretz,* August 4, 2002; Ze'ev Schiff, "Into the Rough," *Ha'aretz,* August 16, 2002.

155. Gideon Alon, "Sharon to Panel: Iraq is Our Biggest Danger," *Ha'aretz,* August 13, 2002. At a White House press conference with President Bush on October 16, 2002, Sharon said: "I would like to thank you, Mr. President, for the friendship and cooperation. And as far as I remember, as we look back towards many years now, I think that we never had such relations with any President of the United States as we have with you, and we never had such cooperation in everything as we have with the current administration." For a transcript of the press conference, see "President Bush Welcomes Prime Minister Sharon to White House; Question and Answer Session with the Press," U.S. Department of State, October 16, 2002. Also see Kaiser, "Bush and Sharon Nearly Identical on Mideast Policy."

156. Shlomo Brom, "An Intelligence Failure," *Strategic Assessment* (Jaffee Center for Strategic Studies, Tel Aviv University), Vol. 6, No. 3 (November 2003), p. 9. Also see "Intelligence Assessment: Selections from the Media, 1998–2003," in *ibid.,* pp. 17–19; Gideon Alon, "Report Slams Assessment of Dangers Posed by Libya, Iraq," *Ha'aretz,* March 28, 2004; Dan Baron, "Israeli Report Blasts Intelligence for Exaggerating the Iraqi Threat," *JTA,* March 28, 2004; Greg Myre, "Israeli Report Faults Intelligence on Iraq," *The New York Times,* March 28, 2004; James Risen, *State of War; The Secret History of the CIA and the Bush Administration* (Simon & Schuster, 2006), pp. 72–73.

157. Marc Perelman, "Iraqi Move Puts Israel in Lonely U.S. Corner," *Forward,* September 20, 2002. This article begins, "Saddam Hussein's surprise acceptance of 'unconditional' United Nations weapons inspections put Israel on the hot seat this week, forcing it into the open as the only nation actively supporting the Bush administration's goal of Iraqi regime change." Peres became so frustrated with the UN process in the following months that in mid-February 2003 he lashed out at the French by questioning France's status as a permanent member of the Security Council. "Peres Questions France Permanent Status on Security Council," *Ha'aretz,* February 20, 2003. On a visit to Moscow in late September 2002. Sharon made it clear to Russian President Putin, who was leading the charge for new inspections, that "the time when these inspectors could have been effective has passed." Herb Keinon, "Sharon to Putin: Too Late for Iraq Arms Inspection," *The Jerusalem Post,* October 1, 2002.

158. Ehud Barak, "Taking Apart Iraq's Nuclear Threat," *The New York Times,* September 4, 2002.

159. Benjamin Netanyahu, "The Case for Toppling Saddam," *The Walt Street Journal,* September 20, 2002. *The Jerusalem Post* was particularly hawkish on Iraq, frequently running editorials and op-eds promoting the war, and hardly ever running pieces against it. Representative editorials include "Next Stop Baghdad." *The Jerusalem Post,* November 15, 2001; "Don't Wait for Saddam," *The Jerusalem Post,* August 18, 2002; "Making the Case for War," *The Jerusalem Post,* September 9, 2002. For some representative op-eds, see Ron Dermer, "The March to Baghdad," *The Jerusalem Post,* December 21, 2001; Efraim Inbar, "Ousting Saddam. Instilling Stability," *The Jerusalem Post,* October 8, 2002; Gerald M. Steinberg, "Imagining the Liberation of Iraq," *The Jerusalem Post,* November 18, 2001.

160. Aluf Benn, "Background: Enthusiastic IDF Awaits War in Iraq," *Ha'aretz,* February 17, 2002. Also see James Bennet, "Israel Says War on Iraq Would Benefit the Region," *The New York Times,* February 27, 2003; Chemi Shalev, "Jerusalem Frets As U.S. Battles Iraq War Delays," *Forward,* March 7, 2003.

161. Indeed, a February 2003 poll reported that 77.5 percent of Israeli Jews wanted the United States to attack Iraq. Ephraim Yaar and Tamar Hermann,

"Peace Index: Most Israelis Support the Attack on Iraq," *Ha'aretz,* March 6, 2003. Regarding Kuwait, a public opinion poll released in March 2003 found that 89.6 percent of Kuwaitis favored the impending war against Iraq. James Morrison, "Kuwaitis Support War," *The Washington Times,* March 18, 2003.

162. Gideon Levy, "A Deafening Silence," *Ha'aretz,* October 6, 2002.

163. Sec Dan Izenberg, "Foreign Ministry Warns Israeli War Talk Fuels US Anti-Semitism," *The Jerusalem Post,* March 10, 2003, which makes clear that "the Foreign Ministry has received reports from the US" telling Israelis to cool their jets because "the US media" is portraying Israel as "trying to goad the administration into war." There is also evidence that Israel itself was concerned about being seen as driving American policy toward Iraq. See Benn, "PM Urging U.S. Not to Delay Strike"; Perelman, "Iraq Move Puts Israel in Lonely U.S. Corner." Finally, in late September 2002, a group of political consultants known as the "Israel Project" told pro-Israel leaders in the United States "to keep quiet while the Bush administration pursues a possible war with Iraq." Dana Milbank. "Group Urges Pro-Israel Leaders Silence on Iraq," *The Washington Post,* November 27, 2002.

164. The influence of the neoconservatives and their allies is clearly reflected in the following articles: Joel Beinin, "Pro-Israel I lawks and the Second Gulf War," *Middle East Report Online,* April 6, 2003; Elisabeth Bumiller and Eric Schmitt, "On the Job and at Home, Influential Hawks' 30–Year Friendship Evolves," *The New York Times,* September 11, 2002; Kathleen and William Christison, "A Rose by Another Name: The Bush Administration's Dual Loyalties," *Counter Punch,* December 13, 2002; Robert Dreyfuss, "The Pentagon Muzzles the CIA," *The American Prospect,* December 16, 2002; Michael Elliott and James Carney, "First Stop, Iraq," *Time,* March 31, 2003; Seymour Hersh, "The Iraq Hawks," *The New Yorker,* Vol. 77, issue 41 (December 24–31, 2001), pp. 58–63; Glenn Kessler, "U.S. Decision on Iraq Has Puzzling Past," *The Washington Post,* January 12, 2003; Joshua M. Marshall, "Bomb Saddam?," *The Washington Monthly,* June 2002;

Dana Milbank, "White House Push for Iraqi Strike Is on Hold," *The Washington Post,* August 18, 2002; Susan Page, "Showdown with Saddam: The Decision to Act," *USA Today,* September 11, 2002; Sam Tanenhaus, "Bush's Brain Trust," *Vanity Fair,* July 2003. Note that all these articles are from before the war started.

165. See Mortimer B. Zuckerman, "No Time for Equivocation," *U.S. News & World Report,* August 26/September 2, 2002; Idem, "Clear and Compelling Proof," *U.S. News & World Report,* February 10, 2003; Idem, "The High Price of Waiting," *U.S. News & World Report,* March 10, 2003.

166. "An Unseemly Silence," *Forward,* May 7, 2004. Also sec Gary Rosenblatt, "Hussein Asylum," *Jewish Week,* August 23, 2002; Idem, "The Case for War against Saddam," *Jewish Week,* December 13, 2002.

167. Just before the U.S. military invaded Iraq, Congressman James P. Moran (D-VA) created a stir when he said, "If it were not for the strong support of the Jewish community for this war with Iraq, we would not be doing this." Spencer S. Hsu, "Moran Said Jews Are Pushing War," *The Washington Post,* March 11, 2003. Moran misspoke, however, because there was not widespread support for the war in the Jewish community. He should have said, "If it were not for the strong support of the neoconservatives and the leadership of the Israel lobby for this war with Iraq, we would not be doing this."

168. Samuel G. Freedman, "Don't Blame Jews for This War," *USA Today,* April 2, 2003. Also see Ori Nir, "Poll Finds Jewish Political Gap," *Forward,* February 4, 2005.

169. It is no exaggeration to say that in the wake of 9/11, the neoconservatives were not just determined, but were obsessed with removing Saddam from power. As one senior administration figure put it in January 2003, "I do believe certain people have grown theological about this. It's almost a religion—that it will be the end of our society if we don't take action now." Kessler, "U.S. Decision on Iraq Has Puzzling Past." Kessler also describes Colin Powell returning from White House meetings on Iraq, "rolling his eyes" and saying, "Jeez, what a fixation about

Iraq." Bob Woodward reports in *Plan of Attack* (Simon and Schuster, 2004), p. 410, that Kenneth Adelman "said he had worried to death as time went on and support seemed to wane that there would be no war." Also see *ibid.*, pp. 164–165.

170. The first letter (January 26, 1998) was written under the auspices of the Project for the New American Century and can be found on its website. The second letter (February 19, 1998) was written under the auspices of the Committee for Peace and Security in the Gulf and can be found on the Iraq Watch website. Also see the May 29, 1998, letter to Speaker of the House Newt Gingrich and Senate Majority Leader Trent Lott written under the auspices of the Project for the New American Century and found on its website. The neoconservatives, it should be emphasized, advocated invading Iraq to topple Saddam. See "The End of Containment," *The Weekly Standard*, December 1, 1997, pp. 13–14; Zalmay M. Khalizad and Paul Wolfowitz, "Overthrow Him," in *ibid.*, pp. 14–15; Frederick W. Kagan, "Not by Air Alone," in *ibid.*, pp. 15–16.

171. See Clinton's comments after he signed the "Iraq Liberation Act of 1998." Statement by the President, White House Press Office, October 31, 1998.

172. One might think from the publicity and controversy surrounding two books published in 2004—Richard Clarke's *Against All Enemies: Inside America's War on Terror* (Free Press, 2004) and Ron Suskind, *The Price of Loyalty: George W Bush, the White House, and the Education of Paul O'Neill* (Simon and Schuster, 2004)—that Bush and Cheney were bent on invading Iraq when they assumed office in late January 2001. However, this interpretation is wrong. They were deeply interested in toppling Saddam, just as Bill Clinton and Al Gore had been. But there is no evidence in the public record showing that Bush and Cheney were seriously contemplating war against Iraq before 9/11. In fact, Bush made it clear to Bob Woodward that he was not thinking about going to war against Saddam before 9/11. See *Plan of Attack*, p. 12. Also see Nicholas Lehmann, "The Iraq Factor," *The New Yorker*, Vol. 76, issue 43 (January 22, 2001), pp. 34–48; Eric Schmitt and

Steven Lee Meyers, "Bush Administration Warns Iraq on Weapons Programs," *The New York Times*, January 23, 2001. And Cheney had defended the decision not to go to Baghdad throughout the 1990s and during the 2000 campaign. See Timothy Noah, "Dick Cheney, Dove," *Slate.com*, October 16, 2002; "Calm after Desert Storm," An Interview with Dick Cheney, *Policy Review*, No. 65 (Summer 1993). In short, even though the neoconservatives held important positions in the Bush administration, they were unable to generate much enthusiasm for attacking Iraq before 9/11. Thus, *The New York Times* reported in March 2001 that "some Republicans" were complaining that Rumsfeld and Wolfowitz "are failing to live up to their pre-election advocacy of stepping up efforts to overthrow President Hussein." At the same time, a *Washington Times* editorial asked, "Have Hawks Become Doves?" See Jane Perlez, "Capitol Hawks Seek Tougher Line on Iraq," *The New York Times*, March 7, 2001; "Have Hawks Become Doves?," *The Washington Times*, March 8, 2001.

173. Woodward, *Plan of Attack*, pp. 25–26. Wolfowitz was so insistent on conquering Iraq that five days later Cheney had to tell him to "stop agitating for targeting Saddam." Page, "Showdown with Saddam," According to one Republican lawmaker, he "was like a parrot bringing [Iraq] up all the time. It was getting on the President's nerves." Elliot and Carney, "First Stop, Iraq." Woodward describes Wolfowitz as "like a drum that would not stop." *Plan of Attack*, p. 22.

174. Woodward, *Plan of Attack*, pp. 1–44.

175. Regarding the neoconservatives' influence on Cheney, see Elliott and Carney, "First Stop, Iraq"; Page, "Showdown with Saddam"; Michael Hirsh, "Bernard Lewis Revisited," *Washington Monthly*, November 2004, pp. 13–19; Frederick Kempe, "Lewis's 'Liberation' Doctrine for Mideast Faces New Tests," *The Wall Street Journal*, December 13, 2005; Carla Anne Robbins and Jeanne Cummings, "How Bush Decided that Hussein Must Be Ousted from Atop Iraq," *The Wall Street Journal*, June 14, 2002. On Cheney's critical role in the decision-making process, see Glenn Kessler and Peter Slevin, "Cheney is Fulcrum of Foreign

Policy," *The Washington Post,* October 13, 2002; Barbara Slavin and Susan Page, "Cheney Rewrites Roles in Foreign Policy." *USA Today,* July 29, 2002.

176. *The New York Times* reported shortly after 9/11 that, "Some senior administration officials, led by Paul D. Wolfowitz . . . and I. Lewis Libby . . . are pressing for the earliest and broadest military campaign against not only the Osama bin Laden network in Afghanistan, but also against other suspected terrorist bases in Iraq and in Lebanon's Bekaa region." Patrick E. Tyler and Elaine Sciolino, "Bush Advisers Split on Scope of Retaliation," *The New York Times,* September 20, 2001. Also see William Safire, "Phony War II," *The New York Times,* November 28, 2002. Woodward succinctly describes Libby's influence in *Plan of Attack* (pp. 48–49): "Libby had three formal titles. He was chief of staff to Vice President Cheney: he was also national security adviser to the vice president; and he was finally an assistant to President Bush. It was a trifecta of positions probably never held before by a single person. Scooter was a power center unto himself. . . . Libby was one of only two people who were not principals to attend the National Security Council meetings with the president and the separate principals meetings chaired by Rice." Also see *ibid.,* pp. 50–51, 288–292, 300–301, 409–410; Bumiller and Schmitt, "On the Job and at Home"; Karen Kwiatkowski, "The New Pentagon Papers," *Salon.com,* March 10, 2004; Patrick E. Tyler and Elaine Sciolino, "Bush Advisers Split on Scope of Retaliation," *The New York Times,* September 20, 2001. On Libby's relationship to Israel, an article in *Forward* reports that "Israeli officials liked Libby. They described him as an important contact who was accessible, genuinely interested in Israel-related issues and very sympathetic to their cause." Ori Nir, "Libby Played Leading Role on Foreign Policy Decisions," *Forward,* November 4, 2005.

177. This letter was published in *The Weekly Standard,* October 1, 2001.

178. Robert Kagan and William Kristol, "The Right War," *The Weekly Standard,* October 1, 2001; Charles Krauthammer, "Our First Move: Take Out the Taliban," *The Washington Post,* October 1, 2001. Also see "War Aims," *The Wall Street Journal,* September 20, 2001.

179. Even before the dust had settled at the World Trade Center, pro-Israel forces were making the case that Saddam was responsible for 9/11. See Michael Barone, "War by Ultimatum," *U.S. News & World Report,* October 1, 2001; Bill Gertz, "Iraq Suspected of Sponsoring Terrorist Attacks," *The Washington Times,* September 21, 2001; "Drain the Pond of Terror," *The Jerusalem Post* editorial, September 25, 2001; William Safire, "The Ultimate Enemy," *The New York Times,* September 24, 2001.

180. See James Bamford, *A Pretext to War* (Doubleday, 2004), chaps. 13–14; Woodward, *Plan of Attack,* pp. 288–292, 297–306.

181. Woodward, *Plan of Attack,* p. 290.

182. See Bamford, *Pretext to War,* pp. 287–291, 307–331; David S. Cloud, "Prewar Intelligence Inquiry Zeroes In On Pentagon," *The Wall Street Journal,* March 11, 2004; Seymour M. Hersh, "Selective Intelligence," *The New Yorker,* Vol. 79, issue 11 (May 12, 2003), pp. 44–50; Kwiatkowski, "New Pentagon Papers"; Jim Lobe, "Pentagon Office Home to Neo-Con Network," *Inter Press Service News Agency,* August 7, 2003; Greg Miller, "Spy Unit Skirted CIA on Iraq," *The Los Angeles Times,* March 10, 2004; Paul R. Pillar, "Intelligence, Policy, and the War in Iraq," *Foreign Affairs,* Vol. 85, No. 2 (March-April 2006), pp. 15–27; James Risen, "How Pair's Finding on Terror Led to Clash on Shaping Intelligence," *The New York Times,* April 28, 2004; Eric Schmitt and Thom Shanker, "Threats and Responses: A C.I.A. Rival: Pentagon Sets Up Intelligence Unit," *The New York Times,* October 24, 2002.

183. The Office of Special Plans relied heavily on information from Ahmed Chalabi and other Iraqi exiles and it had close links with various Israeli sources. Indeed, *The Guardian* reports that it "forged close ties to a parallel, ad hoc intelligence operation inside Ariel Sharon's office in Israel specifically to bypass Mossad and provide the Bush administration with more alarmist reports on Saddam's Iraq than Mossad was prepared to authorize." Julian Borger, "The Spies Who Pushed for War," *The Guardian,* July 17, 2003.

184. See, for example, Douglas J. Feith, "The Inner Logic of Israel's Negotiations: Withdrawal Process, Not Peace Process," *Middle East Quarterly.* March 1996. For useful discussions of Feith's views, see Jeffrey Goldberg, "A Little Learning: What Douglas Feith Knew and When He Knew It," *The New Yorker,* Vol. 81, issue 12 (May 9, 2005), pp. 36–41; Jim Lobe, "Losing Feith, or is the Bush Team Shedding Its Sharper Edges?," *The Daily Star,* January 31, 2005; James J. Zogby, "A Dangerous Appointment: Profile of Douglas Feith. Undersecretary of Defense under Bush," Middle East Information Center, April 18, 2001; "Israeli Settlements: Legitimate, Democratically Mandated, Vital to Israel's Security and, Therefore, in U.S. Interest," The Center for Security Policy, Transition Brief No. 96–T 130, December 17, 1996. Note that the title of the latter piece, which was published by an organization in the lobby, says that what is in Israel's interest is therefore in America's national interest. In "Losing Feith," Lobe writes: "In 2003, when Feith, who was standing in for Rumsfeld at an interagency 'Principals' Meeting' on the Middle East, concluded his remarks on behalf of the Pentagon, according to the Washington insider newsletter. *The Nelson Report,* [National Security Adviser Condoleezza] Rice said, Thanks Doug, but when we want the Israeli position we'll invite the ambassador.'"

185. The "Clean Break" study was prepared for The Institute for Advanced Strategic and Political Studies in Jerusalem and published in June 1996. A copy can be found on the Institute's website.

186. Akiva Eldar, "Perles of Wisdom for the Feithful," *Ha'aretz,* October 1, 2002.

187. "Rally Unites Anguished Factions under Flag of 'Stand with Israel'," *Forward,* April 19, 2002; "Forward 50," *Forward,* November 15, 2002.

188. John McCaslin, "Israeli-Trained Cops," *The Washington Times,* November 5, 2002; Bret Stephens, "Man of the Year," *The Jerusalem Post* (Rosh Hashana Supplement), September 26, 2003; Janine Zacharia, "Invasive Treatment," in *ibid.* Other useful pieces on Wolfowitz include Michael Dobbs, "For Wolfowitz. A Vision May Be Realized," *The Washington Post,* April 7, 2003; James Fallows, "The Unilateralist," *The Atlantic Monthly,* March 2002, pp. 26–29; Bill Keller, "The Sunshine Warrior," *The New York Times Magazine,* September 22, 2002; "Paul Wolfowitz, Velociraptor," *The Economist,* February 9–15, 2002.

189. According to Feith's former law partner, L. Marc Zell, Chalabi also promised to re-build the pipeline that once ran from Haifa in Israel to Mosul in Iraq. See John Dizard, "How Ahmed Chalabi Conned the Neocons," *Salon.com,* May 4, 2004. In mid-June 2003, Benjamin Netanyahu announced that, "It won't be long before you will see Iraqi oil flowing to Haifa." Reuters, "Netanyahu Says Iraq-Israel Oil Line Not Pipe-Dream," *Ha'aretz,* June 20, 2003. Of course, this did not happen and it is unlikely to happen in the foreseeable future.

190. Matthew E. Berger, "New Chances to Build Israel-Iraq Ties," *Jewish Journal,* April 28, 2003. Also see Bamford, *Pretext to War,* p. 293; Ed Blanche, "Securing Iraqi Oil for Israel: The Plot Thickens," Lebanonwire.com. April 25, 2003. Nathan Guttman reports that "the American Jewish community and the Iraqi opposition" had for years "taken pains to conceal" the links between them. "Mutual Wariness: AIPAC and the Iraqi Opposition," *Ha'aretz,* April 8, 2003.

191. Nir, "FBI Probe," On the eve of the war, Bill Keller, who is now the executive editor of *The New York Times,* wrote: "The idea that this war is about Israel is persistent and more widely held than you think." Keller, "Is It Good for the Jews?" *The New York Times,* March 8, 2003.

192. In an op-ed written in mid-2004, Hollings asked why the Bush administration invaded Iraq when it was not a direct threat to the United States. "The answer," which he says, "everyone knows," is "because we want to secure our friend Israel." Senator Ernest F. Hollings, "Bush's Failed Mideast Policy Is Creating More Terrorism," *The Charleston Post and Courier*, May 6, 2004; "Sen. Hollings Floor Statement," Not surprisingly, Hollings was called an antisemite, a charge he furiously rejected. See Matthew E. Berger, "Not So Gentle Rhetoric from the Gentleman from South Carolina," *JTA,* May 23, 2004; "Senator Lautenberg's

Floor Statement in Support of Senator Hollings," June 3, 2004, at http://lautenberg.senate.gov/newsroom/video.cfm; Hsu, "Moran Said Jews are Pushing War." A handful of other public figures—Patrick Buchanan, Maureen Dowd, Georgie Anne Geyer, Gary Hart, Chris Matthews, and General Anthony Zinni—have either said or strongly hinted that pro-Israel forces in the United States were the principal movers behind the Iraq war. See Aluf Bonn, "Scapegoat for Israel," *Ha'aretz,* May 13, 2004; Matthew Berger, "Will Some Jews' Backing for War in Iraq Have Repercussions for All?," *JTA,* June 10. 2004; Patrick J. Buchanan, "Whose War?," *The American Conservative,* March 24, 2003; Ami Eden, "Israel's Role: The 'Elephant' They're Talking About," *Forward,* February 28, 2003; "The Ground Shifts," *Forward,* May 28, 2004; Nathan Guttman, "Prominent U.S. Jews, Israel Blamed for Start of Iraq War," *Ha'aretz,* May 31, 2004; Lawrence F. Kaplan, "Toxic Talk on War," *The Washington Post,* February 18, 2003; E. J. Kessler, "Gary Hart Says 'Dual Loyalty' Barb Was Not Aimed at Jews," *Forward,* February 21, 2003; Ori Nir and Ami Eden, "Ex-Mideast Envoy Zinni Charges Neocons Pushed Iraq War to Benefit Israel," *Forward,* May 28, 2004.

193. Michael Kinsley, "What Bush Isn't Saying about Iraq," *Slaie.com,* October 24, 2002. Also see idem, "J'Accuse."

194. Robert S. Greenberger and Karby Leggett, "President's Dream: Changing Mot Just Regime but a Region: A Pro-U.S., Democratic Area Is a Goal That Has Israeli and Neoconservative Roots," *The Wall Street Journal,* March 21, 2003. Also see George Packer, "Dreaming of Democracy," *The New York Times Magazine,* March, 2, 2003. Although not all neoconservatives are Jewish, most of the founders were and virtually all were strong supporters of Israel. According to Gal Beckerman in *Forward,* "If there is an intellectual movement in America to whose invention Jews can lay sole claim, neoconservatism is it." See "The Neoconservative Persuasion," *Forward,* January 6, 2006.

195. See, for example, *Rebuilding America's Defenses: Strategy, Forces and Resources for a New Century.*

A Report for the New American Century, September 2000, p. 14.

196. Martin Indyk, "The Clinton Administration's Approach to the Middle East," Speech to Soref Symposium, Washington Institute for Near East Policy, May 18, 1993. Also see Anthony Lake, "Confronting Backlash States," *Foreign Affairs,* Vol. 73, No. 2 (March/April 1994), pp. 45–53.

197. Barbara Conry, "America's Misguided Policy of Dual Containment in the Persian Gulf," Foreign Policy Briefing No. 33, CATO Institute, November 10, 1994; Gregory F. Gause III, "The Illogic of Dual Containment," *Foreign Affairs,* Vol. 73. No. 2 (March/April 1994), pp. 56–66; Zbigniew Brzezinski and Brent Scowcroft, *Differentiated Containment: U.S. Policy Toward Iran and Iraq,* Report of an Independent Study Group on Gulf Stability and Security, Council on Foreign Relations, New York, 1997.

198. Brzezinski and Scowcroft, *Differentiated Containment,* p. 6.

199. Brzezinski and Scowcroft, *Differentiated Containment,* p. 130.

200. For example, *The Jerusalem Post* noted in an editorial (September 9, 2002) that "according to Middle East expert Bernard Lewis, a post-Saddam Iraq is one that would be more likely to make peace with Israel, defang Arab radicalism, and perhaps even catalyze revolutionary forces in present-day Iran." Similarly, Michael Ledeen wrote on August 6, 2002 in *National Review Online* ("Scowcroft Strikes Out"). "If ever there was a region that richly deserved being cauldronized, it is the Middle East today. If we wage the war effectively, we will bring down the terror regimes in Iraq. Iran and Syria and either bring down the Saudi monarchy or force it to abandon its global assembly line to indoctrinate young terrorists." On August 19, Joshua Muravchik argued in *The New York Times* ("Democracy's Quiet Victor"), "Change toward democratic regimes in Tehran and Baghdad would unleash a tsunami across the Islamic world." Also see Marina Ottaway et al., "Democratic Mirage in the Middle East," *Policy Brief #20* (Carnegie Endowment for International Peace, October 2002).

201. Charles Krauthammer, "Peace through Democracy," *The Washington Post*, June 28, 2002.

202. Benn, "Background." Also, *The New York Times* reported that Halevy gave a speech in Munich in February 2003 in which he said, "The shock waves emerging from post-Saddam Baghdad could have wide-ranging effects in Tehran, Damascus and in Ramallah." The *Times* article went on to say that Israel "is hoping that once Saddam Hussein is dispensed with, the dominoes will start to tumble. According to this hope . . . moderates and reformers throughout the region would be encouraged to put new pressure on their own governments, not excepting the Palestinian Authority of Yasir Arafat." Bennet, "Israel Says War on Iraq Would Benefit the Region." This same theme is reflected in a *Forward* article from early March 2003, which said that "Israel's top political, military and economic echelons have come to regard the looming war as a virtual deus ex machina that will turn the political and economic tables and extricate Israel from its current morass." Shalev, "Jerusalem Frets." Finally, this line of thinking was apparent in former Prime Minister Ehud Barak's previously discussed September 4, 2002, op-ed in *The New York Times*. Barak maintained that "putting an end to Saddam Hussein's regime will change the geopolitical landscape of the Arab world." He claimed, "An Arab world without Saddam Hussein would enable many from this generation [leaders about to come into power] to embrace the gradual democratic opening that some of the Persian Gulf states and Jordan have begun to enjoy." Barak also maintained that toppling Saddam would "create an opening for forward movement on the Israeli-Palestinian conflict."

203. See Seymour M. Hersh, "The Syrian Bet," *The New Yorker*, Vol. 79, issue 20 (July 28, 2003), pp. 32–36; Molly Moore, "Sharon Asks U.S. to Pressure Syria on Militants," *The Washington Post*, April 17, 2003; Ori Nir, "Jerusalem Urges Bush: Next Target Hezbollah," *Forward*, April 11, 2003; Idem, "Sharon Aide Makes the Case for U.S. Action against Syria,'" *Forward*, April 18, 2003; Marc Perelman, "Behind Warnings to Damascus: Reassessment of Younger Assad," *Forward*, April 18, 2004; Daniel Sobelman and Nathan Guttman, "PM Urges U.S. to Keep Heat on Syria, Calls Assad 'Dangerous,'" *Ha'arelz*, April 15, 2003.

204. Moore, "Sharon Asks U.S."

205. Nir, "Sharon Aide." Also see Karen DeYoung, "U.S. Toughens Warnings to Syria on Iraq, Other Issues," *The Washington Fast*. April 15, 2003.

206. Nir, "Sharon Aide." Also see Perelman, "Behind Warnings." In their efforts to demonize Syria and bait the United States into attacking it, Israelis have said that Damascus was harboring high-level Iraqis from Saddam's regime and even worse, hiding Iraq's WMD. Perelman, "Behind Warnings"; Laurie Copans, "Israeli Military Boss Claims Iraq Had Chemical Weapons," Associated Press news release, April 26, 2004; Ira Stoll, "Saddam's WMD Moved to Syria, An Israeli Says," *The New York Sun*, December 15, 2005; Idem, "Iraq's WMD Secreted in Syria, Sada Says," *The New York Sun*, January 26, 2006. In August 2003, when a suicide truck bomber blew up UN headquarters in Baghdad, Israel's UN ambassador caused a diplomatic spat by suggesting that Syria had provided the truck, thereby implying that Syria was partly responsible. Michael Casey, "Israeli Ambassador Believes Truck Used in UN Bombing Came from Syria," Associated Press news release, August 21, 2003; "Israeli Envoy Links Syria to UN Blast, Stirs Flap," Reuters news release, August 21, 2003. Itamar Rabinovich, the former Israeli ambassador to the United States, told Seymour Hersh that he "wondered… whether, given the quality of their sources, the Syrians had had advance information about the September 11th plot—and failed to warn the United States." Hersh, "The Syrian Bet." There was little evidence to support these charges, but Israel's willingness to make them shows how eager they were to get the United States embroiled with yet another Arab regime.

207. Syria had been in the lobby's gunsights well before 9/11. In fact, Syria, not Iraq, was the main target in the "Clean Break" study that Feith, Perle and Wurmser wrote for Netanyahu in 1996. And Daniel Pipes and Ziad Abdelnour, the head of the U.S. Committee for a Free Lebanon (USCFL), had co-authored a 2000 report calling for the United States to use military threats to force Syria to remove its troops from Lebanon, get rid

of any WMD it might have, and stop supporting terrorism. ("Ending Syria's Occupation of Lebanon: The U.S. Role," Report of the Middle East Study Group, Middle East Forum, May 2000.) The UCSFL is a close cousin of the lobby, and it includes numerous neoconservatives (Abrams, Feith, Ledeen, Perle and Wurmser) among its "official core supporters." Jordan Green, "Neocons Dream of Lebanon," *ZNet,* July 23, 2003; David R. Sands, "Hawks Recycle Arguments for Iraq War against Syria," *The Washington Times,* April 16, 2003. Except for Ledeen, they all signed the 2000 report, as did pro-Israel Congressman Eliot Engel (D-NY), another core supporter of UCSFL.

208. Nathan Guttman, "Some Senior U.S. Figures Say Syria Has Crossed the Red Line," *Ha'aretz,* April 14, 2004; Michael Flynn, "The War Hawks: The Right Flexes Muscle with New U.S. Agenda," *The Chicago Tribune,* April 13, 2003. In addition to Perle and Wolfowitz, John Bolton pushed hard from inside the administration for regime change in Syria. He had told Israeli leaders a month before the Iraq war that the Bush administration would deal with Syria, as well as Iran and North Korea, right after Saddam fell from power. Flynn, "The Right Flexes Muscle." In pursuit of that goal, Bolton reportedly prepared to tell Congress in mid-July that Syria's WMD programs had reached the point where they were a serious threat to stability in the Middle East and had to be dealt with sooner rather than later. However, the CIA and other government agencies objected, claiming that Bolton's analysis greatly inflated the Syrian threat. Consequently, the administration did not allow Bolton to give his testimony on Syria at that time. Douglas Jehl, "New Warning Was Put Off on Weapons Syria Plans," *The New York Times,* July 18, 2003; Marc Perelman, "State Department Hawk under Fire in Intelligence Flap over Syria," Forward, July 25, 2003; Warren P. Strobel and Jonathan S. Landay, "Intelligence Data on Syria Now Disputed," *The Philadelphia Inquirer,* July 17, 2003. Yet Bolton was not put off for long. He appealed before Congress in September 2003 and described Syria as a growing threat to U.S. interests in the Middle East. Nathan Guttman, "US: Syria Supporting

Terror. Developing Weapons of Mass Destruction," *Ha'aretz,* September 16, 2003.

209. Quoted in Robin Wright, "U.S. Insists Syria Alter Its Course," *The Los Angeles Times,* April 14, 2003. Also see Martin Indyk's and Dennis Ross's tough rhetoric about Syria in Hersh, "The Syrian Bet."

210. Lawrence F. Kaplan, "White Lie," *The New Republic,* April 21 & 28, 2003. Also see William Kristol and Lawrence F. Kaplan, *The War over Iraq: Saddam's Tyranny and America's Mission* (Encounter Books, 2003).

211. DeYoung, "U.S. Toughens Stance." There was a story in *Ha'aretz* ("NY Congressman Says Will Push Bill to Pressure Syria") on August 19, 2003, which reported that Engel had just met with Sharon in his Jerusalem Office for 90 minutes, and the Israeli leader had endorsed Engel's efforts to push the Syria Accountability Act. Regarding the specifics of that legislation, see Zvi Bar'el, "Deciphering the Syrians, *Ha'aretz,* July 9, 2003; "The Return of the Syria Accountability Act," www.NewsMax.com, April 19, 2003; Claude Salhani, "The Syria Accountability Act: Taking the Wrong Road to Damascus," *Policy Analysis,* No. 512, CATO Institute, March 18, 2004. Not surprisingly, Richard Perle called on Congress to pass the Syria Accountability Act shortly after Engel reintroduced the legislation. Sands, "Hawks Recycle Arguments."

212. Ron Kampeas, "Bush, Once Reluctant on Sanctions, Prepares to Take a Tough Line with Syria," *JTA,* March 16, 2004.

213. Salhani, "The Syria Accountability Act," p. 5.

214. Julian Borger, "Bush Vetoes Syria War Plan," *The Guardian,* April 15, 2003; Kampeas, "Bush, Once Reluctant."

215. See Hersh, "The Syrian Bet." Other pieces discussing the advantages for the United States of cooperating with Syria include Spencer Ackerman, "Rough Trade," *The New Republic,* January 13, 2003; Susan Taylor Martin, "Experts Disagree on Dangers of Syria" *The St. Petersburg Times,* November 3, 2002; Salhani, "The Syria Accountability Act"; Stephen Zunes, "Bush Has Clear Run at Syria," *Asia Times Online,* March 2, 2005.

216. Two articles that appeared in *Forward* after Baghdad fell describe the driving forces behind

the new U.S. policy toward Syria. In a piece in mid-April, the author noted: "A sudden flurry of U.S. warnings to Syria in recent days indicates that Washington has undertaken what Israel and its supporters here have been urging for months: a comprehensive reassessment of Syrian ruler Bashar Assad." Perelman, "Behind Warnings." A few months later in mid-July, another author noted: "During the past several months, top Israeli officials have warned their American counterparts and audiences about Assad's unreliability. American officials have echoed the stance and press reports have speculated about possible American military intervention in Syria." Marc Perelman, "Syria Makes Overture over Negotiations," *Forward,* July 11, 2003.

217.   Quoted in Alan Sipress. "Israel Emphasizes Iranian Threat," *The Washington Post,* February 7, 2002. This article, which was written as Sharon was arriving in Washington, makes clear that Tel Aviv was "redoubling its efforts to warn the Bush administration that Iran poses a greater threat than the Iraqi regime of Saddam Hussein." Also see Seymour Hersh, "The Iran Game," *The New Yorker,* Vol. 77, issue 38 (December 3, 2001), pp. 42–49; Peter Hirschberg, "Background/Peres Raises Iranian Threat," *Ha'aretz,* February 5, 2002; David Hirst, "Israel Thrusts Iran in Line of US Fire," *The Guardian,* February 2, 2002; "Israel Once Again Sees Iran as A Cause for Concern," *Ha'aretz,* May 7, 2001.

218.   Stephen Farrell, Robert Thomson and Danielle Haas, "Attack Iran the Day Iraq War Ends, Demands Israel." *The Times* (London), September 5, 2002; Stephen Farrell and Robert Thomson, "The Times Interview with Ariel Sharon," in *ibid.*

219.   "Ambassador to U.S. Calls for 'Regime Change' in Iran, Syria," *Ha'aretz,* April 28, 2003. Ten days later *The New York Times* reported that Washington was growing increasingly concerned about Iran's nuclear ambitions, and that there is "a lot of hammering from the Israelis for us to take this position seriously," Steven R. Weisman, "New U.S. Concerns on Iran's Pursuit of Nuclear Arms," *The New York Times,* May 8, 2003. Shimon Peres then published an op-ed in *The Wall Street Journal* on June 25 entitled, "We Must Unite to

Prevent an Ayatollah Nuke." His description of the Iranian threat sounded just like his earlier description of the threat from Saddam, even including a ritual reference to the lessons of appeasement in the 1930s. Iran, he emphasized, must be told in no uncertain terms that the United States and Israel will not tolerate its going nuclear.

220.   In late May 2003. Inter Press Service reported that, "The neo-cons' efforts to now focus US attention on 'regime change' in Iran has become much more intense since early May and already has borne substantial fruit." Jim Lobe, "U.S. Neo-Cons Move Quickly on Iran," Inter Press Service, May 28, 2003. In early June, *Forward* reported, "Neoconservatives inside and outside the administration have been urging an active effort to promote regime change in Tehran. Reports of possible covert actions have surfaced in recent weeks." Marc Perelman, "Pentagon Team on Iran Comes under Fire," *Forward,* June 6, 2003. Also see idem, "White House Is Aiming to Raise Iranian Nukes at U.N. Security Council," *Forward,* May 9, 2003; Idem, "New Front Sets Sights on Toppling Iran Regime," *Forward,* May 16, 2003. Finally, the lobby has established close relations with Reza Pahlavi, the son of the late shah of Iran. He is even reported to have had meetings with Netanyahu and Sharon. This relationship is similar to the lobby's relationship with Ahmed Chalabi. Specifically, pro-Israel forces promote Pahlavi, and in return, he makes clear that if he comes to power in Iran, it will have good relations with Israel. Connie Bruck, "Exiles: How Iran's Expatriates Are Gaming the Nuclear Threat," *The New Yorker,* Vol. 82, issue 2 (March 6, 2006), pp. 48–63; Perelman, "New Front."

221.   The flyer advertising the conference, which was entitled "The Future of Iran: Mullahcracy, Democracy and the War on Terror," can be found at a number of sites on the web. Also see Green, "Neocons Dream of Lebanon"; Lobe, "U.S. Neo-Cons Move Quickly."

222.   William Kristol, "The End of the Beginning." *The Weekly Standard,* February 12, 2003. Others writing articles at the time include Daniel Pipes and Patrick Clawson, who wrote a piece on May 20

for *The Jerusalem Post* entitled, "Turn up the Pressure on Iran." They called for the Bush administration to support the Mujahedeen-e-Khalq, a terrorist organization based in Iraq that was bent on overthrowing the ayatollahs running Iran. Lawrence Kaplan argued in the *New Republic* ("Iranamok") on June 9 that the United States needed to get tougher with Iran over its nuclear programs, which he feared were further along than most American policymakers recognized. Michael Ledeen, one of the leading hawks on Iran, wrote in *The National Review Online* ("The Others") on April 4: "There is no more time for diplomatic 'solutions.' We will have to deal with the terror masters, here and now. Iran, at least, offers us the possibility of a memorable victory, because the Iranian people openly loathe the regime, and will enthusiastically combat it, if only the United States supports them in their just struggle."

223. For evidence of the lobby's intensified efforts to get the Bush administration to deal with the Iranian nuclear problem, see Stewart Ain, "Israel Urging U.S. to Stop Iran Nukes." *Jewish Week*, October 7, 2005: Efraim Inbar, "The Imperatives to Use Force against Iranian Nuclearization," BESA Center [Bar-Ilan University, Israel] *Perspectives*, Number 12, December 1, 2005; Martin S. Indyk, "Iran's Bluster Isn't A Bluff," *The Los Angeles Tunes*, November 1, 2005; Ron Kampeas, "With Time Short on Iran Nukes, AIPAC Criticizes Bush Approach," *JTA*, December 2, 2005; Charles Krauthammer, "In Iran, Arming for Armageddon," *The Washington Post*, December 16, 2005; Dafna Linzer, "Pro-Israel Group Criticizes White House Policy on Iran," *The Washington Post*, December 25, 2005; Ori Nir, "New Sanction Bill Loses Momentum as Administration Presses Diplomacy," *Forward*, June 10, 2005;

Idem, "Jewish Groups Push for Iran Sanctions," *Forward*, September 23, 2005; Idem, "Israeli Aides Warn U.S. Not to Drop Ball on Iran," *Forward*, December 9, 2005; Michael Rubin et al., "War Footing: 10 Steps America Must Take to Prevail in the War for the Free World," American Enterprise Institute, November 30, 2005; Rowan Scarborough, "Israel Pushes U.S. on Iran Nuke Solution," *The Washington Times*, February 21, 2005.

224. Some neoconservatives even welcome this outcome. For example. Robert Kagan and William Kristol wrote in the aftermath of 9/11, "Afghanistan will prove but an opening battle, . . . this war will not end in Afghanistan. It is going to spread and engulf a number of countries in conflicts of varying intensity. It could well require the use of American military power in multiple places simultaneously. It is going to resemble the clash of civilizations that everyone has hoped to avoid." "The Gathering Storm," *The Weekly Standard*, October 29, 2002. Also see Eliot A. Cohen, "World War IV," *The Wall Street Journal*, November 20, 2001; Phil McCombs, "The Fire This Time," *The Washington Post*, April 13, 2003; Norman Podhoretz, "How to Win World War IV," *Commentary*, February 2002; Idem, "World War IV: How It Started, What It Means, and Why We Have to Win," *Commentary*, September 2004; Brian Whitaker, "Playing Skittles with Saddam," *The Guardian*, September 3, 2002.

225. The imbalance of influence in Israel's favor was again demonstrated after the outbreak of fighting in Lebanon. See Laurie Goodstein, "As Mideast Churns. U.S. Jews and Arabs Alike Swing Into Action," *The New York Times*, July 28, 2006.

226. Ron Kampeas, "After Restructuring, AIPAC Plans to Focus on Wider Range of Issues," *JTA*, September 26, 2005.

Twilight of the Republic

ANDREW J. BACEVICH

In this critique Bacevich argues that U.S. foreign policy has never been about idealism, but rather about pragmatic self-interest and opportunism. He contends that the U.S.A.'s declining power in the 21st century is primarily the result of internal problems, such as rampant corruption, moral weakness, profligate spending, and a soaring national debt. Thus, the greatest threats to American strength emanate from internal failings, not external enemies.

In his 2005 inaugural address, President George W. Bush declared the promulgation of freedom to be "the mission that created our nation." Fulfilling what he described as America's "great liberating tradition" required the United States to devote itself to "ending tyranny in our world."

Many Americans find such sentiments compelling. Yet to credit the United States with possessing a "liberating tradition" is like saying that Hollywood has a "tradition of artistic excellence." The movie business is just that—a business. Its purpose is to make money. If once in a while the studios produce a film of aesthetic value, that may be cause for celebration; but profit, not revealing truth and beauty, defines the purpose of the enterprise.

Something of the same can be said of the enterprise launched on July 4, 1776. The hard-headed lawyers, merchants, farmers, and slaveholding plantation owners gathered in Philadelphia that summer did not set out to create a church. They founded a republic. Their purpose was not to save mankind. It was to guarantee for people like themselves "life, liberty, and the pursuit of happiness."

In the years and decades that followed, the United States achieved remarkable success in making good on those aims. Yet never during America's rise to power did the United States exert itself to liberate others absent an overriding perception that the nation itself had large security or economic interests at stake.

From time to time, although not nearly as frequently as we like to imagine, some of the world's unfortunates managed as a consequence to escape from bondage. The Civil War did produce emancipation. Yet to explain the conflagration of 1861–65 as a response to the plight of enslaved African Americans is to engage in vast oversimplification. Near the end of World War II, GIs did liberate the surviving inmates of Nazi death camps. Yet for those who directed the American war effort of 1941–45, the fate of European Jews never figured as more than an afterthought.

Crediting America with a "great liberating tradition" sanitizes the past and obscures the actual motive force behind American politics and U.S. foreign policy. It transforms history into a morality tale and thereby provides a rationale for dodging serious moral analysis. To insist that the liberation of others has never been more than an ancillary motive of U.S. policy is not cynicism; it is a prerequisite to self-understanding.

America Ascendant

If the young United States had a mission, it was not to liberate but to expand. "Of course," declared Theodore Roosevelt in 1899, as if explaining the self-evident to the obtuse, "our whole national history has been one of expansion." He spoke truthfully. The Founders viewed stasis as tantamount to suicide. From the outset, Americans evinced a compulsion to acquire territory and to extend their commercial reach abroad.

How was expansion achieved? On this point, the historical record leaves no room for debate: by any means necessary. Depending on the circumstances, the United States relied on diplomacy, hard bargaining, bluster, chicanery, intimidation, or naked coercion. We infiltrated land belonging to our neighbors and then brazenly proclaimed it our own. We harassed, filibustered, and, when the situation called for it, launched full-scale invasions. We engaged in ethnic cleansing. At times, we insisted that treaties be considered sacrosanct. On other occasions, we blithely jettisoned agreements that had outlived their usefulness.

As the methods employed varied, so did the rationale offered to justify action. We touted our status as God's new Chosen People, erecting a "city upon a hill" destined to illuminate the world. We acted at the behest of providential guidance and responded to the urgings of our "manifest destiny." We declared our obligation to spread the gospel of Jesus Christ and to uplift Little Brown Brother. With Woodrow Wilson as our tutor, we shouldered our responsibility to "show the way to the nations of the world how they shall walk in the paths of liberty." Critics who derided these claims as bunkum— the young Lincoln during the war with Mexico, Mark Twain after 1898, Robert LaFollette in 1917— scored points but lost the argument. Periodically revised and refurbished, the concept of American Exceptionalism (which implied exceptional American prerogatives) persisted.

Meanwhile, when it came to action rather than talk, the architects of U.S. policy, even the most idealistic, remained fixated on one overriding aim: enhancing American influence, wealth, and power. The narrative of American foreign relations from the earliest colonial encounters with Native Americans until, say, the end of the Cold War reveals a record that is neither uniquely high-minded nor uniquely hypocritical and exploitive. In this sense, interpretations of America's past offered by George W. Bush and by Osama bin Laden fall equally wide of the mark. As a rising power, the United States adhered to the iron laws of international politics,

which allow little space for altruism. If the tale contains a moral theme, that theme is necessarily one of ambiguity.

To be sure, America's ascent did not occur without missteps: opéra bouffe incursions into Canada; William McKinley's ill-advised annexation of the Philippines; complicity in China's "century of humiliation"; disastrous interwar economic policies that paved the way for the Depression; Harry Truman's decision in 1950 to send U.S. forces north of Korea's 38th parallel, to name only some. Most of these mistakes Americans have long since shrugged off. A few, like Vietnam, we find impossible to forget even as we persistently disregard their implications.

Yet, however embarrassing, these missteps pale in significance when compared to the masterstrokes of American statecraft. In purchasing Louisiana from the French, Thomas Jefferson may have overstepped the bounds of his authority and in seizing California from Mexico, James Polk may have perpetrated a war of conquest, but their actions ensured that the United States would one day become a great power. To secure the isthmus of Panama, Theodore Roosevelt orchestrated an outrageous swindle. The result affirmed America's hemispheric dominion. In collaborating with Josef Stalin, FDR made common cause with an indisputably evil figure. But in doing so he destroyed the murderous Hitler while simultaneously vaulting the United States to a position of unquestioned economic supremacy. A similar collaboration forged by Richard Nixon with the murderous Mao Zedong helped bring down the Soviet empire, thereby elevating the United States to the self-proclaimed position of sole superpower.

The achievements of these preeminent American statesmen derived not from their common devotion to a liberating tradition but from boldness unburdened by excessive scruples. Notwithstanding the high-sounding pronouncements that routinely emit from the White House and the State Department, the defining characteristic of U.S. foreign policy is not idealism. It is pragmatism, sometimes laced with pragmatism's first cousin, opportunism.

This remained true after 9/11 when President Bush declared without qualification that "America's vital interests and our deepest beliefs are now one." In practice, this dictum allowed the Bush administration to hector Iran or North Korea about their undemocratic ways while giving a pass to Egypt and Pakistan. It provided a rationale for military intervention in energy-rich Iraq, but found no application in Darfur, Burma, and Zimbabwe. (On a flight, shortly after the U.S. invasion of Iraq, I sat beside a retired Zimbabwean supreme court justice. Lamenting the dire situation in his country, he remarked, "Ah, if only we had oil. Then you would come rescue us.")

Bush's critics charged him with abandoning principles that long governed American statecraft. A fairer judgment would credit him with having seized on 9/11 to reinterpret those principles, thereby claiming for the United States new prerogatives (such as waging preventive war) while shedding constraints (such as respect for the sensibilities of key allies) that had seemingly lost their utility. In this regard, the president was adhering to a well-established tradition.

In the annals of history, the rise of the United States to the pinnacle of world power is an epic story worthy of Thucydides or Tacitus. It represents a stunning achievement. Yet those who see America's ascent as an affirmation of virtue are indulging in self-deluding sentimentality. Although sentimentality may sell greeting cards, it ill becomes a great nation that, having reached that pinnacle, now finds itself beset with challenges.

Land of the Free

For those fortunate enough to be Americans, this rise to global power yielded rich rewards. Expansion made the United States the land of opportunity. From expansion came abundance. Out of abundance came substantive freedom. Documents drafted in Philadelphia promised liberty. Making good on those promises required a political economy that facilitated the creation of wealth on an enormous scale.

Writing over a century ago, Frederick Jackson Turner made the essential point. "Not the Constitution, but free land and an abundance of natural resources open to a fit people," he argued, made American democracy possible. A half-century later, the historian David Potter discovered a similar symbiosis between affluence and liberty. Potter credited "a politics of abundance" with creating the American way of life, "a politics which smiled both on those who valued abundance as a means to safeguard freedom and those who valued freedom as an aid in securing abundance."

In short, American prosperity underwrote American freedom. The relationship between the two was reciprocal. Especially as the Industrial Revolution took hold, Americans looked to material abundance to ameliorate domestic tensions and anesthetize the unruly. Money became the preferred lubricant for keeping social and political friction within tolerable limits. As Reinhold Niebuhr once observed, "we seek a solution for practically every problem of life in quantitative terms," certain that more is better. Over time, prosperity also recast freedom, modifying the criteria for eligibility and broadening its claims.

Running in tandem with the chronicle of American expansion abroad is a second narrative of expansion. The theme of this second narrative relates to the transformation of freedom at home. It too is a story of epic achievement overlaid with ambiguity.

Who merits the privileges of citizenship? The answer prevailing in 1776—white male freeholders—was never satisfactory. By the stroke of a Jeffersonian pen, the Declaration of Independence had rendered such a definition untenable. Pressures to amend that restricted conception of citizenship emerged almost immediately.

Until World War II, progress achieved on this front was real but fitful. During the years of the postwar economic boom, and especially during the 1960s, the floodgates opened. Barriers fell. The circle of freedom widened appreciably. The percentage of Americans marginalized as "second-class citizens" dwindled.

Political credit for this achievement lies squarely with the Left. Abundance sustained in no small measure by a postwar presumption of American "global leadership" made possible the expansion of freedom at home. Possibility became reality thanks to progressive political activism.

Pick the group: blacks, Jews, women, Asians, Hispanics, working stiffs, gays, the disabled—in every case, the impetus for providing equal access to the rights guaranteed by the Constitution originated among radicals, pinks, liberals, and bleeding-heart fellow-travelers. When it comes to ensuring that every American should get a fair shake, the contribution of modern conservatism has been essentially nil. Had Martin Luther King in the 1950s and 1960s counted on William F. Buckley and his *National Review* to take up the fight against racial segregation, Jim Crow would still be alive and well.

Granting the traditionally marginalized access to freedom constitutes the central theme of American politics since World War II. It does not diminish the credit due to those who engineered this achievement to note that their success stemmed in part from the fact that the United States was simultaneously asserting its claim to unquestioned global leadership. The reformers who pushed and prodded for racial equality and women's rights did so in tacit alliance with the officials presiding over the postwar rehabilitation of Germany and Japan, with oil executives pressing to bring the Persian Gulf into America's sphere of influence, and with defense contractors promoting expensive new weapons programs.

The creation of what became by the 1950s an informal American empire of global proportions was not a conspiracy designed to benefit the few. Postwar foreign policy derived its legitimacy from the widely shared perception that the exercise of power abroad was making possible a more perfect union at home. In this sense, a proper understanding of contemporary history requires that we acknowledge an ironic kinship linking cold warriors like Curtis LeMay to feminists like Betty Friedan. General LeMay's Strategic Air Command—both as manifestation of American might and as central component of the postwar military-industrial complex—helped to foster the conditions from which Friedan's National Organization for Women emerged.

Cultural Revolution

During the same postwar period, but especially since the 1960s, the nation's abiding cultural preoccupation focused on reassessing what freedom actually means. The political project was long the exclusive preserve of the Left (although belatedly endorsed by the Right). From the outset, the cultural project has been a collaborative one to which both Left and Right contributed, albeit in different ways. The very real success of the political project lies at the heart of the Bush administration's insistence that the United States offered a proper model for other nations—notably those in the Islamic world—to follow. The largely catastrophic results of the cultural project belie that claim.

The postwar political project sought to end discrimination. The postwar cultural project focused on dismantling constraints, especially on matters touching however remotely on sexuality and self-gratification. "Men are qualified for civil liberty," Edmund Burke once observed, "in exact proportion to their disposition to put moral chains upon their appetites." In the aftermath of World War II, Americans rejected that counsel and set out to throw off their manacles. Freedom came increasingly to imply unfettered self-indulgence.

The Left contributed to this effort by promoting a radical new ethic of human sexuality. Removing chains in this regard meant normalizing behavior once viewed as immoral, unnatural, or inconsistent with the common good. On the cutting edge of American culture, removing impediments to the satisfaction of sexual desire emerged as an imperative.

Laws, traditions, and social arrangements impeding the fulfillment of this imperative became obsolete. As a direct consequence, homosexuality, abortion, divorce, out-of-wedlock pregnancies, and children raised in single-parent homes—all once viewed as problematic—lost much of their stigma. Pornography—including child pornography—reached epidemic proportions. Pop culture became a titillating arena for promoting sexual license and celebrating sexual perversity. And popular music became, in the words of cultural critic Martha Bayles, a "masturbatory fantasy."

Some Americans lament this revolution. Many others view it as inevitable or necessary or positively swell. Regardless, the foreign-policy implications of the sexual revolution loom large. The ideals that President Bush eagerly hoped to propagate throughout the Islamic world—those enshrined in Jefferson's Declaration and in the Bill of Rights—today come packaged with the vulgar exhibitionism of Madonna and the debased sensibility of Robert Mapplethorpe.

Note, however, that the metamorphosis of freedom has had a second aspect, one that has proceeded in harmony with—and even reinforced—the sexual revolution. Here the effect has been to foster a radical new conception of freedom's economic dimension. Increasingly, during the decades of the postwar boom, citizens came to see personal liberty as linked inextricably to the accumulation of "stuff."

Here, the enthusiasm for throwing off moral chains came from the Right. The forces of corporate capitalism relentlessly promoted the notion that liberty correlates with choice and that the key to human fulfillment (not to mention sexual allure and sexual opportunity) is to be found in conspicuous consumption—acquiring a bigger house, a fancier car, the latest fashions, the niftiest gadgets.

By the end of the twentieth century, many Americans had concluded, in the words of the historian Gary Cross, that "to consume was to be free." The events of 9/11 did not dislodge that perception. In early 2006—with the nation locked in what President Bush insisted was an epic confrontation with "Islamofascism"—an article in the *New York Times Magazine* posed the question "Is Freedom Just Another Word for Many Things to Buy?" In the conduct their daily affairs, countless Americans, most of them oblivious to Bush's war, answered that question in the affirmative.

Along the way, consumption eclipsed voting or military service as the nearest thing to an acknowledged civic obligation. If citizenship today endows "the sovereign shopper with the right to select from store shelves," Cross comments, it also imposes "the duty to spend for the 'good of the economy.'" Americans once assessed the nation's economic health by tallying up the output of the nation's steel mills or

the tons of bullion locked away in Fort Knox. Today, consumer demand has emerged as the favored metric of overall economic wellbeing. In recent years "Black Friday" has taken its place among notable dates on the national calendar—the willingness of consumers to open their pocketbooks on the day after Thanksgiving having become a key indicator of economic vigor. Woe betide the nation, should holiday shoppers spend less this year than last.

American globalism did little to foster this radical change in American culture. But the cultural revolution—both the sexual liberation demanded by the Left and the conspicuous consumption promoted by the Right—massively complicated our relations with those beyond our borders, who see reigning American conceptions of freedom as shallow and corrosive.

Empire of Red Ink

Still, this consumer's paradise retained considerable appeal for outsiders looking in. The many millions from south of the border or across the seas seeking entry testified to this fact. In the eyes of the typical Third Worlder, to be American was to be rich, pampered, and profligate. Entrance into the United States implied the prospect of being well-fed, well-housed, and well-clothed—to walk where streets are paved with gold.

But how real were our riches? In his 2006 book *Among Empires*, Charles Maier, professor of history at Harvard, chronicled the shift from what he calls America's postwar Empire of Production—when U.S. factories made the steel, the cars, and the TVs—to today's Empire of Consumption—when goods pour in from Japan and China. The implications of this shift for foreign policy were only dimly appreciated but likely to be profound. If Americans were still paving their streets with gold, they were doing so with someone else's money.

In paradise, it turned out, the books didn't balance. After 9/11, the federal budget had tipped into the red and stayed there, deficits getting ever larger as the Bush administration progressed. Much the same applied to current account balance—U.S. imports had routinely exceeded exports for decades.

During the first decade of the twenty-first century, the trade imbalance grew by leaps and bounds. So too did the national debt, which now exceeds $15 trillion—larger than the total size of the U.S. economy. Economic theorists have argued that any nation with a debt-to-GDP ratio exceeding 90 percent is courting big trouble, with prolonged stagnation one likely consequence. The United States today seems hell-bent on testing that proposition.

Despite these alarming trends, we Americans refused to live within our means. We discarded old-fashioned notions of thrift, deferred gratification, and putting up for a rainy day. We forgot how to save. We studiously ignored questions of how to pay for ever-more costly entitlements now viewed as our birthright. We adamantly ignored what President Bush himself referred to as our "addiction" to foreign oil—the president echoing warnings expressed by each of his predecessors going back to Richard Nixon. To sustain the Empire of Consumption we acquired a mountain of debt, increasingly owed to foreign countries such as China. The unspoken assumption was that the American credit line is endless and that the bills won't ever come due.

Once upon a time, Americans would have dismissed such thinking as twaddle. No more. Having made a fetish of freedom-as-consumption, we became beholden to others. Dependence, wrote Jefferson two centuries ago, "begets subservience and venality, suffocates the germ of virtue and prepares fit tools for the design of ambition." As American dependence deepened, the autonomy that from 1776 through the 1950s ranked as the nation's greatest strategic asset withered away. Although periodically bemoaning this slide toward dependence, political leaders in Washington did little to restore our economic house to order.

In 2008, the chickens came home to roost with a vengeance. With the onset of the most severe economic crisis since the Great Depression, unemployment sky-rocketed, at one point exceeding 10 percent. As real estate prices collapsed, millions lost their homes to foreclosure. Yet although the political atmospherics changed—Republicans in Congress who had not hesitated to indulge George W.

Bush's penchant for profligacy suddenly rediscovered the need for fiscal constraint when Democrat Barack Obama became president—in matters of substance things mostly remained the same. In practice, ensuring the uninterrupted flow of foreign oil and borrowing from abroad to feed the consumer's insatiable appetite for cheap imports had become categorical imperatives. Back in 1992, when the immediate issue related to curbing greenhouse gases, President George Herbert Walker Bush had cut to the heart of the matter: "The American way of life is not up for negotiation." Compromise, accommodation, trimming back the expectations implied by that way of life—none of these were to be countenanced. The Great Recession left that diktat intact.

Yet dependence has large foreign-policy consequences. It circumscribes freedom of action. A week after 9/11, Donald Rumsfeld had spelled out the implications. In formulating a response to the terrorist attack, the United States had only two options. "We have a choice," Rumsfeld remarked, "either to change the way we live, which is unacceptable, or to change the way that they live, and we chose the latter."

More Than a Comma

The global "war on terror" launched toward in the end of 2001 represented the Bush administration's effort to do just that—to change the way that they live. "They," of course, referred to the 1.4 billion Muslims who inhabit an arc stretching from North Africa to Southeast Asia.

The overarching strategic aim of that war was to eliminate the Islamist threat by pacifying the Islamic world, with particular attention given to the energy-rich Persian Gulf. Pacification implied not only bringing Muslims into compliance with American norms. It also required the establishment of unassailable American hegemony, affirming beyond the shadow of a doubt the superiority of U.S. power and thereby deterring attempts to defy those norms. Hegemony necessarily entailed presence, evidenced by the proliferation of U.S. military bases throughout strategically critical regions of the Islamic world. Seen in relation to our own history, the global "war on terror" signified the latest phase in an expansionist project that is now three centuries old.

This effort to pacify Islam foundered in Iraq. The Bush administration's determination to change the way Iraqis live landed the United States in a quagmire. For years, trying to salvage something positive from the Iraq debacle consumed the foreign-policy apparatus—while consuming as well thousands of lives and many billions of dollars. The attention lavished on Iraq stemmed from the Bush administration's conviction that events there would powerfully affecting the overall "war on terror," not to mention America's status as sole superpower. Expressing confidence that all was certain to come out well, President Bush insisted that historians would eventually see the controversies surrounding his Iraq policy as little more than a comma.

Rather than seeing Iraq as a comma, we ought to view it as a question mark. The question posed, incorporating but also transcending the "war on terror," is this: As part of some larger effort to "change the way that they live," has the Iraq War preserved or distorted the American way of life? To put it another way, will further such efforts to enforce American dominion abroad enhance the values we profess? Or has the United States now reached a point where expansion merely postpones an inevitable reckoning with the cultural and economic contradictions to which our pursuit of freedom has given rise?

If after Iraq—and in the midst of the Arab Spring—the survival of American freedom does require pacification of the Islamic world, then this must be said: Exertions made up to this point in have been laughably inadequate. Changing the way they live presumes a seriousness hitherto lacking on the part of the American people or their elected representatives.

If the requirement is to transform not only Iraq, but also Afghanistan, Syria, Iran, Pakistan, and Saudi Arabia (among others), then prudence dictates that we stop kidding ourselves that the intended beneficiaries of our ministrations will welcome us with open arms. Why bamboozle ourselves with claims of righteousness that few others

believe? Better to acknowledge, as the hawkish military analyst Ralph Peters has done, that the United States is actually engaged "in an effort to keep the world safe for our economy and open to our cultural assault." Doing so will prevent us from being surprised by the intensity of resistance that awaits us as if we insist on enforcing any so-called Freedom Agenda across the broad expanse of Islam.

Mounting such a campaign implies mobilization, commitment, sacrifice, and reordering national priorities with the prerequisites of victory rising to first place. It will necessarily require the allocation of additional resources to satisfy the mushrooming requirements of "national security." We will have to hire many more soldiers. A serious attempt to pacify the Islamic world means the permanent militarization of U.S. policy. Almost inevitably, it will further concentrate authority in the hands of an imperial presidency.

This describes the program of the "faster, please" ideologues keen to enlarge the scope of U.S. military action. To paraphrase Che Guevara, it is a program that calls for "one, two, many Iraqs," ignoring the verdict already rendered by the actually existing Iraq. Yet the fact is that events in Iraq and at home have definitively exposed the very real limits of American hard power, financial reserves, and will. Leviathan has shot his wad.

Some may argue that President Obama, who inherited the shambles of the Freedom Agenda, understands this. Obama did finally succeed in extricating U.S. forces from Iraq. After ratcheting up the U.S. military presence in Afghanistan, he promises to do the same there. Yet Obama has also shown a marked willingness to broaden the American military effort, extending it by means overt and covert into Pakistan, Yemen, Somalia, and Libya. While toning down the rhetoric, Obama remains committed to the project that Bush began. In all but name, the global war on terrorism continues, with no end in sight.

Expecting further muscle-flexing abroad to provide an escape from the predicament facing the Americans at home points toward bankruptcy and the dismantling of what remains of the American republic. Genuine pragmatism—and the beginning of wisdom—lies in paying less attention to "the way that they live" and more attention to the way we do. Ultimately, conditions within American society determine the prospects of American liberty. As Randolph Bourne observed nearly a century ago, ensuring that authentic freedom will flourish at home demands that we attend in the first instance to "cultivating our own garden."

This does not imply assuming a posture of isolationism, although neoconservative and neoliberal proponents of the "global leadership" will be quick to level that charge. Let us spare no effort to track down anyone daring to attack our land or our people. But let us give up once and for all any pretensions about an "indispensable nation" summoned to exercise "benign global hegemony" in the midst of a uniquely opportune "unipolar moment." For too long now these narcissistic and fallacious claims, the source of the pretensions expressed by President Bush since September 2001, have polluted our discussion of foreign policy, and thereby prevented us from seeing ourselves as we are.

Cultivating our own garden begins with taking stock of ourselves. Thoughtful critics have for decades been calling for just such a critical self-examination. Among the very first canaries to venture into the deteriorating mineshaft of postwar American culture was the writer Flannery O'Connor. "If you live today," she observed with characteristic bluntness a half-century ago, "you breathe in nihilism."

O'Connor correctly diagnosed the disease and other observers bore witness to its implications. Her fellow southerner Walker Percy wondered if freedom American-style was not simply becoming the "last and inalienable possession in a sick society." The social critic Christopher Lasch derided "the ideology of progress" manipulated by elites contemptuous of the ethnic, social, and religious traditions to which ordinary folk subscribed. Lasch

foresaw an impending "dark night of the soul." From his vantage point, Robert Nisbet detected the onset of what he called "a twilight age," marked by "a sense of cultural decay, erosion of institutions . . . and constantly increasing centralization—and militarization—of power." In such an age, he warned, "representative and liberal institutions of government slip into patterns ever more imperial in character. . . . Over everything hangs the specter of war." Towering above them all was Pope John Paul II who, in a message clearly directed toward Americans, pointedly cautioned that a democracy bereft of values "easily turns into a thinly disguised totalitarianism."

Our own self-induced confusion about freedom, reflected in our debased culture and our disordered economy, increases America's susceptibility to this totalitarian temptation even as it deadens our awareness of the danger it poses. Escaping its clutches will require something more than presidents intoning clichés about America's historic mission while launching crusades against oil-rich tyrants on the other side of the globe. We are in difficult straits and neither arms (already fully committed) nor treasure (just about used up) will get us out. Our corrupt age requires reformation.

Shedding or at least discrediting the spurious conceptions of freedom to which Americans have lately fallen prey qualifies as a large task. Still, when compared to the megalomania of those who under the guise of "eliminating tyranny" are intent on remaking the entire Islamic world, the restoration of our own culture appears to be a positively modest goal. At the end of the day, as William Pfaff has observed, "The only thing we can remake is ourselves."

And who knows? Should we, as a consequence of such a reformation, actually live up to our professed ideals—restoring to American freedom something of the respect that it once commanded—we may yet become, in some small way, a model worthy of emulation.

Andrew J. Bacevich is professor of history and international relations at Boston University. This is an updated version of an essay that originally appeared in Commonweal. © 2013 Commonweal Foundation, reprinted with permission. For more information, visit www.commonwealmagazine.org.

A Framework for Strengthening U.S. Intelligence

LOCH K. JOHNSON

> Johnson provides a basic overview of the processes of U.S. intelligence gathering and analysis. He explains basic concepts such as the intelligence cycle and the nature of the national intelligence bureaucracy. Johnson analyzes the consequences of catastrophic failures of U.S. intelligence, including the devastating attacks of September 11th, 2001. He also explores the flaws in the intelligence process during the lead up to the Iraq War, examining the specious arguments made about Baghdad's weapons of mass destruction. Finally, he discusses concrete proposals for comprehensive reform of the U.S. intelligence process.

The main purpose of intelligence is to provide accurate, timely, and comprehensive information to the president and other policymakers to inform decision making. The task of providing useful information to government officials is a complex matter with many opportunities for error. Uncertainty and ambiguity dominate the environment in which key decisions are made. Accordingly, the numerous pitfalls that exist in the conduct of intelligence make some degree of failure inevitable.[1] Despite the inherent impossibility of perfect intelligence, reforming U.S. intelligence agencies can improve their performance and reduce the frequency of failure.

The U.S. intelligence community faces new challenges as its most pressing targets—particularly terrorist organizations—are structured to elude many of the tools of information-gathering that have proven successful in the past. Weaknesses exist in each step of the intelligence cycle, from planning and direction to collection, processing, analysis, and dissemination.[2] The mobilization of U.S. intelligence against these new threats requires not only redirected resources toward increased human intelligence but also a realignment of attitudes within and among the intelligence bureaucracies. The U.S. intelligence apparatus is constrained by miscommunication between analysts and policymakers resulting from sourcing, packaging, and sometimes distorting information.

The intelligence shortcomings in advance of the September 11 attacks and the war in Iraq offer lessons for reform. Investments in new sources of human intelligence and data-mining can help boost U.S. information-gathering capabilities, though genuine intelligence reform will only be possible if the national director of intelligence is invested with the authority to override the bureaucratic turf wars among U.S. intelligence agencies.

The Intelligence Cycle

The planning and direction phase must account for a world with 191 states and a plethora of groups, factions, and gangs—some of which have adversarial relationships with the United States. Speaking just after the end of the Cold War, R. James Woolsey, director of central intelligence (DCI) during the Clinton administration, observed that, "We live now in a jungle filled with a bewildering variety of poisonous snakes."[3] At some point the degree of danger posed by an adversary can become painfully evident, as in the case of al-Qaeda after its attacks against New York City and Washington, D.C., on September 11, 2001. Unfortunately, no one can predict exactly when and where danger will strike, in part because we live in a world filled with secrets and mysteries.

By secrets, intelligence experts refer to information the United States might be able to discern even though it is concealed by another nation or group. For example, the numbers of Chinese tanks and nuclear submarines are discoverable but concealed by the Chinese government. In contrast, mysteries are events no one can know about until they happen because they lie beyond the limited human capacity to foresee. For example, no one knows who will be the next president of Russia. As former Secretary of State Dean Rusk liked to say, "Fate has not given mankind the capacity to pierce the fog of the future."[4]

Within this environment, intelligence agencies are faced with the task of determining intelligence priorities, a process known as threat assessment. Experts and policymakers gather periodically to evaluate the perils that confront the United States and establish a ladder of priorities from the most dangerous (Tiers 1A and 1B) to the least (Tier 4). Bias and guesswork enter the picture, along with the limitations caused by the uncertainty that surrounds the future. Where should one place China in the threat assessment? What about Russia, or Cuba? The outcome of these debates shapes the priorities for some $44 billion worth of intelligence spending each year. It also determines the areas U.S. spies will infiltrate, sets the orbits for surveillance satellites, and establishes the flight patterns of reconnaissance aircraft.

To improve the threat assessment process, the United States has undertaken nine major inquiries into its intelligence apparatus since the end of the Cold War. Each has concluded that policymakers failed to clarify during the planning-and-direction phase of the intelligence cycle exactly what kinds of information they needed. Consequently, intelligence officers often remain ignorant of the data desired by policy officials, who in turn tend to assume that the intelligence agencies will divine the issues that await action at the White House, the State Department, and other important offices in Washington.

Among policy officials, the president and his top aides are the most important consumers of intelligence in the executive branch. These aides include members of the cabinet who deal with foreign and national security issues, along with the staff of the

National Security Council (NSC). These men and women are pulled in many different directions by the demands of their daily schedules. As a result, they are reluctant to devote much time, if any, to updating their intelligence priorities.

Adding to this problem is spotty communication between analysts and decision makers. Sometimes NSC staffers, on the job for a year or more, have never spoken with experienced intelligence analysts on the National Intelligence Council who cover the same areas. This breakdown in communication stems from inadequate liaison relationships between the government's policy departments and the intelligence agencies. The lack of synchronization causes frustration on both sides. All too often policymakers scrawl "irrelevant" or "OBE" (overtaken by events) in ink across intelligence reports.

The collection phase, which follows planning and direction in the intelligence cycle, faces challenges as well. Even a superpower like the United States is unable to cover the globe with expensive surveillance platforms (hardware), such as reconnaissance aircraft, satellites, and ground-based listening posts. During the Cold War, satellite photography monitored the missiles and armies of opponents, rendering a surprise attack like Pearl Harbor unlikely. Today however, cameras on satellites and airplanes are unable to peer inside al-Qaeda tents or into the deep underground caverns where North Korea constructs nuclear weapons. Though they comprise a high percentage of the funds allocated in the annual intelligence budget, costly hardware is of questionable value in tracking many contemporary U.S. security concerns.

Many of the best contributions from spy machines come from relatively inexpensive unmanned aerial vehicles, notably the Predator, which has proven effective at scouring the Iraqi and Afghan countryside in search of insurgents. On occasion, the far more costly surveillance satellites have demonstrated their value by intercepting revealing telephone conversations among terrorists and other enemies (a method known as signals intelligence, the capture of communications from one person or group to another). Moreover, satellite images of Russian and Chinese missile sites, or North Korean troop movements, remain valuable to the security of the United States. Still, in the case of terrorism, it would be more advantageous to have a human agent well placed inside the upper reaches of al-Qaeda. Such an agent, or asset, would be worth a dozen multibillion-dollar satellites.

Yet human intelligence has its limitations as well. Against closed societies like North Korea, Iran, and Saddam Hussein's Iraq, local assets are difficult to recruit. This is especially so because the United States focused for decades on the communist world and largely ignored the study of the languages, history, and culture necessary to operate in such places as the Middle East and Asia. Few U.S. citizens have mastered the nuances of Pashto, Arabic, or Farsi; fewer still are willing to work in perilous locations overseas for government wages.

Even if successfully recruited, indigenous assets can be unreliable. They are known to fabricate reports, sell information to the highest bidder, and scheme as false defectors or double-agents. Intelligence assets are not boy scouts or nuns; they are often driven by avarice and travel without moral compasses. "Curveball," the prophetically code-named German agent, provides a typical illustration of the risks involved in human intelligence. Spying inside Iraq in 2002, Curveball convinced the German intelligence service that weapons of mass destruction (WMD) existed in Saddam's regime. The Central Intelligence Agency, in turn, took the bait through its liaison with the Germans.

Not every human intelligence asset turns out to be as deceptive as Curveball. Now and then a foreign spy provides extraordinarily useful information to the United States, as did the Soviet military intelligence officer Oleg Penkosky during the Cold War. Information from Col. Penkosky, coupled with photographs taken by U-2 reconnaissance aircraft, helped the CIA identify the presence of Soviet nuclear missiles in Cuba in 1962. With occasional successes like Penkosky in mind, the United States and most other countries continue their search for reliable and productive assets, even if the cost-benefit ratio has been disappointing.

Whether collected by machines or human agents, intelligence must be converted into usable information. For example, intercepted telephone conversations in Farsi must be translated into English. Messages may have to be decoded. This is done during the processing phase of the intelligence cycle. Each day, over four hundred satellite images, along with thousands of telephone intercepts, some in difficult codes, are collected by intelligence agencies. Yet the United States lacks sufficient translators, photo-interpreters, and code-breakers. In response to a query about the major problems facing U.S. intelligence, a recent director of the National Security Agency (NSA), Vice Admiral J. M. McConnell, identified three: "processing, processing, and processing."[5]

As the public now knows, the day before the September 11 attacks the NSA intercepted a telephone message in Farsi from a suspected al-Qaeda operative. The message, translated on September 12, proclaimed, "Tomorrow is zero hour." As it stands, the vast majority of information gathered by the intelligence agencies is never examined. This is a supreme challenge for the government's information technology specialists—improving the capacity of the United States to mine intelligence data more rapidly, separating the noise from the vital signals that decision makers need to know.

The heart of the intelligence cycle is the analysis phase, where the task is to bring insight to the information that has been collected and processed. The method is straightforward: hire qualified people to sift through all the available information in an attempt to predict what events may happen next in the world. Given the limitations of human forecasting, Dean Rusk suggested that all intelligence reports ought to start off with the caveat: "Damned if I know, but if you want our best guess, well, here it is."[6]

The intelligence cycle concludes with the dissemination phase. Perhaps the greatest paradox of U.S. intelligence is that so much effort and funding go into gathering information for policymakers only for them to ignore it. Some of the best assistant secretaries of defense and state have conceded that they spent, at best, five minutes a day scanning intelligence reports; they were simply too overwhelmed with other obligations.[7] Officials even higher in the policy hierarchy have even less time read intelligence reports. The first challenge of dissemination, then, is to catch the attention of busy leaders, which is why marketing is a critical part of the intelligence cycle.

In marketing their products to consumers, the intelligence agencies confront several potential obstacles. Policymakers may choose to manipulate intelligence to fit their own political views or ideological predispositions—distortion by politicization.[8] Intelligence officers themselves may succumb to the temptation to slant information to suit the needs of policymakers as a way of advancing their career, delivering "intelligence to please." Fortunately, analysts rarely succumb to this temptation, because most of them are imbued with a sense of professional ethics that shuns twisting information to please politicians.

More common is politicization on the consumer side, when policymakers bend the facts. Speaking truth to power is a notoriously difficult endeavor. Those in power often do not want to hear information that runs counter to their policy preferences; hence, they sometimes distort intelligence reports. Decision makers may cherry-pick snippets of information and analysis from intelligence reports that uphold their stated policy positions, ignoring contrary facts or conclusions. More blatant still, government officials have been known to discount entire intelligence reports, as President Lyndon B. Johnson did with CIA analyses that provided a dismal prognosis for U.S. military success in the Vietnam War, or as the second Bush administration did with CIA reports that found no connections between al-Qaeda and Saddam Hussein's regime in Iraq. In such instances, the unenviable but vital responsibility of intelligence managers is to call policy officials to account for their distortions, publicly if necessary.

As this examination of the intelligence cycle indicates, many opportunities for error and distortion present themselves as intelligence makes its way from the field into the hands of decision makers. Nonetheless, U.S. intelligence agencies have some advantages in their quest for information. Willing to spend vast sums of money on

espionage, the United States enjoys the largest, most sophisticated information-gathering apparatus in the world. This bureaucracy brings in a torrent of information from across the globe, some of which has been invaluable for defending U.S. overseas interests and homeland security. The intelligence agencies are expert, as well, in packaging and delivering their assessments of international affairs to the right people in government in a timely manner. Even so, intelligence failures continue to happen. Perhaps nothing illustrates this reality so clearly as two recent cases: the attacks of September 11, 2001, and the misjudgment about the presence of weapons of mass destruction in Iraq.

The 9/11 Intelligence Failure

U.S. intelligence agencies performed in a more credible manner to warn the nation of the terrorist threat before September 11, 2001, than is usually acknowledged. As early as 1995, the CIA's Counterterrorism Center (CTC) cautioned the White House that "aerial terrorism seems likely at some point—filling an airplane with explosives and dive-bombing a target."[9] The warning erred only in its failure to comprehend that hijacked commercial aircraft, with their highly volatile jet fuel, would be powerful missiles without added explosives. Analysts in the CTC had good reason to be concerned about aerial terrorism during the 1990s. Frequent reports had surfaced in the media about terrorist schemes to fly an airplane into the Eiffel Tower or into CIA headquarters. The CTC's warnings on this topic appeared in high policy circles with regularity between 1995 and 2001.

Yet the CTC never provided officials with precise information about the timing or location of the anticipated hijackings, the kind of actionable intelligence that would have allowed U.S. authorities to intercept the terrorists before they boarded the airplanes. Moreover, the intelligence agencies flooded officials with dire warnings about other possible threats, from trucks filled with dynamite exploding in urban tunnels to attacks against the nation's railroad system, crops, livestock, computer infrastructure, and water supplies. Missing in these reports was a sense of priority or probability among the threats, as well as the degree of specificity necessary to take timely protective measures.

Moreover, government inquiries have discovered that the intelligence agencies failed to coordinate and act on the few shards of specific information they did have regarding the September 11 operatives.[10] For instance, the agencies proved unable to track two of the nineteen terrorists, despite warnings from the CIA to the Federal Bureau of Investigation about the terrorists' arrival in San Diego. Furthermore, the FBI failed to respond to warnings from its own agents in Phoenix and Minneapolis about suspicious flight training undertaken by foreigners in those cities. And the Department of Defense smothered warnings from the "Able Danger" group of military intelligence officers who had apparently discovered the presence of sixty foreign terrorists in the United States almost two years before the September 11 attacks.[11] Among the sixty were four of the September 11 hijackers, including their Egyptian-born leader, Mohamed Atta.

At a deeper level, September 11 was an intelligence failure because the CIA had no assets within al-Qaeda, because the National Security Agency (NSA) fell far behind on translating relevant signals intelligence intercepts involving suspected terrorists, and because all of the intelligence agencies lacked sufficient language skills and understanding about nations in the Middle East and South Asia and the objectives and likely motivations of al-Qaeda.

Yet September 11 was more than an intelligence failure; it was a policy failure too. Despite the CIA's warnings about aerial terrorism, for example, neither the Clinton nor the second Bush administrations took meaningful steps to tighten airport security, warn pilots, seal off cockpits, field air marshals, or even alert top officials in the Department of Transportation about the terrorist danger.

Iraqi Weapons of Mass Destruction

The intelligence failures regarding Iraqi weapons of mass destruction were in some ways even more troubling than those that preceded the September 11 attacks. The National Intelligence Estimate

(NIE) of October 2002 concluded, as did most intelligence agencies and outside analysts, that unconventional weapons were most likely present in Iraq. This assessment was based on several inaccurate sources of information. First, since the intelligence community had no significant human assets in Iraq during the interwar years, analysts in the United States extrapolated from what they knew when the United States last had "boots on the ground"—after the first Persian Gulf War in 1991. At that time, the CIA learned that its pre-war estimates regarding Iraqi WMD were inaccurate; Iraq's weapons program had advanced far beyond what the CIA's analysts had projected. After U.S. troops departed Iraq in 1991, the CIA lacked reliable sources on the ground. Thus, in the run-up to the second Persian Gulf War, CIA analysts compensated for earlier underestimates by overestimating the probability of Iraqi WMD.

The available human intelligence proved problematic. Reports from the German asset Curveball, whose reliability was vouched for by the Germans, also factored into the CIA's miscalculations. Only recently have the Germans conceded that the Iraqi exile was in fact lying. Moreover, the confessions of a captured al-Qaeda member, Ibn al-Shaykh al-Libi, interrogated by the Defense Intelligence Agency (DIA), also proved to be fabrications.[12] In addition, the Iraqi National Congress, led by another Iraqi exile, Ahmed Chalabi, claimed knowledge of Iraq's activities and informed U.S. intelligence agencies and the second Bush administration that Saddam Hussein was pursuing nuclear weapons. Chalabi's reliability has since been called into question. Critics maintain that his purpose may have been chiefly to push for a U.S. invasion so that he might advance his personal political agenda and replace Hussein as president of Iraq.

CIA analysts were also aware that British intelligence was concerned about the existence of Iraqi WMD. Yet British government inquiries into this matter, notably the Butler Report, disclosed that the worries of British intelligence analysts focused on a possible Iraqi use of tactical chemical or biological weapons on the battlefield by Hussein if he faced an invasion, as opposed to strategic WMD that could directly strike the United Kingdom, the United States, or even their military forces in the Middle East away from the battle field.

It is often claimed that the second Bush Administration pressured intelligence analysts to write an NIE that emphasized the probability of weapons of mass destruction in Iraq. Such a finding would have supported a policy to invade Iraq and overthrow Hussein's regime, which some argue was the administration's desired course of action regardless of whether the Iraqi dictator had an unconventional weapons program. Vice President Dick Cheney visited CIA headquarters an unprecedented eight times prior to the publication of the 2002 NIE, pressing analysts on their conclusions whenever they strayed from his conviction that Iraq was pursuing capabilities in weapons of mass destruction. The CIA analysts whom Cheney visited assert, however, that they felt no sense of intimidation by his presence; on the contrary, they were pleased to have such unusual high-level attention paid to their work.[13]

Then-Secretary of State Colin Powell also visited with CIA officials to probe the strength of evidence concerning WMD in Iraq, especially on the eve of his appearance before the United Nations on February 3, 2003, to make the case that Saddam Hussein was a great danger. During his preparation, Powell encountered some disagreement among intelligence analysts, including dissent within his own intelligence organization, the Department of State's Bureau of Intelligence and Research (INR). He also learned of other pockets of dissent inside the Department of Energy's intelligence unit and the Air Force's intelligence service. Yet, the analytic behemoths of the intelligence community, most notably the CIA and the DIA, maintained that Iraq probably did possess weapons of mass destruction. Their reasoning pivoted on Iraq's purchase of 60,000 high-strength aluminum tubes, which, they argued, seemed designed for a uranium centrifuge and a nuclear weapons program.[14] Moreover, then-DCI George Tenet, vigorously backed the majority opinion. Secretary Powell deferred to this powerful coalition, even though analysts in INR and the Department of Energy pointed out that the aluminum

tubes were more likely combustion chambers for conventional rockets. For the most part, though, these were internal disputes that took place outside the hearing of the American public. The dissenting views of the smaller agencies were largely dismissed by the larger and more powerful agencies.

President George W. Bush himself questioned Tenet directly about his confidence in the October 2002 NIE. As reported by Bob Woodward of the *Washington Post,* the intelligence director assured the president that the presence of weapons of mass destruction in Iraq was a "slam dunk."[15] A careful reading of the NIE indicates, however, that the analysts who wrote the assessment hardly claimed perfect knowledge about the state of Saddam Hussein's unconventional weapons program. The odds favored finding WMD, but analysts inserted caveats into the estimate regarding the "softness" of the data.

This softness is precisely what Tenet should have underscored for the president. The DCI should have pointed out that the NIE was not a definitive report—indeed, it was a rushed job prepared in only three weeks—that additional on-the-ground fact-finding was sorely needed, and that the CIA felt uneasy provided by Curveball, al-Libi, and Chalabi. A briefing along these lines from Tenet to the president would have highlighted the need for a delay in the invasion plans until UN weapons inspectors had cleared up the intelligence ambiguities. Instead, the White House appears to have been all too ready to accept the convenient findings of some intelligence agencies that happened to run parallel to its own policy ambitions, namely, regime change in Iraq. As a result, Tenet evidently fell into a trap that awaits every U.S. spymaster: the snare of White House politics. Caught up in the administration's euphoria for war against Saddam Hussein, the pursuit of democracy in the Middle East, and a demonstration of U.S. military might as a warning to adversaries, Tenet's reassurance provided an intelligence linchpin for the president to confirm his argument in favor of an Iraqi invasion.

Earlier, Tenet had failed to set the record straight at another important moment in the WMD debate. Inserted into the State of the Union address in 2003 was an assertion that Iraq had attempted to purchase 500 tons of yellowcake uranium from Niger, indicating that Hussein was indeed pursuing a nuclear weapons program. The CIA looked into this allegation by sending former U.S. Ambassador to Niger Joseph C. Wilson IV to make direct inquiries. The ambassador, however, found no evidence to support the hypothesis and the CIA reported this conclusion to the deputy national security advisor, Steven H. Hadley, well in advance of the State of the Union address. Yet the speech included the yellowcake claim anyway, which was now cloaked with the legitimacy of the president's own word in a nationally televised address. Tenet later claimed that he had not seen an advance copy of the speech and was therefore unable to amend the text. The "eighteen words" regarding Nigerian yellowcake have since become a focus of war critics, as has the outing of Wilson's wife, Valerie Plame, as an undercover CIA operative.

The unwillingness of the CIA to confront policy officials who exaggerated intelligence reporting has been perhaps the most disquieting aspect of the WMD intelligence debates. Throughout these distortions, the CIA mostly stood mute. One exception occurred when analysts complained publicly, through anonymous media leaks, that Vice President Cheney was in error to insist that a significant tie existed between al-Qaeda and the Iraqi government. Intelligence reporting had concluded that no such connection existed, though CIA analysts warned that a bond might be forged between global jihadists and Baghdad—or insurgent remnants—if the West were to invade Iraq. Despite the CIA's findings to the contrary, Cheney continued to state publicly that al-Qaeda and the Hussein regime were secretly allied.

Proposals for Reform

The American public must come to understand that intelligence agencies, like any human enterprise, will always have their share of failures. Nevertheless, much can be done to reduce the chance of mistakes. At the planning and direction phase, policy officials must define information needs with greater precision. Collection has been too broad and requires a sharper focus. What exactly do decision makers need to know? On what specific topics should the intelligence agencies focus? The tasking of intelligence agencies is often vaguely spelled out, if at all, and the result is an overly diffuse global intelligence collection effort.

Within the collection phase, renewed concentration on human intelligence is critical. Since 1947, technical intelligence such as signals intelligence and satellite imagery has dominated the U.S. intelligence budget at the expense of human intelligence. The intelligence budget is just beginning to shift funds toward human intelligence. Funding, however, is only the first step. Spy rings are relatively inexpensive to set up; the more difficult challenge is to develop among intelligence officers the language skills and knowledge of foreign cultures necessary for the effective recruitment of assets abroad. This effort cannot succeed overnight; it is bound to take at least ten to fifteen years. The creation of government scholarships to attract top students into the intelligence agencies, such as the Pat Roberts Intelligence Scholars Program, is a step in the right direction. In return for service in an intelligence agency for a period of time, usually two to three years, the government covers college tuition for students studying foreign languages and cultures.

The intelligence agencies must also do more to recruit U.S. citizens with ethnic heritages germane to strategic areas such as the Middle East, South Asia, and other regions largely ignored during the Cold War. For example, Arab-Americans, who face enhanced scrutiny, need to be recruited into the intelligence agencies in much larger numbers and should not be shunned as prima facie security risks. Once cleared through the normal background security checks, Arab-Americans who wish to work in the government should be actively recruited.

Equally important will be efforts to expand the CIA's use of what are called NOCs—U.S. citizens under non-official cover—who operate within a local society, say, as an investment banker in Egypt, a hotel manager in Dubai, or an oil rigger in Bahrain. Moving intelligence officers out of embassies and into the field will make them more likely to meet potential assets and understand the undercurrents of foreign societies. In light of the added hardships and risks of a NOC career, salaries and bonuses should be considerably higher for those who select this path, and more effort will have to be put into crafting their covers, their methods of communication with CIA headquarters, and their rescue if they find themselves in jeopardy overseas.

Furthermore, the United States must examine anew the relationship between the FBI and the Foreign Intelligence Surveillance Court. Established by the Foreign Intelligence Surveillance Act (FISA) of 1978, this court reviews warrant requests for national security wiretaps and other forms of electronic surveillance, as well as physical searches. As a safeguard against intelligence agencies overstepping their powers, as occurred with the FBI in the 1960s and is a subject of current inquiry with the NSA, the FISA Court stands as a vital check on the merits of surveillance requests.[16] Yet steps must also be taken to ensure that warrants can be acquired with dispatch in properly documented cases of national security threats. This did not happen in the case of a suspected al-Qaeda member in Minneapolis prior to the September 11 attacks. When information is collected by the CIA or other intelligence agencies regarding terrorists traveling toward or operating within the United States, the FBI must be alerted quickly and clearly so that it can conduct follow-up surveillance.

At the processing phase, the intelligence agencies are behind the curve on data-mining. Here, too, the federal government must pay higher salaries and bonuses to attract top talent who can assist the intelligence agencies in overcoming information technology deficiencies. By setting up a quasi-government company in Silicon Valley called "In-Q-Tel," the CIA has already reached out to some of the nation's top computer talent. Further outreach and more money are critical. The intelligence agencies desperately need to bring in IT expertise to integrate their systems, while at the same time enhancing firewalls to protect sensitive intelligence from theft by outside hackers and foreign intelligence services. The FBI in particular has lost credibility among Capitol Hill appropriators, having spent over $580 billion on a non-functioning computer system.[17] A reputable outsider recruited into a senior intelligence management position might be able to restore congressional confidence and attract the necessary appropriations to achieve seamless integration among intelligence agencies. The central technological challenge has two elements. First, as information is gathered by the intelligence agencies from around the world, sophisticated machine-sorting techniques are necessary to separate key signals from the high percentage of surrounding "noise" that streams into the secret agencies. Second, useful intelligence must be rapidly shared among the intelligence agencies in Washington, as well as with law enforcement and intelligence officials at the state and local levels. This requires an effective integration of computer networks, both horizontally (in the nation's capital) and vertically (downward to state and local counterterrorism officials).

During the analytical phase, intelligence officers will need to be more careful about including caveats and nuances in their reporting, as well as making clear just how good—or bad—their sources are. For their part, the president and other policymakers must let it be known to intelligence managers and analysts that vague generalities will not be accepted in NIEs and other reports.

One high-level intelligence briefer told the Aspin-Brown Commission in 1996 that North Korea "might have one or two nuclear weapons or it might not have any."[18] Missing was a sense of what analysts believed were the probabilities of a North Korean nuclear weapon within the next year. When an analyst presents a list of threats without any sense of which ones are most likely, the result is paralysis among policymakers.

Intelligence collectors and analysts must also be more thorough in vetting their sources. When the Germans balked at allowing the CIA to conduct its own interviews with the asset Curveball, the CIA's analysts should have downgraded the quality of this source to a low level or declined to use the source at all. Important, too, are efforts to ensure that policymakers understand the reasons behind dissents voiced by intelligence agencies or individual analysts. Their arguments must be showcased, along with the prevailing majority opinions, so that policymakers have a full understanding of the key points of contention. During the Iraqi WMD debate, the contrary views of the Department of Energy, the State Department's Bureau of Intelligence and Research, and the Air Force were insufficiently underscored.

At the dissemination phase, analysts and intelligence managers should be trained to resist more effectively pressures from policymakers to "cook" intelligence. A self-imposed wall must separate analysts from an administration's policy ambitions. Further, analysts must be determined to set the record straight for the public if intelligence reports are twisted for policy purposes by government officials. Intelligence officers, particularly the nation's intelligence director, must be brutally candid with respect to the limits of the reports they have prepared, warning the president and other officials about the extent to which conclusions are based on conjecture more than empirical indicators, such as unambiguous imagery. Those parts of reports that are largely speculative must be carefully delineated from the fact-based findings.

Fresh incentives can be established to encourage the maintenance of a wall between analysts and policymakers, one that will not prevent them from communicating with one another but that erects a barrier against the coloration of intelligence to suit policy objectives. One stick would be to fire analysts who violate the norms of objectivity. Carrots would include promotions, bonuses, and special recognition to those analysts who display exemplary professional conduct. Though rarely used, A-team, B-team exercises in competitive analysis are a useful means for validating objectivity, as long as the teams are staffed with unbiased experts. Above all, the integrity of the analytic process depends on the recruitment of honest men and women into the intelligence agencies.

Critical, too, is the need for constructing better bridges between policymakers and intelligence agencies. The best approach is for the agencies to gain permission to place liaison officers in policy departments so they can attend staff meetings, periodically discuss with decision makers their information needs, and learn from the inside how they can help with timely factual information and objective analysis. With this approach, intelligence is more likely to be relevant to the immediate agendas of government leaders.

Over the years, the Department of Defense (DoD) has skillfully resisted the idea of creating a DNI, jealously guarding its military intelligence prerogatives against the possible encroachment of a civilian intelligence chief. Finally, in 2004, with the passage by Congress of the Intelligence Reform and Terrorism Prevention Act, the 9/11 Commission seemed to have achieved the impossible: the establishment of a robust DNI. Yet a close look at the statute reveals that the DoD and its allies in Congress have managed to dilute and obfuscate the authority of the new intelligence director.[19] As a result, the inaugural DNI, Ambassador John D. Negroponte, faces an uphill battle to consolidate his control over the entire intelligence establishment. His most important challenge will be to persuade the intelligence agencies to pool their information more effectively. In light of the DoD's opposition to a strong DNI, the ambassador's chances for gathering together the reins of a set of agencies so obviously fissile appear slim—unless President Bush or his successor demands a genuine leader for U.S. intelligence, not just a figurehead.

Over the objections of the secretary of defense, a president would have to insist that the DNI be given the authority to hire and fire all intelligence personnel, as well as determine—in consultation with their senior management teams—the budgets of each agency. With these prerogatives, the DNI would finally serve as a hoop to bind together the fifteen staves of the intelligence "community."

The absence of consistent presidential leadership to strengthen the U.S. intelligence shield is unfortunate. The need to bring unity and coordination to the nation's intelligence agencies is a matter of enormous importance. The security of the United States rides heavily on the outcome of this struggle now unfolding in Washington. If the government proves unwilling or unable to make the necessary improvements to protect the nation, citizens will have to demand change through public lobbying or, if necessary, the ballot box.

Notes

1. See Williamson Murray and Mark Grimsley, "Introduction: On Strategy," *The Making of Strategy: Rulers, States, and War,* eds. Williamson Murray, Alvin Bernstein, and MacGregor Knox (New York: Cambridge University Press, 1994), 1–23; and Richard K. Betts, "Analysis, War and Decision: Why intelligence Failures Are Inevitable," *World Politics* 31 (October 1978): 61–89.
2. On the intelligence cycle and the structure of the U.S. intelligence community, see Loch K. Johnson, *America's Secret Power* (New York: Oxford University Press, 1989); *Secret Agencies* (New Haven: Yale University Press, 1996); and Mark M. Lowenthal, *Intelligence: From Secrets to Policy,* 2nd edition (Washington, DC: CQ Press, 2003).
3. Quoted in "Indiana Jim and the Temple of Spooks," *The Economist,* 20 March 1993, 34.
4. Dean Rusk, interview with author, Athens, Georgia, 21 February 1988.
5. J. M. McConnell quoted by senior NSA official, interview with author, Washington, DC, 14 July 1994.
6. Dean Rusk, interview with author, Athens, Georgia, 21 February 1988.
7. See, for example, Loch K. Johnson, *Bombs, Bugs, Drugs, and Thugs: Intelligence and America's Quest for Security* (New York: New York University Press, 2000), 194.
8. See Loch K. Johnson and James J. Wirtz, eds., *Strategic Intelligence: Windows into a Secret World* (Los Angeles: Roxbury, 2004), 167–218.
9. See Loch K. Johnson, "The Aspin-Brown Intelligence Inquiry: Behind the Closed Doors of a Blue Ribbon Commission," *Studies in Intelligence* 48 (Winter 2004): 12.
10. See National Commission on Terrorist Attacks Upon the United States, The 9/11 Commission Report, *Final Report of the National Commission on Terrorist Attacks upon the United States* (New York: Norton, 2004).
11. Louis Freeh, "Why Did the 9/11 Commission Ignore 'Able Danger'?" *Wall Street Journal,* 17 November 2005, A16.
12. Douglas Jehl, "Report Warned Bush Team About Intelligence Doubts," *New York Times,* 6 November 2005, A14. The report in the title refers to a DIA analysis prepared and circulated to government officials in February 2002.
13. CIA analysts, interviews with author, Washington, DC, June 15, 2005.
14. See the account in David Barstow, William J. Broad, and Jeff Gerth, "How the White House Used Disputed Arms Intelligence," *New York Times,* 3 October 2004, Al, A16–18.
15. Bob Woodward, *Plan of Attack* (New York: Simon & Schuster, 2004), 249.
16. See Loch K. Johnson, "Congressional Supervision of America's Secret Agencies: The Experience and Legacy of the Church Committee," *Public Administration Review* 64 (January 2004): 3–14.
17. See Daniel Benjamin and Steven Simon, *The Next Attack: The Failure of the War on Terror and a Strategy for Getting It Right* (New York: Times Books/Henry Holt & Company, 2005).
18. Member of the Aspin-Brown Commission, interview with author, Washington, DC 22 March 1997.
19. See, for example, the critique by John Brennan, "Is This Intelligence?" *Washington Post,* 20 November 2005, Bl.

Loch K. Johnson, Yale Journal of International Affairs, Winter/Spring 2006.

QUESTIONS FOR READERS

Part Three: Institutions and Processes

Lawrence R. Jacobs and Benjamin I. Page, Who Influences U.S. Foreign Policy?

1. Explain the concept of *epistemic communities*. To what extent do these experts influence the course of U.S. foreign policy?
2. How influential is public opinion in the formation of U.S. foreign policy? Explain why this is the case.
3. Which of the various interest groups discussed in the article seems to have the greatest influence on policy formation? Explain. What are the consequences for the conduct of U.S. foreign policy?

Patrick J. Haney, Foreign-Policy Advising: Models and Mysteries from the Bush Administration

1. What does Haney mean by the *new institutionalism*?
2. Has presidential control over U.S. policy toward Cuba weakened or intensified since the 1960s? What are the implications of this change for the U.S. embargo?
3. Articulate the difference between a neoconservative strategy and a Realist strategy with regard to U.S. policy toward Iraq in 2003.
4. How might pre-existing *images* of "the other" compromise rational decision making? Did this occur after the September 11th attacks? What were the consequences?
5. Using the bureaucratic politics model, explain the Bush Administration's decision to invade Iraq. Is this model more compelling than its competitors? Explain.

Matthew A. Baum and Philip B. K. Potter, The Relationships between Mass Media, Public Opinion, and Foreign Policy: Toward a Theoretical Synthesis

1. Baum and Potter argued that political elites have used conflict to manipulate public opinion, in a

wag the dog scenario. Can you think of two examples of this type of manipulation?
2. Baum and Potter argued that *the CNN effect* (the 24-hour news cycle) has not made a significant impact on public opinion. Do you agree? Explain.
3. How do increasing casualties transform the role of the public in its relation to the media?
4. What do Baum and Potter mean by the *elasticity of reality*? Is this a useful concept in the domain of foreign policy analysis? Explain.
5. To what degree would "niche" media networks (FOX, MSNBC) exacerbate partisanship and preclude consensus? Can you provide examples of this phenomenon?

John J. Mearsheimer and Stephen M. Walt, The Israel Lobby and U.S. Foreign Policy

1. At what level of analysis does the argument that lobbying groups affect foreign policy decision making operate?
2. Mearsheimer and Walt argued that "the lobby" drove the U.S. into war with Iraq in 2003. Is their argument compelling? What other explanations would you offer?
3. Mearsheimer and Walt are both renowned proponents of Realism. How does the argument herein contrast with Realist assumptions?
4. Mearsheimer and Walt argued that (in this case) domestic level explanations of U.S. support for Israel are more compelling than systems level explanations. Is their argument compelling? Explain.

Andrew J. Bacevich, Twilight of the Republic

1. Bacevich argued that U.S. foreign policy is essentially pragmatic and opportunistic, and not idealistic. Do you agree? Provide three examples to support your conclusion.
2. Do you agree with Bacevich's claim that America now equates freedom with "self-indulgence"

and "materialism"? If so, how have these norms affected our foreign policy? Give specific examples.

3. Having become the "Empire of Consumption," to what degree does America's increasing dependence on foreign money to finance our debt, foreign oil, and foreign products, undercut our foreign policy?

4. Bacevich argued that the expansion of U.S. power abroad entails a distortion of U.S. domestic freedoms. Do you agree?

5. Do you agree with Bacevich's argument that growing internal weakness undermines our capacity to project power on a global scale? Explain.

6. To what degree do U.S. domestic problems, combined with recent foreign interventions and

wars, undercut U.S. soft power? How does this contrast with Joseph Nye's article? Which position do you find more compelling?

Loch K. Johnson, A Framework for Strengthening U.S. Intelligence

1. What are the advantages of focusing on developing U.S. human intelligence (*humint*) capacities?

2. Johnson argued that policymakers may distort intelligence to suit their own political agenda. Provide historical examples of this phenomenon.

3. Describe three components of U.S. intelligence failure in the period before the September 11th attacks by al Qaeda.

4. How was intelligence "distorted" in the run up to the 2003 invasion of Iraq?

The U.S. and the World

This section provides a collection of essays on U.S. foreign relations with countries and regions of the world that are central to U.S. foreign policy in the early 21st century. Many of these nations are valuable allies to the U.S.A. in the promotion of democracy, human rights, and international commerce. Other polities discussed herein may represent either minor challenges or significant threats to U.S. interests abroad. In each case it is imperative to understand U.S. relations with these other nations by asking, how do these other nations perceive their own national and international interests, and their security environment?

The section begins with Robert Pastor's analysis of the relations between the NAFTA partners through the lens of political economy and informed by a continental perspective, followed by Castañeda's critical analysis of U.S. relations with the nations of Central and South America. Ikenberry then provides his Liberal analysis of the complexity of Sino-U.S. relations, arguing that the future need not be based on the supposition of conflict between these two powers. Feigenbaum then considers the rise of India to superpower status, its deepening alliance with the U.S.A., its altered perception of threat in South Asia, and the implications of these changes for U.S. interests.

The section continues with challenges to U.S. interests, beginning with Legvold's article on the complexities of the Obama Administration's pursuit of a "strategic partnership" with an increasingly authoritarian Russia. Rubin and Rashid then argue that the complex conflict in Afghanistan can only be resolved by dealing with the increasingly problematic involvement of Pakistan in supporting the Afghan insurgency. The discussion then shifts to focus on those "rogue states" that have had persistently strained relationships with the U.S.A., notably Iran. Milani provides a complex analysis of the dynamics of U.S.-Iranian relations, elaborating on Tehran's perception of threats, and focusing Iranian perceptions of U.S. activity in the region.

The Future of North America

Replacing a Bad Neighbor Policy

ROBERT A. PASTOR

Pastor discusses the progressive integration of the United States with Canada and Mexico through the lens of international political economy. He advocates that the U.S.A. pursue a continental approach with its neighbors, one resulting in the formation of an integrative North American Community.

On January 20, 2009, if not before, a new national security adviser will tell the incoming president of the United States that the first two international visitors should be the prime minister of Canada and the president of Mexico. Almost every new president since World War II has followed this ritual, because no two countries in the world have a greater impact economically, socially, and politically on the United States than its neighbors. The importance of Canada and Mexico may, however, come as a surprise to most Americans, as well as to the new president. In the presidential campaign, instead of discussing a positive agenda for North America's future, the candidates have focused critically on two parts of that agenda, the 14-year-old North American Free Trade Agreement (NAFTA) and immigration. And overall, one could conclude from listening to the campaign that Iraq is key to U.S. national security, China is the United States' most important trading partner, and Saudi Arabia and Venezuela supply most of the United States' energy.

None of these propositions is true. For most of the past decade, Canada and Mexico have been the United States' most important trading partners and largest sources of energy imports. U.S. national security depends more on cooperative neighbors and secure borders than it does on defeating militias in Basra.

The new president will take office at a low moment in U.S. relations with its neighbors. The percentage of Canadians and Mexicans who have a favorable view of U.S. policy has declined by nearly half in the Bush years. The immigration debate in Congress and the exchange between the two leading Democratic presidential candidates on who dislikes NAFTA more has left a bitter taste in the mouths or Canadians and Mexicans. The ultimatum issued by Senators Hillary Clinton (D-N.Y.) and Barack Obama (D-Ill.) to Canada and Mexico—renegotiate NAFTA on U.S. terms, or else—hardly displayed the kind of sensitivity to the United States' friends that they have promised. On the other side, Senator John McCain (R-Ariz.) has offered such an unvarnished defense of NAFTA that it would appear he feels nothing more is needed. Moreover, although an author of legislation on immigration reform, McCain retreated from such reform after being harshly criticized. CNN's LOU Dobbs' reports on the disastrous effects of illegal immigration and trade seem to have had a more profound effect on the national debate than many people have thought. Indeed, the candidates seem to have accepted Dobbs' variation on Hobson's choice—either reject NAFTA or suffer decline as a candidate and as a nation.

Sadly, the United States' leaders are looking backward at NAFTA rather than forward by articulating a new vision of shared continental interests. NAFTA has become a diversion, a piñata for pandering pundits and politicians—even though it succeeded in what it was designed to do. It dismantled trade and investment barriers, and as a result, U.S. trade in goods and services with Canada and Mexico tripled—from $341 billion in 1993 to more than $1 trillion in 2007—and inward foreign direct investment quintupled among the three countries and increased tenfold in Mexico between 1990 and 2005. North America, not Europe, is now the largest free-trade area in the world in terms of gross product.

The new U.S. administration needs to replace a bad neighbor policy with a genuine dialogue with Canada and Mexico aimed at creating a sense of community and a common approach to continental problems. The new president must address the full gamut of North American issues not covered by NAFTA, as well as the governance issues arising from the successful enlargement of the market. North America's leaders should deepen economic integration by negotiating a customs union. They should establish a North American investment fund to narrow the income gap between Mexico and its northern neighbors. This would have a greater effect on undocumented immigration to the United States than so-called comprehensive immigration reform. And they should create a lean, independent advisory commission to prepare North American plans for transportation, infrastructure, energy, the environment, and labor standards.

For the last eight years, North America's experiment in integration has stalled. The new president needs to restart the engine.

The North American Disadvantage

No president has met with his counterparts in Canada and Mexico more and yet accomplished less than George W. Bush. Between February 2001 and April 2008, President Bush met the Mexican president 18 times and the Canadian prime minister 21 times. All three huddled together 12 times.

What have they accomplished? They have devised a North American game of Scrabble with intergovernmental committees meeting periodically to spell new acronyms that purport to be initiatives. NAFTA set the precedent with 29 working groups. President Bush brought the Scrabble game to a higher level, inventing and discarding new acronyms with great abandon. In his first visit to Mexico in February 2001, he announced the goal of building an NAEC (North American economic community). Seven months later, during a visit by the Mexican president to the White House, Bush abandoned the community in favor of the P4P (Partnership for Prosperity). To deal with security fears arising from 9/11 and economic fears that a more formidable border would reduce trade, the United States signed separate "smart border" agreements with Canada and Mexico. These gave birth to still more working groups and initiatives, including FAST (Free and Secure Trade), PIP (Partners in Protection), C-TPAT (Customs-Trade Partnership Against Terrorism), WHTI (Western Hemisphere Travel Initiative), IBETS (Integrated Border Enforcement Teams), ACE (Automated Commercial Environment). SENTRI provided a fast-lane approach to the U.S.-Mexican border, and NEXUS did the same for the U.S.-Canadian border. No one explained why they could not do this with one, rather than two, acronyms—or rather one agency and procedure rather than two.

In March 2005, the SPP, the Security and Prosperity Partnership of North America, replaced the P4P. This was another bureaucratic exercise aimed at delivering "measurable results" to make North America more competitive and secure. It initially listed 300 goals, almost all technical—for example, to harmonize regulations on jelly beans or eliminate "rules of origin" regulations, which tax the part of each product that is not made in North America. After three years, officials still have not harmonized jelly-bean labels, but they have removed "rules of origin" provisions on $30 billion of goods. That may sound like a lot, but it represents less than the growth of annual trade in North America. A year later, in 2006, the three North American leaders invited a group of CEOs from some of the largest corporations in North America to establish the NACC (North American Competitiveness Council). They focused on 51 recommendations, which included eliminating pesky regulations, and agreed on the need to work "under the radar screen" of public attention.

If you measure progress by examining the growth in trade, the reduction in wait times at the borders and the public's support for integration, all of these initiatives have failed miserably. The growth in trade in the Bush years has been less than one-third of what it was in the previous seven years—three percent versus 9.8 percent. The wait times have lengthened, and public opinion toward the rest of North America in all three countries has deteriorated, in part because the United States failed to comply with NAFTA on issues (for example, trucking and softwood lumber) of great importance to Canada and Mexico.

North American integration has stalled in the Bush years for several reasons, beginning with 9/11, which led to intense security inspections on the two borders, creating giant speed bumps for commerce. A study of the U.S.-Canadian border found a 20 percent increase in border delays crossing southbound and a 12 percent increase in delays northbound since 9/11.

Second, although North American trade has tripled, and 80 percent of the goods from that trade is transported on roads, there has been little investment in infrastructure on the borders and almost none for roads connecting the three countries. Thus, the delays are longer and more costly than before NAFTA. The steel industry recently estimated that wait times for their shipments, which are generally 5–6 hours, result in annual losses of $300–$600 million. Another study estimated that delays added a cost of 2.7 percent to the goods.

Third, trucks are still impeded from crossing the U.S.-Mexican border. Despite NAFTA's mandate that Mexican trucks be allowed to enter the United States starting in 1995, the first trucks—beginning with 55—crossed in March 2008, on a pilot project that Congress has tried to stop. (As a point of reference, about 4.2 million Mexican trucks bring their products to the border each year.) Each year, more than four billion pounds of fruits and vegetables are placed on trucks in the Mexican state of Sonora. When the trucks reach the border crossing at Mariposa, the produce is unloaded in a warehouse, then retrieved by another truck that takes it several miles into Arizona, where it is unloaded again into another warehouse and then retrieved by an American carrier. With 280,000 trucks coming to the Arizona border each year, think of the inefficiency and cost of transferring fresh produce three times to cross one border.

Fourth, complying with the "rules of origin" provisions takes so long that many firms simply use the standard tariff that NAFTA was intended to eliminate. Finally, North American integration stalled because China joined the World Trade Organization in 2001, and its exports to all three North American countries grew so fast that in 2007 it overtook Mexico as the United States' second-largest trading partner. In 2001, the United States imported more textiles and garments from Mexico than from China, but by 2006 it imported almost four times as much from China as from Mexico. (The United States still exports 60 percent more to Mexico than to China.)

Intraregional exports among the three North American countries as a percent of their global exports increased from 43 percent in 1990 to 57 percent in 2000—a level of integration almost matching that of the European Union after five decades of integration. Since then, intraregional integration in North America has not changed. Auto parts for one car cross the borders eight times in the course of being assembled. With added security, inadequate infrastructure, and the interruption of trucking from Mexico, the transaction costs now not only exceed the tariff that was eliminated but also are much higher than the tariffs imposed on foreign cars that need to enter the United States only once, as a completed product. In short, the North American advantage has turned into the North American disadvantage.

A Two-Front Storm

Assaults from both ends of the political spectrum have transformed the debate on North America in recent years. From the right have come attacks based on cultural anxieties of being overrun by Mexican immigrants and fears that greater cooperation with Canada and Mexico could lead down a slippery slope toward a North American Union. Dobbs, among others, viewed a report by a 2005 Council on Foreign Relations task force (which I co-chaired), *Building a North American Community*, as the manifesto of a conspiracy to subvert American sovereignty. Dobbs claimed that the CFR study proposed a North American Union, although it did not. From the left came attacks based on economic fears of job losses due to unfair trading practices. These two sets of fears came together in a perfect storm that was pushed forward by a surplus of hot air from talk-show hosts on radio and television. In the face of this criticism, the Bush administration was silent, and the Democratic candidates competed for votes in the rustbelt states, where unions and many working people have come to see NAFTA and globalization much as Dobbs does.

The debate in the United States became so insular that Americans essentially reversed roles with their neighbors. For nearly two centuries, many in Canada and Mexico built walls to limit U.S. influence. Within two decades of their decision to dismantle the walls, the United States is being pressed by anti-North American Union populists to rebuild the barriers to keep out its neighbors. The idea that the United States should fear being taken over by its weaker neighbors is bizarre, but it is becoming a staple of the populist critique.

During the NAFTA debate, people in all three countries had anxieties and reservations. Canada and Mexico feared U.S. investors would take over their industries, and Americans feared that Canadians and Mexicans would take their jobs. None of this happened. Canadians invested at a more rapid pace in the United States than U.S. firms invested in Canada, and although foreign investment in Mexico soared—from $33 billion in 1993 to $210 billion in 2005—the percentage coming from the United States declined by ten percent.

Meanwhile, all three economies became more connected. Many national firms became North American, producing and marketing their products in all three countries. The international sector of all three economies grew (and export-oriented firms pay wages 13–16 percent higher than the national average). Needless to say, as the market expanded and the competition grew more intense, there were more winners and losers, but as consumers, all North Americans benefited from more choices, lower prices, and higher-quality products.

In an econometric analysis of the effects of NAFTA, the World Bank estimated that by 2002 Mexico's GDP per capita was 4–5 percent higher, its exports 50 percent higher, and its foreign direct investment 40 percent higher than they would have been without NAFTA. NAFTA's effects on the United States, given the much larger size of its economy, are much smaller and harder to measure. Still, the first seven years of NAFTA, from 1994 to 2001, were a period of great trade expansion and job creation in the United States! NAFTA does not deserve the credit for all or even much of this job growth, but it surely cannot be blamed for serious job losses. If one focuses only on jobs, U.S. employment grew from 110 million jobs in 1993 to 137 million in 2006 (and in Canada, from 13 million to 16 million). And U.S. manufacturing output increased by 63 percent between 1993 and 2006.

These benefits have not yielded a positive consensus in part because they have not been equitably shared with those who paid a price. On this, North America's different voices are audible. One is the strident and angry voice, personified by Dobbs, which argues that Mexicans have little in common with Americans, that free trade hurts workers and the economy, and that the United States can solve the "immigration problem" by building a wall. This voice has echoes in Canada and Mexico, and it resonates among those who are uneasy or fearful about trade and integration. Another voice represents those who welcome integration and are willing to experiment with new forms of partnership.

Public opinion surveys suggest that the latter voice represents the majority, even if few leaders speak for them today.

There are many surveys of public opinion conducted in North America, and they have found that values in all three countries are similar and converging. Americans, Canadians, and Mexicans like and trust one another more than they do people from almost any other country, even though Canadian and Mexican views of U.S. policy have grown negative in the past seven years. Thirty-eight percent of the people in all three countries identify themselves as "North American," and a majority of these publics would even be in favor of some form of unification if they thought it would improve their standards of living without harming the environment or diminishing their national identities. A majority believes that free trade is good for all three countries, although respondents also believe that free trade has benefited the other countries in North America more than it has theirs. A majority of the publics in all three countries would prefer "integrated North American policies" rather than independent national policies on the environment and border security, and a plurality feel the same way about transportation, energy, defense, and economic policies.

Given these surveys, the obvious question is why the current presidential candidates believe that the American public is anti-Mexican and supports protectionism. There are several possible explanations. Support for free trade is evident over an extended period, but the degree of support varies over time and space, depending on the state of the economy and the size of the trade deficit. A CNN national poll conducted in October 2007 found that more Americans believed foreign trade was an opportunity than believed trade was a threat. But exit polls of Democrats voting in the Ohio primary on March 4, 2008, showed that 80 percent blamed trade for job losses. In a tight race, the candidates responded to the negative view, which was more intense than the hopes reflected in the public opinion surveys. For that reason, and because no political leader is contesting him in the marketplace of ideas, Dobbs is shaping the debate, and the unions are shaping the policy prescription.

North America faces a Dobbsean choice—between reversing and accelerating integration, between putting up barriers and finding new ways to collaborate. Ironically, the Dobbs view has strengthened just as economic integration in North America has weakened.

A Continental Approach

It is clear that the Bush administration's incremental, quiet, business-based approach has not succeeded in promoting economic integration or closer collaboration with the United States' neighbors. Instead, it has raised some legitimate concerns and provoked a nativist backlash. It was a mistake to allow CEOs to be the only outside advisers on deregulation and the harmonization of remaining regulations. Civil society and legislatures must be heard on these issues, which are less about business than about how to pursue environmental, labor, and health goals. More broadly, free trade is clearly not enough. Those groups that pay the price of increased competition need to share the benefits and need to have a safety net that includes wage insurance, education and trade adjustment assistance, and health care. Nor is free trade all that is needed to help Mexico enter the developed world.

The dual-bilateral strategy (U.S.-Canada, U.S.-Mexico) is also failing. It exacerbates the defining and debilitating characteristic of the United States' relations with its neighbors—asymmetry. It leads Washington to ignore them or impose its will, and it causes Ottawa and Mexico City to either retreat or be defensive. Given the imbalance in power and wealth, a truly equal relationship may be elusive, but it is in the long-term interests of all three countries to build institutions that will reduce the imbalance. The genius of the Marshall Plan was that the United States used its leverage not for short-term gain but to encourage Europe to unite. That kind of statesmanship is needed to step beyond short-term and private interests and construct a North American Community.

There are other reasons for a North American approach. If three governments rather than two sit at the table, they are more likely to focus on rules than on power, on national and continental interests rather than on the interests of specific companies or unions. On issues such as transportation and the environment, a three-sided dialogue could produce North American plans. Even on border issues, the three nations could benefit from comparing procedures and borrowing from one another the ones that work the best.

A North American approach needs a vision based on the simple premise that each country benefits from its neighbors' success and each is diminished by their problems or setbacks. With such a vision, it becomes logical to consider a North American investment fund to reduce the income disparity between Mexico and its neighbors. Without such a vision, the governments will continue to grapple with one issue, one country at time, reinforcing old stereotypes, such as that of Mexico as a corrupt, drug-dealing, immigrant-sending problem. With a vision of a community, all three governments should see one another as part of the transnational problem and essential to a solution.

The first step is to deepen economic integration by eliminating the costly and cumbersome "rules of origin" regulations, allowing all legitimate goods to move seamlessly across the borders, and permitting border officials to concentrate on stopping drugs and terrorists. To eliminate the rules of origin, the three governments will need to negotiate a common external tariff at the lowest levels. This will not be easy, as there are other free-trade agreements that would need to be reconciled, but it will make the North American economy more efficient. A smaller measure, which could have as large an economic impact, would be to comply with NAFTA and harmonize the three countries' regulations on truck safety so as to permit trucks to travel in all three countries.

Other decisions could harness the comparative advantage of each country to mutual benefit. For example, more Americans live and retire in Mexico than in any other foreign country. If the United States certified hospitals in Mexico and allowed retirees to use Medicare there, both countries would benefit. The second step is to secure national borders and the continental perimeter. The best approach would be to train Canadian, Mexican, and U.S. officials together to avoid duplication, share intelligence, and secure the borders as a team.

Another challenge is to narrow the gap in income that separates Mexico from its northern neighbors by creating a North American investment fund. The fund should target $20 billion a year to connect central and southern Mexico to the United States with roads, ports, and communications. With the goal of building a North American Community, all three governments should commit to narrowing the income gap, with each deciding how it could best contribute. Since it will benefit the most, Mexico should consider contributing half of the money for the fund and also undertake reforms—fiscal, energy, and labor—to ensure that the resources would be effectively used. The United States should contribute each year 40 percent of the fund's resources—less than half the cost each week of the war in Iraq—and Canada, 10 percent. Since NAFTA was put into place, the northern part of Mexico has grown ten times as fast as the southern part because it is connected to the Canadian and U.S. markets. North America can wait a hundred years for southern Mexico to catch up, or it can help accelerate its development—which would have positive consequences in terms of reducing emigration, expanding trade, and investing in infrastructure to help Mexico enter the developed world.

North America's model of integration is different from Europe's. It respects the market more and trusts bureaucracy less. Still, some institutions are needed to develop continental proposals, monitor progress, and enforce compliance. The three leaders should institutionalize summit meetings at least annually, and they should establish a North American commission composed of independent and distinguished leaders from academia, civil society, business, labor, and agriculture and with an independent research capacity. The commission should offer continental proposals to the three leaders. The leaders would continue to be staffed by their respective governments, but they would respond to a continental, rather than a dual-bilateral, agenda. The commission should develop a North American plan for transportation and infrastructure and plans on labor, agriculture, the environment, energy, immigration, drug trafficking, and borders.

The three heads of state must also commit to building a new consciousness, a new way of thinking about one's neighbors and about the continental agenda. Americans, Canadians, and Mexicans can be nationals and North Americans at the same time. Indeed, an appreciation of one's neighbors as part of a compelling North American idea could enhance the prestige of each country. To educate a new generation of students to think North American, each country should begin by supporting a dozen centers for North American studies. Each center should educate students, undertake research, and foster exchanges with other North American universities for both students and faculty.

This is a formidable agenda that could transform North America and each of its states. It is not possible without a vision, and it is not feasible without real leadership and credible institutions. But with all three, a North American Community can be built. The existence of such a community would mean that the United States would consult its neighbors on important issues that affected them. It would mean that Canada would work closely with Mexico to build rule-based institutions and to develop a formula for closing the development gap. It would mean that Mexico would undertake reforms to make good use of the additional resources.

This is a very different agenda than seeking to improve working conditions and the environment by rewriting NAFTA and threatening to increase tariffs. Labor and environmental issues should be part of the North American dialogue working to improve the continent, but there is no evidence that foreign investors move to Mexico in order to take advantage of lax labor and environmental rules. Quite the contrary: Mexico's labor laws are so rigid that they often discourage foreign investors. Moreover, they incorporate the eight core international labor standards, whereas the United States has not approved six of them. As for its environmental laws, Mexico maintains standards that are quite good; the problem is that it lacks funds for enforcement or cleanup.

The immigration issue also needs to be addressed in this broader context. A fence is needed in some places, but building a 700-mile wall would be more insulting than effective. If the United States is going to try to forge a community, it needs to articulate an approach that acknowledges that it is complicit in the immigration problem in hiring illegal immigrants, who work harder for less. More important, if the United States were to join with Mexico in a serious commitment to narrow the income gap, then cooperation over other issues would become possible. The best place to enforce immigration policy is in the workplace, not at the border, but national, biometric identification cards will be needed for everyone to make the policy effective, and a path to legalization will be needed to make it just.

A North American Community

It would be desirable for Canada and Mexico to join in making a comprehensive proposal for a North American Community, but Canada's aloofness from Mexico makes that unlikely. Therefore, the responsibility for defining North America's future will lie with the new U.S. president. If the next administration seeks to renegotiate NAFTA, presses for enforceable labor and environmental provisions, and allows special interests, such as the Teamsters Union and the trucking industry, to prevent competition and avoid compliance with the agreement, the United States' neighbors may look back on the Bush years with nostalgia. Canada and Mexico would be under pressure to seek their own exemptions to NAFTA, and they would likely remind Washington that when it comes to enforceable sanctions, the United States has been more guilty of noncompliance than they have. Renegotiating NAFTA would require a significant investment of the new administrations time and political capital without, in the end, helping workers or the environment much, if at all.

The alternative approach needs to start with a vision of a North American Community and some institutions—quite different from Europe's—designed to pursue a bold agenda that includes a customs union, a North American commission, a North American investment fund, and a common team of customs and border guards to man the borders and the continental perimeter.

This is a very ambitious agenda, but on the eve of NAFTA's 15th anniversary, Americans are looking for a fresh approach, and no set of foreign policies would contribute more to U.S. prosperity and security than those devoted to building a North American Community. If the United States wants to compete, it cannot march backward, nor can it stand in place without falling behind. The new president—working with counterparts in Canada and Mexico—has the opportunity to redefine the face of North America for the twenty-first century. If the principal foreign policy challenge for the next administration is to restore trust in the United States, then the first step is to demonstrate to the world that it can work with and respect its neighbors.

Morning in Latin America

The Chance for a New Beginning

JORGE G. CASTAÑEDA

Castañeda discusses the U.S.A.'s foreign relations with other countries in Latin America, tackling thorny issues that are common throughout the region including immigration reform, drug enforcement, free trade, and relations with Cuba. Castañeda argues that the United States, in its relations with Cuba, must change the patterns of existing procedures and policies (such as the long-standing embargo) that have failed.

Fixing the mess inherited from the Bush administration will be no simple task for the next U.S. administration. In Latin America, it will be particularly arduous. The reason is simple but paradoxical. George W. Bush raised expectations greatly when he took office and announced that he was making the relationship with Latin America in general and Mexico in particular a priority. He kept his promise for seven and a half months—until 9/11, after which the United States, understandably enough, concentrated all its energies and attention on al Qaeda and Iraq. What was less understandable was that this lasted seven years. And because of this neglect of the rest of the world and the relentless focus on Iraq and terrorism, Bush has become more unpopular in Latin America than any other U.S. president in recent memory. This is all the more paradoxical since Bush has in fact been less interventionist and less aggressive toward Latin America than any other U.S. president in recent memory.

As president, Barack Obama, will enjoy a honeymoon with Latin America (and with the rest of the world), both because of his predecessor's dismal legacy and because of the nature of the most critical pending issues in the hemispheric relationship. Four challenges clearly stand out: what to do about the imminent or ongoing Cuban transition or succession; what to do about immigration reform, which is the single most important bilateral issue for a dozen nations in Latin America; what to do about the continuing ascent of the "two lefts" in the region; and, finally, if, as seems likely, the U.S.-Colombian free-trade agreement is not approved by a lame-duck session of Congress (and Obama continues to insist on revisiting the North American Free Trade Agreement, or NAFTA), how to deliver on campaign promises while deepening, rather than weakening, these undeniably defective trade covenants.

The next U.S. administration will have to deal with these issues—and others, such as drug enforcement—regardless of the priority it attaches to them. It will prove successful if it recalls that Latin America is living in a moment that combines the best and the worst aspects of its history: growing at a pace unheard of since the 1970s, democratic and respectful of human rights like never before, with poverty and inequality at long last diminishing, but more divided, polarized, and involved in greater internecine and intraregional conflicts than ever before. Washington can help enormously by working to consolidate the positive trends while neutralizing the negative ones.

Healing with Havana

In Cuba, the passing of Fidel Castro from the scene, as he nears the 50th anniversary of his triumphant entry into Havana and into history, represents an immense challenge for Washington, for Miami, for Cuba, and for all of Latin America. Matters on the island have never been a strictly Cuban affair, and

although the evolution of the Castro regime under Fidel's younger brother, Raul, is unpredictable, the terms of Washington's predicament are quite clear. On the one hand, the United States cannot, as Obama has quite rightly proclaimed, continue with the failed policies of the past half century. Demanding a full-fledged democratic transition as a precondition for normalizing U.S.-Cuban relations is not only a recipe for further failure but also totally unrealistic and unpalatable to Latin America; a large majority of its governments correctly believe Washington should unilaterally lift the embargo, together with travel and remittance restrictions. On the other hand, as McCain has made clear, Washington cannot set aside the question of democracy and human rights in Cuba while it awaits the departure of the second Castro.

Realpolitik and fear of another exodus of Cuban refugees across the Straits of Florida may tempt Washington to pursue a "Chinese," or "Vietnamese," solution to the relationship with Cuba: that is, normalizing diplomatic relations in exchange for economic reforms while leaving the question of internal political change until much later. It should not do this, chiefly because of the regional implications. Over the past few decades, the United States, Canada, the European Union, and Latin America have patiently constructed a regional legal framework to defend and encourage democratic rule as well as respect for human rights in the hemisphere. These values have been enshrined in conventions, charters, and free trade-agreements, from the Inter-American Democratic Charter, the Inter-American Commission on Human Rights, and the Inter-American Court of Human Rights to the American Convention on Human Rights and the labor and environmental chapters of free-trade agreements, as well as in the democratic clauses of the economic agreements between Chile and the EU and between Mexico and the EU. These mechanisms are not perfect, and they have not truly been tested. But to waive them in the interests of simply guaranteeing stability in Cuba and ensuring an exodus-free succession instead of a democratic transition—that is, creating once again a "Cuban exception" for reasons of pure pragmatism—would be unworthy of the enormous efforts every country in the hemisphere has made to deepen and strengthen democracy in the Americas. Cuba must return to the regional concert of powers, but accepting this concert's rules. To allow it to proceed otherwise would weaken democracy and encourage authoritarian traditions in the hemisphere—and lay the groundwork for other exceptions that would justify their existence by invoking the Cuban precedent.

Still, the United States must change its policy toward Cuba for three reasons: because the existing policy has not worked; because with the Cold War now over for nearly 20 years, that policy has lost its primary raison d'être; and because, however slowly and painfully, Cuba is beginning to emerge from its long night of distress. The change in U.S. policy must combine values and principles with realism and effectiveness, eventually leading to both the normalization of relations with and the establishment of democracy in Cuba. Holding free and fair elections may not be the primary issue, but nor is it one that should be shelved in the interests of stability. If elections are placed at the front of the agenda, Washington will remain right where it started half a century ago: setting a precondition that will lead nowhere. Although Washington cannot evade the issue of free and fair elections in its discussions with the Cuban leadership, insisting that those elections take place before anything else—trade, tourism, unlimited remittances and family travel—is unrealistic. Elections must instead be part of a comprehensive process of normalization: they can be neither a deal breaker nor a nonissue. Exactly where in the process these elections take place is something that negotiations between Washington and Havana should address in order to make those elections the mutually accepted culmination of diplomacy, not a precondition for initiating it.

Lifting the embargo, as well as travel and remittance restrictions, should be a unilateral act on the part of the United States. Reestablishing full diplomatic relations; addressing the claims on confiscated Cuban property made by Cubans living in Miami; helping Cuba reenter the World Bank, the International Monetary Fund, the Inter-American Development Bank, and the Organization of American States; and granting it totally normal economic ties with its neighbor across the straits should be conditional on Havana's initiating a cooperative and fully-mapped-out process for resolving all the issues on the table with Washington and others. Elections should be one of the steps in this process, even if not the first step or even an early one.

Migrant Nations

Although many Americans believe that immigration is a domestic issue that should be excluded from any international negotiation, such an approach is neither a U.S. tradition nor the view held by other nations in the hemisphere. The United States negotiated its first immigration deal in 1907 (the so-called Gentlemen's Agreement with Japan), had a controversial treaty with Mexico for more than two decades (the so-called Bracero Agreement, between 1942 and 1964), and has kept up immigration talks and made deals with none other than Fidel Castro ever since the early 1960s. And for a significant number of Latin American nations today, immigration is the single most important issue on their agendas with Washington.

This is true not just for Mexico. Although the United States' southern neighbor receives the greatest amount of remittances from its expatriates north of the border of any Latin American country (about $25 billion a year), sends more legal and illegal migrants to the United States than any other country (around 500,000 a year), and has the greatest number of nationals living en el norte (probably around 15 million), it is by no means the only country of the hemisphere for which immigration is a crucial issue. In the Caribbean, Cuba (even now, to say nothing of later), the Dominican Republic, Haiti, and Jamaica all have a similarly high proportion of their citizens residing in the United States and depend as much on remittances. The same is true for much of Central America: El Salvador has the largest share of its citizenry living abroad of any country in Latin America (more than 20 percent, compared with 12 percent for Mexico), and remittances are by far its most important source of hard currency. Nor is South America exempt from this trend. Eighteen percent of Ecuadorians reside abroad, and large and growing numbers of Colombians, Paraguayans, Peruvians, and Venezuelans live in the United States.

These countries are deeply affected by the current immigration climate in the United States, and they would benefit greatly from the type of comprehensive immigration reform that both McCain and Obama have supported. The Bush administration's regrettable decision to build fences along the U.S.-Mexican border, raid workplaces and housing sites, detain and deport foreigners without papers, and, more recently and more tragically, launch criminal proceedings against workers with false or stolen papers and subsequently sentence them to several months in jail before deportation is seen in Latin America as a hypocritical and vicious offense against societies and governments that harbor some of the most favorable feelings toward the United States in the world. These actions are accurately perceived as futile, nasty, and unfair, and, worst of all, they are conducive to growing anti-American sentiment in many countries. They play straight into the hands of the "anti-imperialist" faction of the Latin American left.

The issue is all the more painful and disappointing since most Latin American foreign ministries know full well that these positions are purely the result of politics. The White House needed, understandably, to beef up the law enforcement and security chapters of the two immigration reform proposals (the McCain-Kennedy bill, introduced in 2005, and the "Grand Bargain" of 2007) in order to achieve passage, but once they were defeated, the concessions to the right wing remained and were put into effect, while the substance of the reforms disappeared. Latin America found itself facing the worst of both worlds. This is considered an even greater grievance now because of the slowdown in the U.S. economy, which is dragging many Latin American economies down with it.

Defining and passing comprehensive immigration reform is not rocket science; it requires straightforwardly intelligent substance and skillful politics. The substantive elements necessary are well-known: tightening security at the border but also including gates in the walls currently being built; legalizing, with expeditious and sensible fines and conditions, the 15 million or so foreigners now present in the United States illegally; establishing what Obama has called a "migrant worker program" and what McCain has labeled a "temporary-worker program" that allows a sufficient number of foreigners (they will be mainly Latin Americans, and among them, mainly Mexicans) to satisfy the growing needs of the U.S. economy and American society, with paths both to regular visits home and to U.S. permanent residence. All of the proposals put on the table by think tanks, commissions, and lawmakers over the past ten years say essentially this. The nuances will involve the sequencing, the amount of the fines imposed, and the exact requirements for legalization and for paths to eventual citizenship.

The second component is political will and timing. Bush had it right at the beginning: his willingness to negotiate an immigration agreement with Mexico at the very start of his term was probably the only way to get it done. Backing off, first because of 9/11, then because of the war in Iraq, then because of the 2004 elections, and finally in order to wait for the Senate to produce its own bill, proved disastrous: by the time the two bills were voted on, Bush could no longer deliver the conservative faction of his own party, dooming both.

The final component of a bold and viable immigration proposal entails Latin American cooperation and a serious U.S. effort to obtain it. The sending countries in the region—democracies now, thanks in part to U.S. policies—can help curtail illegal immigration with statesmanlike, courageous strategies, if they can show their constituencies that they are getting something for doing so. In addition to U.S. immigration reform itself, that something should include the type of intensive support for development that Robert Pastor described in a recent article in these pages and that the EU offers to its new members. Such support would be in the United States' best interest, not a sacrifice imposed on Washington by shakedown artists south of the border. It would help build up Mexican, Caribbean, and Central American infrastructure, education, rule of law, and security, in an effort to spur growth rates and employment increases that, with time—not overnight—will slow immigration to a level more consonant with the needs of the United States.

The Future of the Two Lefts

Much has been written about the ascent of the left in Latin America over the past decade. In fact, there are two lefts in the region: a modern, democratic, globalized, and market-friendly left, found in Brazil, Chile, Uruguay, parts of Central America, and, up to a point, Peru; and a retrograde, populist, authoritarian, statist, and anti-American left, found in Bolivia, Cuba, Ecuador, El Salvador, Mexico, Nicaragua, and Venezuela and, to a lesser extent, in Argentina, Colombia, and Paraguay. (It has been argued that the roots of this division are historical: the reformist moderate left springs, paradoxically, from a revolutionary past, whereas the radical left springs from populist, nationalist, nonrevolutionary origins.) Some of these "lefts" are in power; some barely missed attaining it but may still do so. Over the past two years, it has become increasingly evident that the "modern," or "soft," left is, all in all, governing quite well: Luiz Inácio Lula da Silva was reelected in Brazil, as was Leonel Fernández in the Dominican Republic; Daniel Astori is likely to succeed his fellow Frente Amplio member Tabaré Vázquez in Uruguay, as is Martin Torrijos' handpicked successor in Panama; and although Michelle Bachelet has disappointed many in Chile with occasional self-destructive stances, this is only in contrast to her predecessors on the reformist left. Conversely, the other left—represented by Raul Castro in Cuba, Hugo Chávez in Venezuela, Rafael Correa in Ecuador, Cristina Fernández de Kirchner in Argentina, Fernando Lugo in Paraguay, Evo Morales in Bolivia, and Daniel Ortega in Nicaragua—has proved to be more extreme and erratic than many anticipated. It is no coincidence that the "soft" left rules in countries largely devoid of immigration to the United States and the "hard" left is present precisely where immigration is crucial: Mexico, El Salvador, Nicaragua, Ecuador, Bolivia.

Herein lies a dilemma, how to address the clear rift between the two lefts in a way that improves U.S.-Latin American relations, fortifies the modern left, and weakens the retrograde left without resorting to the failed interventionist policies of the past. Even with Bush's record of not meddling in the region (with the possible but unproved exception of dabbling in the failed April 2002 coup attempt against Chávez), the United States under Bush is more unpopular in Latin America than it has been under any recent administration. (It is worth recalling that, other than Jimmy Carter, every U.S. president since Dwight Eisenhower, including Bill Clinton, has interfered in the domestic affairs of one country or another in the region.)

It will not be easy for Obama to repair the damage to Latin America in Latin America: the most effective steps would be to withdraw from Iraq and return to respecting multilateralism. The next best, strictly Latin America-focused steps, are self-evident, if not easily achievable. They require strengthening those governments of the modern left or those of the center or center-right threatened by the retrograde left and simultaneously making it clear to the retrograde left that there is a significant cost to be paid for straying out of line—that is, violating the basic tenets of democracy, a respect for human rights, and the rule of law.

Fortunately, the conditions for repairing the damage are propitious. Unfortunately, the nations of the Western Hemisphere are deeply divided today, among themselves and within themselves. At the same time, however, never in recent times has Latin America been doing so well politically, economically, and even socially, as economic growth and representative democracy are helping many nations reduce poverty and even inequality, the region's traditional bane. One of the explanations for this contradiction stems from the ideological and geopolitical battle under way in Latin America and what this battle could mean for the issues of particular concern to Washington: oil, arms, guerrillas, drugs. The conflict could easily escalate and force a major crisis in U.S.—Latin American relations, particularly as Chávez's rule becomes increasingly precarious at home and his policies become increasingly extremist abroad—especially as no one in the Americas seems willing to stand up to him.

There exists a fundamental asymmetry between the two lefts and, more broadly, between the governments (left or right) in the region that subscribe to macroeconomic orthodoxy, representative democracy, and maintaining a modus vivendi with Washington, on the one hand, and those of the "swashbuckling" left (as the Brazilian minister for strategic affairs, Roberto Mangabeira Unger, has labeled it), on the other. The former are timid and cautious to the extreme; it is no coincidence that it was King Juan Carlos of Spain, rather than a Latin American leader, who finally lost his temper with Chávez ("Why don't you shut up!" he demanded at the November 2007 Ibero-American summit in Chile). These regimes feel no urge to "export" their "model" and seem to be concerned that they could be faulted for flaunting its virtues. Brazil, true enough, seeks to expand its influence in the region and in the world, but this is for geopolitical motives rather than ideological ones. In contrast, the other side has an export strategy and the means to implement it. The retrograde left today can realize a version of Che Guevara's old dream: not "two, three…many Vietnams" but "two, three…many Venezuelas"—winning power by the ballot, conserving and concentrating it through constitutional changes and the creation of armed militias and monolithic parties. It can finance all of this with funds provided by the Venezuelan state oil company, PDVSA, implementing social policies that are misguided over the long run but seductive in the short run, especially when carried out by Cuban doctors, teachers, and instructors and backed, in theory and increasingly in practice, by arms sent from Russia to Caracas.

The hard left also offers a narrative that is convincing but wrong: the persistence of poverty and inequality can be blamed on recurrent U.S. aggression or negligence, the venality of the private sector, and the corruption and incompetence of prior governments and entrenched elites; the Bolivarian alternative is the solution. Education and health services are brought to the poorest sectors of society via the so-called missions and Cuban cadres. Bountiful funds are available, whether through nationalized natural-resource companies and utilities (Venezuela's oil, Bolivia's gas and telecommunications, Ecuador's telecommunications and oil) or by levying higher taxes or fees on foreign or national businesses (fees on soybean exports in Argentina, the higher electricity rates Paraguay seeks from the Itaipu and Yacyretá dams). Price reductions, subsidies, and controls are imposed—with threats of expropriation—on products of mass consumption (gasoline, building materials, flour, bread, beverages). This narrative presents a diagnosis and an apparently easy solution. The message works; it is false but plausible. The other side, meanwhile, remains reluctant to utter its own counterargument, if it even has one to offer.

Another reason no government that is capable of standing up to Cuba or Venezuela—Colombia, Costa Rica, Mexico, Peru, perhaps Chile—wants to is because all are terrified of being left hanging by Washington. President Felipe Calderon in Mexico could have refrained from his unfortunate reconciliation with Chávez if he had felt the White House was behind him in pursuing a course of ideological confrontation. President Alvaro Uribe in Colombia could have taken the treasure trove of incriminating evidence found in the captured computers of the Revolutionary Armed Forces of Colombia, or FARC, guerrillas and accused Chávez of aiding and abetting terrorism in Latin America; he also refrained, harboring doubts about Washington's backbone. President Alan Garcia in Peru could have shut down the Chavista Casas del ALBA in his country and expelled the Venezuelan activists, but with no allies to support him, he preferred to avoid a spat with Chávez.

Washington has also not been forthcoming with other kinds of support for its friends in the region who could use its backing to take on Havana and Caracas politically. Three examples stand out: the Mérida Initiative for Mexico, retaining the tariff on ethanol imports (applicable mainly to Brazil) in the 2008 version of the farm bill, and the free-trade agreement with Colombia.

In the first case, Calderon went out on a limb by breaking with Mexico's anachronistic stance of neither requesting nor receiving large-scale drug-enforcement aid from the United States. He was promised, in theory, a lot of money very quickly and with no strings—relating to human rights or anticorruption—attached at a summit meeting with Bush in Mérida, Mexico, in March 2007. This subsequently morphed into a three-year, $1.4 billion package with some fig-leaf conditionality; in turn, this pledge was transformed by the U.S. Congress into a one-year appropriation of $400 million worth of, among other things, low-grade technology (no Black Hawk helicopters) with four significant (and sensible) human rights and anticorruption conditions. Calderon found himself in a singularly uncomfortable position; either reject U.S. support and thereby undercut his commitment to fighting a no-holds-barred war on the drug cartels or accept what the traditional Mexican political elite, of which Calderon is a distinguished member, considered humiliating and unacceptable conditions. In the end, a compromise was reached, one that saved face for everyone but left no one happy. Either Bush misled Calderon or the latter's aides misled their boss, but in either case, the beleaguered Mexican president was embarrassed and forced to resort to obsolete nationalist rhetoric to regain his balance. If anything, the incident made Calderon even more wary of waging the battle of ideas against Chávez and the Castro brothers.

A similar misstep took place with Lula, who has taken remarkably bold steps in reaching out to the United States, especially for a former left-wing union leader. He has welcomed Bush to his country twice, visited him at Camp David, and signed a biofuel cooperation agreement with Washington. Lula knew Bush could not repeal the existing 54-cents-per-gallon tariff on ethanol imports into the United States, but he expected that Bush would surely attempt to exclude it when the 2001 farm bill came up for reauthorization in 2008. As a major sugar-based ethanol producer, Brazil is eager to enter the world's largest energy market, but the tariff makes Brazilian ethanol entirely uncompetitive in that highly protected market. Once again, a Latin American leader who took courageous risks in trying to fashion a functional relationship with Washington was let down by his American interlocutor, who was simply unable to deliver.

With Friends Like These . . .

The free-trade agreement with Colombia is in the same category. Bush undeniably fought for it, and Uribe lobbied personally for it in Washington, but at best it will be approved during a lame-duck session of Congress at the end of the year, and perhaps not even then. Strictly speaking, this unfortunate outcome is not the White House's fault. Nonetheless, when the Bush administration finally got down to forcing a vote on it, Bush found he lacked the political leverage to deliver his own party, let alone members of Congress from across the aisle. This stands in stark contrast to when Clinton sought to push through NAFTA, which was approved largely with Republican votes.

One reason for the difference lies in the timing. The defeat of the trade agreement with Colombia came close to the end of the Bush administration; victory for Clinton came at the end of the first year of his first term. But another reason—the main one—has to do with priorities. Clinton made NAFTA one; Bush did not, because for most of Bush's term there has been only one foreign policy priority—Iraq. Also, Bush was ultimately unwilling to accept that or to persuade Uribe that concerns about human rights in Colombia, expressed mainly by Democrats and nongovernmental organizations, were real and sincere, even if some specific accusations were off base. Bush and Uribe just did not get it. As a result, Congress delivered an undeserved slap to the face of the otherwise highly successful Colombian president— and an unwitting pat on the back to his Venezuelan neighbor. What better proof could Chávez offer of U.S. perfidy than the betrayal of its best friend in the hemisphere? No wonder Uribe is reluctant to resort to regional or international institutions to deal with the FARC. If Washington were to support him on that as halfheartedly as it did on trade, such an attempt would be foolhardy indeed.

The free-trade issue with Colombia leads to a broader discussion of trade, the fourth issue Washington can learn some lessons from the EU'S practices. First, clear and explicit human rights and democracy clauses should be tacked onto the agreements, as addenda rather than as new chapters, along the same lines as similar clauses in the

Mexican and Chilean free-trade agreements with the EU. Second, more specific labor, environmental, gender-rights, and indigenous-rights clauses should be included, as well as antitrust, regulatory, and judicial-reform provisions—for reasons of both principle and political expediency. Without them, these agreements will soon become, more than ever, targets of nongovernmental organizations and grass-roots and political opposition. Although there have been enormous improvements in Latin America in most of these fields in recent years, their remains a huge agenda, particularly with regard to breaking up or regulating the enormous monopolies—public, private, commercial, labor-union -based—that plague nearly every country in the region, beginning with its largest ones, Brazil and Mexico.

Third, and perhaps most important, the agreements should include bold, enlightened provisions for infrastructure and "social-cohesion" funds, since these can make the difference between mediocre muddling through and true success with free trade. Free-trade advocates should view Obama's demand that U.S. trade deals be revisited not as a mistake but rather as an opportunity to improve and deepen them; improving infrastructure, education and the rule of law in Mexico and Central America and improving drug-enforcement efforts and respect for labor laws and human rights in Colombia and Peru—all are in the United States' interest, and free-trade agreements can help, rather than harm, such efforts.

The Opportunity of a Lifetime

The next U.S. president has a unique chance to bring up to date a relationship that is ready to be substantially transformed for the first time since Franklin Roosevelt's Good Neighbor Policy (John F. Kennedy's Alliance for Progress was a good idea, but just that). Latin America today is growing at a faster pace than at any time since the 1970s; it has consolidated and deepened its democratic roots like never before and is more willing than ever to play a responsible role on the world stage. The United States needs the region dearly, as resistance to its world hegemony springs up everywhere and with greater virulence than at any time since the end of World War II.

The Rise of China and the Future of the West

Can the Liberal System Survive?

G. JOHN IKENBERRY

Contrary to the much recent pessimism about the decline of U.S. power, Ikenberry argues that the rise of China does not truly threaten U.S. dominance of the international system. He argues that China will seek to work cooperatively with the United States within the existing framework of international norms and institutions. Ikenberry concludes that even though the U.S.A. cannot prevent the rise of China to great power status, it can help to ensure that China works with other countries in a cooperative manner.

The rise of China will undoubtedly be one of the great dramas of the twenty-first century. China's extraordinary economic growth and active diplomacy are already transforming East Asia, and future decades will see even greater increases in Chinese power and influence. But exactly how this drama will play out is an open question. Will China overthrow the existing order or become a part of it? And what, if anything, can the United States do to maintain its position as China rises?

Some observers believe that the American era is coming to an end, as the Western-oriented world order is replaced by one increasingly dominated by the East. The historian Niall Ferguson has written that the bloody twentieth century witnessed "the descent of the West" and "a reorientation of the world" toward the East. Realists go on to note that as China gets more powerful and the United States' position erodes, two things are likely to happen: China will try to use its growing influence to reshape the rules and institutions of the international system to better serve its interests, and other states in the system—especially the declining hegemon—will start to see China as a growing security threat. The result of these developments, they predict, will be tension, distrust, and conflict, the typical features of a power transition. In this view, the drama of China's rise will feature an increasingly powerful China and a declining United States locked in an epic battle over the rules and leadership of the international system. And as the world's largest country emerges not from within but outside the established post-World War II international order, it is a drama that will end with the grand ascendance of China and the onset of an Asian-centered world order.

That course, however, is not inevitable. The rise of China does not have to trigger a wrenching hegemonic transition. The U.S.-Chinese power transition can be very different from those of the past because China faces an international order that is fundamentally different from those that past rising states confronted. China does not just face the United States; it faces a Western-centered system that is open, integrated, and rule-based, with wide and deep political foundations. The nuclear revolution, meanwhile, has made war among great powers unlikely—eliminating the major tool that rising powers have used to overturn international systems defended by declining hegemonic states. Today's Western order, in short, is hard to overturn and easy to join.

This unusually durable and expansive order is itself the product of farsighted U.S. leadership. After World War II, the United States did not simply establish itself as the leading world power. It led in the creation of universal institutions that not only invited global membership but also brought democracies and market societies closer together. It built an order that facilitated the participation and integration of both established great powers and newly independent states. (It is often forgotten that this postwar order was designed in large part to reintegrate the defeated Axis states and the beleaguered Allied states into a unified international system.) Today, China can gain full access to and thrive within this system. And if it does, China will rise, but the Western order—if managed properly—will live on.

As it faces an ascendant China, the United States should remember that its leadership of the Western order allows it to shape the environment in which China will make critical strategic choices. If it wants to preserve this leadership, Washington must work to strengthen the rules and institutions that underpin that order—making it even easier to join and harder to overturn. U.S. grand strategy should be built around the motto "The road to the East runs through the West." It must sink the roots of this order as deeply as possible, giving China greater incentives for integration than for opposition and increasing the chances that the system will survive even after U.S. relative power has declined.

The United States' "unipolar moment" will inevitably end. If the defining struggle of the twenty-first century is between China and the United States, China will have the advantage. If the defining struggle is between China and a revived Western system, the West will triumph.

Transitional Anxieties

China is well on its way to becoming a formidable global power. The size of its economy has quadrupled since the launch of market reforms in the late

1970s and, by some estimates, will double again over the next decade. It has become one of the world's major manufacturing centers and consumes roughly a third of the global supply of iron, steel, and coal. It has accumulated massive foreign reserves, worth more than $1 trillion at the end of 2006. China's military spending has increased at an inflation-adjusted rate of over 18 percent a year, and its diplomacy has extended its reach not just in Asia but also in Africa, Latin America, and the Middle East. Indeed, whereas the Soviet Union rivaled the United States as a military competitor only, China is emerging as both a military and an economic rival—heralding a profound shift in the distribution of global power.

Power transitions are a recurring problem in international relations. As scholars such as Paul Kennedy and Robert Gilpin have described it, world politics has been marked by a succession of powerful states rising up to organize the international system. A powerful state can create and enforce the rules and institutions of a stable global order in which to pursue its interests and security. But nothing lasts forever: long-term changes in the distribution of power give rise to new challenger states, who set off a struggle over the terms of that international order. Rising states want to translate their newly acquired power into greater authority in the global system—to reshape the rules and institutions in accordance with their own interests. Declining states, in turn, fear their loss of control and worry about the security implications of their weakened position.

These moments are fraught with danger. When a state occupies a commanding position in the international system, neither it nor weaker states have an incentive to change the existing order. But when the power of a challenger state grows and the power of the leading state weakens, a strategic rivalry ensues, and conflict—perhaps leading to war—becomes likely. The danger of power transitions is captured most dramatically in the case of late-nineteenth-century Germany. In 1870, the United Kingdom had a three-to-one advantage in economic power over Germany and a significant military advantage as well; by 1903, Germany had pulled ahead in terms of both economic and military power. As Germany unified and grew, so, too, did its dissatisfactions and demands, and as it grew more powerful, it increasingly appeared as a threat to other great powers in Europe, and security competition began. In the strategic realignments that followed, France, Russia, and the United Kingdom, formerly enemies, banded together to confront an emerging Germany. The result was a European war. Many observers see this dynamic emerging in U.S.-Chinese relations. "If China continues its impressive economic growth over the next few decades," the realist scholar John Mearsheimer has written, "the United States and China are likely to engage in an intense security competition with considerable potential for war."

But not all power transitions generate war or overturn the old order. In the early decades of the twentieth century, the United Kingdom ceded authority to the United States without great conflict or even a rupture in relations. From the late 1940s to the early 1990s, Japan's economy grew from the equivalent of five percent of U.S. GDP to the equivalent of over 60 percent of U.S. GDP, and yet Japan never challenged the existing international order.

Clearly, there are different types of power transitions. Some states have seen their economic and geopolitical power grow dramatically and have still accommodated themselves to the existing order. Others have risen up and sought to change it. Some power transitions have led to the breakdown of the old order and the establishment of a new international hierarchy. Others have brought about only limited adjustments in the regional and global system.

A variety of factors determine the way in which power transitions unfold. The nature of the rising state's regime and the degree of its dissatisfaction with the old order are critical: at the end of the nineteenth century, the United States, a liberal country an ocean away from Europe, was better able to embrace the British-centered international order than Germany was. But even more decisive is the character of the international order itself—for it is the nature of the international order that shapes a rising state's choice between challenging that order and integrating into it.

Open Order

The postwar Western order is historically unique. Any international order dominated by a powerful state is based on a mix of coercion and consent, but the U.S.-led order is distinctive in that it has been more liberal than imperial—and so unusually accessible, legitimate, and durable. Its rules and institutions are rooted in, and thus reinforced by, the evolving global forces of democracy and capitalism. It is expansive, with a wide and widening array of participants and stakeholders. It is capable of generating tremendous economic growth and power while also signaling restraint—all of which make it hard to overturn and easy to join.

It was the explicit intention of the Western order's architects in the 1940s to make that order integrative and expansive. Before the Cold War split the world into competing camps, Franklin Roosevelt sought to create a one-world system managed by cooperative great powers that would rebuild war-ravaged Europe, integrate the defeated states, and establish mechanisms for security cooperation and expansive economic growth. In fact, it was Roosevelt who urged—over the opposition of Winston Churchill—that China be included as a permanent member of the UN Security Council. The then Australian ambassador to the United States wrote in his diary after his first meeting with Roosevelt during the war, "He said that he had numerous discussions with Winston about China and that he felt that Winston was 40 years behind the times on China and he continually referred to the Chinese as 'Chinks' and 'Chinamen' and he felt that this was very dangerous. He wanted to keep China as a friend because in 40 or 50 years' time China might easily become a very powerful military nation."

Over the next half century, the United States used the system of rules and institutions it had built to good effect. West Germany was bound to its democratic Western European neighbors through the European Coal and Steel Community (and, later, the European Community) and to the United States through the Atlantic security pact; Japan was bound to the United States through an alliance partnership and expanding economic ties. The Bretton Woods meeting in 1944 laid down the monetary and trade rules that facilitated the opening and subsequent flourishing of the world economy—an astonishing achievement given the ravages of war and the competing interests of the great powers. Additional agreements between the United States, Western Europe, and Japan solidified the open and multilateral character of the postwar world economy. After the onset of the Cold War, the Marshall Plan in Europe and the 1951 security pact between the United States and Japan further integrated the defeated Axis powers into the Western order.

In the final days of the Cold War, this system once again proved remarkably successful. As the Soviet Union declined, the Western order offered a set of rules and institutions that provided Soviet leaders with both reassurances and points of access—effectively encouraging them to become a part of the system. Moreover, the shared leadership of the order ensured accommodation of the Soviet Union. As the Reagan administration pursued a hard-line policy toward Moscow, the Europeans pursued detente and engagement. For every hard-line "push," there was a moderating "pull," allowing Mikhail Gorbachev to pursue high-risk reforms. On the eve of German unification, the fact that a united Germany would be embedded in European and Atlantic institutions—rather than becoming an independent great power—helped reassure Gorbachev that neither German nor Western intentions were hostile. After the Cold War, the Western order once again managed the integration of a new wave of countries, this time from the formerly communist world. Three particular features of the Western order have been critical to this success and longevity.

First, unlike the imperial systems of the past, the Western order is built around rules and norms of nondiscrimination and market openness, creating conditions for rising states to advance their expanding economic and political goals within it. Across history, international orders have varied widely in terms of whether the material benefits that are generated accrue disproportionately to the leading state or are widely shared. In the Western system, the barriers to economic participation are low, and the potential benefits are high. China has already discovered the massive economic returns that are possible by operating within this open-market system.

Second is the coalition-based character of its leadership. Past orders have tended to be dominated by one state. The stakeholders of the current Western order include a coalition of powers arrayed around the United States—an important distinction. These leading states, most of them advanced liberal democracies, do not always agree, but they are engaged in a continuous process of give-and-take over economics, politics, and security. Power transitions are typically seen as being played out between two countries, a rising state and a declining hegemon, and the order falls as soon as the power balance shifts. But in the current order, the larger aggregation of democratic capitalist states—and the resulting accumulation of geopolitical power—shifts the balance in the order's favor.

Third, the postwar Western order has an unusually dense, encompassing, and broadly endorsed system of rules and institutions. Whatever its shortcomings, it is more open and rule-based than any previous order. State sovereignty and the rule of law are not just norms enshrined in the United Nations Charter. They are part of the deep operating logic of the order. To be sure, these norms are evolving, and the United States itself has historically been ambivalent about binding itself to international law and institutions—and at no time more so than today. But the overall system is dense with multilateral rules and institutions—global and regional, economic, political, and security-related. These represent one of the great breakthroughs of the postwar era. They have laid the basis for unprecedented levels of cooperation and shared authority over the global system.

The incentives these features create for China to integrate into the liberal international order are reinforced by the changed nature of the international economic environment—especially the new interdependence driven by technology. The most farsighted Chinese leaders understand that globalization has changed the game and that China accordingly needs strong, prosperous partners around the world. From the United States' perspective, a healthy Chinese economy is vital to the United States and the rest of the world. Technology and the global economic revolution have created a logic of economic relations that is different from the past—making the political and institutional logic of the current order all the more powerful.

Accommodating the Rise

The most important benefit of these features today is that they give the Western order a remarkable capacity to accommodate rising powers. New entrants into the system have ways of gaining status and authority and opportunities to play a role in governing the order. The fact that the United States, China, and other great powers have nuclear weapons also limits the ability of a rising power to overturn the existing order. In the age of nuclear deterrence, great-power war is, thankfully, no longer a mechanism of historical change. War-driven change has been abolished as a historical process.

The Western order's strong framework of rules and institutions is already starting to facilitate Chinese integration. At first, China embraced certain rules and institutions for defensive purposes: protecting its sovereignty and economic interests while seeking to reassure other states of its peaceful intentions by getting involved in regional and global groupings. But as the scholar Marc Lanteigne argues, "What separates China from other states, and indeed previous global powers, is that not only is it 'growing up' within a milieu of international institutions far more developed than ever before, but more importantly, it is doing so while making active use of these institutions to promote the country's development of global power status." China, in short, is increasingly working within, rather than outside of, the Western order.

China is already a permanent member of the UN Security Council, a legacy of Roosevelt's determination to build the universal body around diverse great-power leadership. This gives China the same authority and advantages of "great-power exceptionalism" as the other permanent members. The existing global trading system is also valuable to China, and increasingly so. Chinese economic interests are quite congruent with the current global economic system—a system that is open and loosely institutionalized and that China has enthusiastically embraced and thrived in. State power today is ultimately based on sustained economic growth, and China is well aware that no major state can modernize without integrating into the globalized capitalist system; if a country wants to be a world power, it has no choice but to join the World Trade Organization (WTO). The road to global power, in effect, runs through the Western order and its multilateral economic institutions.

China not only needs continued access to the global capitalist system; it also wants the protections that the system's rules and institutions provide. The WTO's multilateral trade principles and dispute-settlement mechanisms, for example, offer China tools to defend against the threats of discrimination and protectionism that rising economic powers often confront. The evolution of China's policy suggests that Chinese leaders recognize these advantages: as Beijing's growing commitment to economic liberalization has increased the foreign investment and trade China has enjoyed, so has Beijing increasingly embraced global trade rules. It is possible that as China comes to champion the WTO, the support of the more mature Western economies for the WTO will wane. But it is more likely that both the rising and the declining countries will find value in the quasi-legal mechanisms that allow conflicts to be settled or at least diffused.

The existing international economic institutions also offer opportunities for new powers to rise up through their hierarchies. In the International Monetary Fund and the World Bank, governance is based on economic shares, which growing countries can translate into greater institutional voice. To be sure, the process of adjustment has been slow. The United States and Europe still dominate the IMF. Washington has a 17 percent voting share (down from 30 percent)—a controlling amount, because 85 percent approval is needed for action—and the European Union has a major say in the appointment of ten of the 24 members of the board.

But there are growing pressures, notably the need for resources and the need to maintain relevance, that will likely persuade the Western states to admit China into the inner circle of these economic governance institutions. The IMF's existing shareholders, for example, see a bigger role for rising developing countries as necessary to renew the institution and get it through its current crisis of mission. At the IMF's meeting in Singapore in September 2006, they agreed on reforms that will give China, Mexico, South Korea, and Turkey a greater voice.

As China sheds its status as a developing country (and therefore as a client of these institutions), it will increasingly be able to act as a patron and stakeholder instead. Leadership in these organizations is not simply a reflection of economic size (the United States has retained its voting share in the IMF even as its economic weight has declined); nonetheless, incremental advancement within them will create important opportunities for China.

Power Shift and Peaceful Change

Seen in this light, the rise of China need not lead to a volcanic struggle with the United States over global rules and leadership. The Western order has the potential to turn the coming power shift into a peaceful change on terms favorable to the United States. But that will only happen if the United States sets about strengthening the existing order. Today, with Washington preoccupied with terrorism and war in the Middle East, rebuilding Western rules and institutions might to some seem to be of only marginal relevance. Many Bush administration officials have been outright hostile to the multilateral, rule-based system that the United States has shaped and led. Such hostility is foolish and dangerous. China will become powerful: it is already on the rise, and the United States' most powerful strategic weapon is the ability to decide what sort of international order will be in place to receive it.

The United States must reinvest in the Western order, reinforcing the features of that order that encourage engagement, integration, and restraint. The more this order binds together capitalist democratic states in deeply rooted institutions; the more open, consensual, and rule-based it is; and the more widely spread its benefits, the more likely it will be that rising powers can and will secure their interests through integration and accommodation rather than through war. And if the Western system offers rules and institutions that benefit the full range of states—rising and falling, weak and strong, emerging and mature—its dominance as an international order is all but certain.

The first thing the United States must do is reestablish itself as the foremost supporter of the global system of governance that underpins the Western order. Doing so will first of all facilitate the kind of collective problem solving that makes all countries better off. At the same time, when other countries see the United States using its power to strengthen existing rules and institutions, that power is rendered more legitimate—and U.S. authority is strengthened. Countries within the West become more inclined to work with, rather than resist, U.S. power, which reinforces the centrality and dominance of the West itself.

Renewing Western rules and institutions will require, among other things, updating the old bargains that underpinned key postwar security pacts. The strategic understanding behind both NATO and Washington's East Asian alliances is that the United States will work with its allies to provide security and bring them in on decisions over the use of force, and U.S. allies, in return, will operate within the U.S.-led Western order. Security cooperation in the West remains extensive today, but with the main security threats less obvious than they were during the Cold War, the purposes and responsibilities of these alliances are under dispute. Accordingly, the United States needs to reaffirm the political value of these alliances—recognizing that they are part of a wider Western institutional architecture that allows states to do business with one another.

The United States should also renew its support for wide-ranging multilateral institutions. On the economic front, this would include building on the agreements and architecture of the WTO, including pursuing efforts to conclude the current Doha Round of trade talks, which seeks to extend market opportunities and trade liberalization to developing countries. The WTO is at a critical stage. The basic standard of nondiscrimination is at risk thanks to the proliferation of bilateral and regional trade agreements. Meanwhile, there are growing doubts over whether the WTO can in fact carry out trade liberalization, particularly in agriculture, that benefits developing countries. These issues may seem narrow, but the fundamental character of the liberal international order—its commitment to universal rules of openness that spread gains widely—is at stake. Similar doubts haunt a host of other multilateral agreements—on global warming and nuclear nonproliferation, among others—and they thus also demand renewed U.S. leadership.

The strategy here is not simply to ensure that the Western order is open and rule-based. It is also to make sure that the order does not fragment into an array of bilateral and "minilateral" arrangements, causing the United States to find itself tied to only a few key states in various regions. Under such a scenario, China would have an opportunity to build its own set of bilateral and "minilateral" pacts. As a result, the world would be broken into competing U.S. and Chinese spheres. The more security and economic relations are multilateral and all-encompassing, the more the global system retains its coherence.

In addition to maintaining the openness and durability of the order, the United States must redouble its efforts to integrate rising developing countries into key global institutions. Bringing emerging countries into the governance of the international order will give it new life. The United States and Europe must find room at the table not only for China but also for countries such as Brazil, India, and South Africa. A Goldman Sachs report on the so-called BRICs (Brazil, Russia, India, and China) noted that by 2050 these countries' economies could together be larger than those of the original G-6 countries (Germany, France, Italy, Japan, the United Kingdom, and the United States) combined. Each international institution presents its own challenges. The UN Security Council is perhaps the hardest to deal with, but its reform would also bring the greatest returns. Less formal bodies—the so-called G-20 and various other intergovernmental networks—can provide alternative avenues for voice and representation.

The Triumph of the Liberal Order

The key thing for U.S. leaders to remember is that it may be possible for China to overtake the United States alone, but it is much less likely that China will ever manage to overtake the Western order. In terms of economic weight, for example, China will surpass the United States as the largest state in the global system sometime around 2020. (Because of its population, China needs a level of productivity only one-fifth that of the United States to become the world's biggest economy.) But when the economic capacity of the Western system as a whole is considered, China's economic advances look much less significant; the Chinese economy will be much smaller than the combined economies of the Organization for Economic Cooperation and Development far into the future. This is even truer of military might: China cannot hope to come anywhere close to total OECD military expenditures anytime soon. The capitalist democratic world is a powerful constituency for the preservation—and, indeed, extension—of the existing international order. If China intends to rise up and challenge the existing order, it has a much more daunting task than simply confronting the United States.

The "unipolar moment" will eventually pass. U.S. dominance will eventually end. U.S. grand strategy, accordingly, should be driven by one key question: What kind of international order would the United States like to see in place when it is less powerful?

This might be called the neo-Rawlsian question of the current era. The political philosopher John Rawls argued that political institutions should be conceived behind a "veil of ignorance"—that is, the architects should design institutions as if they do not know precisely where they will be within a socioeconomic system. The result would be a system that safeguards a person's interests regardless of whether he is rich or poor, weak or strong. The United States needs to take that approach to its leadership of the international order today. It must put in place institutions and fortify rules that will safeguard its interests regardless of where exactly in the hierarchy it is or how exactly power is distributed in 10, 50, or 100 years.

Fortunately, such an order is in place already. The task now is to make it so expansive and so institutionalized that China has no choice but to become a full-fledged member of it. The United States cannot thwart China's rise, but it can help ensure that China's power is exercised within the rules and institutions that the United States and its partners have crafted over the last century, rules and institutions that can protect the interests of all states in the more crowded world of the future. The United States' global position may be weakening, but the international system the United States leads can remain the dominant order of the twenty-first century.

India's Rise, America's Interest

The Fate of the U.S.-Indian Partnership

EVAN A. FEIGENBAUM

Feigenbaum argues that India has abandoned its former position of nonalignment to become a major ally of the United States since 2002. He explores the ramifications of India's potential rise to superpower status, as fueled by its rapidly expanding economy. Feigenbaum deals with U.S.-Indian interactions on a spectrum of issues including climate change, economic development, prospects for an Indian seat on the U.N. Security Council, and India's capacity to project power. Finally, he examines the complex interplay between the U.S.A., India and other countries in South Asia and East Asia, including Afghanistan, Pakistan, and China.

Until the late 1990s, the United States often ignored India, treating it as a regional power in South Asia with little global weight. India's weak and protected economy gave it little influence in global markets, and its nonaligned foreign policy caused periodic tension with Washington. When the United States did concentrate on India, it too often fixated on India's military rivalry with Pakistan.

Today, however, India is dynamic and transforming. Starting in 1991, leaders in New Delhi—including Manmohan Singh, then India's finance minister and now its prime minister—pursued policies of economic liberalization that opened the country to foreign investment and yielded rapid growth. India is now an important economic power, on track (according to Goldman Sachs and others) to become a top-five global economy by 2030. It is a player in global economic decisions as part of both the G-20 and the G-8 + 5 (the G-8 plus the five leading emerging economies) and may ultimately attain a permanent seat on the United Nations Security Council. India's trajectory has diverged sharply from that of Pakistan.

With economic growth, India acquired the capacity to act on issues of primary strategic and economic concern to the United States. The United States, in turn, has developed a growing stake in continued Indian reform and success—especially as they contribute to global growth, promote market-based economic policies, help secure the global commons, and maintain a mutually favorable balance of power in Asia. For its part, New Delhi seeks a United States that will help facilitate India's rise as a major power.

Two successive Indian governments have pursued a strategic partnership with the United States that would have been unthinkable in the era of the Cold War and nonalignment. This turnaround in relations culminated in 2008, when the two countries signed a civil nuclear agreement. That deal helped end India's nuclear isolation by permitting the conduct of civil nuclear trade with New Delhi, even though India is not a party to the Nuclear Nonproliferation Treaty. Important as the agreement was, however, the U.S.-Indian relationship remains constrained. For example, although U.S. officials hold standing dialogues about nearly every region of the world with their counterparts from Beijing, Brussels, and Tokyo, no such arrangements exist with New Delhi.

The future scope of the U.S.-Indian relationship will depend, then, on choices made in both Washington and New Delhi: the United States looks to India to sustain its economic and social change while still embracing a partnership with Washington, and India looks to the United States to respect Indian security concerns. And the countries will need to carefully manage looming disagreements between them, including on Afghanistan, Pakistan, and China.

A Transformed Relationship

U.S. President Barack Obama and Indian Prime Minister Manmohan Singh can pursue an enduring partnership because they do not face any of the three principal obstacles that constrained U.S.-Indian cooperation in the past: Cold War politics, a stagnant commercial relationship, and disagreements over India's nuclear program.

During the Cold War, India's policy of non-alignment struck many in the United States as tantamount to alignment with the Soviet Union, especially after the Indian-Soviet treaty of friendship was signed in 1971. And nonalignment was as deeply rooted in India as it was lamented in Washington: the policy dated back to India's first prime minister, Jawaharlal Nehru, who viewed non-alignment as a way for India to exercise international leadership after the end of British rule. But after the collapse of the Soviet Union—one of its largest trading partners and its primary security partner—India began to reassess its priorities, and opportunities emerged for greater cooperation with the United States.

Yet even after India began to abandon nonalignment, there was little economic exchange between the two countries. Until the reforms of the 1990s, India was not well integrated into the global economy. It pursued protectionist policies, such as bars to foreign investment in many sectors, that made trade with the United States difficult. As recently as 2002, Robert Blackwill, then the U.S. ambassador to India, complained that U.S. trade flows to India

were as "flat as a chapati" (chapati is a thin Indian bread). For all of India's growth in manufacturing and increased trade volume over the 1990s, the country remained disconnected from the global supply and production chains that linked so many Asian economies to the United States. But further reforms in recent years have made India one of the United States' fastest-growing commercial partners. Annual two-way trade more than doubled between 2004 and 2008, from just under $30 billion to $66 billion. And investment has begun to flow both ways. According to the Office of the U.S. Trade Representative, Indian direct investment in the United States reached $4.5 billion in 2008, just over a 60 percent increase from 2007.

Still, the thorniest obstacle to U.S.-Indian cooperation was India's nuclear program. In the years after India's first nuclear test, in 1974, Washington imposed sanctions on India that severely restricted its access to technology, fuel supplies, and technical assistance in the nuclear field. After India's subsequent tests, in 1998, the United States cut off direct foreign assistance, commercial export credits, and certain technology transfers. As U.S.-Indian relations began to warm in subsequent years, Indians of all political persuasions condemned the United States as hypocritical for seeking a strategic partnership with India while simultaneously targeting it with punitive sanctions. The United States abandoned this approach during George W. Bush's first term and had completed a total reversal by the end of his second, when the civil nuclear agreement lifted restrictions on nuclear commerce. Although negotiated by a Republican administration, the deal passed a Democratic-controlled Congress with overwhelming bipartisan backing (including the votes of then Senators Joe Biden, Hillary Clinton, and Obama), demonstrating that support for strengthened U.S.-Indian relations extends across party lines in Washington, much as it does in India. Also bolstering the relationship are both American and Indian businesspeople, the nearly 100,000 Indian students currently studying in U.S. schools, some three million Indian Americans, and the tens of millions of Indians with relatives in the United States.

Through their civil nuclear negotiations, the United States and India developed unprecedented habits of cooperation. To earn the approval of the nearly 50 other countries on the International Atomic Energy Agency's Board of Governors and in the Nuclear Suppliers Group, the United States and India coordinated more closely than ever before on their diplomatic and political strategies. Partly as a result, officials in Washington and New Delhi can now work better together on vital issues such as counterterrorism, defense, and intelligence cooperation—as demonstrated by the joint U.S.-Indian response to the November 2008 terrorist attacks in Mumbai.

Still, a number of hurdles remain before the United States and India can build a more enduring, strategic, and global partnership. First, India needs to bolster its emergence as a major power—not least by sustaining high rates of economic growth. This will require India to further open its economy to competition and investment and advance ongoing reforms aimed at relieving inequality, expanding the middle class, and strengthening the country's physical infrastructure.

Second, India's emerging global influence will be sustainable only if India develops new doctrines and diplomatic capacities. The country has moved beyond nonalignment, to be sure, but has not yet coalesced around a new foreign policy vision. And although New Delhi may ultimately settle on a strategy that is conducive to a more open and global partnership with the United States, that is not assured.

Third, the United States needs to be sensitive to Indian concerns in a number of areas that directly affect Indian interests. Differences loom between Washington and New Delhi regarding U.S. policy toward Afghanistan and Pakistan, China, climate change, and other issues. Managing such disputes—by reaching agreement or at least by mitigating the effects of disagreement—will be vital to effective cooperation.

India's Pivotal Transformations

Just as Indian reforms in the 1990s paved the way for the recent transformation of U.S.-Indian relations,

Indian policy choices in the coming years will shape both the country's rise and its relationship with Washington going forward. The most consequential factor of all may be whether India grows economically and integrates further with the world's other major economies. Unless it does so, India is unlikely to exert decisive influence on international economics or politics.

It is fitting, then, that Singh's government—which earned a fresh mandate and expanded its parliamentary majority in elections last year—is focused almost entirely on domestic considerations. The government's top priority is to restore the nine percent annual growth rate that India enjoyed before the recent global economic crisis. As the crisis was unfolding, many Indians argued that their economy was safely decoupled from global trends because it did not depend heavily on foreign demand for Indian exports and its relatively closed financial sector had little exposure to toxic assets. But during the crisis, exports collapsed, capital left the country, and corporate India lost access to many sources of overseas financing. Although Singh's government adopted a fiscal stimulus plan in December 2008 that included heavy capital and infrastructure spending, Indian growth slowed from nine percent in 2007–8 to 6.7 percent in 2008–9, which is around where it is likely to remain until at least 2011, according to the Organization for Economic Cooperation and Development.

To win votes and broaden public support for growth-inducing reforms, India's government is seeking to expand various welfare measures. In the past, Indian voters have punished both major political parties for enacting reforms that appeared to benefit elites disproportionately. This was one reason why the Indian National Congress, after coming to power in 2004, pursued expanded welfare programs alongside measures to increase economic growth, especially in rural India. When the party won reelection in 2009, many commentators credited the Congress-led government's rural employment guarantee and debt waivers for farmers as the principal reasons for its larger-than-expected margin of victory. Now, party leaders are all the more dedicated to raising the incomes of poor and rural Indians: the government's first postelection budget extended the rural debt waiver, boosted spending on the ongoing rural employment guarantee by 144 percent, and hiked the rural infrastructure program by 45 percent.

To facilitate the kind of growth it seeks, India is also improving its physical infrastructure. Just two percent of Indian roads are highways, even though most freight and nearly all passenger traffic are carried by road. Rutted highways, old airports, decaying ports, and chronic electricity shortages weaken nearly every aspect of India's economy: the roads between India's four largest cities are poor, New Delhi's showpiece high-tech district of Gurgaon has gone dark and hot, and power for lights and air conditioning often fails even in state capitals. For India to sustain high GDP growth, Singh told Parliament in 2008, it will have to increase its electricity generation by eight to ten percent annually. By 2012, the government aims to increase infrastructure-related spending from four percent of GDP to nine percent, on par with the rate that gave China the world's third-largest road and rail networks. India's plans include completing construction on the Golden Quadrilateral, a multibillion-dollar superhighway linking New Delhi, Kolkata, Chennai, and Mumbai. India's success or failure in developing its physical infrastructure will say much about its broader potential, because the stakes are high and the obstacles are many. State seizures of land are difficult, cost overruns and political horse-trading are endemic, and violence between the dispossessed and the land-takers is increasingly common.

A further impediment to India's economic ambitions is social: although the country has world-class talent in some areas, such as information technology, it still faces daunting challenges in its labor market and in its education system. Indian labor is disproportionately rural and heavily concentrated in unorganized activities and sectors. Manish Sabharwal, chair of the country's leading temporary-employment agency, has described a series of transitions that would strengthen the Indian work force: from farm to nonfarm, rural to urban, unorganized to organized, school to work, subsistence to a decent wage, and job preservation to job creation. But whether these transitions take place will depend in part on India's education system. Demand for education, especially from the growing middle class, vastly outstrips supply, and 160 million Indian children are out of school. And a UNESCO index recently ranked India 102 out of 129 countries on the extent, gender balance, and quality of its primary education and adult literacy. Thus, as Europe, Japan, and others pay a price for their aging work forces, India risks missing the opportunity to benefit from its significantly younger population.

Finally, there is the challenge of domestic security. The November 2008 attacks in Mumbai dominated headlines around the world, but other major Indian metropolises were bombed throughout 2008: Jaipur in May, Ahmadabad and Bangalore in July, and New Delhi's most famous shopping area, Connaught Place, in September. Indian security is challenged not only by the threat of terrorism—which often emanates from inside Pakistan—but also by the domestic insurgency of the leftist Naxalites. India's effectiveness in combating these threats is weakened by the highly federalized structure of its government. Indian intelligence and law enforcement have weak traditions of cooperation; policing is largely a state, not a federal, matter; and there is insufficient coordination among the states. The government is working to centralize aspects of the security system, promote coordination, expand personnel, and boost budgets, but the situation is improving only slowly.

Although these security threats could greatly affect India's fate, its economic and social choices will be the principal determinant of its success. And choices about economics, infrastructure, and human capital, in turn, will largely determine India's capacity for global influence and thus the potential scope of U.S.-Indian cooperation.

Between G-20 and G-77

Ever since India's growing economic weight began yielding new strategic possibilities, Indians have been debating their evolving interests. One still unresolved question—which is politically explosive to many in India—is how best to pursue partnerships with the advanced industrial countries, especially the United States.

The issue of climate change has brought this debate to the fore. In a memo leaked last October, India's environment minister, Jairam Ramesh, argued that India should curb its emissions without regard to whether advanced industrial countries provide India with the technology and funding to do so—a reversal of long-standing Indian policy. The reason, said Ramesh, was that India should act "in self interest" and "not stick with G77 [a group of developing countries, including India] but be embedded in G20 [a grouping of the world's major economies, also including India]." The memo prompted a political firestorm. Although the interests of a more powerful and economically integrated India are increasingly overlapping with those of the United States and other G-20 countries, many Indians do not believe that their interests lie primarily with the world's developed countries. Faced with a backlash from politicians, including some of his colleagues, Ramesh backtracked at the Copenhagen summit on climate change in December, and Indian negotiators aligned themselves closely with China and other G-77 partners.

The 2008 civil nuclear deal with the United States ignited even broader debates about what sort of international company India should keep. As Shiv Shankar Menon, who served as Indian foreign secretary during the U.S.-Indian nuclear negotiations, said in 2009, the deal was "about the merits of trusting the [United States] or the consequences of a particular line of policy rather than about the substance of the agreements themselves." India's Communists opposed the deal largely for this reason; Prakash Karat, the head of India's leading communist party, argued in 2007 that as a result of the deal, "India would be locked into a strategic tie-up which would have a long lasting impact on India's foreign policy and strategic autonomy." Even some stalwarts of the ruling Indian National Congress were skeptical of the deal. Yet in order to overcome its nuclear isolation, the Congress-led government moved forward with the agreement, aligning itself overtly with the United States.

Indeed, many of India's recent foreign policy decisions have been unprecedented: It has backed three U.S.-supported resolutions against Iran in the International Atomic Energy Agency and is enforcing UN Security Council sanctions against Tehran. It stopped a North Korean ship in Indian waters in August 2009 and inspected its cargo, a move supportive of U.S. (and United Nations) nonproliferation objectives. It is the fifth-largest donor of reconstruction assistance to Afghanistan. It is participating in nearly every U.S.-supported multinational technology initiative for tackling climate change, including projects on hydrogen, carbon sequestration, and nuclear fusion. It has harmonized its export controls with the guidelines of the Nuclear Suppliers Group and the Missile Technology Control Regime and has committed to adhere to future changes in these guidelines. It provided tsunami relief to Indonesia in 2004 through an ad hoc naval partnership with the United States and two of Washington's closest military allies, Australia and Japan. Its military has conducted exercises with every branch of the U.S. armed services. And it has engaged in trilateral military exercises with the United States and Japan, despite Chinese protests. For a country that long cherished its nonalignment policy, such public associations with the United States represent a break from long-standing reflexes. Whether the break will be enduring will depend on the outcome of wider debates over India's foreign policy vision.

A Tale of Influence

India's global aspirations are constrained by its geography. Although India is the most stable country in South Asia, events in less stable neighboring countries threaten to occupy its attention and derail its aspirations: Pakistan is confronting institutional weakness and growing extremism; Nepal may fail as its elites jockey for power and struggle to integrate former Maoist insurgents into the political mainstream; Sri Lanka is struggling with ethnic and constitutional challenges; and Bangladesh and Myanmar (also known as Burma) are yielding unwelcome exports, such as economic migrants, refugees, and extremists.

India's relationship with Pakistan is particularly worrying, as it has deteriorated significantly in recent years. In the early years of this century, India made substantial strides in its relationship with Pakistan, including a cease-fire in 2003, enhanced trade and travel links, and a back-channel dialogue with the government of Pervez Musharraf that arrived at broad parameters of understanding on the most contentious issues, including Kashmir. But politics in both countries, especially Pakistan, were not conducive to normalizing relations, much less reaching a final peaceful settlement. Major terrorist attacks on India planned in Pakistan, particularly the November 2008 attacks in Mumbai, soured the atmosphere for negotiations. And today, political power in Pakistan is splintered, and extremism is spreading to major Pakistani cities from the tribal areas bordering Afghanistan. Thus, even as India's interests increasingly reach beyond South Asia, these dangers may force New Delhi to focus less on global issues than on priorities closer to home.

To become a bigger player on the world stage, New Delhi will need to achieve two major goals: first, break the confining shackles of South Asia and become a truly Asian power that is integrated into the East Asian economic system and influential throughout the wider region; and second, project its power and influence globally, whether by assuming a role in protecting the global commons, shaping international finance, becoming a more significant aid donor, or leveraging its seat in the G-20 and other leading international institutions.

India is already beginning to meet the first challenge. Having played an insignificant strategic and economic role in East Asia from the 1960s through the mid-1990s—partly because it rejected the successful model of export-led growth that linked other Asian economies to the United States during the Cold War—India is now more involved in East Asia. One reason for this is that many in the region (and in India) are wary of China's growing strength and view a large, wealthy India as a buttress for the region's balance of power. In recent years, New Delhi has signed free-trade agreements with Singapore, South Korea, and the Association of Southeast Asian Nations (ASEAN) and has joined regional institutions, such as the East Asia Summit and the ASEAN Regional Forum. India has also deepened its defense ties with Australia, Japan, Singapore, and Vietnam—four countries that are also wary of China's rise and maintain close, or have deepening, security ties with the United States. But the economic dimension of India's integration is lagging: India constitutes just 2.7 percent of ASEAN's total trade volume, whereas China constitutes 10.4 percent.

India's second challenge may prove tougher still. Although New Delhi has increased its profile in the Persian Gulf, Africa, and (to a lesser extent) Central Asia, its ability to project influence globally will depend on how it integrates its various efforts into a coherent strategy. The principal challenge will be to leverage its economic strength for strategic gain, as China has. So far, India's record of global power projection has been mixed.

One example is foreign aid, which both China and Japan have used to gain influence in Africa. India recently joined the fray by increasing its annual aid to Africa and offering $5 billion in credit at the 2008 Indian-African summit. But such aid has produced few strategic or commercial gains for India. Nor has it made India more powerful in Africa-focused institutions: India has been a member of the African Development Bank since 1982 but has less voting weight than nearly every other non-Western donor, including China, Japan, Saudi Arabia, and South Korea.

Various leading or emerging powers—including China, the European Union, Japan, and even Russia—demonstrate their strength by providing public goods, joining clubs of leading economies, leveraging their voting weight in international financial institutions, or deploying economic and financial tools to move global markets. India does less in these areas than Beijing, Brussels, or Tokyo. Consider the global commons. Although Indian interests are growing on the seas and in space and its antipiracy activities off the Horn of Africa are unprecedented, India remains more a beneficiary of public goods than a producer of them, especially when it comes to security. Likewise, India is now part of some of the world's most exclusive clubs, including the G-20, but some Indian decision-makers remain wary of other institutions that would welcome greater Indian involvement, including the

International Energy Agency, which coordinates global oil stockpiles. India's quest to join the world's most exclusive club, the UN Security Council, has so far been stymied.

Over the next five years, India is likely to make its mark on international financial institutions and global markets. At the G-20 conference last September, the members increased developing countries' representation in the International Monetary Fund and the World Bank, giving India greater clout in two important global institutions. India is also beginning to move markets and prices. Corporate India has gone global, acquiring leading brands, including Jaguar, Land Rover, and the aluminum maker Novelis. And the Indian government's purchase of 200 tons of gold from the IMF in 2009 signaled that Asian central banks were beginning to diversify their U.S. dollar holdings, boosting gold prices by as much as 2.2 percent.

A final challenge in India's drive for global influence will be for New Delhi to strengthen its ability to implement its foreign policy. As the former State Department official Daniel Markey has written, India's foreign policy "software" is underdeveloped and risks underperforming: India's foreign service is tiny; seniority often trumps other criteria for promotion in the foreign service; and think tanks and university area-studies programs are underfunded and small. Improvements in these domains will be important if India is to fashion and implement more global strategies.

Looming Disagreements

Although India's choices in domestic and foreign policy will be the most important factors affecting its power, stature, and partnerships in the coming years, decisions made by the United States will also matter greatly. This is especially true in areas that tangibly bear on Indian interests, such as Afghanistan. Washington and New Delhi must sustain momentum on the issues they have made progress on over the last decade, including cooperation on defense, trade, energy, the environment, and education. The tougher challenge will be to manage looming disagreements on five potentially divisive strategic issues: Afghanistan-Pakistan strategy, China policy, arms control, climate change, and high-technology

cooperation. Washington and New Delhi need to move their disagreements toward compromise, without reverting to the acrimony that characterized an earlier era in their bilateral relations.

Indians are asking three questions about the Obama administration's policy toward Afghanistan and Pakistan: Will the United States stay and fight in Afghanistan over time? Will it apply sustained pressure on Islamabad to crack down on groups and individuals that target India? And will it resist the temptation to call for Indian concessions to Pakistan, in the hope that this will encourage the Pakistani government to change its priorities and focus on defeating terrorism?

Obama's decision to deploy 30,000 additional troops to Afghanistan should reassure those Indians who view the fight there as a test of U.S. staying power in South Asia. But many Indians are concerned with Obama's emphasis on setting a timeline for withdrawal, scheduled to start in 2011. Washington's approach to Pakistan is even less reassuring to many Indians. How would the United States respond if another Mumbai-like attack occurred on Indian soil and New Delhi asked Washington to step up its pressure on Islamabad? And what if India responded militarily? Since the 2008 Mumbai attacks, the United States has increased its pressure on Pakistan to crack down on militant groups that target India; still, many in India want even greater U.S. pressure and fear that Washington might revert to its historical focus on the groups that target U.S. interests more directly.

There is a broad perception in India's strategic community that despite the many new elements of U.S.-Indian cooperation, the United States has recently been tilting toward Pakistan by ramping up its aid to the country and its military-to-military cooperation with Pakistan. Particularly concerning to many Indians is the suggestion made by some influential U.S. commentators that Washington should push New Delhi to alter its military posture toward Pakistan—or even make lasting concessions on Kashmir—in the hope that Pakistan would then remove resources from its eastern border and focus them instead on fighting al Qaeda and the Taliban.

Most Indians see this approach as blaming the victim. They also view it as unnecessary and unwelcome U.S. interference in what had been, until recently, a constructive back-channel negotiating process between India and Pakistan. Such U.S. pressure would be flatly rejected in New Delhi and would set back U.S.-Indian relations. It might also undermine the Indian-Pakistani peace process. And it would be unlikely to persuade Pakistan to redeploy its forces: after all, even during the period of greatest progress between New Delhi and Islamabad—which ended with the terrorist attacks in India in 2006 and then the fall of Musharraf's government in 2008—Pakistan did not substantially alter its priorities or redeploy its forces from east to west.

China poses additional challenges to India and the U.S.-Indian partnership. Many in India believe that the Obama administration has tilted its policy toward Beijing in a way that undermines Indian interests. Yet Obama's China policy is broadly consistent with that of every U.S. president since Richard Nixon. This Indian concern is based on a fear that China's increasing weight could lead Washington to pursue a U.S.-Chinese condominium—a G-2, some have called it—which would sideline New Delhi even on issues of direct concern to India. Given China's close relations with Pakistan and continuing claims on Indian territory (including Arunachal Pradesh, a state twice as large as Switzerland), India does not view Beijing as an honest broker. And as U.S. officials are devoting increasing time and energy to cultivating the U.S.-Chinese relationship, Indians are asking whether Washington envisions a role for India in maintaining a balance of power in Asia, or whether the Obama administration views India as tangential to U.S. priorities there. More concretely, Indians worry that Washington may be unwilling to help India relieve the pressure from China if, for instance, tensions were ratcheted up further along the Chinese-Indian border.

China is particularly important because it has begun to replace Pakistan at the center of Indian defense planning. Although China considers India a third-tier security priority at best—far behind internal insecurity and challenges in the East Asian littoral—India views China as a first-tier priority. Developments in Chinese-Indian relations are central to India's internal debate about the reliability of

its strategic deterrent and whether to test nuclear weapons again.

This is one important reason why arms control is another potential source of tension between Washington and New Delhi. The Obama administration is preparing to renew U.S. efforts to ratify the Comprehensive Nuclear Test Ban Treaty. If China does so, too, India will be pressured to follow suit. But many Indians argue that the country cannot sign the CTBT in light of its nuclear competition with China; several Indian nuclear scientists have even sought to prod the government into conducting new nuclear tests by raising questions about whether India's 1998 tests really succeeded. For now, India is unlikely to conduct new tests. But it is equally unlikely to sign the CTBT or similar treaties, even if the Obama administration pressures it to do so.

Climate change is another potentially divisive issue. Both Washington and New Delhi support investment in green technologies, but internationally mandated and monitored emissions reductions are political dynamite in India, where they are often seen as a drag on growth and an affront to Indian sovereignty. India has agreed to emissions goals that would be subject to international "consultation and analysis" but not scrutiny or formal review. It has also offered to allow international monitoring of those of its mitigation activities that are supported by international funds or technologies but not of those that are domestically funded. Thus, although the United States and India may continue to cooperate on green technologies, their general approaches will likely limit the range of possible cooperation in global climate negotiations (as was evident at Copenhagen).

Finally, issues surrounding the transfer of technology (including for clean energy) are also contentious. India's government and its industrial sector have long complained that the United States' emphasis on national security export controls and intellectual property protection has excessively restricted licenses and transfers. Indians expect that if Washington views India as a partner, it should stop denying India so many dual-use and defense-related technologies. This complaint will almost certainly bleed into discussions of climate change and commercial cooperation on technology.

One way to mitigate the debilitating effects of these differences between the United States and India is to enrich bilateral cooperation in areas in which there is mutual agreement. On trade, for example, on which most discussions dwell on the failed Doha Round of multilateral trade talks, the United States and India could instead focus on completing their negotiations for a bilateral investment treaty. Although the United States is India's largest trading partner in goods and services, India ranks only 18th among trading partners of the United States, on par with Belgium. If the Doha negotiations remain a slog, a bilateral treaty with new investor protections would at least help enhance trade between the two countries.

So, too, would removing structural impediments on both sides. India complains about strict U.S. export controls and visa policies; the United States complains about Indian caps on foreign investment in the sectors of greatest interest to U.S. firms, including insurance and retail. New policies on both sides could spur commerce and insulate the bilateral relationship amid multilateral disagreements.

Washington and New Delhi could also enhance the level of transparency in their relationship. U.S. officials could brief their Indian counterparts on relevant talks between Washington and Beijing, for example, and India could brief U.S. diplomats on developments at its BRIC summits, meetings among Brazil, Russia, India, and China. And closer cooperation on counterterrorism would mean closer coordination on developments regarding Pakistan as well.

The United States and India share important interests: both seek to restore global growth, protect the global commons, enhance global energy security, and ensure a balance of power in Asia. They must therefore increase the scope, quality, and intensity of their cooperation at every level. But the ultimate test of their relationship will be whether Washington and New Delhi can turn their common interests into complementary policies around the world.

The Russia File

How to Move toward a Strategic Partnership

ROBERT LEGVOLD

Legvold notes the recent lack of strategic rivalry between these two great powers since the Cold War era. He argues that the Obama Administration is pursuing a "strategic partnership" with Russia, based around mutual reductions in nuclear weapons, a partnership between energy producers and consumers, and collaboration to manage issues such as the rise of powers as China and India while integrating them into the existing international order. Finally, he discusses collaboration between Washington and Moscow in their quest to limit nuclear proliferation.

Reversing the collapse of U.S.-Russian relations is one of the great tests facing the Obama administration. Among the major powers, Russia is the hard case. And the stakes involved in getting U.S.-Russian relations right are high—much higher than the leadership of either country has acknowledged or perhaps even realized so far. If the Obama administration can guide the relationship onto a more productive path, as it is trying to do, it will not only open the way for progress on the day's critical issues—from nuclear security and energy security to climate change and peaceful change in the post-Soviet area—but also be taking on a truly historic task. One of the blessings of the post-Cold War era has been the absence of strategic rivalry among great powers, a core dynamic of the previous 300 years in the history of international relations. Should it return, some combination of tensions between the United States, Russia, and China would likely be at its core. Ensuring that this does not happen constitutes the less noticed but more fateful foreign policy challenge facing this U.S. president and the next.

Washington has scant chance of mustering the will or the energy to face this challenge, however, without a clearer sense of the scale of the stakes involved. Every tally of the ways in which Russia matters begins, and rightly so, with nuclear weapons. Because the United States and Russia possess 95 percent of the world's nuclear arsenal, they bear the responsibility for making their stocks safer by repairing the now-shattered strategic nuclear arms control regime. Their cooperation is also crucial if the gravely imperiled nuclear nonproliferation regime is to be saved. Then comes energy. Russia has 30 percent of the world's gas reserves and sits astride the transport grid by which energy flows from the entire post-Soviet zone to the rest of the world. More recently, tensions have arisen over the Arctic's hydrocarbon reserves—which are said to amount to 13 – 20 percent of the world's total—not least because of the aggressive way in which Russia has asserted its claims over a large share of them. If the United States and Russia compete, rather than cooperate, over energy in Eurasia and add a military dimension to their disputed claims in the Arctic, as they have begun to do, the effects will be negative for far more than the prices of oil and gas. There is also the struggle against global terrorism, which will be sure to flag without strong collaboration between Washington and Moscow. And it has become clear that the help of Russia is needed if anything approaching stability is to have a chance in Afghanistan, Iraq, and Pakistan.

Other issues are also critical but not always recognized as such. Making real progress toward coping with climate change, including during negotiations at the 2009 UN Conference on Climate Change, will depend on whether the three countries that emit 45 percent of the world's greenhouse gases—the United States, Russia, and China—can cooperate. Any effort to mitigate trafficking in humans, small arms, drugs, endangered species, counterfeit goods, and laundered money must focus on Russia, since these often come from or through that country. Blocking cyberattacks, keeping space safe for commerce and communications, and averting the return of the kind of military air surveillance common during the Cold War will involve Russia, first and foremost. And attempts to reform international financial and security institutions will be optimized only if Russia is given a chance to contribute constructively.

If the United States' interests in a relationship with Russia are this many and this great and if, as Undersecretary of State William Burns said of Washington and Moscow in April, "more unites us than divides us," then the Obama administration will need to turn a page, and not simply tinker at the edges, as it redesigns U.S. policy toward Russia. Turning a page means setting far more ambitious goals for the relationship than is currently fashionable and then consciously devising a strategy to reach them. It also means integrating the well-intentioned symbolic gestures Washington has made toward Russia recently, as well as progress on concrete issues, such as arms control, Iran's nuclear program, and Afghanistan, into a larger design.

Ready, Set, Reset

Positive as President Barack Obama's opening moves toward Russia have been, it is not yet clear how far he and key U.S. policymakers are ready to go to mend relations with Moscow.

In a joint communiqué issued on April 1, Obama and Russian President Dmitry Medvedev promised to work together to reach a "legally binding" agreement to succeed the first Strategic Arms Reduction Treaty (START I), launch "a comprehensive dialogue on strengthening Euro-Atlantic and European security," boost the Global Initiative to Combat Nuclear Terrorism, and find a "comprehensive diplomatic solution" to the Iran problem.

So far, the Obama administration's steps toward a healthier relationship with Russia have been earnest but cautious, consistent with the president's deliberate approach to major policy choices. First, Obama altered the tone of the relationship: hence, Vice President Joe Biden's metaphor about hitting the reset button, the recasting of Washington's position on Iran's nuclear program and Washington's attempt to link the issue to its decision to place a ballistic missile defense system in central Europe, an apparent readiness to repeal the Jackson-Vanik amendment (which still denies Russia most-favored-nation status because of Soviet-era restrictions on Jewish emigration, which were lifted long ago), and the businesslike bonhomie of Obama's first meeting with Medvedev. In short order, Washington then set about addressing concrete and urgent issues: drafting a successor agreement to START I; intensifying the dialogue between Washington and Moscow over the Iranian nuclear threat; and exploring closer cooperation on Afghanistan.

This is a good start. But it still leaves open the fundamental question of which of three basic strategies toward Moscow the Obama administration will adopt. Obama and his people clearly reject the first approach: the urge to "call things by their name," as the Russians say—that is, the urge to see Russia as an authoritarian, bullying, and aggressive power and admit that a new Cold War is on and act accordingly. But it is less clear which of the other two approaches the Obama administration favors.

A second option assumes that despite some important areas of potential cooperation, various impediments make a genuine partnership an illusion. Russia's readiness to contest many aspects of U.S.

foreign policy and its indifference to values that Americans consider important create a fundamental barrier. According to this view, the best strategy combines selective engagement with selective containment and calibrates the two in ways that enhance engagement while softening the edges of containment. U.S. policy has more or less evolved in this direction over the last several years, albeit without a well-formulated design, and much of the U.S. political establishment and the U.S. media seem to have endorsed it.

The third approach is more ambitious. A rush of recent commission reports, studies, and essays by Russia specialists—Anders Åslund, Thomas Graham, Andrew Kuchins, and Steven Pifer, among others—have argued that the relationship should be put on a distinctly different footing. They note that Russia is not the entity it was in the 1990s (no longer prostrate and struggling to be like the West, let alone part of it) and neither is the world (no longer dominated by a United States that could tackle scattered secondary security threats with just a little help from a few friends). Much of this work recognizes the difficulties of dealing with Russia's edgy and assertive leaders but maintains that the U.S.-Russian agenda is too important to be delayed until after Washington's doubts and frustrations have been eased. And it contends that engagement, even reconciliation, is possible with Moscow on a wide range of issues—if with considerable effort.

However, moving in this direction, as Obama and his Russian policy team appear tempted to do, requires a strategic vision, and they have not yet begun to formulate one. Rather than simply tackle practical problems and hope that incremental progress on those will eventually produce a different kind of U.S.-Russian relationship, the administration needs to develop a clear and coherent image of where it wants the relationship to be four to six years from now—not a rose-colored image but a set of plausible aspirations by which to orient and discipline day-to-day policy. And then it should think carefully about what is required to get there.

Such a vision needs an anchor, and the notion of building a "strategic partnership" provides that. The concept inspires few adherents these days, but this is largely because in the past it was thought through too little and tossed about too lightly. Because of the concept's enormous potential benefits, its content should be contemplated far more seriously. There is no logical reason why the two countries with the lion's share of the world's nuclear weapons cannot create a tighter regime to shrink their own arsenals and pave the way toward arrangements that render safer the programs of other nuclear powers, why the world's largest energy producer and its largest energy consumer cannot fashion a genuine energy partnership, why they cannot work together to mitigate instability in and around the vast territory of the former Soviet Union, or why they cannot collaborate to ease the integration of rising powers such as China and India into a revamped international order. These goals may not be imminently attainable, but they suggest what could and should be the essence of a strategic partnership.

Such a working relationship can only come about step by step and if it is reinforced by the parties' behavior. Washington's wish list is long and so deserves to be designed with some sense of priority. Russia's investment in promoting progressive change in its neighborhood, as well as its openness to U.S. efforts that do the same, belong toward the top of it. So, presumably, does Washington's desire to see Moscow adopt a cooperative, perhaps even joint, approach to the rational exploitation of and the protection of the global commons, beginning with the Arctic and space. And it is important that Russia's leadership make its economic activity abroad more transparent and Russia itself more open to foreign investment.

Finally, just as Russia has the right to wish for a U.S. foreign policy less given to unilateralism, less enamored of the military option, and more attuned to the security interests of other states, the United States has the right to hope that Russia will gradually understand that it is in its national interest to deal with its neighbors by adopting a strategy of reassurance rather than a crude one of wielding carrots and sticks, particularly sticks.

The View from Moscow

None of this will happen easily or quickly. And it will not happen unless the United States continues to lead the effort, because Russia's inertia and skepticism are too great. Too many Americans mistakenly believe that Russia's leaders are incorrigibly antidemocratic and bent on bludgeoning Russia's neighbors, blackmailing Europeans, and causing trouble for the United States. But Moscow's mood and its behavior really are constraints. Although many Russian leaders, beginning with Medvedev, want to see a more constructive U.S.-Russian relationship, they are limited by a dour, pinched notion of what is possible. Over the last decade, they have allowed their suspicion of Washington to fester to the point where they now view almost anything the U.S. government does—from promoting the construction of oil and gas pipelines out of the Caspian Sea region to supporting civil society in states that neighbor Russia—as part of a conscious and coherent strategy to weaken Moscow. Russia's leaders justifiably demand to be treated as equals, to be given a real voice in critical international deliberations, and to be allowed to define Russia's national interests themselves. Yet they are unwilling to treat their most immediate neighbors as equals or to respect their independent voices.

Mood is not the only problem. Russia's institutionally amorphous political landscape also stands in the way, for neither the current diarchy formed by Medvedev and Prime Minister Vladimir Putin nor the system's broader semi authoritarian power structure is stable. Predicting long-term political trends in Russia, or even who or what will ultimately shape them, is a fool's endeavor. Moreover, the twists and turns likely to mark Russian foreign policy over the next few years will only reinforce these ambiguities.

Then there is Russia's conflicted profile. Russia's traumatic experience over the last two decades has given an intense emotional edge to its relations with the outside world, accentuating the gap between the international status Russia desires and the wherewithal it would need to obtain it. This underlying tension leaves its leaders either unwilling or unable to compose a clear vision of Russia's place and role in the world. Those who speak for Russia have made plain what they oppose but not what they propose instead. Their preference for multipolarity over unipolarity, their exhortations to "democratize" international relations and "strengthen multilateralism," and their calls for a new European security framework are vague appeals. At a more fundamental level, the Russian leadership shies away from deciding with whom to tie the country's fate—the West or rising powers such as China and India—or whether to settle for playing the field.

Still, the chances for a fresh start are better now than they have been in more than a decade, for two reasons. U.S.-Russian relations soured not only because of frictions between Washington and Moscow over issues such as NATO enlargement, the status of Kosovo, and Washington's plans to place a ballistic missile defense system in central Europe. Russia's antipathy toward the general thrust of the Bush administration's foreign policy, particularly what Putin and his entourage came to see as Washington's excessive unilateralism and disposition to use force, also did more than its share of damage. Thus, if the style and substance of Obama's foreign policy change as much as he and his team have suggested they will, the context for U.S. policy toward Russia will improve no matter what happens on the specific issues that set the two countries at odds.

Second, the economic crisis that began engulfing Russia last September has thus far softened the Russian leadership's demeanor. The swagger in its foreign policy is less pronounced, and its speeches are more tempered. Some Russians close to Medvedev openly acknowledge that the social bargain of the last eight years—"the limiting of civil rights in exchange for economic well-being," to use the phrase of Medvedev's confidant Igor Yurgens—has sundered. Thus, as Medvedev himself has acknowledged, a more respectful dialogue between the leadership and the public is required. The Kremlin no longer boasts of turning Russia into the world's fifth-largest economy or Moscow into a leading financial center. "Patience" and "sacrifice" have become the new watchwords.

Russia's leaders have also begun to shed the skepticism they displayed during the first weeks of the Obama administration and are attiring themselves in more optimistic raiment. But because they still insist that it is the Americans, more than they, who need to shift positions on the issues that agitate them—NATO enlargement, ballistic missile defense in central Europe, and the failure to ratify the Conventional Forces in Europe Treaty—the real proof of the economic crisis' bracing effect will only be clear when they soften their own less-than-accommodating attitude. Already, one does notice Moscow's new emphasis on the need for economic cooperation, including on how to refashion the international financial architecture, and its greater diffidence when it comes to issues for which Russia's leaders once pretended to have the better solutions, such as how to build more effective security arrangements in Europe or how to build a fairer global economic order. Now, when they introduce radical ideas, for example, creating a supranational reserve currency, they acknowledge that it is not, as the French say, "for tomorrow." And when they reprise notions that raise eyebrows in the West, such as the claim that Russia has "privileged interests" in the post-Soviet area, they are at pains to moderate their significance. Short of an economic crisis that spirals out of control—in which case, all bets are off—it is reasonable to expect Russia's foreign policy to be less assertive and testy for the time being. The leadership's realization that Russia's near-term economic future will entail low or negative growth (not the seven percent annual increase once projected), that its security depends more on economic transformation at home than on fending off external threats, and that further delaying internal reforms is no longer an option suggests that going forward, Russia will be less inclined to brandish its refurbished power and more likely to welcome relief from quarters it previously scorned.

In the Beginning

Given the level of mistrust between Washington and Moscow, the Obama administration has rightly started to address the disrepair by taking concrete steps. Doing so has not been easy, as the president and senior officials have learned. Often, particularly in the early going, no matter what Washington offered to Moscow, those Russian leaders with divided minds reacted hesitantly and those with their minds made up looked for traps and suspected ulterior motives. Persistence matters. It will take time for those in the impacted upper circles of Russian power who want a more constructive U.S.-Russian relationship to exert themselves.

Symbolic steps by Washington are important in launching the process and none more so than repealing the Jackson-Vanik amendment swiftly, without fanfare or horse-trading. The Obama administration understands this and has placed the task high on its agenda. But it also needs to understand that given the reluctance of some members of Congress to forsake any lever with Moscow, nothing will happen unless the White House takes the lead in pushing for its repeal. In April, Obama promised Medvedev that he would speed efforts to bring Russia into the World Trade Organization, secure ratification of the Comprehensive Nuclear Test Ban Treaty, revive the U.S.-Russian Civilian Nuclear Cooperation Agreement, and advance the treaty ending the production of fissile material for nuclear weapons. The symbolic effect of these measures will generate a powerful impetus toward improving relations—provided, first, that Washington follows through and, then, that Moscow reciprocates with symbolic gestures of its own.

Whatever the first steps, however, real and lasting progress will depend on the two sides' ability to advance the relationship's substantive agenda. The place to start is with the three issues that the Obama administration has singled out in its early efforts to reengage Moscow: arms control (controlling strategic nuclear arms and strengthening the nuclear nonproliferation regime), Iran, and Afghanistan. As both sides recognize, the first priority is reaching an agreement bridging the gap between the end of START I in December and the creation of a more ambitious strategic arms control accord that would pick up where the two sides left off 12 years ago in preparing negotiations for START III. Chances are good, based on the progress achieved so far, that Washington and Moscow can agree on further reductions in their warhead count (without yet having to resolve the spoiler issue of ballistic missile defense), simplified monitoring and verification procedures, and mutually acceptable counting rules.

The issue of Iran and its nuclear program is the second major question that needs to be addressed. Judging by the language they now use to frame the issue, the two sides already seem closer than they once were. And although Medvedev has strenuously resisted the Obama administration's efforts to link the United States' plans to deploy missiles in central Europe to progress on the Iran issue, the atmosphere surrounding the U.S.-Russian dialogue has improved, and Moscow seems ready to work on the issue more intensively.

Admittedly, this apparent goodwill does not guarantee success with Moscow, let alone Tehran. Progress depends, first, on whether Russia's leaders can persuade themselves that the importance of preventing Iran from becoming a nuclear power outweighs the risks of harming their many other interests involving Tehran, such as gaining access to Iranian oil and gas, dividing up Caspian Sea resources, selling arms, and stemming Islamist extremism in the North Caucasus and Central Asia.

This highlights the need for Washington to make a conscious effort to convince Moscow that by collaborating with Washington on containing Iran's nuclear aspirations, Moscow would be ensuring that its interests are respected even if Iran starts normalizing relations with the West. But this is unlikely to be enough, either. To convince Russia to toughen its diplomacy, the United States, along with France, Germany, and the United Kingdom (the three states that have led the European effort), will almost certainly have to offer Iran a deal that is acceptable to Tehran. Either Iran should be allowed to have a nuclear-fuel-cycle capability of its own, provided that the facilities are under International Atomic Energy Agency controls and that the enrichment and reprocessing of fuel occurs outside Iran. Or, better, Iran should be induced to join an international fuel-service center. In either case, Russia's role will be crucial: in the first instance, because Russia would likely be the primary source of nuclear fuel and reprocessing, and in the second, because the international fuel-service center in Angarsk, Russia, would likely be the one with which Tehran would partner.

The third essential and urgent item on the U.S.-Russian agenda is dealing with the mounting crisis in Afghanistan. Russian leaders know it is not in their national interest to see the West's efforts to stabilize Afghanistan fail; were that to happen, Russia's southern border would be subjected to the threat of an Afghanistan in a shambles or in the grip of the Taliban. But they are torn between doing what they can to ensure a successful outcome there and indulging their urge to expel the U.S. military from Central Asia. Russia's readiness to allow the transit across its territory of nonmilitary supplies to U.S. troops in Afghanistan helps, but military goods should also be permitted to move along this corridor, a step the Russians have signaled they are prepared to take. Ultimately, however, the United States should reach out to Russia, China, and other members of the Shanghai Cooperation Organization and encourage them to contribute more to the coalition of states active in Afghanistan. The Obama administration was wise to participate in the SCO conference on Afghanistan last March, because its subject, the fight against drug trafficking out of Afghanistan, is important. But the move only scratches the surface of what should be a larger U.S.-Russian collaboration in addressing the turbulence in and around Afghanistan and its potential reverberations in Central Asia.

Far and Wide

Ultimately, in order for the U.S.-Russian relationship to move forward on a fundamentally different footing, something far more innovative will be needed. If the Obama administration hopes to overcome the bickering that surrounds nearly every issue on the current agenda and reduce the poisonous suspicion with which Moscow regularly greets U.S. initiatives, let alone transform the relationship into a strategic partnership, it must strive sooner rather than later to establish a deep and far-reaching dialogue with Moscow.

There are several reasons why. First, if Washington does not get to the root of the problems that generate tensions and impede progress in negotiations, the future will almost certainly resemble the recent past: mistrust will grow, and the parties will retreat,

convulsively and emotionally, at each new point of trouble. Second, by openly airing and then dealing with the deeper impulses that shape their behavior, the two governments will increase their chances of clearing away the misapprehensions that often prevent sensible outcomes. Third, if it commits to a serious discussion of the most basic issues in the relationship, the Obama administration will increase the likelihood that U.S. policy toward Russia will be more comprehensive, coherent, and well integrated—the qualities most absent in the past.

This is not an original idea. Previous U.S. administrations have attempted something approximating a strategic dialogue with their Russian counterparts. But these experiments were either short-lived or, as in the case of the Gore-Chernomyrdin Commission (which was set up in the 1990s to support bilateral cooperation on space, energy, and technology), more focused on resolving operational concerns than on deeply plumbing the assumptions underlying each side's position. Still, they offer lessons. The first and central one is that in order to succeed, a strategic dialogue must be led by no more than three or four principals on each side—people detached from government bureaucracies but who enjoy the full confidence of their respective presidents. Past efforts were undone either because the process grew too bureaucratic and lost the flexibility necessary to get at the fundamental source of the problems or because the delegations were no longer led by an interlocutor with direct access to the president. A second lesson from the best of prior experience is that the two sides need to agree on paper, at the outset of negotiations, to the principles that will guide them—including the understanding that no topic will be off the table. Reflecting a third lesson, Moscow and Washington are now creating ways to guarantee regular high-level contact, maintain an active agenda, and task and discipline their bureaucracies. To succeed, this effort will have to be organized around a presidential checklist—that is, concrete tasks approved by the two presidents must be assigned to specific agencies with designated dates by which progress achieved is to be reported and then reviewed at presidential summits.

Obama's people understand this well. But that alone cannot ensure success: unless an effective process by which key agencies are held accountable is devised and the U.S. president empowers a senior member of his administration to put teeth into the process, the sum of Washington's efforts will be considerably less than the parts. It is also unclear whether the mechanism currently under consideration, as elaborate as it is, is intended to serve as the basis for a dialogue that gets at the deep underpinnings of the U.S.-Russian relationship.

Yet this is a necessity, for the heart of this strategic dialogue is the agenda itself. Four areas dominate all others, and they represent four of the twenty-first century's preeminent security concerns: European security, security in and around the Eurasian landmass (especially the post-Soviet area), nuclear security, and energy security. Not coincidentally, these also frame the most friction-laden aspects of the U.S.-Russian relationship, namely, the future relationship of Georgia and Ukraine with NATO, the role of ballistic missile defense in central Europe, the U.S.-Russian interaction in the post-Soviet area, and the jockeying over oil and gas pipelines.

Each of these issues needs to be approached at a fundamental level. Thus, the dialogue about European security should start with each side's assessment of the core threats facing Europe. It should then evolve into an open-ended discussion of how Europe's existing security institutions might be improved to better address these threats, mitigate the insecurity felt by states left outside these institutions (such as Georgia and Ukraine), and create an overarching framework in which NATO and parallel organizations in the Commonwealth of Independent States could address various security challenges together. Although this must be a conversation among Americans, Russians, and Europeans, a bilateral dialogue between Washington and Moscow would offer a crucial basis for testing the potential of a broader European security dialogue.

The issue of mutual security in and around the post-Soviet area will be the most difficult to tackle, but it cannot be avoided; no question cuts more deeply to the core of the current tension in the U.S.-Russian relationship. The starting point for this discussion should be a frank and practical look at how each side sees its own and the other's concerns, interests, and role in the post-Soviet area. However awkward and tense this discussion gets, it must address the specific sources of friction: NATO's activities, the claims and counterclaims surrounding the separatist conflicts in Moldova and the Caucasus, the role of Western nongovernmental organizations in the region, Russia's leverage over its neighbors, and competition over oil and gas. The dialogue must especially explore ways in which the United States and Russia can work together to manage the two most explosive issues: the future of Ukraine and the way toward a more stable and constructive Russian-Georgian relationship.

The topic of nuclear security consists of five challenges, each one critical, all of them linked. First, the fundamental question is how best to strengthen the nuclear nonproliferation regime and, most immediately, how to prevent Iran and North Korea from further eroding it. Second, intimately connected to this challenge is the need to minimize the risk of nuclear proliferation as more and more states look to nuclear power to meet their energy needs—sometimes as an excuse or a cover for developing nuclear weapons programs—thereby giving themselves the potential ability to enrich uranium. That effort will require working with suppliers in the nuclear power industry to develop reactors less easy to use for weapons development and concentrating nuclear fuel services in facilities monitored by the International Atomic Energy Agency. This, in turn, will require close cooperation between the United States and Russia—a reason to revive the stalled negotiations for a so-called 123 agreement, which would promote peaceful commercial nuclear activities between the two countries. Third, if Obama and Medvedev are serious about moving toward a world without nuclear weapons, as they affirmed in their joint statement in April, they need to decide how they intend to go about it. Fourth, in their own nuclear relationship, the United States and Russia are no longer like "two scorpions in a bottle," but if left unregulated, their choices—about whether to pursue ballistic missile defense, weaponize space, introduce nuclear weapons into conventional war doctrines—could still be destabilizing. And fifth, the United States and Russia will have to lead any effort to establish a broader multilateral arms control regime designed to reduce the hazardous aspects of the nuclear postures of the other nuclear powers, particularly those weapons systems in China, India, and Pakistan that blur the line between conventional and nuclear attacks.

Finally, there is the question of energy security. The United States and Russia have long toyed with the idea of having an energy dialogue. They launched one in 2002, let it languish, and then partially revived it during the last year of the Bush administration. Useful as the discussion of potential projects and practical measures may be, however, the two sides need to push the dialogue deeper. Discussing ways to bring Russian oil and liquefied natural gas to the North American market and to enhance cooperation within the consortia developing Caspian Sea oil, while vigorously pursuing dueling pipeline projects, raises the core question: Do the two countries intend for the relationship to be cooperative or competitive?

Addressing the enormously complex issues surrounding the politics of oil and gas from Russia and the Caspian Sea basin only makes sense as part of a three-way dialogue among the United States, Russia, and Europe (Europe is Russia's largest oil and gas market, and Russia is far and away Europe's largest supplier). This does not mean, however, that a serious and well-conceived U.S.-Russian dialogue should neglect the subject or shun the chance to find out precisely what Putin meant in Davos in February when he urged states "to work out a new international legal framework for energy security." "If implemented," he added, it "could have the same economic impact as the treaty establishing the European Coal and Steel Community" and could "unite consumers and producers in a common energy partnership that would be real and based on clear-cut international rules." Similarly, Medvedev has called for developing a far more expansive energy convention than the current Energy Charter contains, a document that neither Russia nor the United States has signed.

A Fresh Start

Outlining the agenda of an ambitious strategic dialogue is not to assume that agreement will come soon or easily or even at all. National interests will clash even when the issues have been stripped of emotion and misunderstandings. And issues subject to the warping effect of domestic politics will not submit to the most well-intentioned international dialogue. At root, the purpose of a strategic dialogue is to take the realm of what was impossible and shrink it and the realm of the barely possible and enlarge it.

Finally, nothing in this approach prejudices, much less precludes, a strong and independent U.S. policy toward Georgia, Ukraine, and the other states of the former Soviet Union. It is in the U.S. national interest—not least because it is in the interest of global stability—that as many states in the region as possible emerge as peaceful, stable, prosperous, and self-confident democratic societies. But it is also in the United States' long-term interest to avoid promoting this goal in ways that intentionally or unintentionally encourage these states to balance against Russia or that treat Russian-sponsored institutions in the region as inherently suspect, rather than as potential complements (with some adjustments) to parallel structures in the West.

Nor does this approach suggest that the often roiling subject of clashing U.S. and Russian political values or U.S. concerns over political trends within Russia should be soft-pedaled or ignored. These issues need to be a part of the relationship, not because Washington has the right to judge Moscow or instruct the Russians and their leaders but because any durable and deeper partnership depends on a minimally kindred sense of what the two societies stand for and will defend. The two sides must also find a way to discuss these matters in a civil, constructive manner. Rather than putting Russia in the pillory, the United States should identify areas in which both countries face common challenges and have come up short: say, the problem of illegal immigration or the tension between the struggle against terrorism and the protection of civil rights. Washington and Moscow ought to prove that they can have a productive conversation and only then move on to more sensitive subjects.

One final suggestion: it has been more than 16 years since U.S. President Bill Clinton, speaking on the eve of his first summit with Russian President Boris Yeltsin, delivered the last major U.S. presidential address on U.S.-Russia policy. The time is right for Obama to share with his administration, the American people, and an intensely interested Russian audience his strategic vision for U.S.-Russian relations and where he would like these to be several years from now. He should then invite the Russian side to join in a frank, wide-ranging discussion of how to get there.

Tehran's Take

Understanding Iran's U.S. Policy

MOHSEN M. MILANI

Milani's article is a complex examination of Iranian-U.S. relations from the perspective of Tehran. He argues that Iran perceives the United States as its greatest existential threat, and is therefore pursuing defense strategies that are based on low-intensity asymmetrical warfare, and the development of a nuclear deterrent. Milani contends that while the U.S.A. has been pursuing a policy of containment toward Iran, the Iranians are simultaneously engaged in a policy of deterrence. He concludes that Iran has sought to counterbalance the U.S.A. by not only moving closer to the European Union, but also by courting China and Russia.

Although a great it deal has been written about the United States' policy toward Iran, hardly anything comprehensive has been produced about Iran's policy toward the United States. Given Washington's concerns that the United States faces "no greater challenge from a single country than from Iran," as the 2006 National Security Strategy put it, this lack of serious attention is astonishing. What does exist is sensationalistic coverage about Iran's nuclear ambitions and about mad mullahs driven by apocalyptic delusions and a martyr complex.

That picture suggests that Iran's policy consists of a series of random hit-and-run assaults on U.S. interests and that its leaders, being irrational and undeterrable, must be eliminated by force.

In fact, Tehran's foreign policy has its own strategic logic. Formulated not by mad mullahs but by calculating ayatollahs, it is based on Iran's ambitions and Tehran's perception of what threatens them. Tehran's top priority is the survival the Islamic Republic as it exists now. Tehran views the United States as an existential threat and to counter it has devised a strategy that rests on both deterrence and competition in the Middle East.

To deter any possible military actions by the United States and its allies, Iran is improving its retaliatory capabilities by developing the means to pursue asymmetric, low-intensity warfare, both inside and outside the country; modernizing its weapons; building indigenous missile and antimissile systems; and developing a nuclear program while cultivating doubts about its exact capability. And to neutralize the United States' attempts to contain it, the Iranian government is both undermining U.S. interests and increasing its own power in the vast region that stretches from the Levant and the Persian Gulf to the Caucasus and Central Asia. Although it is being cartful to avoid a military confrontation with the United Scares, Tehran is maneuvering to prevent Washington from leading a united front against it and strategically using Iran's oil and gas resources to reward its friends.

Iranian foreign policy today is as U.S.-centric as it was before the 1979 revolution. Mohammad Reza Shah Pahlavi relied on Washington to secure and expand his power; today, the Islamic Republic exploits anti-Americanism to do the same. Policy has been consistent over the years partly because it is determined by the supreme leader, who is also the commander of the security and armed forces and serves for life. Iran's defiance has in some ways undermined the country's national interests, but it has paid huge dividends to the ruling ayatollahs and helped them survive three tumultuous decades in power.

Today, Ayatollah Sayyid Ali Khamenei is the supreme leader, and he makes all the key policy decisions, usually after Iran's major centers of power, including the presidency, have reached a consensus. President Mahmoud Ahmadinejad and his two major reformist rivals, Mir Hossein Mousavi and Mehdi Karroubi, have all supported engaging in negotiations with Washington—a political taboo just a few years ago. Ahmadinejad would be less likely to compromise than his more moderate competitors, but, thanks to the support he has among major anti-American constituencies inside and outside the Iranian government, he would be in a better position

to institutionalize any shift in policy. Although Iran's president can change tactical aspects of the country's foreign policy, he cannot single-handedly alter its essence. Only Khamenei, the ultimate decider, can do that. And he will do that only if a fundamental change in policy would not undermine his own authority and if it enjoys broad support from among the major centers of power.

The Hungry Wolf and the Fat Sheep

The roots of anti-Americanism in Iran—really, an opposition to U.S. policies—can be traced to the 1953 coup against Mohammad Mosaddeq, which was hacked by the CIA and MI6. Anti-American sentiment was strengthened when in 1964 Ayatollah Ruhollah Khomeini, who would become Iran's first supreme leader after the revolution, opposed a treaty granting legal immunity to U.S. military advisers in Iran and declared that Iran had become a "U.S. colony." By 1979, the revolutionaries were portraying the Iranian monarch as "America's shah" and had made "independence" a defining slogan of their movement. After the taking of hostages at the U.S. embassy in Tehran that year, anti-Americanism became an enduring feature of the state's Islamic ideology. Since then, Iran's leaders have deftly linked the survival of the Islamic Revolution to Iran's independence, depicting the United States as antithetical to both. No one has drawn this link more vividly than Khomeini: he called the United States "the great Satan" and compared U.S. relations with Iran to those between a hungry wolf and a fat sheep. As hostility between the two stares intensified, a Manichaean security paradigm developed in both of them. Each one came to perceive the other as a mortal enemy in a zero-sum game. Anti-Americanism and anti-Iranian feelings became two sides of the same coin.

For decades, the Iranian regime has used anti-Americanism to crush its opponents at home and expand its power abroad. After 1979, documents selectively released by the radical students who occupied the U.S. embassy were invoked to establish links between opponents of the Islamic Republic and the U.S. government. Hundreds of people were consequently defamed, jailed, or exiled. In the

1980s, when the young regime was simultaneously struggling to consolidate its rule and fighting a war with Iraq, allegations that the U.S. government was attempting to stage coups in Tehran and prevent Iran from winning the war strengthened the sentiment.

Over time, anti-American constituencies in Iran have proliferated and gained ground in various institutions. Some of them oppose the United States for purely ideological reasons. Others have substantial economic interests in preventing the normalization of relations between Tehran and Washington: they profit from domestic black markets and international trade routes established to bypass U.S. sanctions. Moreover, the foreign organizations that Iran supports throughout the Middle East, and that Washington considers to be terrorist groups, have created effective lobbies in Iran that thrive on the animosity.

Yet now, as under Khomeini, the intensity of the anti-Americanism prevailing in Iran is ultimately determined by the supreme leader. As president, Khamenei declared in 1981, "We are not like [Salvador] Allende [a Chilean president ousted by a coup allegedly backed by Washington], liberals willing to be snuffed out by the CIA." Today, Khamenei still considers the United States to be an existential threat. Washington surrounds Iran with bases in Bahrain, Kuwait, and Qatar and massive troop buildups in Afghanistan and Iraq. It makes friends with the leaders of Iran's neighbors. And its nuclear-equipped naval carriers patrol the Persian Gulf. Khamenei sees the United State as isolating Iran, strangling it with economic sanctions, sabotaging its nuclear program, and beating the drums of preemptive war. He thinks Washington is pursuing regime change in Tehran by funding his opponents, inciting strife among Iran's ethnic minorities, and supporting separatist organizations such as the Baluchistan-based Sunni insurgent group Jundallah, which has killed scores of Revolutionary Guard members.

Prefer to Deter

Tehran has responded to Washington's policy of containment with a strategy of deterrence. Tehran first developed this strategy against Iraq after Iraq invaded Iran in September 1980 and then, as the 1980s unwound and the menace of Iraq faded, redirected it toward the United States. Today, this approach is the result both of Iran's perception of its vulnerabilities and of the constraints that the international community has imposed on the country.

Iran's deterrence strategy has four components. The first is developing the means to fight an asymmetric, low-intensity war, inside and outside the country. In recent years, particularly after U.S. troops arrived in Afghanistan and Iraq, the Revolutionary Guards have played an increasingly important role in maintaining internal order. They have also improved Iran's retaliatory capability in case of an invasion or surgical strikes against its nuclear facilities or the headquarters of its security forces. Khamenei's recent decision to decentralize the command-and-control structure of the Revolutionary Guards serves this purpose. So do the alleged ability of Iran's troops to transform themselves into nonconventional forces within days and Iran's thousands of small Iranian-made assault boats, which could create havoc for the U.S. Navy, as well as its thousands of motorcycles equipped with light artillery, which could impede the advances of an invading army. Iran's support tor terrorist actions against U.S. interests in the Middle East is part and parcel of its strategy of asymmetric warfare. For example, in 1983, during the civil war in Lebanon, a group associated with the Iranian-hacked Hezbollah killed 220 U.S. marines.

The modernization of Iran's weapons systems is the second component of its deterrence strategy. Decades of arms embargoes from the West have left Iran with limited access to advanced weapons, and Iran has consequently purchased relatively small arms supplies. Between 2002 and 2006, it spent $31 billion on military purchases, compared with $109 billion for Saudi Arabia and a total of $48 billion for Bahrain, Kuwait, Oman, and the United Arab Emirates—four states with a combined population smaller than that of the city of Tehran. The embargoes have also caused an indigenous military-industrial complex to develop, controlled and financed by the state. It employs thousands of people and is connected to the country's major universities and think tanks. Most important, it is in charge of research and development for Iran's missile and nuclear technologies.

Developing indigenous missile and antimissile systems is the third leg of Iran's deterrence strategy. Tehran began building missiles during the Iran-Iraq War and accelerated its program after the "war of cities," in 1988, when both states showered the other's cities with missiles. Iran has used technical support from China and Russia to develop its missile technology. Now, it manufactures its own missiles and claims that two types, the Shahab and the Ghadr, can reach Israel. These missiles are known for their inaccuracy and limited offensive application. But they give Iran the power to retaliate against attacks, particularly in the Persian Gulf, where it could readily upset international navigation.

The fourth component of Iran's, deterrence strategy is its nuclear program. The Iranian government claims that its program is designed for peaceful purposes—using nuclear weapons would violate Islamic law, it says—but Washington (and much of the West) accuses it of having a secret program to build the bomb. So far, the International Atomic Energy Agency has found no smoking gun or any evidence that Iran has diverted its unclear program toward military purposes. But nor has it been able to confirm Tehran's peaceful intentions, because the Iranian government has refused to answer some major questions, Now that Iran has joined, a small club of countries that can enrich uranium to a low level of purity, it seems unlikely to cave in to international pressure and accept zero enrichment in the future.

Why, given all the sanctions imposed by the United Nations, does Iran not cry uncle and stop its nuclear program? For one thing, by insisting that its nuclear project is essential for the country's domestic energy needs and scientific development, Tehran has effectively turned U.S. opposition to its program into a nationalist cause, pointing to it as proof that Washington intends to hold Iran back. (In an attempt to awaken national pride, the government has had the atom symbol printed on 50,000 rial bills.) For another, the nuclear impasse

creates an excellent bargaining chip for Tehran in future negotiations. This may be the reason that Iran's leaders are cultivating uncertainty about the country's actual capability. It does appear, however, that they have decided to develop the infrastructure to build the bomb but not yet the bomb itself. (Former President Ali Akbar Hashemi Rafsanjani claimed in 2005, "We possess nuclear technology that is not operationalized yet. Any time we decide to weaponize it, we can do so rather quickly.") Iran and the United States seem to be engaged in a game of poker, with Tehran not showing its cards about its nuclear capabilities and Washington refusing to exclude the possibility of attacking Iran. Washington has the better hand, but the better hand does not always win.

Countercontainment

For three decades, the United States has sought to contain Iran and has imposed on it a variety of sanctions in an effort to do so. To try to neutralize these measures' effects, Iranian leaders have played major powers off against one another, forged alliances of convenience, and asserted Iran's interests at the regional and global levels.

First, Iran has tried to create a wedge between the United States and the United States' European allies. Iran's leaders believe that increased trade with the European Union will allow them to exploit differences among the organization's 27 members and discourage it from supporting regime change in Tehran, the total containment of Iran, or a military attack. In other words, they see the EU as, a potential counterweight to the United States. After Iran restarted its uranium-enrichment activities in 2003, the EU ended its "constructive engagement" policy and imposed limited sanctions on Iran to tame its nuclear ambitions. Although these restrictions have prevented both Iran from gaining access to advanced technologies and European firms from making substantial investments in Iran, they have had a negligible impact on the overall volume of trade. The EU remains Iran's leading trading partner, accounting for about 24 percent of Iran's total international trade: the EU's total imports from Iran (mostly energy) increased from 6.3 billion euros in

2003 to 12.6 billion euros in 2007, and its exports to Iran (mostly machinery) remained the same, at about 11.2 billion euros, during that period. On the other hand, the fact that France, Germany, and the United Kingdom supported the referral of Iran's case from the International Atomic Energy Agency to the UN Security Council in 2005 proved the limits of Iran's wedge policy. The move, which highlighted the determination of the major Western powers to tame Iran's nuclear ambitions, was a major defeat for Tehran and a major victory for Washington.

The second component of Iran's strategy to undermine the United States' containment measures is to move closer to states that could counterbalance the United States. Iran has signed major economic and military agreements with China and Russia. It sees these two countries as natural allies, since they oppose the United States' unilateralism and its efforts to isolate Iran and have only reluctantly backed the sanctions against Iran. But the fact that they have supported the UN sanctions at all has proved to Tehran that when pressed, Beijing and Moscow are more likely to gravitate toward Washington than toward Tehran. Russia has not yet finished building the Bushehr nuclear reactor, which it had committed to completing by 2006, and Moscow may be willing to pressure Tehran to change its nuclear policies if the Obama administration decides not to build antimissile systems in Russia's neighborhood.

But Iran continues its efforts. With little alternative but to rely on China and Russia as counterweights to the United States, it recently asked to upgrade its status in the Shanghai Cooperation Organization, a six-party security organization that includes China and Russia, from observer to full member so that is would receive assistance from other members if it were ever attacked. It has also become much more active in trying to popularize and-Americanism within the Non-aligned Movement and the Organization of the Islamic Conference, and it has solidified its ties with Washington's most vocal opponents in the United States' backyard: Bolivia, Cuba, Ecuador, Nicaragua, and Venezuela.

The third facet of Iran's countercontainment strategy is to use its energy resources to reward its allies. No country in the region is as well endowed with energy resources as Iran is, not even Saudi Arabia: Iran's oil reserves total about 1,384 billion barrels, and its natural gas reserves total about 26.5 trillion cubic meters. (Although Saudi Arabia's oil reserves, which total approximately 267 billion barrels, are larger than Iran's, its natural gas reserves, which total about 7.2 trillion cubic meters, are much smaller.) Oil diplomacy has long been a strategy of Tehran's, of course. During the Rafsanjani presidency, it briefly served as a means to start normalizing relations with Washington. In that spirit, Iran signed in early 1995 a $1 billion oil deal with the U.S. energy company Conoco, the largest contract of its kind since 1979. But the deal was soon terminated when, under pressure from the U.S. Congress and U.S. interest groups opposed to any opening toward Iran, President Bill Clinton issued an executive order banning U.S. companies from investing in Iran's energy sector. A year later, the Iran-Libya Sanctions Act was passed, which penalizes foreign companies that invest more than $20 million in Iran's energy industry. In reaction, in 1997 Tehran signed a $2 billion deal with the French oil and gas company Total.

Meanwhile, many Western companies that have continued to want to do business in Iran have struggled to bid for its huge and untapped natural gas reserves. And to immunize itself against the effects of the sanctions and any potential boycott by the West, Iran has shifted its oil trade from the West to new markets. Before the 1979 revolution, the top five importers of Iranian oil were, in decreasing order, France, West Germany, the United Kingdom, Italy, and Japan. By 2008, they were Japan, China, India, South Korea, and Italy. Iran has also recently helped open up the Persian Gulf to China and Russia, signing multibillion-dollar contracts with the Chinese company Sinopec and granting Russia major concessions and access to the Azadegan oil field. Khamenei has even proposed forming with Russia a natural gas carrel modeled after OPEC.

Despite U.S. opposition, Iran has also made good progress on the construction of a so-called peace pipeline that would carry gas from the Persian Gulf to India through Pakistan, a project that would strengthen Iran's position as a major source of energy for those two countries. Nor should one underestimate the negative long-term implications for U.S. interests of China's and Russia's increasing involvement in the Persian Gulf, which Iran has facilitated, or of Tehran's recent move to use the euro in its international transactions, which has weakened the dollar. On the other hand, the sanctions have hurt Iran badly. Its plan for gas and oil pipelines that would connect the Persian Gulf to the Caspian Sea has stalled because of the restrictions. And its oil industry has been deprived of access to important modern technologies: as a result, Iran's oil production today remains significantly below what it was in 1979. In other words, the sanctions have been a lose-lose economic proposition for both the United States and Iran.

Rising in the Region

After three decades of Washington's containment policies, Iran has nonetheless emerged as a regional power. The collapse of the Soviet Union allowed Tehran to expand its influence in the former Soviet republics, many of which it shares historical ties with. A decade later, the United States accelerated the process by overthrowing the Taliban and Saddam Hussein, Iran's neighboring nemeses. And by failing to reactivate the Arab-Israeli peace process and mismanaging the occupation of Iraq, Washington created enticing opportunities for Iran to expand its power. For the first time in a long while, Iran's influence now radiates west, north, and east. Iran now rightly considers itself an indispensable regional player.

These ambitions pit Tehran against Washington. As Mohsen Rezai, a former commander of the Revolutionary Guards, stated in 2007, "It is our principal and indisputable right to become a regional power," and the United States "would like to prevent us from playing such a role." According to a March 2007 article in *The New York Times,* a recent UN sanctions package against Iran's nuclear program was passed in order to rein in what U.S. officials saw as "Tehran's ambitions to become the dominant military power in the Persian Gulf and across the broader Middle East.

A pivotal element of Iran's strategy of neutralizing the United States' containment policy is to create spheres of influence in Syria, Lebanon, and among the Palestinians, as well as in Afghanistan and Iraq, by supporting pro-Iranian organizations and networks there. (As Rezai put it, "Iran has no meaning without Iraq, Lebanon, Palestine, and Syria.") An especially controversial part of this strategy is Iran's support for Syria, Hezbollah, Palestinian Islamic Jihad, and Hamas—the rejectionist front in the Arab-Israeli conflict. Iran's, three-decade-long alliance with Syria is one of the most enduring alliances between Middle Eastern Muslim countries since the end of World War II. Iran's support of the Shiites of Lebanon and the Palestinians goes back many years. Rafsanjani was incarcerated in the 1960s for translating a pro-Palestinian book into Persian; Khomeini condemned the shah in 1964 for his de facto recognition of Israel; Khomeini also authorized Hassan Nasrallah, the leader of Hezbollah, to collect religious taxes on his behalf in support of the Lebanese Shiites; and many of Iran's current leaders received training in Lebanon in the 1960s and 1970s. At first, Iran's support for Hezbollah and the Palestinians had an ideological basis; now, is has a strategic rationale. It gives Tehran strategic depth in the heart of the Sunni Arab world and in Israel's backyard, which translates into a retaliatory capacity against Israel, as well as bargaining power in any future negotiations with the United States. Moreover, after centuries of using its influence mostly to defend Shiites, Iran is now increasingly trying to transcend the sectarian divide by supporting the Sunni groups Hamas and Palestinian Islamic Jihad. This, in turn, has undermined the regional position of such powerful Sunni countries as Egypt and Saudi Arabia.

That said, Iran's financial and logistical support for Hamas and Islamic Jihad should not be exaggerated. Tehran remains a peripheral player in the Arab-Israeli conflict. It has no compelling national interest in the dispute and is simply taking advantage of the failure of the peace process between Israel and the Palestinians. What makes Iran an influential player is not its financial support alone—Saudi Arabia and other Arab countries contribute substantially more to the Palestinians—but also the model of resistance it champions. Iran has helped Hezbollah develop an approach that combines Islamic solidarity, populism, some trappings of democracy, strict organizational discipline, extensive economic and social support for the needy masses, and pervasive anticolonial and anti-Western sentiments—all in an effort to mobilize the streets of the Islamic world against Israel and the United States and expand its own power. The effectiveness of that model, and of its asymmetric strategies, was on display during Hezbollah's 34-day war with Israel in 2006. The group's use of antitank missiles and portable rockets, which Israel claimed Iran had provided—a charge Iran has denied—inflicted enough damage on Israeli cities to create havoc and mass fear. Hezbollah appeared to have won because Israel could not score a decisive victory against it; the conflict marked the first time that an Arab force was not humiliatingly defeated by Israel. It boosted Hezbollah's popularity in many Sunni countries, gave Iran more credibility in the region, and undermined Washington's traditional allies, such as Egypt and Saudi Arabia, which had not supported Hezbollah. The war, along with the chaos in Afghanistan and Iraq and what the Iran expert Vali Nasr has called "the Shiite revival," has convinced Tehran that a new order is emerging in the Middle East: the United States no longer dominates, and Iran now plays a major role.

Where the Hard Things Are

The complicated nature of the U.S.-Iranian relationship is most evident in Afghanistan and Iraq, where the convergences and divergences of the two sides" interests are the clearest. After the Soviet occupation of Afghanistan in 1979, Tehran became intensely engaged with its neighbor, and Iran subsequently became home to some two million Afghan refugees. Gradually, throughout the 1980s, it built new alliances and new networks with Shiite and Persian- and Dari-speaking minorities. (As the Afghanistan expert Barnett Rubin has put it, during

that period, "ironically, the United States was indirectly aligned with 'fundamentalists' while Iran courted the "'moderates.'") Then, in the 1990s, while Pakistan and Saudi Arabia were providing critical support to the Taliban government, which itself backed al Qaeda, Tehran created a sphere of resistance in Afghanistan by supporting the Northern Alliance—a force that cooperated with the invading U.S. troops in 2001 in order to liberate Afghanistan from the Taliban. In helping dismantle the Taliban, in other words, Tehran effectively sided with the U.S. government—even providing Washington with intelligence.

Tehran maintained its policy toward Afghanistan even after U.S. President George W. Bush said Iran belonged to "an axis of evil," Today, still, it entertains close relations with the pro-U.S. government of Afghan President Hamid Karzai. And the convergence between Tehran's interests and Washington's interests in Afghanistan remains substantial. Both want to keep the country stable and prevent the Taliban's resurgence. Both want to control and possibly eliminate drug trafficking, the economic backbone of the region's terrorists and warlords. Both want to defeat al Qaeda (which considers Shiism to be a heresy). And both want to eventually rebuild Afghanistan.

At the same time, Iran's heavy involvement in the reconstruction of Afghanistan has allowed it to create a sphere of economic influence in the region around Herat, one of the most prosperous regions in the country. This, in turn, has helped stabilize the area by preventing al Qaeda and the Taliban from infiltrating it. Iran has also empowered the historically marginalized Afghan Shiites, such as the Hazara and the Qizilbash, who constitute about 20 percent of the Afghan population. At a donors' conference in Tokyo in January 2002, Iran pledged $560 million for Afghanistan's reconstruction, or approximately 12 percent of the total $4.5 billion in international reconstruction assistance that was promised then. During a donors' conference in London in 2006, it pledged an additional $100 million. And unlike many other donors, it has delivered most of its promised assistance. The bulk of the funds are targeted at developing projects for infrastructure, education, agriculture, power generation, and telecommunications. Iran hopes to become a hub for the transit of goods and services between the Persian Gulf and Afghanistan, Central Asia, and possibly also China.

This quest for influence in Afghanistan pits Iran against the United States, in some ways. For example, Tehran opposes the establishment of permanent U.S. bases in Afghanistan. And to ensure that Washington will not be able to use Afghanistan as a launching point for an attack on Iran, Tehran is pressuring Kabul to distance itself from Washington. Uncertain about Afghanistan's future and Washington's intentions in the country, Iran is keeping its options open and trying to increase all its possible retaliatory capabilities against the United States. It maintains close ties with the Northern Alliance, as well as with warlords such as Ismail Khan, various Shiite organizations, and the insurgent leader Gulbuddin Hekmatyar and other anti-American fighters. It is turning the region around Herat into a sphere of influence: the bazaars there are loaded with Iranian goods, the area receives the bulk of Iran's investments in the country, and the Revolutionary Guards are reportedly visible and active.

The United States and Iran have tried to strike a fine balance in Iraq as well, but with much less success. If anything, Iraq has become center stage for their rivalry; there they have some common goals but also many more diverging ones. Iran's top strategic priority in Iraq is to establish a friendly, preferably Shiite government that is sufficiently powerful to impose order in the country but not powerful enough to pose a serious security threat to Iran, as Saddam did, Iran was the first country in the region to recognize the post-Saddam government in Baghdad. Since then, it has provided Baghdad with more support than even the staunchest of the United States' allies. It has a close relationship with the two parties that dominate the government of Prime Minister Nouri al-Maliki, as well as with the two major Kurdish parties, like Washington, Tehran supports Iraq's stability, its new constitution, and its electoral democracy, albeit

in the parochial interest of ensuring the dominance of the country's Shiite majority. Like Washington, Tehran opposes Iraq's Balkanization, in its case partly for fear that such fragmentation could incite secessionist movements within Iran's own ethnically rich population. And like Washington, Iran considers al Qaeda in Iraq to be an enemy and seeks to eliminate it.

But as in Afghanistan, Iran is eager to engage in Iraq's reconstruction mainly in order to create an economic sphere of influence in the country, especially in the predominantly Shiite south, where many people of Persian descent live. It has pledged to spend more than $1 billion for Iraq's reconstruction. Tehran seem to believe that with its existing influence in southern Iraq, including close ties to the major Shiite seminaries in Najaf, it can transform the region into a kind of southern Lebanon, creating a ministate within a state.

And then there are some major disagreements between Tehran and Washington. Tehran is determined to keep Washington mired in Iraq and prevent it from scoring a clear victory there. During the sectarian violence in 2004-7, Tehran supplied weapons to Shiite insurgents in Iraq, who then used them against U.S. troops. It supported the Mahdi Army and its founder, Muqtada al-Sadr, the radical Shiite cleric who opposes the U.S. presence in Iraq. Tehran is also vehemently opposed to the establishment of permanent U.S. bases in Iraq, for fear, as with those in Afghanistan, that the United States could use them to attack Iran. The status-of-forces agreement signed by the United States and Iraq in 2008 does seem to have diminished some of Iran's concerns, however. The agreement stipulates that U.S. forces will withdraw from Iraq no later than December 31, 2011, and that "Iraqi land, sea, and air shall not be used as a launching or transit point for attacks against other countries."

Iran's, policies toward Iraq in the past few years suggest that when Iran feels threatened and its legitimate security needs and national interests are ignored or undermined, it tends to act more mischievously than when it feels secure. Its Iraq policy, therefore, is directly correlated with its perception of the threat posed by the United States. The security talks between Tehran and Washington launched at the urging of the Iraqi government in 2005 are thus very important. After these meetings began, and after the U.S. government launched its "surge" strategy in Iraq, the level of violence in Iraq subsided. Iran played a role in stabilizing the situation by pressuring its allies, including the Mahdi Army, to refrain from violence against Sunnis or U.S. troops. The simple fact that Baghdad is a close ally of both Tehran and Washington offers a chance for those two governments to build on their interests in Iraq.

Full Engagement

Anti-Americanism is not an insurmountable obstacle to normalizing relations with Iran. For one thing, Iran's elites are heterogeneous; they consist of two rival factions, both of which have come to favor, like a significant portion of the population, normalizing relations with the United States. For another, *maslebat*, or "expediency," is a defining feature of Iranian politics. Even the most ideological of Iran's leaders favor a cost-benefit approach to decision-making. According to the 2007 U.S. National Intelligence Estimate, Iran halted its nuclear weapons program in 2003, based on a cost-benefit calculation. Although the accuracy of that conclusion is debated, there is no question that Tehran has often resorted to that approach. When Iran needed advanced weapons during the Iran-Iraq War, Khomeini approved secret dealings with Israel and the United States, culminating in the Iran-contra fiasco. Despite its general opposition to the presence of U.S. troops in the region, Tehran remained actively neutral during the 1991 Persian Gulf War, seeing it as an opportunity to weaken its archenemy Saddam and improve relations with the West. The Revolutionary Guards, the most ideological group in the Iranian armed forces, rubbed shoulders with U.S. forces when they assisted the Northern Alliance in overthrowing the Taliban in 2001. Far from being a suicidally ideological regime, Tehran seeks to ensure the survival of the Islamic Republic while advancing the country's interests through negotiations.

Iranian policy toward the United States has a logic. It is a logic driven not by a single faction or a single issue but by a stable and institutionalized system of governance with both authoritarian and democratic features, with domestic constituencies and long-standing international alliances. It is a logic that made Iran into a regional power with substantial influence in Afghanistan, Iraq, Lebanon, and the Palestinian territories, and among millions of Muslims around the world. And it is a logic that, despite mounting international pressure, has made it possible for Iran to make advances in asymmetric warfare, nuclear technology, uranium enrichment, and missile and satellite technologies. Now, Iran legitimately demands that Washington recognize these advances and Tehran's new role as a major regional power.

Unless Washington understands that Tehran's U.S. policy has a rationale, it will not be able to develop a reasonable long-term strategy toward Iran. Invading the country is not a viable option. Nor are so-called surgical strikes against Iran's nuclear facilities, which would most likely lead to a protracted retaliation by Iran; a Tehran more defiant and more determined to become a nuclear weapons power, more terrorism; greater instability in Afghanistan, Iraq, Lebanon, said the Persian Gulf; and higher oil prices.

The challenge for the U.S. government is to give Iran incentives to reevaluate its strategy toward the United Suites. A carrot-and-stick approach designed to stop progress on Iran's nuclear program is unlikely to work. Focusing on a few contentious issues, such as Iran's uranium-enrichment activities, would do little to change the fundamental logic of Iran's U.S. policy. Moreover, the stick part of that approach would only strengthen the anti-American constituencies in Iran while hurting its people. Nor will democracy promotion work. More a feel-good fantasy than a viable strategy, this approach misleadingly assumes that a democracy can be exported, like cars, or imposed by force and that a democratic Iran would no longer have any serious conflicts with the United States or pursue nuclear ambitions. Iran was considerably more democratic under Mosaddeq than under the shah, and yet its relations with the United States, were much worse then.

A better approach is a strategy of full engagement, one predicated on gradually increasing economic, educational, and cultural exchanges between the two countries; exploiting the commonalities shared by their governments; and establishing concrete institutional mechanisms to manage their remaining differences. Washington must recognize that there is no diplomatic magic wand that can fix its "Iran problem" overnight; normalizing U.S.-Iranian relations will be a long and difficult process. Unless Tehran and Washington make a strategic decision to normalize relations, the many forces that continue to pull them apart are likely to detail the process.

As a first step, the United States should allay Iran's fears about regime change. It can do this by explicitly recognizing that Khamenei is the center of gravity in Iran's decision-making process and establishing a line of communication with his office. Holding-direct, comprehensive, and unconditional negotiations with the Iranian government is Washington's least bad option. The two countries' negotiating teams must meet face-to-face to learn firsthand about each other's priorities and interests on all the important issue and break the psychological barriers that have kept the parties apart for three decades. Meanwhile, Washington should provide assurances to Israel and its Arab allies that they should not fear its rapprochement with Tehran and that Iran's nuclear policy will remain the main item on the United States' Iran agenda.

As the Obama administration reviews its options when it comes to Iran, it would do well to examine how, three decades ago, President Richard Nixon brought China back into the community of nations. It took almost eight years after the secret trip by Henry Kissinger, then U.S. national security adviser, to Beijing in 1971 for the United States and China to establish diplomatic relations. Anti-Americanism under Mao Zedong, China's support for North Vietnam, and China's arsenal of nuclear weapons were infinitely more threatening to the United States then than Iran's policies are now. Yet Nixon and Kissinger had the foresight to map out a new strategic landscape for Beijing. They did not punish it for its policies of the past; they gave it a reason to want something better in the future. And then the two countries built a better relationship on their common recognition of the threat posed by Soviet expansionism. Washington can, and should, do something similar with Tehran today and finally end three decades of hostility by highlighting the two governments' shared interests in defeating al Qaeda and stabilizing Afghanistan and Iraq. Tehran, for its part, must recognize that without some kind of understanding with Washington over the issues that matter to the U.S. government, it will not be able to fully benefit from its recent ascent as a regional power—and could even lose much of what it has gained.

From Great Game to Grand Bargain

Ending Chaos in Afghanistan and Pakistan

BARNETT R. RUBIN AND AHMED RASHID

Rubin and Rashid discuss the range of problems that the United States faces in Afghanistan and its neighbor Pakistan. The spectrum of issues they discuss includes terrorism, corruption, narcotics, and the weak governance throughout the region. The authors argue that the conflict in Afghanistan has spread into Pakistan, and that the Pakistani military has been aiding the Taliban against the U.S.A. and the Karzai government. They include a complex discussion of Pakistan's military and intelligence services, and Pakistan's perception of regional threats. Rubin and Rashid contend that the only way to resolve the Afghan war must include a discussion of Pakistan's role in the perpetuation of that conflict.

The Great Game is no fun anymore. The term "Great Game" was used by nineteenth-century British imperialists to describe the British-Russian struggle for position on the chessboard of Afghanistan and Central Asia—a contest with a few players, mostly limited to intelligence forays and short wars fought on horseback with rifles, and with those living on the chessboard largely bystanders or victims. More than a century later, the game continues. But now, the number of players has exploded, those living on the chessboard have become involved, and the intensity of the violence and the threats it produces affect the entire globe. The Great Game can no longer be treated as a sporting event for distant spectators. It is time to agree on some new rules.

Seven years after the U.S.-led coalition and the Afghan commanders it supported pushed the leaderships of the Taliban and al Qaeda out of Afghanistan and into Pakistan, an insurgency that includes these and other groups is gaining ground on both the Afghan and the Pakistani sides of the border. Four years after Afghanistan's first-ever presidential election, the increasingly besieged government of Hamid Karzai is losing credibility at home and abroad. Al Qaeda has established a new safe haven in the tribal agencies of Pakistan, where it is defended by a new organization, the Taliban Movement of Pakistan. The government of Pakistan, beset by one political crisis after another and split between a traditionally autonomous military and assertive but fractious elected leaders, has been unable to retain control of its own territory and population. Its intelligence agency stands accused of supporting terrorism in Afghanistan, which in many ways has replaced Kashmir as the main arena of the still-unresolved struggle between Pakistan and India.

For years, critics of U.S. and NATO strategies have been warning that the region was headed in this direction. Many of the policies such critics have long proposed are now being widely embraced. The Bush administration and both presidential campaigns are proposing to send more troops to Afghanistan and to undertake other policies to sustain the military gains made there. These include accelerating training of the Afghan National Army and the Afghan National Police; disbursing more money, more effectively for reconstruction and development and to support better governance; increasing pressure on and cooperation with Pakistan, and launching cross-border attacks without Pakistani agreement to eliminate cross-border safe havens for insurgents and to uproot al Qaeda; supporting democracy in Pakistan and bringing its Inter-Services Intelligence (ISI) under civilian political control; and implementing more effective policies to curb Afghanistan's drug industry, which produces opiates equal in export value to half of the rest of the Afghan economy.

Cross-border attacks into Pakistan will not provide security. Advancing reconstruction, development, good governance, and counternarcotics efforts and building effective police and justice systems in Afghanistan will require many years of relative peace and security. Neither neglecting these tasks, as the Bush administration did initially, nor rushing them on a timetable determined by political objectives, can succeed. Afghanistan requires far larger and more effective security forces, international or national, but support for U.S. and NATO deployments is plummeting in troop-contributing countries, in the wider region, and in Afghanistan itself. Afghanistan, the poorest country in the world but for a handful in Africa and with the weakest government in the world (except Somalia, which has no government), will never be able to sustain national security forces sufficient to confront current—let alone escalating—threats, yet permanent foreign subsidies for Afghanistan's security forces cannot be guaranteed and will have destabilizing consequences. Moreover, measures aimed at Afghanistan will not address the deteriorating situation in Pakistan or the escalation of international conflicts connected to the Afghan-Pakistani war. More aid to Pakistan—military or civilian—will not diminish the perception among Pakistan's national security elite that the country is surrounded by enemies determined to dismember it, especially as cross-border raids into areas long claimed by Afghanistan intensify that perception. Until that sense of siege is gone, it will be difficult to strengthen civilian institutions in Pakistan.

U.S. diplomacy has been paralyzed by the rhetoric of "the war on terror"—a struggle against "evil," in which other actors are "with us or with the terrorists." Such rhetoric thwarts sound strategic thinking by assimilating opponents into a homogenous "terrorist" enemy. Only a political and diplomatic initiative that distinguishes political opponents of the United States—including violent ones—from global terrorists such as al Qaeda can reduce the threat faced by the Afghan and Pakistani states and secure the rest of the international community from the international terrorist groups based there. Such an initiative would have two elements. It would seek a political solution with as much of the Afghan and Pakistani insurgencies as possible, offering political inclusion, the integration of Pakistan's indirectly ruled Federally Administered Tribal Areas (FATA) into the mainstream political and administrative institutions of Pakistan, and an end to hostile action by international troops in return for cooperation against al Qaeda. And it would include a major diplomatic and development initiative addressing the vast array of regional and global issues that have become intertwined with the crisis—and that serve to stimulate, intensify, and prolong conflict in both Afghanistan and Pakistan.

Afghanistan has been at war for three decades—a period longer than the one that started with World War I and ended with the Normandy landings on D-day in World War II—and now that war is spreading to Pakistan and beyond. This war and the attendant terrorism could well continue and spread, even to other continents—as on 9/11—or lead to the collapse of a nuclear-armed state. The regional crisis is of that magnitude, and yet so far there is no international framework to address it other than the underresourced and poorly coordinated operations in Afghanistan and some attacks in the FATA. The game has become too deadly and has attracted too many players; it now resembles less a chess match than the Afghan game of buzkashi, with Afghanistan playing the role of the goat carcass fought over by innumerable teams. Washington must seize the opportunity now to replace this Great Game with a new grand bargain for the region.

The Security Gap

The Afghan and Pakistani security forces lack the numbers, skills, equipment, and motivation to confront the growing insurgencies in the two countries or to uproot al Qaeda from its new base in the FATA, along the Afghan-Pakistani border. Proposals for improving the security situation focus on sending additional international forces, building larger national security forces in Afghanistan, and training and equipping Pakistan's security forces, which are organized for conflict with India, for domestic counterinsurgency. But none of these proposals is sufficient to meet the current, let alone future, threats.

Some additional troops in Afghanistan could protect local populations while the police and the administration develop. They also might enable U.S. and NATO forces to reduce or eliminate their reliance on the use of air strikes, which cause civilian casualties that recruit fighters and supporters to the insurgency. U.S. General Barry McCaffrey, among others, has therefore supported a "generational commitment" to Afghanistan, such as the United States made to Germany and South Korea. Unfortunately, no government in the region around Afghanistan supports a long-term U.S. or NATO presence there. Pakistan sees even the current deployment as strengthening an India-allied regime in Kabul; Iran is concerned that the United States will use Afghanistan as a base for launching "regime change" in Tehran; and China, India, and Russia all have reservations about a NATO base within their spheres of influence and believe they must balance the threats from al Qaeda and the Taliban against those posed by the United States and NATO. Securing Afghanistan and its region will require an international presence for many years, but only a regional diplomatic initiative that creates a consensus to place stabilizing Afghanistan ahead of other objectives could make a long-term international deployment possible.

Afghanistan needs larger and more effective security forces, but it also needs to be able to sustain those security forces. A decree signed by President Karzai in December 2002 would have capped the Afghan National Army at 70,000 troops (it had reached 66,000 by mid-2008). U.S. Secretary of Defense Robert Gates has since announced a plan to increase that number to 122,000, as well as add

82,000 police, for a total of 204,000 in the Afghan National Security Forces (ANSF). Such increases, however, would require additional international trainers and mentors—which are, quite simply, not available in the foreseeable future—and maintaining such a force would far exceed the means of such a destitute country. Current estimates of the annual cost are around $2.5 billion for the army and $1 billion for the police.

Many have therefore proposed long-term international financing of the ANSF; after all, even $5 billion a year is much less than the cost of an international force deployment. But sustaining, as opposed to training or equipping, security forces through foreign grants would pose political problems. It would be impossible to build Afghan institutions on the basis of U.S. supplemental appropriations, which is how the training and equipping of the ANSF are mostly funded. Sustaining a national army or national police force requires multiyear planning, impossible without a recurrent appropriation—which would mean integrating ANSF planning into that of the United States' and other NATO members' budgets, even if the funds were disbursed through a single trust fund. And an ANSF funded from those budgets would have to meet international or other national, rather than Afghan, legal requirements. Decisions on funding would be taken by the U.S. Congress and other foreign bodies, not the Afghan National Assembly. The ANSF would take actions that foreign taxpayers might be reluctant to fund. Such long-term international involvement is simply not tenable.

If Afghanistan cannot support its security forces at the currently proposed levels on its own, even under the most optimistic economic scenario, and long-term international support or a long-term international presence is not viable, there is only one way that the ANSF can approach sustainability: the conditions in the region must be changed so that Afghanistan no longer needs such large and expensive security forces. Changing those conditions, however, will require changing the behavior of actors not only inside but also outside of the country—and that has led many observers to embrace putting pressure on, and even launching attacks into, Pakistan as another deus ex machina for the increasingly dire situation within Afghanistan.

Borderline Insecurity Disorder

After the first phase of the war in Afghanistan ended with the overthrow of the Taliban in 2001 (and as the United States prepared to invade Iraq), Washington's limited agenda in the region was to press the Pakistani military to go after al Qaeda; meanwhile, Washington largely ignored the broader insurgency, which remained marginal until 2005. This suited the Pakistani military's strategy, which was to assist the United States against al Qaeda but to retain the Afghan Taliban as a potential source of pressure on Afghanistan. But the summer of 2006 saw a major escalation of the insurgency, as Pakistan and the Taliban interpreted the United States' decision to transfer command of coalition forces to NATO (plus U.S. Secretary of Defense Donald Rumsfeld's announcement of a troop drawdown, which in fact never took place) as a sign of its intention to withdraw. They also saw non-U.S. troop contributors as more vulnerable to political pressure generated by casualties.

The Pakistani military does not control the insurgency, but it can affect its intensity. Putting pressure on Pakistan to curb the militants will likely remain ineffective, however, without a strategic realignment by the United States. The region is rife with conspiracy theories trying to find a rational explanation for the United States' apparently irrational strategic posture of supporting a "major non-NATO ally" that is doing more to undermine the U.S. position in Afghanistan than any other state. Many Afghans believe that Washington secretly supports the Taliban as a way to keep a war going to justify a troop presence that is actually aimed at securing the energy resources of Central Asia and countering China. Many in Pakistan believe that the United States has deceived Pakistan into conniving with Washington to bring about its own destruction: India and U.S.-supported Afghanistan will form a pincer around Pakistan to dismember the world's only Muslim nuclear power. And some Iranians speculate that in preparation

for the coming of the Mahdi, God has blinded the Great Satan to its own interests so that it would eliminate both of Iran's Sunni-ruled regional rivals, Afghanistan and Iraq, thus unwittingly paving the way for the long-awaited Shiite restoration.

The true answer is much simpler: the Bush administration never reevaluated its strategic priorities in the region after September 11. Institutional inertia and ideology jointly assured that Pakistan would be treated as an ally, Iran as an enemy, and Iraq as the main threat, thereby granting Pakistan a monopoly on U.S. logistics and, to a significant extent, on the intelligence the United States has on Afghanistan. Eighty-four percent of the materiel for U.S. forces in Afghanistan goes through Pakistan, and the ISI remains nearly the sole source of intelligence about international terrorist acts prepared by al Qaeda and its affiliates in Pakistan.

More fundamentally, the concept of "pressuring" Pakistan is flawed. No state can be successfully pressured into acts it considers suicidal. The Pakistani security establishment believes that it faces both a U.S.-Indian-Afghan alliance and a separate Iranian-Russian alliance, each aimed at undermining Pakistani influence in Afghanistan and even dismembering the Pakistani state. Some (but not all) in the establishment see armed militants within Pakistan as a threat—but they largely consider it one that is ultimately controllable, and in any case secondary to the threat posed by their nuclear-armed enemies.

Pakistan's military command, which makes and implements the country's national security policies, shares a commitment to a vision of Pakistan as the homeland for South Asian Muslims and therefore to the incorporation of Kashmir into Pakistan. It considers Afghanistan as within Pakistan's security perimeter. Add to this that Pakistan does not have border agreements with either India, into which Islamabad contests the incorporation of Kashmir, or Afghanistan, which has never explicitly recognized the Durand Line, which separates the two countries, as an interstate border.

That border is more than a line. The frontier between Pakistan and Afghanistan was structured as part of the defenses of British India. On the

Pakistani side of the Durand Line, the British and their Pakistani successors turned the difficulty of governing the tribes to their advantage by establishing what are now the FATA. Within the FATA, these tribes, not the government, are responsible for security. The area is kept underdeveloped and overarmed as a barrier against invaders. (That is also why any ground intervention there by the United States or NATO will fail.) Now, the Pakistani military has turned the FATA into a staging area for militants who can be used to conduct asymmetric warfare in both Afghanistan and Kashmir, since the region's special status provides for (decreasingly) plausible deniability. This use of the FATA has eroded state control, especially in Pakistan's Northwest Frontier Province, which abuts the FATA. The Swat Valley, where Pakistani Taliban fighters have been battling the government for several years, links Afghanistan and the FATA to Kashmir. Pakistan's strategy for external security has thus undermined its internal security.

On September 19, 2001, when then Pakistani President Pervez Musharraf announced to the nation his decision to support the U.S.-led intervention against the Taliban in Afghanistan, he stated that the overriding reason was to save Pakistan by preventing the United States from allying with India. In return, he wanted concessions to Pakistan on its security interests.

Subsequent events, however, have only exacerbated Pakistan's sense of insecurity. Musharraf asked for time to form a "moderate Taliban" government in Afghanistan but failed to produce one. When that failed, he asked that the United States prevent the Northern Alliance (part of the anti-Taliban resistance in Afghanistan), which had been supported by India, Iran, and Russia, from occupying Kabul; that appeal failed. Now, Pakistan claims that the Northern Alliance is working with India from inside Afghanistan's security services. Meanwhile, India has reestablished its consulates in Afghan cities, including some near the Pakistani border. India has genuine consular interests there (Hindu and Sikh populations, commercial travel, aid programs), but it may also in fact be using the consulates against Pakistan, as Islamabad claims.

India has also, in cooperation with Iran, completed a highway linking Afghanistan's ring road (which connects its major cities) to Iranian ports on the Persian Gulf, potentially eliminating Afghanistan's dependence on Pakistan for access to the sea and marginalizing Pakistan's new Arabian Sea port of Gwadar, which was built with hundreds of millions of dollars of Chinese aid. And the new U.S.-Indian nuclear deal effectively recognizes New Delhi's legitimacy as a nuclear power while continuing to treat Islamabad, with its record of proliferation, as a pariah. In this context, pressuring or giving aid to Pakistan, without any effort to address the sources of its insecurity, cannot yield a sustainable positive outcome.

Big Hat, No Cattle

Rethinking U.S. and global objectives in the region will require acknowledging two distinctions: first, between ultimate goals and reasons to fight a war; and, second, among the time frames for different objectives. Preventing al Qaeda from regrouping so that it can organize terrorist attacks is an immediate goal that can justify war, to the extent that such war is proportionate and effective. Strengthening the state and the economy of Afghanistan is a medium- to long-term objective that cannot justify war except insofar as Afghanistan's weakness provides a haven for security threats.

This medium- to long-term objective would require reducing the level of armed conflict, including by seeking a political settlement with current insurgents. In discussions about the terms of such a settlement, leaders linked to both the Taliban and other parts of the insurgency have asked, What are the goals for which the United States and the international community are waging war in Afghanistan? Do they want to guarantee that Afghanistan's territory will not be used to attack them, impose a particular government in Kabul, or use the conflict to establish permanent military bases? These interlocutors oppose many U.S. policies toward the Muslim world, but they acknowledge that the United States and others have a legitimate interest in preventing Afghan territory from being used to launch attacks against them. They claim to be willing to support an Afghan government that would guarantee that its territory would not be used to launch terrorist attacks in the future—in return, they say, for the withdrawal of foreign troops.

The guarantees these interlocutors now envisage are far from those required, and Afghanistan will need international forces for security assistance even if the current war subsides. But such questions can provide a framework for discussion. To make such discussions credible, the United States must redefine its counterterrorist goals. It should seek to separate those Islamist movements with local or national objectives from those that, like al Qaeda, seek to attack the United States or its allies directly—instead of lumping them all together. Two Taliban spokespeople separately told *The New York Times* that their movement had broken with al Qaeda since 9/11. (Others linked to the insurgency have told us the same thing.) Such statements cannot simply be taken at face value, but that does not mean that they should not be explored further. An agreement in principle to prohibit the use of Afghan (or Pakistani) territory for international terrorism, plus an agreement from the United States and NATO that such a guarantee could be sufficient to end their hostile military action, could constitute a framework for negotiation. Any agreement in which the Taliban or other insurgents disavowed al Qaeda would constitute a strategic defeat for al Qaeda.

Political negotiations are the responsibility of the Afghan government, but to make such negotiations possible, the United States would have to alter its detention policy. Senior officials of the Afghan government say that at least through 2004 they repeatedly received overtures from senior Taliban leaders but that they could never guarantee that these leaders would not be captured by U.S. forces and detained at Guantánamo Bay or the U.S. air base at Bagram, in Afghanistan. Talking with Taliban fighters or other insurgents does not mean replacing Afghanistan's constitution with the Taliban's Islamic Emirate of Afghanistan, closing girls' schools, or accepting other retrograde social policies. Whatever weaknesses the Afghan government

and security forces may have, Afghan society—which has gone through two Loya Jirgas and two elections, possesses over five million cell phones, and has access to an explosion of new media—is incomparably stronger than it was seven years ago, and the Taliban know it. These potential interlocutors are most concerned with the presence of foreign troops, and some have advocated strengthening the current ANSF as a way to facilitate those troops' departure. In November 2006, one of the Taliban's leading supporters in Pakistan, Maulana Fazlur Rahman, publicly stated in Peshawar that the Taliban could participate as a party in elections in Afghanistan, just as his party did in Pakistan (where it recently lost overwhelmingly), so long as they were not labeled as terrorists.

The End of the Game

There is no more a political solution in Afghanistan alone than there is a military solution in Afghanistan alone. Unless the decision-makers in Pakistan decide to make stabilizing the Afghan government a higher priority than countering the Indian threat, the insurgency conducted from bases in Pakistan will continue. Pakistan's strategic goals in Afghanistan place Pakistan at odds not just with Afghanistan and India and with U.S. objectives in the region, but with the entire international community. Yet there is no multilateral framework for confronting this challenge, and the U.S.-Afghan bilateral framework has relied excessively on the military-supply relationship. NATO, whose troops in Afghanistan are daily losing their lives to Pakistan-based insurgents, has no Pakistan policy. The UN Security Council has hardly discussed Pakistan's role in Afghanistan, even though three of the permanent members (France, the United Kingdom, and the United States) have troops in Afghanistan, the other two are threatened by movements (in the North Caucasus and in Xinjiang) with links to the FATA, and China, Pakistan's largest investor, is poised to become the largest investor in Afghanistan as well, with a $3.5 billion stake in the Aynak copper mine, south of Kabul.

The alternative is not to place Pakistan in a revised "axis of evil." It is to pursue a high-level diplomatic initiative designed to build a genuine consensus on the goal of achieving Afghan stability by addressing the legitimate sources of Pakistan's insecurity while increasing the opposition to its disruptive actions. China, both an ally of Pakistan and potentially the largest investor in both Afghanistan and Pakistan, could play a particularly significant role, as could Saudi Arabia, a serious investor in and ally of Pakistan, former supporter of the Taliban, and custodian of the two holiest Islamic shrines.

India would also need to become more transparent about its activities in Afghanistan, especially regarding the role of its intelligence agency, the Research and Analysis Wing. Perhaps the ISI and the RAW could be persuaded to enter a dialogue to explore whether the covert war they have waged against each other for the past 60 years could spare the territory of Afghanistan. The contact group could help establish a permanent Indian-Pakistani body at the intelligence and military levels, where complaints could be lodged and discussed. The World Bank and the Asian Development Bank could also help set up joint reconstruction programs in Afghanistan. A series of regional conferences on economic cooperation for the reconstruction of Afghanistan have already created a partial framework for such programs.

Then there is Iran. The Bush administration responded to Iranian cooperation in Afghanistan in 2001 by placing Tehran in the "axis of evil" and by promising to keep "all options on the table," which is understood as a code for not ruling out a military attack. Iran has reacted in part by aiding insurgents in Afghanistan to signal how much damage it could do in response. Some Iranian officials, however, continue to seek cooperation with the United States against al Qaeda and the Taliban. The next U.S. administration can and should open direct dialogue with Tehran around the two countries' common concerns in Afghanistan. An opening to Iran would show that the United States need not depend solely on Pakistan for access to Afghanistan. And in fact, Washington and Tehran had such a dialogue until around 2004. In May 2005, when the United States

and Afghanistan signed a "declaration of strategic partnership," Iran signaled that it would not object as long as the partnership was not directed against Iran. Iran would have to be reassured by the contact group that Afghan territory would not be used as a staging area for activities meant to undermine Iran and that all U.S. covert activities taking place from there would be stopped.

Russia's main concern—that the United States and NATO are seeking a permanent U.S.-NATO military presence in Afghanistan and Central Asia—will also need to be assuaged. Russia should be assured that U.S. and NATO forces can help defend, rather than threaten, legitimate Russian interests in Central Asia, including through cooperation with the Shanghai Cooperation Organization. Russia and the Central Asian states should be informed of the results of legitimate interrogations of militants who came from the former Soviet space and were captured in Afghanistan or Pakistan.

To overcome the zero-sum competition taking place between states, ethnic groups, and factions, the region needs to discover a source of mutual benefit derived from cooperation. China—with its development of mineral resources and access roads in Afghanistan and Pakistan, the financial support it gave to build the port of Gwadar, and its expansion of the Karakoram Highway, which links China to northern Pakistan—may be that source. China is also a major supplier of arms and nuclear equipment to Pakistan. China has a major interest in peace and development in the region because it desires a north-south energy and trade corridor so that its goods can travel from Xinjiang to the Arabian Sea ports of Pakistan and so that oil and gas pipelines can carry energy from the Persian Gulf and Iran to western China. In return for such a corridor, China could help deliver much-needed electricity and even water to both countries. Such a corridor would also help revive the economies of both Afghanistan and Pakistan.

More Than Troops

Lowering the level of violence in the region and moving the global community toward genuine agreement on the long-term goals there would provide the space for Afghan leaders to create jobs and markets, provide better governance, do more to curb corruption and drug trafficking, and overcome their countries' widening ethnic divisions. Lowering regional tensions would allow the Afghan government to have a more meaningful dialogue with those insurgents who are willing to disavow al Qaeda and take part in the political process. The key to this would be the series of security measures the contact group should offer Pakistan, thereby encouraging the Pakistani army to press—or at least allow—Taliban and other insurgent leaders on their soil to talk to Kabul.

Part Four: The U.S. and the World

Robert A. Pastor, The Future of North America: Replacing a Bad Neighbor Policy

1. According to Pastor how does North American integration lead to enhanced national security for the United States?
2. Do U.S. border regulations with Canada and Mexico undermine U.S. economic efficiency? Explain.
3. Is Pastor's argument for an egalitarian North American approach, instead of the current bilateral approach, compelling? Explain.
4. Pastor argued for the creation of a North American investment fund to enable the economic development of Mexico. What are the strengths or weaknesses of this argument?

Jorge G. Castañeda, Morning in Latin America

1. Castañeda argued that the "Chinese model" of engagement should be avoided by the U.S.A. in its relations with Cuba. Do you agree? Explain.
2. Should the U.S.A. lift the embargo on Cuba? Explain.
3. Is Latino immigration a threat to the U.S. economy and/or to U.S. national security? Explain.
4. To what degree does Venezuela, enriched by oil wealth, threaten the geopolitical interests of the United States?
5. Does the structure of the U.S. federal government undermine the nation's capacity to cooperate with other countries? If so, provide examples.

G. John Ikenberry, The Rise of China and the Future of the West; Can the Liberal System Survive?

1. Are the U.S. and China involved in a classic *power transition*? Is the system then moving to a bipolar or multipolar order? Explain.

2. Ikenberry argued that Realists are wrong to assume that China's rise means inevitable war with the U.S.A. Do you agree? Explain.
3. Does China have an interest in challenging the existing international order? Explain.
4. Ikenberry argued that U.S.-led order is more liberal than imperial, and thus more legitimate than the world orders that preceded it. Do you agree? Explain.
5. Do you accept Ikenberry's logic that war between the Great Powers is largely impossible due to the existence of nuclear weapons? Explain.
6. Why should institutions be crafted behind Rawls' "veil of ignorance"?

Evan A. Feigenbaum, India's Rise, America's Interest: The Fate of the U.S.-Indian Partnership

1. On the issue of global climate change, should India continue to side with the G-77 nations, or integrate their position with the G-20 nations? Explain.
2. India abandoned its former stance of nonalignment to become increasingly allied with the U.S.A. since 2002. Explain this dramatic diplomatic turn in U.S.-Indian relations.
3. Should India be represented by a permanent seat on the U.N. Security Council?
4. Explain how the U.S. military campaign in Afghanistan affects U.S. relations with India.
5. How does the U.S. relationship with Pakistan affect U.S.-Indian relations?
6. How does Washington's relationship with Beijing complicate U.S. relations with India?

Robert Legvold, The Russia File: How to Move toward a Strategic Partnership

1. Legvold argued that the Obama Administration has not articulated a grand strategy in general, nor a specific strategy toward Moscow. To what degree does Legvold's claim ring true? Explain.

2. What does Legvold mean by a "strategic partnership" between Washington and Moscow? What are the key areas underpinning such a partnership?
3. Legvold argued that Russia's security depends more on internal economic growth than on guarding against external threats. Is this argument compelling? Explain.
4. What is the Jackson–Vanik Amendment, and why is it seen as such an impediment to U.S.-Russian relations?

Mohsen M. Milani, Tehran's Take: Understanding Iran's U.S. Policy

1. What are the four components of Tehran's strategy to deter the United States?
2. To what degree does the domestic level of analysis explain relations between Iran and the United States?
3. Has Iran succeeded in creating a coalition of states to balance against the United States?
4. Has the Iran-Libya Sanctions Act had any significant effect on relations between Washington and Tehran?

5. How does the *security dilemma* influence U.S.-Iranian relations?
6. Is the U.S.A.'s containment policy toward Iran working? Explain.
7. How has Iran complicated the U.S. intervention in Afghanistan?

Barnett R. Rubin and Ahmed Rashid, From Great Game to Grand Bargain: Ending Chaos in Afghanistan and Pakistan

1. During 2011 Osama bin Laden was discovered and killed in Pakistan by U.S. military forces. How did this incident affect relations between Washington and Islamabad?
2. Has framing the conflict in Afghanistan through the lens of the "war on terror" been advantageous or problematic for the United States? How has it affected U.S. relations with other polities in South and Central Asia?
3. What are the U.S.'s two principal strategic goals in the Afghan conflict? Is Washington close to realizing them? Explain.

New Domains

This final section examines important new domains for U.S. foreign policy in the 21st century, vital new areas that are often poorly understood by policymakers. The section opens with a discussion of challenges and opportunities in the realm of political economy. Altman argues that the processes of globalization are now slowing, primarily as a result of the global economic crisis of 2008. He argues that U.S. leadership is waning, international organizations are crippled and ineffective, and that international cooperation is declining. His article is followed by Hopkins' provocative and critical piece on capitalism and imperialism, in which he argues that the forces of globalization allowed for the nationalistic, conservative revival in the United States that propelled the neoconservative invasion of Iraq.

Following that article, Victor and Yueh analyze challenges to the energy security of the United States, including price volatility, stagnant global production, and China's increasingly statist behavior in this domain. Miller and Sagan provide a forthright analysis of the proliferation of nuclear technologies, nuclear weapons, and the utility of international organizations and international law. Borgerson then tackles the issue of global climate change, and addresses the geopolitical consequences of Arctic warming. Borgerson argues that the "great melt" will provide opportunities for exploitation of the Arctic's minerals (notably oil and gas), but that it also raises the specter of competition over those resources between the nations of the Arctic.

Deibert and Rohozinski follow with a trenchant examination of the emerging domain of cybersecurity and the rise of cyberthreats to the United States, particularly from state actors (e.g., China), and global criminal/terrorist networks. Taleb and Blyth follow with their analysis of discontinuities, or Black Swans, clearly evident in the turbulence associated with the Arab Spring transformations of 2011. This is followed by McCants' article regarding the geopolitical implications of the Arab Spring revolutions of 2011. He argues that the rise of Islamic democracy in the Arab world undermines violent jihadist networks enemies such as al Qaeda, and will prove beneficial to U.S. interests in the Islamic world. We conclude with Pape's provocative argument that the United States has in fact become an Empire, subject to the dynamics of imperial overstretch, and that we are now witnessing the decline of American power.

Globalization in Retreat

ROGER C. ALTMAN

In this article Altman makes the controversial argument that the era of deregulation and unbridled capitalism is largely over following the global economic crash of 2008. He argues that the popularity of the U.S. model is in decline while China's model of state-centric hybrid capitalism is growing, and that processes of globalization are slowing or in decline. Altman also warns that unipolarity is at an end, and therefore, we are witnessing a decline in the capacity of the United States to lead.

Further Geopolitical Consequences of the Financial Crisis

It is now clear that the global economic crisis will be deep and prolonged and that it will have far-reaching geopolitical consequences. The long movement toward market liberalization has stopped, and a new period of state intervention, reregulation, and creeping protectionism has begun.

Indeed, globalization itself is reversing. The long-standing wisdom that everyone wins in a single world market has been undermined. Global trade, capital flows, and immigration are declining. It also has not gone unnoticed that nations with insulated financial systems, such as China and India, have suffered the least economic damage.

Furthermore, there will be less global leadership and less coordination between nations. The G-8 (the group of highly industrialized states) and the G-20 (the group of finance ministers and central bank governors from the world's largest economies) have been unable to respond effectively to this crisis, other than by expanding the International Monetary Fund (IMF). The United States is also less capable of making these institutions work and, over the medium term, will be less dominant.

This coincides with the movement away from a unipolar world, which the downturn has accelerated. The United States will now be focused inward and constrained by unemployment and fiscal pressures.

Much of the world also blames U.S. financial excesses for the global recession. This has put the U.S. model of free-market capitalism out of favor. The deserved global goodwill toward President Barack Obama mitigates some of this, but not all of it.

In addition, the crisis has exposed weaknesses within the European Union. Economic divergence is rising, as the three strongest EU nations—France, Germany, and the United Kingdom have disagreed on a response to the crisis and refused pleas for emergency assistance from eastern Europe. The absence of a true single currency has proved inhibiting. And the European Central Bank has emerged as more cautious and less powerful than many expected.

Such lack of strength and unity in the West is untimely, because the crash will increase geopolitical instability. Other already unstable nations, such as Pakistan, could disintegrate. And poverty will rise sharply in a number of African countries. All this implies a less coherent world.

The one clear winner is China, whose unique political-economic model has come through un- scathed. This will automatically enhance its global position. Yes, its growth has slowed, but to still en- viable rates. And measured by financial reserves, it is the world's wealthiest country. China's astute leadership is already making strategic investments that others cannot make.

The expected prolonged severity of the global recession is central to understanding these likely geopolitical impacts. The world's three largest economies, will not be able to generate a normal cyclical recovery. The pervasive financial damage will prevent it. As a result, nations dependent on those markets for growth, such as those in Eastern Europe, will also face a long recovery. And many of the developing economies, which depend on for- eign capital, have been hardest hit.

Anatomy of a Crisis

Start with the United States, whose GDP is still nearly double that of any other country. Whereas most recessions follow a sequence of rising infla- tionary pressures, monetary tightening to counter them, and a slowdown in response to higher inter- est rates, this one is a balance-sheet-driven reces- sion. It is rooted in the financial damage to households and banks from the housing and credit- market collapse.

U.S. households lost 20 percent of their net worth in just 18 months, dropping from a peak of $64.4 trillion in mid-2007 to $51.5 billion at the end of 2008. Approximately two-thirds of this reduc- tion involved lower financial asset values, and one- third was tied to home values. This is a big drop when juxtaposed against a median family income of $50,000 (which has been shrinking in real terms since 2000) and unprecedented household debt (which reached 130 percent of income in 2008).

That debt surged because Americans spent beyond their means. This reflected the wealth effect—households feeling wealthier on account of rising asset values and thus spending more. But consumers are now shell-shocked, and so that effect has been reversed. Household outflows are down, producing the unusual surge in personal savings

rates that is now evident. This is why personal con- sumption expenditures fell by record rates in the last quarter of 2008. But consumer spending domi- nates the U.S. economy (at 70 percent of GDP). The core question is, when can spending resume grow- ing at cyclically normal levels? With home values still falling and equity prices still 45 percent below their 2007 peak, the answer is not soon.

The other key constraint is the financial sector. Since the crisis broke, global financial institutions (mostly Western ones) have reported $1 trillion of losses on U.S.-originated assets. And the IMF re- cently estimated that ultimate losses will reach a staggering $2.7 trillion. These losses directly reduce banks' underlying capital and thus their capacity to lend. This explains why U.S. lending volumes have continued to decline and why the lending levels needed to support a normal cyclical recovery are not possible.

The recovery in Europe will be even weaker. Al- though the United States is expected to register marginal growth in 2010-Goldman Sachs is fore- casting 1.2 percent—the Eurozone may contract again, by an estimated 0.3 percent. This reflects Eu- rope's more exposed banking systems, historical factors, and the region's weaker policies.

Europe entered the recession later than the United States did and, logically, will emerge later. The housing and credit markets imploded in the United States, and then this implosion moved east. For example, Europe was still growing in early 2008, whereas the United States was not. Europe's banking system is proportionately larger than the United States,' and its banks were more exposed to weakening emerging markets in Eastern Europe and Latin America. And to date, European banks have recognized a smaller share of total likely write- downs than U.S. banks have.

Furthermore, the European policy response has been much weaker. Washington adopted a $787 bil- lion fiscal stimulus program (involving tax cuts and spending increases), representing five percent of GDP. This is expected to raise 2009 GDP (over four quarters) by two percent above the level that would otherwise have prevailed. By contrast, the European Economic Recovery Plan is targeted to provide a stimulus equal to only about 1.5 percent of the EU's GDP. The resulting boost will be smaller.

When it comes to monetary policy, there has been a similar disparity. The U.S. Federal Reserve lowered the federal funds target interest rate—the rate at which banks lend to one another overnight—to zero percent. Together with the U.S. Treasury and the FDIC, the Federal Reserve has provided an astonishing $13 trillion of support to the financial system. This includes guarantees of commercial paper, money-market-fund investments, specific groups of bank assets, and the like. In contrast, however, the European Central Bank has lowered its rates more slowly, only reaching 1.25 percent in April 2009. The comparable figure for overall credit support is 115 billion euros of capital injection for banks and 217 billion euros of funding guarantees—a fraction of what Washington has spent.

There are numerous reasons for this weaker European response. Some have to do with the stronger social security nets across much of Europe and the lesser need for special protection now. Others involve a historical aversion to steps with potentially inflationary consequences. And there is also the inherent difficulty of reaching agreement among multiple nations. The overall implication is that Europe's recovery will be even slower than the United States.'

The developing world has been hit hardest. Inflows of investment and financing have plunged, exports are very weak, and commodity prices are way down. The countries of central and Eastern Europe are particular victims, as they ran large balance-of-payments deficits and depended on external borrowing to finance them. Several of them, including Hungary and Poland, have resorted to emergency loans from the IMF. Meanwhile, Africa has seen capital inflows nearly come to a halt.

The overall picture is a grim one: a deep, truly global, and destabilizing downturn, with world GDP falling for the first time in the postwar period. Given rising populations, such an outright contraction is stunning. As of this writing, it may have bottomed out, but the next three years will be painfully slow. The geopolitical consequences are now coming into view, and they will be profound.

After Globalization

First, the era of laissez-faire economics has ended. For 30 years, the Anglo-Saxon model of free-market capitalism spread across the globe. The role of the state was diminishing, and deregulation, privatization, and the openness of borders to capital and trade were rising. Much of central and Eastern Europe adopted this model, as did swaths of East Asia and diverse nations from Ireland to Mexico.

This movement reflected the economic primacy of the United States. Its growth, soaring standards of living, and conservative economic policies were widely admired. Countless societies preferred this model and supported governments that espoused it. The state-centered models, such as the French and German ones, were in retreat.

Now, a page has been turned. The Anglo-Saxon financial system is seen as having failed. The global downturn, and all its human devastation, is being attributed to that failure. Throughout the world, including in the United States, this has turned the political tide in a new direction. The role of the state is expanding again, together with a reregulation of markets. This is evident in the United States, where President Obama has moved toward more activist and bigger government. The quasi-nationalization of the banking and automotive industries, as well as the pending reform of the financial system, makes this clear. It is also clear in Ireland, the United Kingdom, and elsewhere, where nationalizations have gone even further. And it is clear in statements made by such leaders as French President Nicolas Sarkozy, who recently celebrated "the return of the state" and "the end of the ideology of public powerlessness."

Second, globalization is in retreat, both in concept and in practice. Much of the world now sees it as harmful. Those nations, especially developing ones, that embraced increased capital flows and open trade have been particularly injured. Those that insulated themselves, such as India, have been less scarred. The global spread of goods, capital, and jobs is reversing. Global exports are falling sharply. The World Bank reports that exports from China, Japan, Mexico, Russia, and the United States fell by

25 percent or more in the year leading up to February 2009. Furthermore, financial and trade protectionism are spreading. Both the World Bank and the World Trade Organization recently reported a movement toward higher tariffs, higher nontariff barriers, and an increase in antidumping actions, designed to protect domestic jobs. Brazil, India, Russia, and numerous other states were cited. Moreover, various states' fiscal stimulus plans include subsidies for exporters and "buy domestic" provisions. And discriminatory actions against foreign workers are spreading. Immigrant workers, who are particular victims of this crisis, are returning home in waves. Japan and Spain are offering them cash to leave, and Malaysia is forcing them out.

Third, the world may be entering a new global phase marked by less leadership, less coordination, and less coherence. The world was already moving away from its post-Berlin Wall, unipolar condition, but this crisis has accelerated that process. The United States has turned inward, preoccupied with severe unemployment and fiscal pressures. Its economic model also is now out of favor. President Obama has made a triumphant overseas tour and is hugely popular everywhere. But his attention and political capital must be reserved for domestic issues, such as stabilizing the banking industry, handling the budget, and reforming health care.

Other nations have been rising, especially China. Although the United States' capacity to lead is now diminished and will continue to be so over the medium term, none of these rising powers is capable of full leadership. The outlook for effective multilateral approaches is also cloudy. The G-8 and the G-20 are relatively ineffective, as evidenced by the recent London summit. Yes, the IMF was expanded there, and that is important, but on the more challenging issues—a coordinated global stimulus, global financial oversight, and Afghanistan—the summit failed. Fundamentally, the G-8 an anachronism—China is not a member—and the G-20 is too large. On urgent political matters, such as Iran and the Arab-Israeli conflict, multilateralism is in retreat. The economic crisis is requiring most nations, including the United States, to focus inward. Also, other nations' responsiveness to U.S.

initiatives has been muted. The case of Pakistan makes that clear: a failed state with nuclear weapons would threaten many nations, and yet only U.S. diplomacy is fully active there.

Fourth, this crisis likely will increase geopolitical instability. Dennis Blair, the U.S. director of national intelligence, has asserted that the downturn already has produced low-level instability in a quarter of the world. The IMF has warned that millions will be pushed into unemployment, poverty, rising social unrest, or even war.

Countries in Africa have been hardest hit of all, and instability will likely rise there. Fragile states, such as the Democratic Republic of the Congo and the Central African Republic, have seen their social problems exacerbated by the crisis. Foreign reserves in the region have dwindled. The Congolese government will soon be unable to import essentials, such as food and fuel. The Central African Republic is already unable to pay the salaries of its civil servants. Private capital inflows could fall by nearly 90 percent, and the Overseas Development Institute, a British think tank, has projected that official aid will decline by $20 billion, as donors retrench. The commodity price crash, combined with the related slowdown in growth, the cutoff of private capital inflows, and diminished official assistance, has pushed the continent's collective current account surplus of four percent to a deficit of six percent in just two years. A World Bank study estimated that 53 million people living in emerging markets will fall back into absolute poverty. More frightening, according to the same study, up to 400,000 more children will die each year through 2015 on account of this economic crisis.

The Chinese Model

All of this is enhancing China's geopolitical standing. The West is experiencing a severe economic crisis, seen as its own making, whereas China is not. The Chinese leadership is well aware of this relative advantage, even though its priorities are always domestic. Apart from its coal supplies, China is resource poor. But it has recently been making offshore investments in natural resources of a kind that others no longer can make—such as securing future oil supplies from Russia and Venezuela.

It is increasingly clear that the U.S.-Chinese relationship will emerge as the most important bilateral one in the world. The two nations have similar geopolitical interests. Neither wants Iran to acquire nuclear weapons, North Korea to be destabilized, or Pakistan to become a failed state. There is no reason, therefore, why their relationship cannot be a cooperative and globally stabilizing one.

This economic crisis is a seismic global event. Free-market capitalism, globalization, and deregulation have been rising across the globe for 30 years; that era has now ended, and a new one is at hand. Global economic and financial integration are reversing. The role of the state, together with financial and trade protectionism, is ascending.

Capitalism, Nationalism, and the New American Empire

A. G. HOPKINS

Hopkins argues that the U.S. invasion of Iraq in 2003 was driven by a neoconservative agenda that transformed patriotic fervor into a nationalism that advocated the projection of hard power after the attacks of September 11, 2001. Thus, the invasion of Iraq was the product of nationalism, not capitalism, and ran counter to the tides of globalization that were dominant in the early 21st century.

Empires are once again big business. The United States is said to be building one in the Middle East, or at least making the attempt, and the word itself has become obligatory for titles of books dealing with contemporary international relations.

Most of the now innumerable books on this subject deal with the unfolding issues of the day and lack a wider focus. The much smaller that seeks to place current events in a larger perspective occupy a range of positions, through including many of the most influential, are those placed on the right and left of the political spectrum. The literature on the right, associated mainly with the neoconservatives but not confined to them, has promoted a vision of a democratic and pacific world order, which the United States is destined to bring into being through the exercise of its supreme power, including its military power.[2] According to this view, the invasion of Iraq was intended to be to first of a series of decisive interventions that would enable the United States to realize its providential mission. The literature on the left has advanced an alternative vision of a more equitable society, which will arise after the contradictions inherent in capitalism have conspired to bring the system down.[3] From this perspective, imperialism expresses the growing power of giant monopolies and world finance at a particular stage in the development of late capitalism. The invasion of

Iraq can be seen, and has been seen, as a measure taken to incorporate the economy, essentially its oil resources, into the world capitalist system.[4]

These opposed positions have the merit of painting big pictures that enable us to place Iraq in a global framework. But they have the disadvantage of fitting the invasion of Iraq into predetermined designs, and they also suffer from significant empirical deficiencies. The radical right makes its policy recommendations on behalf of a national entity, the United States, and is cast in an idealist, political mould that fails to relate foreign policy to the domestic socio-economic order. The radical left engages with internal developments but is hampered by the fact that an analysis based on class loses explanatory power in a country where politics is not primarily a function of class conflict.[5] Nevertheless, commentators on the right have identified one of the most important elements in understanding the foreign policy of imperial America: political nationalism. Commentators on the left have identified the other: capitalism. What is lacking is a means of fitting them together.

One way of joining the two is by returning to a neglected classic: Vilfredo Pareto's theory of elites. Pareto formulated his theory in 1901,[6] partly in response to Marx's emphasis on class relationships and partly in reaction to the way that Italy's democratic institutions had functioned since unification in the 1860s. Pareto's disillusion with the mass of the electorate, which he thought was easily manipulated and inclined to act irrationally, led him to emphasise the importance of sentiments in determining human actions. From this starting point he moved on to consider the character of governing elites and the strategies they used to perpetuate their dominance. The two most important types of elite are those he referred to as lions and foxes.[7] Lions are conservatives who possess "the persistence of aggregates" and stand for tradition and the use of force, if necessary, to uphold it. Foxes are innovators who have the "instinct for combining" and promote their interests by persuasion and guile.[8] When lions predominate, the government is more inclined to favour coercive means; when foxes are in control, negotiation and co-option are

the preferred techniques. Pareto then described how elites tend to exaggerate their dominant characteristics by recruiting like-minded members and by drawing strength from external influences: war and depression favour lions; peace and prosperity help foxes. The conditions that produce success, however, also prepare the way for failure. Uneven recruitment eventually creates an imbalance in the resources needed for governing. Lions have insufficient skill in negotiation; foxes are less adept at the use of force. The resulting unstable equilibrium is resolved by transferring dominance from one group to another, whether by the ballot box or through revolution. The ensuing circulation of elites is the motor of the political system.

Pareto's interest in ruling elites was shared by notable contemporaries, such as Mosca, Michels and Sorel, which suggests that he had identified an issue that was widely applicable to the Europe of the day. His insights into the history of elites also extended well beyond his own time. His anthropomorphic references to lions and foxes drew on an Italian tradition reaching back to Machiavelli, whose princes were either warriors in the heroic mould of Achilles or confidence tricksters possessed of cunning and subtlety.[9] Pareto's younger compatriot, Antonio Gramsci, pursued the question of how ruling classes maintained their dominance by developing his concept of moral hegemony, which is now as well-known as Pareto himself is neglected.

A further connection can be made between Pareto's ideas and the classical theories of imperialism. Pareto himself was not concerned to make the link;[10] studies of the new American empire have not done so either. Taking this step, however, makes it possible to place the actions of the United States in Iraq in a much longer perspective, and thus to begin to make it a subject of history. Radical theories of imperialism, as formulated by Cobden, Hobson and Veblen, emphasised the role of non-capitalist elites in promoting war and imperialism, and the contrasting commitment of the bulk of business interests in maintaining peace.[11] The danger, as they saw it, was that militant elements, supported by special interests (such as the armaments industry) and driven along by irrational nationalist fervour, would take control and destroy the modern capitalist system. The foxes might fail to tame the lions; they might also be drawn into aggressive behavior. Schumpeter, writing in 1919, took this interpretation to its highest stage by arguing that capitalism was indeed inherently pacific and that imperialism was the product of atavistic forces that had outlived their usefulness but were still able to influence policy.[12] Three years earlier, Lenin had produced a theory of imperialism that emphasised the opposite view, namely that the bourgeois order would be driven to war by contradictions in the capitalist system.[13] Foxes, so to speak, were really lions in disguise.

These now distant writers formulated the basic arguments that have resurfaced today in two sharply opposed claims: on the one hand, the view that the invasion of Iraq had non-economic causes, whether strategic, political or even personal; on the other, the notion that capitalism is driven by economic imperatives that produce war, conquest and destruction. Pareto's discussion of elites builds a bridge between the two.[14] The connection made here, briefly put, suggests that the decision to invade Iraq can be seen as marking a historic divergence between the rapid development of capitalism and the lagging development of the nation state. Profound changes in the structure of the economy of the United States in the late twentieth century created important new interests that depend on maintaining amicable relations with the wider world and call for largely fox-like attitudes. The nation-state, on the other hand, represents a constellation of embedded, lion-like interests, ranging from declining industries to populist nationalism, which incline towards a mixture of defensive isolationism at home and assertive action abroad. The two interests are not as estranged as this summary statement suggests because they share an underlying ideology of conservative patriotism that is capable, given the right circumstances, of overlaying their differences. Foxes had no direct interest in occupying Iraq, but they were co-opted by the lions in the administration, who succeeded in the aftermath

of 9/11 in transforming domestic patriotism into forceful nationalism.

The capitalist element in the story can be followed by tracing the evolution of the military-industrial complex—a term launched by President Eisenhower in his Farewell Address and revived today by the debate over the causes of the Iraq war.[15] Eisenhower's concern was that the expansion of the military-industrial complex would lead to what he called "unwarranted influence" in the "councils of government." Although an old lion himself, Eisenhower feared that an excessive growth in the number of lions would lead to the "disastrous rise of misplaced power" that would "endanger our liberties or democratic processes." Eisenhower's remedy—in fact his main message—was to urge that government policies should result from balanced deliberation. Sound judgement at home called for "an alert and knowledgeable citizenry"; sound judgment abroad involved diplomacy as well as force. "The conference table," Eisenhower said, "though scarred by many frustrations, cannot be abandoned for the certain agony of the battlefield." In other words, balance could be achieved only if fox-like qualities of persuasion and flexibility were incorporated into government policies to a degree that would rein in the assertive tendencies of the lion-like interests who managed the military-industrial complex.

Eisenhower's thoughts were his own, but they undoubtedly reflected a much wider preoccupation of the time. A few years earlier, C. Wright Mills had published an account of what he called *The Power Elite*, a study that was widely discussed at the time and is regarded now as a modern classic. Mills did not use the term "military- industrial complex," nor, curiously, did he make use of Pareto, though he was influenced by Veblen, and saw himself as updating his theory of the leisure class.[16] Nevertheless, Mills produced the most comprehensive study of the elites of the day, and what he called the "warlords and their business associates featured prominently in it. Mills used the term "power elite" to refer a cluster of elites—economic, political and military—who came together in "often uneasy coincidence" to run the country.[17] Competition among elites in the "higher circles" was conducted within a framework set by shared values derived from common educational and social backgrounds. Their grip on power had grown as a result of the rise of the large corporation, the expansion of government (during the Roosevelt years and in the course of the Second World War) and "the development of a permanent military establishment."[18] In Mills's view, the citizenry at large were being steadily excluded from the decision-making processes that affected their lives, and the notion that imbalances in power would correct themselves automatically no longer held.

Mills's discussion of what he called "the theory of balance" echoes Pareto's notion of equilibrium and connects even more readily to Eisenhower's emphasis on the need for a counterweight to the military-industrial complex. Unlike Pareto, however, Mills did not offer an account of how elites would transform themselves. Indeed, his analysis suggested that the power elite was able to contain its internal differences and present a generally united front to the rest of society. The result, in his rather bleak assessment, was government by a plutocratic oligarchy consisting of both lions and foxes.

Mills's study has been much discussed and his conclusions and wider judgements have been both assaulted and defended.[19] But his general picture of the changes that had taken place during the previous half century is still regarded as being broadly accurate. As the United States became united, so the "command posts" of power, as Mills called them, had shifted from local societies to the national stage. As institutional hierarchies, private and public, had grown, so too had the power of those who directed them. As clusters of national elites distanced themselves from the population at large, transparency and accountability were reduced and the gap between rulers and ruled grew ever wider. These views were shared by many writers on the radical left whose work became particularly influential in the 1960s and 1970s. For example, William Appleman Williams, one of the most prominent historians of the time, regarded American foreign policy as an imperial policy driven primarily by internal forces that were bound up with the rise of state and corporate capitalism and the expansion of the military interest.[20]

This line of thinking has been applied to the invasion of Iraq where, so it has been held, oil was the primary motive and the military-industrial complex the main agent.[21] This claim needs careful evaluation. There is no doubt of the continuing importance of the complex, though it is not easily measured, either today or in the 1950s.[22] The best proxy is probably annual defence expenditure, which ran at about 5-6 percent of GDP during the era of the Cold War, dropped to about 3.5 per cent in the 1990s and is now back up to about 5 per cent. But of course the GDP is much larger now than it was in the 1950s, and annual expenditure in (constant) dollars is correspondingly greater.[23] This sum, which is currently over $400bn., is greater than that spent on defence by the rest of the world as a whole. Illustrative evidence of links between armaments firms, the military and Congress is also readily available, as are stunning examples of pork barrel politics, including one where the Air Force requested five C-130 aircraft and was voted funds for 25-6.[24] Bringing home the bacon is particularly important for localities where employment has become dependent on defence contracts: Boeing in Seattle and Lockheed Martin in Bethesda (Maryland) are well-known examples, but there are many other centres, scattered across the United States, that would suffer if the defence budget were cut significantly.

At the same time, it is important to recognize that the composition of the military-industrial complex has changed considerably since the 1950s. On the military side, the most significant development has been the introduction of precision-guided weapons, which have reduced the need for a huge air-force and cut the demand for manpower in the army. One consequence has been a fall in employment in the old, metal-working industries and a corresponding increase in links between new, "high-tech" industries and defence.[25] Military research programmes fund the development of semiconductors, software and sensors; military contractors buy back the resulting products cheaply because they have also been mass-produced for the consumer market. A second consequence has been the decline of the tradition of the "citizen-soldier" and the creation of a professional army that is increasingly removed from the wider society it is contracted to represent.[26] The Constitution remains unaltered, but the abolition of the draft has in practice diminished a powerful check on the use of the military.

By the end of the twentieth century, the industrial component of the military-industrial complex had also changed.[27] The new, "high-tech" industries that helped to produce precision weapons were part of a much broader trend representing a shift away from long-established industries. Textiles and steel are in the final stages of a protracted and painful decline; the motor vehicle industry is in serious difficulties, too, as the desperate state of General Motors' finances demonstrates.[28] Manufacturing accounted for about 30 per cent of GDP in 1953 but only around 15 percent in 2000 and ceased to generate new jobs after 1980.[29] The complement to this trend has been the expansion of the service economy, assisted by new digital information technology, in response to the demand for education, health care, entertainment and financial, legal and personal services: in 1948 its share of GDP stood at 45 percent; by 2000 it had reached 66 percent.[30]

These developments were accompanied by increasing integration with the outside world, and by a shift in economic gravity within the United States from the north east to the south and west.[31] Commodity exports grew from about 4 per cent of GDP in 1950 to around 15 percent in 2000; imports moved in parallel fashion until 1976, since then they have risen rapidly, thus producing a persistent and swelling deficit in the balance of trade. Exported services, on the other hand, not only expanded but also generated a growing surplus, though this was insufficient to close the gap on the current account, which was met by borrowing from abroad. Foreign holdings of United States treasury securities and corporate stocks and bonds have increased rapidly since the 1980s, as has foreign direct investment in the United States. There was a corresponding, though slightly greater, growth in American investment overseas as multinational corporations shifted operations abroad—a phenomenon known today as outsourcing. The American economy still consists of a vast internal market, especially if Canada and Mexico (its NAFTA partners) are included, but over the last 30 years it has also been joined more firmly to other parts of the world, especially to Western Europe, Japan and China.[32] This new orientation has been made possible by reduced trade barriers, deregulation and greater financial integration, and carries with it a general commitment to free trade.[33] Agriculture and the older industries, on the other hand, are more inclined to support protection because they fear foreign competition.[34] The foxes promote globalisation; the lions seek shelter.

Evidently, the relationship between the economy and the American presence abroad is far more complicated today than it was in the 1950s, when Williams advanced the view that the chief purpose of foreign policy was to secure markets for manufacturers.[35] It is hard to sustain this argument today and harder still to relate it to the invasion of Iraq. The limited information currently available suggests that the military-industrial complex played a minor part in the decision to go to war in 2003. The best evidence concerns the military itself, which was determined above all to avoid another Vietnam experience.[36] From the 1970s onwards the chiefs of staff tried to steer clear of marginal wars, guerrillas and potential quagmires. These priorities were reinforced by President Bush's secretary of state, Colin Powell, who wanted to ensure that future wars were limited to those that were absolutely necessary and clearly winnable.[37] Even in these eases, the Powell Doctrine held that the army ought not to be deployed unless it had overwhelming force and a defined exit strategy. Powells aim was to create an army that was highly valued, well funded and rarely deployed, and to erect barriers that would prevent politicians from misusing the massive military power at their disposal. The lions had not lost their appetites, but they had learned by experience when to hunt and when to conserve their energies.[38]

With regard to the industrial component, it has yet to be argued that industries linked to defence agitated for war. The old defence industries undoubtedly lost ground to new "high-tech" firms, but the trend would not have been altered by successful war-mongering, and might even have accentuated it. A number of specialised "high-tech" companies were closely involved with the military, but the overwhelming interest of the industry as a whole lay in the civilian market both at home and abroad. Moreover, many of the new suppliers were small, scattered and not as readily mobilised for political purposes as the older, giant corporations, while the significant (and little publicised) participation of foreign-owned companies in defence contracts meant that the new industries could not easily present themselves as being part of the national interest, even if they wished to do so.[39]

This leaves firms that were linked to the military-industrial complex without being confined by it, the most important, of course, being the great oil companies and their close associates.[40] It is self-evident that the American presence in the Middle East is dominated by oil (and Israel), and that the oil companies have a permanent interest in ensuring that supplies flow through them at required levels and appropriate prices.[41] It is also well-known that President Bush and his some of his senior associates have close ties to the oil industry.[42] Moreover, there is no doubt that the development of oil in the Middle East and the political involvement of foreign powers in the region are closely related.[43] This was true of the period of British dominance; it applies equally to the extension of the American presence from the 1940s.[44] Added to this, some commentators have claimed that the oil companies were keen to secure Iraq's rich oil reserves at a time when demand was beginning to outstrip supply.[45] Taken together, these arguments have led to the widespread belief that the invasion of Iraq was prompted primarily by the desire to control its oil resources.[46]

The case is attractive. Foxes, too, can bite when threatened, and the oil companies have been involved in various political interventions in the past. But the evidence relating to the invasion of 2003 is at present circumstantial and will remain so until the records are available. Meanwhile, there are grounds for an alternative view. In the first place, there was no immediate supply crisis in the years immediately before the invasion, and prices since the first Gulf War had followed the normal course of supply and

demand.[47] The question of long-term reserves had long been debated within the oil industry, and had produced judgements and strategies other than resorting to war, which risked massive disruption to plant as well as threatening to destabilise the region as a whole.[48] Above all, the oil companies had long accepted that the days of gun-boat diplomacy had come to an end. By the 1970s, the demise of the Western empires, combined with the rising value of oil exports, had shifted power to the independent states of the Gulf.[49] The oil companies came to terms with this development by reaching an accommodation with the various authoritarian regimes in the region. There is no indication in 2003 that they wished to abandon the relationships they had carefully built up since the formation of OPEC in 1960 and, more particularly, the oil crisis of 1973.

On the contrary, it is now known that the oil industry opposed the administration's plan, devised shortly before the invasion in March 2003, to privatise the oil fields and to destroy the OPEC cartel by selling Iraq's oil above the quota allocated.[50] The oil companies defeated the scheme and devised an alternative in 2004 calling for the formation of a state-owned oil company that would support OPEC. Philip Carroll, the former CEO of Shell Oil USA who took control of Iraq's oil production for the American government after the invasion, made a revealing (and rare) public comment on the episode: "Many neo-conservatives are people who have certain ideological beliefs about markets, about democracy, about this, that and the other. International oil companies, without exception, are very pragmatic commercial organizations. They don't have a theology."[51] Shortly after the invasion, the Chairman of PFC Energy, one of the leading advisory companies to the industry, offered the following judgement: "I don't think we went there for the oil and I don't think we went there for the things the White House said we went there for either. The main reason was to consolidate our position as a superpower."[52] The interest of the oil companies lay in upholding the political *status quo* while negotiating contracts for new investments once the sanctions imposed by the United Nations Security Council were removed.[53] They were well aware that the stability of the Middle East was precarious, that their own presence as foreign firms was a sensitive matter and that, accordingly, discretion—not valour—was called for.[54]

The lions in this affair were not the pride of the military-industrial complex but an alliance of assorted political idealists, commonly known as neo-conservatives, and assertive nationalists, whose influence has now been subjected to detailed scrutiny.[55] The word "nationalist" is appropriate here, even though discussion of America's role in the world since 9/11 has referred almost exclusively to "patriotism," presumably because this term is thought to be untainted and free from dangers of excess. In the present context, however, it is useful to draw a distinction between the two while also recognising the link between them. Patriots have an affiliation to what is and what has been; nationalists have an additional sense of destiny that is shaped to a greater extent by relations with the outside world.[56] The neo-conservatives were nationalists who wished to realise a messianic mission abroad. They traced their intellectual lineage to Wilsonian idealism and they endorsed in particular Wilson's vision of spreading democracy throughout the world. But they disowned important elements of his programme, such as multilateralism and disarmament, and advocated instead unilateral action and the expansion of the military. Their allies were nationalist realists who agreed on the need for an assertive foreign policy but took a more pragmatic view of how to advance America's interests abroad.

The disaffection of the neo-conservatives in particular was enhanced during the Clinton years by the growing conviction that prosperity had distracted the United States from its historic mission of spreading freedom and democracy, and that by promoting globalisation the administration had embraced a weak foreign policy that was a further symptom of moral decline.[57] The nationalists who did not regard themselves as being neoconservatives had a less messianic outlook and were ambivalent about the free-trading implications of globalisation, but concurred that American interests abroad needed to be represented more assertively.[58]

Following the collapse of the Soviet Union, the United States had become the undisputed supreme power. It had the means to impress itself on the world, but not, so it seemed, the will. Caged lions could only watch as foxes gambled with America's future.

Nevertheless, the neo-conservative and nationalist alliance was determined not to allow a unique opportunity to pass. As is now well-known, its leading figures devised a plan for a decisive and awe-inspiring demonstration of American power, and they also selected a recipient: Saddam Hussein.[59] The aim was to remake the Middle East, beginning with Iraq, on the heroic assumption that installing democratic forms of government would produce states that were both pacific and friendly to the United States.[60] A new Iraq also held out the prospect of repositioning the United States in the Middle East by extracting it from the now tainted authoritarian regime of Saudi Arabia.[1] The election of George W. Bush in 2000 was a move in the right direction because it delivered a president who had no expertise in foreign affairs and who was open to the influence of those who claimed that they did, especially if the argument was capable of being expressed in clear-cut moral terms, which it was. 9/11 presented the opportunity that the neo-conservatives had long waited for. It was the mother of all wake-up calls, rallying the nation to its duty and setting the stage for a display of martial virtues that would redirect the country and reshape the world. A huge professional army stood ready. Success in the first Gulf War had boosted its reputation; its ethos, which emphasised discipline and order and a commitment to defend American values, if need be, to the death, embodied all the qualities that civil society seemed to have abandoned.[61] Spreading democracy abroad was the international arm of a policy that was also designed to rehabilitate society at home. The lions had been lionised. The only problem was that they did not want to fight.

Fight they did, however, and for two main reasons. After 9/11, the relatively small group of neo-conservatives and nationalist activists was able to sound an alarm that rang throughout the United

States. In the first place, their call resonated with longstanding and deeply-held conservative beliefs embodied in the notion of American exceptionalism, which held that the United States was the ultimate custodian of liberty and democracy and had a duty to defend them against assailants at home and abroad.[62] The events of 9/11 ensured that there would be a rapid and widespread response to an appeal to rally round the flag and to launch what was called, briefly, a 'crusade' against terrorism. Equally, it was an opportunity to undertake at home the moral rearmament that the right-wing alliance thought was so badly needed.

The second reason why 9/11 stirred up the forces of popular nationalism lies in more recent history. Globalisation, as we have seen, had caused the United States to be increasingly integrated with the rest of the world in the second half of the twentieth century, and especially from the 1980s. In doing so, it had set in train a process of uneven development that amplified socio-economic disparities within the country. Although average incomes have grown during the last 20 years, median incomes have been flat or declining.[63] This divergence has been reflected in the rapid increase in inequality between the top 1 per cent and the bottom 90 per cent of income-earners and in gathering worries about the prospects for upward mobility. Those who gained, such as the new rich in California's high-tech industries, favoured globalisation and in general had little economic incentive to adopt a nationalist approach to geo-political issues.[64] Those who suffered either lost their jobs in the older industries or faced new uncertainties, as companies moved to short-term contracts and cut benefits in an attempt to stay competitive.[65] Anxiety about employment prospects caused by outsourcing was intensified by substantial inflows of immigrants, especially from Mexico and Central America.

Economic change was accompanied by growing socio-cultural anxieties. The old, Anglo-Saxon assimilationist model of society no longer held, but multiculturalism, intensified by expanding immigration, raised doubts about what it was to be American, and increased geographical and social mobility shifted established boundaries, including those governing relations between men and women.[66] These swirling uncertainties help to explain the rise and politicisation of evangelical faiths, which provided material support for those who were losing their place and spiritual guidance for those who were losing their way.[67] The evangelicals propounded an assertive form of Christianity that fitted into secular patriotism and provided validation for it.[68] This programme appealed to at least some of those who were well on their way to realising the American dream of permanent affluence, as well as to those made susceptible by failure. Success in a highly individualistic consumer society imperilled a sense of community and raised questions about the sources of moral authority. Conservative values, stiffened by evangelical teaching, provided unambiguous and reassuring answers.[69] Increasingly, too, they found expression in the Republican Party. As the Republicans improved their position in the southern states in the closing decades of the twentieth century, so the south infused the party with its own style of tradition, religion and patriotism.[68]

In other circumstances, this mix of economic discontent and social unease might have been channelled into class conflict; in the United States it was grouped in support of the traditional values represented by faith, family and flag. The trauma of 9/11 called for national solidarity, which was achieved by promoting shared values and endowing them with an appeal that took the form of a renewed commitment to freedom and democracy, and so rose above party and special interests. Republicans were more successful than Democrats in presenting themselves as guardians of the homeland and in basing their manifesto on fundamental moral values. They succeeded, too, in turning public opinion against the "liberal elite" by characterising it as being weak on defence and strong on big government.[70] The neo-conservative and nationalist alliance succeeded in implementing its assertive foreign policy not only because it was well entrenched in the corridors of power but also because, in the aftermath of 9/11, it was able to convert conservative patriotism across the United States into assertive nationalism. The warfare state was to supplant the welfare state; martial qualities would stiffen the moral fibre of the nation at home and promote a powerful yet benign *imperium* abroad.[71]

Machiavelli wrote his masterpiece, *The Prince*, at a time when the Italian states were torn by internal dissension and beset by external enemies.[72] In his estimation, exceptional circumstances called for an exceptional leader who, by combining the force of lions and the cunning of foxes, would restore internal order and scare off foreign predators. Pareto, writing at a time when, as he saw it, Italy was squandering the opportunities presented by unification, concluded that the state was suffering from the excesses of a plutocratic elite of foxes and needed to be rebalanced by adding lion-like discipline and the weight of traditional values. The United States is neither Renaissance Florence nor Italy after the Risorgimento, but it has been beset by external enemies, and it is also under considerable internal socio-economic strain. Arguably, too, it is characterised by what Pareto termed a "demagogic plutocracy," in which huge wealth is a necessary qualification for governing, and the exercise of power relies heavily on purchasing support and manipulating the core ideologies associated with American exceptionalism.[73] Here Pareto's emphasis on the power of sentiment rather than reason in influencing behaviour is highly relevant to understanding the fear generated by the threat of alien invasion and the heavy stress placed on moral values in restoring social stability—both of which featured so prominently in the presidential election of 2004.

Influential explanations of America's role as a world power have either emphasised its benign, selfless motives in spreading freedom and democracy or focused on its malign consequences as an agent of capitalism in crisis. The first view treats ideology as an unproblematic and transparent influence that is largely removed from economic considerations. The second view regards ideology as masking the fundamental economic forces of an industrial order wrestling with ever deepening contradictions. The argument put here has tried to draw these two lines of thought together by investigating the relationship between the ideology of patriotism-turned-nationalism and the transformation of the American economy in the second half of the twentieth century. The governing elite has been placed at the centre of the enquiry because it directed the traffic at the intersection of nationalism and capitalism. Giving prominence to human agency provides a means of animating otherwise impersonal forces. It also underlines the importance of relating America's presence abroad to developments at home rather than relying on the assumption that foreign policy is determined by the workings of an abstraction beyond its shores called the international regime.[74]

This line of enquiry leads to the conclusion that American imperialism, as illustrated by the invasion of Iraq, was the product of nationalism rather than of capitalism. On current evidence, neither the military-industrial complex nor Big Oil was pushing for war. Nevertheless, an understanding of the evolution of the capitalist system in the United States is still central to the analysis of the forces favouring invasion, despite the fact that specific interests connected to defence and oil were not directly implicated. In the second half of the twentieth century American capitalism experienced profound changes that led to greater integration with the outside world. The most important of these ties were with Europe, the Far East and the other members of NAFTA. None of these regions was a suitable candidate for empire-building or even for the bullying brand of diplomacy advocated by warrior-commentators. The success of the new American capitalism rested instead on promoting fox-like qualities of innovation, guile and persuasion that were needed to manage business relationships across cultures and countries. These qualities were also manifested in the attitude of the oil companies, which decided from the 1970s to work with rather than against nationalists in the Middle East.

The progressive globalisation of the economy, however, also generated economic and social dislocation. An important consequence was the creation of a sense of uncertainty about cultural identity and moral purpose that encompassed those who were gaining from economic change as well as to those who were suffering from it. The main difference was that the winners held to a patriotic conservatism that was consistent with globalisation and free trade, whereas the losers were more inclined to turn to isolationist and protectionist forms of nationalism. The sense that society was drifting from its anchorage lay behind the conservative revival that began as a reaction to what were seen to be liberal excesses in the 1960s and 1970s, and gathered strength in the 1980s from anxieties generated by the character and pace of economic development and the rapidity of social change. In Pareto's terms, the fox-like character of the dominant elite and the morality it endorsed inspired a movement to restore traditional lion-like values. But when these values were extended to the conservative foreign policies advanced in the 1990s, one isolationist and the other assertive, they departed from the developing, international interests of American capitalism; when patriotism was converted into nationalism following the shock of 9/11, the disjunction was complete.

The argument put here that the developing interests of American capitalism were at variance with the decision to go to war suggests that, in this instance at least, Marxist and radical-left interpretations of imperialism have limited explanatory power. Notwithstanding the business connections of senior members of the administration, the military-industrial complex was not agitating for war, still less for the creation of a new formal empire. Schumpeter's view that imperialism was the product of non-capitalist forces seems, on this occasion, to be closer to the mark, though the elites who directed policy in the United States cannot be regarded simply as atavistic residues because the conservative values they represented fitted the capitalist society from which they sprang.

The contest between these interpretations, however, needs to be related to time and place. Economic explanations of imperialism have greater purchasing power where there is a close fit between the development of capitalism and the direction of overseas expansion. This was the case, so it has been argued, with the growth of the British empire in the nineteenth century.[75] International trade was characterised by the exchange of manufactures from the metropole for raw materials from the colonies and semi-colonies; expansion was managed by an elite of lions and foxes who had enough in

common to ensure both cohesion and continuity. Economic integration does not necessarily bring peace, as Cobden and many subsequent commentators assumed, and it is evident that the frontiers of finance and trade were often moved on in the nineteenth century by political and military action. If this interpretation holds, then Schumpeter's view that capitalism was invariably a pacific force also needs modification. What can be said is that the particular type of integration associated with contemporary globalisation makes open conflict among the powers concerned a highly costly and counterproductive exercise. The main lines of capitalist development today join countries in the advanced and rapidly advancing countries of the world. These relationships do not lend themselves to colonial ventures, which are either irrelevant or impossible. Elsewhere, as the United States has so painfully discovered in Iraq, foreign occupation, however benign its intent, provokes intense resentment and determined resistance that draws its inspiration, in a post-colonial era, from the right of self-determination that President Wilson himself did so much to promote. The implication of this argument is clear: empire is indeed an anachronism in the twenty-first century, despite the renewed call to arms that has been sounded in recent years.[76]

As the disjunction between nationalism and capitalism clearly shows, the United States has globalized the world but not itself. The economy is becoming international; politics remains local. The divorce was well illustrated in 2006 by the debate over the attempt by a Dubai company to buy the management business of six major ports in the United States, and by the larger controversy over immigration.[77] In both cases, the administration was caught on its own barbed wire: economic advantage pointed towards globalization, but fear of foreign invaders, stirred up in the aftermath of 9/11, called for the rebuilding of fortress America.[78] These conflicting interests were replicated on a much larger scale in the invasion of Iraq, which represented the triumph of combative nationalism over economic internationalism and caused the United States to attempt to found an empire and, momentarily at least, to lose a role.

Notes

1. Bonner and Wiggin, *Empire of Debt.*
2. The literature is now huge. Dorrien, *Imperial Designs* provides a valuable introduction and numerous further references.
3. Representative commentary can be found in the *Monthly Review, New Left Review* and the *Socialist Register,* especially, Panitch and Leys (eds.), *New Imperial Challenge* and *The Empire Reloaded.*
4. For example, Foster, "Imperial America," 11–12.
5. Lipset and Marks, *It Didn't Happen Here.*
6. The most penetrating of several introductions to Pareto's theory of elites remains Pareto, *Sociological Writings.*
7. It need hardly be said that this is a simplification of Pareto's complex typology. Pareto identified a total of six elements, which he called "residues," each with various subclasses. Residues represented the more or less permanent springs of human action, and were found, notably, in tendencies to conserve (lions) and innovate (foxes). Derivations, in Pareto's terminology, refer to attitudes and beliefs that people express. These may reflect or conceal underlying residues.
8. Combination is a direct translation of *combinazioni,* which means "inventive cunning, foresight, and guile." See Powers, *Vilfredo Pareto,* 73.
9. "[T]he lion cannot defend himself from traps, and the fox cannot defend himself from wolves. It is therefore necessary to be a fox to recognize traps and a lion to frighten the wolves." Machiavelli, *The Prince,* 75.
10. Pareto was opposed to nearly all "isms" (including imperialism), which he saw as devices to manipulate the mass of the people.
11. See Cain, *Hobson and Imperialism* and "Capitalism, Internationalism." Hobson's theory is commonly over-summarized as an example of the influence of financial interests, but he also laid great emphasis on the role of what he called "pride and pugnacity."
12. Schumpeter, *Imperialism.*
13. Lenin, *Imperialism.*
14. It is unnecessary for present purposes to explore here the complexities that Pareto added to his theory over the years. These have been much discussed by sociologists and political scientists and lead in many different directions.
15. 17 Jan. 1961, Public Papers of the Presidents, Dwight D. Eisenhower, 1035–40, readily available on the World Wide Web.
16. *Theory of the Leisure Class.* Mills wrote an introduction to the Mentor edition of Veblen's study (1953) that drew a connection between *The Theory of the Leisure Class* and his own work, *The Power Elite,* which was to appear three years later. Mills referred to Pareto very briefly in ch. 1, ns. 3–4; Mosca is mentioned on 172, n.7 in the 2000 ed.
17. Mills, *Power Elite,* 278.
18. Ibid., 19.
19. Ibid., 380–81 for a brief guide to the literature produced since 1956.
20. See especially *The Tragedy of American Diplomacy.*
21. Representative examples include: Paul, "Oil Companies in Iraq"; Everest, *Oil, Power and Empire.*
22. Johnson, *Sorrows of Empire,* Bacevich, *New American Militarism,* and Priest, *The Mission,* document the military side. As yet, there is no full study of the industrial component.
23. Hartung, "Eisenhower's Warning," 1–2. In real terms the expenditure projected for 2006 is greater than in any year of the Cold War except 1952. See Benjamin, "Pentagon Papers."
24. Hartung, "Eisenhower's Warning"; Flake, "Earmarked Men."
25. Huber, "Military-Industrial Complex," 1.
26. Bacevich, *New American Militarism,* 26–28.
27. The most recent compilation is Kozmetsky and Yue's comprehensive study, *Economic Transformation.*
28. Peters, "GM Loss."
29. Kozmetsky and Yue, *Economic Transformation,* 470. The figures for the goods-producing sector as a whole (manufacturing, agriculture, fishing, forestry, mining and construction) were 44 percent in 1948 and 23 percent in 2000. Ibid., 297.
30. Ibid., 297, 468, 471–75; Bosworth and Triplett, *Productivity in the US Services Sector.*
31. Kozmetsky and Yue, *Economic Transformation,* 272–85.
32. This development is not confined to the outsourcing of manufacturing jobs. Wal-Mart is expanding abroad rapidly: it has 56 stores in China and intends to hire an extra 150,000 Chinese employees during the next five years. See BBC News, 20 March 2006.

33. Cox and Skidmore-Hess, *U.S. Politics and the Global Economy.*

34. Bergstrom, "The United States"; Smitka, "Foreign Policy"; Goodman, Spar, and Yoffie, "Foreign Direct Investment."

35. Williams, *Tragedy of American Diplomacy.*

36. Bacevich, *New American Militarism,* ch. 2. General Anthony Zinni, former head of the U.S. Central command, claims that the invasion of Iraq was a war that the politicians, not the military, wanted: "I can't speak for all generals, certainly. But I know we felt that this situation was contained. Saddam was effectively contained. The no-fly, no-drive zones. The sanctions that were imposed on him." CBS News, "60 Minutes," 21 May 2004.

37. Secretary of State, 2001–05, and before that Chairman of the Joint Chiefs of Staff, 1989–93 and National Security Advisor, 1987–89. Powell's well-known disagreements with the hawkish Vice-President, Dick Cheney, are recorded by Woodward in *Plan of Attack.*

38. Opposition to the war in Iraq was openly expressed in 2006 by a number of newly-retired senior officers. Shane, "Generals Break with Tradition."

39. At the latest count, no fewer than 98 foreign-owned firms had agreements with the Pentagon to have access to classified government defense programs. See McCarthy, "Foreign Firms a Mainstay." Procurement has also been globalized. The army uses Italian-made Berettas; police forces in the USA, as well as in Iraq, are armed with pistols manufactured by Glock, an Austrian company.

40. The leading associates are Halliburton, which is the largest oil-services company in the United States, and Bechtel, which holds most of the reconstruction contracts for Iraq. On the distribution of the spoils see, among many possible illustrations, Weisman and Reddy, "Spending on Iraq." There is no reliable information about whether these firms favored the invasion or, if they did, what influence their representations had on the decision.

41. Two sober and well-informed assessments, written shortly before the invasion, are: Graham-Brown and Toensing, "Why Another War?";

Cable (former Chief Economist for Shell Oil), "Economic Fallout."

42. President Bush and his father both owned oil companies in Texas; Vice President Dick Cheney is the former CEO of Halliburton; Secretary of State Condoleezza Rice is a former director of Chevron Texaco.

43. The literature is vast. An accessible guide is Yergin, *The Prize.*

44. For example, Heiss, *Empire and Nationhood;* Vitalis "Black Gold." Stoff has shown in *Oil, War, and American Security* how the administration came to rely on the oil companies to represent national interests in the Middle East in the period 1941–47.

45. Simmons, *Twilight in the Desert.* The starting point for this literature is the concept of Hubbert's Peak, on which see the concise survey by Semple, "The End of Oil." An extension of this argument, which cannot be discussed here, holds that the invasion was motivated by the need to ensure that Iraq continued to price its oil in dollars. The case has been put by Clark, *Petrodollar Warfare.* The issue is clearly important for the future of the dollar as the world's premier currency, but there is no evidence that it motivated the invasion of Iraq.

46. See n. 30.

47. WTRG Economics. A balanced guide is Retort, "Blood for Oil?"

48. For the alternative, optimistic view of energy supplies, see Yergin, "It's Not the End."

49. Especially Vitalis, "The Closing of the Arabian Oil Frontier."

50. Palast, "Secret Plans."

51. Ibid. The full transcript is at http://www.greg-palast.com.

52. Vahan Zanoyan, quoted in O'Brien, "Just What Does America Want." It is of course possible that these claims are merely covers for the real, oil-based motive, but the case has to be demonstrated, not simply inferred. It is also worth noting that Lee Raymond, the chief executive of the Exxon Mobil, the world's largest oil company, until 2006, held consistently to a long-term political and economic strategy in the Middle East. See Bartiromo, "Lee Raymond."

53. Graham-Brown and Toensing, "Why Another War?," 15. On sanctions, see Graham-Brown, *Sanctioning Saddam.*

54. This conclusion agrees with that of Yergin, "The Fight over Iraq's Oil." On the disastrous consequences of the invasion on oil production, see Negus, "Oil Ministry the Key." While high oil prices benefit the oil companies in the short term, they also increase the power of producers to adjust the gains in their favor. See Mouawad, "As Profits Surge."

55. In President Bush's administration, the former included Paul Wolfowitz and Richard Perle; the latter Dick Cheney and Donald Rumsfeld. The categories can only be approximate because they overlapped and the attitudes of individuals evolved. Full accounts of all the leading figures can be found in Dorrien, *Imperial Designs,* and Mann, *Rise of the Vulcans.*

56. According to Irving Kristol, one the founding figures of American neoconservatism: "Patriotism springs from love of the nation's past; nationalism arises out of hope for the nation's future, distinctive greatness." Quoted in Lieven, *America Right or Wrong*, 6.

57. See the perceptive essay by Robin, "How 9/11 Unified Conservatives."

58. The two groups came together in the Project for a New American Century, a Washington think tank founded in 1997.

59. There is now a large literature detailing the influence of the neoconservatives and nationalists on foreign policy since 2001. See especially Halper and Clarke, *America Alone*; Mann, *Rise of the Vulcans*; Lieven, *America Right or Wrong*; Daalder and Lindsay, *America Unbound*; Woodward, *Plan of Attack*; Bamford, *Pretext for War*; Packer, *Assassins' Gate*; Gordon and Trainor, *Cobra II.* As it became clear that the invasion of Iraq was both a blunder and a quagmire, the hawks started to break ranks. By 2005 their influence was slipping, and in 2006 they began to blame President Bush for mismanaging their (still unimpeachable) plan for transforming the Middle East. The most highly publicized defection was that of Francis Fukuyama, *America at the Crossroads.*

60. The proposition (derived from Kant) that democratic societies were also pacific, or, more precisely that they did not fight one another, has generated a huge industry among political scientists during the past 20 years and provided much of the intellectual basis for promoting democracy throughout the world. The latest study, published (unfortunately) after the decision to promote democracy in Iraq by force, argues that, while mature democracies may not fight one another, new democracies can and sometimes do. See Mansfield and Snyder, *Electing to Fight.*

61. Bacevich, *New American Militarism,* provides an extensive treatment of this theme.

62. Liberty was present "at the creation"; democracy was added in the twentieth century. On the relation between ideology and foreign policy see Hunt, *Ideology and U.S. Foreign Policy,* and Stephanson, *Manifest Destiny.*

63. The trend dates from the 1980s. See Lee, "Wage Inequality." Recent data are summarized by Luce, "Out on a Limb."

64. In 2006 big business (including oil) and finance opposed proposals that would have checked the flow of investment into the USA. See Kirchgaessner, "Business Lobby."

65. Uchitelle, *Disposable American*; Levy, "New Corporate Outsourcing."

66. The war of 1898 (so it has been argued) also gave expression to gender politics. See Hoganson, *Fighting for American Manhood.*

67. Entry points to what is now a large literature include: Halper and Clarke, *America Alone,* Ch. 6; Lieven, *America Right or Wrong,* ch. 4. Phillips, *American Theocracy,* offers an appropriately apocalyptic account of the dangers of excessive religiosity.

68. On the perfect union, see Blumenthal, "Credo of Joel Osteen."

69. McGirr's analysis of Orange County in *Suburban Warriors* complements Frank's widely publicized book, *What's the Matter with Kansas?* Although the communities studied had widely different economic circumstances, they shared a common sociocultural outlook, which derived from the fact that the majority of the new conservatives in

Orange County had migrated from the Midwest. See also n. 87.

70. Frank's account of this process in *What's the Matter with Kansas?* shows how "market populism" enabled business interests, which favored the cheap labor that came with immigration, to win the support of wage-earners (and voters), even though such policies affected them adversely.

71. Widely publicized examples of muscular, military approaches to the problems of the world include: Boot, *Savage Wars of Peace;* Kagan, *Of Paradise and Power;* and Frum and Perle, *An End to Evil.*

72. Plague and the French both descended on Florence 1494.

73. We await a new C. Wright Mills to deal with these issues in the case of the United States. Meanwhile, valuable information has been put together by Phillips, *Wealth and Democracy* and *American Dynasty.*

74. Trubowitz, *Defining the National Interest,* provides a powerful analysis of the role of (regional) domestic forces in shaping foreign policy.

75. Cain and Hopkins, *British Imperialism.*

76. Kinzer, *Overthrow,* catalogues a series of interventions and their consequences.

77. Gross, "Globalization Offered Two Ways." "Uncle Sam Says Yes," 67, notes that America's huge external deficit points to the wisdom of adopting a friendly attitude towards foreign investors. On immigration see, Pew Research Center, "America's Immigration Quandary"; Maddox, "US Immigration."

78. And protectionist talk was amplified. See Stelzer, "America Puts Security before Free Trade." Signs of a revival of isolationist sentiment were already present, as a Pew survey in the fall of 2005 showed. See Bortin, "Survey Shows a Revival of Isolationism."

References

Bacevich, Andrew J. *The New American Militarism.* Oxford: Oxford University Press, 2005.

Bamford, James. *A Pretext for War: 9/11, Iraq and the Abuse of America's Intelligence Agencies.* New York: Doubleday, 2004.

Bartiromo, Maria. "Lee Raymond: Exit Interview." *Business Week* 20 Feb. 2006.

BBC News, 20 March 2006. Available at: http://news.bbc.uk/go/pr/fr/-/2/hi/business/4824786.stm.

Benjamin, Daniel. "The Pentagon Papers." *Washington Post* 14 May 2006.

Benjamin, Daniel, and Steven Simon. *The Next Attack: The Failure of the War on Terror and a Strategy for Getting it Right.* New York: Times Books, 2005.

Bergstrom, Fred C. "The United States and the World Economy." *Annals of the American Academy of Political and Social Science* 460 (1982): 11–20.

Blumenthal, Ralph. "Credo of Joel Osteen, Pastor of Lakewood Church: Eliminate the Negative, Accentuate Prosperity." *New York Times* 30 March 2006.

Bonner, William, and Addison Wiggin. *Empire of Debt: The Rise and Fall of an Epic Financial Crisis.* Hoboken, NJ: Wiley, 2005.

Boot, Max. *The Savage Wars of Peace: Small Wars and the Rise of American Power.* New York: Basic Books, 2002.

———. "What the Heck is a Neocon?" *Wall Street Journal* 30 Dec. 2002.

Bortin, Meg. "Survey Shows a Revival of Isolationism among Americans." *New York Times* 17 Nov. 2005.

Bosworth, Barry P., and Jack E. Triplett. *Productivity in the US Services Sector: New Sources of Economic Growth.* Washington, DC: Brookings Institute, 2004.

Briggs, Laura. *Reproducing Empire: Race, Sex, Science and US Imperialism in Puerto Rico.* Berkeley, CA: University of California Press, 2002.

Buchanan, Patrick J. *Where the Right Went Wrong: How Neoconservatives Subverted the Reagan Revolution and Hijacked the Bush Presidency.* New York: Thomas Dunne, 2004.

Cable, Vincent. "Economic Fallout from a War in Iraq." *The World Today* Feb. 2003.

Cain, Peter. "Capitalism, Internationalism, and Imperialism in the Thought of Richard Cobden." *British Journal of International Studies* 3 (1979): 229–47.

———. *Hobson and Imperialism: Radicalism, New Liberalism and Finance, 1887–1938.* Oxford: Oxford University Press, 2002.

Cain, P. J., and A. G. Hopkins. *British Imperialism, 1688-2000*. London: Longman, 2002.

CBS News, "60 Minutes." 21 May 2004. Available at: http://www.cbsnews.com/stories/2004/05/21/60minutes/printable618896.shtml

Clark, William R. *Petrodollar Warfare: Oil, Iraq and the Future of the Dollar*. Gabriola Island, BC: New Society Publishers, 2005.

Cox, Ronald W., and Daniel Skidmore-Hess. *U.S. Politics and the Global Economy: Corporate Power, Conservative Shift*. Boulder, CO: Lynne Rienner, 1999.

Daalder, Ivo H., and James M. Lindsay. *America Unbound: The Bush Revolution in Foreign Policy*. Washington, DC: Brookings Institute, 2004.

Dorrien, Gary. *Imperial Designs: Neoconservatism and the New Pax Americana*. New York: Routledge, 2004.

Eland, Ivan. *The Empire Has No Clothes: US Foreign Policy Exposed*. Oakland, CA: Independent Institute, 2004.

Everest, Larry. *Oil, Power and Empire: Iraq and the US Global Agenda*. Monroe, ME: Common Courage Press, 2004.

Feldman, Murray. *The Neoconservative Revolution: Jewish Intellectuals and the Shaping of Public Policy*. Cambridge: Cambridge University Press, 2005.

Flake, Jeff. "Earmarked Men." *New York Times* 9 Feb. 2006.

Foster, John Bellamy. "Imperial America and War." *Monthly Review* 55 (2003): 11–12.

Frank, Thomas. *What's the Matter with Kansas? How Conservatives Won the Heart of America*. New York: Metropolitan Press, 2004.

Frum, David, and Richard Perle. *An End to Evil: How to Win the War on Terror*. New York: Random House, 2004.

Fukuyama, Francis. *America at the Crossroads: Democracy, Power, and the Neoconservative Legacy*. New Haven, CT: Yale University Press, 2006.

Goodkind, Terry. *Naked Empire*. New York: Tor, 2003.

Goodman, John B., Debora Spar, and David Yoffie. "Foreign Direct Investment and the Demand for Protection in the United States." *International Organization* 50 (1996): 565–91.

Gordon, Michael R., and Bernard E. Trainor. *Cobra II: The Inside Story of the Invasion and Occupation of Iraq*. New York: Pantheon, 2006.

Gorenberg, Gershom. *The Accidental Empire: Israel and the Birth of the Settlements, 1967–1977*. New York: Times Books, 2006.

Graham-Brown, Sarah. *Sanctioning Saddam: The Politics of Intervention in Iraq*. London: I. B. Tauris, 1999.

Graham-Brown, Sarah, and Chris Toensing. "Why Another War? A Background on the Iraq Crisis." *Middle East Research & Information Project* Dec. 2002.

Grazia, Victoria de. *Irresistible Empire: America's Advance through Twentieth-Century Europe*. Cambridge, MA: Belknap Press, 2005.

Gross, Daniel. "Globalization Offered Two Ways: A la Carte and Prix Fixe." *New York Times* 12 March 2006.

Halper, Stefan, and Jonathan Clarke. *America Alone: The Neo-Conservatives and the Global Order*. Cambridge: Cambridge University Press, 2004.

Hartung, William D. "Eisenhower's Warning: The Military-Industrial Complex Forty Years Later." *World Policy Journal* 18 (2001): 1–2.

Heiss, Mary Ann. *Empire and Nationhood: The United States, Great Britain, and Iranian Oil, 1950- 1954*. New York: Columbia University Press, 1997.

Hoganson, Kristin L. *Fighting for American Manhood: How Gender Politics Provoked the Spanish American and Philippine-American Wars*. New Haven, CT: Yale University Press, 1998.

Horsley, Richard A. *Jesus and Empire: The Kingdom of God and the New World Disorder*. Augsburg, Minneapolis. MN: Fortress Press, 2003.

Huber, Peter. "Military-Industrial Complex, 2003." *Forbes Global* 5 Dec. 2003: 1.

Hunt, Michael H. *Ideology and U.S. Foreign Policy*. New Haven, CT: Yale University Press, 1987.

Johnson, Chalmers A. *The Sorrows of Empire: Militarism, Secrecy and the End of the Republic*. New York: Metropolitan Books, 2004.

Kagan, Robert. *Of Paradise and Power: America and Europe in the New World Order*. New York: Knopf, 2003.

Kennedy, Paul M. *The Rise and Fall of the Great Powers: Economic Change and Military Conflict from 1500 to 2000.* New York: Random House, 1989.

Khalidi, Rashid. *Resurrecting Empire: Western Footprints and America's Perilous Path in the Middle East.* Boston, MA: Beacon Press, 2004.

Kinzer, Stephen. *Overthrow: America's Century of Regime Change from Hawaii to Iraq.* New York: Times Books, 2006.

Kirchgaessner, Stephanie. "Business Lobby Targets Senate on Review of Foreign Deals." *Financial Times* 24 March 2006.

Klein, Naomi. "Baghdad Year Zero: Pillaging Iraq in Pursuit of a Neo-Con Utopia." *Harper's* Sept. 2004: 1–22.

Kozmetsky, George, and Piyu Yue. *The Economic Transformation of the United States, 1950-2000.* West Lafayette, IN: Purdue University Press, 2005.

Lee, David S. "Wage Inequality in the United States during the 1980s: Rising Dispersion or Falling Minimum Wages?" *Quarterly Journal of Economics* 114 (1999): 977-1023.

Lenin, V. I. *Imperialism, the Highest Stage of Capitalism: A Popular Outline.* New York: International Publishers, 1969, 1939.

Levy, Clifford J. "The New Corporate Outsourcing." *New York Times* 29 Jan. 2006.

Lieven, Anatol. *America Right or Wrong: An Anatomy of American Nationalism.* New York: Oxford University Press, 2004.

Lipset, Seymour Martin, and Gary Marks. *It Didn't Happen Here: Why Socialism Failed in the United States.* New York: Norton, 2005.

Luce, Edward. "Out on a Limb: Why Blue-Collar Americans see their Future as Precarious." *Financial Times* 3 May 2006.

Machiavelli, Niccolo. *The Prince,* in *The Prince and Other Writings,* edited by Wayne A. Rebhorn. New York: Barnes & Noble, 2003.

Maddox, Bronwen. "US Immigration is a New Mass Movement." *The Times* 28 March 2006.

Mann, Jim. *Rise of the Vulcans: The History of Bush's War Cabinet.* New York: Viking, 2004.

Mann, Michael. *Incoherent Empire.* London: Verso, 2003.

Mansfield, Edward D., and Jack Snyder. *Electing to Fight: Why Emerging Democracies Go to War.* Cambridge, MA: MIT Press, 2005.

McCarthy, Ellen. "Foreign Firms a Mainstay of Pentagon Contracting." *Washington Post* 18 March 2006.

McGirr, Lisa. *Suburban Warriors: The Origins of the New American Right.* Princeton, NJ: Princeton University Press, 2001.

Micklethwaite, John, and Adrian Wooldridge. *The Right Nation: Conservative Power in America.* New York: Penguin, 2004.

Mills, C. Wright. *The Power Elite.* New York: Oxford University Press, 1956.

Mosher, Steven W. *Hegemon: China's Plan to Dominate Asia and the World.* San Francisco, CA: Encounter Books, 2000.

Mouawad, Jad. "As Profits Surge, Oil Giants Find Hurdles Abroad." *New York Times* 6 May 2006.

Negus, Steve. "Oil Ministry the Key to Unlocking Paralysis in Iraq." *Financial Times* 6 May 2006.

Nelson, Eric D. *The Complete Idiot's Guide to the Roman Empire.* Indianapolis, IN: Alpha, 2001.

O'Brien, Timothy L. "Just What does America Want to do with Iraq's Oil?" *New York Times* 8 June 2003.

Packer, George. *The Assassins' Gate: America in Iraq.* New York: Farrar, Straus & Giroux, 2005.

Palast, Greg. "Secret Plans for Iraq's Oil." BBC News, 17 March 2003. Available at: http:// news.bbc. co.uk/2/hi/programmes/newsnight/4354269.s.

Panitch, Leo, and Colin Leys (eds.). *The New Imperial Challenge.* London: Merlin Press, 2003.

———. (eds.). *The Empire Reloaded.* London: Merlin Press, 2004.

Pareto, Vilfredo. *Sociological Writings,* edited by S. E. Finer. New York: Praeger, 1966.

Paul, James A. "Oil Companies in Iraq: A Century of Rivalry and War." *Global Policy Forum* Nov. 2003.

Peters, Jeremy W. "GM Loss for 2005 is Steeper." *New York Times* 17 March 2006.

Pew Research Center. "America's Immigration Quandary." 30 March 2006.

Phillips, Kevin. *Wealth and Democracy: A Political History of the American Rich.* New York: Broadway Books, 2002.

———. *American Dynasty: Aristocracy, Fortune and the Politics of Deceit in the House of Bush.* New York: Viking, 2004.

———. *American Theocracy: The Peril and Politics of Radical Religion, Oil and Borrowed Money in the Twenty-First Century.* New York: Viking, 2006.

Powers, Charles H. *Vilfredo Pareto.* Newbury Park, CA: Sage, 1987.

Priest, Dana. *The Mission: Waging War and Keeping Peace with America's Military.* New York: Norton, 2003.

Retort. "Blood for Oil?" *London Review of Books* 21 April 2005.

Robin, Corey. "How 9/11 Unified Conservatives in Pursuit of Empire." *Washington Post* 2 May 2004.

Schumpeter, Joseph A. *Imperialism and Social Classes: Two Essays.* New York: Meridian Books, 1955.

Semple, Robert. "The End of Oil." *New York Times* 1 March 2006.

Shane, Scott. "Generals Break with Tradition over Rumsfeld." *New York Times* 15 April 2006.

Simmons, Matthew R. *Twilight in the Desert: The Coming Oil Shock and the World Economy.* Hoboken, NJ: Wiley, 2005.

Smitka, Michael. "Foreign Policy and the US Automotive Industry." *Business and Economic History* 28 (1999): 277–85.

Stelzer, Irwin. "America Puts Security before Free Trade." *The Times* 19 March 2006.

Stephanson, Anders. *Manifest Destiny: American Expansionism and the Empire of Right.* New York: Hill & Wang, 1995.

Stoff, Michael B. *Oil, War, and American Security: The Search for National Policy on Foreign Oil, 1941–1947.* New Haven, CT: Yale University Press, 1980.

Trubowitz, Peter. *Defining the National Interest: Conflict and Change in US Foreign Policy.* Chicago, IL: University of Chicago Press, 1998.

Uchitelle, Louis. *The Disposable American: Layoffs and their Consequences.* New York: Knopf, 2006.

"Uncle Sam Says Yes." *The Economist* 6–12 May 2006.

Veblen, Thorstein. *The Theory of the Leisure Class.* New York: Mentor Edition, New American Library, 1953.

Vitalis, Robert. "The Closing of the Arabian Oil Frontier and the Future of the Saudi-American Relations." *Middle East Report* 204 (1997): 15–21.

———. "Black Gold, White Crude: An Essay on American Exceptionalism, Hierarchy, and Hegemony in the Gulf." *Diplomatic History* 26 (2002): 185–213.

Weisman, Jonathan, and Anitha Reddy. "Spending on Iraq Sets off Gold Rush." *Washington Post* 9 Oct. 2003.

Williams, William Appleman. *The Tragedy of American Diplomacy.* 2nd ed. New York: Dell, 1972.

Woodward, Bob. *Plan of Attack.* New York: Simon & Schuster, 2004.

WTRG Economics. Available at: http://www.wtrg.com/prices.htm.

Yergin, Daniel. *The Prize: The Epic Quest for Oil, Money, and Power.* New York: Simon & Schuster, 1991.

———. "The Fight over Iraq's Oil." BBC News, 14 March 2003. Available at: http://news.bbc.co.uk/l/hi/business/2847905.s.

———. "It's Not the End of the Oil Age." *Washington Post* 31 July 2005.

A.G. Hopkins, "Capitalism, Nationalism and the New American Empire," Journal of Imperial & Commonwealth History 35:1 (2007), pp. 95–117. Reprinted by permission of Taylor & Francis Ltd. (http://www.tandf.co.uk/journals).

The New Energy Order

Managing Insecurities in the Twenty-first Century

DAVID G. VICTOR AND LINDA YUEH

Victor and Yueh argue that the global energy system is changing, as demand for fossil fuels increasingly comes from the developing world rather than the OECD countries. Even though China increasingly resorts to bilateral practices in locking up oil supplies, and rejects market-based approaches, the authors argue that this actually enhances the global energy supply. They argue that international institutions that guarantee energy security (such as the IEA, OPEC, and G-20) are becoming increasingly dysfunctional and ineffective.

The last decade has seen an extraordinary shift in expectations for the world energy system. After a long era of excess capacity, since 2001, prices for oil and most energy commodities have risen sharply and become more volatile. Easy-to-tap local fuel supplies have run short, forcing major energy consumers to depend on longer and seemingly more fragile supply chains. Prices have yo-yoed over the last 18 months: first reaching all-time highs, then dropping by two-thirds, and after that rising back up to surprisingly high levels given the continuing weakness of the global economy. The troubles extend far beyond oil. Governments in regions such as Europe worry about insecure supplies of natural gas. India, among others, is poised to depend heavily on coal imports in the coming decades. For these reasons, governments in nearly all the large consuming nations are now besieged by doubts about their energy security like at no time since the oil crises of the 1970s. Meanwhile, the biggest energy suppliers are questioning whether demand is certain enough to justify the big investments needed to develop new capacity. Producers and consumers, each group unsure of the other, cannot agree on how best to finance and manage a more secure energy system.

A crisis is looming, and it will be difficult to resolve because it will strike as two radically new changes are making it harder for governments to manage the world energy system. The first is a shift in the sources of consumption. The era of growing demand for oil and other fossil fuels in the industrialized countries is over; most of the future growth in demand will come from the emerging-market countries, notably China and India. The International Energy Agency (IEA) has projected that by 2030, China will depend on imports for at least two-thirds of its oil, and India, for even more. These countries, especially China, are choosing to secure their energy supplies less by relying on commercial interests—the standard approach for all the biggest industrial energy users over the last two decades—than by locking up supplies in direct bilateral deals with producing countries. For instance, China's push into Africa, Central Asia, and other energy-rich regions, which usually involves special government-to-government deals, is a rejection of the reigning market-based approach to energy security. And because oil, gas, and coal are global commodities, these exclusive, opaque deals make it harder for the markets to function smoothly, thus endangering the energy security of all nations. They also complicate efforts to hold energy suppliers accountable for protecting human rights, ensuring the rule of law, and promoting democracy.

The other big shift in the world energy system is growing concern about the environmental impact of energy use, especially emissions of carbon dioxide, an intrinsic byproduct of burning fossil fuels with conventional technology and the leading human cause of global warming. Worries about climate change are one reason why the major stimulus packages passed since the global financial crisis began in 2007 have included hefty green-energy measures: by some accounts, these have made up 15 percent of global fiscal stimulus spending. Some believe that such green-tinted stimulus measures will spur a revolution pushing for cleaner and more secure energy. Perhaps. But there is no doubt that energy systems are in for a major change. Curbing global warming will likely require cutting emissions of carbon dioxide and other greenhouse gases by more than half over the next few decades, and that goal cannot be achieved by just tinkering at the margins.

In the face of these new realities, the international and national institutions that were created to help promote energy security over the last three decades are struggling to remain relevant. The most important one, the IEA, has made little headway in involving the new giant energy consumers in its decision-making. That means that it is struggling even to fulfill one of its hallmark functions—to stand ready to coordinate government responses to energy shocks—because a large, and growing, fraction of oil consumers fall outside its ambit and are wary of market-based approaches to energy security. Other institutions are doing no better. European states that depend on gas imported from Russia have signed a treaty and created an organization aimed at making those supplies more secure, but the practical effect of both steps has been nil. It was a good thing for the G-20 to announce a cut in energy subsidies at a summit in Pittsburgh last September—energy subsidies encourage excessive consumption, harming both energy security and the environment—but the G-20 has no plan for actually implementing that policy, and it has too many competing issues on its agenda. The big oil producers in OPEC have mobilized around the goal of promoting what they call "demand security," but the cartel has no power to guarantee demand for its products. Likewise, the institutions charged with

addressing new environmental challenges are barely effective: the Kyoto Protocol has had little impact on emissions, and the disputes that arose at the international climate conference in Copenhagen in December over how to craft a successor treaty are making it hard for investors to justify spending the massive capital needed for cleaner energy systems. Despite the existence of many international institutions attending to energy matters today, dangerous vacuums in governance have appeared.

The traditional solution of creating big new institutions, such as a world energy organization to replace the more exclusive IEA, will not work. What is needed instead is a mechanism for coordinating: hard-nosed initiatives focused on delivering energy security and environmental protection. To be effective, those measures will have to advance the interests of the most important governments, of importers and exporters alike, and they will have to align with the needs of the private and state firms that provide most of the investment in energy infrastructure.

A model for these efforts exists in international economic law. Once saddled with too many institutions and too little governance, the world economic system developed a series of ad hoc arrangements during the last several decades that have evolved into an effective management system. Although the system is still imperfect, it now governs most international trade and a growing proportion of finance and banking. The Financial Stability Board, which issues standards for judging the adequacy of banks' capitalization, is a particularly apt example of the system's success. Its so-called Basel standards, created after the Asian financial crisis of the late 1990s, have been highly effective: many countries and banks have adopted them on the understanding that it is in their interests to run well-governed financial sectors that conform to widely recognized criteria.

A similar Energy Stability Board could be created to help governments and existing international institutions better manage today's energy problems. It could work with the major new energy consumers, such as China, to set investment standards that both align with their interests and are consistent with the market rules that govern most trade in energy commodities and have worked well for some time now. It could also help the governments that are spending the most on green energy coordinate their efforts; without better governance, these green stimulus programs risk triggering trade wars and wasting vast sums of money. Following the example of economic law, success with these initiatives would undoubtedly help the existing energy institutions do a better job and could also spawn broader norms for governing energy security.

Economic Models

The last three decades have not been kind to efforts to create international institutions. One bright spot has been international economic law, now a set of useful general principles that has grown from practical, bottom-up experience. Its most successful aspects have been rooted in national interests: when governments find it pragmatic to comply with their obligations, broader sets of legal principles and institutions designed to ensure compliance develop.

The most visible of these institutions is the World Trade Organization. The WTO consists not only of rules that promote global trade but also of mechanisms to clarify existing trade rules and encourage the creation of new ones. The WTO's members, be they weak or strong, tend to comply even with inconvenient WTO rulings because they usually have a greater interest in the orderly functioning of the global trade system, which the WTO's rules buttress, than in promoting their narrow interests. Even the sore points of the day, such as the stalling of the Doha Round of international trade talks, are signs of the institutions relevance. The WTO has been so effective at creating useful trade rules that the remaining barriers—such as agricultural subsidies on the Doha agenda—are the ones that are nearly impossible to clear, and this is because of political hurdles in some of the most powerful WTO members.

Governments have also built international institutions to govern finance and investment. The Asian financial crisis of 1997–98 led to the creation of the Financial Stability Forum within the Bank for

International Settlements in order to restore order in world banking. Despite a glut of global forums pretending to help, such as the G-8 there was no body that included all the key players. Notably, the Asian states were left out—precisely the countries that, despite strong economic fundamentals, were being destabilized by flows of speculative, short-term portfolio capital, which prevented them from setting credible exchange rates or managing their balance of payments and even threatened pivotal banks and firms with insolvency. The contagion quickly spread to Russia, Turkey, and Latin America, leading to the bailouts of various governments and even the large U.S. hedge fund Long-Term Capital Management. The creation of the Financial Stability Forum was a quick response to the crisis. It explicitly included members beyond the G-8 and relied on the Bank for International Settlements, a credible forum for gathering central bankers, to coordinate the world's increasingly interlinked markets. After these efforts proved successful, the Financial Stability Forum was reconstituted as the Financial Stability Board and expanded to include all members of the G-20.

The Financial Stability Board's greatest achievement has been the creation of the Basel standards to assess the adequacy of bank capitalization. These have been widely adopted in emerging economies. Their application in China, for example, has helped reassure both foreign investors, who were wary of mismanagement by local banks, and the Chinese government, which was wary of intrusion on its sovereignty.

And the benefits of adhering to transparent global standards were overwhelming: China launched a series of successful initial public offerings drawing foreign banks into investing widely in Chinas banking system. Today, these standards are honored throughout most of the world's banking system. Participants understand that since no country alone can regulate banking, it makes sense to entrust the Financial Stability Board with helping governments craft and implement sensible, workable guidelines that suit rich and poor nations alike. To be sure, the global financial crisis has exposed remaining governance problems. But the crisis would have been much worse if capital standards for banks had not been shored up and mechanisms for coordinating financial policy had not already existed.

One lesson from this experience is that any effort to coordinate global energy policy must include all the most powerful players. Yet today, the most visible institutions for governing energy do not do this. Efforts to expand the IEA have been hobbled by the requirement that the agency's members also belong to the Organization for Economic Cooperation and Development, or OECD. Thus, the 28-strong IEA includes many countries with small and shrinking energy needs but excludes emerging giant energy consumers, such as China and India. Partial solutions have been devised—granting various states observer status, conducting joint studies with the IEA's highly competent secretariat—but they have not resolved the fundamental problem: when the IEA coordinates responses to an energy crisis, important players with large oil stockpiles, which could be the most helpful, have no voice. The only comprehensive solution would be to rewrite the IEA's membership rules. But this idea is a nonstarter partly because it would mean turning the organization into an even bigger forum, and existing members fear that their power would be diluted, as happened to the members of the G-8 when the G-20 grew more important.

Another lesson to be drawn from the success of global economic governance is that cooperation must have broad appeal, beyond the most important players. Global trade talks have made the most progress when they have focused on actions, such as the reduction of tariffs, that have a big impact on trade, are rooted in mutual interests, and are easy to enforce. Such successes then set the stage for governments to extend existing trade rules to many more countries and to take on harder tasks, such as building the WTO's dispute-resolution system. Similarly, the G-20' snorms against tax havens have spread more widely following success in such states as Liechtenstein and Switzerland. Since the financial crisis broke, many governments have seen the benefit of curtailing tax havens, not least because these havens have supported a shadow banking system that is hard to govern. That awareness, along with pressure on a few holdouts, explains why the last two years have seen much more effective tax enforcement worldwide.

Applying these lessons to energy means realizing that no system will be effective unless it starts with the countries that matter most—the large consumers and the large producers—and serves their interests. Success will require both that those countries reap practical benefits from cooperation and that the rules be designed so that they can spread widely as their legitimacy increases.

The Impotent Crowd

There is no shortage of institutions in today's energy markets; what is missing, however, is a practical strategy for setting effective norms to govern the global energy economy. The IEA plays an essential part, but it has had a hard time finding its voice. Although OPEC serves a special role for oil producers, it is not designed to take on broader functions. A promising dialogue between members of OPEC and members of the IEA, aimed partly at bringing more transparency to oil markets by providing data on oil production and trade, is under way through the ad hoc International Energy Forum, but so far this body has taken very few concrete actions. The International Atomic Energy Agency is tackling the difficult problem of nuclear proliferation with aplomb. Yet there is no path from success on that front to broader cooperation on distinct energy problems.

Beyond these specialized institutions is a landscape of wreckage. Europe's Energy Charter Treaty has had no practical impact on energy markets, despite its bold vision for integrating the energy systems of eastern and western Europe. One problem is that the treaty violates the first rule of effective institution building: it alienates the most important player. Russia, Europe's pivotal energy supplier, sees no benefit in subjecting itself to oversight by an intrusive Western institution and so has ensured the treaty's irrelevance.

The institutions working on climate change, including the UN Framework Convention on Climate Change, would do well just to survive going forward after the summit in Copenhagen last December. The

G-8 has placed climate and energy issues high on its agenda nearly every year for the last decade, but it has not done much beyond issuing grand and often empty proclamations: it has announced a need to limit global warming to just a two-degree increase over the coming century, despite current trends that almost guarantee the planet will blow through that target. Although efforts to expand the G-8 to include the main developing countries (Brazil, China, India, Mexico, and South Africa)—including the creation of the G-8 + 5—are well intentioned, they have been pursued entirely on the G-8's terms, and the G-8 has failed to seriously engage those pivotal countries. The G-20, which played the pivotal role in crafting new financial regulations after the Asian financial crisis, seemed to be a promising forum for addressing energy and climate issues as well, but topics such as the global economic meltdown of 2008 have crowded them out at the top of the agenda. A special forum for the world's largest emitters of greenhouse gases, which met in London last October, offered the hope of a flexible setting for negotiating limits on emissions, but that effort has also stalled: its most recent meeting ended in no new agreements nor any other progress.

Investors Abhor a Vacuum

Fixing these problems should begin not with grand attempts to build still more institutions but with a practical focus on filling the most important governance vacuums in the world's energy system: those regarding how to promote investment to develop urgently needed supplies of today's main energy sources, oil and gas, and how to support the climate-friendly technologies that will transform the energy system over the next several decades.

The security of oil and gas supplies is in question not only because the existing supplies are depleting quickly but also because investors are wary of pouring money into finding new resources. The problem is not geology: technological innovation is more than amply offsetting the depletion of conventional fossil fuels. The problem lies in the massive economic and political risks inherent in new projects, particularly those that supply energy across national borders and thus face a multitude of political uncertainties. Suppliers worry that there will not be enough demand to justify the investments, especially now that growing concerns about climate change have cast doubt on the future of fossil fuels without offering a clear alternative.

Creating the right incentives to supply oil and gas requires efforts on several fronts. But the area in which governance is both the weakest and the most important concerns China, the world's fastest-growing energy user, and its major energy suppliers in Africa, Central Asia, Latin America, and the Middle East. The grants, special loans, and infrastructure development projects that the Chinese government routinely offers to its resource-rich business partners have generated criticism in the West. That criticism, in turn, has fanned fears in China that the energy supplies essential to sustaining the Chinese economic miracle will be hard to obtain. So long as China and the West lock horns on this issue, it will be hard to convince China that its energy security, like that of the large Western energy consumers, is best ensured by transparent, well-functioning markets governed by effective international institutions, not opaque special deals.

Before they can engage China, the governments of the major Western countries will have to realize that the Chinese deals of today are neither exceptional nor necessarily bad. Throughout history, many of the biggest international energy supply projects stemmed from special agreements that tied financing to a particular customer who could guarantee demand over a predetermined period. When the Chinese bankroll the production of new energy resources—often at a cost that others are unwilling to bear—they are also bringing more supplies onto the global market, which generally benefits all consumers. As with banking, so with the global energy market: China, along with other states, has an interest in the existence of accepted and practical norms; when markets work smoothly, China's energy security improves. And China is learning that flows of new supplies will be more reliable if they come from countries with well-functioning governments; China's scramble for resources since the late 1990s has backfired in many places, including Sudan, which has become a political quagmire for Beijing rather than a reliable long-term supplier. The key task is for China, its major energy suppliers, and the other large players in the world energy market to craft investment standards that align China's interest in securing steady energy supplies with Western norms of well-functioning markets and good governance. This effort could begin with the creation of new standards for the next wave of Chinese investments in countries where the oil sector is well managed, such as Angola; that would set an example for what could be done elsewhere in the future.

Support for new green technology is a second area regarding which a vacuum in governance has made it hard for governments to achieve their common interests. The energy sector is one of the most exciting technological frontiers today. This is partly because climate change is transforming what societies expect from energy supplies, but it is also, and most immediately, because of the role that governments hope investments in energy infrastructure will play in economic recovery. Over the past year, governments have talked a great deal about coordinating their efforts to revive economic activity worldwide. Yet for the most part, each state is making decisions on its own, even though the International Monetary Fund, among other international institutions, has argued that a better-coordinated effort would do more to boost the global economy.

The problem is most obvious regarding the "green" part of the $2.5 trillion that is being spent globally to stimulate the world economy. The United States and China alone are spending $1.5 trillion, including a large fraction on energy projects. South Korea has devoted 85 percent of its stimulus package to green investments, promoting energy efficiency and low-emissions power plants. The British government has set aside hundreds of millions of pounds to support research and development in green industries. Coordination is needed, however, because the market for green-energy technology is global; ideas promoted in one country can quickly spread to the rest of the world through the marketplace. For example, U.S. spending on renewable sources of energy can invigorate U.S., Chinese, and European firms that supply solar cells and wind

turbines, boosting all three economies at the same time. And Chinese spending on new power grids can benefit the Western companies, as well as the Chinese ones, that develop the requisite technology.

Coordinating these green-technology programs offers the prospect of a viable new global industry in clean technology, at least in theory. In practice, however, such stimulus plans are prone to economic nationalism. The United States' program, for example, includes rules that favor U.S. suppliers, and one of the results, to cite an ongoing example, is that a Chinese company trying to bring Chinese technology to a wind farm in Texas will find itself in a hostile investment climate. Yet a true energy revolution cannot happen if technologies are nationalized; indeed, all the best and most competitive energy technologies have been improved by global competition. One way to get coordination started would be to require the leading spenders on green technology—in decreasing order, the United States, the European Union, Japan, and China—to offer periodic assessments of how their own programs are working and where new efforts, including joint ones, are needed. And with the right forum for coordination in place, such early endeavors could eventually spread more widely.

Aboveboard

Existing institutions cannot fill these vacuums. A small, nimble body is needed: an Energy Stability Board modeled after the Financial Stability Board in the banking sector. The Energy Stability Board could gather together the dozen biggest energy producers and users. For its administration, it might rely on the secretariat of the IEA—by far the most competent international energy institution at present—much like the Financial Stability Board drew on help from the Bank for International Settlements to catalyze cooperation in the global financial markets. At first, the Energy Stability Board's activities would need to be ad hoc so that other institutions, such as OPEC and one or more of the Asian security organizations, could easily join its efforts; it would need to be especially welcoming to China, India, and the other important countries, which have been left on the sidelines of energy governance systems so far. Although the list of needed efforts is long, a priority should be engaging China (and other large new energy consumers) in developing standards for overseas investments and in coordinating the green-energy investments that constitute a large proportion of many governments' economic stimulus programs. In both those cases, initiatives by a small number of states, all rooted in these states' national interests, could have a large practical impact.

A key test for the Energy Stability Board would be for it to prove its ability to engage businesses. Firms will not provide the trillions of dollars needed to develop energy infrastructure in the coming decades without credible signals that governments are serious about instituting policies that will allow the private sector to cash in on such investments. One way to reassure these companies would be to allow them to cooperate with governments in performing some of the Energy Stability Board's tasks. For example, leading firms could formally assess governments' green stimulus programs and identify those areas in which governments need to coordinate more effectively. (Governments usually are not effective coordinators of leading-edge technologies on their own because they have neither the energy issues but the necessary knowledge nor the necessary control over investment.) The Energy Stability Board could also become a forum for privately owned firms to work with state-owned companies, which control access to most of the world's oil and gas resources and a large fraction of the world's electric power grid, especially in developing countries. These national enterprises are pivotal in the world energy system yet have not been well integrated into international energy institutions.

Success at these steps would create the right conditions to bring about cooperation in other important areas. Governments have repeatedly failed to establish a multilateral agreement on investment to govern foreign investments of all types, largely because they have taken on too many diverse and contentious topics. A sharper focus on energy infrastructure is more likely to succeed. Another disappointment has been the failure of the world's

leading governments to invest adequately in energy research and development. (Despite the world's growing energy problems, the proportion of global economic output devoted to energy research and development is lower today than it was in the early 1980s.) Just as the Financial Stability Board, after it had proved itself, was asked to take on new tasks, such as devising internationally acceptable rules for bankers' compensation in light of the global financial crisis, the Energy Stability Board could be asked to issue guidelines for how to handle research and development and other issues that are difficult to keep on the agenda of existing institutions yet crucial to the long-term development of the energy system. The board could also help build support for important initiatives, such as the new U.S.- and Chinese-led efforts to build a more secure system for nuclear fuel.

Getting started will require leadership. Only the United States and China can play the part, given their dominant roles as the world's largest energy consumers. But although the two countries have long-professed their common desire to cooperate on energy issues, they have struggled to do anything practical. Moreover, strictly one-on-one dealings cannot solve the world's most pressing energy problems; the United States and China cannot set the agenda entirely on their own. Working in tandem through the Energy Stability Board, however, would give their bilateral efforts more credibility with other important actors and with international institutions. The United States and China know that such cooperation would serve their interests. Beijing's current strategy of locking up energy supplies is not sustainable without strong norms to make these investments seem less toxic politically to other important countries, especially the key Western ones. Working through the Energy Stability Board would serve the United States' interests, too: Washington will achieve very little of what it wants to get done in the world of energy, such as a more effective scheme for cutting greenhouse gas emissions worldwide, without giving a prominent role to other major energy consumers and other potential technology suppliers. An effective mechanism for engaging China would also give the

Obama administration the political cover it needs to pass national legislation on global warming. One of the biggest hurdles in doing so has been its inability to convince a skeptical American public that China, India, and other major developing countries are also willing to play useful roles.

Although energy commodities and technologies are traded globally, the system for governing the markets for these important goods is fragmented and increasingly impotent. As the experience with global financial and trade regulation shows, that need not be the case. Nor is it necessary to devise grand new institutions to fix the problem. A nimble energy agency focused on practical approaches to the new realities of the world energy market can fill the gaps.

Alternative Nuclear Futures

STEVEN E. MILLER AND SCOTT D. SAGAN

Miller and Sagan discuss the challenges to international security resulting from the spread of civilian nuclear power programs. They evaluate the positive role that international institutions (e.g., the IAEA) and international law play in impeding the proliferation of nuclear weapons. They discuss the consequences of the spread of nuclear weapons to nations in the developing world, particularly in reference to the future of the Nuclear Non-Proliferation Treaty.

The global nuclear order is changing, but where is it headed? Will the expected expansion of nuclear power in many regions around the world lead to increased dangers of nuclear terrorism and increased risks of nuclear weapons proliferation? It depends on how quickly and how widely nuclear power spreads to new countries; it depends on the domestic political and governance characteristics of the new nuclear power states; it depends on whether terrorists' plans to attack nuclear sites or steal nuclear materials succeed or fail; and, crucially, it depends on the steps taken by the international community to improve the safety mechanisms, physical protection standards, and nonproliferation safeguards that make up the tapestry of agreements that we call the nonproliferation regime.

Our crystal ball is not clear enough to predict with confidence whether the global nuclear future will be characterized by peace and prosperity or by conflict and destruction. But we do believe that the choices made in the coming few years will be crucial in determining whether the world can have more nuclear power without more nuclear weapons dangers in the future. Here we first briefly outline five major security challenges posed by the potential expansion and spread of nuclear power. Second, we discuss the major players whose decisions and interactions will determine which policies are adopted and which are rejected as the international community seeks solutions to these five security challenges. Finally, we sketch a number of alternative nuclear futures to demonstrate the truly momentous nature of the political and technical decisions that will soon be made by critical national and international actors.

What specific challenges to international security are created by the anticipated expansion and spread of civilian nuclear power? Five serious, interrelated problems appear on the horizon: safety, sabotage, terrorist theft or purchase of a weapon or nuclear materials, nuclear weapons proliferation, and destruction of nuclear facilities in a conventional war. Each of these challenges must be addressed if the global expansion of nuclear power is to evolve in desirable directions.

First, will it be possible to ensure that high levels of *safety* are created and maintained in each new power plant as nuclear power spreads? Even the most established and experienced nuclear power states—including the United States, Japan, and Russia—have had accidents in their nuclear facilities. These incidents led to the creation of both safer reactor technology and national and international institutions, such as the Institute of Nuclear Power Operators (INPO) and the World Association of Nuclear Operators (WANO), to encourage organizational learning and best safety practices.[1] The stakes here are high, for unless the nuclear power newcomers do even better in maintaining safety than did previous new nuclear power states, we can expect periodic minor accidents and rare but occasional serious incidents. Rapid construction of power plants, weak national regulatory systems, and shortages of trained personnel may exacerbate concerns about safety in the future. Constant vigilance and a high degree of cooperation among all governments and operators will be necessary, as a major accident anywhere would have global repercussions.

Second, will adequate standards for the protection of nuclear facilities against sabotage be adopted and implemented as nuclear power spreads? Sabotage can be a gray area since it could be initiated by a disgruntled worker striking out against his or her employer but not meaning to harm coworkers; by an anti-nuclear environmentalist seeking to shut down a power plant; or by a terrorist organization seeking to create a release of radiation and spread fear and panic. All three of these scenarios have occurred in the past, and we see no reason to expect that future sabotage attempts can be eliminated entirely. Fortunately, some measures, such as strong containment vessels and effective personal reliability programs, protect against both accidents and sabotage. The protection of nuclear installations has always been a concern, but the revelation that the 9/11 al Qaeda aircraft hijackers initially considered crashing a jumbo jet into a nuclear power plant heightened the alarm. Continued terrorist interests in targeting nuclear power plants—to create panic, economic damage, and civilian casualties—was demonstrated in the "Toronto 18" case in 2006, in which an Islamic fundamentalist group apparently planned a truck bomb attack against a nuclear power plant in Ontario.[2]

Third, will there be adequate standards of physical protection against a terrorist theft or purchase of a nuclear weapon or the materials necessary to make a nuclear bomb or radiological device? Former International Atomic Energy Agency (IAEA) Director General Mohamed ElBaradei has highlighted this danger: "The gravest threat the world faces today, in my opinion, is that extremists could get hold of nuclear or radioactive materials."[3] The urgency of the physical security problem is well established, as al Qaeda leaders, including Osama bin Laden, have announced their desire to get nuclear weapons and al Qaeda operatives, such as the British terrorist Dhiren Borat, have been apprehended with plans on how to make and use radiological "dirty bomb" devices.[4] There is currently no international agreement about what physical protection standards are considered adequate and how much spending is justified in the name of physical security.[5] For some nuclear utilities, security activities too often are seen as a trade off against profit, even though in the long term strong security can prevent successful terrorist incidents that would be incredibly harmful to both company profits and national security. Even in the United States, with more than six decades of nuclear experience, there is still intense and unsettled debate about whether existing standards of physical security are sufficient given the threats that are now thought to exist. As nuclear facilities are built in more states, especially in countries that may have high degrees of corruption and poor regulatory competence, it will be crucial to promote better international standards and implementation of strong physical security measures. New international institutions, such as the World Institute for Nuclear Security (WINS), will need to play an absolutely critical role in promoting best physical security practices between the existing nuclear power states and new states that construct nuclear power plants.

Fourth, will the spread of nuclear power lead to further *nuclear weapons proliferation*? The link between nuclear power and nuclear weapons has been a serious worry throughout the nuclear age. The expansion of nuclear power can lead to the dissemination of expertise and technology that is useful in the weapons context. This will be true particularly if nuclear newcomers acquire the full panoply of technology associated with nuclear power, including fuel cycle technologies that have direct weapons applications. This risk can be limited if the acquisition of uranium enrichment or plutonium reprocessing technologies is discouraged or prohibited. These technologies are, however, also indispensable for the production of fuel for nuclear reactors. Hence, states have to be persuaded that reliable external sources of supply exist before they will agree to forsake the option of national fuel cycle capabilities. States that doubt whether they can trust international suppliers of reactor fuel (whether commercial or multinational) are more likely to think it necessary to acquire their own fuel cycle infrastructure—which means that they will possess a latent nuclear weapons capability. The more states that acquire their own national enrichment or reprocessing capability, the more worrisome the nuclear future will be.

Fifth, there is legitimate concern that a nuclear power plant could be attacked during a *conventional war*, potentially leading to an environmental catastrophe, if, for example, the containment vessel was breached or the spent fuel was attacked and dispersed. Fortunately, some states are acutely aware of this danger and have attempted to mitigate it: India and Pakistan, for example, have agreed not to target each other's nuclear facilities in the event of armed conflict and, as a confidence-building measure, routinely exchange information about their commercial nuclear facilities. Other states, in contrast, have engaged in dangerous attacks during conflicts: during the 1991 Gulf War, for example,

Iraq launched a SCUD missile attack against the Dimona nuclear reactor in Israel, but fortunately lacked the accuracy to hit the intended target. Future "no-targeting" agreements, like the confidence-building measures that India and Pakistan have signed, between new states that have both nuclear power plants and an enduring military rivalry, may be useful.

These five challenges are not the only consequential questions associated with the growth of nuclear power. Questions of finance, of nuclear waste, and of human capital are also important and will have great bearing on decisions about whether states pursue or expand nuclear power, by how much and how quickly. But from a global security perspective, the degree to which the future nuclear order promotes safe, secure, proliferation-resistant, and effectively monitored and governed nuclear power is of paramount importance.

Given these concerns, there are some experts (including some in this special issue[6]) who oppose the further spread of nuclear power on security grounds. There are other experts[7] who are skeptical about the wisdom of expanding nuclear power worldwide, on grounds that other renewable energy resources will be more effective in combating global climate change. Here we are agnostic on the question of whether there *should be* an expansion and spread of nuclear power in the future. Instead, we simply assume that there *will be* some degree of growth in the use of nuclear energy, including some new states acquiring nuclear power plants. Who will determine which states acquire nuclear technology and how the resulting security concerns are addressed? The fact is that the Nuclear Non-Proliferation Treaty (NPT) regime is, first and foremost, a system of states. Within the governments of those states, however, there are often diverse bureaucratic and political interests affecting nuclear issues. And within those states, the innovators, the providers, the owners, the operators, the sellers, and the exporters of nuclear technology are often found in the private sector.

Accordingly, it is in central governments and corporations around the world where the fundamental decisions are being made that will play the largest role in shaping the future global nuclear order. To be sure, these decisions are not wholly independent of one another. The relevant actors are often influenced by the nuclear policies and programs of others. They are often at least indirectly connected and constrained by varying levels of engagement with the international nuclear marketplace. They are typically participants in the international institutions created to provide some structured governance of the world's nuclear affairs—whether the IAEA and the Nuclear Suppliers Group (NSG) for states or WANO for corporations. They all operate in the context of existing treaty obligations, legal constraints, regulatory requirements, export control guidelines, and normative expectations, however imperfectly the rules-based regime may operate at times. And in a substantially integrated and highly mobile globalized world, the intellectual infrastructure for thinking about nuclear power and nuclear weapons can spread worldwide and produce many common or overlapping frameworks for addressing nuclear issues. Rarely will nuclear decisions be made in complete isolation from these wider realities.

Within this web of potential constraints and influences, however, governments and companies will decide and act on the basis of their own self-defined perceptions, preferences, policies, and calculations of self-interest. They will make their own judgments about the desirability or unattractiveness of nuclear power as a component of their overall approach to energy. Their choices will determine how fast and how widely nuclear power expands and spreads. As part of its long-term energy strategy, China, for example, has chosen to pursue a policy that will more than double its nuclear power capacity within a decade and that aims to increase that capacity by fivefold or sixfold by 2050. (China currently has 17 nuclear power reactors under construction.) Countries such as Egypt, Jordan, and the United Arab Emirates have already decided to acquire nuclear power plants and other regional powers may follow suit, with the result that the Middle East will become a much more nuclear region.[8] Similar decisions by other states (so-called nuclear aspirant states) will gradually but eventually change the strategic geography of nuclear power on a global scale.

States and firms will also determine, within the constraints of the politicized international nuclear marketplace, which technology paths to follow in developing their nuclear programs. A crucial question for the future is whether the spread of nuclear power reactors will be accompanied by the spread of sensitive fuel cycle technologies that can produce bomb material as well as reactor fuel. There may be international norms and pressures against the acquisition of such worrisome technologies, but ultimately states will choose for themselves. For example, proponents of the nonproliferation regime have long argued that countries like Iran or Brazil do not need, and should not seek, independent uranium enrichment capabilities; however, both of those governments, at least thus far, have decided otherwise. Similarly, the feasibility of proposed international or multinational nuclear fuel cycle arrangements intended to discourage the spread of sensitive weapons-usable technologies will depend on whether states embrace or reject such schemes. Washington, for example, may believe that it is a good idea for Iran to have its nuclear fuel produced in Russia or Western Europe, but Tehran has yet to find the proposal acceptable.

In short, national governments play the central role in shaping the governance of global nuclear affairs. They decide which rules to accept and which to reject, which to respect and which to violate, which are enforced and which are ignored. Whatever constraints or restrictions for strengthening the NPT regime may seem obvious or desirable to the international community of nonproliferation experts, they have no hope of acceptance unless they are found agreeable by the overwhelming majority of states. Similarly, the IAEA is an international organization comprised of member states that provide its funding, oversee its policies, and determine its powers. If the IAEA is to be given additional resources and greater investigative powers, it will be because states have agreed that this should happen.

Within those states, however, different actors often hold different views about which nuclear policies their governments should adopt at home and support abroad. The evolving nonproliferation regime will therefore be strongly influenced by whether supporters of international cooperation and compromise or supporters of national fuel cycle facilities win the debate at home. Fortunately in many states the central government and industry leaders are committed to the cause of nonproliferation and will act in support of a stronger NPT regime.

Six conclusions follow from this analysis. First, as nuclear power spreads, a growing number of states will become active players in the NPT system. Their investment in nuclear power will mean that they can be directly affected by the functioning of the regime. Moreover, they will be different states. Once, nuclear power was, with a few exceptions, found in the wealthy industrial nations: the United States, Japan, France, and Britain, among others. In the future, many developing countries—Egypt, Iran, Malaysia, Indonesia, and many others—will be in the nuclear power club and will have interests to be defended in the NPT regime. Their views will no doubt sometimes be different from those of the established nuclear power states. The mix of states active in NPT diplomacy will be different than in the past, and these states' decisions will help determine the future global nuclear order.

Second, in an NPT system of 189 states that relies on voluntary commitments by members and that operates generally on a consensus principle, inclusive diplomacy is an imperative if progress is to be made. States need to be persuaded that new rules or reinterpreted norms are desirable and in their interests. The perceptions and preferences of nuclear newcomers need to be understood and taken into account; outreach is essential. States need to believe that they have a stake and a voice in the system or they are unlikely to invest much effort in preserving and strengthening it. This need for broad participation and cooperation is why occasions such as the periodic NPT Review Conferences are so important, despite all their well-known difficulties and problems. They represent the sort of inclusive diplomacy that is necessary if the NPT regime is to be strengthened and if states are to be convinced to choose nuclear policies that are compatible with the needs of the NPT system.

Third, any deviations from the principle of consensus within the NPT regime must be perceived by the majority of states as being legitimate if they are to be effective. This is true regarding both new interpretations of NPT rules and any future efforts to enforce them. It is possible that future NPT Review Conferences may adopt a resolution to strengthen the NPT regime, overriding the votes of one or more member states; this could be highly disruptive unless there are widespread perceptions that any such resolutions are fair and legitimate.[9] In his April 2009 speech in Prague, President Obama also emphasized the importance of enforcing nonproliferation commitments:

> Rules must be binding. Violations must be punished. Words must mean something. The world must stand together to prevent the spread of these weapons.[10]

Enforcement decisions, in the UN or in other international institutions are, almost by definition, not consensus decisions, since those states being punished will dissent. The degree to which the vast majority of states, however, views any resulting sanctions or military actions as legitimate and fair enforcement of commitments (as opposed to being raw coercion) will help determine whether the act strengthens or weakens the overall NPT regime in the long term.

Fourth, the points discussed so far highlight, the importance of the IAEA and other international organizations. Will the IAEA be able to cope effectively with a world in which there is more nuclear technology spread across more countries? In the design of the nonproliferation regime, the IAEA is intended to play a crucial role in reassuring the international community that civil nuclear programs are not contributing to weapons acquisition. Through a scheme of inspections and safeguards, the IAEA is meant to bring transparency to the world's peaceful nuclear activities and thus to serve as a buffer between peaceful nuclear programs and possible development of nuclear weapons. Across time, the IAEA increasingly has been expected to fulfill the additional role of investigating concerns about the possible existence of clandestine nuclear weapons programs, an issue of obvious importance in judging compliance with the NPT. The IAEA attempts to perform these pivotal roles with limited (many would say inadequate) resources and many political and legal constraints on its ability to act. In his remarkably candid farewell address, IAEA Director General ElBaradei stated, "Our ability to detect possible clandestine nuclear material and activities depends on the extent to which we are given the necessary legal authority, technology, and resources. *Regrettably, we face continuing major shortcomings in all three areas, which, if not addressed, could put the entire nonproliferation regime at risk.*[11] As nuclear power spreads, the IAEA's challenge will become even more demanding and the shortfalls could become even more acute. A crucial question for the future of the nuclear order is whether the member states that fund the IAEA and determine its legal mandate will be prepared to strengthen the Agency so it is adequate to its responsibilities in a more nuclear world. If not, one of the principal barriers between energy production and weapons programs will be seriously weakened.

Fifth, an important determinant of future proliferation will be the degree to which the spread of the nuclear power industry produces civilian nuclear power bureaucracies in different states that want to maintain peaceful programs and oppose turning civilian energy programs into nuclear weapons programs. Indeed, how best to ensure that civilian nuclear power bureaucracies maintain a strong interest in opposing nuclear weapons proliferation may be the $64,000 question for estimating the effect of the global spread of nuclear power on the likelihood of nuclear weapons proliferation. This is ironic, for although some nonproliferation specialists may not want more countries to start nuclear power programs, once those states do so, it will be important for nonproliferation that their nuclear power programs are successful. The leaders and bureaucratic organizations that run successful nuclear power enterprises will want to maintain strong ties to the global nuclear power industry, to international capital and technology markets, and to global regulatory agencies—and hence will be more likely to cooperate with the nuclear nonproliferation regime. Leaders of less successful or struggling nuclear power enterprises, in contrast, might be more likely to support clandestine or breakout nuclear weapons development programs as tools to justify their existence, prestige, and high budgets within their state. Research on Japan and South Korea, for example, has shown that the

liberalizing governments supported maintaining their close relationship to global markets and institutions and that this decision influenced the capability and willingness of nuclear bureaucracies to push for weapons programs. In the case of India, by contrast, the power and autonomy of the state's "strategic enclave," coupled with the record of failure in producing nuclear energy, strongly encouraged the leaders of India's nuclear bureaucracies to lobby Indira Gandhi to test a weapon in 1974, to encourage the Bharatiya Janata Party (BJP) to test another set of weapons in 1998, and to oppose constraints on their ability to test new nuclear weapons today.[12]

Sixth, and finally, a critical factor shaping our nuclear future will be whether leaders in the non-nuclear-weapons states (NNWS) see the NPT merely as an effort to get the nuclear-weapons states (NWS) to disarm, or whether they conceive of the NPT as a solution to a collective action problem. This clearly was part of how leaders conceived of the NPT when they signed and ratified it in the late 1960s and subsequently. The Treaty and the IAEA inspection regime it created were valued because they provided a sense of confidence that other states in the region were not developing nuclear weapons and that, therefore, the state in question could renounce nuclear weapons as well. But over time, that vision was lost, and many NNWS began to see the NPT as merely an unfair constraint on them and as a largely unsuccessful goad to encourage nuclear disarmament in the NWS. The possibility of international control of the nuclear fuel cycle, and the accompanying constraint on national nuclear fuel production programs, will be more likely if all nuclear power states see a danger in their neighbors operating sensitive nuclear fuel facilities. This perceived fear may make states more willing to accept international control of the nuclear fuel cycle, and the constraints on their national programs that come along with it, in exchange for constraints on their neighbors' programs.

Many possible outcomes could arise from the complicated, unpredictable, decentralized process of nuclear decision-making. Expectations have often been confounded and predictions have often been wrong. The notion of nuclear electricity "too cheap to meter," for example, has long ago faded into history. Forecasts that there would be dozens of nuclear-armed states have fortunately proven wrong (so far). Previous predictions that there would be a rapid expansion of nuclear power around the globe turned out to be wildly off the mark. Though we can see today features of the nuclear landscape that will materialize well into the future, it is not easy to predict what the global nuclear order will be. A long legacy of incorrect predictions should keep us humble and remind us that we, too, can be wrong. It is possible, however, to envision how things might turn out if things go well or badly.

The most optimistic vision of the future sees the substantial expansion and spread of nuclear energy use around the globe, but with effective constraints placed on the potential adverse security consequences. There would be many more nuclear reactors on a global scale, contributing to the mitigation of climate change and to energy security, but fuel cycle capabilities would not have spread. Nuclear newcomers would rely on international arrangements for the fuel to run their reactors and would use international or regional repositories to store spent fuel, rather than hold it or reprocess it at home. In this way, the link between nuclear power and nuclear weapons could be limited. Ideally, further reassurance about the purely peaceful applications of the world's additional investments in nuclear power would be provided by a larger, stronger, better funded IAEA, presiding over a regime that institutionalized high levels of transparency and empowered the IAEA with sufficient investigative powers to produce confidence that cheaters will not undermine the regime. If the international governance of the world's nuclear affairs can evolve and strengthen, then it may be possible to establish and promote compliance with high common standards for safety and physical security—for example, through the refinement, and enforcement of UN Security Council Resolution 1540, which already calls on states to ensure "appropriate and effective" levels of security at their nuclear facilities (but without ever defining what steps meet that standard). It will never be possible to eliminate all

risk, of course; but the world would be a safer place if all states possessing nuclear technology were not only obliged to accept desirable standards, but made more genuine and monitored efforts to meet those standards. A system that possessed this set of attributes would be a robust nonproliferation regime that would allow the wide exploitation of nuclear power while circumscribing the potential risks and problems associated with nuclear power.

The likelihood of reaching this nuclear future would be increased if steps were taken to delegitimize and marginalize nuclear weapons and if the NWS were judged to be making sincere efforts to move toward nuclear disarmament in fulfillment of their obligations under Article VI of the NPT.[13] It is difficult to dampen the appetite for nuclear weapons when existing NWS enshrine those weapons at the center of their security policies, tout the unique and indispensable security contributions of these weapons, and proclaim their intention to retain nuclear weapons for the indefinite future. It is also difficult to credibly call for a strictly enforced rules-based nonproliferation system when the NWS are seen to be flouting their own obligations under the nonproliferation regime. It is too soon to tell where the arms control initiatives launched by President Obama, notably in his nuclear disarmament speech in Prague in April 2009, may lead, but even the first small steps seem to have had a positive impact on the climate of opinion in nuclear affairs. If there is progress toward deeper cuts in nuclear forces, if the NWS begin to reduce their reliance on nuclear weapons, and if there is success in putting into place other measures such as the Comprehensive Test Ban Treaty and the Fissile Material Cutoff Treaty, then nuclear weapons would seem less valuable and the incentive for new states to acquire them would diminish. This shift would be a useful buttress to a more extensive and effective nuclear nonproliferation regime.

A much more negative vision of the future finds that the global, expansion of nuclear power has produced an array of undesirable consequences. If nuclear newcomers lack confidence in the international market for nuclear fuel, however it is configured, some will surely seek to master the nuclear fuel cycle themselves (as Iran has done) in order to ensure a reliable supply of reactor fuel for their nuclear programs and, perhaps, to maintain a weapons option for the future. Neighboring states will be nervous, great powers will be alarmed, and friction is likely to ensue—as evidenced in the past decade in the cases of Iraq, Iran, Libya, and North Korea. Coping with this problem will be even worse if the standing of the IAEA were to erode and its ability to provide transparency and reassurance were undermined. It is certainly possible that in the future the IAEA, hobbled by inadequate resources, handicapped by its limited legal mandate, partially blinded by the lack of its own intelligence capabilities, tainted by the political maneuverings of member states, harmed by past failures, and crippled by the defiance of troublesome states, would be judged insufficient, incapable of addressing the challenges of a more nuclear world. The IAEA has its critics even today, but its problems could easily be compounded in the future. If the IAEA were no longer regarded as an effective tool in the nonproliferation regime, this would weaken another barrier that stands between nuclear power and nuclear weapons. In the event that the nonproliferation system seems to be breaking down, institutionalized efforts to provide global governance in the nuclear realm are also likely to decay or fail. In a world in which states are aggressively pursuing their own nuclear interests and the institutions and mechanisms of nonproliferation are weakening, rules are less likely to be accepted, respected, or enforced. The evolution toward universal high standards for safety and physical security would be stifled and the result could be very uneven safety and security efforts in national nuclear programs—meaning higher risk of accident or incident.

The most disturbing variant of this negative vision for the nuclear future would be one in which the norm against acquisition of nuclear weapons is fractured and new NWS emerge. States that determined for their own self-interested reasons to acquire nuclear weapons could defy or ignore the NPT/IAEA system or simply withdraw from the NPT (as North Korea did). In conflict-prone regions in which fuel cycle capabilities exist in multiple

states, there arises the possibility of the competitive pursuit of nuclear weapons (as occurred in South Asia between India and Pakistan). If enrichment and reprocessing are more widely distributed across states, acquisition of nuclear weapons by one power could more easily trigger nuclear acquisition by others. In the past, rapid cascades of proliferation—though sometimes predicted—have not occurred and are not certain to occur in the future.[14] But the dynamic could well be different if the nonproliferation regime is thought to be eroding and more NNWS possess the latent capability to manufacture nuclear weapons. The reassuring record of a past era marked by few NWS, a sturdy norm against acquisition, a reasonably sound nonproliferation regime, very infrequent spread of nuclear weapons to new states, and possession of fuel cycle capabilities by only a few states may not be a reliable guide to the future if trends slide in a negative direction. Decades ago, Henry Rowen and Albert Wohlstetter famously worried about the dangers of "life in a nuclear-armed crowd."[15] Decades hence, we could find ourselves living in that world if unwise choices and unfortunate preferences lead us down an undesirable nuclear path.

Momentum toward a proliferated world would be reinforced if the current MWS fail to move away from reliance on nuclear weapons. The notable cooling in U.S.-Russia relations could plausibly lead to a restoration of their nuclear rivalry and to a resurrection of nuclear deterrence as the centerpiece of the strategic relationship between the world's two largest nuclear powers. Indeed, both powers retained substantial nuclear arsenals postured at least in part to "hedge" against the possibility that hostility would resume in their bilateral relationship. The nuclear obsession that marked the Cold War could return. But even if that does not happen, both the United States and Russia have continued to embrace nuclear weapons and to adopt doctrines and defense policies that accord a prominent role to nuclear weapons, If the arms control process sputters and breaks down, if multilateral agreements founder and fail to enter into force because of strenuous opposition within

NWS, if the articulated commitments to nuclear disarmament come to be regarded as false promises, then relations between nuclear haves and have-nots are likely to be difficult and the international atmosphere will be more conducive to the spread of nuclear weapons.

A third vision of the nuclear future would involve a collapse of the expected nuclear renaissance and a possible contraction of the role of nuclear power. It would not be the first time that, an expected nuclear renaissance did not happen. This could come about in two ways, one benign and the other dystopian. It is possible that the economic costs and security challenges will in the end outweigh the incentives to expand nuclear power. Perhaps alternative energy sources will develop more rapidly than expected or some technological innovation will make nuclear power seem less necessary or less competitive. Perhaps it will be possible to address the world's energy and climate change challenges without additional exposure to the risks and challenges associated with nuclear power. This would be the benign route to a more circumscribed future for nuclear power.

The darker scenario involves failure to contain successfully the risks of nuclear power. The anticipated expansion and spread of nuclear technology could be derailed if something horrible happens. The catastrophic reactor accident, at Chernobyl set back the nuclear sector by decades in some countries; another large accident would likely have similar effects. A breach of physical security at a nuclear installation that resulted in a serious sabotage incident or terrorist possession of nuclear materials or weapons undoubtedly would dampen the enthusiasm for nuclear power expansion and cause some recalculation of the cost-benefit equation. And then there is the most horrible scenario of all: the use of nuclear weapons. A nuclear detonation in a city or against any other target would clearly alter the global nuclear debate and produce a more constrained nuclear power future.

The global nuclear future is highly uncertain, and there is no reason to assume that a desirable nuclear order will arise automatically or spontaneously. Men make their own history, but they do not make it entirely as they please, Karl Marx famously noted. Governments, the nuclear industry, and international institutions will make our nuclear future, but their complex interactions may not produce the nuclear world that each of them seeks. This is why it is so important to think hard now about where we may be headed, what desirable outcomes we should seek, and what steps should be taken now to increase the likelihood of a safer and more secure nuclear order in the years ahead.

Notes

1. Richard A. Meserve, "The Global Nuclear Safety Regime," *Dædalus* 138 (4) (Fall 2009): 100–111.
2. See Colin Perkel, "Terror Cell Co-leader Pleads Guilty," *The Canadian Press,* October 8, 2009, http://ca.news.yahoo.com/s/capress/terror_guilty_plea; and Melissa Leong, "Fertilizer, Remote Detonators Figure in Terror Plot," *Canwest News Service,* May 30, 2008.
3. Mohamed ElBaradei, "Statement to the Sixty-Fourth Regular Session of the United Nations General Assembly," November 2, 2009.
4. See U.S. Regulatory Commission, "Backgrounder on Dirty Bombs," July 30, 2009. http://www.nrc.gov/reading-rm/doc-collections/fact-sheets/dirty-bombs-bg.html.
5. Matthew Bunn, "Reducing the Greatest Risks of Nuclear Theft & Terrorism," *Dædalus* 138 (4) (Fall 2009): 112–123.
6. Robert H. Socolow & Alexander Glaser, "Balancing Risks: Nuclear Energy & Climate Change," *Dædalus* 138 (4) (Fall 2009): 31–44.
7. Harold A. Feiveson, "A Skeptic's View of Nuclear Energy," *Dædalus* 138 (4) (Fall 2009): 60–70; and José Goldemberg, "Nuclear Energy in Developing Countries," *Dædalus* 138 (4) (Fall 2009): 71–80.
8. See *Nuclear Programmes in the Middle East: In the Shadow of Iran* (London: International Institute for Strategic Studies, 2008).
9. See Jayantha Dhanapala, "The Management of NPT Diplomacy," in this volume. See also, Cecilia Albin, *Justice and Fairness in International Negotiation* (Cambridge: Cambridge University Press, 2001).
10. U.S. President Barack Obama speaking in Prague, April 5, 2009.

11. ElBaradei, "Statement to the Sixty-Fourth Regular Session of the United Nations General Assembly," emphasis added.

12. See Etel Solingen, *Nuclear Logics: Contrasting Paths in East Asia and the Middle East* (Princeton, N.J.: Princeton University Press, 2007); and Itty Abraham, *The Making of the Indian Atomic Bomb: Science, Secrecy and the Postcolonial State* (London: Zed Books, 1998). See also George Perkovich's essay, "Global Implications of the U.S.-India Deal," in this volume.

13. See Scott D. Sagan, "The Case for No First Use," *Survival* 51 (3) (2009): 163–182.

14. See William C. Potter's essay, "The NPT & the Sources of Nuclear Restraint," in this volume.

15. See Albert Wohlstetter, Thomas A. Brown, Gregory Jones, David McGarvey, Henry Rowen, Vincent Taylor, and Roberta Wohlstetter, "Moving Toward Life in a Nuclear Armed Crowd?" Report for the Arms Control and Disarmament Agency, April 22, 1976, http://vvwvv.npec-web.org/Frameset.asp ?PageType=Single&PDFFile=19751204-AW-EtAl-MovingTo\vardsLifeNuclearArmedCrowd&PDF Folder=Essays.

Arctic Meltdown

The Economic and Security Implications of Global Warming

SCOTT G. BORGERSON

Borgerson discusses the implications of global climate change for the interests of Arctic nations. He posits that the melting of the Arctic may generate increasing competition between the Arctic powers over the region's resources and trade routes. Borgerson contends that in a region devoid of norms and overarching political and legal structures, U.S. interests would be best served by ratification of the Law of the Sea (UNCLOS), and the development of cooperative agreements with Canada.

The arctic ocean is melting, and it is melting fast. This past summer, the area covered by sea ice shrank by more than one million square miles, reducing the Arctic icecap to only half the size it was 50 years ago. For the first time, the Northwest Passage—a fabled sea route to Asia that European explorers sought in vain for centuries—opened for shipping. Even if the international community manages to slow the pace of climate change immediately and dramatically, a certain amount of warming is irreversible. It is no longer a matter of if, but when, the Arctic Ocean will open to regular marine transportation and exploration of its lucrative natural-resource deposits.

Global warming has given birth to a new scramble for territory and resources among the five Arctic powers. Russia was the first to stake its claim in this great Arctic gold rush, in 2001. Moscow submitted a claim to the United Nations for 460,000 square miles of resource-rich Arctic waters, an area roughly the size of the states of California, Indiana, and Texas combined. The UN rejected this ambitious annexation, but last August the Kremlin nevertheless dispatched a nuclear-powered icebreaker and two submarines to plant its flag on the North Pole's sea floor. Days later, the Russians provocatively ordered strategic bomber flights over the Arctic Ocean for the first time since the Cold War. Not to be outdone, Canadian Prime Minister Stephen Harper announced funding for new Arctic naval patrol vessels, a new deep-water port, and a cold-weather training center along the Northwest Passage. Denmark and Norway, which control Greenland and the Svalbard Islands, respectively, are also anxious to establish their claims.

While the other Arctic powers are racing to carve up the region, the United States has remained largely on the sidelines. The U.S. Senate has not ratified the UN Convention on the Law of the Sea (UNCLOS), the leading international treaty on maritime rights, even though President George W. Bush, environmental nongovernmental organizations, the U.S. Navy and U.S. Coast Guard service chiefs, and leading voices in the private sector support the convention. As a result, the United States cannot formally assert any rights to the untold resources off Alaska's northern coast beyond its exclusive economic zone—such zones extend for only 200 nautical miles from each Arctic state's shore—nor can it join the UN commission that adjudicates such claims. Worse, Washington has forfeited its ability to assert sovereignty in the Arctic by allowing its icebreaker fleet to atrophy. The United States today funds a navy as large as the next 17 in the world combined, yet it has just one seaworthy oceangoing icebreaker—a vessel that was built more than a decade ago and that is not optimally configured for Arctic missions. Russia, by comparison, has a fleet of 18 icebreakers. And even China operates one icebreaker, despite its lack of Arctic waters. Through its own neglect, the world's sole superpower—a country that borders the Bering Strait and possesses over 1,000 miles of Arctic coastline—has been left out in the cold.

Washington cannot afford to stand idly by. The Arctic region is not currently governed by any comprehensive multilateral norms and regulations because it was never expected to become a navigable waterway or a site for large-scale commercial development. Decisions made by Arctic powers in the coming years will therefore profoundly shape the future of the region for decades. Without U.S. leadership to help develop diplomatic solutions to competing claims and potential conflicts, the region could erupt in an armed mad dash for its resources.

Go North, Young Man

The Arctic has always experienced cooling and warming, but the current melt defies any historical comparison. It is dramatic, abrupt, and directly correlated with industrial emissions of greenhouse gases. In Alaska and western Canada, average winter temperatures have increased by as much as seven degrees Fahrenheit in the past 60 years. The results of global warming in the Arctic are far more dramatic than elsewhere due to the sharper angle at which the sun's rays strike the polar region during summer and because the retreating sea ice is turning into open water, which absorbs far more solar radiation. This dynamic is creating a vicious melting cycle known as the ice-albedo feedback loop.

Each new summer breaks the previous year's record. Between 2004 and 2005, the Arctic lost 14 percent of its perennial ice—the dense, thick ice that is the main obstacle to shipping. In the last 23 years, 41 percent of this hard, multiyear ice has vanished. The decomposition of this ice means that the Arctic will become like the Baltic Sea, covered by only a thin layer of seasonal ice in the winter and therefore fully navigable year-round. A few years ago, leading supercomputer climate models predicted that there would be an ice-free Arctic during the summer by the end of the century. But given the current pace of retreat, trans-Arctic voyages could conceivably be possible within the next five to ten years. The most advanced models presented at the 2007 meeting of the American Geophysical Union anticipated an ice-free Arctic in the summer as early as 2013.

The environmental impact of the melting Arctic has been dramatic. Polar bears are becoming an endangered species, fish never before found in the Arctic are migrating to its warming waters, and thawing tundra is being replaced with temperate forests. Greenland is experiencing a farming boom, as once-barren soil now yields broccoli, hay, and potatoes. Less ice also means increased access to Arctic fish, timber, and minerals, such as lead, magnesium, nickel, and zinc—not to mention immense freshwater reserves, which could become increasingly valuable in a warming world. If the Arctic is the barometer by which to measure the earth's health, these symptoms point to a very sick planet indeed.

Ironically, the great melt is likely to yield more of the very commodities that precipitated it: fossil fuels. As oil prices exceed $100 a barrel, geologists are scrambling to determine exactly how much oil and gas lies beneath the melting icecap. More is known about the surface of Mars than about the Arctic Ocean's deep, but early returns indicate that the Arctic could hold the last remaining undiscovered hydrocarbon resources on earth. The U.S. Geological Survey and the Norwegian company StatoilHydro estimate that the Arctic holds as much as one-quarter of the world's remaining undiscovered oil and gas deposits. Some Arctic wildcatters believe this estimate could increase substantially as more is learned about the region's geology. The Arctic Ocean's long, outstretched continental shelf is another indication of the potential for commercially accessible offshore oil and gas resources. And, much to their chagrin, climate-change scientists have recently found material in ice-core samples suggesting that the Arctic once hosted all kinds of organic material that, after cooking under intense seabed pressure for millennia, would likely produce vast storehouses of fossil fuels.

The largest deposits are found in the Arctic off the coast of Russia. The Russian state-controlled oil company Gazprom has approximately 113 trillion cubic feet of gas already under development in the fields it owns in the Barents Sea. The Russian Ministry of Natural Resources calculates that the territory claimed by Moscow could contain as much as 586 billion barrels of oil—although these deposits are unproven. By comparison, all of Saudi Arabia's current proven oil reserves—which admittedly exclude unexplored and speculative resources—amount to only 260 billion barrels. The U.S. Geological Survey is just now launching the first comprehensive study of the Arctic's resources. The first areas to be studied are the 193,000-square-mile East Greenland Rift Basins. According to initial seismic readings, they could contain 9 billion barrels of oil and 86 trillion cubic feet of gas. Altogether, the Alaskan Arctic coast appears to hold at least 27 billion barrels of oil.

Although onshore resources, such as the oil in Alaska's Arctic National Wildlife Refuge, have dominated debates about Arctic development in Washington, the real action will take place offshore, as the polar ice continues to retreat. An early indication of the financial stakes and political controversies involved is a lawsuit that was filed against Royal Dutch/Shell in the U.S. Ninth Circuit Court. Filed jointly by an unusual alliance of environmental groups and indigenous whalers, the case has held up the development of Shell's $80 million leases in the newly accessible Beaufort Sea, off Alaska's northern coast. By 2015, such offshore oil production will account for roughly 40 percent of the world's total. The Alaskan coast might one day look like the shores of Louisiana, in the Gulf of Mexico, lit up at night by the millions of sparkling lights from offshore oil platforms.

Polar Express

An even greater prize will be the new sea-lanes created by the great melt. In the nineteenth century, an Arctic seaway represented the Holy Grail of Victorian exploration, and the seafaring British Empire spared no expense in pursuing a shortcut to rich Asian markets. Once it became clear that the Northwest Passage was ice clogged and impassable, the Arctic faded from power brokers' consciousness. Strategic interest in the Arctic was revived during World War II and the Cold War, when nuclear submarines and intercontinental missiles turned the Arctic into the world's most militarized maritime space, but it is only now that the Arctic sea routes so coveted by nineteenth-century explorers are becoming a reality.

The shipping shortcuts of the Northern Sea Route (over Eurasia) and the Northwest Passage (over North America) would cut existing oceanic transit times by days, saving shipping companies—not to mention navies and smugglers—thousands of miles in travel. The Northern Sea Route would reduce the sailing distance between Rotterdam and Yokohama from 11,200 nautical miles—via the current route, through the Suez Canal—to only 6,500 nautical miles, a savings of more than 40 percent. Likewise, the Northwest Passage would trim a voyage from Seattle to Rotterdam by 2,000 nautical miles, making it nearly 25 percent shorter than the current route, via the Panama Canal. Taking into account canal fees, fuel costs, and other variables that determine freight rates, these shortcuts could cut the cost of a single voyage by a large container ship by as much as 20 percent—from approximately $17.5 million to $14 million saving the shipping industry billions of dollars a year. The savings would be even greater for the megaships that are unable to fit through the Panama and Suez Canals and so currently sail around the Cape of Good Hope and Cape Horn. Moreover, these Arctic routes would also allow commercial and military vessels to avoid sailing through politically unstable Middle Eastern waters and the pirate-infested South China Sea. An Iranian provocation in the Strait of Hormuz, such as the one that occurred in January, would be considered far less of a threat in an age of trans-Arctic shipping.

Arctic shipping could also dramatically affect global trade patterns. In 1969, oil companies sent the *S.S. Manhattan* through the Northwest Passage to test whether it was a viable route for moving Arctic oil to the Eastern Seaboard. The *Manhattan* completed the voyage with the help of accompanying icebreakers, but oil companies soon deemed the route impractical and prohibitively expensive and opted instead for an Alaskan pipeline. But today such voyages are fast becoming economically feasible. As soon as marine insurers recalculate the risks involved in these voyages, trans-Arctic shipping will become commercially viable and begin on a large scale. In an age of just-in-time delivery, and with increasing fuel costs eating into the profits of shipping companies, reducing long-haul sailing distances by as much as 40 percent could usher in a new phase of globalization. Arctic routes would force further competition between the Panama and Suez Canals, thereby reducing current canal tolls; shipping chokepoints such as the Strait of Malacca would no longer dictate global shipping patterns; and Arctic seaways would allow for greater international economic integration. When the ice recedes enough, likely within this decade, a marine highway directly over the North Pole will materialize. Such a route, which would most likely run between Iceland and Alaska's Dutch Harbor, would connect shipping megaports in the North Atlantic with those in the North Pacific and radiate outward to other ports in a hub-and-spoke system. A fast lane is now under development between the Arctic port of Murmansk, in Russia, and the Hudson Bay port of Churchill, in Canada, which is connected to the North American rail network.

In order to navigate these opening sea-lanes and transport the Arctic's oil and natural gas, the world's shipyards are already building ice-capable ships. The private sector is investing billions of dollars in a fleet of Arctic tankers. In 2005, there were 262 ice-class ships in service worldwide and 234 more on order. The oil and gas markets are driving the development of cutting-edge technology and the construction of new types of ships, such as double-acting tankers, which can steam bow first through open water and then turn around and proceed stern first to smash through ice. These new ships can sail unhindered to the Arctic's burgeoning oil and gas fields without the aid of icebreakers. Such breakthroughs are revolutionizing Arctic shipping and turning what were once commercially unviable projects into booming businesses.

The Coming Anarchy

Despite the melting icecap's potential to transform global shipping and energy markets, Arctic issues are largely ignored at senior levels in the U.S. State Department and the U.S. National Security Council. The most recent executive statement on the Arctic dates to 1994 and does not mention the retreating ice. But the Arctic's strategic location and immense resource wealth make it an important national interest. Although the melting Arctic holds great promise, it also poses grave dangers. The combination of new shipping routes, trillions of dollars in possible oil and gas resources, and a poorly defined picture of state ownership makes for a toxic brew.

The situation is especially dangerous because there are currently no overarching political or legal structures that can provide for the orderly development of the region or mediate political disagreements over Arctic resources or sea-lanes. The Arctic has always been frozen; as ice turns to water, it is not clear which rules should apply. The rapid melt is also rekindling numerous interstate rivalries and attracting energy-hungry newcomers, such as China, to the region. The Arctic powers are fast approaching diplomatic gridlock, and that could eventually lead to the sort of armed brinkmanship that plagues other territories, such as the desolate but resource-rich Spratly Islands, where multiple states claim sovereignty but no clear picture of ownership exists.

There are few legal frameworks that offer guidance. The Arctic Council does exist to address environmental issues, but it has remained silent on the most pressing challenges facing the region because the United States purposefully emasculated it at birth, in 1996, by prohibiting it from addressing security concerns. Many observers argue that UNCLOS is the correct tool to manage the thawing Arctic. The convention provides mechanisms for states to settle boundary disputes and submit claims for additional resources beyond their exclusive economic zones. Furthermore, UNCLOS sets aside the resources in the high seas as the common heritage of humankind, it allows states bordering ice-covered waters to enforce more stringent environmental regulations, and it defines which seaways are the sovereign possessions of states and which international passages are open to unfettered navigation.

However, UNCLOS cannot be seamlessly applied to the Arctic. The region's unique geographic circumstances do not allow for a neat application of this legal framework. The Arctic is home to a number of vexing problems that, taken in their entirety, make it a special case. These unresolved challenges include carving up the world's longest uncharted and most geologically complex continental shelf among five states with competing claims, resolving differences between Canada and the rest of the world over how to legally define the Northwest Passage, demarcating maritime borders between the United States and Canada in the Beaufort Sea and between Norway and Russia in the Barents Sea, and regulating vessels shielded behind flags of convenience (which obscure the true origin and ownership of the vessels) as they travel across numerous national jurisdictions. Finally, increased oil and gas exploration and the trans-Arctic shipping that comes with it will pose serious environmental risks. Oil tankers present a particularly grave environmental threat, as illustrated by three recent oil spills in the much safer waters of the San Francisco Bay, the Black Sea, and the Yellow Sea.

There are also a handful of unresolved issues at play in the Arctic that are not covered under UNCLOS. Between 1958 and 1992, Russia dumped 18 nuclear reactors into the Arctic Ocean, several of them still fully loaded with nuclear fuel. This hazard still needs to be cleaned up. Furthermore, the Arctic region is home to one million indigenous people, who deserve to have a say in the region's future, especially as regards their professed right to continue hunting bowhead whales, their safety alongside what will become bustling shipping lanes, and their rightful share of the economic benefits that Arctic development will bring. With the prospect of newfound energy wealth, there is also growing talk of Greenland petitioning Denmark for political independence. Finally, there has been an explosion in polar tourism, often involving ships unsuited for navigation in the region. Last year, 140 cruise ships carried 4,000 intrepid travelers for holidays off Greenland's icy coast, a dangerous journey in largely uncharted waters.

Although it is tempting to look to the past for solutions to the Arctic conundrum, no perfect analogy exists. The 1959 Antarctic Treaty, which froze all territorial claims and set aside the continent for scientific research, provides some lessons, but it concerns a continent rather than an ocean. Moreover, Antarctica is far removed from major trade routes, and negotiations unfolded in the entirely different context of the Cold War. As a body of water that links several large economies, the Mediterranean Sea is somewhat similar to the Arctic Ocean, but its littoral states have always had clearer historical claims, and it has never been covered with ice, at least not in human history. There is simply no comparable historical example of a saltwater space with such ambiguous ownership, such a dramatically mutating seascape, and such extraordinary economic promise.

The region's remarkable untapped resource wealth and unrealized potential to become a fast lane between the Atlantic and Pacific Oceans makes it a key emerging pressure point in international affairs. At this critical juncture, decisions about how to manage this rapidly changing region will likely be made within a diplomatic and legal vacuum unless the United States steps forward to lead the international community toward a multilateral solution.

Northern Exposure

Until such a solution is found, the Arctic countries are likely to unilaterally grab as much territory as possible and exert sovereign control over opening sea-lanes wherever they can. In this legal no man's land, Arctic states are pursuing their narrowly defined national interests by laying down sonar nets and arming icebreakers to guard their claims. Russia has led the charge with its flag-planting antics this past summer. Moscow has been arguing that a submarine elevation called the Lomonosov Ridge is a natural extension of the Eurasian landmass and that therefore approximately half of the Arctic Ocean is its rightful inheritance. The UN commission that is reviewing the claim sent Russia back to gather additional geological proof, leading Artur Chilingarov, a celebrated Soviet-era explorer and now a close confidant of Russian President Vladimir Putin, to declare, "The Arctic is ours and we should manifest our presence" while leading a mission to the North Pole last summer.

Naturally, other Arctic states are responding. Norway submitted its claim for additional Arctic resources to the commission in 2006, Canada and Denmark are now doing their homework in order to present their own claims. Ottawa and Copenhagen are currently at odds over the possession of Hans Island, an outcropping of desolate rocks surrounded by resource-rich waters in the Nares Strait,

between Canada's Ellesmere Island and Greenland. Even the United States, despite its refusal to ratify UNCLOS, has for the past few summers dispatched its sole icebreaker to the Arctic to collect evidence for a possible territorial claim in the event the Senate eventually ratifies the treaty.

There are also battles over sea-lanes. Canada has just launched a satellite surveillance system designed to search for ships trespassing in its waters. Even though the Northern Sea Route will likely open before the Northwest Passage, the desire to stop ships from passing through the Canadian archipelago—especially those from the U.S. Coast Guard and the U.S. Navy—is the cause of much saber rattling north of the border. "Use it or lose it," Canadian Prime Minister Harper frequently declares in reference to Canada's Arctic sovereignty—an argument that plays well with Canadians, who are increasingly critical of their southern neighbor. So far, the delicate 1988 "agreement to disagree" between the United States and Canada over the final disposition of these waters has remained intact, but the United States should not underestimate Canadian passions on this issue.

The ideal way to manage the Arctic would be to develop an overarching treaty that guarantees an orderly and collective approach to extracting the region's wealth. As part of the ongoing International Polar Year (a large scientific program focused on the Arctic and the Antarctic that is set to run until March 2009), the United States should convene a conference to draft a new accord based on the framework of the Arctic Council. The agreement should incorporate relevant provisions of UNCLOS and take into account all of the key emerging Arctic issues. With a strong push from Washington, the Arctic states could settle their differences around a negotiating table, agree on how to carve up the region's vast resource pie, and possibly even submit a joint proposal to the UN for its blessing.

But even as it pushes for a multilateral diplomatic solution, the United States should undertake a unilateral effort to shore up U.S. interests in the Arctic. The few in the United States who still stubbornly oppose U.S. accession to UNCLOS claim that by ratifying the treaty Washington would cede too much U.S. sovereignty and that customary international law and a powerful navy already allow the United States to protect its Arctic interests. But these are not enough. The United States is the only major country that has failed to ratify UNCLOS, and Washington is therefore left on the outside looking in as a nonmember to various legal and technical bodies. In addition to becoming a party to the convention, the United States must publish an updated Arctic policy, invest in ice-mapping programs, and breathe new life into its inefficient, uncompetitive shipyards, thus enabling it to update the country's geriatric icebreaker fleet, as soon as possible.

The United States should also strike a deal with Canada, leading to a joint management effort along the same lines as the 1817 Rush-Bagot Agreement, which demilitarized the Great Lakes and led to the creation (albeit more than a century later) of the nonprofit St. Lawrence Seaway Development Corporation to manage this critical, and sometimes ice-covered, national waterway. In the same spirit, the United States and Canada could combine their resources to help police thousands of miles of Arctic coastline. Washington and Ottawa now work collaboratively on other sea and land borders and together built the impressive North American Aerospace Defense Command, or NORAD, system. They are perfectly capable of doing the same on the Arctic frontier, and it is in both countries' national interests to do so.

There is no reason that economic development and environmental stewardship cannot go hand in hand. To this end, Canada could take the lead in establishing an analogous public-private Arctic seaway management corporation with a mandate to provide for the safe and secure transit of vessels in North American Arctic waters while protecting the area's sensitive environment. Shipping tolls levied by this bilateral management regime could pay for desperately needed charts (much of the existing survey information about the Northwest Passage dates to nineteenth-century British exploration), as well as for search-and-rescue capabilities, traffic-management operations, vessel tracking, and similar services that would guard life and property. Such a jointly managed Arctic seaway system could establish facilities for the disposal of solid and liquid waste, identify harbors of refuge for ships in danger, and enforce a more rigorous code for ship design in order to ensure that vessels traveling through the Northwest Passage have thicker hulls, more powerful engines, and special navigation equipment. The captains and crews of these vessels could also be required to have additional training and, if the conditions warrant, to take aboard an agency-approved "ice pilot" to help them navigate safely.

This bilateral arrangement could eventually be expanded to include other Arctic countries, especially Russia. The United States and Russia, as an extension of the proposed Arctic seaway management corporation, could develop traffic-separation schemes through the Bering Strait and further invest in the responsible development of safe shipping along the Northern Sea Route. Eventually, a pan-Arctic corporation could coordinate the safe, secure, and efficient movement of vessels across the Arctic. Japan, which is vitally dependent on the Strait of Malacca for the overwhelming majority of its energy supplies, would be a natural investor in such a project since it has an interest in limiting the risk of a disruption in its oil supply.

It's Easy Being Green

In 1847, a British expedition seeking the fabled Northwest Passage ended in death and ignominy because Sir John Franklin and his crew, seeing themselves as products of the pinnacle of Victorian civilization, were too proud to ask the Inuit for help. At the height of its empire, the United States sometimes sees itself as invincible, too. But the time has come for Washington to get over its isolationist instincts and ratify UNCLOS, cooperate with Canada on managing the Northwest Passage, and propose an imaginative new multilateral Arctic treaty.

Washington must awaken to the broader economic and security implications of climate change. The melting Arctic is the proverbial canary in the coal mine of planetary health and a harbinger of how the warming planet will profoundly affect U.S. national security. Being green is no longer a slogan just for Greenpeace supporters and campus activists; foreign policy hawks must also view the environment as part of the national security calculus. Self-preservation in the face of massive climatic change requires an enlightened, humble, and strategic response. Both liberals and conservatives in the United States must move beyond the tired

debate over causation and get on with the important work of mitigation and adaptation by managing the consequences of the great melt.

Risking Security

Policies and Paradoxes of Cyberspace Security

RONALD J. DEIBERT AND RAFAL ROHOZINSKI

Deibert and Rohozinski argue that the rapid evolution of computer technologies, and increasing integration of governments and economies with cyberspace, present a spectrum of novel threats and opportunities to nations, notably the United States. They contend that many states are unable to control the risks that arise in the domain of cyberspace, and that the disruption of cyberspace poses a threat to both the global economy and to the security interests of the U.S.A. They discuss a range of cybertechnology risks including dark nets, resistance nets, and cybercrime.

Globalization is generating new security challenges. Modern societies confront a myriad of risks that threaten economic prosperity, undermine the safety and security of citizens, and cause significant disruption to society and politics. These risks range from empowered and militant nonstate actors to technological and human-made processes, such as environmental degradation and global warming. Risk mitigation has become a routine matter of good public policy.

Cyberspace represents a special category of risk.[1] A term once found only in science fiction novels, cyberspace describes the human-made domain for action that exists as a consequence of an interconnected and interdependent global communications and computing infrastructure. Cyberspace connects more than half of all humanity and is an indispensable component of political, social, economic, and military power worldwide. In strategic terms, cyberspace is accepted now as a domain equal to land, air, sea, and space.

Predictably, in the post-9/11 era, cyberspace is the focus of security concerns as states weigh the risks and benefits of omnipresent global connectivity. However, cyberspace presents special security challenges, for a variety of reasons. First, and most importantly, it is a communication network that is organized transnationally and not through the institutional structures of the state system. Although states and individuals may claim sovereignty or ownership over segments of cyberspace, particularly parts of its material infrastructure, or even opt out of it entirely, once in they are never fully *in control*. Cyberspace has emergent properties, in other words, that elude state control.

Second, and closely related, cyberspace is operated as a mix of public and private networks. Governance of cyberspace, like its architecture, is distributed, and does not take place within a singular forum or point of control (Dutton and Peltu 2007).

Even the Internet Corporation for Assigned Names and Numbers (ICANN), that is most often associated with Internet governance issues, is only narrowly concerned with domain and routing management and not with the full panoply of cyberspace governance issues (Mueller 2002). There are instead numerous sites of cyberspace governance, from spectrum allocation to copyright and intellectual property regulation to content filtering and cybercrime (among many others). Each of these sites involves numerous stakeholders, including governments, businesses, and civil society networks. In addition, private sector actors from multiple countries operate most of the core infrastructural components of cyberspace. What James Der Derian (2003) calls "heteropolarity" perhaps best characterizes the state of cyberspace governance.

Third, unlike other domains, such as the sea, land, air, or space, cyberspace is a human-made domain in constant flux based on the ingenuity and participation of users themselves. One of the core design features of cyberspace is the end-to-end principle, which allows for generative technologies to be introduced into cyberspace by end users as long as they conform to the basic protocols of interconnectivity (Saltzer, Reed, and Clark 1984). The latter introduces not only great variation and constant innovation, but also new and unforeseen security risks (Zittrain 2007). It also creates major problems for regulation, insofar as regulators are always chasing a moving target. In other words, cyberspace is a domain of constant transformation and a high degree of complexity.

Fourth, cyberspace is comprised of both a material and a virtual realm—a space of *things* and *ideas*, structure and content. Theorists and observers of cyberspace often focus on one of these elements to the exclusion or diminution of the other, but both are important and interdependent. Cyberspace is indeed a "consensual hallucination" as Gibson (1984) famously defined it, but one that could not exist without the physical infrastructure that supports it. Attempts to control and monitor the virtual realm of cyberspace often begin with interventions in the physical infrastructure, at key Internet chokepoints (Deibert, Palfrey, Rohozinski, and Zittrain 2008). However, these efforts are never entirely comprehensive; once released into cyberspace, the distributed properties of the network help ideas and information circulate, duplicate and proliferate. Even radical measures, such as disconnecting the Internet entirely as was done recently in Burma and Nepal, can only limit, but not entirely contain the flow of ideas.

In this paper, we examine processes of securing cyberspace and their wider implications. Drawing from the sociologist Ulrich Beck, we do so by first disaggregating cyberspace security into two related but distinct dimensions, articulated as "risks": risks to the physical realm of computer and communication technologies and their associated networks (risks *to* cyberspace, commonly known as critical infrastructure protection); and risks that arise from cyberspace and are facilitated or generated by its associated technologies, but do not directly target the infrastructures per se (risks *through* cyberspace). As we show, there is a robust international consensus, growing communities of practice, and even an emerging normative regime around critical infrastructure protection. Even in military areas, where states compete for strategic advantage and have developed doctrines for operations in cyberspace, there is, for the moment, a reluctance to employ overt computer-based attacks against other state's national information infrastructures and a mutual deterrent norm is slowly developing, albeit in fits and starts.

This is less the case when it comes to risks *through* cyberspace. While states do collaborate around some policy areas where consensus and mutual interests can be found (for example, "piracy," and to a lesser degree child pornography), cooperation declines as the object of risk becomes politically contestable and where national interests can vary widely. These include the nature of political opposition and the right to dissent or protest, minority rights and independence movements, religious belief, cultural values, or historical claims.

The contrast between policies around these two domains has led to contradictory tendencies. States seek policy coordination and regulations so as to make cyberspace a more secure, safe, and predictable environment recognizing its strategic importance to economic and social development. These efforts to combat risks to the network are driven by a desire to sustain-through-security a friction-free and distributed global communications environment. At the same time, regime type and legitimacy varies greatly between states, and actions taken in response to *risks through cyberspace* can have the opposite effect, introducing friction in the form of filtering of undesirable content, intimidation and self-censorship through pervasive surveillance, and even the disabling or disconnection of critical infrastructures in an attempt to neutralize the risks posed by networked political or social actors.

This paper examines the larger implications of these seemingly paradoxical tendencies. We suggest that securing cyberspace is not a simple balkanization of the Internet or a "return of the state," as some have suggested (Goldsmith and Wu 2006). Rather, it is a complex process entwining both the development of universally accepted norms and ever-expanding "rules of the game," state regulation of issues of vital domestic, political and cultural concern, privatization of risk mitigation, and the internationalization of public policy.

Risk Society

In a globalizing world, risk mitigation has become a routine matter of politics, good public policy, and a major market segment in its own right. Politicians employ risk in lieu of ideology as a justification for policies ranging from economic and social development to national security and international aid. Risk mitigation, management, and governance are now widely studied, propagated and institutionalized techniques of governance.

The German sociologist Ulrich Beck (1992) first teased out the connections between "risks" and modern industrialism and globalization organized around a historical narrative of modern social development.

There are several elements of Beck's risk society thesis that pertain to our analysis and from which we draw inspiration. First, and most importantly, is the notion of "risk" itself, and the social redistribution of risks. According to Beck, the central principle of industrial society is the distribution of goods and services, while the central principle of the risk society is the distribution of "bads," or risks. In general terms, risk is simply defined as the possibility of incurring loss. Analyzing how risks are distributed tells us much about the functioning and politics of particular societies. One of the more remarkable aspects of securing cyberspace is the way in which some risks are distributed by states to private actors and the consequences that flow from that, redistribution.

Like Beck, we place a great deal of emphasis on unintended and often paradoxical consequences of risk mitigation.[2] For Beck, a central characteristic of reflexive modernization is the tendency for risk mitigation to beget further risk, and so on, until the mitigation of risk becomes the central element of politics and public policy. Each risk mitigation strategy breeds new uncertainty and unpredictable consequences, which in turn require further mitigation, often undermining risk mitigation strategies in other sectors of society. As the title of our paper suggests, there is a paradox at the heart of some of the ways in which states are securing cyberspace, which leads to an insecurity of a different sort.

To understand that paradox, the two different conceptions of risks emerging from cyberspace need to be unpacked and evaluated separately: risks *to* cyberspace and risks *through* cyberspace.

Risks to Cyberspace: Critical Infrastructure Protection

As the Internet was specifically designed to be a resilient communications network, security vulnerabilities have always been a major factor with which to contend and are at the core of the network's distributed architecture. These vulnerabilities have become more pronounced, however, as cyberspace has grown from an experimental network, to a university-based research network, to an integral part of the global political economy on which all modern societies exist (Kleinrock 2008). Cyberspace is the domain through which electronic clearances take place, irrigation systems are controlled, hospitals and educational systems interconnect, and governments and private industries of all types function. It can be found aboard nuclear submarines and bicycles, watches and air traffic control systems—it is ubiquitous and pervasive, and is most acutely felt when it is absent.

The vulnerability of cyberspace to malicious or accidental disruption came to light in several high profile incidents, including the infamous 1988 Morris Worm in which a virulent program was mistakenly released on the Internet, causing worldwide traffic to come to a standstill. Beginning in the 1990s, it became more common to hear scenarios involving actors targeting the Internet (and cyberspace more broadly) to bring about widespread havoc—famously coined an "electronic pearl harbor" by President Clinton's National Cyber-Security Advisor, Richard Clarke (Denning 2000). Whether through cyberterrorism, or through accident, a growing recognition of all advanced societies' increasing dependence on cyberspace has brought, about ever more pronounced efforts at cyberspace securitization. Although there have been many that have been rightly skeptical of the scope of the claims made, as well as the interests served by the articulation of threats, there has been a growing consensus among advanced industrialized states around defining cyberspace as a key national asset and critical infrastructure to be secured.

There are numerous policy documents, legislative and institutional initiatives, and analyses around securing critical infrastructures (Dunn Cavelty 2008; Lewis 2008). Rather than attempt to be comprehensive, our aim here is instead to highlight several crosscutting characteristics of these initiatives. A growing number of states have created new institutions or re-tasked existing ones with the mandate to either oversee critical infrastructure security and/or make recommendations as to how the security should be undertaken. In almost all cases, a similar justification is employed pointing to society's growing dependence on information and communication technologies, the vulnerabilities that exist in these systems, and the steps that need to be taken to secure cyberspace to keep it functioning as the infrastructure of the global political economy, either from deliberate attack or disruption through accident (Lewis 2008). The latter is the area with, not surprisingly, the greatest scope for policy divergences among states. Generally speaking, though, among advanced industrialized economies, like Canada, the United States, and the countries of Europe and parts of Asia, there is recognition of the significant role played by private actors in the constitution of cyberspace and the need for public-private partnerships. Many countries are unwilling, or their constituencies would not tolerate, heavy-handed regulations that impose requirements on private actors from the state.

Second, and related, is that there is a particular ideological notion of cyberspace that is supported by these policies, one closely related to the functioning of global capitalism. This may seem self-evident, but it is important to underscore and scrutinize. Although discussions of Internet security are often couched in technical-functional terms, the political economy of critical infrastructure is never absent and broad values always inform security policies. The often unspoken logic of securing critical infrastructures is to support and sustain a friction- free communications environment in which ideas/data/purchase orders/financial transactions move freely and with as much speed as possible across borders and around the word (Deibert 2002). Disruption to critical infrastructures means, first and foremost, disruption to global capital markets.

Third, there is a delicate matter of balancing the security requirements of critical infrastructure protection with national security imperatives, and in particular the collection of intelligence. In many states, the main agency charged with critical infrastructure protection is also the central agency charged with signals intelligence and actionable electronic information (Bronk 2008). In part, this is a vestige of the critical assurance role played by these agencies for governments' communications and increasingly for businesses. Both the Communications Security Establishment Canada (CSEC) and National Security Agency (NSA) provide due diligence for government encryption standards, for example, a role that has continued and in fact broadened to include private actors.

Although prima facie this may seem appropriate, the risk distribution creates a significant tension for a variety of reasons. First, many of these organizations operate in secrecy and with limited public accountability, and have both a track record and putative interest in having covert access to private communications. Since much of the operation of critical infrastructures is in private hands, it creates a tension between the interests of national security agencies and private actors and raises major privacy concerns, particularly as many of the companies themselves are constituted as multi-national or transnational joint ventures. Second, and as will be explained in more detail below, the effort to secure cyberspace by these agencies has been used to justify a massive expansion of surveillance powers, and even in some cases an alteration to the very framework of that which is to be protected.[3]

Third, although national critical infrastructure initiatives are the most common, there is a slow but steady internationalization of critical infrastructure protection initiatives, policy coordination, and legislation. These include initiatives at the regional, inter-state, and global levels. The G8, APEC, CoE, the OECD, NATO, and the ITU (IMPACT) all have cyber-security initiatives of some sort (Hosein 2008; ITU 2008). These initiatives are noteworthy for a variety of reasons. First, they suggest a growing international consensus and norm around the importance of securing critical infrastructures along the lines of the principles outlined earlier. Second, they represent a nascent "internationalization" of public policy, particularly in areas of early warning, notification, harmonization of law enforcement, data retention, and best security practices. Third, the mix of private and public actors involved in these initiatives gives them an *embeddedness* (and thus stickiness) in state-society relations and across multiple

jurisdictions. Fourth, and most importantly, they represent a growing recognition of the mutual interdependence generated by cyberspace. Although protection of *national* assets is obviously first priority among states worldwide, there is also acknowledgment that cyberspace cannot truly be secured single-handedly and that the definition of "national assets" itself is problematic for this very reason.

The emerging norm around securing critical infrastructures, and the recognition of mutual interdependence of cyberspace, can be seen most clearly in the limits that shape states' offensive operations in cyberspace. A growing number of states have developed or are exploring doctrines around offensive operations in cyberspace. These doctrines are a legacy of a variety of factors: the "revolution in military affairs," a greater understanding of the vulnerabilities of cyberspace and ways to exploit those vulnerabilities, the natural imperatives of defense organizations whose mandate is to pursue military technologies to their fullest limits, and also a growing recognition of, and need to counteract, the risks through cyberspace that are described in more detail below. However, the limits to these actions are also widely acknowledged and a variety of legal and technical factors prohibit offensive operations (Kelsey 2008). For example, during the 2003 invasion of Iraq, the full range of offensive computer network attack capabilities was constrained by both legal restrictions and the fears of a cascading effect on European financial institutions.[4]

Risks Through Cyberspace: Dealing with Dark and Resistance Nets[5]

Cyberspace, in particular the Internet, has made networking between like-minded individuals and groups possible on a global scale and has contributed to a massive explosion of civic networks. Powerful, easy-to-use search technologies, media of self-expression, like blogs, and communicative systems make it easy to form virtual communities, connect causes, and organize political activities. Global civic networks have consistently been the earliest adopters of Internet technologies for their collective activities, and oftentimes have been at the forefront of innovative uses of new media, like SMS,

VoIP, Facebook, Twitter, and blogs. The medium's constitutive architecture—distributed, decentralized, and relatively cheap and easy to employ—"fits" with the organizational and political "logic" of global chic networks (Naughton 2001). Local causes seek and find moral and financial support on a global basis and consequently, local politics can now play to a global audience.

But the technological explosion of civil society has not emerged without unintended and even negative consequences, particularly for nondemocratic, authoritarian, and competitive authoritarian states (Way and Levitzsky 2002). Cyberspace has enabled new, nimble and distributed challenges to these regimes, manifest in vigorous, mobilized opposition movements, protests, and in some cases, even revolutionary challenges to political authority. In many countries, cyberspace presents the only medium of expression not rigidly or traditionally controlled by the state. Activists in even the most tightly controlled societies, like Uzbekistan, Burma, Iran, China, Vietnam, Belarus, Tunisia, and Vietnam, are able to find links across borders and mobilize support for their cause through the medium of cyberspace. For these regimes, these movements represent a new, fluid, and very formidable security risk. We call these risks through cyberspace that challenge nondemocratic, authoritarian, and competitive authoritarian regimes, *resistance networks.*

Even among democratic states, the explosion of civic networks has presented serious challenges, though of a slightly different nature. Just as progressive and social justice groups have made use of the Internet to advance global norms, so too have a wide variety of militant groups, extremists, criminal organizations, and terrorists to serve more ulterior purposes. Cyberspace has facilitated their activities in much the same way as it has for more benign civil society networks that often get more attention, but the aims of these groups are often criminal, covert, and sometimes violent. We call these risks through the network *dark nets,* of which there are two different sorts (Deibert and Rohozinski 2008).

The most well-known of the dark nets are armed social movements, which can represent a multiplicity of local causes, but whose ability to share tactics, contacts, and at times, drink from the same ideological well, make them appear as a unified global network. In the post-9/11 era, al Qaeda and the Jihad movements represent the most visible manifestation of this kind of armed social movement. However, they are by no means the first and only networks of this kind. Many of the "new wars" (as Mary Kaldor calls them) that, occurred during the 1990s were fought essentially as transnational civil wars where participants pursued both guerilla and conventional warfare against government and rival groups (Kaldor 1999). In conflicts that included Sri Lanka, Somalia, former Yugoslavia, West Africa and Chechnya, "new wars" demonstrated that armed social movements are capable of challenging and at times defeating state actors without the need of state-based patrons or backers.

More importantly, this new generation of armed social actors has also increasingly embraced cyberspace (Rohozinski 2004). They recognize the capacity afforded by cyberspace to "effect" both their supporters and opponents. Significantly, it was these groups, rather than militaries of the First World War, that were the first to leverage cyberspace as means to wage information operations redefining the main battlefield away from the military and towards the political sphere (Weimann 2006b). Beginning with the first Chechen war, the video taping of attacks on the Russian military became more important than the military significance of the attacks themselves. When shown to supporters, as well as the Russian public (via rebroadcast in Russian television, and later on the Internet) their shock value was enough to convey the impression that the Russian military was being defeated. Similar tactics were adopted and further refined by Hezbollah in its resistance against Israeli occupation of Southern Lebanon prior to their withdrawal in 2001, and again in the 2006 summer war. Attacks were documented and produced in the form of music videos, that were both broadcast across Hezbollah's terrestrial TV station, (al Manar) as well as made available for download from a website, the movement established as part of its strategic communications and information warfare strategy (Pahlavi 2007; Wehrey 2002).

These video shorts proved highly effective, and have since undergone several significant evolutions, paralleling the spread and popularity of such online resources as YouTube and Twitter that are used by "civil" networks. They are now one of the key instruments used by these movements to attract interest in their causes and are a significant feature of the more than 4,500+ active jihad websites, chat rooms, and forums (Weimann 2006a; Kimmage 2008). As the resources necessary for producing multimedia technologies continue to fall, and access to inexpensive digital cameras and computers increases, the threshold and number of video and other multimedia products in circulation has grown exponentially, while the age of the producers has declined. During the early months of the second Intifada, for example, several of the more compelling PowerPoint slides circulating on the Internet depicting the brutality of the Israeli reoccupation of the West bank were produced by a 14-year-old living in a refugee camp in Lebanon.

In addition to changing the nature of the conflicts, cyberspace has also served to change the nature of the movements themselves. They have eliminated the need for strict command and control, especially for smaller and more marginal movements who can now claim legitimacy for their actions by "virtually" piggy-backing on the perceived effectiveness and success of others. It also gives the impression of a unity and scale among groups that in reality, simply does not exist. As a result, much as the discourse of human rights and other universal issues provides an intellectual center that binds many civil networks together, the depictions, forums, and shared virtual spaces of resistance, wrapped in religious undertones, provide a means for smaller, more local struggles to identify with and benefit from a broader ideological pool that, serves to demonstrate that resistance is not only possible, but positively effective (Kohlmann 2008).

Cyberspace is only one domain used by armed social movements in the pursuit of their cause, but it is certainly the one that, because of its largely unregulated character and relative freedom of access, causes the greatest concern for states under threat from such actors. It is seen, at least in part, as the

sea in which global militants find sanctuary of the kind that Mao postulated in his classical treatise on people's war. The difficulty, then as it is now, is how to effectively separate the insurgents from the people, or armed social movements from cyberspace, in a manner that does not destroy the latter. In this study again the unintended and paradoxical consequences or risk mitigation strategies becomes apparent.

Transnational criminal networks are a second form of dark nets. These actors, who can be large or small, local or transnational, exploit the relative anonymity offered by cyberspace as well as the absence of harmonized national laws defining cybercrime, to circumvent or avoid prosecution. Cybercrime is typically broken down into two distinct realms: *old crimes,* such as fraud, child pornography, and theft (including digital "piracy"), which have been adapted to the new possibilities offered by the emergence of the e-economy (Brenner 2001); and *new crimes* that are unique to cyberspace, such as phishing attacks, spam, or the use of malware, cyberespionage, and distributed denial-of-service attacks (DDoS), which would not have emerged without it (Brenner 2005; Wall 2005). In both cases, jurisdictions with poorly functioning or nonexistent laws are used to hide otherwise criminal activities out of the reach of authorities in jurisdictions where they are clearly criminalized (Wall 2007). What Michael Froomkin (1997) characterized as "regulatory arbitrage" allows cybercriminals to exploit the lowest state denominators as safe harbors, electronically moving to lax jurisdictions when the net tightens or laws are progressively harmonized.

Globally, the incidence of cybercrime is reported to be increasing in both developed and developing economies. In Russia, for example, acknowledged as a source of some of the most imaginative forms of cybercrime, incidences reportedly grew by almost 300% between 2003 and 2006. Yet, accurate comparative statistics makes measuring global cybercrime difficult. For example, in the United States—an economy where the economic losses caused by cybercrime were cited by one Treasury Board official as exceeding $105 billion—only in 2006 did the Department of Justice belatedly begin the process of establishing a base-line for measuring cybercrime. In part, the absence of reliable statistics belies the difficulty faced by local police and justice institutions when faced with having to police activities that may not be defined or considered criminal in their jurisdiction (or against which they have few tools). Indeed, the very concept of jurisdiction itself is confused in cyberspace.

Securing Risks Through Cyberspace

The state responses to risks through the network are much more diverse, competitive, and characterized by self-help policies than are risks to the network, where an emerging norm and growing international cooperation can be discerned. Even in areas where one might anticipate international cooperation—control of child pornography, for example—the primary responses have been nationally based. In other areas, such as dealing with extremists, militants, and anti-regime resistance networks, perceptions of threats and national interests vary too widely for there to be any meaningful policy coordination and national controls predominate. Indeed, in certain cases, states support, illicitly or otherwise, the dark and resistance nets that pose challenges to other states as part of inter-state competition. Self-help policies also tend to predominate because the policy instruments deployed—filtering, surveillance, and information warfare attacks—tend to be highly secretive, lack transparency and accountability and fall within the realm of national security and military strategy. Significantly, some of the policies taken to secure risks through cyberspace are having the paradoxical outcome of undermining the very object of security in the *risks to cyberspace* domain.

The one risk through cyberspace where there is significant policy coordination is cybercrime, and in particular dealing with theft of intellectual property and fraud, although even here the coordination is limited mostly to industrialized countries. The most far-reaching is the Council of Europe's Cybercrime Convention, signed and ratified by 15 states, and signed but not yet ratified by a further 28 in Europe and elsewhere (Weber 2003). Among

other things, the convention harmonizes policies around dealing with crimes in cyberspace, including those relating to data retention and information sharing for law enforcement and intelligence. Outside of the convention's regime, however, national policies and, most importantly, stale *capacities* differ widely, allowing criminal organizations to triage among jurisdictions and find safe harbor within corrupt and failed states or where legal enforcement of existing laws is lax. Criminal networks, therefore, are able to continue to multiply and expand into new regions and activities. Russian hackers are implicated with identity theft and credit card fraud in the United States and Europe. Nigerian gangs have become omnipresent in a variety of scams and wire fraud, whereas Chinese, Iranian, Malaysian, Thai, Peruvian and Israeli networks preside over a global distribution network of pirated DVDs and software (USTR 2008).

Filtering, Surveillance, and Information Attacks

Several self-help and competitive strategies are employed by states to deal with risks through cyberspace, introducing friction and disruption to cyberspace. The starkest example is Internet filtering. Once thought impossible in cyberspace, Internet content filtering is now a widespread global practice. Solid comparative research around Internet filtering practices is generally lacking. A notable exception is the research of the Open Net Initiative (ONI), which has documented the growth in scope, scale and sophistication of Internet filtering practices since 2002 (Deibert et al. 2008, 2010).[6] Whereas in the early 2000s, there were only a handful of states blocking access to information, the latest research of the ONI has documented more than 40 countries. Filtering technologies are installed at key Internet chokepoints, and work by preventing requests for URLs, IPs, or domain names of banned content from being carried through (Villeneuve 2006). Although methods vary widely, most states implement Internet filtering practices by imposing upon Internet service providers (ISPs) responsibility for blocking access to a pre-determined list of websites, IP addresses, and services, while others impose nationwide uniform controls at international gateways. Other filtering systems can be implemented at more local levels, such as Internet cafes. The countries that are described by the ONI as "pervasive" filterers of Internet content—China, Burma, Vietnam, Thailand, Iran, Syria, Saudi Arabia, UAE, Bahrain, Uzbekistan, Turkmenistan, Ethiopia—routinely block access to the websites, forums, and blogs of political opposition, human rights, independence, minority rights, alternative faiths, and cultural groups. Almost all of them do so without public accountability or transparency.

There are related questions around the involvement of search engines and other Internet service companies that collude with governments that violate human rights. In order to gain a toehold in such jurisdictions, companies have been required lo filter access to information on search engines, or comply with "local laws" that contain none of the safeguards around due process and privacy that are typically found in liberal democratic regimes (Maclay 2010). In one of the most egregious cases, the American Internet company Yahoo! turned over email records to the Chinese government leading to the arrest of three people, Jiang Lijun, Shi Tao, and Li Zhi. In testimony before the U.S. Congress, Yahoo! said that they had no choice but to comply with the request, that "Yahoo! China was legally obligated to comply with the requirements of Chinese law enforcement . . ." or face the possibility of "criminal charges, including imprisonment. Ultimately, US Companies in China face a choice: comply with Chinese law, or leave."[7] These cases illustrate the ways in which the distribution of risk mitigation strategies to private actors can create serious accountability gaps, and ultimately pervert the very service being delivered. Ironically, the best and brightest of Silicon Valley, once heralded by their own advertisements as "wiring the world" and "connecting individuals," are here being asked to do precisely the opposite.

Next-generation control strategies, such as just-in-time blocking, can include an even more pernicious example of self-help policies to deal with risks through the network: covert or semi-covert support of dark and resistance networks. China, Russia, Burma, Iran, Belarus (among others) have been accused of supporting criminal organization and third parties to denigrate resistance networks, although determining the exact, involvement of the government in each case is difficult. For example, China's adversaries—the U.S. government, Tibetan groups, the Falun Gong, pro-democracy groups—have all experienced increasingly sophisticated information warfare attacks, including distributed denial-of-service (DDoS) attacks, the use of Trojan horses and viruses, cyberespionage, and targeted malware. Using forensic investigative techniques, researchers have been able to trace back some of these attacks and espionage networks to control servers in mainland China, the most famous of which being the "GhostNet" system (Information Warfare Monitor 2009). However, determining whether the Chinese government itself is responsible for the attacks has not been possible given the ease by which such attacks can be launched through anonymous means or launched by private actors for commercial or illicit gain. It is instructive to note in this respect that part of China's explicit information warfare strategy is to enlist the "people's" support, and there is a very vibrant nationalist-patriotic hacker community in China that erupts in defense of the Chinese regime whenever domestic political incidents arise. Likewise, several recent conflicts involving adversaries of Russia have experienced massive DoS attacks, including Estonia and Georgia. However, researchers have not been able to conclusively determine whether the Russian government is the source of the attacks, whether the attacks were contracted out to criminal organizations, or whether they originate from patriotic hackers, or some combination. We might infer that such outsourcing to private actors may in fact become more common because of the attractions of plausible deniability it affords to the regimes involved.

The risks posed by both dark and resistance networks have contributed to a massive expansion of electronic surveillance among all countries, a significant portion of it carried out through extra-legal means and/or downloaded to private companies. The attacks of 9/11 were a definite watershed in this regard. Following upon revelations that the hijackers employed cyberspace as an organizational domain to carry out the attacks, there was widespread support for more enhanced monitoring powers for law enforcement and intelligence. The United States quickly adopted wide-ranging legislation, in the form of the PATRIOT Act, which expanded the scope for electronic surveillance. Numerous countries around the world then passed legislation similar to the United States PATRIOT Act, requiring lawful access provisions for law enforcement to be undertaken by private ISPs.

Some non-democratic countries have used the excuse of the war on terror and followed the normative lead of the United States tolegitimize their surveillance of opposition and minority. In several countries, notably Egypt, a combination of surveillance and selective prosecution is used to effectively curtail bloggers, and specific minority groups (especially the gay and lesbian community). In 2008, Russia expanded the powers previously established by SORM-II, which obliged ISPs to purchase and install equipment that would permit local FSB offices to monitor the Internet activity of specific users. The new legislation makes it possible to monitor all Internet traffic and personal usage without specific warrants. The legislation effectively brings into the open covert powers that, were previously assigned to FAPSI, with the twist of transferring to the entire ISPs the costs. In many countries, Internet cafes are monitored by secret police both physically and through remote surveillance technologies. The measures present a clear warning to anyone seeking the anonymity of cyberspace to voice political criticism or express alternative lifestyles: you can be found, and you can be prosecuted.

Although far from exhaustive, the previous section highlights some of the ways in which states are attempting to secure against risks through cyberspace. Of particular note is the extent to which self-help policies predominate, transparency and accountability are rare, risk mitigation includes outsourcing to third parties and illicit networks, and competition is often fierce. In attempting to neutralize risks through cyberspace, states are turning to filtering, blocking, surveillance, and information warfare tactics. These tendencies point to an increasingly competitive cyberspace commons where states, individuals, civil society and dark and resistance nets jostle for agency and advantage, often at the expense of cyberspace itself.

The Paradoxes of Risking Security

Securing cyberspace has become one of the major global policy areas of the 21st century. A growing-international norm has emerged that sees cyberspace as vital to economics, government, society, and culture. Policies have focused on securing systems that support a friction-free global communications environment in which commerce can flourish, data can be exchanged without corruption, and infrastructures can operate without significant downtime or disruption.

Risks through the network involve much wider divergence among states, an emphasis on national policies and self-help, and most significantly policies whose outcome are having the opposite effect, of those associated with risks to cyberspace. Ironically, in other words, security policies in response to risks through cyberspace are creating insecurities around cyberspace itself. The responses to the two "risks" operate at cross-purposes. The aim of "risks to" is to secure a friction-free, distributed and resilient global communications network. The aim of "risks through," on the other hand, is to introduce friction and disruption through filtering, surveillance, and computer network attacks. Whether and how these two risk domains will co-exist into the future, and what implications will follow for international security, are areas worthy of further investigation.

Securing cyberspace has definitely entailed a "return of the state" but not in ways that suggest a return to the traditional Westphalian paradigm of state sovereignty. First, efforts aimed at combating risks to the network are supporting a worldwide, interconnected domain of communications that, in turn, is facilitating a rapid expansion of transnational non-state actor activities. Second, many of the policies described above entail devolution of responsibilities and authority to private actors. This includes the imposition of surveillance, mining, and data retention responsibilities to ISPs and other cyberspace service companies (search engines, cellular phone operators) in both democratic and nondemocratic environments. Privatization of a different sort is also implicated in the outsourcing of computer network attacks to illicit networks and criminal organizations. Privatization of security has become an area of active investigation among some theorists lately; this analysis suggests privatization of intelligence and computer network attacks should be added to that area. Lastly, the efforts taken to combat cybercrime, to harmonize laws across state jurisdictions, and to facilitate international policing and intelligence can be seen as an internationalization of the state, albeit among a core group of industrialized states.

Together these trends suggest that the paradoxes of securing cyberspace will ensure the continuation of a complex and multifaceted domain, one that defies simple and extreme characterizations. Cyberspace will continue to be tugged in heteropolar directions: from the ingenuity of end users who develop technologies that have system-wide effects; from states who intervene to try to shape, limit and disable adversarial sources of information; from major commercial providers centralizing information and communication in "cloud" computing systems; to anonymous tunneled networks hardened by advanced encryption technologies. This domain, like others before it, is an object of geopolitical contestation that at once shapes and constrains the nature of that contestation. Unlike sea, land, air and space, though, it is a domain entirely created, sustained and ultimately transformed by ongoing human interaction and competition.

Notes

1. There are perennial debates about how to define cyberspace and distinguish it from related concepts, like the Internet. The latter is typically defined as "a worldwide network of computer networks that use the TCP/IP network protocols to facilitate data transmission and exchange." Although this definition is important and at the core of the subject matter under investigation in this paper, it is primarily focused on the material infrastructure of networked devices while excluding from consideration other important non-physical elements and characteristics. In this paper, we adopt the definition of cyberspace recently put forward by the U.S. Department of Defense. According to the U.S. Department of Defense's National Strategy for Military Operations in Cyberspace (2006:3), cyberspace is defined as "a domain characterized by the use of electronics and the electromagnetic spectrum to store, modify, and exchange data via networked systems and associated physical infrastructures." There are several benefits of this broader definition: First, it covers more than just networked computers, and includes cellular technologies, space-based systems, and other technologies that are not at first blush usually associated with the Internet. Second, the reference to cyberspace as a "domain" allows for inclusion of non-physical elements, such as ideas and virtual realities, which are increasingly the subject of securitization today.

2. Anthony Giddens (1990:153) best describes the dynamics in this regard: "Design faults and operator failure clearly fall within the category of unintended consequences, but the category includes much more. No matter how well a system is designed and no matter how efficient is the operators, the consequences of its introduction and function, in the contexts of the operation of other systems and of human activity in general, cannot be wholly predicted. One reason for this is the complexity of systems and actions that make-up world society. Bui even if it were conceivable—as in practice it is not—that the world (human action and the physical environment) could become a single design system, unintended consequences would persist. The reason for this is the circularity social knowledge, which affects in the first instance the social rather than the natural world. In conditions of modernity, the social world can never form a stable environment in terms of the input of new knowledge about its character and functioning. New knowledge (concepts, theories, findings) does not simply render the social world more transparent, but alters its nature, spinning it off in novel directions."

3. Here we see starkly an illustration of how risk mitigation and distribution begets further risk, in this case to privacy. One example of this is the

recent exploration at a UN working group, supported by both the Chinese and U.S. national security agencies, for an end to anonymity online through an infrastructural alteration to cyberspace to allow for Internet Protocol (IP) tracebacking (McCullagh 2008).

4. One rather perverse outcome of the constraints is that they may create an incentive for states to offload or outsource computer operations to third parties or criminal organizations and thus allow for plausible deniability. For example, in several recent instances involving DDoS computer network attacks on adversaries of the Russian state, there was unverified, but circumstantially compelling evidence connecting criminal organizations involved in the attacks with Russian security forces. It is noteworthy that China's doctrine of establishing the people, and nationalist fervor, in offensive computer network attacks is compatible with such an incentive structure. Such offloading and outsourcing allow plausible deniability although capitalizing on some of the limited outcomes of offensive computer network operations, examples of which are picked up in more detail in subsequent sections of this article.

5. The following section draws from Deibert and Rohozinski (2008).

6. The authors are two of four founders and principal investigators. The other two are John Palfrey and Jonathan Zittrain. The ONI's methodology combines technical and contextual research. Two lists of websites are checked in each of the countries tested: a global list (constant for each country) and a local list (different for each country). The global list is composed of internationally relevant websites with provocative or objectionable content in English. The local lists are designed individually for each country to unearth unique filtering and blocking behavior. In countries where Internet censorship has been reported, the local lists also include those sites that were alleged to have been blocked. These lists, however, are not meant to be exhaustive. The actual tests are run front within each country using specially designed software. Where appropriate, the tests are run from different locations to capture the differences in blocking behavior across ISPs and across multiple days and weeks to control for normal connectivity problems. The completion of the initial accessibility testing is just the first step in our evaluation process. Additional diagnostic work is performed to separate normal connectivity errors from intentional tampering. There are a number of technical alternatives for filtering the Internet, some of which are relatively easy to discover. Others are difficult to detect and require extensive diagnostic work to confirm.

7. Testimony of Michael Callahan, Senior Vice President and General Counsel, Yahoo! Inc., before the Subcommittees on Africa, Global Human Rights and International Operations, and Asia and the Pacific, February 15, 2006. Recently, several major Internet services companies have entered into a self-regulation pact called the Global Network Initiative (GNI). The effectiveness of such self-regulation is untested and still questionable.

References

Adler, Emmanuel. 2005. *Communitarian International Relations: The Epistemic Foundations of International Relations.* London: Routledge.

Beck, ulrich. 1992. *Risk Society: Towards a New Modernity,* trans. Mark Ritter. London: Sage.

Brenner, Susan W. 2001. Is There Such a Thing as Virtual Crime? *California Criminal Law Review* 4 (1): 105–11.

Brenner, Susan W. 2005. Distributed Security: Moving Away from Reactive Law Enforcement. *International Journal of Communications Law & Policy* 9: 1–43.

Brenner, Susan W., and Bert-Jaap Koops. 2004. Approaches to Cybercrime Jurisdiction. *Journal of High Technology Law* 4 (1): 3–44.

Bronk, Christopher. 2008. Webtapping: Securing the Internet to Save Us from Transnational Terror? *First Monday* 13 (11).

Buzan, Barry, Oie Waever, and Jaap de Wilde. 1998. *Security: A New Framework of Analysis.* Boulder, CO: Lynne Rienner.

Deibert, Ronald J. 2002. Circuits of Power: Security in the Internet Environment. In *Information Technologies and Global Politics: The Changing Scope of Power and Governance,* ed. James M. Rosenau and J. P. Singh. Albany: State University of New York.

Deibert, Ronald J., And Rafal Rohozinski. 2008. Good for Liberty, Bad for Security? Global Civil Society and the Securitization of the Internet. In *Access Denied: The Practice and Policy of Global Internet Filtering*, edited by Ronald J. Deibert, John Palfrey, Rafal Rohozinski and Jonathan Zittrain. Cambridge, MA: MIT Press.

Deibert, Ronald J., John Palfrey, Rafal Rohozinski, and Jonathan Zittrain (Eds.) 2008. *Access Denied: The Practice and Policy of Global Internet Filtering*. Cambridge, MA: MIT Press.

———. (Eds.). 2010. *Access Controlled: The Shaping of Power, Rights, and Rule in Cyberspace*. Cambridge, MA: MIT Press.

Denning, Dorothy E. 2000. Activism, Hacktivism, and Cyberterrorism: The Internet as a Tool for Influencing Foreign Policy. *Computer Security Journal* 16 (3): 15–35.

Der Derian, James. 2003. The Question of Information Technology in International Relations. *Millennium: Journal of International Studies* 32 (3): 441–56.

Dunn Cavelty, Myriam. 2008. *Cyber-Security and Threat Politics: US Efforts to Secure the Information Age*. London: Routledge.

Dutton, William H., and Malcom Peltu. 2007. The Emerging Internet Governance Mosaic: Connecting the Pieces. *Information Polity* 12 (1–2): 63–81.

Froomkin, Michael. 1997. The Internet as a Source of Regulatory Arbitrage. In *Borders in Cyberspace*, ed. Brian Kahin and Charles Nesson. Cambridge, MA: MIT Press.

Gibson, William. 1984. *Neuromancer*. New York: Ace Books.

Giddens, Anthony. 1990. *The Consequences of Modernity*. Stanford, CA: Stanford University Press.

Goldsmith, Jack L., and Tim Wu. 2006. *Who Controls the Internet? Illusions of a Borderless World*. Oxford: Oxford University Press.

Hosein, Ian. 2008. Creating Conventions: Technology Policy and International Cooperation in Criminal Matters. In *Governing Global Electronic Networks*, ed. William J. Drake and Ernest J. Wilson, III. Cambridge, MA: MIT Press.

Information Warfare Monitor. 2009. Tracking Ghost. net: Investigating a Cyber Espionage Network. Available at http://www.scribd.com/doc/13731776/Tracking-GhostNet-Investigating-a-Cyber-Espionage-Network.

International Telecommunications Union (ITU). 2008. ITU Global Cybersecurity Agenda (CGA) High-Level Experts Group (HLEG) Global Strategic Report. International Telecommunications Union. Available at http://www.itu.int/cybersecurity/gca.

Kaldor, Mary. 1999. *New and Old Wars: Organised Violence in a Global Era*. Cambridge, MA: Polity Press.

Kelsey, Jeffrey T. G. 2008. Hacking into International Humanitarian Law: The Principles of Distinction and Neutrality in the Age of Cyber Warfare. *Michigan Law Review* 106 (7): 1428–50.

Kimmage, Daniel. 2008. *The Al-Qaeda Media Nexus*. Washington, DC: Radio Free Europe. Available at http://docs.rferl.org/en-US/AQ_Media_Nexus.pdf.

Kleinrock, Leonard. 2008. History of the Internet and Its Flexible Future. *IFE Wireless Communications* 15 (1): 8–18.

Kohlmann, Evan F. 2008. Homegrown Terrorists: Theory and Cases in the War on Terror's Newest Front. *The Annals of the American Academy of Political and Social Science* 618 (1): 95–109.

Lewis, James. 2008. *Securing Cyberspace for the 44th Presidency: A Report of the CSIS Commission on Cyber-security for the 44th Presidency*. Washington, DC: Center for Strategic and International Studies.

Maclay, Colin. 2010. Protecting Privacy and Expression Online: Can the Global Network Initiative Embrace the Character of the Net? In *Access Controlled: The Shaping of Power, Rights, and Rule in Cyberspace*, ed. Ronald. J. Deibert, John G. Palfrey, Rafal Rohozinski, and Jonathan Zittrain. Cambridge, MA: MIT Press.

McCullagh, Declan. 2008. U.N. Agency Eyes Curbs on Internet Anonymity. *CNET*, Available at http://news.cnet.com/8301-13578_3-10040152-38.html.

Mueller, Milton L. 2002. Ruling the Root: Internet Governance and the Taming of Cyberspace. Cambridge, MA: MIT Press.

Naughton, John. 2001. Contested Space: The Internet and Global Civil Society. In *Global Civil Society*, ed. Helmut Anheier, Marlies Glasius, and Mary Kaldor. London: Sage.

Office of the United States Trade Representative. 2008. 2008 Special 301 Report. Available at http://www.ustr.gov/assets/DocumentJLibrary/Rcpom_publications/2008/2008.Special_301_Report/asset_upload_file553_14869.pdf.

Pahlavi, Pierre. 2007. The 33 Day War; An Example of Psychological Warfare in the Information Age. *Canadian Army Journal* 10 (1): 12–24.

Rohozinski, Rafal. 2004. Bullets to Bytes: Reflections on ICTs and Local Conflict. In *Bombs and Bandwidth: The Emerging Relationship Between Information Technology and Security*, ed. Robert Latham. New York: Free Press.

Saltzer, Jerome H., David P. Reed, and David D. Clark. 1984. End-to-End Arguments in System Design. *Transactions on Computer Systems* 2 (4): 277–88.

Stritzel, Holger. 2007. Toward a Theory of Securitization: Copenhagen and Beyond. *European Journal of International Studies* 13 (3): 357–83.

United States Department of Defense. 2006. The National Military Strategy for Cyberspace Operations. Available at http://www.dod.mil/pubs/foi/ojcs/07-F-2105docl.pdf.

Villeneuve, Nart. 2006. The Filtering Matrix: Integrated Mechanisms of Information Control and the Demarcation of Borders in Cyberspace. *First Monday* 11 (1–2) Available at http://firstmonday.org/htbin/cgiwrap/bin/ojs/index.php/fm/ariicle/view/1307/122.

———. 2009. Breaching Trust: An Analysis of Surveillance and Security Practices on China's TOM-Skype Platform. Information Warfare Monitor/ONI-Asia. Available at http: //www.nartv.org/mirror/breachingt.rust.pdf.

———. (2010) Barriers to Cooperation: An Analysis of the Origins of International Efforts to Protect Children Online. In *Access Controlled: The Shaping of Power, Rights, and Rule in Cyberspace*, ed. Ronald J. Deibert, John Palfrey, Rafal Rohozinski, and Jonathan Zittrain. Cambridge, MA: MIT Press.

Wall, David S. 2005. Digital Realism and the Governance of Spam as Cybercrime. *European Journal on Criminal Policy and Research* 10 (4): 309–35.

———. 2007. Policing Cybercrimes: Situating the Public Police in Networks of Security within Cyberspace. *Police Practice & Research* 8 (2): 183–205.

Way, Lucan, and Steven Levitzsky. 2002. The Rise of Competitive Authoritarianism. *Journal of Democracy* 13 (2): 51–65.

Weber, Amalie M. 2003. The Council of Europe's Convention on Cybercrime. *Berkeley Technology Law Journal* 18 (1): 425–46.

Wehrey, Fredrick M. 2002. A Clash of Wills: Hizbullah's Psychological Campaign Against Israel in South Lebanon. *Small Wars and Insurgencies* 12 (3): 53–74.

Weimann, Gabriel. 2006a. Virtual Disputes: The Use of the Internet for Terrorist Debates. *Studies in Conflict and Terrorism* 29 (7): 623–39.

———. 2006b. *Terror on the Internet: The New Arena, The New Challenges*. Washington, DC: United States Institute of Peace.

Zittrain, Jonathan. 2007. *The Future of the Internet and How to Stop It*. New Haven, CT: Yale University Press.

The Black Swan of Cairo

How Suppressing Volatility Makes the World Less Predictable and More Dangerous

NASSIM NICHOLAS TALEB AND MARK BLYTH

Taleb and Blyth posit that the United States is frequently caught off guard by "discontinuities" (such as attacks and revolutions) because of our static mind-set, which does not allow us to anticipate rapid and nonlinear changes. They argue that the U.S. should curtail its support for all authoritarian governments. Taleb and Blyth also argue against intervention by the U.S. government to ensure "stability," both domestically and in the affairs of other nations.

Why is surprise the permanent condition of the U.S. political and economic elite? In 2007–8, when the global financial system imploded, the cry that no one could have seen this coming was heard everywhere, despite the existence of numerous analyses showing that a crisis was unavoidable. It is no surprise that one hears precisely the same response today regarding the current turmoil in the Middle East. The critical issue in both cases is the artificial suppression of volatility—the ups and downs of life—in the name of stability. It is both misguided and dangerous to push unobserved risks further into the statistical tails of the probability distribution of outcomes and allow these high-impact, low-probability "tail risks" to disappear from policymakers' fields of observation. What the world is witnessing in Tunisia, Egypt, and Libya is simply what happens when highly constrained systems explode.

Complex systems that have artificially suppressed volatility tend to become extremely fragile, while at the same time exhibiting no visible risks. In fact, they tend to be too calm and exhibit minimal variability as silent risks accumulate beneath the surface. Although the stated intention of political leaders and economic policymakers is to stabilize the system by inhibiting fluctuations, the result tends to be the opposite. These artificially constrained systems become prone to "Black Swans"—that is, they become extremely vulnerable to large-scale events that lie far from the statistical norm and were largely unpredictable to a given set of observers.

Such environments eventually experience massive blowups, catching everyone off-guard and undoing years of stability or, in some cases, ending up far worse than they were in their initial volatile state. Indeed, the longer it takes for the blowup to occur, the worse the resulting harm in both economic and political systems.

Seeking to restrict variability seems to be good policy (who does not prefer stability to chaos?), so it is with very good intentions that policymakers unwittingly increase the risk of major blowups. And it is the same misperception of the properties of natural systems that led to both the economic crisis of 2007-8 and the current turmoil in the Arab world. The policy implications are identical: to make systems robust, all risks must be visible and out in the open—*fluctuat nec mergitur* (it fluctuates but does not sink) goes the Latin saying.

Just as a robust economic system is one that encourages early failures (the concepts of "fail small" and "fail fast"), the U.S. government should stop supporting dictatorial regimes for the sake of pseudostability and instead allow political noise to rise to the surface. Making an economy robust in the face of business swings requires allowing risk to be visible; the same is true in politics.

Seduced By Stability

Both the recent financial crisis and the current political crisis in the Middle East are grounded in the rise of complexity, interdependence, and unpredictability. Policymakers in the United Kingdom and the United States have long promoted policies aimed at eliminating fluctuation—no more booms and busts in the economy, no more "Iranian surprises" in foreign policy. These policies have almost always produced undesirable outcomes. For example, the U.S. banking system became very fragile following a succession of progressively larger bailouts and government interventions, particularly after the 1983 rescue of major banks (ironically, by the same Reagan administration that trumpeted free markets). In the United States, promoting these bad policies has been a bipartisan effort throughout. Republicans have been good at fragilizing large corporations through bailouts, and Democrats have been good at fragilizing the government. At the same time, the financial system as a whole exhibited little volatility; it kept getting weaker while providing policymakers with the illusion of stability, illustrated most notably when Ben Bernanke, who was then a member of the Board of Governors of the U.S. Federal Reserve, declared the era of "the great moderation" in 2004.

Putatively independent central bankers fell into the same trap. During the 1990s, U.S. Federal Reserve Chair Alan Greenspan wanted to iron out the economic cycle's booms and busts, and he sought to control economic swings with interest-rate reductions at the slightest sign of a downward tick in the economic data. Furthermore, he adapted his economic policy to guarantee bank rescues, with implicit promises of a backstop—the now infamous "Greenspan put." These policies proved to have grave delayed side effects. Washington stabilized the market with bailouts and by allowing certain companies to grow "too big to fail." Because policymakers believed it was better to do something than to do nothing, they felt obligated to heal the economy rather than wait and see if it healed on its own.

The foreign policy equivalent is to support the incumbent no matter what. And just as banks took wild risks thanks to Greenspan's implicit insurance policy, client governments such as Hosni Mubarak's in Egypt for years engaged in overt plunder thanks to similarly reliable U.S. support.

Those who seek to prevent volatility on the grounds that any and all bumps in the road must be avoided paradoxically increase the probability that a tail risk will cause a major experiment a man placed in an artificially sterilized environment for a decade and then invited to take a ride on a crowded subway; he would be expected to die quickly. Likewise, preventing small forest fires can cause larger forest fires to become devastating. This property is shared by all complex systems.

In the realm of economics, price controls are designed to constrain volatility on the grounds that stable prices are a good thing. But although these controls might work in some rare situations, the long-term effect of any such system is an eventual and extremely costly blowup whose cleanup costs can far exceed the benefits accrued. The risks of a dictatorship, no matter how seemingly stable are no different, in the long run, from those of an artificially controlled price.

Such attempts to institutionally engineer the world come in two types: those that conform to the world as it is and those that attempt to reform the world. The nature of humans, quite reasonably, is to intervene in an effort to alter their world and the outcomes it produces. But government interventions are laden with unintended—and unforeseen—consequences, particularly in complex systems, so humans must work with nature by tolerating systems that absorb human imperfections rather than seek to change them.

Take, for example, the recent celebrated documentary on the financial crisis, *Inside Job,* which blames the crisis on the malfeasance and dishonesty of bankers and the incompetence of regulators. Although it is morally satisfying, the film naively overlooks the fact that humans have always been dishonest and regulators have always been behind the curve. The only difference this time around was the unprecedented magnitude of the hidden risks and a misunderstanding of the statistical properties of the system.

What is needed is a system that can prevent the harm done to citizens by the dishonesty of business elites; the limited competence of forecasters, economists, and statisticians; and the imperfections of regulation, not one that aims to eliminate these flaws. Humans must try to resist the illusion of control: just as foreign policy should be intelligence-proof (it should minimize its reliance on the competence of information-gathering organizations and the predictions of "experts" in what are inherently unpredictable domains), the economy should be regulator-proof, given that some regulations simply make the system itself more fragile. Due to the complexity of markets, intricate regulations simply serve to generate fees for lawyers and profits for sophisticated derivatives traders who can build complicated financial products that skirt those regulations.

Don't be a Turkey

The life of a turkey before Thanksgiving is illustrative: the turkey is fed for 1,000 days and every day seems to confirm that the farmer cares for it—until the last day, when confidence is maximal. The "turkey problem" occurs when a naive analysis of stability is derived from the absence of past variations. Likewise, confidence in stability was maximal at the onset of the financial crisis in 2007.

The turkey problem for humans is the result of mistaking one environment for another. Humans simultaneously inhabit two systems: the linear and the complex. The linear domain is characterized by its predictability and the low degree of interaction among its components, which allows the use of mathematical methods that make forecasts reliable. In complex systems, there is an absence of visible causal links between the elements, masking a high degree of interdependence and extremely low

predictability. Nonlinear elements are also present, such as those commonly known, and generally misunderstood, as "tipping points." Imagine someone who keeps adding sand to a sand pile without any visible consequence, until suddenly the entire pile crumbles. It would be foolish to blame the collapse on the last grain of sand rather than the structure of the pile, but that is what people do consistently, and that is the policy error.

U.S. President Barack Obama may blame an intelligence failure for the government's not foreseeing the revolution in Egypt (just as former U.S. President Jimmy Carter blamed an intelligence failure for his administration's not foreseeing the 1979 Islamic Revolution in Iran), but it is the suppressed risk in the statistical tails that matters—not the failure to see the last grain of sand. As a result of complicated interdependence and contagion effects, in all man-made complex systems, a small number of possible events dominate, namely, Black Swans.

Engineering, architecture, astronomy, most of physics, and much of common science are linear domains. The complex domain is the realm of the social world, epidemics, and economics. Crucially, the linear domain delivers mild variations without large shocks, whereas the complex domain delivers massive jumps and gaps. Complex systems are misunderstood, mostly because humans' sophistication, obtained over the history of human knowledge in the linear domain, does not transfer properly to the complex domain. Humans can predict a solar eclipse and the trajectory of a space vessel, but not the stock market or Egyptian political events. All man-made complex systems have commonalities and even universalities. Sadly, deceptive calm (followed by Black Swan surprises) seems to be one of those properties.

The Error of Prediction

As with a crumbling sand pile, it would be foolish to attribute the collapse of a fragile bridge to the last truck that crossed it, and even more foolish to try to predict in advance which truck might bring it down. The system is responsible, not the components. But after the financial crisis of 2007–8, many people thought that predicting the subprime meltdown would have helped. It would not have, since it was a symptom of the crisis, not its underlying cause. Likewise, Obama's blaming "bad intelligence" for his administration's failure to predict the crisis in Egypt is symptomatic of both the misunderstanding of complex systems and the bad policies involved.

Obama's mistake illustrates the illusion of local causal chains—that is, confusing catalysts for causes and assuming that one can know which catalyst will produce which effect. The final episode of the upheaval in Egypt was unpredictable for all observers, especially those involved. As such, blaming the CIA is as foolish as funding it to forecast such events. Governments are wasting billions of dollars on attempting to predict events that are produced by interdependent systems and are therefore not statistically understandable at the individual level.

As Mark Abdollahian of Sentia Group, one of the contractors who sell predictive analytics to the U.S. government, noted regarding Egypt, policy-makers should "think of this like Las Vegas. In BLACKJACK, if you can do four percent better than the average, you're making real money." But the analogy is spurious. There is no "four percent better" on Egypt. This is not just money wasted but the construction of a false confidence based on an erroneous focus. It is telling that the intelligence analysts made the same mistake as the risk-management systems that failed to predict the economic crisis—and offered the exact same excuses when they failed. Political and economic "tail events" are unpredictable, and their probabilities are not scientifically measurable. No matter how many dollars are spent on research, predicting revolutions is not the same as counting cards; humans will never be able to turn politics into the tractable randomness of blackjack.

Most explanations being offered for the current turmoil in the Middle East follow the "catalysts as causes" confusion. The riots in Tunisia and Egypt were initially attributed to rising commodity prices, not to stifling and unpopular dictatorships. But Bahrain and Libya are countries with high GDPs that can afford to import grain and other commodities. Again, the focus is wrong even if the logic is

comforting. It is the system and its fragility, not events, that must be studied—what physicists call "percolation theory," in which the properties of the terrain are studied rather than those of a single element of the terrain.

When dealing with a system that is inherently unpredictable, what should be done? Differentiating between two types of countries is useful. In the first, changes in government do not lead to meaningful differences in political outcomes (since political tensions are out in the open). In the second type, changes in government lead to both drastic and deeply unpredictable changes.

Consider that Italy, with its much-maligned "cabinet instability," is economically and politically stable despite having had more than 60 governments since World War II (indeed, one may say Italy's stability is because of these switches of government). Similarly, in spite of consistently bad press, Lebanon is a relatively safe bet in terms of how far governments can jump from equilibrium; in spite of all the noise, shifting alliances, and street protests, changes in government there tend to be comparatively mild. For example, a shift in the ruling coalition from Christian parties to Hezbollah is not such a consequential jump in terms of the country's economic and political stability. Switching equilibrium, with control of the government changing from one party to another, in such systems acts as a shock absorber. Since a single party cannot have total and more than temporary control, the possibility of a large jump in the regime type is constrained.

In contrast, consider Iran and Iraq, Mohammad Reza Shah Pahlavi and Saddam Hussein both constrained volatility by any means necessary. In Iran, when the shah was toppled, the shift of power to Ayatollah Ruhollah Khomeini was a huge, unforeseeable jump. After the fact, analysts could construct convincing accounts about how killing Iranian Communists, driving the left into exile, demobilizing the democratic opposition, and driving all dissent into the mosque had made Khomeini's rise inevitable. In Iraq, the United States removed the lid and was actually surprised to find that the regime did not jump from hyperconstraint to something like France. But this was impossible to predict ahead of time due to the nature of the system itself. What can be said, however, is that the more constrained the volatility, the bigger the regime jump is likely to be. From the French Revolution to the triumph of the Bolsheviks, history is replete with such examples, and yet somehow humans remain unable to process what they mean.

The Fear of Randomness

Humans fear randomness—a healthy ancestral trait inherited from a different environment. Whereas in the past, which was a more linear world, this trait enhanced fitness and increased chances of survival, it can have the reverse effect in today's complex world, making volatility take the shape of nasty Black Swans hiding behind deceptive periods of "great moderation." This is not to say that any and all volatility should be embraced. Insurance should not be banned, for example.

But alongside the "catalysts as causes" confusion sit two mental biases: the illusion of control and the action bias (the illusion that doing something is always better than doing nothing). This leads to the desire to impose man-made solutions. Greenspan's actions were harmful, but it would have been hard to justify inaction in a democracy where the incentive is to always promise a better outcome than the other guy, regardless of the actual, delayed cost.

Variation is information. When there is no variation, there is no information. This explains the cia's failure to predict the Egyptian revolution and, a generation before, the Iranian Revolution—in both cases, the revolutionaries themselves did not have a clear idea of their relative strength with respect to the regime they were hoping to topple. So rather than subsidize and praise as a "force for stability" every tin-pot potentate on the planet, the U.S. government should encourage countries to let information flow upward through the transparency that comes with political agitation. It should not fear fluctuations per se, since allowing them to be in the open, as Italy and Lebanon both show in different ways, creates the stability of small jumps.

As Seneca wrote in *De clementia*, "Repeated punishment, while it crushes the hatred of a few, stirs the hatred of all . . . just as trees that have been trimmed throw out again countless branches." The imposition of peace through repeated punishment lies at the heart of many seemingly intractable conflicts, including the Israeli-Palestinian stalemate. Furthermore, dealing with seemingly reliable high-level officials rather than the people themselves prevents any peace treaty signed from being robust. The Romans were wise enough to know that only a free man under Roman law could be trusted to engage in a contract; by extension, only a free people can be trusted to abide by a treaty. Treaties that are negotiated with the consent of a broad swath of the populations on both sides of a conflict tend to survive. Just as no central bank is powerful enough to dictate stability, no superpower can be powerful enough to guarantee solid peace alone.

U.S. policy toward the Middle East has historically, and especially since 9/11, been unduly focused on the repression of any and all political fluctuations in the name of preventing "Islamic fundamentalism"—a trope that Mubarak repeated until his last moments in power. This is wrong. The West and its autocratic Arab allies have strengthened Islamic fundamentalists by forcing them underground, and even more so by killing them.

As Jean-Jacques Rousseau put it, "A little bit of agitation gives motivation to the soul, and what really makes the species prosper is not peace so much as freedom." With freedom comes some unpredictable fluctuation. This is one of life's packages: there is no freedom without noise—and no stability without volatility.

Al Qaeda's Challenge

The Jihadists' War With Islamist Democrats

WILLIAM McCANTS

> McCants provides a history of the rise of al Qaeda, and details the attacks it carried out against the United States and other nations. He contends that the Arab Spring revolutions may actually be problematic for Islamic jihadist networks, as formerly oppressed peoples now find it possible to express their frustrations through the democratic political process. Thus, the revolutions of the Arab Spring have empowered nonviolent factions, not violent networks such as al Qaeda. As a result of the death of Osama bin Laden and the rise of the Arab Spring, McCants concludes that al Qaeda's power is now in decline.

The Arab Spring and the death of Osama bin Laden represent a moment of both promise and peril for the global jihadist movement. On the one hand, the overthrow of secular rulers in the heartland of the Muslim world gives jihadists an unprecedented opportunity to establish the Islamic states that they have long sought. On the other hand, jihadists can no longer rally behind their most charismatic leader, bin Laden. And the jihadist flagship that he founded, al Qaeda, may lose its relevance in the Muslim world to rival Islamist groups that are prepared to run in elections and take power through politics.

The last time jihadists faced such a crossroads was at the end of the Cold War. The Soviet Union's withdrawal from Afghanistan and subsequent collapse emboldened jihadist strategists. Convinced that they had defeated a global superpower, they plotted to overthrow secular Arab governments and replace them with Islamic states, with the goal of eventually uniting them under a single caliphate. At the same time, however, the Soviet Union's demise opened up the Arab world to U.S. influence. Having been long constrained by the Soviet presence in the region, the United States quickly asserted itself by spearheading the coalition against the Iraqi dictator Saddam Hussein, thus increasing its military presence in the Arab world. As a result, jihadists—and al Qaeda in particular—concluded that Washington now enjoyed virtually unchecked power in the Middle East and would use it to prevent the creation of the Islamic states they desired.

Several established Islamic organizations, such as the Muslim Brotherhood, shared this belief with al Qaeda. But al Qaeda rejected the Brotherhood and like-minded groups because of their willingness to work within existing systems by voting for and participating in legislative bodies. Such tactics would fail to establish Islamic states, bin Laden and his comrades asserted, because they involved pragmatic political tradeoffs that would violate the principles of such future states and leave them susceptible to U.S. pressure. Only attacks on the United States, al Qaeda argued, could reduce Washington's regional power and inspire the masses to revolt.

Two decades later, bin Laden's long-sought revolutions in the Arab world are finally happening, and the upheaval would seem to give al Qaeda a rare opportunity to start building Islamic states. But so far at least, the revolutions have defied bin Laden's expectations by empowering not jihadists but Islamist parliamentarians—Islamists who refuse to violently oppose U.S. hegemony in the region and who are willing to engage in parliamentary politics. In Tunisia, the Islamist Renaissance Party leads in the polls ahead of legislative elections in October. In Egypt, the Freedom and Justice Party, the new faction created by the Muslim Brotherhood, is likely to gain a large number of seats in parliament in elections this fall. Should countries that have experienced more violent revolutions also hold elections, such as Libya, Syria, and Yemen, Islamist parliamentarians are well positioned to compete in those nations as well.

Al Qaeda and its allies will not support these Islamists unless they reject parliamentary politics and establish governments that strictly implement Islamic law and are hostile to the United States. The Islamist parliamentarians are unlikely to do either. Having suffered under one-party rule for decades and wary of rival Islamist parties, the Arab world's Islamist parliamentarians (like their secular counterparts) will be unwilling to support such a system in the future. And although they will certainly seek to implement more conservative social laws, the Islamist parliamentarians will likely come to accept that their countries require the economic and military aid of the United States or its allies.

Unable to make progress in countries where Islamist parliamentarians hold sway, such as Egypt, al Qaeda will instead attempt to diminish Washington's clout by attacking the United States and focus on aiding rebels in Libya, Syria, and Yemen. But even in those countries, it will need to make compromises to work with existing rebel groups, and these groups, like their fellow Islamists elsewhere, may accept some level of U.S. support should they take power. What all this means is that despite the seemingly opportune moment, al Qaeda is unlikely to make much progress toward its ultimate goal of establishing Islamic states in the Arab world.

Islamism Rises

Both al Qaeda and today's Islamist parliamentarians are outgrowths of the Islamism that arose in the nineteenth century as a response to the colonial domination of Muslim lands. Islamists believed that Muslims' abandonment of their faith had made them vulnerable to foreign rule. In response, they advocated for independent Muslim rulers who would fully implement Islamic law, or sharia. A large number of these Islamists adhered to Salafism, a revivalist ideology that sought to purge Islam of Western influence and supposedly improper legal innovations by returning to the religious instruction of the first generations of Muslims, or *Salaf.* Pan-Islamic sentiment intensified after World War I, when France and the United Kingdom created colonies out of the ruins of the Ottoman Empire. Sunni Muslims were further outraged when the new secular government in Turkey abolished the caliphate, a largely symbolic institution that nonetheless had represented the unity of the Muslim empire under a single leader (or caliph) in the religion's early days.

When nationalist movements succeeded in ending the direct rule of foreign powers in the Middle East, beginning when Egypt gained independence from the United Kingdom in 1922, Islamist activists sought to replace the secular laws and institutions governing the newly independent states with systems based on sharia. Perhaps the most famous of the Islamist organizations of this period was the Muslim Brotherhood, founded in Egypt in the 1920s. Yet when it tried to compete in Egypt's parliamentary elections in 1942, the Egyptian government, under British pressure, forced it to withdraw. Although they failed to achieve their aims through parliamentary politics, some Brotherhood activists turned to peaceful social activism, whereas others, such as Sayyid Qutb, who was one of the group's most prominent members, developed an ideology of violent revolution. Qutb rejected the idea of man-made legislation and held that Muslim-led governments that made their own law, as opposed to adopting sharia, were not truly Muslim. Qutb encouraged pious Muslims to rebel against such regimes; his writings have inspired generations of Sunni militants, including the founders of al Qaeda.

Islamists continued to focus on domestic matters until the Soviet Union invaded Afghanistan in 1979. In a burst of pan-Islamic spirit, thousands of young Arab men flooded into Pakistan hoping to battle the Soviets. Among them was bin Laden, who recruited men, procured equipment, and raised money for the cause. His training camps in Afghanistan, and others like it, gave jihadists of all backgrounds a shared identity and mission. In doing so, they served as early incubators of global jihadism. When the Soviets withdrew from Afghanistan nearly a decade later, the jihadists believed that they had helped defeat a superpower.

Al Qaeda, which was created in 1988, grew out of those camps. Ayman al-Zawahiri, an Egyptian Islamist who merged his organization, Egyptian Islamic Jihad, with al Qaeda in 2001, explained al Qaeda's mission in 2010 as providing a "base for indoctrination, training, and incitement that gathered the capabilities of the *ummah* [universal Islamic community], trained them, raised their consciousness, improved their abilities, and gave them confidence in their religion and themselves." This base, Zawahiri said, involved "large amounts of participation in jihad, bearing the worries of the *ummah*, and seizing the initiative in the most urgent calamities confronting the *ummah*." In other words, al Qaeda envisioned itself as a revolutionary vanguard and special operations unit working to defend the Muslim world.

Bin Laden's Days of Promise

Al qaeda's early years seemed full of possibility. The collapse of the Soviet Union created new opportunities for radicals in the empire's former client states. Islamists took control of Sudan in 1989, and Saddam's invasion of Kuwait in 1990 galvanized Islamist political protests in Algeria, culminating in an Islamist victory in the country's elections the following year. When the secular Algerian military nullified the results and retained power, it only underscored the perceived need for a committed Muslim vanguard.

Iraq's invasion of Kuwait turned al Qaeda's attention to the United States. Bin Laden offered to send al Qaeda operatives to Saudi Arabia to help protect the country from attack by Saddam. But the Saudis rejected his proposal and instead invited the U.S. military to lead an assault on Iraq from their territory. The decision insulted bin Laden and raised his fears about the growth of unchecked U.S. power in the Middle East. Bin Laden's concerns grew the following year, when the United States deployed peacekeeping troops to Somalia soon after he had moved al Qaeda's headquarters to Sudan—although he celebrated the U.S. withdrawal following the infamous "Black Hawk down" ambush (in which al Qaeda operatives claim to have participated). By 1993, al Qaeda members began identifying U.S. targets in East Africa, and in 1994 they sent explosives to Saudi Arabia to attack an unspecified U.S. facility.

Bin Laden returned to Afghanistan in 1996 after Islamist-controlled Sudan expelled him at Washington's behest. He viewed his exile as further evidence that Arab Islamists could not build Islamic states until Western power in the region was diminished. In a public declaration that same year, he announced that he was turning his gaze from Africa to the Persian Gulf and urged Muslims to launch a guerrilla war against U.S. troops in Saudi Arabia. Bin Laden not only resented the Saudis for refusing his help in the Gulf War and banning him from the kingdom but also could not tolerate the continued presence of U.S. forces in the country. If jihadists inflicted enough damage on the United States, he argued, the U.S. military would withdraw from Saudi soil, a move that would allow the Islamists to confront the deviant Saudi royal family directly. Although bin Laden did not have the resources to carry out his threat, his statement infuriated the Saudi government, which instructed its clients in Afghanistan, the ruling Taliban, to restrict his activities.

But bin Laden only escalated his rhetoric against the United States. In 1998, in a joint fatwa with the leaders of other militant organizations, he called on every Muslim to murder Americans. Soon thereafter, al Qaeda made good on this threat by bombing the U.S. embassies in Kenya and Tanzania. Bin Laden later described these attacks in his will and testament as the second of three "escalating strikes" against the United States—the first being Hezbollah's bombing of the U.S. Marine barracks in Lebanon in 1983 and the third being 9/11—all of which would "lead to the withdrawal [from the Middle East] of the United States and the infidel West, even if after dozens of years."

In fact, 9/11 did not mark the logical culmination of the Lebanon and Africa bombings, as bin Laden suggested. Instead, it represented a subtle but significant shift in al Qaeda's strategy. Before 9/11, al Qaeda had targeted U.S. citizens and institutions abroad, never attacking U.S. soil. The idea behind a mass-casualty attack against the U.S. homeland arose only after the Africa bombings. Two months before 9/11, Zawahiri, who had become al Qaeda's second-in-command, published *Knights Under the Banner of the Prophet*, which offers insight into why al Qaeda decided to attack the United States within its borders. In it, he stated that al Qaeda aimed to establish an Islamic state in the Arab world:

> Just as victory is not achieved for an army unless its foot soldiers occupy land, the mujahid Islamic movement will not achieve victory against the global infidel alliance unless it possesses a base in the heart of the Islamic world. Every plan and method we consider to rally and mobilize the *ummah* will be hanging in the air with no concrete result or tangible return unless it leads to the establishment of the caliphal state in the heart of the Islamic world.

Achieving this goal, Zawahiri explained elsewhere in the book, would require a global jihad:

> It is not possible to incite a conflict for the establishment of a Muslim state if it is a regional conflict. . . . The international Jewish-Crusader alliance, led by America, will not allow any Muslim force to obtain power in any of the Muslim lands. . . . It will impose sanctions on whomever helps it, even if it does not declare war against them altogether. Therefore, to adjust to

this new reality, we must prepare ourselves for a battle that is not confined to a single region but rather includes the apostate domestic enemy and the Jewish-Crusader external enemy.

To confront this insidious alliance, Zawahiri argued, al Qaeda had to first root out U.S. influence in the region, which it could best accomplish by attacking targets on U.S. soil. Zawahiri predicted that the United States would react either by waging war against Muslims worldwide or by pulling back its forces from Muslim lands. In other words, the United States would either fight or flee. A successful direct strike against U.S. centers of power, he believed, would force this choice on the United States and allow al Qaeda to overcome the obstacles preventing it from rallying the Muslim masses and ending U.S. hegemony in the Middle East: a lack of leadership, the lack of a clear enemy, and a lack of confidence among Muslims. Al Qaeda would soon test that theory on 9/11.

Jihadist State Building

From an operational perspective, the 9/11 attacks succeeded far beyond bin Laden's imagination, killing more than 3,000 civilians and unexpectedly destroying the World Trade Center. But to al Qaeda's dismay, 9/11 did not rally Muslims to its cause. Indeed, the organization lost legitimacy when bin Laden, hoping to avoid angering his Taliban hosts, initially denied responsibility for the attacks. And when the United States retaliated against al Qaeda in Afghanistan, it did so without providing the group with the kind of clear enemy—a large "Crusader" army—the militant Islamists had hoped for. The United States kept its footprint small, using overwhelming airpower and deploying special operations forces and cia agents to work with allied tribes to depose the Taliban and destroy al Qaeda's base of operations.

Although the U.S. military failed to capture bin Laden, it quickly overran the Taliban and toppled what many jihadists considered the only authentic Islamic state. Afghanistan's fall thus represented a huge blow to al Qaeda, whose professed goal, of course, was to establish such states. The majority of al Qaeda's Shura Council had reportedly counseled bin Laden against attacking the United States for fear of precisely this outcome.

Having failed to rally Muslims to his cause or bog down the U.S. military in a protracted ground war, bin Laden fled to Pakistan and refocused his efforts on the U.S. presence in Saudi Arabia. Saudi Arabia had been at the forefront of bin Laden's thoughts since 1994, and he now had the resources to launch a major offensive against the U.S. presence in the kingdom. In early 2002, he sent hundreds of jihadists to Saudi Arabia to organize attacks on U.S. military and civilian personnel in the country. After a year of preparation, bin Laden and Zawahiri impatiently launched these attacks over objections from their Saudi branch that it was not ready. The campaign was a disaster. Although al Qaeda attempted to strike only U.S. targets, it killed many Arab Muslims in the process, turning the Saudi public against the group. In one particularly disastrous example, an al Qaeda attack on a residential compound in Riyadh in November 2003 killed mainly Arabs and Muslims, many of whom were children. After a two-year battle, Saudi forces had stamped out the organization's presence in the kingdom.

Yet al Qaeda's targeting miscalculations were not the only reason for its failure in Saudi Arabia. Despite a series of spectacular attacks, the organization could not compete for attention with the battle in Iraq. The U.S. invasion of that country in 2003 inflamed Muslim opinion worldwide and had finally given jihadists the clear battle they craved. Bin Laden and Zawahiri seized the opportunity to recover from their strategic blunders in Afghanistan and Saudi Arabia and to spark an all-consuming battle between the United States and the Islamic world. They hoped that this struggle would rally Muslims to al Qaeda's cause and, most important, bleed the United States of its resources. As U.S. casualties mounted in Iraq, al Qaeda strategists began citing the lessons of Vietnam and quoting the U.S. historian Paul Kennedy on the consequences of "imperial overstretch." By the end of 2004, bin Laden had begun publicly referring to al Qaeda's "war of attrition" against the United States.

Al Qaeda hoped that Iraq would be the first Islamic state to rise after the loss of Afghanistan. In a 2005 letter to Abu Musab al-Zarqawi, a leader of the Iraqi insurgency who eventually joined al Qaeda and formed the subsidiary group al Qaeda in Iraq, Zawahiri asserted that victory would come when "a Muslim state is established in the manner of the Prophet in the heart of the Islamic world. . . . The center would be in the Levant and Egypt." Zawahiri argued that to expel the United States and establish an Islamic state, jihadists needed "popular support from the Muslim masses in Iraq, and the surrounding Muslim countries." Zawahiri told Zarqawi that gaining this support would be easier while U.S. forces continued to occupy Iraq. But to preserve their legitimacy after a U.S. retreat, Zawahiri said, jihadists would need to avoid alienating the public through sectarianism or gratuitous violence. They had to cooperate with Muslims of all ideological and theological stripes as long as they shared the desire for a state dedicated to sharia. Zawahiri warned Zarqawi that if he declared an Islamic state before al Qaeda had built an effective coalition of Muslim groups and garnered popular approval in Iraq, the state would fail and the jihadists' secular and Islamist opponents would take power.

Zarqawi's followers did not heed Zawahiri's advice. Al Qaeda in Iraq declared the founding of an Islamic state soon after Zarqawi was killed in an air strike in 2006, and, as Zawahiri had warned, the group ended up alienating more moderate Sunnis through its brutal implementation of Islamic law and its relentless assault on Iraq's Shiites. It also lost many of its allies in the insurgency by demanding their obedience and then targeting them and their constituencies if they refused to cooperate. Additionally, the fact that al Qaeda in Iraq's so-called Islamic state controlled so little territory earned the scorn of fellow Sunni militants in Iraq and abroad. Al Qaeda had botched its first real attempt at state building. Even if it had followed Zawahiri's counsel, however, al Qaeda in Iraq, as well as the larger organization, would have faced a new threat on the horizon: Islamist parties with the desire and know-how to enter the political system.

The Islamists Who Vote

Whereas al Qaeda's brutal, sectarian tactics turned the Iraqi populace against it, the Sunni forces willing to engage in parliamentary politics gained the most power. Chief among them was the Muslim Brotherhood, whose Iraqi Islamic Party dominates Sunni politics in Iraq today and regularly supplies one of the country's two vice presidents.

The jihadists, of course, reject this success. Zawahiri has been particularly critical of Abdel Moneim Abou el-Fatouh, a one-time member of the Egyptian Muslim Brotherhood's leadership council who is now an independent candidate for president in Egypt. Abou el-Fatouh stated before the Arab revolutions that the Brotherhood would respect the results of any popular election in Egypt and remain in loyal opposition should its opponents win. This idea was anathema to Zawahiri, who argued that a government's legitimacy derives not from the ballot box but from its enforcement of Islamic law. "Any government established on the basis of a constitution that is secular, atheist, or contradictory to Islam cannot be a respected government because it is un-Islamic and not according to sharia," he wrote in a revision of *Knights* published in 2010. "It is unacceptable that a leader in the Brotherhood evinces respect for such a government, even if it comes about through fair elections."

To be clear, Zawahiri does not oppose all elections; for example, he supports elections for the rulers of Islamic states and for representatives on leadership councils, which would ensure that these governments implemented Islamic law properly. But he opposes any system in which elections empower legislators to make laws of their own choosing. In the second edition of *Knights*, Zawahiri outlined al Qaeda's vision for the proper Islamic state:

We demand . . . the government of the rightly guiding caliphate, which is established on the basis of the sovereignty of sharia and not on the whims of the majority. Its *ummah* chooses its rulers. . . . If they deviate, the *ummah* brings them to account and removes them. The *ummah* participates in producing that government's decisions and determining its direction. . . . [The caliphal state] commands the right and forbids the wrong and engages in jihad to liberate Muslim lands and to free all humanity from all oppression and ignorance.

Bin Laden agreed with Zawahiri's take on elections, stating in January 2009 that once foreign influence and local tyrants have been removed from Islamic countries, true Muslims can elect their own presidents. And like Zawahiri, bin Laden argued that elections should not create parliaments that allow Muslims and non-Muslims to collaborate on making laws.

Although al Qaeda's leaders concurred on elections, they differed on the utility of using nonviolent protest to achieve Islamist goals. In bin Laden's January 2009 remarks, he claimed that demonstrations without weapons are useless. This contradicted a statement made by Zawahiri a week earlier, in which he called on Egyptian Muslims to go on strike in protest of then Egyptian President Hosni Mubarak's blockade of the Gaza Strip. Now that Zawahiri has replaced bin Laden as the leader of al Qaeda, his openness to nonviolent tactics may help the organization navigate the revolutions sweeping the Arab world. Even so, his hostility toward parliamentary politics cedes the real levers of power to the Islamist parliamentarians.

Springtime for the Parliamentarians

Al Qaeda now stands at a precipice. The Arab Spring and the success of Islamist parliamentarians throughout the Middle East have challenged its core vision just as the group has lost its founder. Al Qaeda has also lost access to bin Laden's personal connections in Afghanistan, Pakistan, and the Persian Gulf, which had long provided it with resources and protection. Bin Laden's death has deprived al Qaeda of its most media-savvy icon; and most important, al Qaeda has lost its commander in chief. The raid that killed bin Laden revealed that he had not been reduced to a figurehead, as many Western analysts had suspected; he had continued to direct the operations of al Qaeda and its franchises. Yet the documents seized from bin Laden's home in Abbottabad, Pakistan, reveal how weak al Qaeda had become even under his ongoing leadership. Correspondence found in the raid shows bin Laden and his lieutenants lamenting al Qaeda's lack of funds and the constant casualties from U.S. drone strikes. These papers have made the organization even more vulnerable by exposing its general command structure, putting al Qaeda's leadership at greater risk of extinction than ever before.

Al Qaeda has elected Zawahiri as its new chief, at least for now. But the transition will not be seamless. Some members of al Qaeda's old guard feel little loyalty to Zawahiri, whom they view as a relative newcomer. Al Qaeda's members from the Persian Gulf, for their part, may feel alienated by having an Egyptian at their helm, especially if Zawahiri chooses another Egyptian as his deputy.

Despite these potential sources of friction, al Qaeda is not likely to split under Zawahiri's reign. Its senior leadership will still want to unite jihadist groups under its banner, and its franchises will have little reason to relinquish the recognition and resources that come with al Qaeda affiliation. Yet those affiliates cannot offer al Qaeda's senior commanders shelter. Indeed, should Pakistan become too dangerous a refuge for the organization's leaders, they will find themselves with few other options. The Islamic governments that previously protected and assisted al Qaeda, such as those in Afghanistan and Sudan in the 1990s, either no longer exist or are inhospitable (although Somalia might become a candidate if the militant group al Shabab consolidates its hold there).

In the midst of grappling with all these challenges, al Qaeda must also decide how to respond to the uprisings in the Arab world. Thus far, its leaders have indicated that they want to support Islamist insurgents in unstable revolutionary countries and lay the groundwork for the creation of Islamic states once the existing regimes have fallen, similar to what they attempted in Iraq. But al Qaeda's true strategic dilemma lies in Egypt and Tunisia. In these countries, local tyrants have been ousted, but parliamentary elections will be held soon, and the United States remains influential.

The outcome in Egypt is particularly personal for Zawahiri, who began his fight to depose the Egyptian government as a teenager. Zawahiri also understands that Egypt, given its geostrategic importance and its status as the leading Arab nation, is the grand prize in the contest between al Qaeda and the United States. In his recent six-part message to the Egyptian people and in his eulogy for bin Laden, Zawahiri suggested that absent outside interference, the Egyptians and the Tunisians would establish Islamic states that would be hostile to Western interests. But the United States, he said, will likely work to ensure that friendly political forces, including secularists and moderate Islamists, win Egypt's upcoming elections. And even if the Islamists succeed in establishing an Islamic state there, Zawahiri argued, the United States will retain enough leverage to keep it in line. To prevent such an outcome, Zawahiri called on Islamist activists in Egypt and Tunisia to start a popular (presumably nonviolent) campaign to implement sharia as the sole source of legislation and to pressure the transitional governments to end their cooperation with Washington.

Yet Zawahiri's attempt to sway local Islamists is unlikely to succeed. Although some Islamists in the two countries rhetorically support al Qaeda, many, especially the Muslim Brotherhood, are now organizing for their countries' upcoming elections—that is, they are becoming Islamist parliamentarians. Even Egyptian Salafists, who share Zawahiri's distaste for parliamentary politics, are forming their own political parties. Most ominous for Zawahiri's agenda, the Egyptian Islamist organization al-Gama'a al-Islamiyya (the Islamic Group), parts of which were once allied with al Qaeda, has forsworn violence and recently announced that it was creating a political party to compete in Egypt's parliamentary elections. Al Qaeda, then, is losing sway even among its natural allies.

This dynamic limits Zawahiri's options. For fear of alienating the Egyptian people, he is not likely to end his efforts to reach out to Egypt's Islamist parliamentarians or to break with them by calling for attacks in the country before the elections. Instead, he will continue urging the Islamists to advocate for sharia and to try to limit U.S. influence.

In the meantime, Zawahiri will continue trying to attack the United States and continue exploiting less stable postrevolutionary countries, such as Libya, Syria, and Yemen, which may prove more susceptible to al Qaeda's influence. Yet to operate in these countries, al Qaeda will need to subordinate its political agenda to those of the insurgents there or risk destroying itself, as Zarqawi's group did in Iraq. If those insurgents take power, they will likely refuse to offer al Qaeda safe haven for fear of alienating the United States or its allies in the region.

Thanks to the continued predominance of the United States and the growing appeal of Islamist parliamentarians in the Muslim world, even supporters of al Qaeda now doubt that it will be able to replace existing regimes with Islamic states anytime soon. In a recent joint statement, several jihadist online forums expressed concern that if Muammar al-Qaddafi is defeated in Libya, the Islamists there will participate in U.S.-backed elections, ending any chance of establishing a true Islamic state.

As a result of all these forces, al Qaeda is no longer the vanguard of the Islamist movement in the Arab world. Having defined the terms of Islamist politics for the last decade by raising fears about Islamic political parties and giving Arab rulers a pretext to limit their activity or shut them down, al Qaeda's goal of removing those rulers is now being fulfilled by others who are unlikely to share its political vision. Should these revolutions fail and al Qaeda survives, it will be ready to reclaim the mantle of Islamist resistance. But for now, the forces best positioned to capitalize on the Arab Spring are the Islamist parliamentarians, who, unlike al Qaeda, are willing and able to engage in the messy business of politics.

Empire Falls

ROBERT A. PAPE

Pape argues that the United States has become an Empire, burdened by imperial overstretch, and that it has entered a pattern of long-term decline. He contends that the U.S.A.'s unipolar dominance is a thing of the past, and that we are witnessing the transformation of the international system to a multipolar environment. The erosion of U.S. economic power, coupled with Washington's growing indebtedness to other nations, are the principal causes of the demise of American hegemony. He argues that all hegemons experiencing a decline in power typically engage in preventive wars as they struggle to maintain their position of dominance.

America is in unprecedented decline. The self-inflicted wounds of the Iraq War, growing government debt, increasingly negative current-account balances and other internal economic weaknesses have cost the United States real power in today's world of rapidly spreading knowledge and technology. If present trends continue, we will look back at the Bush administration years as the death knell for American hegemony.

Since the cold war, the United States has maintained a vast array of overseas commitments, seeking to ensure peace and stability not just in its own neighborhood—the Americas—but also in Europe and Asia, along with the oil-rich Persian Gulf (as well as other parts of the world). Simply maintaining these commitments requires enormous resources, but in recent years American leaders have pursued far more ambitious goals than merely maintaining the status quo. The Bush administration has not just continued America's traditional grand strategy, but pursued ambitious objectives in all three major regions at the same time—waging wars in Iraq and Afghanistan, seeking to denuclearize North Korea and expanding America's military allies in Europe up to the borders of Russia itself.

For nearly two decades, those convinced of U.S. dominance in the international system have encouraged American policy makers to act unilaterally and seize almost any opportunity to advance American interests no matter the costs to others, virtually discounting the possibility that Germany, France, Russia, China and other major powers could seriously oppose American military power. From public intellectuals like Charles Krauthammer and Niall Ferguson to neoconservatives like Paul Wolfowitz and Robert Kagan, even to academicians like Dartmouth's William Wohlforth and Stephen Brooks, all believe the principal feature of the post-cold-war world is the unchallengeable dominance of American power. The United States is not just the sole superpower in the unipolar-dominance school's world, but is so relatively more powerful than any other country that it can reshape the international order according to American interests. This is simply no longer realistic.

For the past eight years, our policies have been based on these flawed-arguments, while the ultimate foundation of American power—the relative superiority of the U.S. economy in the world—has been in decline since early on in the Bush administration. There is also good reason to think that, without deliberate action, the fall of American power will be more precipitous with the passage of time. To be sure, the period of U.S. relative decline has been, thus far, fairly short. A healthy appreciation of our situation by American leaders may lead to policies that could mitigate, if not rectify, further decline in the foreseeable future. Still, America's shrinking share of world economic production is a fact of life and important changes in U.S. grand strategy are necessary to prevent the decline in America's global position from accelerating.

Although the immediate problems of war in Iraq and Afghanistan, al Qaeda's new sanctuary in western Pakistan, Iran's continued nuclear program and Russia's recent military adventure in Georgia are high-priority issues, solutions to each of them individually and all of them collectively will be heavily influenced by Americas reduced power position in the world. Most important, America's declining power means that the unipolar world is indeed coming to an end, that major powers will increasingly have the strength to balance against U.S. policies they oppose and that the United States will increasingly face harsh foreign-policy choices. Like so many great powers that have come and gone before, our own hubris may be our downfall.

From Rome, Imperial China, Venice, Spain, France, Great Britain and the Soviet Union to the United States today, the rise and fall of great nations has been driven primarily by relative economic strength. As Paul Kennedy so ably describes in his classic *The Rise and Fall of Great Powers,* the more international commitments a state has, the more its power matters and hence the more relative economic strength it needs.

Although scholars have long debated its nuances, the basic definition of power in international politics is simple: power is the aggregate resources a state has at its disposal to achieve its aims, the most important of which are to defend its national interests, both at home and abroad.[1] But it is not only how much power a state has that matters. It is also how much power a state has relative to other states. This is true in any rough-and-tumble environment. A Ford Explorer is a powerful vehicle—unless it collides with a Mack Truck. In international politics, power does not ensure success. But, power certainly helps.

At any given moment, U.S. power is heavily dependent on the size and quality of its military forces and other current power assets. A successful grand strategy, however, must work for the long haul and so depends on the power a state is able to produce in the future.

Over time, America's power is fundamentally a result of its economic strength. Productive capacity—defined by indicators such as wealth, technology and population size—is a prerequisite for building and modernizing military forces. The United States, like any state, may choose to vary the degree to which its productive capacities are used to create military assets. But it is the economy as a whole that constrains the choice. And the size of the economy relative to potential rivals ultimately determines the limits of power in international politics. Major assessments of this relative position have long turned heavily on a single statistic: America's share of world economic product.

Advocates of extending America's unipolar dominance are well aware of the central importance of the economic foundations of American power and routinely present detailed statistics on the U.S. share of world product. The basic notion is

simple: take U.S. domestic product in any year and divide it by the aggregate total of the gross domestic product of all states in the world. To measure gross domestic product, the unipolar-dominance school prefers to compare every country's output in current-year U.S. dollars, a method that tends to show America is much further ahead of other countries than alternative measures. Indeed, the most recent call for America to exploit its hegemonic position (published in 2008) rests on the presumption of U.S. dominance based on the current-year dollar figures.[2] By this metric, in 2006 the United States had 28 percent of world product while its nearest most likely competitor, China, had 6 percent. Looks pretty good for America, right?

Alas, single-year "snapshots" of America's relative power are of limited value for assessing the sustainability of its grand strategy over many years. For grand-strategic concerns—especially how well the United States can balance its resources and foreign-policy commitments—the trajectory of American power compared to other states is of seminal importance.

For the sake of argument, let us start with the unipolar-dominance school's preferred measure of American hegemony, but look at the trajectory of the data over time. According to GDP figures in current U.S. dollars from the International Monetary Fund (IMF), the United States increased its share of world production during the 1990s, reached its apogee in 2000, and then began to steadily lose ground during the eight years of the Bush administration, with its relative power ultimately falling by

Table 5.1 Percentage of World Product (current-U.S.-dollar measure)

	1990	2000	2006	2008 (est.)	2013 (est.)	Change 2000–13
U.S.A.	26	31	28	23	21	−32%
China	2	4	6	7	9	+144%
Japan	14	15	9	8	7	−55%
Germany	7	6	6	6	5	−11%
UK	5	5	5	5	4	−9%
France	6	4	5	5	4	+6%
Russia	2	1	2	3	5	+455%

Source: IMF World Economic Outlook Database (October 2008).

nearly a quarter in the first decade of the twenty-first century. At the same time, the relative power of China, the state many consider Americas most likely future rival, has grown consistently. If we look out as far as the IMF can see (2013), things get even worse—with the United States expected to continue declining and China to continue rising. The United States has been going through the first decade of the twenty-first century not stronger than before, but substantially weaker.

How good are the numbers? Economists commonly use two other methods to calculate GDP, constant-dollar calculations and purchasing power parity.[3] Although each offers advantages and disadvantages, for our purposes what matters is that they form a lower bound of America's relative decline. And regardless of the metric, the trend is the same. Again using IMF figures, Table 2 shows the trajectory of the share of world product for the United States and China using both alternative measures.

Simply put, the United States is now a declining power. This new reality has tremendous implications for the future of American grand strategy.

The erosion of the underpinnings of U.S. power is the result of uneven rates of economic growth between America, China and other states in the world. Despite all the pro-economy talk from the Bush administration, the fact is that since 2000, U.S. growth rates are down almost 50 percent from the Clinton years. This trajectory is almost sure to be revised further downward as the consequences of the financial crisis in fall 2008 become manifest.

As Table 3 shows, over the past two decades, the average rate of U.S. growth has fallen considerably, from nearly 4 percent annually during the Clinton

years to just over 2 percent per year under Bush. At the same time, China has sustained a consistently high rate of growth of 10 percent per year—a truly stunning performance. Russia has also turned its economic trajectory around, from year after year of losses in the 1990s to significant annual gains since 2000.

Worse, America's decline was well under way before the economic downturn, which is likely to only further weaken U.S. power. As the most recent growth estimates (November 2008) by the IMF make clear, although all major countries are suffering economically, China and Russia are expected to continue growing at a substantially greater rate than the United States.

True, the United States has not lost its position as the most innovative country in the world, with more patents each year than in all other countries combined. However, the ability to diffuse new technology—to turn chalkboard ideas into mass-produced applications—has been spreading rapidly across many parts of the globe, and with it the ultimate sources of state power—productive capacities.

America is losing its overwhelming technological dominance in the leading industries of the knowledge economy. In past eras—the "age of iron" and the "age of steel"—leading states retained their technological advantages for many decades.[4] As Fareed Zakaria describes in his recent book, *The Post-American World*, technology and knowledge diffuse more quickly today, and their rapid global diffusion is a profound factor driving down America's power compared to other countries. For instance, although the United States remains well ahead of China on many indicators of leading technology on a per

Table 5.2 Percentage of World Product (other measures)

Constant 2000 U.S. Dollars	1990	2000	2008	2013	Change 2000–13
USA	31	31	27	24	−22%
China	2	4	6	8	100%
Purchasing Power Parity	1990	2000	2008	2013	Change 2000–13
USA	23	24	21	19	−19%
China	4	7	11	15	104%

Source: Calculations based on IMF World Economic Outlook (October 2008).

Table 5.3 Uneven Growth Rates

Annual GDP Growth Rate (constant prices).

	1993–2000	2001–2008
U.S.A.	3.7	2.2
China	10.6	10.1
Japan	1.1	1.5
Germany	1.7	1.3
UK	3.2	2.4
France	2.2	1.7
Russia	−2.1	6.7

Source: IMF World Economic Outlook Database (October 2008).

capita basis, this grossly under-weights the size of the knowledge economy in China compared to America. Whereas in 2000, the United States had three times the computer sales, five times the internet users and forty times the broadband subscribers as China, in 2008, the Chinese have caught or nearly caught up with Americans in every category in the aggregate.[5] The fact that the United States remains ahead of China on a per capita basis does matter—it means that China, with more than four times the U.S. population, can create many more knowledge workers in the future. So, how much is U.S. decline due to the global diffusion of technology, U.S. economic weaknesses under Bush or China's superior economic performance?

Although precise answers are not possible, one can gain a rough weighting of the factors behind America's shrinking share of world production by asking a few simple counterfactual questions of the data. What would happen if we assumed that the United States grew during the Bush years at the same rate as during Clinton's? What would have happened had the world continued on its same trajectory, but we assume China did not grow at such an astounding rate? Of course, these are merely thought experiments, which leave out all manner of technical problems like "interaction effects." Still, these back-of-the-envelope approximations serve as useful starting points.

The answers are pretty straightforward. Had the American economy grown at the (Clinton) rate of 3.7 percent per year from 2000 to 2008 instead of

the (Bush) rate of 2.2 percent, the United States would have had a bigger economy in absolute terms and would have lost less power relative to others. Assuming the rest of the world continued at its actual rate of growth, America's share of world product in 2008 would have risen to 25.2 percent instead of its actual 23.1 percent.[6] When compared to the share of gross world product lost by the United States from 2000 to 2008—7.7 percent—the assumed marginal gain of 2.1 percent of world product amounts to some 27 percent of the U.S. decline.

How much does China matter? Imagine the extreme case—that China had not grown, and the United States and the rest of the world continued along their actual path of economic growth since 2000. If so, America's share of world product in 2008 would be 24.3 percent, or 1.2 percent more than today. When compared to the share of world product lost by the United States from 2000 to 2008—7.7 percent—the assumed marginal gain of 1.2 percent of world product accounts for about 15 percent of the U.S. decline.

These estimates suggest that roughly a quarter of America's relative decline is due to U.S. economic weaknesses (spending on the Iraq War, tax cuts, current-account deficits, etc.), a sixth to China's superior performance and just over half to the spread of technology to the rest of the world. In other words, self-inflicted wounds of the Bush years significantly exacerbated America's decline, both by making the decline steeper and faster and crowding out productive investment that could have stimulated innovation to improve matters.

All of this has led to one of the most significant declines of any state since the mid-nineteenth century. And when one examines past declines and their consequences, it becomes clear both that the U.S. fall is remarkable and that dangerous instability in the international system may lie ahead. If we end up believing in the wishful thinking of unipolar dominance forever, the costs could be far higher than a simple percentage drop in share of world product.

The United States has always prided itself on exceptionalism, and the U.S. downfall is indeed extraordinary. Something fundamental has changed. America's relative decline since 2000 of some 30 percent represents a far greater loss of relative power in a shorter time than any power shift among European great powers from roughly the end of the Napoleonic Wars to World War II. It is one of the largest relative declines in modern history. Indeed, in size, it is clearly surpassed by only one other great-power decline, the unexpected internal collapse of the Soviet Union in 1991.

Most disturbing, whenever there are major changes in the balance of power, conflict routinely ensues. Examining the historical record reveals an important pattern: the states facing the largest declines in power compared to other major powers were apt to be the target of opportunistic aggression. And this is surely not the only possible danger from relative decline; states on the power wane also have a history of launching preventive wars to strengthen their positions. All of this suggests that major relative declines are often accompanied by highly dangerous international environments. So, these declines matter not just in terms of economics, but also because of their destabilizing consequences.

Tsarist Russia presents the first case in point. Compared to other great powers on the European continent, its power declined the most during the mid-nineteenth century. And, it became the target of opportunistic aggression by the state with the greatest rising power, Great Britain, during the Crimean War (1854–1856). Indeed, the consequences of Russia's decline were not fully recognizable until the war itself. Though Russia was still a great power and the war cost Britain and France more than expected, Russia emerged the clear loser. Russia's inability to defend the status quo in the Crimea confirmed its grand-strategic weaknesses, and ultimately left it worse-off than had it anticipated its vulnerabilities and sought to negotiate a reduction in its military commitments to the region peacefully. Considering that the Crimea conflict left Russia with fairly gaping wounds, and that even its slow 10 percent decline in relative power over twenty years left the country bruised and battered, one might wonder how our far more rapid descent might play out.

Meanwhile, similar destabilization occurred in the two decades before World War I and before World War II, when France and Great Britain were declining European powers. In both instances, France and Britain became targets of opportunistic aggression by one of the strongest rising powers in the region: Germany. And as a small cottage industry of scholarship suggests, Germany's fairly modest relative declines compared to Russia prior to World War I and the Soviet Union prior to World War II encouraged German leaders to wage preventive wars. Again, these declines occurred as another power was concomitantly rising (Germany in the case of France and Britain, and Russia—later the Soviet Union—relative to Germany). Of course, this only served to increase the danger. But again, these rises and falls were less precipitous than America's current losses, and our descent appears far trickier to navigate.

As we look to address our current fall from grace, lest we forget, the United States faced two major declines of its power during the cold war as well. Neither was without risk. The first occurred shortly after World War II, when the devastation of the Soviet, European and many Asian economies, combined with the increasingly productive American economy, left the United States with a far larger share of gross world product—41 percent in 1948—than it even possessed in the age of unipolar dominance beginning in 1991. As the war-torn economies recovered, U.S. share of world product fell 20 percent by 1961 while that of its main rival, the Soviet Union, grew by 167 percent. This relative American decline corresponds to the height of U.S.-Soviet cold-war rivalry in Europe and Asia. Eight of the nine U.S.-Soviet nuclear crises occurred from 1948—1962, all of which involved efforts by the Soviet Union or its allies to revise the political status quo in their favor[7]—that is, all could be reasonably interpreted as instances in which the United States or its allies became the targets of opportunistic aggression.

The second major U.S. relative decline occurred from 1970 to 1980, when the U.S. share of world product fell 27 percent. This decade brought with it challenges to America's position in the world. This was especially true toward the end of the decade with the Soviet invasion of Afghanistan and the Iranian Revolution, which collectively increased concern about Soviet dominance of Persian Gulf oil. However, the 1970s was mainly a period of "détente" between the cold-war protagonists, which corresponds to the fact that the shares of world product for both the United States and the Soviet Union were in decline. In other words, it is reasonable to think that America's decline in the 1970s did not lead to more significant trouble for the United States because its main rival was descending even faster.

Clearly, major shifts in the balance of power in the international system often lead to instability and conflict. And America's current predicament is far more severe. This time, our relative decline of 32 percent is accompanied, not by an even-steeper decline of our near-peer competitor, but rather by a 144 percent increase in China's relative position. Further, the rapid spread of technology and technological breakthroughs means that one great discovery does not buoy an already-strong state to decades-long predominance. And with a rising China—with raw resources of population, landmass and increasing adoption of leading technology—a true peer competitor is looming. America's current, rapid domestic economic decline is merely accelerating our own downfall.

The distinct quality of a system with only one superpower is that no other single state is powerful enough to balance against it. A true global hegemon is more powerful still—stronger than all second-ranked powers acting as members of a counterbalancing coalition seeking to contain the unipolar leader. By these standards, America's relative decline is fundamentally changing international politics, and is fundamentally different from Russia circa 1850 and Great Britain circa 1910.

In current-U.S.-dollar terms—the preferred measure of the unipolar-dominance school—the United States has already fallen far from being a global hegemon and unipolarity itself is waning, since China will soon have as much economic potential to balance the United States as did the Soviet Union during the cold war.

At the beginning of the 1990s, the United States was indeed not only stronger than any other state individually, but its power relative to even the collective power of all other major states combined grew from 1990 to 2000. Although the growth was small, America almost reached the crucial threshold of 50 percent of major-power product necessary to become a true global hegemon. So it is understandable that we were lulled into a sense of security, believing we could do as we wished, whenever and wherever we wished. The instability and danger of the cold war quickly became a distant memory.

Near the time of the Iraq War, it would have required virtually every major power to actively oppose the United States in order to assemble a counterbalancing coalition that could approximate America's potential power. Under the circumstances, hard, military balancing against the United States was not a serious possibility. So, it is not surprising that major powers opted for soft-balancing measures—relying on institutional, economic and diplomatic tools to oppose American military power. And yet we are beginning to see "the conflict of history" repeat itself.

Even with less relative power, in the run-up to the Iraq War, people grossly under-rated the ability of Germany, France, Russia and China, along with important regional powers like Turkey, to soft balance against the United States; for instance, to use the United Nations to delay, complicate and ultimately deny the use of one-third of U.S. combat power (the Fourth Infantry Division) in the opening months of the Iraq War. This is not yet great-power war of the kind seen in centuries past, but it harkens the instability that future unilateral efforts may trigger.

The balance of world power circa 2008 and 2013 shows a disturbing trend. True, the United States remains stronger than any other state individually, but its power to stand up to the collective opposition of other major powers is falling precipitously. Though these worlds depict potential power, not active counterbalancing coalitions, and this type of alliance may never form, nonetheless, American relative power is declining to the point where even subsets of major powers acting in concert could produce sufficient military power to stand a reasonable chance of successfully opposing American military policies.

Indeed, if present trends continue to 2013 and beyond, China and Russia, along with any one of the other major powers, would have sufficient economic capacity to mount military opposition at least as serious as did the Soviet Union during the cold war. And it is worth remembering that the Soviet Union never had more than about half the world product of the United States, which China alone is likely to reach in the coming decade. The faults in the arguments of the unipolar-dominance school are being brought into sharp relief. The world is slowly coming into balance. Whether or not this will be another period of great-power transition coupled with an increasing risk of war will largely depend on how America can navigate its decline. Policy makers must act responsibly in this new era or risk international opposition that poses far greater costs and far greater dangers.

A coherent grand strategy seeks to balance a state's economic resources and its foreign-policy commitments and to sustain that balance over time. For America, a coherent grand strategy also calls for rectifying the current imbalance between our means and our ends, adopting policies that enhance the former and modify the latter.

Clearly, the United States is not the first great power to suffer long-term decline—we should learn from history. Great powers in decline seem to almost instinctively spend more on military forces in order to shore up their disintegrating strategic positions, and some like Germany go even further, shoring up their security by adopting preventive military strategies, beyond defensive alliances, to actively stop a rising competitor from becoming dominant.

For declining great powers, the allure of preventive war—or lesser measures to "merely" firmly contain a rising power—has a more compelling logic than many might assume. Since Thucydides, scholars of international politics have famously argued that a declining hegemon and rising challenger must necessarily face such intense security competition that hegemonic war to retain dominance over the international system is almost a foregone conclusion. Robert Gilpin, one of the deans of realism who taught for decades at Princeton, believed that "the first and most attractive response to a society's decline is to eliminate the source of the problem . . . [by] what we shall call a hegemonic war."

Yet, waging war just to keep another state down has turned out to be one of the great losing strategies in history. The Napoleonic Wars, the Austro-Prussian War, the Franco-Prussian War, German aggression in World War I, and German and Japanese aggression in World War II were all driven by declining powers seeking to use war to improve their future security. All lost control of events they thought they could control. All suffered ugly defeats. All were worse-off than had they not attacked.

As China rises, America must avoid this great-power trap. It would be easy to think that greater American military efforts could offset the consequences of China's increasing power and possibly even lead to the formation of a multi-lateral strategy to contain China in the future. Indeed, when China's economic star began to rise in the 1990s, numerous voices called for precisely this, noting that on current trajectories China would overtake the United States as the world's leading economic power by 2050.[8] Now, as that date draws nearer—indeed, current- dollar calculations put the crossover point closer to 2040—and with Beijing evermore dependent on imported oil for continued economic growth, one might think the case for actively containing China is all the stronger.

Absent provocative military adventures by Beijing, however, U.S. military efforts to contain the rising power are most likely doomed to failure. China's growth turns mainly on domestic issues—such as shifting the workforce from rural to urban areas—that are beyond the ability of outside powers to significantly influence. Although China's growth also depends on external sources of oil, there is no way to exploit this vulnerability short of obviously hostile alliances (with India, Indonesia, Taiwan and Japan) and clearly aggressive military measures (controlling the sea-lanes from the Persian Gulf to Asia) that together could deny oil to China. Any efforts along these lines would likely backfire—and only exacerbate America's problems, increasing the risk of counterbalancing.

Even more insidious is the risk of overstretch. This self-reinforcing spiral escalates current spending to maintain increasingly costly military commitments, crowding out productive investment for future growth.

Today, the cold-war framework of significant troop deployments to Europe, Asia and the Persian Gulf is coming unglued. We cannot afford to keep our previous promises. With American forces bogged down in Iraq and Afghanistan and mounting troubles in Iran and Pakistan, the United States has all but gutted its military commitments to Europe, reducing our troop levels far below the one hundred thousand of the 1990s. Nearly half have been shifted to Iraq and elsewhere. Little wonder that Russia found an opportunity to demonstrate the hollowness of the Bush administration's plan for expanding NATO to Russia's borders by scoring a quick and decisive military victory over Georgia that America was helpless to prevent. If a large-scale conventional war between China and Taiwan broke out in the near future, one must wonder whether America would significantly shift air and naval power away from its ongoing wars in the Middle East in order to live up to its global commitments. If the United States could not readily manage wars in Iraq and Afghanistan at the same time, could it really wage a protracted struggle in Asia as well? And as the gap between America's productive resources and global commitments grows, why will others pass up opportunities to take advantage of America's overstretched grand strategy?

Since the end of the cold war, American leaders have consistently claimed the ability to maintain a significant forward-leaning military presence in the three major regions of the globe and, if necessary, to wage two major regional wars at the same time. The harsh reality is that the United States no longer has the economic capacity for such an ambitious grand strategy. With 30 percent of the world's product, the United States could imagine maintaining this hope. Nearing 20 percent, it cannot.

Yet, just withdrawing American troops from Iraq is not enough to put America's grand strategy into balance. Even assuming a fairly quick and problem-free drawdown, the risks of instability in Iraq, Afghanistan and elsewhere in the region are likely to remain for many years to come. Further, even under the most optimistic scenarios, America is likely to remain dependent on imported oil for decades. Together, these factors point toward the Persian Gulf remaining the most important region in American grand strategy.

So, Washington must think creatively and look for opportunities to make strategic trades. America needs to share the burden of regional security with its allies and continue to draw down our troop levels in Europe and Asia, even considering the attendant risks. The days when the United States could effectively solve the security problems of its allies in these regions almost on its own are coming to an end. True, spreading defense burdens more equally will not be easy and will be fraught with its own costs and risks. However, this is simply part of the price of America's declining relative power.

The key principle is for America to gain international support among regional powers like Russia and China for its vital national-security objectives by adjusting less important U.S. policies. For instance, Russia may well do more to discourage Iran's nuclear program in return for less U.S. pressure to expand NATO to its borders.

And of course America needs to develop a plan to reinvigorate the competitiveness of its economy. Recently, Harvard's Michael Porter issued an economic blueprint to renew America's environment for innovation. The heart of his plan is to remove the obstacles to increasing investment in science and technology. A combination of targeted tax, fiscal and education policies to stimulate more productive investment over the long haul is a sensible domestic component to America's new grand strategy. But it would be misguided to assume that the United States could easily regain its previously dominant economic position, since the world will likely remain globally competitive.

To justify postponing this restructuring of its grand strategy, America would need a firm expectation of high rates of economic growth over the next several years. There is no sign of such a burst on the horizon. Misguided efforts to extract more security from a declining economic base only divert potential resources from investment in the economy, trapping the state in an ever-worsening strategic dilemma. This approach has done little for great powers in the past, and America will likely be no exception when it comes to the inevitable costs of desperate policy making.

The United States is not just declining. Unipolarity is becoming obsolete, other states are rising to counter American power and the United States is losing much of its strategic freedom. Washington must adopt more realistic foreign commitments.

Since 2000, a systemic change has been occurring in the economic foundations of America's relative power, and it may fall even further in the foreseeable future. None of the dramatic consequences for U.S. grand strategy is likely to be immediate, but neither are those effects easily avoidable. For nearly two decades, the United States has experienced tremendous latitude in how it chooses to conduct itself in the world. But that latitude is now shrinking, and American policy makers must face facts. With the right grand strategy, however, America can mitigate the consequences of its relative decline, and possibly even reverse it.

Notes

1. For excellent discussions of the concept of power, see John Mearsheimer, *The Tragedy of Great Power Politics* (New York: W. W. Norton, 2001), ch. 3; and Edward Vose Gulick, *Europe's Classical Balance of Power* (New York: W. W. Norton, 1955), ch 1.

2. Stephen G. Brooks and William C. Wohlforth, *World Out of Balance: International Relations and the Challenge of American Primacy* (Princeton, NJ: Princeton University Press, 2008), 32.

3. For explanations of different measures of gross domestic product, see glossaries for the International Monetary Fund, "World Economic Outlook Database" (October 2008) and World Bank, "World Development Indicators" (2008), both available online.

4. For a classic study of the diffusion of technology in past eras, see David S. Landes, *The Unbound Prometheus: Technological Change and Industrial Development in Western Europe from 1750 to Present* (New York: Cambridge University Press, 1969).

5. See the Global Market Information Database; CIA World Factbook for the above dates; the National Science Board's "Science and Engineering Indicators 2008"; Nationmaster.com; and International Telecommunication Union's "International Communication Statistics, 2007." All were accessed online from August to October 2008.

6. This counterfactual calculation and the one in the next paragraph rely on the current-dollar method preferred by the unipolar-dominance school.

7. Richard K. Betts, *Nuclear Blackmail and Nuclear Balance* (Washington, DC: Brookings Institution Press, 1987).

8. For instance, Richard Bernstein and Ross H. Munro, *The Coming Conflict with China* (New York: Alfred A. Knopf, 1997).

Robert A. Pape, "Empire Falls," The National Interest 99 (2009), pp. 21-34. Reprinted by permission of Center for the National Interest.

Part Five: New Domains

Roger C. Altman, Globalization in Retreat

1. Altman predicted the decline of laissez-faire economics and the return of the state to market intervention. To what extent has this reregulation and state interference in the market come to pass?
2. Altman argued that "globalization" is now in retreat. Do you agree? Explain.
3. To what extent is globalization problematic, or even dangerous? Give examples.
4. Altman argued that the global financial crisis of 2008 accelerated the transformation of the international system to a multipolar environment. Do you agree?

A. G. Hopkins, Capitalism, Nationalism, and the New American Empire

1. Explain the difference between "lions" and "foxes" in Pareto's classic theory of elites.
2. How does the rise of the *military-industrial complex* complicate the conduct of U.S. foreign policy?
3. Hopkins argued that globalization combines with nationalism and thereby promotes imperium and war. Does this logic hold?
4. Have elites augmented the U.S.A.'s tendency to engage in foreign wars? Explain.
5. Is the U.S. governed by a *demagogic plutocracy*? What are the implications for the conduct of U.S. foreign policy?
6. To what extent do domestic forces drive the conduct of U.S. foreign policy?
7. To what degree were capitalism and/or nationalism drivers of the U.S. invasion of Iraq in 2003?
8. Hopkins argued that imperialism was not a driver of the war. Do you agree? Explain.

David G. Victor and Linda Yueh, The New Energy Order: Managing Insecurities in the Twenty-first Century

1. Victor and Yueh critiqued international institutions as largely powerless and ineffective. Do you agree? Explain.
2. Victor and Yueh argued for extensive reforms to the International Energy Agency. Do you concur?
3. Victor and Yueh argued that the international organizations, treaties, and norms that should govern global energy politics are in disarray. What are the implications for the debate between Liberals, Realists, and Constructivists? Which position do you find more compelling in this case?
4. Victor and Yueh argued that China's strategy of pursuing bilateral deals with supplier nations actually enhances global energy security and is a boon to the United States. Do you agree?

Steven E. Miller and Scott D. Sagan, Alternative Nuclear Futures

1. How might international institutions effectively contribute to nuclear security? Provide two examples.
2. How did the Japanese crisis of 2011 affect global perceptions of the safety of nuclear power? Has it affected the spread of nuclear technology and infrastructure?
3. Have international law and international institutions acted as effective checks on the spread of nuclear weapons? What are the implications for global governance and Liberal theory?
4. How will the spread of nuclear weapons to the nations of the developing world affect the Nuclear Non-Proliferation Treaty? What strategy do Miller and Sagan advise?
5. Does the International Atomic Energy Agency (IAEA) possess adequate resources? What are

the resulting consequences for nuclear proliferation? How could the IAEA be strengthened?

Scott G. Borgerson, Arctic Meltdown: The Economic and Security Implications of Global Warming

1. Should the United States ratify the Law of the Sea (UNCLOS)? What are the domestic impediments to doing so?
2. Does a melting Arctic mean increasing competition, perhaps even conflict, between the powers in that region? Explain.
3. How will the "big melt" affect U.S. diplomatic relations with Russia and Canada?
4. Does a warming world qualify as a threat to U.S. vital interests, or to U.S. national security? Explain.

Ronald J. Deibert and Rafal Rohozinski, Risking Security: Policies and Paradoxes of Cyberspace Security

1. Do sovereign states have the capacity to control cyberspace? How are states limited in their attempts to control this domain.
2. What do Deibert and Rohozinski mean by risks "to" and "through" cyberspace? Give two examples of each.
3. Is the disruption of cyberspace, and thus the global economy, truly a threat to U.S. national security? Explain.
4. How did cybertechnology in general, and *resistance nets* in particular, contribute to the Arab Spring revolutions of 2011?
5. How do *dark nets* challenge U.S. interests abroad? Give examples.
6. Is cybercrime a challenge to U.S. foreign interests? To U.S. national security? Explain.

Nassim Nicholas Taleb and Mark Blyth, The Black Swan of Cairo: How Suppressing Volatility Makes the World Less Predictable and More Dangerous

1. Taleb and Blyth argued that volatility is in fact helpful in complex systems, and that governments should not seek to suppress it. Is their logic compelling?
2. What do Taleb and Blyth mean by the *illusion of control*?
3. What are the consequences of complex *interdependence* and *Black Swans* for U.S. intelligence?

William McCants, Al Qaeda's Challenge: The Jihadists' War with Islamist Democrats

1. Does the rise of nonstate actors (such as al Qaeda) challenge certain core assumptions of the Realist theory? Explain.
2. Which of the theories presented in this volume best accommodates the rise of terrorism as a challenge to U.S. foreign policy interests?
3. Did the trajectory of U.S. foreign policy change in a *substantive* manner after the attacks of September 11th?
4. Is the wave of democratization resulting from the Arab Spring a help or hindrance to terrorist groups such as al Qaeda? Does such democratization help or hinder U.S. interests in the Islamic world? Explain your position.

Robert A. Pape, Empire Falls

1. Pape argued that the U.S.A.'s hegemonic power is declining relative to other rising nations, and that the end of unipolarity is at hand? Do you agree?
2. Is economic power truly the core of political power? Explain.
3. Are economic indicators an effective mechanism to measure shifts in relative power between hegemonic contenders?
4. Do shifts in relative power always lead to war between the Great Powers? Is war between the U.S. and China then inevitable? Explain.
5. Pape argued that declining powers find strategies of *preventive war* appealing. Will the U.S. engage in such a strategy against rising powers? What factors diminish the probability of preventive war?

1775, the **American Revolutionary War**: General George Washington leads the colonies against the British.

1776, 4 July, the **Declaration of Independence.**

1783, 3 September, the **Treaty of Paris**: marked the end of the Revolutionary War and the recognition of U.S. boundaries by Britain.

1796, 19 September, **Washington's Farewell Address**: the President warns against the U.S. becoming entangled in European affairs.

1803, 30 April, the **Louisiana Purchase**: the U.S.A. acquires 828,000 square miles of territory from France after Napoleon concludes that France can no longer maintain its control over its American possessions.

1812, 18 June, the **War of 1812**: following the U.S. invasion of Canada, the War of 1812 begins between the U.S. and Britain; ultimately, the peace treaty resulting from this conflict delineated the U.S.A.'s northern border.

1823, 2 December, the **Monroe Doctrine**: the U.S. claims the entire Western Hemisphere as its sphere of influence in an effort to exclude the European powers from the region.

1846, 13 May, the **U.S.–Mexican War**: following this conflict (**1846–1848**) the U.S.A. gained the territories of Texas, California, and New Mexico.

1898, the **Spanish–American War**: following this conflict the U.S.A. gains territories in Guam, Puerto Rico, Cuba, and the Philippines.

1904, 6 December, the **Roosevelt Corollary** to the Monroe Doctrine: the U.S.A. articulated the right to intervene in other countries throughout Latin America in order to "stabilize" them.

1917, 6 April, **U.S.A. Enters World War I**: the entry of the U.S. into the war followed German attacks on U.S. shipping, the sinking of the *Lusitania*, and the Zimmermann Telegram, which sought to fashion a German–Mexican alliance against the United States. The Armistice ending the war was signed on 11 November 1918.

1918, 8 January, **Woodrow Wilson's Fourteen Points**: in a proposal to Congress, President Wilson sought to fashion a postwar order that relied on the self-determination of nations, transparent diplomacy, and a mechanism of collective security.

1919, 14 February, the **League of Nations**: in his proposal to the members of the Paris Peace Conference, President Wilson articulated the first "collective security" mechanism. Ultimately, the U.S. Senate refused to ratify the Treaty and thereby rejected U.S. membership in the League. The League formally came into existence on 19 January 1920, without US membership. The absence of the United States compromised the League's power and permitted the aggression of Fascist Italy, Nazi Germany, and Imperial Japan.

1941, 7 December, the **Attack on Pearl Harbor**: the Japanese attack on Pearl Harbor Naval Base, Hawaii, precipitated the entry of the U.S. into World War II, with President Franklin Delano Roosevelt's declaration of war against Japan. Days later Germany declared war on the U.S.A.

1944, 6 June, the **D-Day Landings at Normandy**: U.S. forces combined with British and Canadian troops push German forces back from the beaches of Northern France; following the establishment of such beachheads, Allied forces pushed on to liberate Paris. Then in combination with Soviet pressure in the East, the Allies ultimately took Berlin in 1945. Germany surrendered on 8 May 1945.

1945, 28 June, the **Rise of the United Nations**: the U.S.A. ratified the Charter of the United Nations on this day, ensuring that the U.S. would be part of the nascent international organization.

1945, 6–9th August, **Hiroshima and Nagasaki, Japan**: the United States drops Nuclear Weapons on these two Japanese cities to bring an end to the War in the Pacific. Japan subsequently sues for peace.

1947, 12 March, **Truman Doctrine**: the U.S.A. declares its support of Greece and Turkey in their resistance to communist infiltration. This marks the onset of the Cold War.

1948, April, the **Marshall Plan**: this massive mobilization of aid by the U.S.A. was an effort to revive those western European economies that had been shattered by the Second World War. The Marshall Plan was also an economic mechanism to bolster western European nations against destabilization by communist forces.

1950–53, the **Korean War**: during this conflict U.S. and U.N. forces fought to support South Korean forces against North Korean and Chinese forces who were given material aid by the Soviets. The Korean War was the first proxy war of the Cold War era. Recent years have seen sporadic outbreaks of aggression by North Korean forces against the South, and a significant U.S. military presence is still deployed in the defense of South Korea.

1961, April, the **Bay of Pigs Affair**: a group of Cuban exiles (trained by the CIA) attempted a landing in Cuba's Bay of Pigs in an attempt to eventually oust the Castro regime. The plot was a dismal failure and an embarrassment to the Kennedy Administration.

1962, October, the **Cuban Missile Crisis**: the crisis began with the Kennedy Administration's discovery of the existence of Soviet medium range ballistic missile bases in Cuba. The U.S. subsequently initiated a naval blockade of the island, prompting Soviet Premier Khrushchev to warn of the possibility of nuclear war between the superpowers. The October Crisis was one of the most dangerous moments in the Cold War.

1964 the **Vietnam War begins**: the U.S. began to significantly increase its military presence in Vietnam as the French retreated from a nationalist uprising against their colonial presence. The U.S. sought to contain the spread of communism reflected in a deepening military involvement since the early 1960s. The war lasted from 1964 until the fall of Saigon to enemy forces in April 1975. Over 58,000 American troops were killed during this conflict.

1972, February, **President Nixon visits China:** during this visit President Nixon met with PRC Chairman Mao Zedong and initiated a period of warming economic and diplomatic interaction between the two nations. Part of Secretary of State Henry Kissinger's realpolitik, the thawing relations between Beijing and Washington, allowed for the former to distance itself from Moscow.

1979, the **Iranian Revolution** results in the **Iran Hostage Crisis** (4 November 1979, 20 January 1981): during this incident Iranian radicals seized the U.S. embassy in Tehran, and held the American embassy staff hostage for 444 days. President Carter's attempt to rescue the hostages by force ended in failure, and the incident tarnished the legacy of the Carter Administration.

1980, 23 January, the **Carter Doctrine**: President Carter proclaims that the U.S.A. will not tolerate any attempt by an external power to gain control of the oil resources of the Persian Gulf, seeing any such attempt as a threat to the U.S.A.'s vital national interests. This bellicose statement was a direct response to the Soviet invasion of Afghanistan in 1979, which many perceived as a move toward the oil fields of the Persian Gulf.

1983, **U.S. invasion of Grenada:** in response to a leftist coup against the government of that small island in the Caribbean.

1986, the **Iran-Contra Affair**: wherein the U.S. sells missiles to Iran (in violation of numerous federal laws) and uses the proceeds to fund the activities of the Contras in Nicaragua. This latter activity was in direct violation of the will of Congress, which had expressly forbidden further funding of CIA/Contra activities against the Sandinistas.

1989, **Operation Just Cause:** U.S. forces invade Panama, seizing Manuel Noriega for the extensive trafficking of narcotics throughout the Americas.

1991, **Operation Desert Storm:** fearing Saddam Hussein's desire for Iraqi hegemony over the oil reserves of the Persian Gulf, and consistent with the Carter Doctrine, the U.S.A. leads U.N. forces in the expulsion of Iraq from Kuwait. This conflict sets the stage for the 2003 invasion of Iraq by U.S. forces.

1992, U.S. Congress ratifies the **North American Free Trade Agreement** (**NAFTA**): the trade agreement goes into effect in January 1994.

1999, March–June, **U.S.-led NATO forces bomb Yugoslavia:** to end Serbian violence against Albanians in the province of Kosovo.

2001, the **September 11th Attacks:** Islamic jihadists commit suicide attacks against New York and Washington, DC resulting in the deaths of over 3,000 U.S. civilians. It was the first significant attack against the continental U.S.

2001, October, the **Afghan War:** the U.S. begins a massive bombing campaign against the Taliban government of Afghanistan, and teams up with the Afghan Northern Alliance forces to win a temporary victory. The Taliban were attacked for sheltering Osama bin Laden and his al Qaeda organization who had committed the September 11th attacks. This marks the start of the Afghan War (2001–present).

2003, March 20, marks the start of the **Iraq War** (**2003–2011**): also known as Operation Iraqi Freedom. The war was initially sold by the Bush Administration as a response to Saddam Hussein's possession of weapons of mass destruction. No such weapons were ever found by U.S. forces. During the invasion U.S. forces enjoyed initial success and toppled the government of Saddam Hussein. Thereafter the U.S. military was bogged down fighting an aggressive insurgency made up of Sunni, Shia, and "al Qaeda in Iraq" forces. On December 15, 2011, Secretary of Defense Panetta declares a formal end to the Iraq War, and the withdrawal of U.S. troops from the country.

2011, March 19, U.S. military forces join NATO in the **Libyan Intervention:** backing rebels in their attempt to oust the oppressive regime of Muammar Gaddafi. NATO forces decisively intervened on the side of the rebels during the Libyan civil war, authorized under U.N. Security Council Resolution 1973.

2011, May 1, **Death of bin Laden:** U.S. forces track down and kill Osama bin Laden in Abbottabad, Pakistan. The fact that bin Laden had apparently been hiding in Pakistan for some time results in a deterioration of U.S.–Pakistani relations.

CONTRIBUTORS

Roger C. Altman
Roger C. Altman is chairman and chief executive officer of Evercore Partners.

Andrew J. Bacevich
Andrew J. Bacevich is professor of international relations and history at Boston University.

Matthew A. Baum
Matthew A. Baum is the Marvin Kalb Professor of global communications and professor of public policy at Harvard University's John F. Kennedy School of Government.

Mark Blyth
Mark Blyth is professor of international political economy in the Department of Political Science at Brown University and a faculty fellow at Brown's Watson Institute for International Studies.

Scott G. Borgerson
Scott G. Borgerson is a cofounder and managing director of CargoMetrics. Previously, he was the visiting fellow for ocean governance at the Council on Foreign Relations and an adjunct senior research scholar at Columbia University's Center for Energy, Marine Transportation, and Public Policy.

Jorge G. Castañeda
Jorge G. Castañeda is a Global Distinguished Professor of politics and Latin American and Caribbean studies at New York University and the former Foreign Minister of Mexico (2000–2003).

Ronald J. Deibert
Ronald J. Deibert is associate professor of political science and director of the Citizen Lab at the Munk Centre for International Studies, University of Toronto.

Evan A. Feigenbaum
Evan A. Feigenbaum is a vice chairman of the Paulson Institute. He is also nonresident senior associate in the Asia Program at the Carnegie Endowment for International Peace.

Richard N. Haass
Richard N. Haass is the president of the Council on Foreign Relations.

Patrick Haney
Patrick J. Haney is professor of political science at Miami University in Oxford, Ohio.

A.G. Hopkins
A.G. Hopkins is professor at the University of Texas, Austin and the Walter Prescott Webb Chair of History.

Samuel P. Huntington
Samuel P. Huntington was professor of political scienceat Harvard University.

G. John Ikenberry
G. John Ikenberry is the Albert G. Milbank Professor of politics and international affairs at Princeton University in the Department of Politics and the Woodrow Wilson School of Public and International Affairs.

Lawrence R. Jacobs
Lawrence R. Jacobs is the Walter F. and Joan Mondale Chair for political studies and director of the Center for the Study of Politics and Governance in the Hubert H. Humphrey Institute and Department of Political Science at the University of Minnesota.

Robert Jervis
Robert Jervis is the Adlai E. Stevenson Professor of International Affairs at Columbia University.

Loch K. Johnson
Loch K. Johnson is the Regents Professor and Josiah Meigs Distinguished Teaching Professor at the University of Georgia, and has been a visiting scholar at Yale University.

Robert Legvold
Robert Legvold is Marshall D. Shulman Professor Emeritus in the Department of Political Science at Columbia University.

William McCants
William McCants is an analyst at CNA's Center for Strategic Studies and an adjunct faculty member at Johns Hopkins University.

John J. Mearsheimer
John J. Mearsheimer is the R. Wendell Harrison Distinguished Service Professor of political science and codirector of the Program on International Security Policy at the University of Chicago.

Mohsen M. Milani
Mohsen M. Milani is the executive director of the Center for Strategic and Diplomatic Studies at the University of South Florida and professor of politics in the Department of Government and International Affairs at the University of South Florida.

Steven E. Miller
Steven E. Miller is director of the International Security Program, editor-in-chief of the quarterly journal, *International Security,* and coprincipal investigator of the Project on Managing the Atom series, Belfer Center Studies in International Security.

Henry R. Nau
Henry R. Nau is professor of political science and international affairs at the Elliott School of International Affairs, the George Washington University.

Joseph S. Nye, Jr.
Joseph S. Nye, Jr. is a University Distinguished Service Professor and former dean of the Kennedy School at Harvard University.

Benjamin I. Page
Benjamin I. Page is the Gordon S. Fulcher Professor of decision making at Northwestern University and a faculty associate at the Institute for Policy Research.

Robert A. Pape
Robert A. Pape is professor of political science and director of the Program for International Security Politics at the University of Chicago.

Robert A. Pastor
Robert A. Pastor is professor of international relations and director of the Center for North American Studies and the Center for Democracy and Election Management at the American University in Washington, DC.

Philip B.K. Potter
Philip B.K. Potter is assistant professor of public policy and political science at the Gerald R. Ford School of Public Policy at the University of Michigan.

Ahmed Rashid
Ahmed Rashid is a Pakistani journalist and writer and a fellow at the Pacific Council on International Policy.

Rafal A. Rohozinski
Rafal A. Rohozinski is principal and chief executive officer of the SecDev Group Ottawa, Canada.

Barnett R. Rubin
Barnett R. Rubin is director of studies and senior fellow at the Center on International Cooperation of New York University.

Scott D. Sagan
Scott D. Sagan is the Caroline S.G. Munro Professor of political science at Stanford University and a senior fellow at the Center for International Security and Cooperation and the Freeman Spogli Institute.

Jack Snyder

Jack Snyder is the Robert and Renée Belfer Professor of international relations in the Department of Political Science and the Saltzman Institute of War and Peace Studies at Columbia University.

Nassim Nicholas Taleb

Nassim Nicholas Taleb is distinguished professor of Risk Engineeringand codirector of the Research Center for Risk Engineering at New York University.

David G. Victor

David G. Victor is professor at the School of International Relations and Pacific Studies and codirector of the Laboratory on International Law and Regulation at University of California San Diego.

Stephen M. Walt

Stephen M. Walt is the Robert and Renée Belfer Professor of international affairs at Harvard University.

Linda Yueh

Linda Yueh is a fellow in Economics at Oxford University and adjunct professor of economics at the London Business School, as well as an economics correspondent for Bloomberg TV.

al Qaeda: Islamic terrorist organization founded and led by Osama bin Laden, carried out the attacks on September 11, 2001; carried out numerous strikes on U.S. and European targets.

Anarchy: The state of the international system where there is no higher power that can compel sovereign states to moderate their behavior. Note that the quality of anarchy may change, from a competitive formulation under Realist theory, to a cooperative mode under Liberal theory.

Appeasement: A policy of concessions to an adversary to maintain peace.

Arab Spring: Refers to the democratic revolutions that began in the Arab states of North Africa in the spring of 2011. The turbulence commenced in Tunisia and then spread to topple authoritarian regimes in Egypt, Algeria, and Libya.

Attribution Theory: Holds that decision makers try to discern attributes of other actors, inferring causes of important events. Decision makers are regarded as problem solvers.

Authoritarianism: Mode of government wherein the rulers demand absolute obedience from the ruled.

Availability Heuristics: Rules of thumb that policymakers typically expect situational outcomes that replicate past experiences.

Balance of Power: A condition in which the distribution of military and political forces among nations means that no one state is sufficiently strong enough to dominate all the others. An attempt at a stable equilibrium in the international system—it may be global, regional, or local in scope.

Bandwagoning: An alliance in which a state, instead of joining a counterbalancing coalition, joins the stronger power or coalition.

Bay of Pigs: A small inlet on the southern coast of western Cuba; the site of an ill-fated invasion on April 17, 1961, when a force of 1,500 U.S.-trained guerrilla troops landed in an attempt to overthrow the government of Fidel Castro. By April 17th, the invasion attempt had collapsed, and it was a great embarrassment to the U.S. in general, and to the Kennedy Administration in particular.

Bilateral: Typically in reference to actions undertaken by two countries to address an issue of mutual interest or concern.

Bipolarity: An international system dominated by two actors of roughly equivalent power.

Black Market: Refers to a type of economic activity that occurs outside of government approved pathways.

Bounded Rationality: Refers to the notion that humans attempt to act in a rational manner, but they are inhibited by cognitive and psychological factors.

Bretton Woods System: The Allies met at the town of Bretton Woods, NH in 1944, to lay the groundwork for a stable postwar economic system. The goal was to avoid repeating the mistakes made during the years between the world wars, namely protectionism, economic nationalism, collapse of trade, and the Great Depression. The new system sought to foster a stable, persistent climate of global free trade and economic interdependence. It resulted in the creation of multilateral lending institutions to stabilize and accelerate the development of national economies, namely the International Monetary Fund (IMF) and the International Bank for Reconstruction and Development (IBFD; World Bank).

Bureaucracy: A body of nonelected government officials distinguished by a hierarchy of authority, specialization of functions, and adherence to fixed rules.

Bureaucratic Politics: Theory that sees outcomes as a result of competition between government agencies. Disputes the idea that decision making is based on rational cost-benefit analysis.

Bush Doctrine: Created by the administration of President George W. Bush, this term refers to the canon of unilateralism and pre-emptive war in defense of U.S. security. It also refers to the spread of democracy by force, and was used to justify the invasion of Afghanistan in 2001 and the invasion of Iraq in 2003.

Capitalism: Idea that the means of production should be privately owned, and that the desire for profit leads to greater efficiency, benefitting both producers and consumers.

Cold War: 1947–1991, the state of political tension and military rivalry between the United States and Soviet Union following World War II. Based on ideological rivalry (capitalism vs. communism), it began in earnest with the Truman Doctrine (1947), where the U.S.A. pledged support to those nations (Greece, Turkey) who were resisting Communist insurgency. During this period both superpowers created opposing alliance structures, the Soviets crafted the Warsaw Pact in Eastern Europe, and the U.S.A. formed NATO. It ended in 1991/92 with the dissolution of the Soviet Union.

Cognitive Consistency: Refers to the fact that people see what they expect to see, so they interpret their perceptions through pre-existing images and beliefs to fit their theories.

Collective Action Problem: A situation where the uncoordinated actions of each player may not result in the best outcome that they could possibly achieve. Example is the Prisoner's Dilemma.

Collective Security: The principle that states will band together in a defensive alliance against an aggressor. The principle was originally developed by Hugo Grotius in the Treaty of Westphalia (1648). Institutions can be regional in nature (NATO) or global (U.N. Security Council). The logic is that the larger community of nations will oppose any aggression by one state against another. The Concert of Europe that followed the Napoleonic Wars, the League of Nations, the United Nations, and NATO are all examples of attempts to institutionalize the principle of collective security.

Colonialism: Policy of one nation extending or maintaining its control over other countries or peoples.

Communism: Organization of a society around a centralized mode of production. It focuses on the equitable distribution of wealth. Mode of government is typically centralized and authoritarian.

Concert of Europe: The informal system of consultation set up by the Great Powers (Austria, Britain, France, Prussia, and Russia) to manage the balance of power at the end of the Congress system.

Constructivism: An approach that sees truth and knowledge as socially constructed and thus based on subjectivity, not objectivity.

Containment: The policy pursued by the U.S. toward the Soviet Union circa 1947–1989, the aim was to halt Soviet expansion. It involved the encirclement of the Soviet Union and its allies by pro-Western forces. It was first articulated by President Truman in 1947.

Cuban Missile Crisis: Soviet missile sites are discovered in Cuba by the United States in October 1962, leading to the "October Crisis." This was the most dangerous moment of the Cold War era. In response, President Kennedy orders a naval blockade to prevent further shipments of Soviet weapons from reaching Cuba. Ultimately the Soviets backed down removing their missiles in return for the U.S. removing its Jupiter missiles from Turkey.

Cult of the Offensive: The widespread belief of strategic planners that the first country to attack would triumph. This encouraged a situation where all the great powers of the time were primed for rapid mobilization, and where every state would try to attack using a first strike. The Cult of the Offensive encourages pre-emptive strikes, and thereby exacerbates the security dilemma because countries fear that their neighbors will strike first. Therefore everybody gets ready to strike first, leading to extreme instability.

Democracy: A government in which the supreme power is vested in the people and exercised by them directly or indirectly through a system of representation usually involving periodically held free elections.

Democratic Peace Theory: The German philosopher Immanuel Kant, in his treatise on Perpetual Peace, established the notion that democracies do not fight each other. However, democracies will actively fight nondemocracies, and authoritarian regimes will fight one another. Theoretically, as the number of democracies expands it creates a "zone of peace," where war becomes impossible.

Dependency Theory: A theory of international political economy based on Marxist ideas. It sees the world as divided between underdeveloped "periphery" states and the industrialized nations of the "core." In this model the core continually exploits the periphery.

Détente: A French term meaning "the relaxation of tensions." It denotes an era during the Cold War in which the superpowers showed enhanced cooperation.

Deterrence: Attempt to prevent war by dissuading a potential aggressor.

Diplomacy: The art or practice of conducting international relations, as in negotiating alliances, treaties, and agreements.

Diplomatic Immunity: Norm of international law that shields diplomats from arrest and prosecution.

Empire: Domination of a single state over other nations to the extent that they are subordinated to the ruling state.

European Union: Created by the Treaty of Rome 1957, it is the most integrated bloc of nations in the international system.

Fascism: Doctrine promoted by the far right, advocates an authoritarian society based on elite rule.

First-Strike Capability: Ability to destroy or critically weaken an opponents strategic forces or prevent a retaliatory strike.

Flexible Response: The Kennedy Administration wanted greater latitude in its ability to deal with the Soviets, so they moved away from the prior doctrine of Mass Retaliation. Under Flexible Response, U.S. forces developed a range of conventional and nuclear forces and strategies to counter the Soviets up and down the ladder of conflict escalation, from the use of conventional force, to battlefield nuclear weapons, and finally to strategic nuclear weapons.

Fundamental Attributional Error: Refers to a double standard in one's conduct. One's own bad behavior is attributed to situational context, but a rival's bad behavior is attributed to poor character and beliefs.

General Agreement on Tariffs and Trade (GATT): 1947, agreement was established to encourage free trade, focused on lowering tariff and nontariff barriers to trade.

Globalism: The policy of placing the interests of the entire world above those of individual nations.

Globalization: Process of intensifying interdependence between the states and societies of the planet.

Gray Market: The business of buying or selling goods, such as imports, at prices below those set by an official regulatory agency.

Group of Eight (G-8): Refers to the Group of Eight nations, which includes the seven richest members of the OECD (United States, Canada, Britain, Germany, Japan, France, Italy) and Russia. The group holds regular summits to coordinate global economic policy and deal with other issues of concern to its members.

Hegemonic Stability Theory: Refers to the notion that the most powerful nation will set the rules of the game for international system to protect its own self-interests. Notion that dominance by one hegemon creates a system that is more stable than one dominated by several great powers. The dominant state provides public goods to the entire system to reinforce stability to protect its power and prosperity. This entails significant costs to the hegemon.

Hegemony: Derived from the Greek word hegemon, which translated into English means "chieftain." Hegemony implies the dominance of one power over others, either within the international system or on a regional level. Thus, a hegemonic power exercises dominance over other powers.

Heuristics and Schemas: Heuristics are rules of thumb or mental shortcuts to process large amounts of information. For example the availability heuristic comes into play when policymakers expect a situation based on past experiences.

Imperialism: Denotes the projection of power by one state to extend the dominion of that state over other nations.

Imperial Overstretch: Concept that an empire can extend itself beyond its ability to protect and fulfill their global interests and obligations.

Insurgency: A condition of revolt against established authority, typically a government.

Interdependence: Refers to the deepening web of connections between states in areas such as commerce and trade, ecology, energy, and so forth.

Countries are becoming increasingly sensitive to what occurs in other nations and regions of the world.

Interest Group: A group of people that share common interests and seek support from the state.

International Law: Body of rules and regulations that moderates the actions of states and other actors, much of it was originally developed by Hugo Grotius.

International Monetary Fund (IMF): International organization created under the Bretton Woods System. Its original purpose was to promote short-term loans so that countries could restore economies shattered by the war. It also was created to deal with balance of payments deficits and ensure systemic liquidity.

International Organization: Institution drawing membership from at least three states, and whose members are held together by a formal agreement.

International Political Economy: Discipline that explores the interaction between economics and political science at global and national levels.

Intifada: Arabic term for "a shaking off," refers to several Palestinian uprisings against Israel.

Irredentism: Any movement or aspiration to recover territory once held by one's own peoples.

Isolationism: A national policy of abstaining from political or economic relations with other countries.

Jihad: Arabic term for a "holy war" waged on behalf of Islam.

Just War: A war held to be justly caused and humanely conducted, the concept was developed by Thomas Aquinas.

Least Developed Country (LDC): Refers to those countries that exhibit the lowest levels of socioeconomic development, and often rank at the very bottom of the Human Development Index (HDI).

(Liberal) Imperialism: The creation and/or maintenance of an unequal economic, cultural, and territorial relationship, usually between states and often in the form of an empire, based on domination and subordination.

Liberalism: Based on the notion of classical free-market liberal economic theory. The international relations theory argues that humans are capable of rising above patterns of base behavior, and that humanity is capable of cooperation—between communities, races, nations, and so forth. Liberals see the quality of anarchy as cooperative and argue that most states will ultimately find it in their best interests to cooperate for mutual gains, creating a "society of states."

Marxism: The system of economic and political thought developed by Karl Marx and Friedrich Engels. Marxism holds that the state is a mechanism for the exploitation of the masses by a dominant class. Posits that class struggle has been the main driver of historical change, and that the capitalist system, containing the seeds of its own decay, will inevitably, after the period of the dictatorship of the proletariat, be superseded by a socialist order.

Massive Retaliation: Strategic doctrine of the Eisenhower Administration, which calls for a nuclear response to any aggressive action by the enemy (in this case the Soviet Union).

Mercantilism: The old economic theory that trade is in fact a zero-sum game, and that to realize profit one had to cheat one's trading partners. Protectionism was widely employed during this era. Mercantilism prompts imperialism, colonial expansion, and restrictive trading practices.

Modernization theory: Theory that key barriers to industrialization are located at the domestic level, and that these are often social and political structures. Advocates argue that industrialization is possible through investments in human, financial, and physical capital and through open markets.

Monopoly: A situation in which a single company owns all or nearly all of the market for a given type of product or service.

Multilateralism: An approach to domains such as international trade, the monetary system, international disarmament and security, or the environment, based on the idea that if international cooperative regimes for the management of conflicts of interest are to be effective, they must represent a broad and sustainable consensus among the states of the international system.

Multinational Corporation (MNC): An enterprise operating in several countries but managed from one (home) country. Generally, any company or group that derives a quarter of its revenue from operations outside of its home country is considered a multinational corporation.

Multipolarity: A form of the international system dominated by more than two great powers.

Mutual Assured Destruction (MAD): Strategic doctrine that guarantees each side in a nuclear exchange would survive a first strike by its opponent with enough arms intact to launch a second-strike sufficient to destroy the aggressor. Therefore, because neither side can survive a nuclear war—the incentive for conflict declines.

Nationalism: First developed in postrevolutionary France. Used by Napoleon to galvanize the French population into mass support for the Napoleonic Wars.

Neoconservativism: In international politics, the theory derived from the thought of Immanuel Kant, aggressively promoting the expansion of democracy, often through the use of force.

Nongovernmental Organization (NGO): Groups not related to governments but take active role in international politics. Examples include humanitarian, religious, and terrorist organizations.

Norms: General rules and principles established to facilitate cooperation among nations.

North American Free Trade Agreement (NAFTA): A treaty between the United States, Canada, and Mexico that ushered in a free-trade area in North America. It went into effect 1 January 1994.

North American Treaty Organization (NATO): Established 1949, the collective security agreement between the U.S.A., Canada, and many nations of Western and Central Europe to counter Soviet aggression.

Nuclear Proliferation: The spread of nuclear weapons to countries that formerly did not possess them.

Offshore Balancing: A strategic concept often used in Realist analysis in international relations. The term describes a strategy where a great power uses favored regional allies to check the rise of potential hostile powers.

Operational Codes: Operate as mental flowcharts that contain sets of rules that are used to help process information, create and evaluate options given uncertainty. They exist as a way to translate moral and political beliefs into actions, so they are both a belief system and a guide to action.

Organization of American States (OAS): Organization that includes many countries of the Western hemisphere, promotes international cooperation on a broad spectrum of issues in the region.

Parity: A roughly equal distribution of power among a group of countries in the international system.

Peace of Westphalia: 1648, refers to peace that resulted from the Treaty of Westphalia that ended the Thirty Years War. It marks the beginning of the modern international system.

Polarity: Denotes the presence of dominant powers in the international system. Unipolar and bipolar systems exhibit greater stability than multipolar systems.

Power Projection: The capacity of a country to deploy its military forces to distant regions.

Pre-emptive Strike: A defensive attack carried out when an assault by an opponent is thought to be imminent.

Prisoner's Dilemma: A model derived from game theory designed to explain the difficulties that states face in cooperating under conditions of anarchy. In this model, if both players act in their self-interest, each will defect, leading to a suboptimal outcome for both.

Protectionism: The government's placing of duties or quotas on imports to protect domestic industries from global competition.

Rational Actor Model: Model of decision making that assumes a perfectly rational decision maker who has access to perfect information, and conducts cost-benefit analyses that result in optimal decision making.

Rationality: Ability of a decision maker to make and rank cost-benefit comparisons among possible options.

Realism: A theory that argues that the distribution of relative power within the international system has a profound influence on how states act. It stipulates that the quality of anarchy is competitive. To ensure their survival, states will maximize their relative power and compete with each other in a zero-sum environment.

Realpolitik: The policy of power politics, the practice or promotion of Realist policies.

Reciprocity: A response in kind, a mutual exchange between two countries.

Regimes: An agreement or formal institution that facilitates cooperation between sovereign states under conditions of international anarchy.

Relative Power: A state power as compared to other countries in the international system.

Rogue State: A state that is considered untrustworthy and is shunned by the international community.

Salafism: An ideology that seeks to rid Islam of Western influence, and to return Islam to its "original" interpretations.

Sanction: A provision of a law enacting a penalty for disobedience or a reward for obedience.

Schemas: Generic concepts stored in a person's memory that help process information rapidly and efficiently. They refer to people, situations, events, and objects.

Schlieffen Plan: Strategy developed by German General Alfred von Schlieffen in 1892 to prevent a two-front war from developing against Germany. Based on the premise that Germany would conduct a rapid first strike against France, subdue Paris, and then use its railway system to quickly redeploy troops to the East to strike Russia.

Security Council: Principle organ of the United Nations responsible for maintaining global peace and security. Role is to oversee collective security operations, peacekeeping missions, and deploy observer missions to troubled regions. The five permanent members (China, France, Russia, United Kingdom, United States) of the Security Council have veto power.

Security Dilemma: Lack of international order that results from anarchy leads a state to feel insecure, and it responds by building up its military capacity. As rivals do the same, an unintended arms race results, adding to the insecurity that each country experiences. Ultimately the security dilemma generates a highly unstable environment that is prone to conflict.

Shi'ite: A member of the branch of Islam that regards Ali and his descendants as the legitimate successors to Muhammad and rejects the first three caliphs.

Socialism: Belief that productive assets should be owned collectively to generate optimal benefits to society.

Sovereignty: Independence from external forces. The principle was developed by the Dutch jurist Hugo Grotius in response to the Thirty Years War between Catholics and Protestants in Europe, and enshrined in the Peace of Westphalia in 1648. The principle dictates that the state possesses ultimate authority over all things occurring within its boundaries and guarantees against external interference in internal affairs.

Sphere of Influence: A region dominated by one great power. The dominant power imposes its will on nearby states, restricting their latitude in decision making.

State: An independent political entity with institutions and authority over a defined territory.

Structural Adjustment Program: Policy undertaken to meet the condition placed on loans from international lenders. Such conditions include cutting government spending, price controls and subsidies, opening markets to imports, the devaluation of currencies, and reducing state ownership of firms.

Subsidies: Government payments to domestic industries that allow producers to price their goods below costs of production.

Sunni: A member of one of the two great religious divisions of Islam, regarding the first four caliphs as legitimate successors of Muhammad and stressing the importance of Sunna as a basis for law.

Sustainable Development: Policies that combine economic growth with effective management of environmental resources, such as protection of biodiversity and reducing air pollution.

Taliban: An Islamist movement that ruled most of Afghanistan from 1996 until 2001, despite having diplomatic recognition from only three countries (the United Arab Emirates, Pakistan, and Saudi Arabia). The most influential members, including Mullah Mohammed Omar, the leader of the movement, were simple village *ulema* (Islamic religious scholars), whose limited education did not include exposure to modern Islamic thought.

Tariff: A tax that is imposed on a selected foreign good. The tariff raises the price of this import, making it more expensive than domestically produced goods. As a result the consumption of imports declines and the consumption of domestically produced goods increases.

Terrorism: The use of violence and threats to intimidate or coerce, especially for political purposes.

Ummah: Is an Arabic word that means *community* or *nation*. It is correctly used to mean the nation of the believers (*Ummah Al-Mu'hmini*) in Islam, thus the whole Muslim world.

Unipolarity: Occurs when the international system is dominated by one Great Power.

Uranium Enrichment: Enriched uranium is a sample of uranium where the abundance of the isotope U-235 is increased above the natural abundance. Nuclear reactors need U-235 to produce a controlled nuclear chain reaction. Enrichment is a prerequisite for making nuclear weapons.

War of Attrition: Strategy of wearing out one's enemy over time. Both the Allies and Central Powers employed this strategy during World War I.

Warsaw Pact: The alliance of Soviet client states in Eastern Europe formed in 1954 by Moscow, largely as a response to the formation of NATO in 1949.

Weapons of Mass Destruction (WMD): Refers to nuclear, biological, and chemical weapons.

World Bank (IBRD): Originally created under Bretton Woods System to facilitate economic reconstruction after the Second World War. It subsequently evolved into the role of a multilateral lending agency to LDCs (least developed countries) financing development projects.

World Trade Organization: The trade organization that replaced the General Agreement on Tariffs and Trade (GATT) as a result of the Uruguay Round in 1994.

World War I: 1914–1918, a devastating conflict in Europe between the Central Powers (Germany and Austria), and the Allies (United States, Great Britain, France, and Russia).

World War II: 1939–1945, the conflict between the Axis powers (Germany, Italy, and Japan) and the Allies (Britain, France, Canada, Australia, United States, and Russia). The immense destruction caused by the conflict gave momentum to the restructuring of the global economy under the Bretton Woods System, and the rise of the United Nations.

Zero-Sum Game: One state's gain is another state's loss—this encourages intense competition between the two powers.

INDEX